NEGRO BAPTIST HISTORY

NEGRO BAPTIST HISTORY, U.S.A.

1750-1930

by
Lewis Garnett Jordan, D.D.

VOLUME II
of
E. C. MORRIS History of National Baptists SERIES

Townsend Press ✝ Nashville, Tennessee
Sunday School Publishing Board
NBC, USA, Inc.
1995

Townsend Press, Nashville 37201-1188
Sunday School Publishing Board of the National
Baptist Convention, USA, Inc.
©1930, 1995 by the Sunday School Publishing Board
Manufactured In The United States of America

Library of Congress Cataloging-in-Publication Data

Jordan, Lewis Garnett, 1854?-1939
     Negro Baptist history U.S.A., 1750-1930 / by Lewis G. Jordan. p.   cm.
     ISBN 0-910683-16-6 (pbk.)
     1. National Baptist Convention of the United States of America--History. 2.
National Baptist Convention of the United States of America--History--Sources. 3.
Afro-American Baptists--History. 4. Baptists--United States--History. 5. Afro-Ameri-
can Baptists--History--Sources. 6. Baptists--United States--History--Sources. I. Title.
BX6456.3.J67 1993
286'.133'09--dc20   93-1767
                                                           CIP

The Baptist people are vindicated in their origin, history and achievement. Their principles are set out with admirable frankness, clearness and in excellent temper.—J. B. Campbell, D.D.

Next to the personal call of the Master, the greatest incentive to young Christians is a record of the glorious victory under the matchless standard of the Cross. We will, therefore, be pardoned if we have pointed with special pride to the magnificent record made by the Negro Baptist army.—An Outline of Baptist History, *N. H. Pius, D.D.*

NEGRO
BAPTIST HISTORY
U. S. A.

1750   **1930**

By
REV. LEWIS G. JORDAN, D.D.
Author of "Up the Ladder in Missions," "Standard Baptist Directory
and Busy Pastor's Guide," "In Our Stead,"
"Pebbles From an African Beach," and other booklets.

Published by
THE SUNDAY SCHOOL PUBLISHING BOARD, N. B. C.
A. M. Towsend, D.D., Secretary
Nashville, Tenn.

To my wife,
Susie Allston Jordan
Whose zeal and faithfulness are a constant source
of inspiration to me.
This book is affectionately dedicated.

REV. GEORGE LEILE

He was set apart May 20, 1775, as the first ordained
Negro Baptist preacher in North America.

THE FIRST CHURCH IN AMERICA

The first Negro Baptist meeting house known in history—
First African Baptist Church, Savannah, Ga.

CONTENTS

The New Testament is the law of Christianity. All the New Testament is the law of Christianity. The New Testament is all the law of Christianity. The New Testament always will be all the law of Christianity. Avaunt, ye types and shadows! Avaunt, Apocrypha! Avaunt, O synagogue! Avaunt, Tradition, thou hoary-headed liar. Hush Be still and listen! All though the Christian ages—from dark and noisome dungeons, from the lone wanderings of banishment and expatriation, from roarings and sickening conflagrations of martyr fires—there comes a voice-shouted here, whispered there, sighed, sobbed, or gasped elsewhere—a Baptist Voice, clearer than a silver trumpet and sweeter than the chime of bells, a voice that freights and glorifies the breeze or gale that bears it. O Earth, hearken to it: the New Testament is the law of Christianity.—B. H. Carroll.

Editor's Preface

It is with great delight that we reintroduce what we believe to be the only genuine history of Negro Baptists in the United States of America. NEGRO BAPTIST HISTORY 1750-1930, Sunday School Publishing Board, Nashville, Tennessee by Dr. Lewis Garnett Jordan is a classic. He was very close to our Negro Baptist beginnings (A.D. 1750) and as for the inception of the National Baptist Convention (A.D. 1880 and 1895), he wrote as an eyewitness. Hence, this publication places us in touch with our forebears and our beginnings in a most profound manner and, to a great extent, comes from an eyewitness point of view.

Dr. Jordan has done for National Baptists what Luke the Physician did for the Christian Church in recording his narrative of the life and teachings of Jesus. Luke begins his Gospel by saying,

> *Forasmuch as many have taken in hand to set forth in order a declaration of those things which are most surely believed among us, even as they delivered them unto us, which from the beginning were eyewitnesses, and ministers of the word; it seemed good to me also, having had perfect understanding of all things from the very first, to write unto thee in order, most excellent Theophilus, that thou mightest know the certainty of those things, wherein thou hast been instructed.*
>
> *Luke 1:1f.*

We are eternally indebted, therefore, to Dr. L. G. Jordan for this great contribution which chronicles the path over which we have trod as Negro Baptists. He is among the rare few among our people who took upon themselves the task of writing our story. Dr. Jacob Tileston Brown once remarked with abrasive irony that "...Negroes may have made and are making glorious history, but they write no history worth while, but leave the other fellow to write all the history and take all the honor and relegate the Negro to the back yard or even give him no place whatever in the plan of religious movements" (THE SUNDAY SCHOOL INFORMER, August 1941, Sunday School Publishing Board, Nashville, Tennessee). Dr. Brown's remarks, written in the course of a series of articles he prepared on "Why the Sunday School Publishing Board Was Ever Started," were correct by and large. Only a few Negroes had written about our sojourn in this country. The absence of such information drawn from original cisterns of our own experience has made us poorer indeed. However, Dr. Jordan saw to it that Negro Baptists would have at least one volume which told our story without the editorial adulteration of the larger culture. According to the editorial staff of the erstwhile THE SUNDAY SCHOOL INFORMER, Dr. Jordan "...perhaps, knew more about Baptist history, the individual personalities of Negro Baptist leaders, and of the intricate problems of missions, than any other man of our group" (THE SUNDAY SCHOOL INFORMER, April 1939, pg. 3, Sunday School Publishing Board, Nashville, Tennessee). Hence, this publication is as true a representation as possible of what happened in our nascent beginnings. Dr. Jordan was one man among a very few of us who knew much of the story of Negro Baptists and wrote so it could be passed on to generations of our children coming behind us.

Dr. Jordan was a man born of humble beginnings. He was born in Lauderdale County, Mississippi between Enterprise and Meridian. The year and date of his birth are washed away into obscurity by the swift and strong currents of time. He never knew his birth date. His mother told him he was born when the corn was in tassel. As a result of this, he chose June 2 as his birthday. As a child, he never knew his name. He responded to "Nig" (short for "Nigger") whenever called. This was all he knew. However, after escaping with his mother to a Yankee camp in the Meridian vicinity, a White teacher from Newark, Ohio asked his name. Stunned at the request, he quickly sought an answer. He remembered two White soldiers who had shown him kindness. One's name was "Lewis" and the other was "Jordan." Thus, he took the name, "Lewis Jordan." Also, he remembered reading of a great Black Presbyterian preacher named Henry Highland Garnett. Remembering that most names had three parts, he took on the name "Garnett" and became "Lewis Garnett Jordan."

Dr. Jordan's educational career is not overly impressive, in the general sense of academic achievements of Blacks today. His résumé did not include Harvard, Yale, Columbia, Vanderbilt, University of Chicago, and the like. In his own personal history, he cited Roger Williams University of Nashville, Tennessee as his academic alma mater. It appears this was the extent of his formal education. The rest was acquired from great Black preachers and his perpetual study and eternal inquiry. Thus, it was his sheer grit and determination to aspire to academic excellence in telling the story of our Baptist beginnings which caused this volume to be set before us with such magnificence in quality and quantity of material.

An eyewitness account of a people's history is most valuable to that people's self-awareness. Knowledge of a people's history is the fuel on which they feed to give strength for contemporary times and momentum for the future. A clear reading of that history is critically important for the development of a viable people.

We are unable to seek that history in the myriad volumes which pour out of the publishing enterprises of the larger White church community. Their attitude toward Black Baptist history is tantamount to that of my American Church History professor at Vanderbilt Divinity School. That attitude amounts to unconscious, but no less damaging, neglect. The professor had gone through the entire semester without making reference to the history of the Black church in America. The class met one hour per session with three sessions held each week. When asked why he had not lectured on the history of the Black church, he remarked that obviously I was absent the day he covered that area. In other words, this erudite professor covered "all" the history of the Black church in one hour's lecture out of an entire semester. The most limited of mental faculties would know you cannot cover the history of the Negro Baptist Church in one hour, let alone the history of "all" Black church communions in that period of time.

In keeping with this unconscious, but no less damaging, neglect approach to Black Baptist history, when I studied the history of Baptists at the American Baptist Theological Seminary in Nashville, the textbook written by R. G. Torbett faintly treated the subject of the history of the Negro Baptist church. It was as though the Negro

Baptist church hardly existed. William Warren Sweet's *The Story of Religion in America*, gives a modest bit of information on the history of the Negro Baptist Church. However, it is woefully inadequate. It is right to conclude that whenever historians of the larger culture have written their versions of Baptist church history in this country, inevitably they have left out the Negro or hidden him deep behind the misty veil of obscurity.

Having studied in a school controlled by Whites and taken two major degrees from another school which is predominantly White, both in Nashville, Tennessee, I can say experientially that the history of the Black Baptist church cannot and will not be written by historians from within the White Baptist church. In all probability, it will be like the response given by Dr. Wayne Oates of Southern Baptist Seminary of Louisville, Kentucky who, while lecturing in the 1960's at the American Baptist Theological Seminary, was asked of the whereabouts of the publications concerning pastoral care in the Negro Baptist church. His response was, in effect, "That will have to come from someone out of the Black Baptist church. White middle class theologians cannot write about pastoral care in the Black Baptist church." It is logical, then, that Black theologians would write the history of the Black Baptist church.

Some attempts have been made in recent years to write respectable histories of the Black Baptist church. Regrettably, these scholars have not relied considerably on Dr. L. G. Jordan's work. Leroy Fitts' work, *A History of Black Baptists*, Broadman Press, Nashville, Tennessee, only courteously refers to Dr. Jordan and his work. However, Dr. Fitts' work has been taken seriously by many to be a good representation of the history of the Black church. Conversely though, there have been serious questions raised concerning the veracity of many assertions of fact in his treatment of the events of some of the early congregations. This lack on Dr. Fitts' part could have been caused by his failure to utilize Dr. Jordan's work more fully. James Melvin Washington's *Frustrated Fellowship: The Black Baptist Quest For Social Power*, Mercer University Press, Macon, Georgia, again only modestly utilizes Dr. Jordan's work. He does, however, applaud him for preserving the "record" of National Baptist activities in history. He cites Dr. Jordan's book as ". . .actually a precious compilation of denominational records. While weak on interpretation, Jordan did preserve several records that would otherwise be lost" (p. 217).

Finally, Evelyn Brooks Higginbotham faintly refers to Dr. Jordan in her crucial contribution to the work of women in the National Baptist Convention, USA, Inc. (see, *Righteous Discontent: The Women's Movement in the Black Baptist Church, 1880-1920*, Harvard University Press, Cambridge, Massachusetts.). However, there is little evidence that she utilized his representation of the history of Negro Baptists.

The one publication which drew heavily from Dr. Jordan's eyewitness account of Negro Baptist beginnings was Dr. Joseph Harrison Jackson's *A Story of Christian Activism: The History of the National Baptist Convention, U.S.A., Inc.*, Townsend Press, Nashville, Tennessee. Throughout this voluminous work, Dr. Jackson utilizes Dr. Jordan's work. Dr. Jackson's is a representable work, in terms of a history of the National Baptist Convention, U.S.A., Inc. This is due, to a great extent, to his dependence on Dr. Jordan's contribution.

It is, then, with great pleasure that the Sunday School Publishing Board, through its Christian Education Department, re-presents Dr. Jordan's work. As we proceed toward a new century, it is important that Negro Baptists have a clear understanding of our roots in history. Dr. L. G. Jordan comes closer than most who have made the effort of giving us a clear reading of our history. We are indebted to him. The least National Baptists can do is to keep his work alive. This is our intention.

As you read Dr. Jordan's work, you will recognize spelling variations throughout. For example, the spelling of the name for George Liele will also be found as "Lisle" and "Leile." J. Q. A. Wilhite may sometimes be found to read "Wilwhite." Similarly, the name Corprew may appear as "Corpew" and DeLamotta may be discovered as "Delamotta" or "DeLamatta." We have allowed to let stand the capitalization of terms such as "Black," "Colored," and "White." However, in deference to current standards, we have eliminated excessive comas in order to facilitate smoother reading.

We convey our most sincere thanks to the staff at the library of Fisk University. Ms. Beth M. Howse, Ms. Ann A. Shockley, and Dr. Jessie Smith were extremely helpful. Our copy of Negro Baptist History: 1750-1930 had become brittle and could not be handled without the danger of destroying the book. Fisk Library had a volume which was strong and intact. This volume was made available to the Sunday School Publishing Board for the process of reproducing what you now hold in your hands.

We must give recognition to the Vanderbilt Divinity School library for valuable assistance. The staff assisted in tracing the titles of some of the very old books mentioned in the publication. Expressions of appreciation are due as well to the Presbyterian Historical Foundation. Also, the Historical Commission of the Baptist Sunday School Board of the Southern Baptist Convention are worthy of our thanks.

Additional panegyrics and praise are due to the Reverend Emmanuel Reid, assistant editor, Christian Education Department-Sunday School Publishing Board, NBC, USA, Inc. Reverend Reid read and reread the manuscript over and again to sweep it clean of editorial glitches. Thanks of enormous magnitude are due to the staff of the PrePress Department-SSPB. The cover design is the work of Ms. Ruth Epps, a creative and diligent worker. Mr. John Bandy and Mrs. Evelyn Campbell are due thanks for piloting the publication through our production system to completion.

In summary, we hope you, the reader, will reap the rich benefits of reading afresh the eyewitness report of the history of our Negro Baptist beginnings by Dr. Lewis Garnett Jordan.

Dr. Amos Jones, Jr.
Christian Education Department
Sunday School Publishing Board
National Baptist Convention, USA, Inc.
April 24, 1995

Introduction

Remarkable, intensely interesting, and history-making has been the life of the author of his book. It was mine to meet the Rev. L.G. Jordan in 1880 while attending school at the Branch Normal College, Pine Bluff, Ark. We were stripling youths and students preparing for the future, he at Old Roger Williams, Nashville, and I in the State School, Arkansas. For all these years I have kept in close touch with him while we pastored, and especially while I pastored in Virginia and he in Philadelphia. He was the first pastor to give national renown to the old Union Baptist Church of Philadelphia, and it was he who gave them the first building erected by themselves. We have worked together in the National Baptist Convention since 1893. It was my pleasure to offer a resolution making Dr. Jordan secretary emeritus of the Foreign Mission Board which gives him a pension of $1200 a year during his lifetime; this resolution was adopted unanimously by more than two thousand delegates at the Chicago session in 1921. He was the first to be thus honored by our group and the only one thus far.

As a result, the National Baptist Convention of the United States of America has appointed Bro. Jordan as their historiographer. He is admirably well-fitted to tell the STORY OF THE NEGRO BAPTISTS, for he has made Baptist history in the pastorate in Mississippi, Texas, and in Pennsylvania.

Dr. Jordan has given the denomination and race a life of service. As corresponding secretary of the Foreign Mission Board, he was called the life and center of our Foreign Mission work for nearly twenty-six years, and it is characteristic of his unselfish nature and generous heart that, when broken in health he resigned, he authorized the Board to collect $600 (one-half of the pension voted him) annually, and use it to advance the cause of foreign missions. In 1926 out of his scanty savings, he contributed $500 in a lump sum to serve as a nucleus of a Fund for Missions and Christian Education—for aiding deserving young people to obtain an education, specifying that six hundred dollars which he donates from his pension is to be added thereto annually. The story of how he has touched men here and there, in this country and abroad, helping to launch careers and opening opportunities to worthy and aspiring youth is too long to be narrated here; his influence and power have done much, under God, to bring to the National Baptist Convention the progress it now enjoys.

The task of the collector of information relative to Negro Baptists is not easy. Men who founded the denomination have passed. Those who stood colossus-like over the gulf that divided slavery from emancipation are passing. They have left little in writing. They had not time to write, although many of them were good scholars. They were building a denomination and shaping a race. But their achievements must not be left unrecorded.

The Republic of Liberia has knighted him for distinctive contributions to the cause of Christianity that have been made in his half century of activity in the Negro church.

Standing as he does midway between the antebellum generation of Baptist preachers and the younger men, Dr. Jordan has been blest with an intimate personal acquaintance with hundreds of Baptist leaders. In this compilation of a history of Negro Baptists, he has turned this advantage to good account. He has brought to his work as historian of the National Baptist Convention the same ardor and earnestness which carried the cause of Foreign Missions up from a board in name only to the place it had attained when he gave up the office to a younger man. And now, in assembling in this book facts which should and will become household words among Baptists of the Negro race, he affirms that this too is but a foundation upon which more youthful historians may build— that here also he is simply a pioneer/pathfinder—but we know that his life will shine as a star of the first magnitude on and on to the end of Kingdom-building on earth.

His comrade and yokefellow,
WESLEY F. GRAHAM,
Philadelphia, Pa.
May the Seventeenth
Nineteen Hundred Thirty

REV. E. J. FISHER, D.D.

Born, La Grange, Ga. Aug. 2, 1858; died, July 31, 1915, in Chicago. Dr. Fisher outgrew his state and became a leader in Tennessee as pastor of old Spruce Street. From there he went to Chicago where as a great preacher he became known in the country as pastor of Olivet Baptist Church. A daughter is city missionary of that church and a son, after teaching in Union University, is pastoring in West Virginia.

MISS LUCY WILMOT SMITH
Louisville, Ky.

Miss Smith, following the organization of the American National Baptist Convention, was a teacher in Simmons University and was made historian for Negro Baptists. If the minutes of that organization could be secured, the reports of Miss Smith which were doubtless printed would give us much information, but if they are in existence we can't find them.

A HISTORY-MAKING EVENT

Foreword

"The largest contribution of the New World to civilization was the principle of the separation of Church and State. Historians ascribe to the Baptists the chief credit for the establishment of this principle in the United States."

"The origin of that sect which acquired the name of Anabaptist by their administering anew the rite of baptism to those who came over to their communion, is hid in the remote depths of antiquity, and is, of consequence, extremely difficult to be ascertained." —*Mosheim*

* * *

For the benefit of those who may not have had access to reliable Baptist history heretofore, and as a befitting approach to the study of what Negro Baptists have achieved for the benefit of their own group and what they have contributed to the Christianization of the world, I am inserting the introductory essay by Rev. J.R. Graves, D.D., to his reproduction of Orchard's Baptist history. In my judgement this treatise includes the very cream of Baptist history as a whole, and will save looking up many books, so we give it here that we may go on with Negro Baptist history. Dr. Graves was an author of large standing and his great debate with Ditzler which is remembered by many persons still living, marks him as an outstanding historian and a great contender for the faith.

The account given in our Bible of "The Beginning" is really one phase of a particular section of the world's history which begins authentically with the Hebrew Bible, in the ancient times of Adam, Noah, and Abraham, who were the fathers of three great families into which the human race is divided. The activities of mankind were not published in books, but rather were preserved through tradition. In other words, men were books.

Adam brought down the story of creation through 930 years, and Noah after him brings it down 950 years more; Noah's family giving it to Abraham's family, from whose careful compilations Moses, by and by, writes the Book of Genesis.

While Abraham was born 2 years after Noah's death, it was, however, some 125 years after Adam's death till the birth of Noah. God in his providence appointed six faithful and much honored men as reliable trustees of all facts in history known by Adam, ordaining these six men to live centuries with Adam and then prolonged their lives so as to enable them also to live centuries with Noah, who was to become the second great father of the human race. So the transmission of facts and histories from Adam to Noah was indeed most satisfactory. The following is a clear presentation of the whole matter of linking Adam to Noah, Adam alone being enabled to re-hearse the fond story of creation to the first world, and Noah alone allowed to bear the same priceless treasure of truth to the inhabitants of the second world of mankind. Please carefully study the following:

1. Enos lived with Adam 695 years. He also lived with Noah 84 years.

2. Cain lived with Adam 605 years. He also lived with Noah 179 years.

3. Mahalaleel lived with Adam 535 years. He also lived with Noah 234 years.

4. Jared lived with Adam 470 years. He also lived with Noah 366 years.

5. Methuselah lived with Adam 243 years. He also lived with Noah 600 years.

6. Lamech lived with Adam 56 years. He also lived with Noah 595 years.

Hence the majority of the lineal forefathers prior to the Flood were born hundreds of years before Adam died, and lived hundreds of years after Noah was born.

How excellent are the plans of the Lord!

Let us transfer this precious information from Noah's day to that of Abraham, and safely lodge it in the custody and keeping of the "Sacred Family."

There were also six men, well approved of the Lord, living contem-poraneously with each other, having their lives so ordered as to live many years with Noah, and subsequently also many years with Abraham. Look at the following facts and behold the great wisdom of God in ordering things:

1. Arphaxad lived with Noah 345 years. He also lived with Abraham 88 years.

2. Salah lived with Noah 313 years. He also lived with Abraham 118 years.

3. Eber lived with Noah 283 years. He also lived with Abraham 175 years.

4. Reu lived with Noah 219 years. He also lived with Abraham 20 years.

5. Serug lived with Noah 18 years. He also lived with Abraham 41 years.

6. Terah lived with Noah 128 years. He also lived with Abraham 75 years.

So the communication between Noah and Abraham is as good as that between Noah and Adam. In fact, much might be added to the above array of invulnerable facts to make the account of creation as given by Moses one of the most plausible narratives that has ever challenged the investigation of men.

For instance, take the following:

Lamech and Methuselah, who lived with Adam also, each of them lived with Shem, Noah's son, for more than 90 years. Now Shem crossed the Flood and lived 500 years after the Deluge which allowed him to be 50 years with Isaac, saying nothing of 150 years he spent with Abraham. So Isaac saw the man who saw the Flood. Here, Adam tells the whole story to Methuselah, who tells it to Noah's son, Shem, whose exceedingly long life allows him to communicate the same to Isaac—making only two men to stand between Isaac and Adam. Thus we have a through "trunk line" of two thousand years, as direct as the Pennsylvania or the Baltimore and Ohio Railroads between Chicago and New York. To summarize Methuselah's living with Adam 243 years, and with Shem 100 years, who also lives 50 years with Isaac, whose birth, being as miraculous as the creation of Adam, doubtless assured Shem (who is no other than Melchizedek) that God had actually begun the great delivery once vouchsafed to Adam in the day of his fall.

In fact, good old Ebal, who lived with Noah 283 years, lived through all of Abraham's day down so late as to see Jacob a lad of nineteen summers.

So Abraham's family is most fully and wonderfully endowed with the history of first things, and also installed as the divinely appointed custodians of all things else thus far developed in the Kingdom of God.

I recall with interest my acquaintance with hundreds of the leaders in our pulpits for the past half century, though "up from slavery" so many of whom were former leaders in forming and fostering Baptist organizations. Following the cruel war, there is one outstanding fact in Negro Baptist history by which very much of our judgment of men past, present, and future, may be gauged—it is that our sources of information are exceedingly meager, and trustworthy data is hard to obtain. Only a few facts of our first 150 years of church life in the New World are recorded, and those by interested White men, who hardly dreamed of this day and this need as we were not allowed to know books. So far as possible, I have drawn on my personal acquaintances, trying to be impartial and accurate.

In preparing this book, I have had occasion to look up the method used by more than a dozen historians, and have been amazed to see with what frankness they have dealt with men and measures as to church affairs.

Where a minister was known to be a lover of intoxicating liquors, to be loose in his morals, a consummate prevaricator, or careless about his debts, all of these facts have been told with great frankness. I suppose this was done as a lesson to the preachers of all times. Naturally this frankness has suggested many things to this writer. Although some of our comrades who have crossed the "divide" have had checkered careers, adverse criticism would be regarded as sacrilegious. I can understand now as never before what our Lord meant when He said that the things that He knew to say could not be borne by his disciples at that time.

I thank God I have lived and wrought in the days of some of the noblest men God ever made. Among them I recall the following:

Alabama—A.N. McEwen, great preacher and witty debater; W.R. Pettiford, a good thinker and banker, who aided in bringing from Africa and educating a son of a former missionary, H.N. Bouey; I knew W.H. McAlpine, learned and pious, who had much to do with organizing the Baptists of his state.

Arkansas—George Robinson, a wise pastor and a good organizer; Jno. T. and Rubin B. White, brothers and good preachers, both of whom had much to do with statecraft, and Elias C. Morris, "the noblest Roman of them all," who was known to so many men who still live, and who held the presidency of our National Baptist Convention for twenty-six years.

Connecticut—W.M. Morton, who was for a long time the most outstanding minister in his state.

District of Columbia—Robert Johnson, reserved and undemonstrative, but a fine preacher; W. Bishop Johnson, regarded as one of our most learned men, and truly a "big brother" to his brother ministers; George W. Lee, sarcastic and biting in speech, but very eloquent as a gospel preacher.

Florida—George W. Rayford, friendly and a real gospel preacher.

Georgia—W. Tilman, whom I knew only a short time; Emanuel K. Love, a born leader of men and a great soldier in any cause he championed; James W. Carr, the evangelist and dignified pastor; Charles T. Walker, widely known among his brothers as a great preacher.

Illinois—Duling; whom I knew in 1888 as the state missionary, active about Bloomington; Richard DeBaptist, regarded as the best statistician among us. The data which he gathered through all the years and which can never be replaced, was used by mistake for kindling in 1908; Elijah J. Fisher, a brotherly pastor and a great contender for the faith.

Kentucky—Geo. W. Dupee, who made a specialty of Hebrew and Greek and sought joint debates with those who attempted to divert the Scriptures, a Baptist through and through; Wm. J. Simmons, a great soul, and a maker of preachers, the founder of the American National Baptist Convention.

Kansas—Willie L. Grant, a poet-preacher, who died all too young.

Louisiana—A.L. Newman, beloved of men, who was whipped in Lumpkins' jail before being sold to Louisiana; A.B. Flood, for a long time president of the Louisiana Convention. E.J. Brown, one of the first pastors whose church made monthly offerings for African Missions; and John Marks, a good preacher who lived to a ripe old age.

Mississippi—Rent Ramsey, a good man and the first preacher I ever saw and heard; also Randall Pollard who continued service with the Negro members when the war scared off the White members in Natchez, and H.P. Jacobs, a missionary of the consolidated American Baptist Convention; H. Bland, one of the most consecrated preachers the state ever produced.

New Jersey—Robt. W. Wynn, witty and eloquent.

New York—James Spillman, a strong leader and once president of the American Baptist Missionary Convention; and Granville Hunt.

Ohio—James Poindexter, who was exclusive, not much for mixing but a great man.

Pennsylvania—T.Doudey Miller, a leader among Northeastern Baptists; Horace Whalan, of the old school and also a leader of men; Eugene Evans, W.H. Phillips, Granville L.P. Taliferro. The last named was editor of the *Christian Banner*, a Baptist paper of large influence for many years. He helped a number of pastors to find their places in the ministerial work; and A.R. Robinson, a great pastor who served as chairman of our Foreign Mission Board for twelve years; Wesley G. Parks was vice-president of the National Baptist Convention for twelve years and a successful pastor.

Rhode Island—Joseph 0. Johnson, earnest and hard-working, who was born in Canada; James H. Presley, who served in Africa as a missionary.

South Carolina—I.P. Brockington, president of the state convention, a good leader. He was reported as dead at one time, and a beautiful eulogy of him appeared in the *Home Mission Monthly* and he read of all the good things said of himself and lived many years longer. And also Hector (Heck) M. Rayford, a good organizer.

Tennessee—Nelson G. Merry, far-seeing, who made a way to attend meetings of Negro Baptists in the North before and during the Civil War. The first convention of a larger kind was held by invitation in his church in 1866; R.B. Vandervall, Jordan Bransford, and A. Buchanan, all of whom I knew personally. They pastored the First Baptist Church, Edgefield (now East Nashville), Mount Zion Baptist Church, and the Summer Street Baptist Church, respectively. These men were well above middle age when I knew them, and they were giants in their day and made the Nashville of this day a strong spiritual Baptist center, which in a large way holds good to this day; and Michael Vann—early in the eighties, Brother Vann rose to great power and place. Eloquent and earnest, he had large influence in his state and national Baptist affairs. He died young. Southern Baptists trusted his judgment touching Negro Baptist affairs, and heard him often in their behalf.

Texas—A. Ryanhart, who was in 1882 the oldest living Baptist pastor in Texas. He often told how in early days men folks sat with their backs to the preacher, and rifles in their hand in order to keep Indians off; Israel S. Campbell, organizer of many churches and associations; I. Toliver, the evangelist, the best we have produced; and Allen R. Griggs, the man of prayer who did much in gathering historical data for the denomination.

All Texas owes much to these men as great preachers and reliable guides.

Virginia—Jas. H. Holmes, D.D., quiet, unassuming, stuttered a bit, but it was little noticed in his preaching. He was among the greatest preachers of his day. A. Binga, Jr., a Canadian by birth, a ripe scholar and fine pastor. Once offended, did not easily forgive. Exerted a large influence over the young preachers about him. John Jasper, of "Sun Do Move" fame, regarded as the most descriptive preacher of his time, and Philip F. Morris, who led in and had much to do with the founding of Virginia Seminary and College, which he deserted when the question arose as to the Negro's ability to be president and run a college. Dr. McVicker, Superintendent of Education of the American Baptist Home Mission Society and Dr. Hovey, President of Virginia Union University, are reported to have said: "It will be a hundred years before a Negro will be competent to be president of a college." And to this, many of the foremost Baptist pastors of Virginia, in a large measure led by Doctors Binga and Morris are said to have subscribed. Prof. J.E. Jones,

A.M., a most lovable character, had much to do with making many of the present day preachers of the state. What shall be said of Gregory W. Haynes, A.M.? He was not a preacher. He was a graduate from Oberlin, a Congregational school, a good Baptist, and a great believer in the possibilities of his people. Virginia Seminary and College, with the largest enrollment of any school of its kind among us, attests his faith and the large way he won Virginia Baptists, and indeed, the Negro everywhere to believe we can do and we will do. All of these men have done their work and passed on. They were all lions in defense of truth in their communities and cities. All were pastors with one exception, of outstanding churches, all owning good church houses, not many of which have been rebuilt even to this day.

West Virginia—"Father Barnett," R.J. Perkins, and Daniel Stratton, pioneers in the religious and educational work of that new state. "For there were giants in those days." Men and women and children, who lived in the days of these religious giants knew them as real benefactors.

My own poor life was enriched by knowing them. Greater things could be said—whole pages of eulogy written for every name given above and a thousand more just as good could be inscribed here, but the living, many of whom are the direct beneficiaries of their sacrificial services, will not cooperate and the following is a most shameful comment on this whole situation:

> "The Negro Baptists, whose figures at best can only be approximated, are nevertheless a mighty host. Their total is set down at 3,110,850, including the constituency of 66,322 affiliated with the various state conventions of the Northern Baptist Convention, and incorporated in that total. Could correct figures be given it would be found that the Negroes' difficult procedure to get Negro returns which are not at all accurate, although each year sees a marked advance on the part of the Negro convention secretaries in proficiency in this endeavor."
>
> —Dr. C.A. Walker, Editor, *American Baptist Year Book.*

Watchman Examiner, Oct. 8, 1925

After nearly seventy years of life, and fifty-four as a preacher, the above quotation states one of the most painful facts I have ever noted—but this is history.

"A man's immortal till his work is done."—David Livingstone.

It is said that a chronicler who narrates the bare events of a series of years does little to advance human knowledge; he contributes still less to the profit of the human race. It is required that he give something more than a record of events, he must discover the connection between one event and another; not only between two events more or less closely united in point of time, but also between events, separated, it may be, by centuries. Thus the events which occurred one thousand years ago are being developed today and we are watching their working out. We in this present day see the outworkings of the immutable laws that have, from "The Beginning," ruled the universe. True many of the pages are dark and bloody but a thread of flame shows God in the humblest as well as in the highest places, "The Unchanging." Over and over we are taught the folly of trying to disarrange cause and effect. We can trace, if we will but see, the path formed by every new idea, every advance, and form our concepts of how they have paved the way for still more progress in God's great plan for the progress of man.

When the author began several years ago the collection of facts concerning Negro Baptists, he remembered that four persons had preceded him in the effort to amass information as to denominational work: Rev. Rufus L. Perry, D.D.; Miss Lucy Wilmot Smith; Rev. Richard DeBaptiste; and Dr. A.R. Griggs. Unfortunately, the most careful and unremitting search for the past five years fails to reveal the slightest trace of the results of their work; questionnaires sent out and advertisements in our race papers have alike been fruitless and unavailing in the hunt for whatever data these former workers may have accumulated. The writer has succeeded, however, in gathering a vast store of facts, tiresome details of chronology, fragmentary and disconnected memoranda of which the matter in the following pages is but a partial summary. He has uncovered some original private letters and some statements corroborated by unimpeachable authority, but some more favored historiographer must give the great summary, the synthesis; must follow the trail of records of sworn testimony or original acts of legal tribunals and make the structure complete. His will be the task of applying scientific methods, of interpreting and drawing conclusions that shall be final. But although this writer has been extreme in condensation and elimination, if any fact of major importance to Negro Baptists has been omitted, the omission has not been intentional. This version could not be entirely neutral; no historian who has participated in the events he portrays can be as impersonal as might be desired. And yet the writer has sought, in stating his personal opinions to stress the tentative character of these views, to present the problems and furnish a point of view for further study. The chief aim of this book is to give a correct impression of the general character and trend of a given period.

He does not claim to possess the equipment which he believes to be necessary for the efficient historian of today; he frankly confesses deficiency in both breadth and minuteness. Satisfactory conclusions require a wide sweep of such research as is not now possible, but the historian builds up his facts in such a way as the truth may be apparent, and while this writer may not have builded well, he has at least endeavored to build faithfully.

Introductory Essay

To the Twelfth Edition of G.H. Orchard's *Concise History of Foreign Baptists*[1]

The comparatively little interest taken by the world, and even by professed Christians in church history, is truly astonishing. In how small a proportion of the homes, not to say libraries, can a book, purporting to be a church history, be found! And in what profound ignorance of the history of Christianity is the world today! That non-professing men should take so little interest in church history is strange, but that Christians should be indifferent to it is unaccountably negligent. An ancient historian justly remarks:

"Nothing can be more becoming a Christian than a general knowledge of Church History. It is a shame, that most of those who profess Christianity should be acquainted not only with the history of their own country, but even with that of the remotest nations, which only serves to satisfy their curiosity; and should at the same time know nothing of Church History, whence they may draw such light as may be conducive to their salvation. What advantage may not be reaped from it? It teaches us religion, it shows us what we are to believe and practice, what errors are to be rejected; what things we are to imitate; it furnishes us with abundance of examples of heroic virtue, and instructs in duty. It is a great abuse that the study of it is so much neglected. Men are very careful to instruct their children in profane history, which very often only serves to spoil their minds and corrupt their manners, and they leave them altogether ignorant of the history of Jesus Christ and His Church. Worldly people read the ancient and modern histories of nations and countries, without casting their eyes upon the gos-

---

[1]This edition was published in 1885. Ed.

pel, the Acts of the Apostles; and those historians who have writ what has happened concerning religion."

Excepting the study of the Bible, the life and teaching of Christ, and the teachings and acts of His apostles, what study can or should be more delightful or more intensely interesting to the Christian than the study of the history of the churches which succeeded those planted in the days of the apostles, and which have existed, preserving a pure faith and a pure practice through centuries of the fiercest persecutions and martyrdoms—unto this time? Are not Christians concerned to know whether that prophecy concerning the kingdom of Christ, spoken by Daniel 2:44, has thus far been fulfilled? If we understand the prophet, he foretells the setting up of a kingdom in the days of the kings of the fourth universal Empire—the Roman—which was never to be broken in pieces—utterly disorganized—or given to another people, but to stand forever and ultimately fill the whole earth. Was there a kingdom set up in the days of the Caesars by the God of heaven? Has that kingdom, or organizations in all respects similar to it, existed from the days of Christ until now? And has it been composed of the same class and character of people during all subsequent ages until this time?

Ought not Christians to interest themselves to learn the fulfillment of those promises of Christ Himself concerning His Church and people? "The gates of hell shall not prevail against it," "Lo, I am with you alway even unto the end...." These promises certainly secure the integrity and perpetuity of churches of Christ in and through all subsequent ages, even into the end of this dispensation. Says Dr. S. Miller, "This promise seems to secure his people that there shall be, in all ages, in the worst of time, a substantially pure church; that is, there shall always be a body of people more or less numerous, who shall hold just the doctrines and order of Christ's house, in some good degree, in conformity with the model of the primitive church." Accordingly, it is not difficult to show that ever since the rise of the "Man of Sin," there has been a succession of those whom the Scriptures style "Witnesses for God"—"Witnesses for the truth," who have kept alive "the faith once declared to the saints," and have in some good degree of faithfulness, maintained the ordinance and discipline which the inspired apostles, in the Master's name committed to the keeping of the church.

The Christian who reads and so understands this promise must feel a painful solicitude touching the history of his brethren—that company of faithful and true witnesses who have preceded him—and especially knowing as he does that the powers of darkness and the gates of hell have ceased not in their attempts to prevail against them; that apostate Rome for nearly

1260 years has employed armies and crusades, inquisitions and tortures, prisons, famine, and the stake to break in pieces this kingdom, and utterly exterminate these witnesses throughout the world: to consummate that work which pagan Rome attempted ages before. Will not the Christian ask, Who have been these suffering witnesses during the past eighteen centuries? In what lands of earth have they been fed for these twelve hundred and sixty prophetic days, and by what countries has the bride of Christ been "nourished...from the face of the serpent;" in the mountains and caves, and forests of what wilderness has she been securely hid by the Savior from their hand?

Will not the Christian desire to know the gracious manner in which the Savior has thus far fulfilled his promise to his followers in the fearful ages of persecutions past? Will not the questions rise within him, "How grievous were the trials, how merciless the persecutions, how intense the sufferings, how many and great the sacrifices which those who kept the testimony of Jesus, have been called upon to undergo, since the days of the last apostles, and what has been the faith and patience of the saints during them all?"

And having ascertained the sources from whence the history of such people can be gathered, will he not be moved, owing to the present distracted state of Christendom and the conflicting claims of modern sects, to belong to the family of Christian churches, to inquire with great carefulness, "What were the peculiar doctrines which in every age distinguished this unbroken body of witnesses? Under what form of church government did they exist? How did they observe the ordinances of God's house? Did they admit of human traditions? Did they recognize human legislation in the churches? And in what light did they regard, and with what measure of charity treat, those persons and powers that opposed them with human and worldly organizations, into which they sought to coerce men?" The right answer to these inquiries would at once determine which one of all the different opposing denominations in this our day, can claim kindredship with those two witnesses, and are therefore the legitimate and only surviving heirs to the promises of the "Lord Messiah," to His Church. Are not these then questions of paramount concern to all denominations since, if not from the New Testament, certainly from the history of these, the form, subject, ordinances, and doctrines of the true churches of Christ can be learned?

If the solutions of the above questions could be ascertained from the pages of church history—and they undoubtedly can from one faithfully written—would they not immensely strengthen the faith of the Christian? Would they not tend to add unmeasurably to their boldness and the faithfulness of their testimony for Christ, to their zeal and sacrificing in the kingdom and patience of the saints? Would not the unshrinking faith, the heroic virtue, and patient sufferings of his brethren the martyrs, through such ages of inconceivable afflictions and wrongs, loudly reprove his own sinful lukewarmness, repinnings and murmurings, when called upon to "endure but a little hardness as a good soldier of Christ?" When he has learned by the light of God's Word and the history of his people, that he is indeed a member of the same household, resting upon the same immutable Rock upon which apostles and martyrs, so securely based, were grounded through ages of such fearful whirlwinds of pagan enmity and papal wrath, will he not feel indeed a thousand-fold more confidence in the immutability of his foundation, and more confidently challenge the malice of devils, and the "gates of hell" to "shake his sure repose?" And will he not, from the mouths and lives of those whom Christ Himself pronounces "faithful and true witnesses," learn how to testify against all informal and corrupt "churches" in this our day—against human traditions, and mutilated and profaned church ordinances, and those who impiously presume to enact laws in place of Christ, and to change the order of His Church?

The study of the history and lives and testimony of those preceding us, who have been accounted "faithful and true" is certainly praiseworthy and of great advantage. Did not Paul recount the faith, and sufferings, and patience of the holy men and prophets who had lived before his day to animate the zeal of his brethren? Did he not intimate that they were, through their whole Christian race, being inspected by that "so great a cloud of witnesses" who, from their blissful seats, were gazing intently down upon them, and ready to receive the victory with triumphant shouts and acclaims of joy? Surely with advantage may we then study the history of the holy men and martyrs through whom the church of Christ, and its doctrines and ordinances, have been transmitted to us in their primitive integrity and purity; and with profit may contemplate their lives and their sufferings, their patience in trials and their triumphs in death—all having been made more than conquerors through him who was with them to the last.

Their history introduces us to the countries—not that they inhabited, not in which were their homes, but in which they were pilgrims and strangers, as it were—in which were their refuges and hiding places from the face of their pursuers. Who can imagine the feelings of the Christian traveler visiting those Alpine valleys in which the witnesses of Jesus were hid and nourished in those fearful times, here and there the foundations decrying upon which, traditions tell him, once stood their houses of worship, and from which they were driven by their enemies—and then gazing upward to the "munitions of rocks," the cloud-capped citadels of the everlasting hills to which they fled for refuge, as into the very bosom of their God! Or wandering through those mountains and deep forests, he enters, perhaps, the very caverns in which they hid, and which they made to echo—not with murmurs and complaining, but with the voice of worship, songs of praise, and "their hymns of lofty cheer." Cold and insensible must be that heart whose piety would not be rebuked, and whose zeal would not be energized by the contemplation of scenes hallowed by such memories! If a visit to the homes of the ancient patriots and philosophers of Athens, the rostrums from which they spoke, the groves in which they taught, and the tombs in which they slept, could so inflame the ardor of Cicero in the imitation of their virtues, how must a visit to the vales of Piedmont, and the mountains of Wales affect the heart and influence the life of a Christian! And yet in all the pilgrimages of modern times to scenes of sacred history, never do we hear of one to the valleys of Pragela, or St. Martins, or Perouse, Argonne, or Lucerne.

The little interest felt in, and the almost universal ignorance of, church history, are attributable to the unfaithfulness of those who have professed to write it. There ever has been more or less anxiety on the part of Christians to inquire into the history of the churches that have preceded them, but while they have asked for bread, they have received a stone, and a scorpion for an egg.

Seventeen centuries of the Christian era have passed, and the history of the Christian church is still unwritten while a thousand works have been palmed upon the world for church histories. The only true history of Christian churches that has been extant during these centuries is the Acts of the Apostles by Luke, and the prophetic history of the church by John the beloved disciple; and were this last but thoroughly understood, no other history would be necessary, unless to show the world with what particularity and faithfulness Christ has fulfilled its predictions. As we have said, tomes and epitomes of books purporting to be church histories have been written, and each year adds to their number, but still, not until within a few years past has a solitary effort been made upon the proper basis or in the right direction. The church histories with which our bookstores are crowded were written by pedobaptists, and they wear a falsehood upon their very title pages, as samples of their contents.

Do pedobaptists regard the Romish church as the church of Christ, or the trunk or even branch of the true church? They certainly do not, if their standards are the exponents of their view.

Since this has lately become a question of vital importance with all pedobaptist sects, we quote the language of Dr. Beman, in the General Assembly of the N.S. Pres. Church,[2] 1854, to establish our position:

> "Our standards declare the Pope to be Antichrist, and that his ministers must be excluded from the Christian ministry. Let us not shrink from the conclusion which flows from this principle; the Scriptures have declared this thing: Rome is the scarlet harlot, riding on the beast with seven heads and ten horns. This church is drunk with the blood of saints."

This is most unquestionably so; all Protestant sects so affirm. Now, if that church has been manifestly Antichrist, since it has been under the jurisdiction of the Pope, then has it been Antichrist since the year 606, when the first bishop of Rome assumed the name of universal bishop, and for the first time begirt himself with both swords. But for full three hundred years before 606—from the time of the Pure Secession—this church was a corrupt secularized hierarchy, without the least claim to be considered a church of Christ. How then do these facts bear upon the subject before us? Evidently the history of this "Man of Sin"—this "Son of Perdition"—THIS "Antichrist"—has been written and palmed off upon the world for the history of the churches of Christ. Was ever anything one-half so preposterous?

Historians acknowledge the New Testament to be an authentic history of the Church until its canon closes, A.D. 100. Commencing with this date, they trace its history down for two centuries, when the first secession took place; when the Puritans, who maintained the primitive simplicity and integrity of church government and of the ordinances, repudiated the claims of the corrupt party to be considered a church although assuming to be *par excellence* the church Catholic. This corrupt party, which called itself, so early as the fourth century, the Catholic Church, in 606 became the Roman Catholic Church, anathematizing all who dissented from it as heretics, and consigning them to destruction. All pedobaptist historians have recognized the impious claims of the Catholics to be the Church, and have written their history for the history of the church of Christ, down to the sixteenth century, and then reformed the churches of Christ out of the bosom of the Mother of Harlots! Examine the standard church histories of our day, and mark, they all include the history of sixteen centuries; thirteen of which belong to the Catholic and Romish churches, and only two of the sixteen to the church of

---

[2]This is in reference to Dr. Nathan Sydney Smith Beman (1785-1871), and the abbreviation "N.S. Pres." is the New School Presbyterian Church which came about as a result of an 1837-38 schism of the Presbyterian church. The New School church was anti-slavery. For a full discussion of this subject, see William Warren Sweet's *The Story of Religion in America*, Harper and Bros., 1930, p. 440. Ed.

Christ. It is no longer strange that the world is so profoundly ignorant of church history. It is not strange that the people are disgusted with the books that purport to be church histories, and have "wandered after the Beast," with whose history they have been surfeited. Do not such histories wear a falsehood on their title pages? Dr. Beman, pursuing this same track, writes a history and calls it a "History of the Church of Christ." His history includes sixteen centuries. You ask him as a historian if his book is a correct history of the church of Christ during these sixteen centuries, and he avers that it is. You ask him as a theologian if this party, the history of which he has written from A.D. 300 to A.D. 1600, is the church of Christ, and he answers you with great warmth and indignation: "No, sir, it is Antichrist; it is the scarlet harlot riding on the beast with seven heads and ten horns; she is drunk with the blood of saints." "Why then, sir, have you written the history of Antichrist, instead of the history of the churches of Christ, for church history?" And what can Dr. Beman, or all the doctors of Presbyterianism in the world, answer? The question is involved in inextricable difficulties. It is a fearful question for them; it devolves awful consequences upon them.

A little history connected with the last N.S. Presbyterian General Assembly, which held its session in Buffalo, May 1854, will illustrate this, and it ought not to be allowed to pass without improvement.

A query was introduced into that body to this effect: "Are Romish baptisms and ordinations valid?" A committee of junior and senior patriarchs was sent out to report an answer. They failed to agree. The majority reported negatively. But there were sundry gray-haired doctors who saw the logical consequences that lay behind such a decision, and indeed any decision they as pedobaptists could make; and those consequences would certainly be precipitated upon them by their Baptist friends and Catholic foes.

The reports were read in the Assembly, and a warm discussion ensued. Unfortunately, very little of that discussion has been given to the public; but the positions taken by the two parties were substantially these:

The majority reported that all ordinances at the hands of Romish priests were invalid because the Romish Catholic Church was no Church of Christ

REV. JERRY J. RIANHART

Navasota, Tex.

Among the first converts in Texas in slavery days. Helped keep Indians off while colonists worshipped.

WINSTON

Germantown, Philadelphia, Pa.

Pastor, preacher and leader.

Rev. W. W. Colley and wife; Rev. J. H. Presley and wife. They were the first missionaries of our present organized work who went to Africa. Only Mrs. Colley remains with us. She lives with a daughter in New York. One or more of the children will attend our Golden Jubilee in Chicago. Mrs. Presley sleeps in African soil.

and no part or branch of Christ's church, but manifest Antichrist—the scarlet harlot, riding on the beast with seven heads and ten horns, drunk with the blood of saints; the baptisms and ordinations of such an apostate body null and void; and to pronounce them valid is to pronounce the Romish church the Church of Christ; and more, to involve Presbyterians and all Protestant sects in the guilt of schism since they rent the body of Christ when they came out of Rome!

But the party who sustained the minority report, or were unfavorable to a decision, urged on the other hand [that] if you deny the church of Rome to be a true church, and decide that her baptisms and ordinations are invalid, then do we to all intents and purposes unchurch ourselves, unless we can baptize the ashes of Luther and Calvin, from whom we have received our baptisms and ordinations! If the baptisms and ordinations of Antichrist, of the Man of Sin, and Son of Perdition are invalid, then Luther and Calvin were unbaptized, as were all the members that composed the first churches of the Reformation! Then were they unordained and consequently had no authority to baptize their followers or ordain other ministers to follow them. In a word, all Protestant societies are unbaptized bodies, and consequently no churches of Christ, since a body of unbaptized persons, however pious, cannot be considered a church; all Protestant ministers are both unbaptized and unordained, and consequently unauthorized to preach officially and administer ordinances.

Thus we see the trilemma into which the query precipitated them.

1. To decide that "Antichrist," "the Man of Sin," "the Mother of Harlots" is a true Church of Christ, would be a monstrous solecism. But this would convict all Protestant sects of sin, and destroy at once every claim they could set up to be churches of Christ; for they confess themselves schismatics.

2. To decide that the Romish apostasy is not the true Church of Christ, is to decide that all her ordinances are invalid, and consequently that all Protestant societies are bodies of unbaptized persons, and therefore not churches of Christ; and all Protestant ministers are both unbaptized and unordained, and consequently unauthorized either to preach or administer the ordinances.

3. To say that we cannot decide a question so manifest will arouse the attention of the people and awaken their suspicion at once; and there is great wrong and a great failure about Protestant churches somewhere.

Finding that they could not extricate themselves from this labyrinth of fatal consequences, they removed an indefinite postponement of the question! Their membership which they have led into their societies, and the world which they are now using every possible effort to entice into their societies, should loudly and constantly demand of them to decide whether the Romish apostasy is a true church of Christ or not, for let Protestant societies decide it affirmatively or negatively, according to their own admissions, they equally cut off all their own claims to be considered Christian churches!

It is "high time" for the history of the Church of Christ to be written. The world has quite long enough wandered after the Beast, with the Church of Christ left in the obscurity of the wilderness. One thing settled by the late discussion in the Presbyterian Assembly is that no Protestant can write the history of the Christian church! Unless he writes the history of the Romish church, he has no church to write about for sixteen centuries, until the Reformation of Luther. He may well be asked, Had Christ no Church, no witnesses in the world during the roll of 1500 years? And if he had, why did not Luther and Calvin unite themselves and their followers to the then existing Christian churches, instead of setting up rival churches, originating new and never before heard of schemes of church governments, and thus distracting Christendom.

If the world is ever favored with a faithful history of Christian churches, it will receive it from Baptists, and that history will rest upon a new basis and will look after communities of Christians from the third to the sixteenth, and down to the nineteenth centuries, far different from Catholics of the former period or the Protestants of the latter.

During the last thirty years, several efforts have been made in the right direction. Robert Robinson in his *History of Baptism and Ecclesiastical Researches*[3] aided in indicating the direction such a work should take. Wm. Jones, with the light thrown upon his path by Paul Perrin and Robinson, did still more and left us not a complete but a valuable church history.

But the most valuable chronological history of the churches of Christ, now extant, and excepting Jones', the only one passing over eighteen centuries that deserves the name of Church History, now before the Christian world, is the one we now present to the American public for the first time, in a reprint. A full, philosophic history it claims not to be, but it does claim to prove, by the most unquestionable authorities, the existence of large com-

---

[3]According to the Library of Congress, this work was originally published in 1790. It was published again posthumously in 1817 by Lincoln and Edmands Press, Boston, edited by David Benedict. Ed.

munities of Baptists in the various countries of Europe and a succession of them from the earliest ages down to the present time; and we think the author has been successful. It has been before the public in England for several years, and if its authority has been questioned we have the fact to learn.

It is a history especially needed by Baptists, to assist them in replying to the taunting interrogations of Pedobaptists, "Where were you before the days of Roger Williams, or before the days of Mercer?"

In the standard denominational publications issuing from their "Book Concerns" and Publication Societies, they teach the world that Baptists originated about the time of the Münster rebellion, and were the ringleaders and chief actors in it! It is time for the public to be so well informed as to be able to give the retailers of such scandal the rebuke they deserve.

The reasons that induced the author to prepare this work—the sources from which he drew his facts; the directions in which he looked for the communities of Christians whose history he has compiled; the principles by which he has determined their religious character; the unshaken confidence he has in his authorities; and the conclusions to which he has arrived—he has briefly set forth in an "advertisement," from which we make the following extracts:

"While on a visit to a friend in Somersetshire, in 1823, a minister of the Independent persuasion panegyrized Dr. Carey to me and others as the individual who raised the Baptists out of obscurity; and further remarked, that `they had no existence before the days of the Commonwealth.' The respectability and age of the minister did not allow me, a young man, and unacquainted as I was with our history, to negative his assertion, only by a relieving hint, `that from the days of John the Baptist, **until now**' I believed our denomination had had an existence. I was resolved to be satisfied on this subject, particularly since this assertion has appeared in print; but there was no volume to which I could be directed, that would meet the inquiries and solicitude of my mind. Mr. Ivimey's work was of the English Baptists; Mr. Crosby's was of the same character; Mr. Danvers enters into the question, but gives no historic connection. I wrote to Mr. Jones, author of the *History of the Christian Church,* and his work (on his recommendation) I procured; and this valuable history gave me **the clue to the church of God**. I had now to ascertain the views the different parties advocated, which cost me very considerable application, and the result fully satisfied my inquiries. After some years' reading and making extracts from authors on the subject of my investigation, I resolved on throwing my materials into chronological order, to exhibit the feature of a connected history. This done, I became fully satisfied and established the proof of what Robinson conjectured, that 'the English Baptists, contending for the sufficiency of Scripture, and for Christian liberty to judge of its meaning can be traced back, in authentic documents, to the first nonconformists and to the apostles.'

"In the course of my reading, materials so accumulated on my hands as to enable me to furnish facts sufficient to make a compendious history of the Baptists in various provinces, from their rise to their being scattered or extinguished; and which facts are submitted in the following pages. Nor do I fear contradiction, since I have taken the most accredited historians and have preferred, in most instances, the testimonies of men hostile to our communion.

"The ensuing facts, with many more, were selected to satisfy my own inquiries; but when I had placed them in a connective form, I thought they might be useful to other similarly circumstanced, conducing, perhaps, to the removal of a portion of that visible ignorance, as to the early features of our denomination; particularly, since it has been said, that 'the Baptists may be considered as the only Christian community which has stood since the times of the apostles; and as a Christian society which has preserved pure the doctrines of the gospel through all ages.' This statement we consider to be proved in the following pages, where authors are quoted, supporting these facts.

"It is stated in the most satisfactory manner, that all Christian communities during the first three centuries were of the Baptist denomination, in constitution and practice. In the middle of the third century, the Novation Baptists established separate and independent societies, which continued till the end of the sixth age; when these communities were succeeded by the Paterines, which continued till the Reformation. The oriental Baptist churches, with their successors the Paulicians, continued in their purity until the tenth century, when these people visited France, resuscitating and extending the Christian profession in Languedoc, where they flourished till the crusading army scattered, or drowned in blood, one million of unoffending professors.

"The Baptists in Piedmont and Germany are exhibited as existing under different names, down to the Reformation; these churches, with their genuine successors, the Mennonites in Holland, are connectedly and chronologically detailed to the present period, for proof of which, see the body of the work.

"The ground of unity and denominational claim to the people whose Christian characters are detailed, is not the harmony of their creeds or views; this was not visible or essential in the first age: but the bond of union, among our denomination in all ages, has been faith in Christ; and that faith publicly expressed, by a voluntary submission to his authority and doctrine in baptism. Wherever this conduct is evident, we claim the disciple as belonging to our communion and of primitive character, at the same time leaving his mind in the full enjoyment of his native and purchased freedom; and in establishing this association, we feel no difficult or dishonor, since almost every denomination has, from their honorable and holy characters, claimed affinity to them in faith and practice, though such claims are not supported by family likeness.

"Most modern historians have been of the pedobaptist persuasion. These writers have, in a general way, suppressed in their details those evidences of believers' baptism, which abound in early writers. This omission in their histories was intended, that the modern practice may not be disturbed, and themselves condemned as innovators, by the records and practice of early churches. These writers, from the Pope to the peasant, have united in suppressing and extinguishing part of the truth; consequently, it was necessary to collate writings, histories, and documents, before the dawn of the German Reformation, in order to get at the whole truth; and strange to say, while ministers of religion for party purposes have suppressed certain denominational features, Voltaire, Hume, Gibbon, and other infidels with deistical writers, have in these respects faithfully and openly recorded events, and have been more impartial in their details than many modern divines.

"The author has found it necessary to use the specific names of the denomination more frequently in this history than might be agreeable to some readers. The reluctancy of some moderns to allow of the early and reputable existence of this class of Christians, made it necessary that the terms Baptist, Anabaptist, etc., should be often mentioned to prevent misconstruction, and the more fully to establish the objects the writer had in view.

"He has also kept unadorned facts prominently forward. These are the stubborn materials of history. In many instances, he has copied the language of able historians, and here he acknowledges his obligations to Mr. Jones' invaluable writings on the Church of Christ. On controverted points he feared to alter statements or clothe ideas in his own language, lest cavilling readers should doubt his veracity. If more verbosity had been given, the work would have been more agreeable to some, but the writer feared weakening the evidence of his work, and of making a large book; he has, therefore, preferred crowding the materials together to make his compilation a reference book in triumph, rather than its contents should be questioned from any accommodating aspect. In its character, it may be considered a rough rampart, planted round the visible camp of the saints, within which fortification they may feel safe, while at the same time, they are furnished with those means of repelling attacks, made with antiquated weapons.

"A refutation we do not fear; this would be a difficult task, since controverted facts are generally given in the words of the historian, and so far as the writer could, a pedobaptist's testimony has had the preference. References could have been increased to a considerable extent, but the support of the statement by one respectable name was deemed sufficient.

"Whatever inadvertence or errors there might be, the writer's best efforts are here offered to the society of which he stands an unworthy member, and if he realizes their approbation, he shall consider it next to the smiles of his Master and feel remunerated for fifteen years' labor; at the same time, his desire, prayer, and efforts are for the promotion of the truth, the whole truth, and nothing but the truth; and his hope is that this heavenly principle will soon universally prevail. Then the precepts of men, traditionary services, and compulsory religion shall be swept away; truth then, in all its legitimate and unrestrained influence, shall have free course, unadorned by human fancy, unchecked by human laws, unaided by human device; then, reinstated in its native dignity, truth shall be found like the beams of the sun alighting and regulating the inhabitants of the world, dispelling darkness and ignorance, conferring on the benighted the blessings of a gospel day, exhibiting their moral condition, awakening new sensations, requiring the "north to give up, the south to keep not back; bring my sons from far, and my daughters from the ends of the earth; then shall we see eye to eye, Jerusalem shall be the joy of the whole earth, and our God shall bless us."

For more than one century, our enemies conjointly have made one continuous effort to depreciate the claims of Baptists to an ancient origin. Like the animal in the manger, that, not being able to eat the hay himself, was determined the oxen should not; so they, satisfied that they cannot claim an origin prior to the days of Luther, they seem determined that no one shall believe that Baptists have a valid claim to a more ancient origin. They allege that the madmen of Münster were Baptists; and that Baptists as such, were the authors of the rebellion and all the excesses of that period; and they point us to Münster, when we speak of our origin and history, and sneeringly say: —"That was your origin and that your early history."

In vindication, we point them to the pages of Mlle. D'Aubigne:

"One point it seems necessary to guard against [is]misapprehension. Some persons imagine that the Anabaptists of the times of the Reformation, and the Baptists of our day are the same. But they are as different as possible."

Fessenden's Encyclopedia (quoted with approbation by D'Aubigne) says:

"Anabaptist! The English and Dutch Baptists do not consider the word as at all applicable to their sect." "It is but justice to observe that the Baptists of Holland, England, and United States are to be essentially distinct from those seditious and fanatical individuals above mentioned; as they profess an equal aversion to all principles of rebellion, or the one for the enthusiasm of the other."— Pre. to His. Ref. p. 10.

We point them to Mosheim, himself a Lutheran, who lived upon the soil, though a bitter enemy to Baptists: he was conversant with all the facts. Does he say that the Baptists had their origin at Münster? Hear him:

"The true origin of that sect which acquired the name of Anabaptists, by their administering anew the rite of baptism to those who came over to their communion, and derived that of Mennotists from that famous man, to whom they owe the greatest part of their present felicity, IS HID IN THE REMOTE DEPTHS OF ANTIQUITY, and is consequently extremely diffi-cult to be ascertained."—Vol. iv. p. 427

We ask Zuingulius, the celebrated Swiss Reformer, who was contem-porary with Luther, Muncer, and Stork, "Is Anabaptism a novelty; did it spring up in your day?"

"The institution of Anabaptism is no novelty, but for 1300 years has caused great disturbance in the church, and has acquired such a strength that the attempt in this age to contend with it appeared futile for a time." This carries our history back to A.D. 225!

But have we not been persecuted and worn down for lo, these 1200 years—has not the Apocalyptic "WOMAN" during all this time, been drunk with our blood and heaven filling with our martyred brethren? We appeal to Cardinal Hosius, president of the Council of Trent (A.D. 1560), the most learned and powerful Catholic of his day. Hear him testify:

"If the truth of religion were to be judged of by the readiness and cheer-fulness which a man of any sect shows in suffering, then the opinion and persuasion of no sect can be truer and surer than that of Anabaptists (Bap-tists) since there have none for these twelve hundred years past, that have been more generally punished, or that have more cheerfully and steadfastly undergone and even offered themselves to the most cruel sorts of punish-ment than these people." This carries our history back to the fourth century.

We appeal to the most eminent scholars and historians of Europe, to the matured verdict rendered by Dr. J.J. Durmont, Chaplain to the King of Hol-land, and to Dr. Ypeig, Professor of Theology in the University of Groningen, who were especially appointed by the king to ascertain if the claims of the

Dutch Baptists had any foundation in the facts of history. These distinguished men did go into the investigation; and what did they report to the king? That Baptists originated at Münster—as we are charged by authors, whose works are now published and sent broadcast over this land by the Methodist Book Concern? This is what they reported, which has never been disproved or attempted to be disproved.

"The Mennonites are descended from the tolerably pure evangelical Waldenses, who were driven by persecution into various countries; and who during the latter part of the twelfth century, fled into Flanders, and into the provinces of Holland and Zealand, where they lived simple and exemplary lives—in the villages as farmers, in the towns by trades, free from the charge of any gross immoralities, and professing the most pure and simple principles, which they exemplified in a holy conversation. They were, therefore, in existence long before the Reformed Church of the Netherlands."

Again, "We have now seen that the Baptists, who were formerly called Anabaptists, and in later times Mennonites, were the original Waldenses; and who have a long history of the church, received the honor of that origin. ON THIS ACCOUNT THE BAPTISTS MAY BE CONSIDERED THE ONLY CHRISTIAN COMMUNITY WHICH HAS STOOD SINCE THE APOSTLES; AND AS A CHRISTIAN SOCIETY WHICH HAS PRESERVED PURE THE DOCTRINE OF THE GOSPEL THROUGH ALL AGES. The perfectly correct external economy of the Baptist denomination tends to confirm the truth disputed by the Romish church; that the Reformation brought about in the sixteenth century was in the highest degree necessary; and at the same time goes to refute the erroneous notion of the Catholics, that their communion is the most ancient."—Encyclopedia Rel. Knowl.

It is an interesting fact that as a consequence of this, the government of Holland offered to the Mennonite churches the support of the State. It was politely but firmly declined, as inconsistent with their fundamental principles.

Finally, and with still greater triumph, we now appeal to the pages of this history, upon which, not our enemies only, but the dredulous and fearful of our brethren may see the clearest and most satisfactory proof, that not in one country alone, but in many kingdoms, successions of Baptist communities have come down to us from the apostles, all striped and scarred and blood covered—a line of martyrs slain by prisons, by fire, and by sword— we hail these as the faithful and true witnesses of Jesus during those fearful ages, when the Man of Sin "sat upon the Seven Hills, and from his throneof darkness ruled the world;" and we may well be proud to be able to claim these as our brethren; would that we were worthier to bear their name.

This picture was made in 1875. Most of this army of gospel warriors have crossed the Divide to be with God. A look into their faces by those who now pastor where they wrought so well and so long, will be inspired and helped in their works.

1. S.P. Young; 2. Thomas Huffman; 3. W.J. Smith; 4. John Johnson; 5. John Morgan; 6. Henry Wathen; 7. John Thompson; 8. Alex Hamilton; 9. A.G. Graves; 10. E.D.D. Walker; 11. A. Taylor; 12. A. McKee; 13. R. Lee; 14. E.J. Anderson; 15. Frank Hinton; 16. H. Davis; 17. W.M. Miller; 18. C. Oldham; 19. L. Smith; 20. Isaac Slaughter. 21. J.M. Harris; 22. C. Stumm; 23. Sam'l Mack; 24. A. Ferguson; 25. W.B. Blackburn; 26. W. Lewis; 27. John P. Wills; 28. Simon Grisby; 29. Allen Allensworth; 30. Eugene Evans; 31. P. Johnson; 32. S.P. Lewis; 33. P. Obannon; 34. W.C. Dabney; 35. E.W. Green; 36. G.W. Dupee; 37. Q.B. Jones; 38. M. Harding; 39. R. Martin, Jr.; 40. Geo. W. Bolling; 41. S.Q. Goodloe; 42. J.F. Thomas; 43. W.W. Taylor; 44. D.A. Gaddie; 45. M.M. Bell; 46. John Vinegar; 47. M. Campbell; 48. Phillip Alexander; 49. J.K. Polk; 50. G.W. Brown; 51. Daniel Martin; 52. Daniel Martin; 53. John Reed; 54. A. Stratton; 55. N.A. Walker; 56. E.P. Marrs; 57. H. Curd; 58. H. Mayfield; 59. J.C. Harrison; 60. W. Fisher; 61. Henry Fry; 62. Chas. Fishback; 63. Louis Lewis; 64. Chas Bates; 65. Richard Jones; 66. Reuben Strauss; 67. W.J. Brown; 68. J. Moran; 69. A.J. Green; 70. Lewis Overall; 71. Robinson Owsley.

Our history is now redeemed from reproach, but are Baptist principles obnoxious to the censure by Americans or of republican Christians anywhere? Through the influence of our religious principles, and the example of our form of church government, republicanism and republican institutions have already been bequeathed to half the world, and are now rocking the other half to its centre, crumbling the thrones of its tyrants and arousing and energizing oppressed humanity, to assert its rights and overthrow its oppressors.

We appeal to the opinion of Jefferson, the most eminent of American statesmen, touching Baptist church government. The following facts were communicated to the Christian Watchman several years ago, by the Rev. Dr. Fishback, of Lexington, Kentucky:

"Mr. Editor—The following circumstance, which occurred in the State of Virginia, relative to Mr. Jefferson, was detailed to me by Elder Andrew Tribble, about six years ago, who since died when ninety-two or three years old. The facts may interest some of your readers.

Andrew Tribble was the pastor of a small Baptist church which held monthly meetings at a short distance from Mr. Jefferson's house, eight or ten years before the American Revolution. Mr. Jefferson attended the meetings of the church several months in succession, and after one of them he asked Elder Tribble to go home and dine with him, with which he complied.

Mr. Tribble asked Mr. Jefferson how he was pleased with their church government? Mr. Jefferson replied that it had struck him with great force, and had interested him much, that he considered it the only form of pure democracy that then existed in the world, and had concluded that it would be the best plan of government for the American colonies. This was seven years before the Declaration of Independence."

We appeal to Judge Story, the most eminent of American jurists:

"To Roger Williams belongs the renown of establishing in this country, in 1636, a code of laws, in which, we read for the first time, since Christianity ascended the throne of the Caesars, the declaration that 'conscience should be free, and man should not be punished for worshipping God in any way they were persuaded he required.'"

We appeal to Bancroft, the most eminent of American historians:

"Roger Williams was then but little more than thirty years of age; but his mind had already matured a doctrine, which secures him immortality of fame, as its application has given religious peace to American world."

We turn to the old world—to Germany, the land of scholars and historians—and ask if the character of Baptist principles' influence upon the world, has not been seen and felt?

Gervinus, the most astute and philosophic historian of this age, in his work entitled, *An Introduction to the History of the Nineteenth Century*, says:

"In accordance with these principles, Roger Williams insisted in Massachusetts upon allowing entire freedom of conscience, and upon entire separation of the Church and the State. But he was obliged to flee, and in 1636 he formed in Rhode Island a small and new society, in which the perfect freedom in matters of faith was allowed, and in which the majority ruled in all civil affairs. Here in a little state, the fundamental principles of political and ecclesiastical liberty practically prevailed, before they were even taught in any of the schools of philosophy in Europe. At that time people predicted only a short existence for these democratic experiments—change of rulers, perfect religious freedom—the Miltonian doctrines of schisms. But not only have these ideas and these forms of government maintained themselves here, but precisely from this little state have they extended themselves throughout the United States. They have conquered the aristocratic tendencies in Carolina and New York, the High Church in Virginia, the Theocracy in Massachusetts, and the monarchy in all America. They have given laws to a continent, and formidable through their moral influence, they **lie at the bottom of all the democratic movements which are now shaking the nations of Europe.**"

Here we might be satisfied to rest, were it not to do justice to the memory of the pastor of the first Baptist church in America,—Dr. John Clarke. The fame that justly belongs to or at least should be divided with him, has been bestowed upon Roger Williams, whose name has been sounded round the whole world as the first great champion of civil and religious freedom. He was indeed a brilliant light in thick darkness; but his was only borrowed light, and he himself but a reflector. The Baptists of England and of the Continent advocated the glorious principles of soul liberty, centuries before Roger Williams was born; as they did during the reigns of James I and Charles I when he was in his boyhood.—

"That Roger Williams cannot be said—in the language of Bancroft—to have been `first in modern Christendom to assert in its plenitude the doctrine of freedom of conscience' would seem to be evident from the very fact that the arguments against persecution, prefixed to Roger Williams' `Bloody Tenet' which called forth an answer to them from Mr. Cotton, are entitled by witness of Jesus Christ, close prisoner in Newgate, against persecution in cause of conscience.' It was added that this prisoner in Newgate was a Baptist; and that the `humble supplication' which he drew up in 1620, and addressed to King James, from which the arguments prefixed to Roger Williams' book are taken, was subscribed `your Majesty's loyal subject, not for fear only; but for conscience's sake, falsely called Anabaptists.'

The history of the life and times of Dr. J. Clarke, and of the organization and rise of the first Baptist church in America, is now in course of preparation, when the proper distinction will be made between the labors and merits of R. Williams and Dr. J. Clarke.

But we are not limited in looking for our brethren to those countries, alone, which Mr. Orchard has explored with such rich results. Could not Baptists be heard of in Africa, in Spain, in Italy, in Piedmont, Bohemia, or Holland? Yet it can be shown upon the most unquestionable authorities, that there has been a succession of Baptist churches in England and Wales, from the days of Paul until now, and it is an established fact that a majority of the churches planted in America from the year 1645-1730, were organized by Welsh Baptists, and constituted upon articles of faith brought over with them from the mother churches. Mr. Orchard informs us in an advertisement at the end of his book, that he is preparing for the press a history of the Baptists of England, Wales, Ireland, Scotland, and America, which will be immediately reprinted so soon as it can be obtained. In the meantime we submit the following facts:

A.D. 63-180

About fifty years before the birth of our Saviour, the Romans invaded the British Isle in the reign of the Welsh king Cassibellan, but having failed—in consequence of other and more important wars—to conquer the Welsh nation, made peace with them and dwelt among them many years. During that period, many of the Welsh soldiers joined the Roman army, and many families from Wales visited Rome; among whom there was a certain woman of the name of Claudia, who was married to a man named Pudens. At the same time, Paul was sent a prisoner to Rome and preached there in his own hired house for the space of two years, about the year of our Lord 63. Pudens and Claudia his wife, who belonged to Caesar's household, under the blessing of God on Paul's preaching, were brought to the knowledge of the truth as it is in Jesus, and made a profession of the Christian religion. These, together with other Welshmen among the Roman soldiers who had tasted that the Lord was gracious, exerted themselves on the behalf of their countrymen in Wales, who were at that time vile idolaters.

That the gospel was extensively spread in Britain during this period, we learn from Tertullian and Origen. In the year 130 there were two ministers by the names of Faganus and Damianus, who were born in Wales but were born again in Rome, and there becoming eminent ministers of the gospel, were sent from Rome to assist their brethren in Wales.

During this year, Lucius the Welsh King was baptized, and was the first king in the world who embraced the Christian religion. During the next century

Christianity made rapid progress in the island, as is evident from the testimony of Tertullian, and from the multitudes of martyrs who suffered in the tenth pagan persecution under Diocletian, which took place about...

300-469

...the year 300. The Saxons in 469 invaded England, overthrew Christianity, and burnt the meeting houses, and drove all who would not submit to them into Cambria, which is now called Wales. During this century the British Christians suffered greatly at the hands of their Saxon foes. Yet we find there were several eminent and faithful ministers among the Welsh Baptists at this period; among whom were Gildas (who was a man of learning), Dyfrig, Dynawt, Teilo, Padaru, Pawlin, and Daniel.

606

Infant baptism was not known to the Welsh Christians until A.D. 596 or 600, when Austin was sent by Gregory, Bishop of Rome, to convert the Saxons. In this he was successful, and according to Fox, he baptized ten thousand **in the River Swale**. He sought and obtained a conference with the Welsh Baptists, near the border of Wales. The main point was that these primitive Christians should acknowledge the usurped authority of the Church of Rome. Fabian, an ancient historian, relates the final demand of Austin in these words, "Sins ye wol not assent to my hests generally, assent to me specially in III things: the first is, that ye keep Ester day in due forme and tyme as it is ordayned. The second, that ye give Christendome to children; and the thirde is that ye preache unto the anglis, word of God as aforetimes I have exhorted you, and all the other deale, I shall suffer you to amende and reforme within yourselves." But these Baptists utterly refused to practice the traditions of Rome for the commands of Christ, when this emissary of Rome threatened them in this wise, "sins ye wol not recave warre and wretch." The Saxons shortly after invaded Wales, it is thought through the influence of Austin, and slaughtered incredible numbers. While infant baptism and the traditions of the son of perdition were enforced by the sword upon the low country, and the rich and more fertile portion of the island, Welsh Baptists contend that the principles of the gospel were maintained pure and unalloyed in the recesses of their mountainous principality, all through the dark reign of popery.

"God had a regular chain of true and faithful witnesses in the country, in every age, from the first introduction of Christianity to the present time, who never received nor acknowledged the pope's supremacy: like the thousands and millions of the inhabitants of the vale of Piedmont, residing on green and fruitful meadows, surrounded by high and lofty mountains, separated from other nations, as if the all-wise Creator had made them on purpose, as places of safety for his jewels that would not bow the knee to Baal."

"Dr. Richard Davis, Bishop of Monmouth, said 'there was a vast difference between the Christianity of the ancient Britons, and that mock Christianity introduced by Austin into England, 596; for the ancient Britons kept their Christianity pure, without any mixture of human traditions, as they received it from the disciples of Christ, and from the church of Rome when she was pure, adhering strictly to the rules of the word of God.'"

"President Edwards of America, said: `In every age of this dark time (of popery), there appeared particular persons in all parts of Christendom, who bore a testimony against the corruptions and tyranny of the church of Rome. There is no one age of Antichrist, even in the darkest times, but ecclesiastical historians mention by name those who manifested an abhorrence of the pope and his idolatrous worship, and pleaded for the ancient purity of doctrine and worship. God was pleased to maintain an uninterrupted succession of many witnesses through the whole time, in Britain, as well as in Germany and France; private persons and ministers; some magistrates and persons of great distinction. And there were numbers, in every age, who were persecuted and put to death for this testimony.'"

"The faith and discipline of the Scottish churches in Ireland were the same with the British churches, and their friendship and communion reciprocal. The ordinances of the gospel in both islands, at this time, were administered in their primitive mode. The venerable Bede says that the supremacy of Rome was unknown to the ancient Irish. The worship of saints and images was held in abhorrence, and no ceremonies used which were not strictly warranted by Scripture. All descriptions of people were not only allowed but desired to consult the sacred writings as their only rule of conduct."

"In short, from what we have stated, and the evidence produced by the learned archbishop Usher, quoted by the Rev. William Hamilton, `We have the strongest reason to conclude that these islands enjoyed the blessings of a pure enlightened piety, such as our Saviour himself taught, unembarrassed by any of the idle tenets of the Romish church.'"

"When we cast our eyes on King Henry II, advancing towards this devoted nation, bearing the bloody sword of war in one hand, and the iniquitous bull of Pope Adrian in the other, we have one of the strongest arguments to prove that this was not originally an island of popish saints, and that the jurisdiction of Rome unquestionably was not established here."

With the above authorities I submit with confidence the subject of Primitive Church Constitution to all candid men.

Rev. Moses Broyles, Indianapolis, Ind. It seems that Rev. Broyles was the third pastor of the Second Baptist Church which came out of the White church and organized in 1848.

J.W. Carr, D.D., the evangelist, and Rev. C.H. Johnson were among his successors, Dr. B.J.F. Wesbrook is serving that church now. They have built one of the most substantial concrete churches in all this land. Dr. Wesbrook is indeed a great pastor and a great leader.

Rev. James M. Foster was born in Franklin, Ky., settled in Montgomery, Ala., 1865, where he labored until tranferred to his heavenly home December, 1891. He was pastor of the First Baptist Church where our national work was organized in 1880. He served as president of the Alabama Baptist Convention, two years as president of the Foreign Mission Convention, U.S.A. He was a great preacher, good organizer and a leader of men.

Rev.?? Lee was born in Virginia; organizer and first pastor of Salem Baptist Church, Jenkinstown, Pa., a pious and good man. Drs. J.C. Jackson and Pinson are among his successors. The present pastor, Rev. Jordan, D.D., is regarded as one of the most outstanding preachers of Pennsylvania.

Rev. George B. Howard, D.D., born in Virginia, died in Pennsylvania. Dr. Howard was among the most exemplary characters in the denomination, served one of the largest churches in Virginia and finally in Pennsylvania. His children have given a good account of themselves, one is an assistant pastor in New York—indeed they have all risen up to call him blessed.

Chapter I

BEGINNINGS OF OUR HISTORY

We have now seen that the Baptists, who were formerly called Anabaptists, and in later times Mennonites, were the original Waldenses; and who have long in history of the church received the honor of that origin. On this the Baptists may be considered as the only Christian community which has stood since the days of the Apostles, and as a Christian society which has preserved pure the doctrines of the Gospel through all ages.—Haynes The Baptist Denomination.[4]

THE BAPTISTS IN HISTORY

Each denomination of Christians has its characteristic type which differs from all the rest, and this type is what it is because the fundamental principles of church life and organization are what they are.

A Baptist Christian is quite different from a Methodist Christian; and the Methodist Christian is different from the Presbyterian; a Disciple Christian differs from either of them, and again a real Christian in the Episcopal or Lutheran church differs from them all. A man who has forty years of experience in the Methodist ministry is a very different man in his thought, his bearing and general air, his style of prayer, and his religious experience from a man who has had a period of training or a service in the Baptist ministry. One who has been familiar with the different denominations can tell without inquiry and with very considerable certainty, to what denomination a minister belongs upon hearing him preach.

It is, moreover, my profound conviction that the foundation principles of our Baptist churches are the right ones, and the more I study them the more I think so; and it is still further my conviction, just as profound, that we have a sacred obligation laid upon us to defend them and to teach them.

But let us first note that the New Testament religion is not a matter of "feeling," but of principle, a question of loyal obedience to Christ. We are not to judge of the "amount of religion" or the piety we may possess by the

---

[4]*The Baptist Denomination*, by Dudley C. Haynes (1809-1888), Sheldon, Blakeman & Co., New York, 1857. Ed.

frequency of states of blissful and ecstatic feeling, but by the readiness with which we obey the commands of Christ and the completeness of our submission to His will. Christ never said, "Ye are my friends if ye feel good," but "if ye do whatsoever I command you." Love and sentiment and gush are not piety, although there is no true piety without love. Obedience to Christ is piety, and an ounce of obedience is worth more than a ton of gush.

However, there must be something to these Baptist people, for see how they prosper, and see how they are coming up in every way in spite of the most strenuous opposition. They are more rigid in their discipline than any other denomination; it is a harder matter to get into their churches than any other, and they refuse many whom others accept. They are unpopular everywhere and always have been, yet what a sweeping growth they have made and what a power they have attained to, and their growth, moreover, had always been just in proportion to the strictness with which they have held to their principles. They have grown in this country, from a half dozen poor, oppressed, outcast, and despised few, to number more than eight millions, and they have wealth and culture of the highest rank. Taking the Baptists, Congregationalists, Methodists and the Presbyterians together for eight years past, the Baptists have, with less than one-fifth the total expenditure of money, sustained nearly one-third of the entire working force and have received more than one-third of the converts.

It is simply this: THE ABSOLUTE SUPREMACY OF CHRIST IN HIS CHURCH.

Notice that we speak of a distinctive principle. Because Baptist churches are not like any other churches, Baptist history cannot be written upon the same plan as any other church history. It would be easy to trace the history of an organization from a fixed, definite beginning by definite steps to the present condition; nor would it be hard to trace a certain name which has always had a definite meaning, but the name Baptist is comparatively modern, and research shows us that the name itself has been applied to those who were actually not Baptists, and, on the other hand many who were really such were known by another name. The records of primitive times are very scant and meager, and a little later persecutions were so abundant and so severe that for generations the Baptists were obliged to conduct their movements in secret; nothing was put down on paper that might betray them to the authorities. Thus a full history of the Baptists can never be written. But the Baptist principles: "Standing for God's Word and His way as shown in His Word" can be traced. Various bodies in those obscure periods held to these principles, sometimes with completeness and sometimes not; sometimes closely connected with other bodies and sometimes isolated and widely scattered. We date back to that Church "called out" by Christ Himself and we must disabuse our minds of the fancy that Baptists are a modern sect founded by Roger Williams or perchance the thought that one Smythe in England, who, about the year 1600, baptized himself, originated the sect; or to identify them with the fanatical Anabaptists (re-baptizers), the "Madmen of Münster." The Baptist principle was tenaciously held and consistently carried out centuries before. The works of Baptist authors, except the modern ones, have perished, and we have for our guidance chiefly the story of their enemies; the description of their beliefs and deeds were written by men who were bitter in their hatred and antagonism; the men who drowned them, tortured and burned them, and their records were burned with their bodies; their books were everywhere sought out and destroyed. No public library would receive and preserve them, so that we know only the titles of their works, and these have been preserved to us only in writings of their enemies.

Therefore as aforementioned, to answer the question, "What is a Baptist in history?" We must look for those who held to the supreme authority of the Bible and discarded the idea of infant baptism; who contended for a spiritual church membership and for the baptism of believers only, for the absolute freedom of conscience, and therefore for entire freedom from the control of the civil government in religious matters.

The Sufferings of Baptists

For generations it was as much a crime to be a Baptist as to be a murderer. They had no protection for life or limb or property. For teaching any of the great truths which we treasure or for baptizing a believing convert, that most glorious privilege of a Baptist minister—for these things they were burned alive, buried alive, even boiled alive. Some were torn to pieces on the rack; some were torn with red-hot tongs; some were hanged on trees, some plunged into the water, some executed with the sword. The accounts of their persecution seem like the memory of some frightful dream. It seems incredible that no less than three million Christians should have been murdered for their faith before the year 312, yet historians tell us of 30,000 Waldensians butchered and thrown into a single heap at the instigation of the Holy Catholic campaign and of 200,000 destroyed in a few months, and this followed by other and still other massacres until the heart grows sick. To get some idea of the awfulness of Baptist sufferings, think how numerous they were: In the year 1530 there was scarcely a village in the Netherlands

3

where they were not found, and in many localities they were the leading influence. Behold their churches in city after city after city and province after province—all over the German empire—yet they were exterminated. They were systematically hunted out, as men hunt wolves with the set purpose of their complete annihilation.

The Electors of Hesse, Germany, commended the zeal of King Henry VIII who had banished Baptists, giving them twelve days to leave his kingdom or pain of death if they disobeyed, in these words: "There are no rulers in Germany, whether they be Baptists or Protestants, that do suffer these men. If they come into their hands all men punish them quickly." And so Peter of Bruys and thousands of his adherents were burned for being Baptist (1126). Felix Manx was executed by drowning in 1527. In 1528 Hubmeyer was burned, and his loyal wife who encouraged him to stand fast in the faith was shortly afterwards thrown into the Danube with her feet tied. Bunyan, the tinker and typical Baptist preacher, languished in Bedford Jail for years, but the world was the richer for the wonderful allegory, "Pilgrim's Progress," written while thus imprisoned. The name of Hubmeyer was honored, his courage and sacrifice vindicated, at the Fourth Congress of the Baptist World Alliance, held in Toronto, Canada, in June, 1928. Thousands of delegates from every section of the globe met to demonstrate their Baptist belief that truth crushed to earth will rise again.

We have seen that hatred of Baptists was not confined to Europe. In England public attention was brought to their meetings and preachings of justification in 1575, and they were persecuted from that time until the law called the Act of Toleration, was passed in 1689, giving them liberty to worship as they pleased.

It was a Baptist, General Thomas, who opposed Cromwell as being "unrepublican," (1657).

Baptists in America

In the New World, Baptists first appear in the records treating of Rev. Roger Williams, who was formerly a clergyman of the Church of England, but who left England in December, 1630, to escape the tyrannical persecutions visited upon those who advocated the religious principles laid down in the New Testament. He met with much opposition, not only in Boston, but throughout New England, wherever he tried to settle. Driven from place to place in mid-winter, and forced to leave his family, he sought refuge among the Indians and soon gained their confidence and friendship. He founded a colony which he called, "Providence" in commemoration of the guidance and provision which God decreed should follow his efforts and desire to obey the Holy Spirit's dictates. After getting established, he was joined by a few friends in what afterward became the State of Rhode Island. Here he was enabled to carry out his twofold plan of acting as both minister and lawgiver. He was the first in America to recognize and insist upon equal rights for all. IT WAS THE PRINCIPLES WHICH HE HAD ENUNCIATED AND LAID DOWN THAT THE 13 STATES ADOPTED WHEN THEY UNITED TO FORM A GOVERNMENT.

These same principles of Baptists' self-government, freedom, and liberty have grown and prospered until mankind the world over has planted sprigs of this wonderful tree.

The record says: "Roger Williams baptized one Ezekiel Holliman and immediately after was himself baptized by Holliman," (March 1639).

In 1658 we have an account of William Wickenden, the Baptist,who was driven out from New York City.

In Massachusetts John Clark, a New England Baptist, asked Governor Endicott, "What law of God or man have I broken?" and was answered "You have denied infant baptism and you deserve death." In Haverhill, Mass., the town sheriff ordered Hezekiah Smith "off the earth."

Massachusetts went so far as to pass laws against Baptists in November, 1644, and the following charge was brought against them:

They would not permit worldly affairs to enter into their religious life. And, in the New World as in the Old, they received abusive treatment at the hands of those who were the governing powers of that day. Their property was seized and sold; their bodies were rended with three-corded whips; they were hanged, tortured, and imprisoned.

Strange to relate the Baptist denomination seems to thrive on difficulties and opposition, for in Virginia where persecution was terrific, their numbers grew exceedingly, but in Maryland where Lord Baltimore's lenient laws gave some form of freedom to all religions, Baptists are, to this day, comparatively few in number.

Taylor, in *Baptists in Virginia*,[5] tells us of their sorrows and yet that no amount of cruelty could turn them aside from that narrow path.

---

[5]By James Barnett Taylor, 1804-1871. Ed.

Chapter II

To the Negro pioneer preachers, many of whom preached the gospel in log cabons with dirt floors, thereby laying the foundation upon which our brick church houses of today stand.
"History of Louisiana Baptists"—By Wm. Hicks, D.D.

Salvation is essential to Baptism and Church membership. Here, if nowhere else, Baptists stand absolutely alone. The foot of no other denomination in Christendom rests on this plank. Blood before water—the altar before the laver. This principal eliminates not only all infant baptism and membership, but locates the adult's remission of sins in the fountain of blood instead of the fountain of water.

PIONEER PREACHERS

The Negro preacher of early days brought to his work a sincerity of Christian character, a grasp of divine truth—"Thus saith the Lord"—a vivid imagination, and a fervid power as a preacher that stirred the heart and commanded respect and recognition from White and Black alike. He had little or no education but possessed strong piety and a keen sense of the dignity of pastoral office and the responsibility thereof, although his discipline was often severe; manifesting the spirit of the disciples in his untiring zeal to save the souls of the unconverted. It is said that Andrew Bryan, whom many historians claim as pastor of the First Negro Baptist church (The First African Baptist Church) could neither read nor write. Another Negro preacher of early days is thus described: "He was uncouth in appearance, his coarse shirt unfastened at the neck, his bare toes revealed through the holes in his heavy shoes, his trousers ragged—but when he had finished, I, with the rest, was in tears, and the sense of my guilt as a sinner never left me until I surrendered my life to Christ."

The list is a long and brilliant one. In antebellum days, it includes names which are immortal in our archives; George Lisle, a Negro, who was the first American Baptist foreign missionary, preceding William Carey, the renowned European missionary, by at least fifteen years. Lisle, though handicapped by the chains of human slavery and hampered by law-enforced ignorance, incurring the penalties of being a Negro, rose above all these degrading circumstances and became the chief human factor in the salvation of Jamaica, the most beautiful island in the Caribbean Sea. Mr. Sharp, the master of Elder Lisle, himself being a deacon of a Baptist church, emancipated this stirring preacher so that he might give himself wholly to the preaching of the gospel. A few years later Mr. Sharp died. The inference is that Lisle had been very outspoken in favor of the British Red Coats which seems plausible from the fact that his former master and benefactor was on that side. As the British prepared to evacuate Savannah, the Sharp children laid their plans to re-enslave Lisle, either as a punishment for his expressed sympathy for the Red Coats, or because of their insatiable love for gold. Whatever the reason for such an ungodly act, the thought of being re-enslaved must have well-nigh crushed this unfettered soul; hence he made a hasty and successful effort to borrow $700 to move himself and family beyond the reach of the children of Deacon Sharp, his former owner, and on reaching the island he lived so economically that he saved enough money to reimburse his benefactor. To Lisle belongs the honor of possibly being the first ordained Negro Baptist preacher in the New World. He preached in Georgia during the Revolutionary War, and his ministry was greatly blessed by a number of converts whom he baptized in the Savannah River. At the close of the war he went to Jamaica as the indentured servant of Col. Kirkland, an English officer. On getting settled in his new home on the island, Lisle was so deeply impressed with the sad conditions of superstition and ignorance in which he found the Negroes of Kingston, that he determined to do something to alleviate this state of affairs. He preached first at the race tracks and on the street but later hired a room at his own expense and organized a little Baptist church consisting of four persons.

Others joined him in forming a church which grew until in less than eight years he had baptized 500 persons.

In 1789 he builded a chapel, and in spite of the relentless storm of persecution which he encountered, during which time he was imprisoned, placed in the stocks, and finally tried for his life, for preaching "sedition." From 1805 to 1814, a law forbidding all preaching to slaves was strictly carried out. One man was hung for preaching and baptizing—but their labor bore fruit and when in 1814 Baptists in England were moved by letters of appeal from Lisle and others to send missionaries, they found the people ready to greet them and cooperate in their work, because of the pioneer mission work established by George Lisle thirty-five years before.

To give our readers a more intimate insight into the life and struggles of our denominational racial group in Jamaica, it should be borne in mind that they (English missionaries) found George Lisle an honest, conscientious Christian man. He borrowed money from one Colonel Kirkland, who it seems, was in Georgia, which paid the passage for himself, wife, and four children in Jamaica. In the face of all sorts of barriers, within two years the last cent of the borrowed money had been paid back.

Personal Letter of George Lisle
(Page 122, N.B.C. Minutes, 1915)

The first Baptist church was organized in 1784, in Kingston. A personal letter written to Dr. Rippen, of London, in 1791, will show more fully the character, work, and struggle of this man.

"I cannot tell what my age is, as I have no account of the time of my birth, but I suppose I am about 40 years old. I have a wife and four children. My wife was baptized by me in Savannah, and I have every satisfaction in life from her. She is much the same age as myself. My eldest son is 19 years, my next son, 17, and the third, 14, and the last child, a girl of 11 years. They are all members of the church. My occupation is a farmer, but as the seasons of this part of the country are uncertain, I also keep a team of horses and wagons for the carrying of goods from one place to another, which I attend myself, with the assistance of my sons, and by this way of life have gained the good will of the public, who recommended me to the business and to some very principal work for the government. I have a few good books, some good old authors and sermons, and one large Bible that was given me by a gentleman. A good many of our members can read, and are all desirous to learn. They will be very thankful for a few books to read on Sundays and other days.

"There is no Baptist church in this country but ours. We have purchased a piece of land at the east end of Kingston, containing three acres, for the sum of $775, and on it we have begun a meeting house, 57 feet in length by 37 feet in breadth. We have raised the brick wall eight feet high from the foundation, and intend to have a gallery.... The chief part of our congregation are slaves, and their owners allow them, in common, but three or four bits a week to feed themselves, and out of so small a sum we cannot expect anything that can be of service from them; if we did, it would soon bring scandal upon religion. The free people in our society are poor, but they are willing, both free and slaves, to do what they can. As for my part, I am too much entangled with the affairs of the world to go on, as I would, with my design in supporting the cause. This has, I acknowledge, been a Great hindrance to the gospel in one way; but I have endeavored to set a good example of good industry before the inhabitants of the land, it has given general satisfaction in another way. And, reverend sir, we think the Lord has put the power of the Baptist societies in England and to help and assist us in completing this building, which we look upon to be the greatest undertaking in this country for the bringing of souls from darkness into the light of the gospel. And as the Lord has put it in your heart to inquire after us, we place all of our confidence in you to make our circumstances known to the several Baptist churches in England, and we look upon you as our father, friend and brother. Within the brick walls we have a shelter in which we worship until our building can be accomplished.

"Your letter was read in the church two or three times, and did a great deal of love and warmness throughout the congregation, and we shouted for joy and comfort to think that the Lord has been so gracious as to satisfy us in this country, with the same kind of religion of our beloved brethren in the old country, according to the Scriptures, and that such a worthy_____[sic] of London could write so loving a letter to such poor worms as we are. And I beg leave to say that the whole congregation sang out they would, through the assistance of God, remember you in their prayers. They all together give their Christian love to you and all the worthy professors of Jesus Christ in your church at London, and beg the prayers of your churches in general and of our congregation wherever it pleases you to make known our circumstances. I remain, with the utmost love, reverend sir, your unworthy fellow laborer, servant and brother in Christ.

—George Lisle.

P.S.—We have chosen twelve trustees, all of whom are members of our church, whose names are specified in the title: the title proved and recorded in the Secretary's office of this island."

A list headed "Native Baptist Preachers" contains seven names, and adds, "Founded by George Lisle."

As a direct fruit of their efforts, in 1842 more than forty Jamaica missionaries left the island to Christianize the heathen in Africa.

Back in America, George Lisle had baptized among many other converts, Andrew Bryan, who was destined to carry on the work which Lisle had begun. Bryan was also a slave and after his conversion, showed such talent for exhorting that his master and some other White friends encouraged him to continue teaching the Bible and holding regular meetings. His success was so remarkable that when, on January 20, in 1788 a pioneer White Baptist minister visited Georgia, he found in Savannah a little group of forty-five believers ready for baptism. He ordained Bryan to the ministry, and as pastor of the infant church Bryan served until his death in 1812. This is the First African Baptist church, which, in spite of many vicissitudes, changes, and trials, has endured to the present.

David George, born a slave in 1742, went to Halifax, Nova Scotia in 1782, with many other Colored and White persons, and organized a church with six members at Shelburne. In his case, as in countless others, misplaced confidence caused the migration. The occasion arose during the Revolutionary War. While the contest was raging, both sides made overtures to the slaves, "If our side win, we will free you in return for your services," said the colonists. "Fight on our side and when we put down the rebellion, you shall be free," promised the British. But when independence came, neither side remembered the past promise.

Jesse Peters, a helper of George Liele, who refused to line up with the British but remained loyal to the American colonists and did not follow the British forces to Nova Scotia, Jamaica, and to freedom. He also helped Rev. Matthew Moore in 1788, in the reorganization of the First African Baptist Church in Savannah, Ga., and who also led the Silver Bluff Church to Augusta, Ga., where it seems to still exist as the Springfield Baptist Church.

It is worthy to note that the first Baptist doctrine ever preached in Louisiana was the gospel as expounded by **Elder Joseph Willis** at the peril of his life, being a Negro and a Baptist. He organized the first association in the state. This, the Louisiana Baptist Association, had a membership of both White and Colored churches. In Alabama, one **Caesar McLemore** was bought by the Alabama Baptist Association in order that he might give his full time to preaching.

In Virginia, a Negro named **Jacob Blackwell** was bought by the Virginia Baptist Association and called to a White church, but as *The Chronicler* naïvely informs us, of course, as might have been expected, this would not do in Virginia.

Leonard Grimes, although born free, was indefatigable in his labors in behalf of the Underground Railroad, working night and day to secure the freedom and security of runaway slaves. Rev. Grimes served as the gifted and faithful pastor of the Twelfth Baptist Church, Boston, Mass., for more than twenty-five years.

Rev. Edmund Kelly deserves special notice from those who would read of our denominational beginnings. Born a slave in Columbia, Tenn., his master hired him out to wait tables in a boarding school where the students took delight in teaching him to read. He was sixteen years old before he learned his letters. Finally, he was able to write a "pass" which was a faithful copy of his master's handwriting, and with its aid, he escaped to Massachusetts. Once in the North, his ready mind found means for further cultivation. He was a splendid organizer and established several churches which still flourish to this day. The Calvary Baptist Church, Haverhill, Mass., bears on its wall a tablet inscribed "Sacred to the memory of Rev. Edmund Kelly, first pastor of Calvary Baptist Church." . . .He was not only a splendid preacher, but was foremost in helping refugees escaping from the South to find friends, work, and economic independence in their new environment. His letters to various newspapers give an appealing picture of the life and thought of the times just preceding and subsequent to the Civil War. In another part of this booklet will be found a few of these communications.

Rev. Kelly speaks in his diary, or scrap book, of the work of the American Baptist Missionary Convention, which was organized in New York.

Lott Carey, "The Father of West African Missions," was another preacher of the old regime, who caught the vision of foreign mission work for the heathen in Africa and was the first to sail from America to that part of the continent. His striking career may be briefly summed up as follows:

Born 1780
Hired in tobacco factory 1804
Converted 1807
Bought freedom for himself and two children $850.00 1813
Organized Missionary Society,
First Baptist Church,Richmond, Va. 1815
Gave up salary of $800.00 per year to go to Africa 1820
Sailed for Liberia, January 23, ... 1821
Organized First Baptist Church, Liberia 1822

Lott Carey was born a slave about the year 1780, thirty miles below the city of Richmond, in the county of Charles City. His father was an eminently pious member of the Baptist denomination, and his mother, although unconnected with any church, gave pleasing evidence that she had passed from death unto life. He was their only child. From the character which his parents sustained, no room is left to doubt that they endeavored to bring him up in the fear and admonition of the Lord.

Nothing can be learned of his early history. Whether in the days of_____[sic] youth he exhibited indications of vigorous intellect, of special seriousness on eternal realities, is not known. In the year 1804, he was removed from his native county to the city of Richmond and employed as a common laborer in the Shockoe Tobacco Warehouse. At that time he had become rather dissipated in his habits, being frequently intoxicated, and allowing himself to indulge in profane swearing. He became increasingly vicious for two or three years after his settlement in Richmond.

Having been led to the discovery of his ruined condition as a rebel against the skies, he turned to the Lord with full purpose of heart, and rejoiced in Christ Jesus as the Savior of sinners. An immediate and remarkable change was discovered in his life. He whose tongue was wont to profane the name of the Most High, was now taught to address him in accents of prayer and praise. He was baptized by Elder John Courtney, and joined the First Baptist Church in the city of Richmond in the year 1807. At this time he was exceedingly ignorant, not knowing even the alphabet. The circumstances which led to the improvement of his mental powers were somewhat remarkable.

Being a regular attendant on the ministry of Elder Courtney, he heard his pastor deliver a discourse on one occasion, on the conversation between Christ and Nicodemus, and became so deeply interested in the rich truths contained in that portion of the sacred pages, that he determined to become qualified to read it for himself. Accordingly he procured a Testament, and commenced learning his letters in the chapter referred to, nor did he rest satisfied until he had accomplished his purpose. Some assistance was rendered by young gentlemen at the warehouse, and in a short time he was able with distinctness to read the third chapter of John. He soon afterwards learned to write.

About this period he began to hold meetings among the Colored people of Richmond, and to exhort them to flee the wrath to come. After a sufficient trial of his capacity to be useful as a public speaker, the church encouraged him to exercise his gifts in preaching the gospel. Not only did he labor among those of his own color in the city of Richmond, but in all the surrounding country. He now applied himself diligently to the improvement of his mind, and for several years made advances in knowledge. His leisure time at the warehouse was employed in reading, and it is said that a gentleman on one occasion taking up a book which he left for a few moments, found it to be Smith's *Wealth of Nations*.[6] While thus engaged in storing his mind with valuable information he was kindly assisted by two or three benevolent individuals, who took a lively interest in his prosperity. While an increasing interest in the work of preaching the gospel was cherished, he became more and more respected, and useful in his services at the warehouse. A brother who was intimately acquainted with him, states that his services at the warehouse were highly estimated, but of their real value no one except a dealer in tobacco can form an idea. Notwithstanding the hundreds of hogsheads that were committed to his charge, he could produce any one the instant it was called for; and the shipments were made with a promptness and correctness, such as no person, White or Black, has equalled in the same situation. For this correctness and fidelity, he was highly esteemed and frequently rewarded by the merchant with a five-dollar note. He was allowed, also, to sell for his own benefit, many small parcels of waste tobacco.

In the year 1813, having by rigid economy accumulated a considerable sum, with the assistance of the merchants to whose interest he had been devoted, he purchased the freedom of himself and two children, for $850. He had previously lost his first wife by death, and about the year 1815, was married a second time. He now received a regular salary, which from time to time was increased; until the year before he left the warehouse, it amounted to $800 per annum. During this period, he also made frequent purchases and shipments of tobacco, on his own account: in one instance to the number of twenty-four hogsheads. Some time about the year 1815 he was, to a great extent, instrumental in awakening among his Colored brethren in the city of Richmond a lively interest on behalf of the spiritual condition of Africa. This was shortly after the formation of the Baptist General Convention. Missionary intelligence was at different times placed within his reach; and his own heart becoming affected by the miserable condition of the heathen world, he soon communicated something of his own feelings to those by whom he was surrounded. This resulted in the origination of the Richmond African Missionary Society, which for several years contributed from $100 to $150 for African missions. But he was not satisfied with these efforts.

The struggle between worldly advantage, and an imperious sense of duty, was long and desperate. On the one hand, he was comfortably settled in his native state; was the possessor of a small farm, and high in the confidence of

---

[6]*An Inquiry into the Nature and Cause of the Wealth of Nations*, by Adam Smith (1723-1790), A. Strahan and T. Caldwell, London, 1786. Ed.

his employers and the public generally, was receiving for his services a handsome salary beside, he was the object of universal affection, as a preacher among his own color; they exercised almost unbounded confidence in him. On the other hand, the facilities for laboring in Africa were far from being numerous; the climate was sickly, and there was a strong probability that he would early fall a victim to the African fever. But none of these things moved him; he was willing to leave all, and to venture all for Christ, and for the sake of those who were perishing for lack of vision, in a far distant land. When a ministering brother inquired why he could determine to quit a station of so much comfort and usefulness, to encounter the dangers of an African climate, and hazard everything to plant a colony on a distant heathen shore;—his reply was to this effect: "I am an African, and in this country, however meritorious my conduct, and respectable my character, I cannot receive the credit due to either. I wish to go to a country where I shall be estimated by my merits, and not by my complexion; and I feel bound to labor for my suffering race." He seemed to have imbibed the sentiment of Paul, and to have great heaviness and continual sorrow in his heart for his brethren, his kinsmen according to the flesh. When it was ascertained by his employers that he was contemplating a removal to Africa, they offered to raise his salary to $1000, if he would remain in this country. But this inducement had no influence in changing his views of duty.

Early in the year 1819, the Journal of Messrs. Mills and Burgess, in their exploring agency for the American Colonization Society, on the coast of Africa, was published; and, also, several letters from Colored residents at Sierra Leone, inviting the free Colored people of the United States to come and join them. These produced an immediate determination in Lott Carey and Collin Teage, to remove to Africa. The following extract of a letter, written by Mr. William Crane to Rev. O.B. Brown, of Washington City—then a member of the board of managers of the American Colonization Society, and also of the Board of the Baptist General Convention—was the means of their becoming connected with both these bodies. It is dated as follows:

"Richmond, March 28th, 1819

"You will probably recollect, that I introduced you to two of our Colored brethren in this place who are accustomed to speak in public: one named Collin Teage, the other Lott Carey. Ever since the missionary subject has been so much agitated in this country, these two brethren, associated with many others, have been wishing they could, in some way, aid their unhappy kindred in Africa; and I suppose you have heard of their having formed a missionary society for this sole purpose. Some letters published in No. VI of the Luminary, have served to awaken them effectually. They are now determined to go themselves to Africa; and the only questions with them are, in what way will it be best for them to proceed? and what previous steps are requisite to be taken? They think it necessary to spend some time in study first. They both possess industry and abilities, such as, with the blessing of providence, would soon make them rich. It is but two or three years since either of them enjoyed their freedom; and both have paid large sums for their families. They now possess but little, except a zealous wish to go and do what they can. Brother Lott has a wife and several little children. He has a place a little below Richmond, that cost him $1500, but will probably not sell for more than $1000, at this time. Brother Collin has a wife, a son of fourteen years of age, and a daughter of eleven, for whom he has paid $1300 and has scarcely anything left. Both their wives are Baptists; their children amiable and docile, have been to school considerably; and I hope, if they go, will likewise be of service. Collin is a saddler and harness maker. He had no early education. The little that he has gained has been by chance and piecemeal. He has judgment, and as much keenness of penetration as almost any man. He can read, though he is not a good reader, and can write so as to make out a letter. The little knowledge he has of figures has been gained by common calculations in business. Lott was brought up on a farm; and for a number of years has been chief manager among the laborers in the largest tobacco warehouse in this city. He has charge of receiving, marking, and shipping tobacco; and the circumstance that he receives $700 a year wages may help you to form an estimate of the man. He reads better than Collin, and is, in every respect, a better scholar. They have been trying to preach about ten or eleven years, and are both about forty years of age.

"They would be glad to receive the patronage of some public body, and wish advice how to proceed. I had thought of addressing the corresponding secretary on their behalf, for the patronage of the American Baptist Mission Society; but again thought that the Colonization Society might be pleased with taking them under their care, and that their mission might bear a more imposing aspect under the auspices of this society than it would with the Baptists alone. But should they go under the Colonization Society, they would feel themselves attached to the mission cause, and would wish some connection with the general board. We are desirous of your thoughts upon the subject. In a little time they can be ready to engage. They would go to Sierra Leone, but will submit that to the decision of their patrons. It would,

I suppose, be somewhere between the tropics, on the western coast. Their object is to carry the tidings of salvation to the benighted Africans. They wish to be where their color will be no disparagement to their usefulness. I suppose the funds of our African Mission Society here, after their next meeting, on Monday after Easter, will probably amount to $600 which I believe the society will be willing to appropriate to the aid of their brethren, should they go. Brother Bryce will also write to you on this subject."

On the presentation of this letter, they were immediately received as emigrants by the board of the Colonization Society, and at the meeting of the board of the Baptist General Convention, in April, they were both recognized as their missionaries; a variety of obstacles, however, prevented their departure till January, 1821. The year 1820 was devoted to study with a view to their future usefulness in Africa. The following brief extract from the instructions of the board of the convention, deserves a place here.

"Philadelphia, January 6, 1821
"The board of managers of the General Convention of the Baptist denomination in the United States, to their Colored brethren, Collin Teage and Lott Carey, present the assurance of their sincere and affectionate esteem. They have heard with pleasure, that by a vessel about to sail from Norfolk to the coast of Africa, an opportunity is presented for accomplishing those benevolent desires which, for many months past, you have been led to entertain. At the same time, they possess a deep anxiety for your preservation, in a country where so many colonists have recently found a grave. They most fervently commend you to the gracious protection of that God in whose hand your breath is, and whose are all your ways. May you make the Lord your refuge, even the Most High your habitation. It is a source of much encouragement, that you will be able to collect useful information from the experience of your predecessors; and it is hoped that, by the advice of your brethren who have already reached the shores of your forefathers you will be enabled to adopt, the most prudent measures for health and safety of yourselves and families.

"The board earnestly recommends, what they cheerfully anticipate, that your conduct before your fellow passengers on the ocean, be pious and exemplary. Endeavor to secure their good will by every office of kindness; and, above all, cherish and discover a solemn concern for their everlasting salvation. Arrived in Africa, you will find much that will require patience, and mutual counsel. You will have to bear with prejudices that have descended on the minds of the inhabitants, after having cherished for ages, and to instill the sacred truths of the gospel with meekness and wisdom. While your conduct shall be without blame, the board advises you, in your ministry, to dwell much on the doctrine of the cross, a doctrine which has been found in every age of the church of Christ, the power of God.

"They pray that the grace of our Lord Jesus Christ may be with you, with your families, and with all who sail or settle with you; and the American Colonization Society and all its sister institutions, may be rendered instrumental in diffusing literary, economical, and evangelical light, from the Mediterranean to the Cape of Good Hope, and from the Atlantic to the Red Sea and Indian Ocean.

By order of the board,
Wm. STARGHTON,
Corresponding Secretary"

Within a few days after the reception of this letter, an opportunity of sailing for the field of their labors occurred. Elder Carey delivered a farewell sermon in the meeting house of the First Baptist Church, Richmond. It was a melting season. His auditors hung with intense earnestness upon his parting words, many of them sorrowing that they should see his face no more. His discourse was founded on Romans 8:32, "He that spared not his own Son, but delivered him up for us all, how shall he not with him also freely give us all things?" His sermon was well arranged throughout, was entirely clear of the senseless rant too common with many pious Colored preachers. He spoke with a deep sense of the weighty character he had assumed—and enlarged particularly, with amazing pathos on the freeness of the salvation disclosed in his text. He urged as an example worthy the imitation of men, the amazing love of God in not withholding his own Son, when a race of miserable sinners were exposed to the curse of his violated law, and dwelt much on the disinterested and immeasurable sacrifice which the Father of spirits had made. It is to be regretted that portions of this discourse could not have been preserved, as it is said by those who were present, that it contained many touches of the true sublime. In the close of his sermon he remarked in substance: "I am about to leave you, and expect to see your faces no more. I long to preach to the poor Africans the way of life and salvation. I don't know what may befall me, whether I may find a grave in the ocean, or among the savage men, or more savage wild beasts on the coast of Africa; nor am I anxious what may become of me. I feel it my duty to go, and I very much fear, that many of those who preach the gospel

17

in this country, will blush when the Saviour calls them to give an account of their labors in his cause, and tells them, 'I commanded you to go into all the world, and preach the gospel to every creature,' and with most thrilling emphasis, looking round on his audience, he exclaimed, The Saviour may ask, Where have you been? what have you been doing? have you endeavored to the utmost of your ability to fulfil the commands I gave you? or have you sought your own gratification, and your own ease, regardless of my commands?"

Collin Teage, who was for many years frequently associated with him in preaching, in and about Richmond, and whose opinion may deserve some weight, was in the habit of saying soberly, that he considered his Brother Carey the greatest preacher he was in the habit of hearing. They were both publicly ordained and set apart as missionaries to Africa, in the First Baptist Church in Richmond, of which church they were both members. A few days before he sailed he wrote, in conjunction with Elder Collin Teage, to the corresponding secretary of the board, as follows:

Richmond, January 11, 1821

"Rev. and Dear Sir:

We have no other way to express our gratitude to the board but through you. We feel very much rejoiced that we have now to communicate to you, that our long beclouded prospect of getting to Africa has opened upon us. We expect to leave here with our families tomorrow morning on our way to Norfolk, there to remain but a very few days, before we shall hoist our sails for Africa in the brig *Nautilus*, with our Bibles, and our utensils, and our hopes in God our Saviour.

"But we must not omit to beg that the board will receive our thanks for the assistance we have received from them, and particularly for the very kind letters we have received from you this day; and we are happy to inform them that through their favor, and the kindness and assistance of our friends here, we think we are supplied with what may be necessary for our comfort for some time, more especially, as we understand, that provisions are supplied by government. We expect to write to you when we arrive at our destined place, and will always be grateful to you for any communications you may send us."

The late Rev. John O. Choules, D.D., of Newport, Rhode Island, who, while attending a Baptist Convention at Richmond, Virginia, had a conversation with an officer of the Baptist church in that city at whose home he was a guest, says: I asked him if he did not apprehend that the slaves would eventually rise and exterminate their master.

"Why God has made a providential opening, a merciful safety valve, and now I do not feel alarmed, in the prospect of what is coming."

"What do you mean," said Mr. Choules, "by Providence opening a merciful safety valve?"

"Why," said the gentleman, "I will tell you. The slave traders come from the cotton and sugar plantations of the South, and are willing to buy up more slaves than we can part with. We must keep a stock for the purpose of breeding, but we part with the most dangerous, and the demand is very constant, and is likely to be so, for when they go to those Southern states, the average existence is only five years."—*The Present State of Things.*

A person who is in good standing in our church, a few months since (in April 1855), sold a member of the church to a Southern slaveholder. Then the poor fellow was delivered to his new owner, they had to tie him, hand and foot, and throw him upon a dray, and sent him in this way to the steamboat that was to convey him to the New Orleans slave market.—*The Present State of Things.*

Drs. Wm. J. Simmons, author of *Men of Mark: Eminent, Progressive, and Rising*,[7] and J.T. White, Senator of Arkansas, entered politics during the period when to be a Negro leader was almost inevitably to be drawn into the complex "Reconstruction" political situations.

Negro Baptists also endured various sorts of hardships and afflictions. In witness of this we cite the records of floggings, of being put in the stocks, of imprisonment, and even the threats of death undergone by George Lisle in Jamaica; in Georgia Andrew Bryan was, with bleeding back, thrust into prison; besides the facts related by historian Holcombe concerning the heart-rending fate which befell our Negro Baptist brethren in Alabama, the whole path which human slavery inflicted upon those who prayed.

Possibly the ugliest blot upon the pages of American history is revealed in the actions of the colonists in employing Negroes to help them drive out the British Red Coats and later rewarding the Black men for their faithfulness and courage by riveting the chains of slavery but the more firmly at the successful termination of the Revolutionary War. A Negro Baptist preacher, whose name we are unable to ascertain, but who was a co-worker in the gospel with George Lisle, was hung for "preaching and baptizing" in Jamaica during the period 1805-1814.

In 1835 the Rev. W.C. Monroe was ordained in New York and went to

---

[7]The 1887 edition was reprinted in 1968 by Arno Press. Ed.

proclaim the Word in Port-au-Prince, Hayti. Here he underwent so many trials, reverses and discouragements that he was forced to give up the work.

In 1842 one Keith, a Negro Baptist, sold "all he possessed except a few clothes" and leaving his beloved wife in this country, worked his passage out to Africa whence he had been stolen years before. He had the satisfaction of preaching the message of salvation on the identical spot where he had been captured.

Many of these preachers were leaders in more than a spiritual sense.

REV. Wm.W. COLLEY, D.D.

Foremost in the organization of the National Baptist Convention; first Corresponding Secretary and first missionary to African fields of that body. Born in Prince Edwards County, Virginia, February 12, 1847. Died in Winston-Salem, N.C., December 24, 1909.

REV. W.H. McALPINE, D.D.

First president of the National Baptist Convention. He served two terms and refused a third election. Founder and second president of Selma University and editor of the *Baptist Pioneer*, a state paper. Born in Buckingham County, Virginia, June, 1847; died in Selma, Ala., 1905.

REV. J.M. ARMSTEAD, D.D.

Born in Lynchburg, Va. Educated in Tennessee and Virginia. President Virginia Baptist Convention for 14 years. First recording secretary of our National Baptist organized work. He served as pastor of Zion Baptist Church, Portsmouth, Va., for 43 years. He died Dec. 1, 1929, full of years and good works.

Chapter III

"The name 'Baptist' has been applied to distinguish us from others, and it serves as a convenient designation. In former times it was Anabaptists, meaning rebaptizers because then, as now, all who were received into our churches on profession of their faith in Christ, were according to his command baptized, whether the ceremony of infant sprinkling had been performed or not."—W. B. Bogg.

"If there be any irregularity in doctrine or practice anywhere, it is the result of ignorance rather than erroneous convictions. The present, and for many years to come, the great work of our ministry must be that of development, particularly along the line of Baptist doctrine and work. Much has been done by the living voice to train and lead the people, but the time has come when the pen must also be employed. Our trained leaders must write."—Edward McKnight Bradley, D.D., The Negro Baptist Pulpit.

PIONEER CHURCHES

The early history of the Negro Baptists in the United States is closely interwoven with that of the White Baptists, and yet from the period following the War of the American Revolution until the present day, there have been distinctive Negro Baptist churches—that is, churches whose members, officers, and pastors were of the Negro race. The first organization of this kind of which there is any record was at Silver Bluff, in Aiken County, S.C. It was formed by eight slaves on the plantation of George Galphin in a settlement on the Savannah River, near Augusta, Ga., and appears to have dated from some years previous to 1776. Two of the slaves who were constituent members of this church became noted preachers. One of them, David George, was pastor until the capture of Savannah by the British in 1778. Subsequently, he founded the First Baptist church at Shelburne, Canada, and went from there to Freetown, Sierra Leone, West Africa, in 1792. The other, Jesse Peters, helped Abraham Marshal (White) reorganize the

First African Baptist Church at Savannah in 1788, where there had already been a Negro Baptist church since 1778, of which it seems George Lisle was pastor at one time. Since then there has always been somewhere in the county of Chatham, Ga., a Negro Baptist church.

The First African Baptist Church of Savannah grew, and in 1802 and 1805, two other churches were organized, the Second Baptist Church and the Ogeechee Baptist Church, both of which are still in existence and are strong and prosperous. In 1805 the Joy Street Baptist Church, the first Negro church in New England, was organized in Boston; in 1808 the Abyssinian Church in New York City; in 1809 the First African Baptist Church in Philadelphia. These three were the first Negro Baptist churches in the North.

The First Baptist Church of Washington, D.C., was organized in 1802, including in its membership many Negro people. In 1833, when the congregation moved to a new edifice, the Negro members were encouraged to continue in the old church which they finally purchased.

Another type of Baptist churches had White pastors. Often the minister was of very high character, zealous, and earnest. Such a man was the pastor of the first Colored church at Richmond, Va., who during his twenty-five-year pastorate baptized more than three thousand souls. Then there was the "Colored Branch" type of church. This, in actual operation, was really two organizations in one. The "Colored Branch" had its own officers and received and disciplined its own members under the purely nominal guidance of the White church members. Some notable examples of this kind of church were: The First Baptist Church of Montgomery, Ala., and churches at Natchez and Jackson, Miss., and Charleston, S.C. They flourished in pre-war days, and when freedom came in 1865, the old "First Church" of Montgomery had nine hundred members; three hundred in the White section, and six hundred in the "Colored Branch." In the vast number of instances the Negroes were always segregated where they belonged to White churches. Occasionally they sat in the body of the church, but mainly they occupied the galleries. When the sacrament was passed the Negroes were served after the Whites had all finished.

Often an arrangement prevailed whereby the White portion of the church met for worship in the morning, and Negroes in the afternoon. With these and many other disadvantages to overcome, it is not strange that they took the first opportunities to do away with this proscription. So it came to pass that in the decade 1870-1880, or little before, nearly all Negro members had left the churches which had formerly had both White and Black communicants. With absolutely no friction or disagreement, they began to build their own church houses, laying no claim to their former houses of worship, which they had had a double share in paying for, viz., by their own direct contributions and offerings and by really earning by the sweat of their brow the money their masters donated.

There is nothing said historically about the salary of these White pastors, but it is inferred that it was paid by these black folk, and that the meeting houses were directly or indirectly paid for by them, also. The money used by the slaves for religious work was the fruit of self-sacrifice earned on rainy days, holidays, or from their little "patch" of corn, tobacco, or cotton cultivated at night. Thus they gave thousands of dollars earned at odd times and in divers ways toward the salary of their White pastors. They also earned that given by the master for his part of the religious work in the community. Just as a shoat, a calf, a few chickens, may be sold today to enlarge the gift to missions, education, or the rally for a new church building, so the slave owner could sell a slave child, woman, or man to raise his part of any fund. A story is told of a Mr. Prior Lee, in Jackson, Miss., who was happily converted in a revival conducted by his slaves. Wishing to do something to show his gratitude for salvation, he put his slaves to work in a brickyard where they made thousands of bricks which the master donated for the building of the church. These slaves received no money for the sweat and toil put into the making of the bricks. Who then actually made the donation to the church?

At the close of the Civil War there were hundreds of Negro preachers unordained, but disciplined; these men soon found a way to become ordained, and embraced this chance to take over and to minister to these flocks. Starting out therefore with no church property whatever, the total value of their present holdings seems fabulous—$306,357,000. Raised entirely through plans laid by Colored people, and executed by them also, these figures express as nothing else can, the wholehearted fervor and devotion of Negroes to their religious services.

Hardly had the smoke of the Civil War lifted from a hundred battle fields and peace been declared when sympathetic friends—men and women through the American Baptist Home Mission Society, the Freedmans Aid Society, the American Missionary Association and kindred organizations—sent men and women as preachers and teachers to the four and one-half million freedmen in all parts of the southland. To them we are grateful and for them we and our children thank God always. The chance given us through the instruction of these devoted friends from pulpit and schoolroom, did much to make us today the most advanced group of Negroes in the world. Our own people through the American Baptist Missionary Convention composed of Negro churches sent strong men in every former slave state. Be it said to their everlasting credit, they did more to help our race consciousness than all our White friends combined.

In those far-off days the deserted soldier barracks, and in one case even an old slave pen, "Lumpkins' Jail," served us as school buildings. The first school of Negro Baptists was Roger Williams University, Nashville, Tenn., organized in 1864. We have now ninety-six schools, some in grade 'A', and many of fairly high grade, maintained for the purpose of training preachers and teachers; and these denominational schools, with an army of 896 teachers, are rendering splendid service. For more than ten years Southern White Baptists advocated the idea of a seminary for the education of Negro Baptist preachers, and the plan met with a favorable reception from leading Colored Baptists.

Finally, a cooperation was effected by means of a joint commission consisting of leaders of both the Southern Baptist Convention and the National Baptist Convention. The National Baptist Convention furnished forty acres of land near Nashville, and the Nashville Chamber of Commerce together with the Southern Baptist Convention gave the buildings, the total equipment representing a value of at least $100,000.

The Revival Period

Such were the cruelties of American slavery that the slaveholders were forced to seek room for its expansion by the securing of more territory for its protection and growth, hence the Missouri Compromise. As the agitation for the abolition of slavery increased, both the slave and his friends turned to God in prayers for deliverance and relief. Finally through the clash of arms and the Emancipation Proclamation, slavery died. Prayers of thanksgiving, songs of praise and gratitude brought four and one-half million freedmen to their knees before God and gave what we call "The Revival Period." Thousands sought and found forgiveness for sins. Churches were organized by the hundreds. The Civil War had an unusual aftermath. History records that rank infidelity and godlessness were rampant after both the Revolutionary War and the War of 1812. We know that the World War has been followed by excesses in crime and law-breaking, in a general letting-down in moral restraint and a lowering of ideals, but no such state of affairs was true following the "war among brothers." The freedmen struggling in ignorance and poverty were forced to look to the God who had loosed their shackles. Both in the North and in the South this example was also followed by the White people. Particularly the Baptist churches grew and multiplied. The gin houses, barns, brush arbors and friendly shade trees were used as places of worship; tan vats, creeks, ponds, and rivers became baptisteries.

1880

The year 1880 found nearly two million of these former slaves in the Baptist churches alone. The following are among the oldest churches known to us from records gathered here and there:

Harrison St. Baptist Church, Petersburg, Va. 1776

First Baptist Church, Richmond, Va. 1780

First Baptist Church, Williamsburg, Va. 1785

First Baptist Church, Lexington, Ky. 1790

Springfield Baptist Church, Augusta, Ga. 1793

Joy St. Baptist Church, Boston, Mass. 1805

Stone St. Baptist Church, Mobile, Ala. 1806

Abyssinian Baptist Church, New York, N.Y. 1808

First African Baptist Church, Philadelphia, Pa. 1809

Calvary Baptist Church, Louisiana 1812

First Baptist Church, Trenton, N.J. 1812

First Baptist Church, St. Louis, Mo. 1823

First African Baptist Church, New Orleans, La. 1826

Union Baptist Church, Cincinnati, Ohio 1827

Fifth Street Baptist Church, Louisville, Ky. 1829

Union Baptist Church, Philadelphia, Pa. 1832

First Baptist Church, Baltimore, Md. 1836

First Baptist Church, Jacksonville, Fla. 1838

19th Street Baptist Church, Washington, D.C. 1839

Chapter IV

"The name 'Baptist' has been applied to distinguish us from others, and it serves as a convenient designation. In former times it was Anabaptists, meaning rebaptizers because then, as now, all who were received into our churches on profession of their faith in Christ, were, according to his command, baptized, whether the ceremony of infant sprinkling had been performed or not."—W. B. Boggs.

If there be any irregularity in doctrine or practice anywhere, it is the result of ignorance rather than of erroneous convictions. The present, and for many years to come, the great work of our ministry must be that of development, particularly along the line of Baptist doctrine and work. Much has been done by the living voice to train and lead the people, but the time has come when the pen must also be employed. Our trained leaders must write."—Edward McKnight Bradley, D.D., "The Negro Baptist Pulpit."

EARLY BAPTIST ORGANIZATIONS

To the Providence Missionary Baptist District Association of Ohio belongs the distinction of being the first independent Negro organization of Baptist churches in this country. It was founded in 1836 and preceded the Wood River Baptist Association of Illinois by about two years. Both bodies were made up of churches whose members were fugitives who had escaped from slavery in the South, and "free men of color" who were unable to endure their condition in that section, who had settled in large numbers in the cities of the West. The Wood River Baptist Association was also a district body, which had its beginning April 27, 1839, when messengers from the Union Baptist Church, Alton, Ill.; Mt. Zion Baptist Church, Ridge Prairie, Ill.; and Salem Baptist Church, Ogle Creek, Madison County, Ill., met in the home of one Samuel Vinson. They adjourned to hold the first annual meeting in the Mt. Zion Church, Ridge Prairie, Ill., on Friday, September 13, 1839. Elder John Livingston was chosen as moderator. At the time of organization all the state of Illinois was included in its territory. The name "Wood River," was said to have been taken either from the town of that name or from the little "Wood River Creek" which flows through the neighborhood.

In order that the reader may get correct ideas of these early Baptist organizations, we print herewith some letters written by Elder Edmund Kelley, who lived and served with them:

Alexandria, Va., August 30, 1865

Mr. Editor:

Having just concluded the twenty-fifth anniversary of the American Baptist Missionary Convention in this city, and as the readers of the Baptist are interested in the cause of missions in connection with convention, I thought I would pen you a few lines, that all interested might be posted.

First, we organized on the 19th inst., in the First Colored Baptist meeting house by the reappointment of Rev. L.A. Grimes, of Boston, as moderator, and Rev. William T. Dixon, of Brooklyn, N.Y., recording secretary, and Rev. T.D. Miller, of Philadelphia, corresponding secretary. The annual sermon was preached the previous evening by Rev. N. Davis, of Baltimore, Md., from Matthew 28:19,20. The delegation was very large, and the meetings were large and interesting, both in a spiritual and in a temporal point of view. Delegates who were before unrepresented were from Virginia, Tennessee, and Georgia. Churches and societies were received from Richmond, Petersburg, Savannah, and Nashville.

The aggregate salaries of the agents and missionaries appointed this year will amount to about $4,500 or $5,000, so, you see, we are in the work this year. Thank God, the state of things has greatly improved in Washington, D.C., and this part of the Old Dominion within a year's time. The Colored people are evidently looking up; all seem cheerful and at work and are getting along finely. The family in which I am staying own two houses in the city, worth about $500 each. They are very intelligent and pious persons. Four years ago they were both slaves near Warrington, Virginia; when they arrived here they were destitute of everything except what they stood in. They are both members of the church of which Rev. Mr. Robinson, who visited our city last winter to get funds to aid in paying for his church edifice, is pastor. It is a neat house, including an apartment for divine service and another for day and Sabbath schools, both of which are in a flourishing condition. The change here has been very great, since the last year. Then we were proscribed to one corner of the boats and the platform of the street cars, but now the reverse is true. In many respects we have more than our rights conceded at times, for we often find ourselves, since the abolition of the prospective regulations, in possession of room enough upon the boats and in the cars for two or three persons, the rebs and their sympathizers either getting up when we take seats or refusing to take seats when they enter the conveyances.

The religious and educational departments are in a flourishing condition. It would do your soul good to be here and witness the great progress and mighty change for the better within the last few years. We have preached twice, and exhorted incessantly since our arrival here. Our text was, first, Luke 9:62; the second, John 9. Before the close of the convention a delegation of fourteen of our members waited upon President Johnson. Of that delegation I had the honor to be one. Our object was threefold: 1st, to pay our respects to the chief magistrate of this great nation; 2nd, to assure him of our hearty cooperation in the right; 3rd, to remind him of the fact that we have not forgotten his promise to be our Moses. Rev. T.D. Anderson, of Washington, acted as our spokesman. About 9 o'clock, a.m., on Friday, we were ushered into the reception room, and formed into a line, all standing. Next came the President, to whom each member of the delegation was separately introduced. All were cordially received by the President, with a shake of the hand, after which our spokesman mentioned the object of our visit, to which the President responded; first expressed his thanks for our interest manifested in him, and secondly, referred us to his former pledges and acts, stating if they were believed by us he reasserted them, but if not, all that he could say would prove unavailing. Towards the close of the interview some one or two of the delegates spoke of the contrast between Massachusetts and the North generally and the South, to which the President responded with energy and recommenced his speech by saying, "Gentlemen, it's no use to conceal the facts, or to build an argument upon false premises." He again reminded us of our alleged overleaning northern proclivity; also of the black laws of some of the states professing so much interest in the Colored people. See, says he, they have but comparatively few Colored people, and yet they disfranchise them. The President was reminded that in Massachusetts it was different, to which he replied, "Even in Massachusetts the reading and writing test was in force." He was informed that the same test applied to White men; he told us that there were a few laws even in Massachusetts for Colored people that did not apply to White men. Now, says the President, if they meant it, they would set us an example.

The President then referred to our present object, namely equality before the law. He said it was in the future, and how it was to be brought about was yet undecided, and whether if it came it was to be developed in

Some of Our Workers in Darkest Africa

REV. J. J. BUCHANAN.
MIDDLE DRIFT, SO. AFRICA.

MISS E. B. DE LANEY.

REV. L. N. CHEEK.
CHIRADZULU BLANTYRE, B.C. AFRICA

REV. MAJOLA AGBEBI, A.M. PH.D.
LAGOS, W. AFRICA.

MOZAMBIQUE CHANNEL

MADAGASCAR

REV. H. N. BOUY, D.D.

REV. E. B. KOTI.
QUEENS TOWN, SO. AFRICA.

REV. JOHN CHILEMBWE.
CHIRADZULU BLANTYRE, B.C. AFRICA

Of this group only Rev. Landon still sojourns among us in
This land, and Rev. E. B. Koti in far away South Africa.

our amalgamated state or in a separate condition, remained to be seen. We have entered on the first step, commencing with emancipation in our midst. If this fails, the second alternative will be a separate colony, where there will be equality under the same government. The President does not seem to make the distinction upon the ground of complexion, but suggests it as a matter of alleged policy in consequence of the different conditions of the different races. As the result of all that I have seen and heard, I believe President Johnson's want of faith in the immutability and ultimate triumph of right over wrong prevents him from giving the Colored people a fair chance in the race, the first division of which, as he stated, we have entered. We do most heartily commend the President to the affectionate remembrance and prayers and well wishes of all Christians, and to the American people; first that he may become a Christian, and secondly that he may be convinced that not anything is expedient that is not right; that to do right is our duty, leaving the consequences with God. In some respects, our interviews with the lamented Lincoln, and the second meeting with Mr. Johnson presented a comparison, and in others a contrast. In the former we were introduced standing, and then all invited to seats by the President, who conversed freely, the good President leading off.

Yours,

EDMUND KELLEY.

REPORT

of the

NINETEENTH ANNIVERSARY

of the

American Baptist Missionary Convention

HELD IN THE MEETING-HOUSE

of the

FIRST BAPTIST CHURCH, NEWBURG, NEW YORK

New Bedford

Friday, August 19, 1859

Standard Steam Printing House, 67 Union Street.

1859

CONSTITUTION

ARTICLE 1. This body shall be called "THE AMERICAN BAPTIST MISSIONARY CONVENTION." It shall hold its sessions annually, at such time and place as shall be agreed upon at each meeting.

ARTICLE 2. It shall be the object of this convention to propagate the gospel of Christ, and to advance the interests of his kingdom, by supplying vacant churches when requested; by sending ministers into destitute regions within our reach; and by planting and building up churches, whenever a favorable opportunity offers. This convention shall in no case interfere with the internal regulation of the churches or associations.

ARTICLE 3. Every Baptist minister who is in good and regular standing in any regular Baptist church, and who is acceptable to the pastor or pastors of said church or churches, provided he or they are members of this convention, may become a life member by contributing one dollar to its funds. Every church, association, or missionary society, contributing three dollars annually, shall be entitled to one representative, and another for every additional three dollars. Any person may become a member by contributing one dollar annually. None but a Baptist in good and regular standing shall be entitled to vote on questions before the convention.

ARTICLE 4. The officers of this convention shall be a president, vice-president, the secretaries, and a treasurer, and they shall be members of the board, and the board shall not exceed nine in number.

ARTICLE 5. The executive committee shall constitute a board, for the transaction of all business during the recess of the convention. They are to apply the funds appropriated by the convention, on approved missionary fields and laborers. Five members of the board shall constitute a quorum, without which number no business shall be transacted.

ARTICLE 6. The treasurer shall give such security as shall be approved by the convention for all moneys committed to his trust. He shall keep a faithful account of all moneys received and expended, and report the same at each annual meeting. No money shall be drawn from the treasury during the recess of the convention, without an order from the corresponding secretary, signed by the president, or vice-president, and regularly ordered by a majority of the executive committee.

ARTICLE 7. The recording secretary shall keep a faithful record of all the doings of the convention; he shall enroll the names of all the members of the convention, from its origin to the time being, and submit the same for examination at each annual meeting.

ARTICLE 8. The corresponding secretary shall conduct the correspondence of the board. All communications from societies, churches, and individuals, relating to the convention, must be made to him. All letters, papers, packages, &c, officially received by him, shall be the property of the convention. He shall present bills of the postage on the same, and shall present the reports of the doings of the board at each annual meeting, for acceptance and payment. He shall draw drafts on the treasurer, according to Article 6 of this convention.

ARTICLE 9. This constitution may be amended by a vote of two-thirds of the members present at any annual meeting, provided that at least three months' notice has been given to the corresponding secretary, who shall report the same to the annual meeting.

CERTIFICATE OF INCORPORATION
of the
American Baptist Missionary Convention

We, the subscribers, persons of full age, and citizens of the United States, and of the state of New York, DO HEREBY CERTIFY that we have associated ourselves with others, for benevolent, charitable and missionary purposes; that the name assumed to distinguish such association, and by which to be known in law, is "THE AMERICAN BAPTIST MISSIONARY CONVENTION"; that the particular object of said convention is to propagate the gospel of Christ, and to advance the interests of his kingdom, by supplying vacant churches when requested, by sending ministers into destitute regions within our reach, and by planting and building up churches whenever a favorable opportunity offers; that the place of business and principal office of said convention is in the city of New York; that the management of the business affairs of the said convention is vested in an EXECUTIVE COMMITTEE or board of NINE MANAGERS; and that the following-named individuals compose said committee or board:

ALBANY, JUNE 26, 1848

I certify that the certificate of incorporation of "The American Baptist Missionary Convention" was this day received and filed in this office.

ARCH. CAMPBELL, *Dep. Sec. of State.*

PLAN OF MINISTERS' WIDOWS' FUND
Unanimously adopted, August, 1845.

In pious and grateful remembrance of our departed brethren in the ministry whose widows and orphans may be left in circumstances of need, the Baptist Missionary Convention *Resolved* to contribute to their relief, as far as our compassionate Saviour may indulge us with ability. In order, therefore, to create a fund for this benevolent purpose, we recommend the following:

MEANS

1. That on the fourth Lord's day in May, in every year, the respective churches composing this convention make a public collection for the purpose of aiding this fund.

2. That a subscription book be opened in every such church and congregation, to receive either annual subscriptions or donations to this desirable object.

OBJECTS

1. Persons intended to receive the benefit of this fund are the widows and orphans of deceased ministers who, at the time of their death, whether *ordained* or licensed, shall have been in good standing in this convention; and no others. As to all the portions of said fund, received or accruing at or after the session of 1847, the trustees of the fund have power, when the case of the applicant seems to be a peculiar one, to extend the advantages of the fund to the family of any deceased minister of good standing who may at any time have belonged to this convention.

2. Relief afforded to widow to continue during their widowhood, and no longer.

3. If there be no surviving widow, and the children, if any, of such deceased minister be under twelve years of age, and in need, they shall

receive the same portion as allowed to a widow, until they arrive at their fifteenth year: provided, also, that should any one of the said children, destitute of both father and mother, be found, by disease or accident, incapable of providing a living for him or herself, the allowance of this fund may continue until such person shall have arrived at twenty years of age.

MANAGERS OF THE FUND

1. That this convention, at their annual meeting, shall elect and appoint out of its members *five* trustees, who shall have the sole management of this fund; one of whom shall be appointed treasurer, and one other as secretary; and that such trustees continue in office three years, and until others are appointed.

2. That this board of trustees, (three of whom shall form a quorum,) shall meet annually, or oftener, as the case may require, for the transaction of business; and that the said board shall have the power to fill any vacancy in their number which may be occasioned by death or otherwise, until the next meeting of the convention.

3. All applications for relief shall be made to the board in *writing*, stating the name, residence and circumstances of the applicant.

4. It shall be the business of this board to receive and keep in charge all moneys collected or otherwise contributed to this fund—to receive and examine all applications for relief, and that they make such allowance of money to the needs as in their opinion the case may require, and the state of the funds may warrant.

5. *It is further resolved,* That the board of trustees, whenever the moneys in hand shall amount to $300, and there be no applicant for immediate relief (be and they are hereby authorized to invest the same in some secure, stock, or loan the same on bond and mortgage, for the purpose of creating a PERPETUAL FUND, the interest of which only shall be employed to relieve the necessitous. And, further, whenever other moneys in their hands successively shall amount to $100, and not be immediately required for use, the said sum shall be added to the *perpetual fund,* which it is presumed will ultimately prove essentially beneficial to the object intended. And, likewise, that the said permanent fund shall in no wise be disposed of, but by the order of three-fourths of this convention.

6. Finally, it is required that the trustees of this board present to this convention, at their annual meeting, a statement of their funds, collections, and disbursements, with whatever else may be combined with this benevolent object, and the performance of their duty.

7. Whereas it is highly probable that benevolent persons will be disposed to remember the *minister's widows' fund* while making their last will and testament, the following form of a bequest is respectfully submitted to their attention:

Form of Bequest to the Ministers' Widows' Fund of the
Baptist Missionary Convention of Baptist Ministers and Churches for
Missionary Purposes

I bequeath to my executors the sum of [ ] dollars, in trust, to pay over the same in [ ] after my decease, to the person, who, when the same is payable, shall act as treasurer of the widows' fund of the American Baptist Missionary Convention, formed in the year one thousand eight hundred and forty-five, to be applied to the aid of widows and orphans of deceased Baptist ministers, as expressed in their constitution.

———————

A majority of the Executive Board made and filed in the office of the Clerk of the City and County of New York, on the eleventh day of December, one thousand eight hundred and fifty, the names of the officers of the convention, inventory of the property, effects and liabilities thereof, with an affirmation of the truth of the same.

RULES OF ORDER
1. The president of the previous year shall call the meeting to order, and preside until another is appointed.
2. The secretary of the last year shall serve until another is appointed.
3. The committee for the nomination of officers for the ensuing year shall be appointed.
4. Immediately after the organization of the convention, the presdent shall read the rules of order.
5. Every sitting of the convention shall be opened and closed with prayer.
6. The usual invitation shall be given to visiting brethren.
7. Appointment of committees, to be nominated by the chair:
    On the admission of churches.
    On the circular letter.
    On the examination of minutes of corresponding bodies.
    On the collection of money for various objects.

Other committees, if any.

8. No subject shall be open for discussion until a motion has been made and seconded.

9. When a motion has been made and seconded, if any member oppose its being discussed, the president shall immediately put the question—Shall this question be discussed? and if negatived, the subject shall be dismissed.

10. Every person speaking on a motion shall arise from his seat and address the president, and shall avoid using personalities in debate.

11. No person shall speak more than twice nor longer than five minutes on any subject, without permission from the president.

12. Motions made and lost shall not be recorded, unless so ordered by the convention.

13. Delegates sent to this convention shall remain until the business is finished, unless excused by the president.

14. All resolutions presented to the convention shall be reduced to writing.

15. Unfinished business of the previous year.

16. Written accounts from the churches, with prayers and singing, as the president may request.

17. Application for admission.

18. Reading the roll of the convention.

19. Reports of committees, in the order of their appointment.

20. Choice of a place for the next meeting of the convention.

21. Choice of a preacher and alternate.

22. Choice of a writer of the circular letter.

23. Business of the relief fund.

24. Miscellaneous business.

STANDING RESOLUTIONS

1. That in view of our profession as ministers of the gospel of Jesus Christ, and the legitimate claims of the people upon us for correct gospel knowledge and instruction, we will devote all the time we can spare from our other labors connected with the ministry to reading the Scriptures and such standard works on divinity and ecclesiastical history as we are able to obtain, and by every means within our reach to improve ourselves; and we will encourage all our ordained and licensed ministers to do the same, thereby elevating the standard of ministerial education, piety and usefulness among us.

2. That the use of intoxicating drinks as a beverage is injurious and most destructive to morals, and we recommend all over whom we have influence immediately to abandon their use.

3. That each minister be requested to use his influence to procure donations from auxiliaries to the convention, and in every laudable respect further the views of this body.

4. That the great destitution at present among the colored population of this country calls loudly upon the members of this convention to use every laudable exertion to supply the perishing with the appointed means of grace.

5. That the Bible, sabbath-school and tract societies are institutions which commend themselves to the confidence of the churches and members of this convention.

6. That the education of young men for the gospel ministry is an object which commends itself to the pastors of the churches and the members of the convention.

7. That the corresponding secretary be requested to furnish each missionary a copy of the following rules:

RULES FOR MISSIONARIES

1. Every missionary shall be required to make a report to the corresponding secretary quarterly, from the time he enters upon his labors, containing the number of sermons preached; the probable number of persons who attend on his ministry; the number of scholars in the sabbath-schools; the different stations occupied by him, and the manner in which his labors are divided amongst them;

2. The present state of the church; the number of members attached to it; the number received, and how, whether by letter, baptism, or experience; the number excluded, and for what; also the number deceased.

3. That appropriations be made quarterly only when the above requisitions are complied with.

OFFICERS OF THE CONVENTION
Rev. CHAUNCEY LEONARD, *President*.
Rev. JESSE F. BOULDEN, *Vice-President*.
Rev. WILLIAM JACKSON, *Recording Secretary*.
Rev. JEREMIAH ASHER, *Corresponding Secretary*.
Bro. JOHN S. JENKINS, *Treasurer*.

MEMBERSHIP

Every church, association, or missionary society, contributing three dollars annually, shall be entitled to one representative, and another for every additional three dollars. Any person may become a member by contributing one dollar annually.

FORM OF A BEQUEST TO THE CONVENTION

I give and bequeath unto "The American Baptist Missionary Convention," incorporated in the city of New York, in the year of our Lord one thousand eight hundred and forty-eight, the sum of [ ] dollars, for the purposes of the said convention.

JOURNAL OF PROCEEDINGS

FIRST DAY

The nineteenth anniversary of the American Baptist Missionary Convention, held in the meeting-house of the First Baptist Church, Newburg, N.Y., commencing Friday evening, August 19th, at 7 1/2 o'clock.

The exercises were commenced by singing the 400th hymn of the Psalmist. Rev. Wm. Jackson, of New Bedford, read a portion of scripture, and Rev. Jeremiah Asher, of Philadelphia, offered prayer. Rev. Edmond Kelley, of West Philadelphia, then preached the introductory sermon, from the 24th chapter of Luke, 46-48 verses: "And thus it behoved Christ to suffer, and to rise from the dead the third day: and that repentance and remission of sins should be preached in his name among all nations," etc.

A collection was taken, amounting to $2.26.

The president called the convention to order. Prayer by Bro. Boulden.

The following brethren appointed a Committee to Nominate Officers for the ensuing year: Brethren White, N.Y.; Jackson, Mass.; Carey, N.Y.; Evans, Va., and Burriss, Philadelphia.

The following brethren were appointed a Devotional Committee: Brethren Jackson, Mass.; Hawkins, N.Y.; and Boulden, Philadelphia.

Adjourned to meet 10 o'clock tomorrow (Saturday) morning. Benediction by the president.

SECOND DAY

AUG. 20th, Morning Session

President in the chair. Opened with singing, and prayer by Bro. Wescott, of N.Y. Minutes of last meeting read and approved.

The committee on Nomination of Officers reported as follows:

For President, Rev. SAMPSON WHITE, Brooklyn, N.Y.

Vice-President, Rev. JESSE F. BOULDEN, Philadelphia, Pa.

Recording Secretary, Rev. WILLIAM JACKSON, New Bedford, Mass.

Corresponding Secretary, Rev. JEREMIAH ASHER, Philadelphia, Pa.

Treasurer, Bro. JOHN S. JENKINS.

Report adopted, and the following committees were appointed by the president:

1st.   *On Reception of Churches*: Brethren Kelley, Vaughn, and Wm. Evans.

2nd.   *On Circular Letter*: Brethren Carey, David Evans, and Kelley.

3rd.   *On Minutes of Corresponding Bodies*: Brethren Cooley, Burroughs, and Francis.

4th.   *On Finance*: Brethren Asher, Leonard, and Carey.

5th.   *On Fields*: Brethren Nicolas, Jenkins, Clayton, Asher, and Leonard.

6th.   *On Obituaries*: Brethren Asher, Leonard, and Hawkins.

The president then gave the usual invitation to ministering brethren, and the following presented their names: Rev. Isaac Wescott, pastor 1st Baptist Church; Rev. Joseph P. Thompson, of Zion M.E. Church; both of this city.

The Devotional Committee presented the following report: That the following order be observed during the session: Meet at 9, adjourned at 12; meet 2, adjourn 3 1/2; and also spend one hour in religious services; also a prayer meeting be held every day during the convention from 6 to 7 o'clock. Also, the following appointments for the sabbath:

First Baptist Church	{ Morning——— Bro. C. Leonard. { Afternoon—— Bro. J. Asher. { Evening—Bro. Wm.E. Walker
Zion A.M.E. Church	{ Afternoon—Bro. M.C. Clayton { Evening—Bro. S.W. Madden
Fishkill	{ Afternoon—— Bro. R. Vaughn { Evening——— Bro. J. Carey

On motion, *Resolved*, We hear the report of the Board. The Secretary then presented and read the report, which was on motion received. The following amendment was presented and adopted: "That the whole matter of the report of the Board be recommitted to the Board; they offering definite recommendations to this convention touching such subjects as they wish adopted."

On motion, *Resolved*, That the names of the annual members deceased be dropped from the records; pending which the hour of adjournment arrived.

On motion, adjourned till Monday morning, 9 o'clock. Prayer by Brother Madden.

THIRD DAY

AUGUST 22nd, Morning Session

President in the chair. Opened with singing. Prayer by Bro. Boulden. Minutes of previous meeting read and approved.

On motion, *Resolved*, That Bro. T.D. Miller, N.Y., be appointed to prepare daily a condensed statement of the doings of the convention, for publication in the "High Chief," of this city.

On motion, *Resolved*, That Bro. T.D. Miller be appointed Assistant Secretary of this convention.

Bro. White tendered his resignation as President of the convention, which was after discussion accepted. On motion, *Resolved*, That Bro. Chauncey Leonard be appointed President, to fill the vacancy occasioned by Bro. White's resignation. On motion, *Resolved*, That Bro. White be appointed to fill the vacancy in the Finance Committee occasioned by the removal of Bro. Leonard.

On motion, *Resolved*, The names of deceased members be retained, with stars annexed indicating their decease.

On motion, *Resolved*, That members' annual membership be continued until they refuse to pay their annual dues.

The President then appointed the following brethren as Auditing Committee: Brethren Dixon, Madden, and Miller.

The Committee on Reception of Churches reported the Salem Baptist Church, New Bedford, Mass., as applying for admission, recommending the same to the convention. Report received, and adopted.

On motion, adjourned. Prayer by Bro. Walker. Benediction by the President.

Afternoon Session

President in chair. Opened with singing. Prayer, by Bro. Kelley.

On motion, *Resolved*, That a committee of three be appointed to prepare business for the action of this convention; and the following brethren appointed as such committee by the president: Brethren Boulden, Vaughan and Asher.

The following resolution was offered, and after discussion laid over till tomorrow morning, 10 o'clock: *Whereas*, The present state of affairs concerning our treasury is quite deplorable: *Resolved*, That an agent be appointed immediately, at such a salary as the convention may decide, for the purpose of raising moneys to augment the funds of the treasury.

The resolution of last year, page 13 on the minutes, was called up for action eliciting considerable discussion, pending which the hour for religious services arrived.

Then listened to a discourse by Rev. Bro. Evans, of Washington, D.C., from John 4:29: "Come, see a man, which told me all things that ever I did," &c.

A collection was taken, amount, $1.04.

Adjourned to 7 1/2 o'clock. Prayer by Bro. Cooley.

Evening Session

Opened with singing. Prayer by Bro. Miller. Then listened to the missionary sermon, by Rev. Sampson White, from Romans 15:20: "Yea, so have I strived to preach the gospel, not where Christ was named, lest I should build upon another man's foundation."

A collection was taken, after a fervent appeal by the president, amounting to $4.53.

Adjourned till 9 o'clock Tuesday morning. Benediction, by the President.

FOURTH DAY

MORNING SESSION, Aug. 23rd

Vice-President in the chair. Opened with singing. Prayer by Bro. Jackson. Minutes of previous meeting read and approved.

The Committee on Nomination of Officers reported the following nominations:

For Treasurer, BRO. JOHN S. JENKINS
For Executive Board: Brethren S. White, W.L. Nicholas, J. Carey, W. Spellman, and R.R. Hubbard.

Report accepted, and laid on table.

These lie buried in "God's acre" in Southern, Eastern
and Western Africa.

The hour having arrived for the discussion on the subject of the agency, on motion, resolutions were taken up for discussion, in which Brethren Walker, Clayton, Asher, White and others participated. On motion, amended so as to read—"An agent be appointed at such a percentage as the Board may decide," &c.; and on motion adopted.

The president appointed the following as a committee to nominate preachers of the introductory sermon, missionary sermon and alternate, widow's fund and alternate, writer circular letter, selection of place for next convention, &c.: Brethren Boulden, Clayton, Burris, Evans, and Jenkins.

After discussion on the appointment of an agent, an agreement was made that the pastors severally pledge $25, when the following responded: Rev. J. Asher, $25; Rev. C. Leonard, $25; Rev. S. White, $25; Rev. J.F. Boulden, $25; while the other pastors, Brethren Jackson, Miller, Kelley, Clayton, &c., promised to raise what they could. The following brethren also responded: Bro. Burriss, $25; Bro. Nicholas, $25; Bro. Jenkins, $5; Bro. Hubbard, $5.

The Committee on Fields presented the following report:

"In view of the low state of our funds, and the importance of the prosecution of the African mission, therefore we recommend that our strength and means be mostly directed to that field till the mission there is established. To the Salem Church, New Bedford, Mass., we recommend an appropriation of $25 be made."

Report accepted. Pending the discussion on motion of adoption, hour of adjournment arrived.

Adjourned, till 2 o'clock. Prayer by Bro. Vaughan. Benediction, by the President.

Afternoon Session

President in chair. Opened with singing. Prayer, by Bro. Burriss.

The reading of the letters from the churches was commenced and completed.

The resolution on page 9 of last year's minutes, relative to Bro. T.D. Miller's essay, was called up. Not being ready, resolutions were ordered to continue over till next year.

Then listened to a discourse by Bro. William Valentine, of Washington, D.C., from Luke 14:22: "Lord, it is done as thou hast commanded, and yet there is room."

A collection was taken, amounting to $.84.

Adjourned to 7 1/2 o'clock. Prayer and benediction, by the president.

Evening Session

Vice-President in chair. Opened with singing. Prayer by Bro. Madden. Then listened to a discourse in behalf of the widows' fund, by Rev. J.F. Boulden, from Matthew 10:8: "Freely ye have received, freely give." Rev. Wm. Jackson followed with an appropriate address.

A collection was taken, amounting to $3.19.

Adjourned to 9 o'clock tomorrow morning. Benediction, by Bro. Jackson.

FIFTH DAY

MORNING SESSION, Aug. 24th

President in chair. Opened with singing. Prayer, by Bro. David Evans. Minutes of previous meeting read and approved.

The resolution of last year, page 13, was taken up, and on motion indefinitely postponed.

The report of the Committee on Fields was taken up, and after discussion on motion adopted.

The report of the Committee on Nominations was taken up for action, and on motion adopted.

The Committee on Circular Letter reported letter incomplete.

The Committee on Minutes of Corresponding Bodies reported none had been submitted to them.

The agents, &c., of widows' fund and societies were reappointed. On motion, *Resolved*, That the name of Wm. Stevens be dropped from the list of licentiates.

The Committee on the Appointments for next year presented the following report, recommending the convention to be held next year with the First Colored Baptist Church, Washington, D.C.

> *Preacher of the introductory sermon*, Rev. T. Doughly Miller; *alternate*, Rev. J. Carey.
> *Missionary sermon*, Rev. Wm. Jackson; *alternate*, Rev. R. Vaughan.
> *Widows' fund*, Rev. M.C. Clayton; *alternate*, Rev. E. Hawkins.
> *Writer of the circular letter*, Rev. W.E. Walker.

Report accepted, and adopted.

Adjourned to 2 o'clock. Prayer, by Brother Clayton.

Afternoon Session

President in chair. Prayer, by Brother Madden.

The report of the Treasurer was called for, when Bro. Asher made a statement of the death of the Treasurer, and gave a report, which was on motion adopted.

On motion, *Resolved*, There be a committee of two appointed to confer with the executors of the late Treasurer, relative to the financial state of the convention, and receive from them the papers, &c., belonging to the convention. The President appointed as such committee Brethren Vaughan and Asher.

The report of the treasurer of the widows' fund was received and adopted.

On motion, *Resolved*, That the treasurer of the widows' fund be requested to inquire of the former treasurer why he did not receive the full amount of money as reported in minutes of 1857.

On motion, *Resolved*, That all money belonging to the widows' fund be placed in such hands where it shall draw interest.

Then listened to a discourse by Bro. Burriss, from John 1:14: "And the Word was made flesh, and dwelt among us, and we beheld the glory," &c.

The hour of adjournment having arrived, on motion, time was extended to 5 o'clock.

The Committee on Obituaries presented the following report: "We are called to record the death of our esteemed brother and fellow-laborer, Dea. Frank Williams, of Philadelphia, Pa., deacon of the Shiloh Church, and for the last four or five years Treasurer of the American Baptist Missionary Convention; who discharged this duty with honor and fidelity. The loss of our brother we deeply deplore, and sympathize both with the church of which he was a member and his deeply afflicted family, and pray that his family may receive comfort, support and consolation of the grace of God, that his place in the church may be supplied with another characterized with an equal degree of patience, perseverance, steadfastness and faith with which he was possessed, and that his place in the convention be filled with another who will perform his duties with equal zeal and fidelity. May this admonition of the providence of God be sanctified to all of us, and we quickened in the discharge of every labor, until we shall go hence to join with our fellow-laborer in that world where remaineth a rest to the people of God." Report received and adopted.

On motion, *Resolved*, That the Secretaries publish one thousand copies of the minutes for the use of the churches, and that the usual appropriation of $10 be made to the secretaries for their services.

On motion, *Resolved*, The convention be authorized to extend the loan on the widows' fund, for a time not exceeding one year. On motion, time further extended 10 minutes.

Adjourned till 7 ½ o'clock. Benediction, by Bro. Jackson.

Evening Session

Vice-President in the chair. Opened with singing. Prayer, by Bro Jackson.

The Assistant Secretary then read the report of the Board. Report received. A discussion followed on the motion of adoption, quite interesting, participated in by Brethren Jackson, Asher, Buriss, White, Walker, and Kelly; after which, adopted with the recommendations.

A collection was taken, amounting to $4.62.

On motion, *Resolved*, That the thanks of this convention are hereby tendered to the First Baptist Church, Newburg, N.Y., for the kind privilege of using their house of worship during the session of our convention; to the Shiloh Baptist Church, and to the citizens generally, for their kind hospitalities shown us during our stay in their midst.

Resolved, That the thanks of this convention be tendered to the Rev. Elisha Hawkins, for his unbounded hospitality in entertaining the members of this convention and friends from a distance, refusing all compensation for the same, implicitly relying upon the promise of God for his reward. In this, his disinterested benevolence, we commend him to the consideration of a generous public as entitled to their utmost confidence and esteem, and to an all-wise and good God who will not let this act of brotherly love and friendship go unrewarded.

Resolved, That these resolutions be published .

Adjourned to 9 o'clock tomorrow morning. Benediction by President.

SIXTH DAY

MORNING SESSION, Aug. 25th

Vice-President in the chair. Opened with singing. Prayer, by Bro. White. Minutes of previous meeting read and approved.

The letters from the First African Church, Philadelphia, and Daughters of Convention of same church, were read.

The following resolutions were presented by Rev. S. White: *Resolved*, That slavery is against the progress of the gospel at home and abroad. *Resolved*, That we use all laudable means to abrogate it. *Resolved*, That no slaveholding minister be invited into the pulpits of any of our churches. A lengthy and interesting discussion followed, participated in by Brethren Asher, Kelley, Walker, Randolph, Clayton, Burriss, Jackson, White, and Evans; after which, on motion, adopted.

On motion, *Resolved*, The roll of ministers, licentiates and annual members be read for correction.

The hour of adjournment having arrived, on motion, *Resolved*, To continue the session until business is completed.

On motion, *Resolved*, The appointment of an agent to go to Africa with Bro. Barnett be referred to the Board.

On motion, *Resolved*, That the partial indebtedness of the convention as presented by the Board, amounting to $178.75, be paid.

The Auditing Committee presented the following report of the Treasurer:

ANNUAL MEMBERSHIP
New York

William T. Dixon	$1.00
Mr. Williams, by Wm. Spellman	1.00
Elizabeth Nichols	1.00
Peter Wilson	1.00
Eliza Jones	2.00
John S. Jenkins	1.00

Philadelphia

James Fells	$1.00
Nelly West	1.00
Nelly Denney	1.00
Ruth A. Miller	1.00
Charlotte Fitterman	1.00
Maria Wilson	1.00
John Kenney	1.00
Pamelia Logan	1.00
Samuel Parker	1.00
Sarah Parker	1.00
Charlotte Underwood	1.00
Jane Green	1.00
Edward Cook	3.00
Jane Scott	1.00
Matilda Duncan	1.00
Susan Singleton	1.00

$25.00

CHURCH MEMBERSHIP

Shiloh, Newburg	$3.00
Saratoga, Baltimore	3.00
Union, Baltimore	3.00
First Colored Baltimore	3.00
Abyssinian, New York	3.00
First Colored Washington	3.00
Concord, Brooklyn	3.00
Oak Street, Philadelphia	3.00
Zion, New Haven	3.00
Shiloh, Philadelphia	3.00
Union, Philadelphia	3.00
Salem, New Bedford	3.00
First Colored African, Phila.	3.00

$39.00

COLLECTIONS

Friday	$2.26
Sabbath morning	6.65
Sabbath afternoon	6.88
Sabbath evening	5.07
Monday afternoon	1.04
Monday evening	4.53
Tuesday afternoon	.84
Wednesday evening	4.62

$31.89

LIFE MEMBERSHIP

William Valentine $1.00
William E. Walker 1.00
S. W. Madden 1.00
Theodore Valentine 1.00

          _____

                    $4.00

AUXILIARY SOCIETIES

First Colored, Washington . $4.00
Union, Philadelphia 3.00
Daughters of Conven., Phila. 3.00
Shiloh 12.36
Daughters of Conv., Balt. ... 3.00
First Colored African, Phila. 7.00

          _____

                  $32.36

MISSIONARY SOCIETIES

First Colored, Washington . $3.00
Union, Philadelphia 5.79
Hamilton Street, Albany
(for African mission) 5.00
Shiloh, Philadelphia 4.22

          _____

                  $18.01

SABBATH-SCHOOL

First Colored, Washington $3.00

WIDOW'S FUND

Sisters Wilson and Nichols,
New York $3.00
Sisters Green and Logan,
Philadelphia 3.00
Eliza Jones, Zion, New York 6.00
Collection, Tuesday evening 3.19

          _____

                    $15.19
Annual membership $25.00
Church membership 39.00
Collections 31.89
Life membership 4.00
Auxiliary societies 32.36
Sabbath-school 3.00
Missionary societies 18.01

          _____

                  $153.26
Widow's fund   15.19

          _____

                  $168.45

Resolved, That the Corresponding Secretary be requested to address circulars to all the churches connected with this body, prior to each annual meeting, to make due preparation for the same, and correspond with Baptist churches which are not connected, or wish to become members of this body.

Resolved, That Rev. Bro. Vaughan and Bro. Burris be confirmed as agents to collect for this convention.

Resolved, That we reconsider the vote adopting that part of the report of Committee on Nominations relative to the place of next convention. Resolved, It be referred to the Board.

Adjourned to meet at the call of the convention through the Corresponding Secretary.

REPORT OF THE WIDOW'S FUND

PHILADELPHIA, August 17, 1859

At the close of the session in 1858, there was in the treasury	$165.61
Amount received during present session	16.62
	$182.23

EXPENSES PAID OUT, AS FOLLOWS:

To Brother Barnett, by Brethren Asher and F. Williams	$75.00
To Widow Burroughs	20.00
To Widow Scott	20.00
To Widow Noflit	20.00
To Widow Serrington	20.00
Postage for the moneys from Boston	.75
Books for treasurer and secretary	.65
	156.40

Balance in treasury 25.83

WM. WILSON MORRIS, *Treasurer*

Jas. Fells, *Secretary*

We have examined the above, and found it to be correct.
Wm. T. Dixon, Saml. W. Madden, Theo D. Miller,
Auditing Committee

ORDAINED MINISTERS

Names	*Post-offices*
*Daniel Scott	
Sampson White	Brooklyn, N. Y.
*John Nepean Evans	
Richard Vaughan	Philadelphia
Moses C. Clayton	Baltimore, Md.
Joseph Henderson	Philadelphia
Jeremiah Asher	Philadelphia
Edmond Kelley, W.	Philadelphia
Jesse F. Boulden	Philadelphia
John T. Raymond	
William Jackson	New Bedford

William Thompson
*James Burroughs
*Stephen Dutton
Cummings Bray
*Thomas U. Allen
James E. Crawford . . . . Nantucket, Mass.
David Miller . . . . Rochester, N. Y.
Noah Davis . . . . Baltimore, Md.
*Thomas Jefferson
*Jeremiah Durham
*John B. Meacham . . . . St. Louis, Mo.
John Carey
B. F. Drayton . . . . Liberia, Africa
Leonard Grimes . . . . Boston, Mass.
*Joseph Lewis
Elisha Hawkins . . . . Newburg, N. Y.
Gustavus Brown . . . . Washington, D. C.
William Spellman . . . . New York
Thomas Henson
Chauncey Leonard . . . . Washington, D. C.
*Wm. B. Serrington
Peter Johnson
Daniel Reese
Joseph Amos . . . . Marshpee, Mass.
Simon Bundick . . . . .Carsville, N. Y.
Robert Pinn . . . . Columbia, Penn.
Daniel Jackson
Leonard Black . . . . Williamsb'g, N. Y.
Charles Satchell . . . . California
Peter Randolph . . . . Newburg, N. Y.
John R. Gones.
N. G. Merry . . . . Nashville, Tenn.
William J. Barnett . . . . Sierra Leone, Af.
David Evans . . . . Kainsville, N. J.
Henry H. Butler . . . . Washington, D. C.
*Washington Christian.
S. Cutting Massachusetts
J. J. Brown . . . . Sierra Leone
William Evans . . . . Alexandria, Va.
Theo. Doughty Miller . . . . New Haven, Ct.

James Underdue . . . . Philadelphia, Penn.
James Hamilton . . . . Williamsb'g, N. Y.
William E. Walker

LICENTIATES

Names	*Post-offices*
David Thomas	Philadelphia
*Henry T. Smith	
*Oscar Taylor	
David H. Crosby	Philadelphia
W. B. Taylor	
*David Noflit	
Malachi Ferald	Philadelphia
William Ferguson	
John Wey	Baltimore, Md.
A. Williams	
Balar Cooley	Staten Isl., N. Y.
Robert Johnson	Boston, Mass.
Champion Hill	
J. E. Carter N.	Bedford, Mass.
Wm. Wilson Morris	Philadelphia
Caleb Burriss	Philadelphia
Frederick Woodson	Philadelphia
J. P. Miles	
Theodore Valentine	
William Valentine	
Samuel W. Madden	Baltimore, Md.

ANNUAL MEMBERS

Ruth Ann Miller.	*Canvas Reynoldson	Samuel P. Doosey
Maria C. Kendall.	*Henry Roach	P. Moore.
*Dea. J. Osborne.	Mary Ann Cooper	Frances Williams
J. O. Bonner.	*John Butler	Ann E. Ferril
W. H. Jackson.	*Dea. George C. Willis	Robert Morris, Esq.

Richard Foan.
Matilda Thomas.
Caroline Gray.
Richard Edwards.
Dea. Pearson
Mary A. Liggins
J. Young.
Dea. Frank Williams
F. Wodson, Sen.
Ann Goines.
William Goines
Samuel Monroe

Luke Goines
Margaret S. Freeman
David Peck

*James Goldham
*Rev. A. T. Driver
*Michael Hall
*Peter Huett
*Edward White
*Martha Clark
*Nancy Manners
W. L. Nichols
A. M. Goines
Dea. Kendrick
Eliza Jenkins
Caroline Carter

F. Woodson, Jr.
Reuben Coots
Julia A. Banks

Henry Johnson, Esq.
Louisa Besselleau
Mr. Preston
Martha Onley
Dea. William Piper
Faustina E. Carter
Thomas Jones
Thomas Reams
Mary A. Leonard
Sarah J. White
Lucy Ashton
Charles H. Brook,
Massachusetts

Jane Scott
Sophia Pollard

THE NINETEENTH REPORT OF THE BOARD
OF THE
AMERICAN BAPTIST MISSIONARY CONVENTION

DEAR BRETHREN:—Another year of anxiety and suffering has passed away, and we are not able to report that measure of success which our prospects seemed to warrant; but we trust that our labors in the Lord have not been in vain. And we hope, notwithstanding the disappointment we have encountered and the consequent embarrassment, never to cease our labors until the object we anticipate is fully realized, viz., to procure a location, and build a chapel, and establish a mission in the region of Sierra Leone, and preach the gospel of the blessed God to the benighted heathen in Africa, and do something in the great work of Africa's redemption. The gospel must first be preached to the untutored heathen, in order to prepare the way for civilization—and we believe the only effectual remedy for the traffic in human flesh on the shores of Africa.

Soon after the close of the last session of the Convention our missionary returned from Waterloo, Africa, and visited most of the churches, reported his labors and success at his station, which seemed to inspire the Board and the churches with increased confidence and renewed vigor to prosecute the work in which we were engaged. This report being satisfactory to the Board, the balance of his salary was paid in full for missionary labors, up to the 23rd Sept., 1858, and he continued in the service of the Convention, as their missionary to Waterloo, at a salary of $200 per annum.

His object while here was, if possible, to persuade the Board to procure a location and build a chapel at Waterloo. He reported thirty-five native converts through his instrumentality, who had professed faith in the Saviour. He proposed, on his return, to organize them into a church, and thus the mission would be established. He left this field in charge of Brother Weeks, of Sierra Leone, who was a licentiate of the Baptist church there, and whose pastor had baptized these candidates at Waterloo. Accordingly the Board, at their meeting in December, resolved to take measures to raise the amount needed to procure a location and build a chapel; and succeeded in raising about four hundred and fifty dollars, from the following churches and individuals:

COLLECTIONS
NORTHERN BAPTIST CHURCH

Philadelphia Baptist Assoc. . . . . $ 69.00
Mrs. Blandina Dudley, Alb. 100.00
Shiloh Baptist Church, Phila. 31.00
A friend 10.00
Oak Street Church, West Phila. 8.00
Mrs. Forbes 1.00
Oliver St. Baptist Church, N.Y. 29.80
A friend 2.00
Concord Street, Brooklyn 7.00
A friend 3.00
Hamilton Street Baptist Church, Albany 27.03
Rev. Dr. Kennedy 3.00
C.M. Lockwood 3.00
State St. Baptist Church, Alb. 21.90
_____ Lockwood 3.00
Subscription, Troy, N.Y. 13.00
Mr. George Vail 10.00
Dea. William Deutez, Albany 100.00
Other friends, amounting to 15.00

When it was thought advisable to suspend the collection, and send Brother Barnett at once to his field of labor:

The following resolution was passed by the Board at their December meeting: *Resolved,* That in view of the feeble health of Rev. J.J. Brown, pastor of the church in Sierra Leone, and he being the only ordained minister there, we deem it expedient to ordain Brother Barnett before sending him back to his station; and Brethren White and Asher be a committee to make the arrangements for the ordination; which took place in the Shiloh meeting-house, Philadelphia, December 23rd, 1858; and on the 26th he sailed in the brig Colvert, from Philadelphia, and arrived at Sierra Leone on the 20th of February, 1859. On his arrival he found the land visited by that scourge, the small-pox, in its worst form—carrying the people off by hundreds—and most of his relations and near connections had fallen victims to the disease.

He commenced to labor in Sierra Leone, in company with Brother Brown, in administering the comforts of religion to the sick and dying, and preaching the gospel there; for he found, to his surprise, that the field at Waterloo had been occupied during his absence, by the Southern Board; and Brother Weeks, whom he left in charge, employed at a salary of two hundred dollars per annum to labor in that field; and also the female teacher which Brother Barnett had hitherto employed. Brother Brown thinks it has been rather providential, for he says Sierra Leone is a field sufficiently large without attempting at present to go further; but as we are anxious to commence a mission ourselves he will do all he can to assist us. We wrote him requesting him to assist Brother Barnett, at Waterloo, in the formation of the church, the selection of a location and the erection of the chapel, and what he would consider would be a compensation for his services. But as we did not succeed in Waterloo he has been to Bullom Shore, just across the river from Sierra Leone, and twenty miles east of Freetown. He says there is a great field for missionary labor, and no missionary has ever been stationed there. He thinks we ought to take possession at once, so as to teach the people the commands of our Saviour. It is a main land, and has an interior of about five hundred miles. He has been to see if a location could be obtained, and arrangements made so that Brother Barnett could proceed, if the Convention approve the measure; but the chief was not at home and he could learn nothing definite about it. He, however, conversed with one of the under chiefs, who seemed pleased with Brother Barnett, and the object of his mission, and wished them to come and preach the word there. He informed them, however, that it was not their custom to sell their land, but to lease it for any length of time required; and promised, when the head chief came home, to send them word, so they can come and meet them and make a selection of land—the quantity required. Brother Brown, in reply to the inquiry of the corresponding secretary, whether he would assist Brother Barnett, says, he superintends the missions at Waterloo, for the Southern Baptist, for two hundred dollars a year, and will do the same for us if we wish him. These questions were important—the Board would take no steps in the premises, but refer the whole matter to the Convention for their deliberation and decision. Or, if be thought best, to send out a brother with power to carry into effect the purpose of the Convention. And we would furthermore suggest the importance of sending an agent to get each church in connection with the Convention to enter into this work with renewed zeal, and, in the early part of this conventional year, raise a certain amount towards the prosecution of the great work of gospel to our brethren in Africa.

A party of missionaries who sailed in company for West Africa in 1920. Dr. Robert M. Sisusa, a native of South Africa with Delia, his wife, also from South Africa and their three children. One of these with Mrs. Sisusa died in 1924. Mrs. Delia Harris, Washington, D. C., Mrs. Priscilla Bryan, a trained nurse, Rev. Nichols of Florida and Miss Hooks with Secretary Jordan made up this party. Dr. Sisusa is still on the West Coast; Mrs. Harris, Rev. Nichols and Miss Hooks have returned to the home field.

Pilgrim Baptist Church, where Rev. S. E. J. Watson showed the Christian mettle out of which he was made. At his death Rev. J. C. Austin was called from Ebenezer Baptist Church of Pittsburgh, and under whose care Pilgrim Church is reckoned as having the third largest membership of any church in the denomination. The Foreign Mission Board put this church down as one of its largest contributors, and it is regarded as a real bee-hive in Christian service.

It is believed that we can do something for the perishing heathen; and if we love the Saviour we will do something, as well as pray that his kingdom may be eternal and his salvation be known to the ends of the earth.

We would also call the attention of the Convention to the present condition of our finances. By reference to the minutes it will be seen that on the 27th of December, after paying our obligations, there remained in the treasury thirty-four dollars and twenty-two cents. This balance is just about the amount required to print the minutes of last year. So that in the commencement of our present undertaking we have not had one dollar in the treasury. The time having arrived that Brother Barnett should return to Sierra Leone, the Board ordered the Corresponding Secretary to loan the treasury twenty-five dollars from the building fund, to pay his passage to Sierra Leone, which money was to be refunded as soon as sufficient means were received in hand. The passage was thus provided. It was also necessary to provide for the first half year of his salary, which was done by assuming the following obligations, which are now due:

On Perry Davis & Son, Providence, R.I. $50.00
Baptist Publication Society, Philadelphia 20.00
Rev. Thomas Smith, at the Baptist Mission House, No. 33 Moorgate Street,
        London, England 35.00
Dr. Granger, Philadelphia 10.00

making one hundred and fifteen dollars. These bills were preferred to the money, for they were obtained so that a large percentage was secured in his favor, and immediately converted into money after his arrival. In addition to the above we shall be in debt to Brother Barnett $85, which will be due on the 23rd of September. It will also be borne in mind that the treasurer of the widows' fund was authorized to loan the Treasurer of the Convention one hundred dollars to defray the expenses of last year. The amount required, however, was but seventy-five dollars. This amount, added to the two hundred dollars for missionary labor and seventy-five dollars from building fund, makes three hundred and fifty dollars to be provided for this session, besides printing minutes, and other incidental expenses.

It is with deep regret that we are called, in the providence of God, to record the death of our lamented and much respected brother and fellow-laborer, Deacon FRANK WILLIAMS, of Philadelphia, a member of the Board, and Treasurer of this body for the last four or five years—respected and beloved by all who knew him, and faithful to the charge committed to his trust. The memory of the just is blessed. We forbear to say more in this connection, leaving it to the Committee on Obituaries, which will not fail to do justice to his character and worth.

In the last communication from Brother Barnett, dated 18th June, he stated that he, in company with Brother Brown, has visited Waterloo, and thinks there is still an opening in that region. They spent seven days there. In the meantime, Brother Barnett baptized six native converts—four females and two males—and visited a small town near Waterloo, named Benguma, and preached the word to them. He says the people are anxious to hear about the Saviour.

They like him. He understands their language. They wish him to locate in their town, and build his chapel. They offer him a piece of land— he says enough for a good farm. He is extremely anxious to go and possess the land at once—but the terms are not mentioned. He says the people are anxious everywhere to have him come and tell them of the love of Jesus. He says he is determined to preach baptism wherever he goes.

Now, brethren, what shall we do? Shall we prosecute this work with vigor? Shall we go right up and possess this land, and, in the name of our God, set up our banner, or shall our hands hang down, the work cease, and we become weary, and leave our brethren to perish in their blindness?

The Board now awaits the action of your body, in order to answer the inquiry of Brother Barnett; and which of the places, Bullom Shore or Benguma, you will occupy, or whether you will leave it to the choice of Brother Barnett.

Now dear brethren, we submit this whole matter to your careful and prayerful consideration. We wish you to look at it in the light of eternity, and with reference to the judgment, when the assembled heathen of Africa, in the language of a convert of Sierra Leone, in a plea for the spread of the gospel among the heathen of Africa, said "Now if we refuse to tell them of a Saviour's love, they will then say to us, 'Now you been seen us going to hell, and never told us.'"

The Board intends prosecuting the work necessary to the purchase of a location and building the chapel, as soon as they can ascertain where you will commence, and the amount required. But we must look to you for means to support the missionaries. It will be seen, therefore, that as little change in the Board as possible will be desired, in order to facilitate the object.

All of which is most respectfully submitted, in behalf of the Board.

JEREMIAH ASHER,
Corresponding Secretary.

After reading the report, on Monday, it was recommitted to the board, requesting them to give specific recommendations respecting the best course to pursue, in order to establish our Mission.

After careful deliberation we submit the following:

In view of the whole matter, we recommend, in the early part of this conventional year, that an agent be employed at the rate of $500 per year, and sent to confer with Brother Barnett in the selection of a suitable location, to purchase of a site to build a chapel, and all the necessary arrangements to establish the African mission under the direction of the American Baptist Missionary Convention on a permanent basis.

J. ASHER
S. WHITE
WM. L. NICHOLAS

The amount which must be provided for and paid, on or before the 22nd of September, 1859, is one hundred and seventy-eight dollars and seventy-five cents, in the following amounts:

Perry Davis & Son	$ 25.00
Publication Society	20.00
Dr. Granger	10.00
Bro. Barnett	100.00
Rev. David Evans	18.75
Revs. J. Asher and Underdue, for superintending publication	5.00
TOTAL	$ 178.75

This convention made a draft on the ordained preachers throughout the North and East, hundreds of whom at various times, and in various ways in the providence of God, had escaped slavery.

A number of them had gone to school and had been fitted for leadership in that golden hour. They were appointed as missionaries and teachers, to come South and work among the freedmen, under the protection of the Union Army. Edmond Kelley reported:

The 23rd Annual Session of the American Baptist Missionary Convention was held in the First Colored Baptist Church, Washington, D.C., from August, 18-23, 1865, and the proceedings were very harmonious. The following officers were elected for the ensuing year: Leonard A. Grimes, Boston, president; Noah Davis, Baltimore, vice president; Daniel C. Muse, Washington, recording secretary; Jeremiah Asher, Philadelphia, corresponding secretary; John Kinney, Philadelphia, treasurer. On Sunday, Rev. E. Kelly, of this city, preached from 2 Kings 4:7.

During the session the delegates in a body visited the freedmen's quarters, and met some brethren with whom they were acquainted while in the land of bondage.

A committee of which Mr. Kelley was a member waited on the President to know what protection their missionaries might have on Southern soil. They were cordially received and on retiring were presented with the following:

Executive Mansion, Washington, D.C.
August 31st 1863

TO WHOM IT MAY CONCERN:
Today I am called upon by a committee of Colored ministers of the gospel, who express a wish to go with our military lines and minister to their brethren there. The object is a worthy one and I shall be glad for all facilities to be afforded them, which may be inconsistent with or of a hindrance to our military operations.
[President] A. LINCOLN

No other single contribution meant so much to us as these men. Being bone of our bone, their dress and mannerism created a model in many ways and proved real character makers, and an inspiration to those preachers, who like ourselves, had been slaves and came with us from bondage. As well as to those who soon entered upon that work.

In order that the leaders of the convention might have an object of appeal to the philanthropists, and sympathetic friends of the millions recently emancipated, they sought to make all churches, no matter how old, nor how strong, or weak numerically, mission stations under the control of the board of this convention, and all ordained preachers in the southland, missionaries of this hastily organized body.

The officers of the convention made several efforts to get the American Baptist Home Mission Society (White), to cooperate with or accept them as a cooperating agency in the distribution of the funds given to help our people, but the offer was never accepted. It were better that they had never asked, as the refusal weakened them with the freedmen and they lost prestige. Thus embittered by what they termed a "very unbrotherly act on the part of the Home Mission Board displaying a lack of confidence in their weaker brethren, they worked for nearly ten years unaided, growing weaker and weaker. Their last meeting was held in Lexington, Ky., 1878.

By making missionaries of the pastors they estranged the most ambitious among us and were soon charged with "demoting the elders," and as Dr. J.M. Armstead says, "Caused them to fall away and enlarge their efforts to organize state conventions and make them popular."

Footnote
Dr. R.L. Perry, an official, says, "At their Twenty-sixth Anniversary, at Richmond, Va., August, 1866, this body united with the Northwestern Convention." The united bodies took the name of the "Consolidated American Baptist Missionary Convention" and did a grand work in the South. Some difference of opinion arose as to jurisdiction and management at Richmond in 1876, which indicated approaching disruption, hence the union with the N.W. and So.

COPY OF AN ARTICLE IN *THE NATIONAL BAPTIST*
PHILADELPHIA, SEPTEMBER 13, 1866, PAGE 2.

Made in the Library of the American Baptist Historical Society,
Chester, Pa., October, 1927

**Consolidation of the Northwestern and Southern,
and the American Baptist Missionary Conventions**

Editor, *National Baptist*:—As many of the friends are repeatedly requesting me to detail to them the nature,object, and outline of the recent consolidation of the two Baptist bodies, the Northwestern and Southern, and the American Baptist Missionary Conventions, commenced at the Nashville anniversary of the former in May last, and consummated at Richmond, Va., August last, at the recent yearly meeting, I would state that it has been thought by many of the brethren that as the dissensions and divisions are so frequent that we would endeavor to become one united body from Maine to the Gulf, not only in sentiment and practice, but as an organic body. The respective terms North and South, as generally used in politics, become mutually objectionable to the different sections of the country, because of the two opposite modes of civilization, the success of the one necessarily involves the destruction of the other. But with us as Baptists there is no need of such uses of the terms other than in a geographical sense, as we are the same the world over, the Bible being our only recognized chart on land and sea. "There is one body and one spirit, even as ye are called in one hope of your calling; one Lord, one faith, one baptism." While we have thus united with a view of concentrating upon one common centre, yet it was with the understanding that we should district the United States into four parts, of about nine states or more each; to have state conventions; in those conventions to have associations; with the design of having the churches report to the district conventions through the associational letters, and through the districts to the general convention.

The time of the meetings is to be fixed in the future. Of course the same roll will be retained of the life and annual members. In the consolidation act, provision was made for a closer and more intimate relation between us and the three societies of Whites at the North, viz., the American Baptist Free Mission Society, the American Baptist Home Mission Society, and the American Baptist Publication Society; they being the recipients of funds for the Colored people as well as Whites, and wishing to expend them to the best advantage, and our Society being already in the field with Colored laborers in the capacity of missionaries and Sabbath-school agents, who we believe, are better adapted to the wants of our people.

We adopted the following plans to be presented to the societies named: That we appoint missionaries and Sabbath-school agents for every state, who shall be amenable to our board; that more or less of the appointees be presented to the society for their endorsal and support; that all who are supported in part or altogether by these societies shall send to them duplicates of their quarterly reports through our corresponding secretary. We feel very hopeful of this plan, because of their repeated generous proffers of aid in our noble work of evangelizing the South and the world. We hope to make a similar proposal to the American Baptist Missionary Union in behalf of Africa. Lord speed the right!

EDMUND KELLY.

THE CONSOLIDATED
AMERICAN BAPTIST MISSIONARY CONVENTION

The CONSOLIDATED AMERICAN BAPTIST MISSIONARY CONVENTION that has been in session in Nashville for the last eight or nine days, is a union of the late Northwestern and Southern Baptist Missionary Convention and American Baptist Missionary Convention. The consolidation was effected at the last annual meeting held a year ago at Richmond, Va. The former of the now united bodies had existed but three or four years, while the latter had existed about six years.

The convention is largely represented, there being near a hundred delegates present from almost every part of the United States, representing in the body nearly a hundred thousand communicants of the Colored Baptist church.

During the past year this convention has had a large number of missionary preachers laboring in the different Southern States with signal and blessed results. One missionary reported as an item among his spiritual doings, over eight hundred baptisms.

The reports of all the missionaries were very encouraging and showed as a general thing, that a wise selection of evangelists was made at the last annual session of the convention.

Meetings of a highly interesting character have been held every evening, while through the day the time was spent in hearing reports from executive boards, reports of committees and in devising ways and means for the more successful prosecution of the legitimate work of the convention.

The Rev. Mr. Merry's church, where the convention is holding its meeting, is filled to its utmost capacity every evening with attendants.

Religious services have been held in most of the Colored churches of the city so, that among the Colored people there has been a week of spiritual feasting.

Five or six hundred dollars have been raised during the session for missionary purposes.

The convention failed to get funds enough the past year to pay the salaries of some of the missionaries, and is now indebted for missionary labor, about sixteen hundred dollars ($1600).

Several other bodies are represented in this convention by special delegates. The American Baptist Home Mission Society is represented by Rev. James French; the American Baptist Publication Society, by Rev. J.R. Stone and Mr. A.B. Thankland; the Af. Civ. Society, by Rev. Rufus L. Perry, of Brooklyn, N.Y.; the American Free Missionary Society, by Rev. R.R. Whittier; and the National Theological Institute, by Rev. A.L. Grimes, of Boston, Mass. These different organizations are all laboring professedly, in the interest of the Colored people of the South.

Reports are yet to be made by the several committees appointed by the convention, to whom have been referred all matters pertaining to the work of the convention for the ensuing year.

The Committee on Nominations of New Officers for the ensuing year consisted of twelve ministers selected from the states of Virginia, Missouri, Alabama, Ohio, Kentucky, Tennessee, Georgia, Louisiana, Arkansas, and Massachusetts. They reported for president, Elder Richard DeBaptiste, of Chicago, Ill.; for vice president, Elder N.G. Merry, of Nashville, Tenn.; for treasurer, Elder Wm. P. Brooks, of St. Louis, Mo.; for recording secretary, Elder Henry L. Simpson, of Cincinnati, Ohio; and for corresponding secretary, Elder Rufus L. Perry, of Brooklyn, N.Y.

Several of the delegates are thoroughly educated, and give every needful evidence of the Black man's capacity to be, act, and rise in intelligence and usefulness as readily and as high as anybody else.

The salvation of the world, the universal brotherhood of man, a perpetual union of the states and civil and political equality are its cherished sentiments.

I have failed to get the amount due me on salary by near $300, though they report that I have under God done a great work as general missionary for the State of Tennessee, and have reappointed me. They recommended my simple forms of church organization and Sabbath school constitutions to the churches and Sabbath schools throughout the United States. After recommending the formation of associations in every state and church representation through associational letters, when equally acceptable to the churches, in consequence of the largeness of the body, they renewed their proffer to co-labor with the above named White societies.

They adjourned to meet at Savannah, Ga., on Thursday before the third Lord's Day in August, 1868.

EDMUND KELLY
Nashville, Tenn., August, 26, 1867

Just here we should state that it appears there was organized somewhere and at some time a convention known as "The African Missionary Convention of America." The only time we read of it is when it was represented at the Foreign Mission Convention held in the Vermont Avenue Baptist Church of Washington, D.C., in 1893. We have no record of its officers, or date of its organization, but we find that at this Washington meeting delegates from three conventions were present; viz., The Foreign Mission Convention of the United States of America, A.R. Griggs, President; the New England Convention, W.I. Dixon, President; and the African Missionary Convention. An agreement was reached whereby the three bodies were to form what they called a "Tri-Party Convention."

The next year in the report of the Foreign Mission Convention made at Montgomery (September, 1894), Mrs. Lucy A. Coles, Corresponding Secretary of the Convention, states that The African Missionary Convention of America had not reported during the conventional year and the trial, when, where, and by whom this Convention was organized, lost. We wrote a number of men who might possibly know, and the only information received was that given by Brother Charles D. Swayne, of Springfield, Ohio, historian of the Western Union Association of Ohio, one of the oldest associations in our country, which is as follows:

Rev. L. G. Jordan, D.D.

I have your letter inquiring for information concerning the African Missionary Convention of America. I have not been able to find among any old records that I have, just who was the head of that organization. It appears first in the minutes of the Western Union Baptist Association of Ohio, through the appointment of a corresponding manager to meet them in October, 1893. In 1894 in October this convention met in Xenia, Ohio. I attended one session and during this meeting in Xenia, the Rev. J.F. Thomas, Pastor at that time of Olivet Baptist Church of Chicago, Ill., was the presiding officer, although on that occasion the Rev. Thomas allowed (as a matter of honor) the Rev. Bishop B.W. Arnett to preside. I do not know who the other officers were, nor the objectives of this convention. It disappears from our minutes and no further relations seemed to be maintained after 1896. The corresponding messengers, either through ignorance or lack of interest, failed in their reports to give any data other than that they went, saw, and had a good time. My own personal recollection of this convention is—that it changed names afterward and was known as the "Western States and Territories Missionary Convention." The Rev. William Balay seemed to be its agent or vice president for Ohio. Balay is now dead."

Now, if Brother Swayne is correct as to the change in name, I can personally shed a little light on this organization. For in 1896 when I became secretary of the Foreign Mission Board of the National Baptist Convention, I met the Western States and Territories Missionary Convention and spoke in the interest of foreign missions at Chicago. I induced them to represent in the National Baptist Convention at the St. Louis meeting that same year, and the result was they officially united with the National Baptist Convention and they have ever since been an integral part of that body.

It will be remembered the Foreign Mission Convention in 1894 is without a missionary, the Educational Convention without a school or student, and the American National Baptist Convention has cast the Purdy or Tennessee fuss overboard. Each of these organizations had tendrils, feeling for something of value to which they might cling, and for which they might work; so they all appointed a separate committee to jointly work out a plan, and arrange a Constitution for a National Baptist Convention, in

Atlanta, Ga., for 1895.

One year later, this commission reported, and the merger obtained, but the Foreign Mission Board of the Foreign Mission Convention, did not report for the second year. Under the new order of things, the three new boards were appointed and domiciled by the convention as follows:—Home Board, Little Rock, Ark.; Foreign Mission Board, Louisville, Ky.; Educational Board, Washington, D.C.

At the first annual meeting of the United Body, September, 1896, in St. Louis, a resolution was passed that a Publishing Committee in charge of the Home Board at Little Rock, Ark., be created, and that there be no longer delay, but that said committee get a series of Sunday school quarterlies and a Baptist Teacher ready for our Sunday schools for the first Sunday in January, 1897. It was done, and I can never forget the feelings against those who in any way aided it. The agents of the Northern societies, being from the Home Mission schools, were in the main the most learned and influential men among us, so they made us quake. So, two schools of thought obtained among us as to the Negroes' ability to write for his own children, and this contention was carried to the Negro Baptist churches, and was so intense that it disturbed the White Baptists North and South. In 1897 for the first time Negro Baptists met in the North.

It will be seen there is no mention of publishing literature or printing of any kind in the preamble or constitution of our reorganized National Baptist Convention in 1895. The next historian will more fully explain this and more.

The idea of gaining wider influence and closer fellowship by organizing "Conventions" with membership composed of churches in two or more states, seems to have existed since the year 1840. From the letters and records left by the principle officers of these organizations it appears that they hoped to have the aid and cooperation of White sympathizers who would help them with their financial burdens. The minutes of the consolidated Convention in particular breathed a note of disappointment and discouragement when this help was not forthcoming.

It is not hard for us of a later day to say they lacked a definite objective and that their aims were perhaps too theoretical to win enthusiastic and practical support, but remember they had undertaken work among four and one-half millions of people without homes, money, church or school houses and 250 years of labor unpaid for. Whatever the cause, they were all short-lived; even when they merged two or three bodies to form a stronger one—as was done in the cause of the Southern and Northern Baptist Convention, they ultimately languished and died. Thus it was that when Rev. W.W. Colley, a missionary of the Southern Board returned to this country and began to travel among the churches of the Southern States, he found willing minds and open hearts to respond to his appeals that American Negroes should launch out in an effort to send the gospel to the heathen. Elder Colley, as far as can be learned from the few surviving friends who met and knew him personally, seems not to have been endowed with any special gifts or eloquence, but he was deeply imbued with the desire to serve by giving the Word of God to "Darkest Africa." He insisted that those who had received the light had a sacred duty to pass on the message to their brethren still in the darkness of that benighted land. From his own experiences he impressed his hearers with the fact that the missionaries who worked under White boards were hampered and restricted by the limitations set for them in dealing with the natives to whom they preached. So graphically did he present the situation that when he issued a general call for a meeting of pastors and leaders, there was no hesitation or evidence of reluctance to undertake the sacrificial task of foreign mission work by Negroes, most of whom had been recently set free from slavery.

Eye witnesses have described to us the feelings of intense emotion which permeated the assembly of 151 persons, mostly ministers and church workers, who met in Montgomery, Ala., on November 24th, 1880, for this holy purpose. They have told us that in spite of the beautiful autumn weather and the brilliant sunshine, nearly every face was bathed in tears even before the meeting had been formally opened, and that on every hand could be heard expressions which indicated the warmth and intensity of feeling that prevailed. They declare that during the session the usual spirit of levity and the jovial greetings of friend to friend was absent. In its place there was a keen sense of the weight and responsibility of the work they were about to begin, and while there was harmony and unanimity in their actions throughout, there was ever present a realization of the importance of the work which was to be done. Their first hymn, "All Hail the Power of Jesus' Name," was chosen with their heathen brethren in mind, it is said. Likewise the sermon for the occasion was based upon a specially selected text: "He that goeth forth with weeping, bearing precious seed, shall doubtless come again with rejoicing, bringing his sheaves with him."

(Excerpts From Minutes)

The Consolidated Convention meets triennially, but the Executive Board meets annually and reports through the official organ, *The National Monitor*.

REV. WM. T. AMIGER, D.D.
Philadelphia, Pa.

He was pastor, World War chaplain, superintendant West African Missions and President American Baptist Theological Seminary, Nashville, Tenn. He was born in Virginia and died in Tennessee, 1929.

REV. A. R. ROBINSON, D.D.

Rev. Robinson pastored Shiloh Baptist Church which was remodeled under his pastorate; a $10,000 organ installed and an old folks' home built. He was for twelve years chairman of the Foreign Mission Board. A fine executive and a workman in the Christian field that needed not to be ashamed. Born in South Carolina, died in Philadelphia, 1922.

The above is the first Missionary Baptist Church building, Kingston, Jamaica, B. W. I. This building was brick, the story of which will be found in the writings of George Leile.

This is a picture of Drs. C. H. Parrish and L. G. Jordan standing on the foundation of the church in Jamaica. This building had been torn away brick by brick and when the commissioner visited the Island in 1917 all that remained of that former great church was the foundation.

In 1876, in New York City, November 30, they reported that forty-six schools [were] aided in more or less measure, and eighteen new schools organized with five hundred baptisms.

These states reported: Pennsylvania, New Jersey, Connecticut and New York in the Northeast; North Carolina, South Carolina, Georgia, Florida, Alabama, Mississippi, Louisiana, Texas, Arkansas and Kansas in the South and Southwest.

The Haytian mission work was flourishing, and the deed to the mission property there is in charge of Shadrach Hoppolyte, who has instructions to hold it for the church. His son Lucius is being educated with the hope of taking the work at Port au Prince.

Officers for the year 1876 were:

President .... Wm. Gray, Mississippi
Secretary .... W.C. Phillips, Chicago
Corresponding Secretary .... R.L. Perry, Brooklyn, N.Y.

The Consolidated Convention held its Twelfth Annual Session at Richmond, Va., October 11, 1877.
Its officers were:

President .... Amos Johnson, Macon City, Mo.
Corresponding Secretary .... R.L. Perry, Brooklyn, N.Y.
Recording Secretary .... Wm. Dixon, Richmond, Va.
Treasurer .... Wm. Troy, Richmond, Va.

Twenty states reported an enrollment of 600,000 Colored Baptist.

Recommendations were passed concerning the work of Hayti:

That this cause be presented to the churches. That the Board be empowered to raise funds to build a church at Port au Prince.

The Committee on Fields has this matter in charge.

The Constitution was so amended as to make the meetings of the Consolidated Convention hold annual meetings, instead of triennial as they are now.

They then adjourned to meet in Lexington, Ky., from October 17 to 22, 1876.

At the Thirteenth Annual Session of the Consolidated Convention, held in Lexington, Ky., October, 1876, the receipts for the year were shown to be $3,614.67. The Committee on Foreign Missions recommended the formation of a "Foreign Board." It was voted that the Rev. Richard DeBaptiste of Chicago be the corresponding secretary of this Board. It was also recommended that in addition to the efforts made in Hayti, we begin work in

Africa at once, accepting C.H. Richardson, now in England or en route to Africa, as our missionary.

The Executive Board was ordered to inquire into the status of the Von Brun Missions among the Bassa people in Liberia, and if it be found feasible, we should also adopt that work.

The report having been adopted, the following persons formed the first Foreign Mission Board:

Revs. J.P. Johnson, R.M. Duling, Amos Johnson; and Brethren W. C. Phillips, W.S. Johnson, with Rev. R. DeBaptiste as corresponding secretary. This Foreign Mission Board is constituted with headquarters at Chicago.

Rev. R.M. Duling and wife were made field agents for all of the states west of the Alleghenies, and Rev. Walter Brooks for all the states east of the same mountains.

In this same year (1878), the Committee on Education reported. This committee urged the need of an educated ministry and commended the institutions of learning, North and South, that were open to such Colored persons as were qualified by training and ability to enter. Officers were elected as follows:

President . . . . Rev. J.W. Patterson
Corresponding Secretary . . . . Rev. R.L. Perry
Recording Secretaries . . . . . . Rev. R. De Baptiste, Rev. W.H. Brooks

The meeting adjourned to meet in Cincinnati, Ohio, August 14, 1879.

Chapter V

In other decades Baptists were better indoctrinated than they are to-day. The environment in which they lived, sometimes inimical of them was conducive to the mastery of their principles. Of later years, a tendency to depreciate doctrinal discussion is easily discernible, and young converts particularly are not rooted and grounded in the faith.—The People Called Baptists—*McDaniel.*[8]

"Praise is as good for a race as for an individual, but flattery is not good for either."—Booker T. Washington, President of Tuskegee, National Baptist Magazine, *July 1896.*

EARLY HISTORIANS' ACCOUNTS OF NEGRO BAPTISTS

History shows that the first African slaves were brought to the colonies in August, 1619, but a long span of 154 years passed before we have the account of the first Negro Baptist church. However, as early as 1624, in Virginia, an Anglican church did receive a Negro babe into fellowship by sprinkling. (Shaf-Herzog Vol. 8) I feel sure a careful perusal of the church records by counties in the older states would reveal much about Negro Baptists during that span of 150 years—but another must do it. This was due to the fact that those who were the first purchasers of the Africans considered themselves as guardians and not masters of these heathen. From a careful reading, it seems that some good men secured these helpless, starved, emaciated Africans from the ships as a sort of missionary work and that they, on becoming Christians, were added to the White churches. All of the old historians among Southern Baptists and other sects record many churches whose membership was three-fourths, one-half, or even wholly made up of Black folk. The right of one Christian to enslave another was a bone of contention—the cancer which ate its way into many a church membership everywhere. But in course of time American slavery became lucrative, became a custom, and was in less than a hundred years legalized, first into a

---

[8]*The People Called Baptists,* by George White McDaniel (1875-1927), The Sunday School Board of the Southern Baptist Convention, Nashville, Tennessee, *circa* 1919. Ed.

system and then into an institution so cruel that the cries of its victims went up to God and returned as a vexing problem to good men and women, one calling for settlement.

John Wesley had denounced human slavery as the "sum of all villainy," and the question of the right and wrong of our enslavement would not down. Wherever men met—at a crossroad, political meeting, or a log-rolling—or wherever women gathered—at a social or quilting party or like occasions—someone always injected this question, which enlarged itself and it was fought out by all bodies of Christians, resulting in the splitting of churches, conferences, conventions, associations, and synods. But in the meantime, the step between guardian and master was so short, it was soon taken; the ward became the slave, the pulpit and press scourged into silence on the subject, and the results were written into the most inhuman laws ever promulgated by a civilized people. However, as the slaves became Christians, some masters being fully conscious of guilt of slave-holding, emancipated their slaves. Others allowed them to "hire their time." In this way many of the children of the former savages in various ways learned to read and began thinking, devising plans and considering ways to be free. When Toussaint L'Ouverture out-generalled Napoleon and freed Haiti, the good news filtered through to thousands of free Negroes and slaves as well, despite the efforts made to keep the slaves from reading of the victory in Haiti. And this information was the inspiration which gave rise to the fanatical Nat Turner Insurrection, resulting in the unsightly pile of sixty White corpses in a single night.

This caused a mortal fear and dread to seize the slaveholders in all the states. Laws forbidding the assembling of slaves for any purpose were passed in all of the slaveholding states; prayer meeting rooms on all of the plantations were closed; chains were tightened and cruelty was the order of the hour. Then a time came when it was unlawful for Negroes to become Christians and when it was unlawful to build any kind of meeting house for them. Hence, it was that 250 long years of cruel enslavement were meted out to these people and their children.

In the meantime, the spirit of abolition was born in the hearts of good men among the colonists, especially being pronounced among Baptists.

The fires of freedom for 250 years continued to glow and to grow, culminating in the Emancipation Proclamation issued by Abraham Lincoln, September 22, 1862, which went into effect January 1, 1863, thereby giving the emancipated slaves an opportunity to serve and worship God without hindrance.

"There are a great number of Colored persons, particularly slaves, who belong to the Baptist church in Alabama, as well as in other states. There are three or four churches, whose members are entirely Colored. And there are many other churches, where one-half or two-thirds of the members are Colored. It is often remarked that the Blacks are so deplorably ignorant, they should not be members of any church. If they had justice done them, they would not be half so ignorant as they are. Notwithstanding, a great number of those who unite with our churches, express themselves in a very visionary manner, yet it must be acknowledged that a goodly number of them are as really pious as their owners, or other members. Some of the most pious and devoted, in number of our churches, are slaves. Many masters even of those who are professors of religion, are very neglectful of their religious instruction. Is this doing as they would be done by? The law forbidding his master to teach his servants to read ought not to prevent his giving them instruction. That law is unjust and unrighteous. Is there no other way to make obedient servants, but to keep them in abject ignorance? There is, certainly."

"Africans in Huntsville united with the association in 1821, their number was then 76. They have had a gradual increase until the present time, and their number now is 265. Their pastor is Wm. Harris, who is a free Colored man, and called a good preacher."

"Job, mentioned in the history of Canaan Association, died in the bosom of this church. He was an African, brought as a slave to Charleston, S. Carolina, in 1806, purchased by Mr. E. Davis, and owned by him as long as he lived. Job professed religion in 1812, soon learned to read, and taught a Sabbath school for two summers, in Abbeville District, under the care of James Thompson, Esq., was licensed to preach in 1818—with his master, until 1833, when Mr. Davis removed to Pickens County. There Job died on the 17th of November, 1835. His wife followed in less than a year afterward. The last words she ever uttered were "O tell me no more, of this world's vain sore," and as soon as she had finished singing the stanza, she closed her eyes on the world. Few better preachers were found in Alabama in those days than Job. He was generally loved and respected by all who knew him. He lived the Christian and died the saint. In 1827 there were about thirty baptized, chiefly Colored."—*History of Alabama Baptists,* by Hosea Holcombs.

The matter of abolishing slavery was first introduced in the Baptist General Committee, at their meeting at Williams' meeting house, in Goochland County, Virginia, March 7, 1788. The subject was regarded of such importance as to demand calm deliberation. It was, therefore, deferred till the meeting in August of next year, that the churches might have time to express their sentiments on the subject. The General Committee convened in Richmond, August, 1789. "The propriety of hereditary slavery was taken up at this session," says Mr. Sample, "and after some time employed in the consideration of the subject, the following resolution was offered by Mr. John Leland, and adopted:

'Resolved, That slavery is a violent deprivation of the rights of nature, and inconsistent with a Republican Government, and we therefore recommend to our brethren, to make use of every legal measure to extirpate this horrid evil from the land, and pray Almighty God that our honorable legislature may have it in their power to proclaim the great jubilee, consistent with the principles of good policy.'"

Here it will be seen the early Baptists of Virginia, in their great general yearly meeting, declared their opposition to, and abhorrence of slavery, in no ambiguous terms. They viewed it as "a violent deprivation of the rights of nature," a "horrid evil," "inconsistent with a Republican Government" and "the principles of good policy." Whatever may be thought by Virginians upon this subject now, it cannot be denied that the Baptists of ninety years ago were strongly opposed to slavery, and ardently desired its abolishment and pledged themselves to make use of every legal measure to secure its extirpation. They are entitled to the honor, or reproach, according to the viewpoint, of being the first religious society in the South to declare explicitly in favor of the abolition of slavery.

* * * *

The first reference to the unlawfulness of slavery, found on the public records of Kentucky Baptists, is contained in the following queries, sent from Rolling Fork Church, in Nelson County, to Salem Association convened at Cox's Creek Church in the same county, on the 3rd of October, 1789:

"Is it lawful in the sight of God for a member of Christ's church to keep his fellow creature in perpetual slavery?" The question was answered thus: "The association judges it improper to enter into so important and critical a matter, at present." (Clack's Annals of Salem Association, p. 4). This answer gave no relief to the church. It soon afterwards withdrew from the association, all except three members, who were advised to dissolve their organization, and join other churches. Lick Creek Church became divided on the subject of slavery, and was denied a seat in the association, till the difficulty should be settled. Mill Creek Church in Jefferson County sent up a query on the subject of slavery, in 1794, and upon the association's refusing to answer it, withdrew from that body. The preachers that headed the anti-slavery party, in this part of the state, were Joshua Carman and Josiah Dodge. Finding that they could accomplish nothing in the association, they withdrew from that fraternity, with Mill Creek and Rolling Fork churches. They also constituted another church, six miles northwest of Bardstown, of such members of Cox's Creek, Cedar Creek and Lick Creek Churches as had adopted their sentiments. This was, probably, the first church of emancipators constituted in Kentucky. They appear to have made no attempt to form an association at this time, however. Meanwhile, Elkhorn Association, at its meeting, in August, 1791, appointed a committee of three to draw up a memorial to the convention to be held on the 3rd day of April next, requesting them to take up the subject of Religious Liberty, and Perpetual Slavery, in the formation of the constitution of this district, and report at the "Crossing," on the 8th of September. Eastin Garrard and Dudley were the committee. At the meeting, at Great Crossing, in September of the same year, the "Memorial on Religious Liberty and Perpetual Slavery was read and approved." This action of the association did not meet the approval of the churches. Accordingly, the next association, which met at Bryants, in December of the same year, and which was probably convened, in extra session, for the express purpose, "Resolved, that the association disapprove of the memorial which the last association agreed to send to the convention, on the subject of Religious Liberty and the Abolition of Slavery." (Manly's Annals Elkhorn Association.)

Even the earnest and laborious William Hickman was carried beyond the limits of prudence. On a fast day of that same year, he preached at Elkhorn Church, of which he was a member, and the pastor. His text was Isa. 58:6: "Is not this the fast that I have chosen to loose the bands of wickedness, to undo the heavy burdens, and to let the oppressed go free, and that ye break every yoke?" "This sermon," says Theodrick Boulware, "was disingenuous and offensive. The speaker declared non-fellowship for all slaveholders. A few days afterwards, he wrote a letter to the church, declaring his withdrawal." (Manly's Annals) Whether he went into the constitution of an emancipation church or not, does not appear.

About the same time, John Sutton led off a party from Clear Creek Church, which united with a faction of Hillsboro Church, under the leader-

75

Monument erected to the memory of the late Rev. E. C. Morris, D.D., by the National Baptist Convention and Arkansas State Convention jointly at Helena, Ark. Dr. Morris served as pastor of Centennial Baptist Church, Helena, Ark., president Arkansas State Convention and president of the National Baptist Convention during his life. He was regarded by his brethren as a farsighted Christian statesman and a big brother without hatred for those who differed from him.

This is made of Italian marble and is in the front yard of the First Bryant Baptist Church, Savannah, Ga. It was unveiled during the session of the National Baptist Convention, 1916, having been arranged for by the Foreign Mission Board A. R. Robinson, D.D., Chairman; J. R. Bennett, D.D., Recording Secretary; W. F. Graham, D.D., Treasurer; L. G. Jordan, Corresponding Secretary.

ship of Carter Tarrant, and formed an emancipation church, called New Hope. This church was located in Woodford County, and was the first abolition church constituted in that region of the state. (*History of Ten Churches*, p. 81).

The excitement extended all over the settled portion of the state. Several churches in Bracken Association fell in with the emancipation scheme. Among these were Licking Locust, Lawrence Creek, Givgaland Bracken. Among the churches that united in the movement, from North District, were Mount Sterling and Bethel. These and a number of other churches effected an organization, in September, 1807, under the name of "The Baptized Licking Locust Association, Friends of Humanity." At their next meeting they resolved that the present mode of associations, or confederation of churches was unscriptural. They then proceeded to form themselves into an Abolition Society. (*History of Ten Churches*, p. 81). We have no means at present, of knowing the number of churches or preachers that went into this organization. Mr. Benedict estimated their number at twelve churches, twelve ministers and 300 members. In 1816 they met at Lawrence Creek meeting house, in Mason County, under the name of "The Association of Baptist, Friends of Humanity."

* * * *

But the sincerity of the movers did not sanctify the movement. It was simply one of those unfortunate mistakes that grew out of the weakness of human judgment. The emancipation movement accomplished little or no good, and a vast amount of evil. It disturbed the Baptist churches in Kentucky for a period of thirty years. It rent in sunder many of the churches, stirred up the bad passions of the people, gendered a spirit of insubordination among the slaves, and almost destroyed the influence and usefulness of a number of excellent preachers.

The board at this time (1844) was burdened with a troublesome debt: The slavery question, also, was becoming a perplexing one. A crisis in respect to this was reached when the Alabama Baptist Convention sent to the board a series of resolutions expressive of the sentiments of the Baptists of that state, and demanding an explicit avowal that slaveholders are eligible and entitled equally with nonslaveholders to appointments by the board either as agents or as missionaries. The Board replied that all members of the convention, whether slaveholders or not, were unquestionably entitled to all the privileges which the constitution granted or permitted; but that the constitution guaranteed to no one the right to be appointed to any office, or mission; that the board had the appointing power, and its members were accountable only to the convention for the proper discharge of their duties. It was added, however, that with reference to the question implied in the resolutions addressed to the board, its members were agreed that "if any one should offer himself as a missionary having slaves, and should insist on retaining them as his property, they could not appoint him." As soon as this answer was made known, the churches in the Southern States withdrew from the convention and organized the Southern Baptist Convention.

* * * *

One of the missionaries of the convention, Rev. J.L. Shuck, of China, entered the service of the Southern Baptist Convention. All the rest remained in the service of the Union.

History of the Baptists in New England
Burrage
Reported in History of Kentucky Baptists, Pages 158, 159, 167

* * * *

The Baptists have no societies in existence expressly for evangelizing the Negroes; although their associations and conventions do from time to time call up the subject and act upon it. There are more Negro communicants, and more churches regularly constituted, exclusively of Negroes, with their own regular houses of public worship, and with ordained Negro preachers, attached to this denomination than to any other denomination in the United States.

It is difficult to collect the direct efforts of this denomination for the instruction of Negroes, as the reports of the associations are not easily obtained, they being printed and circulated chiefly within their respective bounds. If investigation was carefully made it might be found that in many of the associations of this denomination as much attention is paid to the instruction of the Negroes, as in the Sunbury Association, Georgia, already referred to. There are missionaries in destitute settlements who devote a portion of their time to this people. Perhaps in most of the chief towns in the South there are houses of public worship erected for the Negroes alone; there are three, for example, in the city of Savannah. [It has been] a year or two since I preached to the Baptist Negroes in Petersburg, Va., in their own house of worship crowded to suffocation.

* * * *

1792

Towards the close of this year, the first Colored Baptist church in the city of Savannah began to build a place of worship. The corporation of the city gave them a lot for the purpose. The origin of this church—the parent of several others—is briefly as follows:

George Leile, sometimes called George Sharp, was born in Virginia about 1750. His master, some time before the American war, removed and settled in Burke County, Georgia. Mr. Sharp was a Baptist and a deacon in a Baptist church, of which Rev. Matthew Moore was pastor. George was converted and baptized under Mr. Moore's ministry. The church gave him liberty to preach. He began to labor with good success at different plantations. Mr. Sharp gave him his freedom not long after he began to preach: for about three years he preached at Brampton and Yamacraw in the neighborhood of Savannah. On the evacuation of the country, (1782-1783) he went to Jamaica. Previous to his departure he came up from the vessel lying below the city in the river, and baptized an African woman by the name of Kate, belonging to Mrs. Eunice Hogg, and Andrew, his wife Hannah, and Hagar, belonging to the venerable Mr. Jonathan Bryan.

The Baptist cause among the Negroes in Jamaica owes its origin to the indefatigable and pious labors of this worthy man, George Leile. It does not come within my design to introduce an account of his efforts on that island: I shall add only that in 1784 he commenced preaching in Kingston, and formed a church, and in 1791 had gathered a company of 450 communicants and commenced the erection of a commodious meeting house. It finally cost with steeple and bell $40,001. He was alive in 1810 and about sixty years of age.

About nine months after George Leile left Georgia, Andrew, surnamed Bryan, a man of good sense, great zeal, and some natural elocution, began to exhort his Black brethren and friends. He and his followers were reprimanded and forbidden to engage further in religious exercises. He would however pray, sing, and encourage his fellow worshippers to seek the Lord. Their persecution was carried to an inhuman extent. Their evening assemblies were broken up, and those found present were punished with stripes. Andrew Bryan and Sampson his brother, converted about a year after him, were twice imprisoned, and they with about fifty others were whipped.

---

[9]Charles Colcock Jones, 1804-1863. This work was originally published in 1842. Ed.

When publicly whipped, and bleeding under his wounds, Andrew declared that he rejoiced not only to be whipped, but would freely suffer death for the cause of Jesus Christ, and that while he had life and opportunity, he would continue to preach Christ. He was faithful to his vow, and by patient continuance in well-doing, he put to silence and shame his adversaries; and influential advocates and patrons were raised up for him. Liberty was given Andrew by the civil authority to continue his religious meetings under certain regulations. His master gave him the use of this barn at Brampton, three miles from Savannah, were he preached for two years with little interruption. Not long after Andrew began his ministry he was visited by the Rev. Thomas Barton, who baptized eighteen of his followers on profession of their faith. The next visit was from the Rev. Abraham Marshal of Kioka, who was accompanied by a young Colored preacher, by the name of Jesse Peter, from the vicinity of Augusta. On the 20th of January, 1788, Mr. Marshall ordained Andrew Bryan, baptized forty of his hearers and constituted them with others, 69 in number, a church of which Andrew was the pastor. Such was the origin of the first Colored Baptist church in Savannah. Holcombe's *Letters*; *Analytical Repository*; and Benedicts's *History of Baptists*[10]; from which the preceding account has been taken.

* * * *

Before dismissing this notice, I cannot forbear introducing the remarks of Dr. Holcombe on Andrew Bryan, written in 1812:

"Andrew Bryan has, long ago, not only honorably obtained liberty, but a handsome estate. His fleecy and well set locks have been bleached by eighty winters; and dressed like a bishop of London, he rides, moderately corpulent, in his chair, and with manly features, of a jetty hue, fills every person to whom he gracefully bows, with pleasure and veneration, by displaying in smiles even rows of natural teeth, white as ivory, and a pair of fine black eyes, sparkling with intelligence, benevolence, and joy. In giving daily thanks to God for his mercies my aged friend seldom forgets to mention the favorable change that has of late years appeared through the lower parts of Georgia, as well as of South Carolina, in the treatment of servants."

1793

The African church in Augusta, Ga., was gathered by the labors of Jesse Peter, and was constituted this year by Rev. Abraham Marshall and David

---

[10] *A General History of the Baptist Denomination in America*, by David Benedict (1779-1874), Lincoln and Edmans, 1813. Ed.

Tinsley. Jesse Peter was also called Jesse Golfin on account of his master's name—living twelve miles below Augusta.

The number of Baptists in the United States this year was 73,471; allowing one-fourth to be Negroes, the denomination would embrace between eighteen and nineteen thousand.

* * * *

While in Sierra-Leone in 1920, by a fortunate chance we were permitted to see a small out-of-date book, narrating the early stories of that colony. We could not buy or borrow the book, and what we copied from it, during our sojourn in West Africa, was lost. However, we recall very distinctly the following gist of that story: In 1793, Rev. Moses Baker and a number of other former slaves who left the United States for Nova Scotia with the English troops who had been conquered by the colonists, one day attended a case of what we now call peonage, which was being tried in the courts of that Island. These former slaves had become alarmed, and this case had attracted them to the courtroom in large numbers. To their utter dismay the judge among other things said in rendering his decision from the bench: "It is impossible to cultivate this land without slaves." This startling decision threw consternation in the rank of these former slaves who had helped the British in their fight against the colonists and who had followed the British to Nova Scotia where as they thought their freedom would be secure.

It was these forebodings and surroundings which caused Rev. Moses Baker to organize his forces to move on where their freedom might be secure. So they got in touch with the founders of Sierra-Leone and finally set sail for that colony, where on reaching they organized the first Baptist church known to this day as Rowden St. Baptist Chapel. This property is in the heart of Freetown, the capital of the colony, and is very valuable, although there has been no service in it for more than fifteen years. There was a second church organized out of it, known as the Ebo Baptist Church; finally this church went to pieces with only two or three members remaining, they joined a church organized about 1879 known as the Church of God. This sect dipped their candidate three times as follows:

"I baptize thee in the name of the Father—(dip), In the name of the Son—(dip), In the name of the Holy Ghost—(dip)."

This property was finally sold to the United Brethren and the Church of God, the third split in the Baptist church, had only a handful of members in 1920—while only one man still lived who was a member of the original Baptist church organized by Rev. David George in 1798.

Author

"FROM HISTORY OF GEORGIA BAPTISTS
WITH BIOGRAPHICAL COMPENDIUM"[11]

"About two years before the Revolutionary War a Colored man and slave, by the name of George Leile (sometimes spelled Lisle), was converted in Burke County by the preaching of one, Dr. Moore. George Leile was licensed to preach by the church of which Dr. Moore was pastor, and his labors were attended with success among the people of his own color. About the beginning of the Revolutionary War, George Leile, who had been liberated by his master, a Mr. Henry Sharp, went to Savannah and began to preach at Brampton and Yamacraw, near the city and the surrounding plantations, but at the close of the war when the British evacuated Savannah, George Leile, often also called George Sharp, accompanied them to Kingston, Jamaica, where he soon raised a large church. Before leaving for Jamaica he baptized Andrew, his wife, Hannah, and Hagar, slaves of Jonathan Bryan; and Kate, who belonged to Mrs. Eunice Hogg. Nine months afterwards Andrew, commonly called Andrew Bryan, began to preach at Yamacraw, his labors resulting in many converts. Although persecuted by wicked and cruel White people who sought to interrupt their worship and put a stop to their religious meetings, they were sustained by Chief Justice Henry Osborne, James Habersham, and David Montague. After an examination, permission to worship in the day was given them. A barn for a house of worship was granted them at Brampton by Jonathan Bryan, master of Andrew, and his brother Sampson. A number of respectable and influential people befriended them, and by well-doing they at length disarmed and silenced their bitterest persecutors. Andrew learned to read and for two years preached to great numbers without interruption in his master's barn; although neither licensed nor ordained, converts began to increase. Their condition, as being destitute of any one qualified to administer the ordinances, became known at a distance, and they were visited by Rev. Thomas Burton, an aged Baptist minister, who baptized the converts. In 1788, Rev. Abraham Marshall of Kiekee Church visited them in company with Jesse Peter, a young Colored minister of Augusta, and baptized forty-five more. Later, on the 20th of January, he organized them into a church and ordained Andrew Bryan to the ministry as their pastor. Thus was Andrew Bryan fully authorized to preach and administer the ordinances of his church at

---

[11]*History of the Baptist Denomination in Georgia: with Biographical Compendium and Portrait Gallery of Baptist Ministers and other Georgia Baptists . . .*, J. P. Harrison & Co., 1881. Ed.

last properly organized. Permission was granted them to build a large house of worship in the suburbs of Savannah."

In the course of time it became advisable to organize two other churches with members from the mother church, and on the 26th of December, 1802, the second Colored Baptist church of Savannah was formed, with 200 members. A third, called the Ogeechee Colored Baptist Church was constituted on the 2nd of January, 1803 with 250 members. Two new Colored ministers were also ordained—Henry Cunningham on the first of January, 1803 and Henry Francis on the 23rd of May, 1802—the former to become pastor of the Second church and the latter, pastor of the Ogeechee. In April, 1802, the first Colored church united with the White church of Savannah and the Newington Church, twenty miles north of Savannah. The combined membership of the three Colored churches was 850.

"Andrew Bryan died on the 12th of October, 1812. This son of Africa, after suffering inexpressible persecutions in the cause of his divine Master, was at length permitted to discharge the duties of the ministry among his Colored friends in peace and quiet."

In the city of Augusta, also, there was a large and flourishing church of Colored people which, in 1813 held a membership of 588. In 1818 the number of churches was twelve, with membership of 3541, most of whom were Colored.

The session of the Sunbury for 1825 was interesting. Some eminent and useful men belonged to the body at that time. Among them was a very learned man, converted from Presbyterianism by the thesis: "Did John's Baptism Belong to the Old or New Dispensation?" His name was S.S. Law, of Sunbury. Andrew Marshall, pastor of the first Colored church of Savannah, and others were present. While manifesting so much zeal in the education of the Whites, the convention also exhibited a strong interest in the religious instructions of the Colored people. In 1835 the following was adopted by the body: "Resolved, that we recommend to all our brethren a due consideration of the best method of affording religious instructions to the Black population among us; and that such facilities be afforded for this instruction as in their best judgment may be deemed most expedient.

The slaves were all suddenly freed, and many acted in an outrageous manner, though by no means to the extent one would have supposed. The great misfortune, accompanied by loss of so much property broke many a noble southern heart, and here and there all over the state, aged men were gathered to their fathers, unable to bear up under the impending calamities.

All over the state there was an immensity of Colored Baptists many of whom were organized into churches. In the cities they were under the supervision of the Whites, while in the country, they were generally members of the White churches. The Whites invariably assisted their brethren in organizing churches and in building their houses of worship. They even went farther—they advised and aided them in organizing into associations and forming a state convention after the models furnished by the White organizations. The consequence is that a good state of feeling between the White and Colored Baptists of Georgia has continued to exist down to the present day. The present number of Colored Baptists of Georgia, as far as can be ascertained, is twenty-eight associations, nine thousand churches, and 110,000 members. About one-half of the Colored churches maintain Sunday schools.

Every Baptist church is, in itself, a republic in miniature. "The government is with the body," is a sentiment dear to every member of the Baptist denomination. They rejoice that it is not committed to church wardens, preachers in charge, the bishop, ruling elder, presbyteries, conferences, associations, conventions, nor any other body or set of officers, but to the church itself. With them "the church is the highest ecclesiastical authority on earth," and they do not admit the civil courts have any power or right to prescribe regulations regarding worship or dictate who shall or shall not take part in or conduct divine worship. This has been exemplified, even in our day, as late as 1863, when a number of Baptists of Georgia sent to the State Legislature a protest against an enactment in the code of Georgia, which made it unlawful to license a Negro to preach, whether free or a slave. This protest, written by Dr. H.H. Tucker, assisted in procuring the repeal of the obnoxious law, and, in a most able and pointed manner, declared the position of the Baptists of Georgia with reference to the principle of religious liberty, and as such it deserves to be put permanently on record in the history of our people. The following petition was drawn by Rev. H.H. Tucker, formerly professor in Mercer University, and was presented to the Legislature just before its repeal of the section of the New Code, to which reference is made. The Legislature, however, left in full force the old law requiring permission to be obtained from the Inferior Court, before a slave can be licensed to preach:

"To the Honorable Senate and House of Representatives of the State of Georgia"

The petition of the undersigned members of Baptist churches and citizens of Georgia, respectfully showeth, that,

Whereas, His Excellency, the Governor, in his recent message to your Honorable Body did recommend the repeal of Section 1376 of the New Code which section reads as follows; "It shall be unlawful for any church, society or other body or any persons to grant any license or other authority to any slave or free person of color, to preach, or exhort, or otherwise officiate in church matters," and

Whereas the objections to said section are of the gravest possible character, to-wit:

"It is objectionable in the first place, because it virtually unites the church and state. Its very phraseology shows that the legislation embodied therein has reference to 'Church Matters,' and these are matters over which no human tribunal has any jurisdiction. However inexpedient, unwise and improper for churches to authorize unsuitable persons, whether White or Black to preach, it is still more inexpedient, unwise and improper for civil authorities to take cognizance of matters purely ecclesiastical. As Baptists, we desire to put on record our solemn protest against this encroachment of the kingdom of this world upon the Kingdom of Christ.

"The section in question is objectionable, in the second place because it trespasses upon the rights of conscience, and is a violation of religious liberty. To say nothing of the sacred right of the Black to preach, exhort or pray, if God called and commanded him to do either. Cases might arise in which we might feel it our duty as Baptists to license a man of color to preach or otherwise officiate in church matters. To grant such license would then be a part of our religion. But the Code of Georgia forbids our acting according to the dictates of our own consciences, and in this particular, in prescribing what ours **shall** be we protest against this attempt to bind our consciences. Our religion is a matter between us and our God, with which no power on earth has a right to interfere. Soul-liberty is the rightful heritage of all God's moral creatures. Not over the religion of the slave has civil authority any power, nor yet has it over that of the citizen.

"But aside from local or temporary objections, and aside from its attempted despotism over the conscience of men, the most objectionable feature of all in the obnoxious section is its heaven-daring impiety. It trespasses not only on the rights of men, but on the rights of God. It dictates to the Almighty on what color his preachers shall be. The great majority of the human race are of dark complexion. If one of these among us is called by the great Head of the Church to minister in holy things, the Code of Georgia forbids obedience. It stops the preaching of the everlasting gospel on the ground of a police regulation. It says to Omnipotence "Thus far shalt thou go, and no farther." It allows Jehovah to have ministers of a certain complexion and no other, and so exacting and rigid are these regulations imposed on the Almighty, that they not only forbid his having preachers such as he may choose, but also prescribe that none shall even exhort, or in any way whatever officiate in church matters, unless they be approved by this self-exalted and heaven-defying tribunal."

HISTORY OF THE BAPTISTS IN VIRGINIA

The degraded state of the minds of slaves rendered them totally incompetent to the task of judging correctly respecting the business of the church, and in many churches there was a majority of slaves, in consequence of which, great confusion arose. The Association of Mattaponi directed that the subject should be treated in a circular letter. It has sometimes happened among the churches that partial revivals have been granted in which there would be only those of a particular description brought in. A remarkable stir of this kind took place among the Black people in this church in the year 1806. More than one hundred of them were baptized.

Within the limits of the Dover Association in Richmond, the metropolis of Virginia, here, although the Baptists are not the most flourishing sect, they stand upon respectable ground. They have built by public subscription a large brick meeting-house, and probably move on, both as it respects discipline and the conducting of public worship, with as much regularity as any people in the Union. Their pastor, Elder Courtney, took the care in the year 1788, and under his labors they have enjoyed peace and prosperity. This church is now owned by Colored Baptists.

Williamsburg, Virginia

This church is composed almost, if not altogether, of people of color. Moses, a Black man, first preached among them, and was often taken up and whipped for holding meetings. Afterwards, Gowan, who called himself Gowan Pamphlet, moved from Middlesex, where he had been preaching for some time. He became popular among the Blacks and began to baptize as well as to preach. It seems that the association had advised that no person of color should be allowed to preach, on pain of excommunication. Against this regulation many of the Blacks were rebellious, and continued still to hold meetings. Some were excluded, and among this number was Gowan, just mentioned. Continuing still to preach, and many professing faith under his ministry, not being connected with any church himself, he formed a kind of church of some who had been baptized, and, sitting with him, received such as offered themselves. Gowan baptized them, and moreover appointed their pastor. Some of them, knowing how to write, a church book was kept. They increased to a large number so that in the year 1791, when the Dover Association was held in Mathews County, they petitioned for admittance into the association, stating their number to be almost five hundred. The association received them, so far as to appoint persons to visit them and set things in order. These making a favorable report, they were received, and have associated ever since. A few years since, Gowan died.

For seven or eight years Dr. Thomas Chisman was thought by most of his acquaintances to be singularly zealous and pious. He emancipated his slaves and in other respects made great apparent sacrifices, but his day ended in darkness.

Robert Carter, Esq., once a member of the Virginia Executive Council, and on that account commonly called "Counsellor" Carter, was baptized by Mr. Lunsford shortly after he began to preach in this parts. He was one of the richest men in the State of Virginia, having as some say, six or eight hundred Negroes, besides immense acres of land, etc. After being baptized some years he became conscientious about the lawfulness of hereditary slavery. In a letter to Mr. Rippon of London, he said, "The toleration of slavery indicates great depravity of mind." In conformity to this sentiment, he gradually emancipated all that he possessed.

* * * *

Allen's Creek

The gospel was carried here about 1770, and many persons embraced the truth, under the preaching of Mr. John Williams in 1790. They were united and happy until Mr. Williams moved away. Being left destitute

REV. W. H. BOLLING, D.D.
Virginia

REV. ISRAEL S. CAMPBELL
Texas

A persuasive preacher, an organizer and leader of men. Known and respected in the city where he preached as intently interested in the civic betterment of all the people. He built and paid for Bute Street Baptist Church in Norfolk, in a few years. He fell asleep as a sacrifice to the cause which he loved.

First Colored Baptist preacher to ordain other preachers in Texas. Pastored Avenue "L" Baptist Church in Galveston for many years. He was among the Civil War. One or more men of this type came from Canada or the North, to which they or their parents had fled in search of freedom, to every Southern State and were key men for the American Baptist Home Mission Society.

The above is one of the outstanding homes of which there are hundreds of thousands just as good, and many thousands larger and more costly.

of ministerial instruction and having a considerable number of Black people in their society of whom there were some preachers of talent, they commenced the administration of the ordinances without ordination. They were persecuted by some of the community and protected by others, equally respectable. They increased rapidly so that in a few years more than one hundred Blacks were baptized by them.

In 1787 the lawfulness of hereditary slavery was debated in this association. They determined that hereditary slavery was a breach of the divine law. They then appointed a committee to bring in a plan to gradually emancipate them, which was accordingly done. They were treading upon delicate ground. It excited considerable tumult in the churches, and accordingly, in their letters to the next association,remonstrated so decidedly that the association resolved to take no further steps in the business.

The association took up the subject to the general meeting by correspondence at different periods, but in every instance decided against encouraging it. There are, however, within the limits of the district a very respectable party who was favorable to the institution of the general meeting.

* * * *

About 1792 partly from bad health and other causes, Mr. Armstead resigned his charge. After his resignation the church declined greatly. They employed Jacob Bishop, a Black man of considerable talent, to preach for them. This, as might have been expected, could not answer in Virginia.

Mr. Barrow carried his opinions of liberty so far as think it criminal to hold Negroes in slavery. Therefore he emancipated all he had. Although this measure proved his disinterested zeal to do right, it is questionable whether it was not in the end productive of more evil than good. While it embarrassed his affairs at home by lessening his resources for the maintenance of a large family, it rendered him suspicious among his acquaintances, and probably in both ways limited his usefulness.

THE AFRICAN BAPTIST CHURCHES OF MISSOURI

First African Baptist Church, established at St. Louis. "In March 1818, Messrs. Peck and Welch, missionaries of the Baptist General Convention, organized a Sunday school in the village of St. Louis, for Colored people, with fourteen pupils. To accommodate the feelings of the slaveholding community, certificates were required from their masters or owners. By pursuing a conciliatory course, the approbation of the influential citizens of the town and vicinity was gained. In a few weeks the number of attendants, adults and children, averaged ninety to one hundred. They were taught to read and were instructed in the Scriptures. A part of the time was occupied with religious worship. Many became hopefully converted, were baptized, and united with the church. It was soon found expedient and profitable to hold separate meetings for this class. In 1822 they were formed into a separate branch, but still under the supervision of the White brethren. For several years they were visited monthly by J.M. Peak, who exercised supervision over their meetings and guided them in discipline. In 1827 they erected and finished a plain and comfortable brick house for worship, in which they were partially aided by the citizens. John Berry Meachum, a free man of color, became their pastor, with several assistants who exhorted and instructed the people. J.B. Meachum was born a slave, but obtained his freedom by his own industry. The next step was to procure funds by labor and purchase his father, a slave and a Baptist preacher in Virginia. He was then a resident of Kentucky, where he married a slave and where he professed religion. His wife's master, removing to Missouri, Meachum followed her, and arrived in St. Louis with $3.00 in 1815. Being a carpenter and cooper he soon obtained business, purchased his wife and children, commenced preaching, and was ordained in 1825. In the next ten years he purchased, including adults and children, about 20 slaves; he never sold them again. His method was to place them at service and encourage them to form habits of industry and economy and when they had paid for themselves, he set them free. In 1835 he built a steamboat, which he provided with a library and made it a temperance boat. He was then worth about $25,000, nor was he less enterprising and successful in religious matters. Within less than eight years from the time the First African Church became an independent body, which was 1827, it consisted of 220 members, of which about 200 were slaves. A large Sabbath school, a Temperance Society, a deep-toned missionary spirit, uncommon order and correctness among the slave population, and strict and regular discipline in the church was among the fruits of his arduous and persevering labor in St. Louis."—Allen's Register.

Meachum continued pastor of the First African Church for thirty-eight years, and was succeeded by Emanuel Cartwright, who was succeeded by Henry Thompson, who was succeeded by Thomas Jefferson, the pastor in 1880. All of the Colored Baptist churches in St. Louis are the outgrowth of this body.

Second Colored Baptist Church

By the year 1847 the old First Baptist Church had increased to about 800 members, and the same year 22 members withdrew from it and formed what was then called the Second Colored Baptist Church, but now known as the Eighth Street Colored Baptist Church. The first pastor of this new interest was Richard Snethen, once owned by Mrs. Dorcas Duncan, the mother of Elder Lewis Duncan. He was a native of Virginia and was brought to Missouri a slave about the year 1840 or before.

He was succeeded in the pastoral office at the expiration of one year by J.R. Anderson, who continued in this relation until his death in 1862. In 1852 the present church edifice on the corner of Eighth Street and Christy Avenue was erected, its first cost being for the lot $500.00, and for building $3,000.00. In three years the church had increased to 195 members, and by the year 1872 its members numbered 991. One of the prominent constituent members was William. B. Brooks, who subsequently became a preacher and traveled over a larger portion of the state.

William B. Brooks was born in Essex County, Virginia, December 26th, 1826, the slave property of Thomas Pitts, and moved to Missouri in March, 1842. He united with the First African Church, St. Louis, then under the pastoral care of J.B. Meachum. In September 1864, the Northwestern and Southern Colored Baptist Convention was organized in the Eighth Street Colored Baptist Church for the "evangelizing of the Western states and territories." This body at once appointed Wm. B. Brooks, then a licentiate missionary for Missouri. He was instructed to gather the Colored Baptists of the state into churches. In November following, Mr. Brooks was ordained. From his first appointment, he commenced active operations and in September 1865, organized the first Colored Baptist church at Warrensburg. At this time, outside of St. Louis, Colored churches were known to exist only in Hannibal, St. Joseph, Jefferson City, and probably Lexington. In the winter of the same year Rev. Brooks visited Boonville and formed the first Colored Baptist church in that town, consisting of 20, and in the spring of 1866, Chesterfield Church was formed by him, of 25 members. Then following the organization of the first Colored Baptist church of Columbia, of 12 members, in July 1855, the first Colored Baptist church of Louisiana was formed with the same number of members. During the summer of 1866 Mr. Brooks organized the Mt. Zion Church, St. Louis, of members principally from the Eighth Street Colored Church. Tipton Colored Church was the next organized the same summer. In the fall of 1866, he gathered into an organization the Colored Baptist Church of Rosheport, and another in New London in the early spring of 1867. In April, 1867, he formed the first Colored Baptist church of Huntsville, being assisted by W.R. Rothwell. Rev. Brooks had been preaching at this point about a year, during which time nearly 100 had been added to the Baptist members, mostly by baptism. The first Colored Baptist church of Mexico was founded in the summer of 1867 by Elder Brooks, assisted by Elder S.A. Beauchamp, pastor of the White church.

Elder Brooks began his missionary labors early in the year 1866 under the appointment of the American Baptist Home Mission Society. He thus continued until the close of 1867. In January 1868 he was called to the pastoral office of the Chamber Street Colored Baptist Church, St. Louis, to which he gave three-fourths of his time, devoting the other forth to itinerating. He continued at Chamber Street Church six years and nine months, when he returned to the mission field and so continued until 1879.

North Missouri Association

This was the first association of African Baptists in Missouri, having been formed at Chillicothe in September, 1866—the design of which was to embrace all the churches of this order in the state. (Up to this time we have been unable to procure the names of the churches and ministers in this new organization). The object of this organization is thus stated in its constitution:

"Article 2. The object of this association shall be to promote the preaching of the gospel in this state, and the thorough evangelization of the race."

The North Missouri Association continued as a body for five years, when, in 1871, it was divided into two districts, numbers one and two. The preliminary meeting for the formation of the second district having been held at Lexington during the session of the old North Missouri Association, in 1870, at which time a meeting of them was appointed at Independence for September 21, 1871, when the North Missouri Colored Baptist Association, second district, was fully organized. This body was composed of all the churches of the old North Missouri that were south of the Missouri River—eighteen in all, with 2,537 members. In 1878 this association was divided, and another body formed called the

Third District of the North Missouri Colored Baptist Association. This was consummated November 8, 1878, at Cape Girardeau. Its territory was all that portion of the state south of St. Louis County, and East of Franklin County. The Fredericktown, Charleston, Cape Girardeau, Wolf Island, Texas Bend, Bird's Point, Big Lake, and Potosi Colored Baptist Churches were the constituents of this association, in all nine churches, with 144 members. Twenty-seven dollars was collected.

The North Missouri Association, District No. 1, gained strength rapidly and numbered forty-two churches in 1872, only one year after the division. In 1880, having grown to seventy-three churches, it again divided into the Eastern and Western divisions.

The Eastern Division of the North Missouri Association was formed at Columbia, September 13, 1880, at the close of the 16th Annual Session of the Old North Missouri. Its territory embraced the counties of Schuyler, Adair, Macon, Randolph, Scotland, Knox, Shelby, Monroe, Audrain, Boone, Callaway, Clarke, Lewis, Marions, Pike, Ralls, Lincoln, Warren, St. Charles, Montgomery, Putman, and Sullivan.

The Northwestern Division of the North Missouri Baptist Association was organized at the close of the session of the North Missouri Association at Columbia, September 13, 1880, embracing all the counties in Missouri, north of the Missouri River, and west of the territory of the eastern division.

Union (Colored) Baptist Association

This fraternity was organized in 1869, most likely in the old First African Baptist Church, St. Louis. It was composed of churches mainly in Eastern Missouri and south of the Missouri River. Rev. Emanuel Cartwright was the leading spirit and moderator of this body as long as he was able to attend its meetings. In 1871 this association was composed of twenty-five churches, Pleasant Hill and Harrisonville, Cass County, being the only two west of Jefferson City.

In 1880 the Colored Baptists of the state furnished the following statistics:

Total number of churches . . . 147   Ministers 70
Members 10,980

(These are independent churches)
Sarepta Association--Georgia

CHURCHES	COUNTIES	Const.	PASTORS	Baptized	Members
North Newport, Savannah,First African	Chatham	1788	A.Marshall	102	1369
Savannah, 2nd African	Chatham	1802	John Cox	91	841
Savannah, 3rd African	Chatham			15	205
Great Ocheege, African	Chatham	1803			315
Abercorn, African	Chatham			9	78
White Oak, African	Chatham				75
White Bluff, African	Chatham		Guy McQueen	6	146
Oakland African	Chatham			3	43
St. Mary's Branch of African, Savannah	Chatham, Camden				120
St. Catherine's African	Chatham			7	149
Cumberland, African					124
Clifton, African	Chatham			29	57

Colored Baptist Preachers Listed in Georgia

Ardis, Ben	L	Johnson, Peter	
Beall, Frank	L	Jones, Philip	L
Cox, John	P	Key, George	P
Fraser, Garrison	P	Low, Kelly	P
Golphin, Moses	P	Marshall, Andrew	P
Horton, Caesar		McQueen, Guy	P
Johnson, Henry			

P-Pastor.   L-Licensed.

RETURNS FOR 1851
Elkhorn Association—Kentucky

CHURCHES	COUNTIES	Const.	PASTORS	Baptized	Members
Lexington, First African	Fayette	1824	London Ferrell	77	1548
Lexington, Second African	Fayette	1844		4	112
Versailles, African	Woodford	1848		16	105

Long Run Association—Kentucky

Louisville, African	Jefferson	1842	Henry Adams		820
African	Jefferson			39	306

Tate's Creek Association—Kentucky

Tate's Creek and African, Richmond	Madison	1786	T. J. Drane	8	140

CHURCHES	COUNTIES	Const.	PASTORS	Baptized	Members
Mississippi River Association--Louisiana					
New Orleans, Second	Orleans				62
Maryland Union Association--Maryland					
Baltimore, First	Baltimore	1836	Moses C. Clayton		91
Baltimore, Second,	Baltimore	1848	Noah Davis	2	15
Washington, Second	Washington, D. C.	1850		5	19
Missouri Association--Missouri					
St. Louis, First African	St. Louis	1828	J. B. Meacham	33	648
St. Louis, Second	St. Louis	1849	John R. Anderson	15	209
Hudson River Association--South--New York					
Brooklyn, Concord St.	Kings	1847	L. Black	6	50
Philadelphia Association--Pennsylvania					
Philadelphia, First African	Philadelphia	1809	Richard Vaughn	1	197
Philadelphia, Union	Philadelphia	1832	Sampson White	13	254
Blockley, African	Philadelphia	1827		4	80
Washington, First	Washington, D.C.	1838	G. Brown	3	216
Philadelphia, Third	Philadelphia	1841	J. Henderson	3	75
Philadelphia, Shiloh	Philadelphia	1842	Jeremiah Asher	11	114
Dover Association--Virginia					
Williamsburg, African	James City		S. Jones	17	305
Richmond, First African	Henrico	1841	Robert Ryland	151	2763
Richmond, Second African	Henrico		J. Porter	154	560
Middle District Association--Virginia					
Manchester, African	Chesterfield		Levi D. Horner	51	534
Portsmouth Association--Virginia					
Petersburg, African	Dinwiddie	1826		30	1635
Petersburg, Gillfield	Dinwiddie		H. Crowder	19	1361
Petersburg, Third	Dinwiddie		R. R. Overby	104	
Norfolk, First	Norfolk		Robert Gordon	12	643
Norfolk, Bute Street	Norfolk	1849	V. Palin	6	250

Strawberry Association

African	Campbell		James C. Clopton		225

Valley Association

Fincastle, African	Botetourt		A. C. Dempsey	17	118

COLORED MEMBERS
OF BAPTIST CHURCHES PRIOR TO 1850

The minutes of numerous associations report, in part, their Colored members. We have, with much pains, collected the following statistics, imperfect as they are:

State	Church	Members	State	Church	Members
Massachusetts	1	141	Pennsylvania	5	550
Rhode Island	1	53	Maryland	1	105
New York	2	467	District of Columbia	1	195

These are independent Colored churches.

STATES	ASSOCIATIONS	MEMBERS	
Virginia	10 (Associations)	White	17,938
		Colored	28,386
		Total	46,324
North Carolina	4 (Associations)	White	6,271
		Colored	3,248
		Total	9,519
South Carolina	5 (Associations)	White	6,504
		Colored	7,987
		Total	14,491
Georgia	17 (Associations)	White	18,902
		Colored	12,872
		Total	31,774
Alabama	4 (Associations)	White	5,678
		Colored	2,240
		Total	7,918
Mississippi	4 (Associations)	White	18,649
		Colored	2,078
		Total	20,727

Tennessee	1 (Association)	White	31,840
		Colored	636
		Total	32,476
Kentucky	4 (Churches)	White	60,111
		Colored	2,028
		Total	62,139
Missouri	1 (Association)	White	979
		Colored	213
		Total	1,192
Ohio	(Association)	White	24,743
		Colored	1,072
		Total	25,815
Illinois	1 (Association)	White	12,363
		Colored	217
		Total	12,580

The aggregate of Colored members, as above reported in part, in sixteen states, is 62,685. We estimate this number as not more than one-half the actual number in the United States. --*Baptist Almanac, 1849*

Rev. J. Francis Robinson, D.D., who served as field secretary of the Publishing Board for several years and always took part in things pertaining to the group and denomination. He was a fine speaker and much loved by the brethern. He passed to his reward 1929.

SISTER JOANNA P. MOORE
This good woman came among us at the close of the Civil War and what she has been to our women eternity alone will reveal. The Fireside School, Bible Bands and Children's Societies have sprung up at her suggestion throughout our entire Southland.

Rev. W. W. Hay, Pastor of Mt. Gilead Church, Ft. Worth, Texas, and First Independent Baptist Church, Corsicana, Texas.

Rev. DeBaptiste, Pastor Mt. Gilead Baptist Church, Fort Worth, Texas.

Chapter VI

Those who brought this convention into being deserve great praise. It has laid the foundation of a mission work in Africa that will afford material for the use of this convention for all time to come. The seed has been planted. The ripe fruit of converted souls and bright experiences of missionaries, who have suffered persecution, endured hardness, in the midst of tears, blood, agony and death will always afford a field from which eloquent and effective appeals can be made for men, sympathy and money for the work over here. A. R. Griggs, D.D., President The Foreign Convention, 1993.

Just as other races have left their impress upon the world, so must we. All the civilizing forces that touch and mould us are intended to be productive of these results, and we are set down in history as a success or a failure as we do or do not arise to the best of our opportunities.

E. K. Love, D.D.

THE NATIONAL BAPTIST CONVENTION

The inception of our present National Baptist Convention was in Montgomery, Alabama. Before we began this survey, in 1924, we wrote Drs. C.O. Booth then in Detroit, Michigan; T.L. Jordan, of Meridian, Mississippi; H.W. Bowen, of Chicago; A.F. Owens, of Alabama; R. Spiller of North Carolina; J.M. Armstead, of Portsmouth, Virginia; and Mrs. Sheppard, of North Carolina. All of these were at the organizing in Montgomery, Ala., 1880. At that time we had no line-up on any other nationally known organization. Dr. Booth passed to his reward before he had chance to answer; Drs. Jordan and Bowen answered, describing the joyful and yet earnest attitude of the men who gathered, the pleasant weather, and hearty reception they met on reaching Montgomery.

Prompted by a never failing faith in God and a desire to be of greater service to the Master, Rev. W.W. Colley of Virginia, who had served as a missionary in Africa under the Foreign Mission Board of the Southern Baptist Convention, returned to the States in 1879, imbued with the desire of awakening the Colored Baptists to a greater love for God and Africa. He spent much time with the leaders in Virginia, and Washington, D.C., considering the possibilities of organizing these churches into a convention.

He interested the most thoughtful among the pastors and the old Virginia Missionary Society of Richmond, which society took part in sending Lott Carey to Africa, January 23, 1821. By the direction of that society and the advice of leaders, Brother Colley, with his magnetic personality, power of appeal, and knowledge of the field, canvassed the States, arousing the churches and pastors to the need of such an organization.

After months of travel and personally touching hundreds of pastors, the call was sent forth, summoning for the first time Negro Baptists to a well thought out national meeting. These leaders were only fifteen years from bondage; we may imagine their timidity in answering such a call and, indeed, their response was marvelous.

We must remember that the distance between churches was much greater at that time than now; travel was more by water than by rail. Wednesday, November 24th, 1880, the call was answered and we may well recall that only the men in the largest cities and on a few adjoining plantations knew each other intimately. The meeting was hailed with much joy and delight because here the men hoped and expected to meet the representative men of the denomination from all the states, to become better acquainted with one another as of one household of faith. They hoped to know more of each other's work, each other's plans, each other's views and desires; and by counseling one with the other to better carrying forth the work of their common Savior and Lord. Again it was to be the dawn of a brighter day in regard to the question of giving Africa the gospel of Christ.

The call was answered by 151 delegates, representing eleven states, as follows:

ALABAMA

Delegates from State Conventions.—Revs. M. Tyler, C.O. Booth,W.H. Booth, W.H. McAlpine, J. Wilhite, J.P. Barton, A.F. Owens, W.R. Pettiford, A. Cunningham, W.J. Stevens, W. A. Burch, P. Underwood, Wallace Allen, E.K. Love, and P. Matthews... Uniontown Association.—Revs. W.H. McAlpine, S. Dozier ..Muscle Schoals Association and S.S. Convention.—Rev. J.F. Thompson ... Dallas County Association.—Revs. Peter Underwood, D. Boyd, H. Blevens, C.L. Brooks ... Eufaula S.S. Convention.—Rev. J. Wilhite, Antioch Association.—Rev. S. Fanteroy. Colored Bethlehem Association.—Rev. A. Cunningham... Pine Grove Association.—Rev. E. Thornton, C. Thornton.. Alabama District S.S. Convention.—H.A. Loveless, R.M. Tyler. East Alabama S. S. Convention.—Rev. R. Fenn, J.D. Maddox. Shelby Springs Association. —Rev. H.S. Williams. First Church, Birmingham.-Rev. A.C. Jackson ... Mt. Zion Church.—Rev. L.J. Jones.. Mt. Canaan Church.—J.P, Barton ... Alabama District Association.—Rev. M. Tyler, J.A. Foster, George Washington...Mt. Gilead and Pleasant Hill Churches.—Rev. A.A. Scott. New Hope Church, Sherman.—Rev. W.M. Merritt. Marion Church and S.S.— Rev. W.H. McAlpine, J.W. Curtis, R. Nickerson. Everdale Church.—Rev. G.J. Brooks... Friendship, Batesville.—Rev. J.D. Maddox...Midway Church.- Rev. A. Rivers ... Mt. Olive Church and Cedar Fork.—Rev. D. Small ... Bethel.—Rev. G.C. Cosby...Baptist Lily and Mt. Olive.—Rev. C.P. Cain ... Town Creek.—Sidney Ross ... Roxana.—Rev. Smart Taylor ... Old Elma.— Curtis Woods ... First Baptist, Wetumpka.—L.P. Moore ... St. Phillips Street, Selma.—Rev. W.A. Burch ... Bethel and Antioch Churches Rev. Josiah Davidson ... Mt. Clairborn, Union Chapel and Barlow Bend.—Rev. A. Johnson..Mt. Zion S.S. Hawkinsville.— W.M. Boykin ... Marion Baptist Foreign Mission Society.—J.W. Curtis, N.R. Nickerson ... Selma Baptist Missionary Society.—H. Woodsmall, D.T. Gully, D.L. Prentice, Mrs. A.A. Bowie, D.A. May, Eli Adams, M.W. Alston, C.W. Childs, Miss E.F. Cassidy, Mrs. Della Pettiford, Deacon Charles White, Revs. W.A. Burch, C.O. Booth, Charles Goldsby ...Uniontown S.S. Convention.—Rev. W.R. Pettiford.

ARKANSAS
Revs. George Robinson, Pine Bluff; P.H. Hatchett, J. Simms Little Rock.

NORTH CAROLINA
Revs. F.R. Howell, C. Johnson, Raleigh; A. Buck, Charles Smith, Halifax.

GEORGIA
Rev. E.K. Love, Thomasville; C.H. Dwelle, Americus; A.A. Blake, East Point.

FLORIDA
Rev. James Page, Tallahassee.

LOUISIANA
Rev. J. Marks, Miss J.P. Moore.

MISSISSIPPI
Rev. R. Ramsey, Meridian; J. Harvey, Winona; J.W. Muse, Macon; H.W. Bowen, Oxford; A.J. Dent, Pontotoc; G.W. Allen, Okolona; F.E. Plummer,

P.I. Fraxtius, Jackson; Daniel Webster, Meridian; T.L. Jordan, Columbus.

TEXAS
Rev. C.P.Martin, Jefferson; F. Hooks, Texarkana; E. Barnes, W.A. Walton, Navasota.

TENNESSEE
Rev. J.M. Armstead, Knoxville; P. Guinn, Rodgersville Junction; C.P. Hughes, Shelbyville; J.A. Steward, Murfreesboro; W.A. Brinkley, R.N. Countee, Memphis.

VIRGINIA
Revs. J.W. Patterson, Danville; E.G. Corpew, Portsmouth; O.H. Carey, Abingdon; R. Spiller, D. King, Norfolk.

The meetings were held in the First Baptist Church, of Montgomery, Alabama, with Rev. J.M. Armstead of Tennessee, temporary secretary.

Rev. W.W. Colley being the best informed on the subject for which they gathered, called the meeting to order and was made temporary chairman.

The first day's session consisted of enrollment of members, appointment of committees, hearing of welcome addresses and short, pointed addresses by members expressing the status of their respective states in regard to the mission to be accomplished. The first welcome to the delegation was delivered by Rev. W.H. McAlpine; the other welcome by the pastor, Rev. J.A. Foster.

Rev. R. Spiller of Norfolk, Virginia, being introduced preached an able Introductory Sermon, using as his text, "He that goeth forth and weepeth, bearing precious seed, shall doubtless come again with rejoicing, bringing his sheaves with him."

W.H. McAlpine of Alabama, was the first permanent president; and Rev. J.M. Armstead of Tennessee, and G.H. Dwelle of Georgia, secretaries. They organized as the FOREIGN MISSION BAPTIST CONVENTION OF THE UNITED STATES OF AMERICA. In 1886, THE AMERICAN NATIONAL BAPTIST CONVENTION was organized at St. Louis, Mo. with Rev. William J. Simmons, D.D., of Kentucky as president. This organization attempted to exist apart from the Foreign Convention which was only four years old, and its first six missionaries had been in West Africa only one year. However, at its second meeting the American National Baptist Convention sent a committee to the Foreign Mission Convention asking permission to meet with it which was agreed upon. THE BAPTIST NATIONAL EDUCATIONAL CONVENTION was organized in the District of Columbia in 1893. In this same year it was suggested that what was called the "TRIPARTITE UNION" be formed to consist of the New England Convention, organized in 1875; the African Foreign Mission Convention organized..., and the Foreign Mission Convention of America, organized in 1880. But for some unknown reason, the reports made at the Montgomery session in 1894 show that the Tripartite Union plan had failed, as the following will show:

"To the Fifteenth Anniversary of the Baptist Foreign Mission Convention held in the First Baptist Church, Montgomery, Ala., Sept. 13-16, 1894, Rev. Andrew J. Stokes, Pastor. The Fifteenth Annual Report of the Executive Board of the Baptist Foreign Mission Convention of the United States is herewith submitted with a hope that every friend and member of the Convention may unite with the Board in giving thanks to God who has preserved us amid the financial shock under which the world is now staggering. The number of the missionaries on the foreign field is smaller than any of the previous years of the Convention's history.

"THE TRIPARTITE UNION"

The union of the New England Convention, the Baptist African Mission Convention of America, and the Baptist Foreign Mission Convention which was affected at Washington, D.C., one year ago, has not reached the expectations of many. Under the "Tripartite Union," the Board agreed to try and raise the sum of five thousand dollars to plant a new field in the Congo, and to send forth five missionaries to labor therein. Since there is an address to be delivered upon the "Tripartite" it is not deemed wise to make any further statements in relation to the subject in this report. Mrs. Lucy A. Cole acting secretary."

A crisis was reached and all seemed lost. A new line-up was arranged. In 1894 when the "Tripartite" Convention at Montgomery, Ala., failed, the Foreign Mission Convention was only fourteen years old; the American National Baptist Convention was eight years old, and the National Educational Convention was only one year old. Had the New England and the African Foreign Mission Convention met as agreed there would have been in Montgomery, at that time, five conventions; each of them trying to be national, in a way, and all living at a "poor dying rate." Those who led them seemed lost for a program. The Foreign Mission Convention which was the most outstanding of the lot, like the church at Ephesus, had lost its first love. The Foreign Mission work had run down to the point where only one missionary was on the African field; this was the Rev. R.A. Jackson, and he, in a large measure, was on his own resources. The fourteen years of hard work of the Foreign Mission Convention seem to be at an end, with all workers either dead or at home. This was the first time in fourteen years that the Foreign Mission Convention had met where it was originally organized. As stated above, they were all run down and great speech-making and prayerless giving had gotten them nowhere. Was it a love for show, honor, office, or a downright love for money which brought them to this verge? Who was responsible, the Board at Richmond, or the field secretary? All had ceased to look to him from whom all help comes, and who is responsible was the question. In the controversy, Dr. Luke showed that inattention and waste by the Board was responsible for the suffering of the missionaries on the foreign field and also the poor support given among the churches at home. Rev. S.E. Griggs, then a student in the Richmond Theological Seminary and a pastor in the state, was employed by the Board to answer the attacks of Dr. Luke, which he did, greatly softening the blows of public criticism thereby. However the Board became so offended that they did not come to the Montgomery meeting to report the year's work. Here the trained leader was at his best when Dr. Pegues of North Carolina offered the following resolution:

"Whereas the interests and purposes of the three national bodies; namely, The Foreign Mission, National, and Educational Conventions can be conserved and fostered under the auspices of one body; and:

"Whereas the consolidation of the above named bodies will economize both time and money, therefore,

"Resolved, that the Foreign Mission Convention appoint a committee of nine, who shall enter immediately into consultation with the Executive Boards of the National and Educational Conventions, for the purpose of effecting a consolidation of the three bodies upon the following plan:

1. That there shall be one national organization of American Baptists.
2. Under this, there shall be a Foreign Mission Board, with authority to plan and execute the foreign mission work according to the spirit and purpose set forth by the Foreign Mission Convention of the United States.
3. There shall be a Board of Education, and also, a Board of Missions to carry into effect the spirit and purpose of the National and the Educational Conventions, respectively" (See *Journal 1894*, page 15).

This resolution was surely put in this good man's mind by the Lord, and, in the same church where many of the leaders who were at this meeting just fourteen years before, amid songs, prayers, and tears brought forth the Baptist Foreign Mission Convention of the U.S.A. Only fourteen years later, here in the old First Church at Montgomery, they again renewed their vows unto the Lord. Here they began their work all over. Only the love for Africa and others in non-Christian lands, and the urge by a few choice souls, our Convention has lived to be fifty years old. God and the Baptists are marching on. In 1895 at Atlanta, Georgia, after several days of discussion, the report of the committee which was appointed at Montgomery, Ala., in 1894, was adopted. This committee comprised the following persons: Rev. William H. McAlpine, Alabama; Joseph E. Jones, Virginia; A.W. Pegues, Ph.D., N.C.; A.S. Jackson, La.; J.H. Frank, Ky.; A. Hubbs, Texas; Jacob R. Bennett, Ark.; Wesley G. Parks, Tenn.; Andrew J. Stokes, Alabama. By the merging of these bodies whatever had been undertaken by any or either of the individual organizations was rendered null and void unless such purpose or action was definitely set forth in the new constitution. Along this line it is said that a contention arose; some insisting it should be clearly stated in the preamble to the constitution that a part of the work of the convention must be the preparation of their own Sunday school literature by Negro Baptists, through their own Baptist Book Concern; but because of the hostility of many of the prominent members in all of the merging bodies, the statement in regard to this phase of the work was eliminated. Many who took part in that meeting say it was hoped by the more learned, that the idea of printing was stamped out. The reason for this was said to be that all or nearly all who fought the idea were employees of the Northern Societies which were then furnishing literature for the Sunday schools of our churches, and these workers felt that such steps would be construed as enmity against our White brethren and friends who had given so much, and endured so much for us. So in the readjusting of things the following shows the first official roster:

OFFICERS - ELECT
Rev. E.C. Morris, D.D., Arkansas President
Vice-Presidents
Rev. J.L. Barksdale . . . . Virginia
Rev. A.D. Hurt . . . . Tennessee
Rev. R.W. Baylor . . . . South Carolina
Rev. R. Mitchell . . . . Kentucky
Rev. G.B. Howard . . . . West Virginia
Rev. J.P. Robinson . . . . Arkansas
Rev. C.T. Walker . . . . Georgia

Rev. H. Watts . . . . Texas
Rev. W.M. Massey . . . . Texas
Rev. G.L.P. Taliaferro . . . . Pennsylvania
Rev. H.W. Bowen . . . . Mississippi
Rev. L.N. Robinson . . . . Florida
Rev. G.W. Lee . . . . District Columbia
Rev. A.S. Jackson . . . . Louisiana
Rev. C. Johnson . . . . North Carolina
Rev. W.C. Bradford . . . . Alabama

REV. D. A. TOWNSEND, D.D.

Born—Franklin Co., Tenn., September 27, 1848.

Died—Winchester, Tenn., December 23, 1927.

Graduate—Roger Williams University, Nashville, Tenn. Pioneer minister, educator and citizen. Successful pastor for 50 years; aggressive educator, 51 years; faithful clerk Elk River District Association, 50 years.

Member of the National Baptist Convention, and an ardent and loyal supporter of all work of the Convention.

T. J. Searcy was a strong courageous preacher. I knew him when in school and when together we made the bread for the Roger Williams University to help ourselves through school. He continued in this way until he finished and was for a long while among leaders of Tennessee Baptists. He passed to his reward while pastoring Metropolitan Baptist Church in Memphis, Tenn.

Three new Boards were selected by the National Baptist Convention as follows:

The Foreign Mission Board located in Louisville, Ky., Rev. John H. Frank, Chairman; Daniel A. Gaddie, Treasurer; Brother William H. Steward, Recording Secretary; Dr. Luke, Corresponding Secretary. The Home Mission Board, located in Little Rock, Ark., Rev. G.W.D. Gains, Chmn.; Rev. J.A. Booker, Recording Secretary; Rev. R.H. Boyd, Corresponding Secretary. The Educational Board, located in Washington, D.C., Rev. A. Wilbanks, Chairman; Rev. W. Bishop Johnson, Corresponding Secretary.

What The National Baptist Convention Stands For

"Unto whomsoever much is given, of him shall much be required." The principles of Baptists commit them to a large program. The whole gospel for the world is their program. No people profess more by their doctrines. We are under obligations to match professions with practice. The world, Christian and non-Christian, has a right to demand works as proof of our faith. Unless we can show results we must give place to those who can. This is merely a cold commercial rule; it was the acid test of Jesus-"By their fruits, ye shall know them"—*Selected.*

As a denomination, Baptists have some principles—tenets—which distinguish them, set them apart, from all others. Among them are:

(1) That the New Testament, in its entirety, comprises the whole rule and guide for humanity through the light of the Holy Spirit, and not the Old Testament.

(2) That the acts and sayings of Jesus Christ should neither be added to, as in forms, rituals, etc., nor subtracted from by any omissions, from what Christ as Lawgiver practiced and commanded. Baptists, therefore, do not administer circumcision, do not sprinkle, nor do they baptized infants. (See Rev. 22:19.)

(3) Baptists believe in individual responsibility, with no intervention between the soul and its God; that all believers are priests and may come directly to God in confession of their sins, may praise Him and ask for

guidance. They have always opposed the union of church and state for this reason and have contended always for religious freedom, standing up for the right of each individual to worship God as his conscience directs. A child may inherit of his parents, big or small feet, flat or sharp nose, good or bad disposition, but never their religion. Religion is a matter between God and the soul.

(4) That since Christ himself sanctioned the baptism of believers only, the church is only for saved persons, and that infants are not included in this category. They cite the accounts of the households of Cornelius, Crispus, and the jailer (Acts 16:31-34).

(5) That New Testament, not church but churches were independent and self-governing with no general body ruling the local church. Messengers sent from cooperating churches to said general bodies come in a purely advisory capacity. Each church has absolute control over its own membership. Baptist churches of today are the same democratic organizations that the New Testament shows them to be in their origin.

(6) That they know from the New Testament that immersion is baptism, just as they know from the Bible that there is a God. Just as they know that there were believers and churches, even so they know that immersion came before the sacrament.

(7) That baptism is the use of water in one particular way; viz., Immersion, embodying three fundamental ideas—Christ's death—the regeneration of the soul buried with him by baptism and raised to walk with him in the newness of life, and the final resurrection of the body—a prophecy (John 15:14).

(8) That bread and wine used in the sacrament are only as symbols of the body and the blood of Christ, that it simply represents His flesh and blood, and that the only blessing is that which comes from obedience to His command and from thinking upon the significance of these pictures.

(9) That unbaptized persons must not be invited to the Lord's Supper, and members of Baptist churches are not to partake of the sacrament when administered by unbaptized persons. They contend that every time baptism is mentioned it follows immediately after profession of faith and comes before the Lord's Supper. The Samaritans believed Philip and were baptized at once, (Acts. 8:12). Paul was baptized as soon as he received his sight, (Acts 9:18). The jailer was baptized the same hour of the night, (Acts 16:38).

(10) Baptists believe that they should give "the whole gospel to the whole world" and that since they are strong in doctrine fulfilling the law—as does no other denomination—and mightier in numbers, so they are required to be more powerful in deeds of righteousness in home and foreign

lands; giving systematically and weekly as the "Lord has prospered" is just as Scriptural as baptism, for "by their fruits ye shall know them," and "unto whomsoever much is given of him much is required."

Then the National Baptist Convention stands for all the Bible, sanctions as interpreted in the "Articles of Faith" and our "Baptist Church Covenant."

The National Baptist Convention, like Roger Williams and all Baptist forebears, is against the union of the church and state and is in favor of the constitution of our country including the 13th, 14th, 15th, and 18th amendments.

The National Baptist Convention stands for the Christianization of our homeland and the highest efficiency of all the people through the preaching of the gospel and Christian education.

The National Baptist Convention stands for the evangelization of all lands in general, Africa, the West Indies, and Latin America in particular, where it now maintains workers.

The National Baptist Convention stands for the ownership and absolute control of all boards and agencies created or authorized to function in its name. All property acquired by these boards and agencies is secured for and in the name of the National Baptist Convention. All charters, deeds, and contracts must anchor in the National Baptist Convention, U.S.A.

Out of all this controversy in the rise, fall, and merging of conventions were evolved the very men needed for such a time.

The American Baptist Publication Society, at that time headed by that princely man among men, Dr. B. Griffith, which at that time furnished the Sunday school literature in all Baptist schools, tried to satisfy this craving in our group by inviting a number of our leaders among whom were Drs. W.J. Simmons, E.M. Brawley, E.K. Love, Walter H. Brooks, and C.H. Parrish to write for its S.S. Teacher. The reader will recall that the great body of Baptists had split in 1845 over the slavery question and had resolved itself into two factions—one comprised of the churches North and known as the Northern Baptist Societies and the other known as the Southern Baptist Convention comprising the former slaveholding states. The latter had continued to receive most of its literature for churches and schools from the parent body. Though forty-seven years had passed since the division, and twenty-four years since the war which brought freedom to the Negro, yet it was found that Negro writers however learned, would not be accepted as writers for literature which was to be read and studied by Black and White Baptists alike, and to attempt it only served to rekindle old fires of prejudice among our Southern brethren. To the surprise of all Christian people everywhere, leaders among Southern Baptists entered a vigorous protest against using the copy prepared by these Black men for the periodicals of the American Baptist Publication Society. Under this onslaught leaders of the Publication Society weakened and finally withdrew the invitation to our brethren to write, thereby sending a wave of sorrow, disappointment, and resentment to the very fingertips of all organizations among Negro Baptists. However, the decision not to give Negroes recognition came too late to prevent a double-barreled dilemma: The Southern Baptists took this opportunity to rally their forces for enlarging their own publishing interests, and on the other hand the Negro press and pulpit voiced their protest against the treatment accorded their ripest scholars—men from Brown University, Newton, Rochester and Bucknell Seminaries, and other great schools, had been invited to contribute articles for the Society's publications, and then had been set aside so abruptly. In the judgment of some, this was providential; had the Society, seeing the Southern Baptists had the intelligence and money to put their program over, held on to the policy of employing Negro writers, our gratitude for this consideration would doubtless have kept us from organizing for issuing literature to this day.

The years from 1889 to 1895[12] were filled with more history- making transitions than any former six years of our denominational life. The agitation growing out of our disappointment over the actions of the American Baptist Publication Society, had reached the most distant leaders of our denomination and was felt to the farthest end of our organized church and social life. Plans for having our own printing plant were being discussed at association and convention meetings everywhere. The American National Baptist Convention led by Dr. William J. Simmons, held its third annual session in Indianapolis in 1889, as did the Baptist Foreign Mission Convention. A periodical, the *National Baptist Magazine* (monthly), had been planned and among the resolutions adopted by the American National Baptist Convention was the following:

"Shall we, the foremost in numbers and the peers of any in talents and culture, continue to be conspicuously wanting in this arena? Can we, as a denomination, a million and a half strong, with forty-one educational institutions, and an army of able educators, advanced scholars, and able writers, afford not to have a Baptist Magazine? We think not. The loss we sustain by the continued neglect of so imperative a need is not easily calcu-

---

[12]The original of this text had the year "1906," which is obviously more than six years. The year "1895" corresponds with the history-making "six years" stated above, which encompassed events leading to the official beginning of the convention followed by the establishment of a publishing house one year later. Ed.

lated. The cultured minds of our young people will seek other channels through which, to give vent to the pent-up fires that are burning within their souls. If their own denomination will not provide green pasture for their intellectual wants, they cannot be blamed if they seek it of others, and to permit this will be first to lose their respect and ultimately to lose them to the denomination. There are two things that must be provided, and should be provided at this meeting, that the Baptist Magazine may appear at once; First, the money, second, subscribers." (*Journal of the American National Baptist Convention.*)

In the meantime, many of our best among the older men were passing away, and others had been supplanted in our state organizations, by a better prepared and more aggressive set: Brawley in South Carolina; Vann in Tennessee; Pegues in North Carolina; Morris in Arkansas, and one or more, just as aggressive, were appearing on our denominational horizon in each of the states. There had come over Negro Baptists a spirit of adhesion that was interesting indeed. Dr. William J. Simmons, who had become in a large way the idol of the denomination, on October 30th, 1890, passed away. In his last message he said: "I further recommend that it be now understood that a part of our aim is to found a printing house for the purpose of encouraging the publication of the ordinary printing-house business, and the utilizing of our own favored and progressive country that has not a representative of this kind in the literary world."

In 1893 the New England Convention united with the Foreign Mission Convention, and all of the state organizations were growing in interest and increasing in numbers. L.M. Luke passed away in December 1895. This writer, then serving as pastor of the Union Baptist Church, Philadelphia, Pennsylvania, was chosen as Foreign Mission secretary, which he served for nearly twenty-six years. The address delivered by E.K. Love at St. Louis in September 1896, concerning the National Baptist Publishing House fitted us admirably for organizing to print Sunday school literature for our children. Among other inspiring sentences, he said, "As closely connected and as affectionately attached to the American Baptist Publication Society as I am, I could not be so disloyal as to rebel against my race and denomination after the National Baptist Convention had decided by vote to establish a National Baptist Publishing House. I am a loyal Baptist and a loyal Negro. I will stand or fall, live or die, with my race and denomination; where they die, I will die and there will I be buried. There is as strong an argument in favor of a distinctive Negro Publishing House as there is for distinctive Negro churches, schools, or families. It is just as reasonable and fair for

Negroes to want these things to themselves as it is for White people to want them to themselves. If one is necessary and right, the other is equally so. It never was true anywhere, and perhaps never will be, that a Negro can enjoy every right in an institution controlled by White men that a White man can enjoy. There is not as bright and glorious a future before a Negro in a White institution as there is for him in his own. It cannot be denied that we can better marshal our forces and develop our people in enterprises manned by us. We can more thoroughly fill our people with race pride, denominational enthusiasm and activity, by presenting to them for their support enterprises that are wholly ours. A people who man no enterprises show that they have no spirit of progress in them; and a people without this cannot command the recognition of nations and the respect of the world. The world recognized men for the power they have to affect it. If men do nothing, the world recognizes them as being nothing. Negro brain should shape and control Negro thought. Every nation should have its distinct literature. As a people's literature is, so are they."—(W.A. Burch in National Baptist Magazine Bunch.)

The Convention began with a Foreign Mission Board, a Home Mission Board, and an Educational Board, but since that time these working agencies developed until there are now seven boards or agencies engaged in the prosecution of its work. Including those just mentioned, are the Woman's Auxiliary Convention, the Sunday School Publishing Board, the Baptist Young People's Union Board, and the Baptist Ministers' Benefit Board. The Lott-Carey Convention, now chartered as the Lott-Carey Missionary Society, continues its distinctive foreign mission work.

The Home Mission work of the Negro Baptists is carried on chiefly through the Home Mission Board, with headquarters at Atlanta, Georgia. The report for 1929 shows 16 home missionaries employed, 1500 churches aided, and contributed for this work. This Board cooperates with the Southern Baptist Convention and has the tentative promise of similar cooperation from the Northern Baptist for work in their territory.

The Foreign Mission work, under the care of the Foreign Mission Board, located at 701 S. 19th St., Philadelphia, Pa., is carried on in Central, South, and West Africa, the West Indies, and South America. Its first company of missionaries consisted of 6 persons who went to West Africa in 1883. In 1929 there were reported 42 missionaries and 142 native helpers, occupying 88 stations; 21 churches, with 3494 members; schools with 15,311 pupils; and contributions to the amount of $99,615.22. The value of property owned is estimated at $99,263.50.

The Educational Board reports 115 schools, including 31 colleges and academies and 84 secondary schools. Of these, 13 colleges and 10 secondary schools are supported in whole or part by the American Baptist Home Mission Society of New York, while 18 colleges and academies and 66 secondary schools are in cooperation with the National Baptist Educational Board. The total number of students and pupils reported in these schools for 1929 was 14,010, and the amount contributed for their support was $1,637,116.

In 1909 the National Training School for Women and Girls was founded in the District of Columbia, and is conducted by the Woman's Auxiliary of the National Baptist Convention. The object of the school is to provide for the training of women and girls "to the highest level of religious, moral, and industrial efficiency," and it is the largest and best equipped plant conducted by women of the Negro race in the United States. The report for 1929 shows 117 pupils, representing nearly every state in the Union, Africa, South America, and the West Indies. The value of the school property is estimated at $153,357.48, and the amount contributed during the year was $60,173.13.

The Young People's work is under the general supervision of the National Baptist Young People's Union Board, with headquarters at Nashville, Tenn.; it reports 12,550 societies and about 1,750,000 members. The contributions made to the Board in 1929 were $69,979.93, and it has property valued at $25,000.

The National Baptist Convention has a Publishing House at Nashville, Tenn., the largest and best equipped of its kind among the Negro race on Mother Earth. It has property valued at about $1,000,000 and a business at the close of 1929 amounting to $397,467.02.

There are a number of religious and denominational papers in various states. Among these are the *National Baptist Voice* at Nashville, the accredited organ of the denomination; the *Christian Review* of Philadelphia; the *American Baptist* of Louisville, the oldest among the Negro Baptist journals; the *Baptist Leader* of Birmingham, Ala.; *Baptist Vanguard* of Little Rock, Ark.; the *Baptist Record*, Kansas City, Mo.; *The National Baptist Union-Review*, Nashville, Tenn., and more than a score of others giving aid in the publicity of denominational activities.

THE DIVISION AMONG NEGRO BAPTISTS

An account of the dissension which arose among Negro Baptists and culminated after more than a decade of discussion in the separation into two Conventions, each bearing the name, "National Baptist Convention," must necessarily go into much detail. We will show that in truth there has never been any disruption of the National Baptist Convention as such, but that on the contrary only one Board withdrew leaving intact all the other agencies of the Convention; viz., Home Mission Board, Foreign Mission Board, Educational Board, BYPU Board, Church Extension Board, Benefit Board, and the Woman's Auxiliary Convention.

The National Baptist Publishing Board was a unit, an entity in itself. It was in 1915, at the Chicago session of the Convention that the storm in all its fury burst upon us. Though the pre-Convention meeting was being held in Olivet, with Dr. Nabritt of Georgia, the writer attended the pre-Convention meeting held by the opposition on Tuesday night, September 7, in Salem Baptist Church, 30th and LaSalle Sts., which was presided over by Dr. J.E. Wood of Kentucky. The whole atmosphere was filled with venom, poisoned with threats and expressions which foretold the mighty battle that was to be waged on the morrow with Board control as the goal or destruction of the Convention as alternatives. For nearly an hour the writer and other friends endeavored to appeal to this highly excited gathering, but we were not allowed to speak. The truth of the matter was that no one was permitted to participate unless he could be relied upon to add fuel to the already blazing fires of opposition and revolution in preparation for the conflagration of the next day.

Just here it should be stated that at the Philadelphia session in 1914, a meeting had been held in the basement of Zion Baptist Church wherein the secretary and some friends endeavored to lead away the Publishing Board and as many others as could be mustered to form another Convention. The attempt was unsuccessful, for the majority of those present did not favor the move. However, one year later, the opposition was better organized. The opening session of the 1915 Convention was being held in the 18th St. Regiment Armory, Chicago, September 9th. No sooner had the devotions ended than a motion was made to adopt the program.

Then the opposition to the motion threw the meeting into a confusion such as one may witness only once, if at all, in a lifetime. The reassuring circulars sent out by President Morris had disarmed the loyal members of the Convention, and they were not expecting such an onslaught, so all they could do was to keep the more blustering ones from controlling the meeting. The filibustering lasted till after twelve noon, when a motion passed to adjourn, and President Morris declared the Convention adjourned. The opposition thereupon called their friends to order and furthered their plans for disrupting the Convention on the morrow. It was reported $1000 was then offered as a bribe to secure badges from the secretary of the Convention. This move failing, the last resort was an injunction. On Thursday morning, the 10th, all of the preliminaries, including welcome addresses and responses were over. President Morris was reading his annual address when a sheriff arrived with an injunction sworn out by the Secretary of the Publishing Board and friends who followed the sheriff to point out their man. Many of the highly spiritual pastors stood aghast at this proceeding and referred to the whole matter as a miniature picture of Judas at Gethsemane. The secretary of the Publishing Board and his followers had an injunction issued restraining Dr. Morris from acting as president and others from presiding, hoping to stop further proceedings. During the recess between sessions all the belongings of the Board were removed, church furniture, books, periodicals and all, to Salem Baptist Church; the plans for secession were complete and perfect in every detail and as a surprise measure, could not have been executed in a more thorough and disconcerting manner.

When the Board left to organize in Salem Baptist Church, they took from the Armory all records, material, and the members who declared that the secretary's argument in defense of his claim that the Publishing House was his own private property was a perfectly just and reasonable one.

However, the National Baptist Convention continued to hold its sessions in the 18th St. Regiment Armory, the building engaged by the local committee, originally, for the purpose of, with President Morris in the chair and all secretaries of Boards, performing their original duties. But after long years of prosperity and splendid financial returns the Publishing Board had become completely independent and was thus able to defy the wishes of the National Baptist Convention and ignore its edicts. The resultant depression and discouragement of the brethren cannot be adequately portrayed in words. But there was no remedy for the situation.

How the So-called Split Occurred

The sainted E.J. Fisher, D.D., pastor of Olivet in Chicago, had died. One of the strong opposition men from Texas came to the funeral, and it was said, spent two weeks in Chicago with the pastors of Ebenezer and Salem Baptist Churches; laid the plans for the insurrection and secured the use of Salem Church as the place where the organization of the opposition would take place. These plans were known to Prof. M.M. Rodgers, the auditor and two others, who wrote and wired Dr. E.C. Morris the situation; but he doubted that an attempt to disrupt the Convention was to be made. Dr.

Morris did not believe that there lived a man or men so void of principle as to do such a thing. Had he followed the advice of his informers, the Publishing House might have been saved. The following letter explains itself:

Helena, Ark., Aug. 7th, 1915

To the Negro Baptists in the United States, Greetings:

As we near the time for the 35th Annual Meeting of the National Baptist Convention, to be held at Chicago, Ill., September 8-14, 1915, it is fitting we think that the man who has been honored with the presidency of that great organization for twenty-one years, to at least attempt to forecast some of the things to be considered in that meeting and ask the prayerful consideration of them by the leaders.

The editors of our denominational papers are honest, capable men, and most of them predict a peaceable, harmonious meeting, for which we should all labor and pray. But it is evident that some of them have been misinformed; and as molders of public sentiment, they have unintentionally conveyed that misinformation to the general public. The National Baptist Convention is intact, and will hold a harmonious, profitable meeting, unless it should be disturbed by just such persons as were in evidence at the Philadelphia meeting.

The officers of the Convention have but one purpose, and that is the promotion of the best interest of the race and denomination, and they hold firmly to the doctrine that the people must rule; and that principle will be strictly adhered to at Chicago.

The clouds which some would have you believe have gathered over the denomination, to the effect that seven men have arrogated to themselves the authority to incorporate the Convention, and that they are to be the sole owners and controllers of the affairs of the Convention have nothing in them but wind. The president of the Convention never saw a copy of the charter gotten out by the committee, until the 25th of June 1915, and was not consulted as to its form of construction. But he has given some time to a study of it since that time; and no such construction can be rightly given to it by any unbiased man. But to the reverse, the charter places the affairs of the Convention where they rightfully belong—in the hands of the people as represented in their national organization.

Most of the complaint being raised against the seven incorporators are by persons who are themselves members of a corporation, whose charter makes it possible for their perpetuation in office without the consent of the National Baptist Convention, while the seven men mentioned in the charter will not retain their positions except by the will of the Convention. Nor are the conditions of the charter such as to require all meetings to be held in the District of Columbia as reported in the papers. I quote Article 6 "That the annual meetings of said corporation shall be held at such times and places in the United States of America as shall be provided in its by-laws, or shall be fixed by resolution of its Board of Directors." It will be observed that the corporation is the National Baptist Convention, and not the seven directors who may be replaced by the corporation at its option.

Let me beg that all persons who desire that the Convention shall control its own affairs, and that the will of the people shall not be overthrown, to come to Chicago to peaceably adjust all differences, and not allow yourselves to be angered by designing men, who would have you disgrace the race and denomination.

Very truly yours,
E.C. MORRIS, President
National Baptist Convention

The American National Baptist Convention organized in St. Louis in 1886 by Wm. J. Simmons and others was the outburst of a desire for self-determination.

The National Baptist Educational Convention in Washington, D.C., exhibited the desire on the part of the leaders to train young men for the ministry.

Then in 1894, at Montgomery, was indicated the willingness to unite to form one great National meeting, and [this] reflects the desire to have an honest and workable organization through which the churches might work for home and foreign missions as well as Christian education. As yearly the scope increased, a few of the most far-visioned members of the National Baptist Convention saw the importance of safeguarding the holdings of the Convention, for the denomination and coming generations. Professor M.M. Rodgers of Texas, a very capable layman who was at the time auditor of the Convention, was asked to ascertain the proper steps to take towards this end. This letter from an eminent New York lawyer shows the aim and results of the auditor's inquiry:

New York, July 27th, 1912

M.M. Rodgers, Esq.,
Secretary National Baptist Convention
Lagrange, Texas

Replying to yours of the 16th inst., I have to say that I think I fully grasp

MY MOTHER
Marie J. Phillips into whose face the author first looked. Born a slave in Marion, Ala., and reared in Lauderdale County, Miss. She had no knowledge of books or her age. Out of her mother love she helped me all she could. Departed this life in Philadelphia in 1922.

Rev. Wm. L. Craft was born in Bastrop, Texas. He pastored in the state and was made field secretary of the B. Y. P. U. Board where he laboured until his death. He was resourceful, kind and very loyal to those who trusted him. He won for himself a place in the denomination, and passed to his reward.

Mrs. I. M. Terrell, prominent in religious, civic and welfare work for over 37 years; successful education; worker with her husband, Prof. Terrell, in Prarie View College, Prarie View, Texas.

REV. I. A. CARTER
It seems that Dr. Carter pastored the Evergreen Baptist Church in Shreveport for 44 years. He was at one time the president of the Louisiana State Convention and recognized as the leader of the Baptists in that state.

your situation with regards to the affairs of the National Convention, and will do my utmost to aid you in making the very best presentation of your side of matters.

Answering your several questions I would say:

1st: "Can the National Convention by resolution abrogate the charters of all of its incorporated boards?"

A. No resolution of the Convention itself can abrogate a charter of incorporation granted by the laws of state or of the District of Columbia. Such charters must be abrogated or dissolved in the manner provided by the laws of the jurisdiction where incorporated. In Kentucky this may be done by the written consent of a majority of the incorporators. In Tennessee and the District of Columbia an application must be made to the courts, but the Convention has the right by resolution to direct the officers of the incorporated boards to make transfer of all the property of such corporations to the National Convention, when incorporated, and also direct them to take the proper steps in the several states to procure the dissolution of their corporations.

2nd: "Can the National Baptist Convention in the same resolution authorize the parent body to be incorporated, and if so should the incorporators be named in that resolution?"

A. A proper resolution may be drawn embodying the matter of the dissolution of the subordinate corporations, and the incorporation of the parent body, which resolution I have undertaken to draw, and am now sending you. It will not be necessary to name the incorporators in that resolution; that being a matter of detail should be left to the committee in charge of the matter of incorporation referred to in the resolution. The number of that committee may be in number from three to nine as the Convention cares to name.

3rd: "If such a resolution is adopted, will it be necessary for the body to meet and ratify the articles of incorporation before they can be filed and made effective?"

A. No. The committee appointed will have all the power necessary to render the incorporation effective.

4th: "Will it be necessary to get the consent of the incorporators of boards to dissolve them?"

A. The consent of the identical persons who procured the incorporation will not be required, but as in Kentucky where the written consent is required for a dissolution the consent of the active members of a corporation, at the time dissolution is sought, I would imagine would be all that is

119

necessary. That, however, will be a detail which can be complied with after the parent body has been incorporated.

5th: "If the parent body can be incorporated, would you advise its incorporation in one of the states or the District of Columbia?"

A. Under the circumstances, taking in consideration the nature of your work and the personnel of your membership, I am inclined to the District of Columbia as the place of incorporation. While the effect will be the same in law, a charter granted by the District of Columbia under the laws of the U.S.A., it being the seat of the National Government would carry with it the idea of national importance and supreme control, and will generally appeal to the Convention.

The Supreme Lodge of Knights of Pythias was incorporated in the District of Columbia for this very reason.

Coming to the reason why the parent body should be incorporated rather than the several subordinate boards, the following may be suggested:

1st: The necessity of having the title to all the property of the Convention stand in the name of the parent or supreme body rather than in the name of its subordinate boards, which cannot be done unless the parent body is incorporated.

2nd: That in the event of a split in the Convention, or the want of harmony, or if any sort of rebellion should arise, the parent body unincorporated would encounter great difficulty in securing control of the property and interests of the incorporated boards, should they refuse to recognize the claim of the parent body.

3rd: In the event persons charitably inclined should desire to make donation of money or property to the Convention for the purpose of aiding its work by deed or will, such donation would fail unless the Convention were incorporated, as it would have no authority to hold or acquire any property whatever in its present name. True, it could take property in the name of trustees or other officers, but donors might not so easily remember the names of trustees as they would the Convention when desiring to make a gift or a will.

4th: The scope and dignity of the National Baptist Convention requires that it should assume permanent form as a legal creature and being, with full power to exercise control over all its boards and branches throughout the world.

More reasons will occur as you think the matter over, but the foregoing seem to me to be quite sufficient.

Some of these reasons are hinted at already in the preamble to the resolution.

The resolution is given more as a form to guide you than anything else, and you may find it necessary to change its wording altogether to make it conform to your idea of the true situation of Convention matters.

If you succeed in winning the Convention over to the idea of incorporation, I shall be glad to take up the question of terms for the work of incorporating same. This I can do as well in the states as in the District of Columbia.

I shall expect to hear from you again.

Very truly yours,
WILFORD H. SMITH

RESOLUTION

Indianapolis, Indiana, September 9, 1920

WHEREAS, THE NATIONAL BAPTIST CONVENTION OF THE UNITED STATES OF AMERICA, since its organization in 1880, has been carrying on its business and conducting its affairs as an unincorporated voluntary association; and

WHEREAS, the said Convention is national in scope and also in its representation and membership and is constantly seeking to enlarge its territory and

WHEREAS, the said Convention has found it necessary to its efficiency and permanency to establish various subordinate boards under its supervision and control; viz., The National Baptist Publishing Board, the Baptist Young Peoples Union Board, the Foreign Mission Board, the Home Mission Board and the Woman's Board, auxiliary to the National Baptist Convention; and

WHEREAS, without being incorporated the said National Baptist Convention cannot hold or acquire any property in its own name either by deed, gift, or devised, and it is now the sense of the National Baptist Convention of the United States of America, in it Fortieth Annual Session assembled that it would be more in keeping with the dignity and scope of this organization that the same should be incorporated as the supreme and parent body over all its subordinate boards, with power to create and establish such boards, branches, and auxiliaries as in the judgment of the Convention it may deem wise and best so that all such boards, auxiliaries, and branches may be brought under one management and head according to law and so that all the property acquired by said boards will stand in the name of and belong to the said Convention. NOW THEREFORE BE IT RESOLVED: That the charter which has been applied for by the said National Baptist Convention of the United States of America, and granted under the laws and recorded, May 17, 1915 in the office of the Recorder of Deeds, D.C.; and, this day read and considered by the said National Baptist Convention of the United States of America be and the said charter is hereby ratified and adopted.

Respectfully submitted,
M.M. RODGERS

Upon his report a Committee on a Charter was appointed and the charter was gotten out in Washington, D.C.

There were two schools of thought in denominational affairs, the one insisting that the work of the Board should be undisturbed save for the annual report to the Convention; the other denying the right of the Board to hold such power. In an unskillful attempt to make wrongdoers atone and to retain our already-weakened tenure on the property of the Convention, the battle waxed warm to offset sentiment favoring dividing the Publishing Board from the Home Board, the secretary turned the fight on President Morris. Dr. C.T. Walker, one of the most modest, eloquent, and influential men in our ranks, was nominated by the secretary and his friends for the presidency of the Convention at New Orleans in 1913. Because the delegates were so determined to divide their boards, in the belief that by so doing they would break the strangle hold the Publishing Board had on the Convention. Good Dr. Walker was greatly humiliated by the small number of votes received. At New Orleans the Convention was so overwhelming in its determination, the Publishing Board made a complete surrender, and had the delegates followed up that victory the plant might have been saved to the Convention. In good Rooseveltan language, the Publishing Board and its secretary were "whipped to a frazzle." Ominously gathering clouds of dissatisfaction and doubt seen faintly on our horizon at the New Orleans meeting in 1913 grew during the year until, at the Philadelphia session in 1914, there was revealed the insistent determination on the part of the secretary of our Publishing Board and his friends to declare the Publishing House to be a purely private business institution. Naturally this decision was opposed by a group of men who, equally determined, contended that the National Baptist Publishing House had been bought and was being paid for by the donation, patronage, and moral support of the churches, district associations, and state conventions making up the National Baptist Convention. That at St. Louis in 1896 by vote of the parent body, the Publishing Committee was created and the secretary elected; that for nineteen years the report of the secretary and Board presented, had been programmed, listened to, and voted upon by the delegates assembled, and adopted by the National Baptist Convention. That in consequence of these facts the churches, district associations, and state conventions which made up the great National Baptist Convention would either control said plant or it would organize one that it could control. But after long years of prosperity and splendid financial returns from a confiding people, the Publishing Board had become completely independent and was thus able to defy the wishes of the National Baptist Convention and ignore its edicts. Dr. Haynes representing a special committee on this matter received a letter containing among other things the following:

Nashville, Tenn., Dec. 17, 1914

Rev. William Haynes and Others,
Dear Brothers:

It is unnecessary for us to say that we hold ourselves in readiness to give any information to the denomination that will be any benefit to it. The business of the National Baptist Publishing Board has been built up by the Board after many years of labor and hardship. The results of its labors have been, we say with pardonable pride, not only to promote the interest of the denomination, but to demonstrate to the world what our people could do for themselves in this particular way.

We are thoroughly aware of the fact that a large part of our success has been due to the fact that we have received the endorsement and encouragement of our Baptist brethren throughout the country; and in return, we have endeavored at all times, to promote the interests of the denomination, as well as of our race.

In regard to the questions that you ask, we take them up in their order.

Insofar as the purchase of the property of Boyd and Beckham, or the sale of the interest that this Board has in the property, we desire to say that this Board has no control over Boyd and Beckham individually, and could not, if it so desired, coerce them to sell their property.

As to the sale of the option which this Board holds on this property, the Board has not yet determined what course it will pursue. It will necessarily be governed in this matter by the best lights that the members of the Board have, as what will be to the interest of the National Baptist Publishing Board.

2. In reply to the second proposition, namely that we separate all private enterprises from the Publishing Board, we beg leave to say that insofar as this matter is of interest to you, that has always been true since the organization of the separate concerns, except insofar as they have been able to work in cooperation for their mutual interests, without injury to either.

3. In regard to the payment of the mortgage debt, we desire to say that the Board entertains but slight hope that the business will be such for some time to come, as to enable it to pay off this mortgage. However, the Board is not unmindful of the desirability of accomplishing this end.

Signed:

R.H. BOYD

The resultant depression and discouragement of the brethren cannot be adequately portrayed in words. But there was no remedy for the situation.

The judge pronounced them "Splitters" and characterized their body as a "Rump Convention." Thereupon the insurgent secretary and his friends withdrew and met to hold in the Salem Baptist Church a session of what they designated as "The National Baptist Convention, Unincorporated," Dr. E.P. Jones of Mississippi was chosen as the first president. They created Boards modelled after those of the original Convention. It will be seen they did not include our seceding Board but made a Publishing Board of their own. It was voted that their Publishing Board should take up its headquarters in Nashville to look after the orthodoxy of the literature issued by our seceding Board. Note further this Board was instructed that it was in no way to interfere with the property or the management of the property of our rebellious Board—the "Old Publishing Board." The reason assigned for this stipulation was given; viz., they had put no money into it, thereby declaring the institution to be property of the secretary of the Publishing Board and managed by a committee who were to be chosen and appointed by him or themselves. The following excerpt taken from the closing paragraph of their "Exhibit C" is the expression made by the "Unincorporated Convention" in 1915, concerning this question of "Who owns the Publishing House?"

"You are aware that the National Baptist Publishing Board of the National Baptist Convention is an incorporated institution, a legal entity created under the laws of the State of Tennessee, and that the National Baptist Convention has no record known to us where the National Baptist Convention owns any property interest, or invested any money in said corporation; therefore you will not be expected to enter litigation for possession of the property, or the removal of any of the incorporators but you will demand in the name of the National Baptist Convention, Unincorporated, of the United States of America, free and full advisory supervision as to the doctrine, dictation and policy of all Baptist publications furnished by them to our churches and Sunday schools under the resolution passed by this Convention."

Signed
REV. E. P. JONES, President
REV. T. J. KING, Secretary
National Baptist Convention

(See *National Baptist Convention Journal*, Page 34, 1916)

This organization, dubbed by Judge Smith a "Rump Convention," has survived, and from year to year many of the good men who made up its personnel have, for various reasons, returned to the original body. Both the president, Dr. E.P.Jones, and the seceding secretary have gone to their reward. It is said that the property is no longer as prosperous and flourishing in appearance as in the days when it was considered to belong to the National Baptist Convention, and visitors to Nashville often comment on the signs of decay and neglect that are evident everywhere. The "Rump Convention" was the second group to secede during the past years of the existence of the National Baptist Convention. A spirit of bitterness among the brethren arose as the result of the dissemination of halftruths and even utter falsehoods by those who believed in Board control, which divided families and friends, causing much sorrow among Baptists. But time, the great healer, invariably softens men's hearts and gives them better judgment. In less than a year after this ever-to-be-regretted affair, Negro Baptists began to ask themselves: "Am I wise in helping to build private institutions, or should I unite with the brethren in projecting enterprises to be owned and controlled by the National Baptist Convention? Would it not be infinitely better to aid in founding institutions that may be passed on to my children and to other young Baptists—institutions which shall be centers of economic, social, and religious activities—on down through the ages, when as a united Baptist group they shall be called upon to do their share of the world's work?" Thus reasoning, it has come about that same, thoughtful consideration has caused many to heed Paul's advice: "Mark them which cause divisions and offenses, contrary to the doctrine which ye have learned, and avoid them."

Rev. A.R. Griggs offered a resolution directing that all records of the Home Mission Boards now in the hands of the former secretary, Dr. R.H. Boyd, be turned over to the new secretary, Dr. J.A. Booker. The rules were suspended and the resolution was adopted, after eliminating the feature asking for the appointment of a committee by the Southern Baptist Convention.

WHEREAS, It has been reported to this Convention, by the corresponding secretary of the Home Mission Board of the National Convention, Rev. J.A. Booker, D.D., that when the office of corresponding secretary was vacated by his predecessor, not one scratch of a pen in way of records or accounts covering a period of nearly eighteen years was turned over to him.

WHEREAS, The Southern White Baptist Home Mission Board has been cooperating with this Convention financially in helping to support our Home Mission work to the extent of about ten thousand dollars a year for the last ten years. Therefore be it

RESOLVED, That we advise the Home Mission Board of this Convention to investigate this whole matter of how one hundred thousand dollars expended by the Home Mission Board was disposed of through Rev. R.H. Boyd, and demand that he turn the books and records of the office of the Home Mission Board over to his successor, Rev. J.A. Booker, D.D.

This resolution failed in its purpose, for the books were never given to Secretary Booker.

WHEREAS, Certain brethren, including Dr. R.H. Boyd, formerly secretary of the National Baptist Publishing Board, have made a futile attempt to enjoin perpetually the officers of the National Baptist Convention and officers of its Foreign Mission, B. Y. P. U., and Educational Boards from filling their places as officers of said Convention and its Board for the evident purpose of getting control of the Convention and its property irregularly and

WHEREAS, These brethren have withdrawn and separated themselves from the National Baptist Convention in a manner contrary to all Baptist usage as well as contrary to the laws of the land; and

WHEREAS, The Publishing Board is chartered as a domestic corporation in the State of Tennessee, which fact may cause delay in getting possession of its plant and property, both real and personal in Nashville, Tenn., and elsewhere through its proper agency; therefore be it

RESOLVED, That the National Baptist Publishing Board of the National Baptist Convention, be and is hereby instructed to immediately take such steps as may be necessary to get possession and control of the Publishing plant and property at Nashville, Tenn., or elsewhere, amicably or at law, or in equity; and to quiet any unrest on the part of our loyal churches and Sunday schools, etc., as to Sunday school periodicals and other religious literature, or by directing them in the matter of obtaining supplies of this nature in any way the said Board may deem feasible and wise.

R.M. CAVER,
R.A. WILLIAMS,
J.P. BURDETTE

The "Old Publishing House" lost forever to organized Negro Baptists, they proceeded to take steps that would forbid a repetition of this unfortunate affair, and forever prevent a diversion of the people's property, built up and fostered by the Convention, to private use and ownership. In brief, by means of well-nigh incredible struggles the denomination has succeeded in building a magnificent structure, occupying a lot which measured 92 by 155 ft., and [the lot] costing $37,500. It is located at the intersection of Fourth Avenue and Cedar Street, in Nashville, Tennessee. Counting the basement the "New Publishing House" is six stories high. Negro architects drew the plans for this edifice, and a Negro contractor erected the house with Negro labor. Built of steel, concrete, and stone, it has with equipment cost $750,000, and is financed almost entirely with Negro capital. But best of all, it is the property of Negro Baptists and will be passed on to their posterity. Standing on the site of a hotel which in antebellum days was the favored resort of slave traders and owners, within sight of the spot where the slave auction block stood, the descendants of the slaves who built the old hostelry used in their mortar some of the crumbled bricks which Black hands molded in servitude, a striking commentary on the vicissitudes of time and an example of the fact that "God moves in a mysterious way, His wonders to perform."

The property is deeded to the National Baptist Convention absolutely, and every Baptist has equity in it, for this reason. About four hundred employees are needed in all departments, and it serves as a constant inspiration to the youth of the race who may be available as printers, editors, proofreaders, typesetters, linotype operators, clerks, bookkeepers, book-binders, salesmen, stenographers, laborers, and the like. It is easily the greatest thing built by Negroes since we built the Sphinx and the Pyramids.

After the defection of Secretary Boyd, the National Baptist Convention chose lawyer S. P. Harris, nephew by marriage of President Morris, of Arkansas, for secretary of this Board, which has ever since been called the Sunday School Publishing Board of the National Baptist Convention.

As a second beginning, the B.Y.P.U. housed the Publishing Board, 409 Gay St., where it remained for one and one-half years. Because of some differences between Secretary Harris and the auditor, he served only one year. Exactly one year after the upheaval, and dissolution of our old Publication Board in Chicago, many of our leaders including the veteran secretary of the B.Y.P.U. Board, Dr. E. W. D. Isaac; Dr. S. E. Griggs, editor of the *Beacon Light;* and Rev. L.K. Williams, president of the Texas Baptist State Convention, were imbued with the idea that Rev. L.G. Jordan, then secretary of the Foreign Mission Board, could fill this place to the great advantage of the Convention. They insisted that Dr. Jordan, being a contemporary and personal friend of Dr. Boyd, would know best how to quell the turmoil into which the former secretary had plunged our Convention. Accordingly at the Savannah, Georgia, meeting of the Convention, 1916, the Publishing Board elected Dr. Jordan to succeed Attorney Harris. This action did not meet with favor from President Morris who expressed his opinion that the Foreign Mission work would suffer if its secretary were taken away at this period in its activities. Hence, under great pressure from President E.C. Morris and from an aspirant to the position and the field secretary of the American Baptist Publication Society as well, the National Baptist Convention urged the Publishing Board to rescind its actions and to allow Dr. Jordan to continue with the Foreign Mission Board. Thereupon Dr. Jordan withdrew, throwing his strength to Rev. Wm. Haynes of Tennessee, who was elected. Dr. Haynes brought to the office much influence and personal credit in the business world. He was a successful pastor, the treasurer of Roger Williams University and an alumnus of that institution. Within four years Secretary Haynes had accomplished a vast amount of work in so organizing the Board as to secure more adequate headquarters and to meet the growing demand for Sunday school supplies. It must be kept in mind, the courts gave the seceding Board everything we had gathered for eighteen years even to our name. So, without a pencil or mailing list, the Convention started all over again. Dr. A. M. Townsend, the present secretary, a cultured and scholarly man, trained for both the medical and ecclesiastical professions, was elected in Indianapolis, Indiana, 1920. He has been remarkably successful in his work of bringing to reality the National Baptist Convention's dream of an ideal publishing house. His efforts have been untiring to build and place on a sound financial basis the "New Publishing House," the wonderful structure aforementioned. Dr. Townsend possesses all of the qualities of intellect

REV. P. JAMES BRYANT, D.D.

Dr. Bryant, as a yong man, succeeded Rev. W. H. Tilman as pastor of the Wheat Street Baptist Church about 1895, where he remained until his death. He did not live to finish the building for "Greater Wheat Street Baptist Church" but his plans were so well laid that they will be carried out. He served as chairman of the B.Y.P.U. Board from its origanization until his death, and was known as one of the most outstanding characters of his day. With a splendid voice, a fine vocabulary, he was one of the denomination's great preachers and public speakers.

REV. H. K. HILL, D.D.

A leader of large mold in Florida and National Baptist affairs. He delivered a sermon for our women in Kansas City, in 1929, and died in Colorado without returning to his home at Orlando, Florida.

and the courage required to perform the heroic undertaking which he has so efficiently executed. Many believed we have built too costly a structure, but until now we are going and growing.

An interesting fact came to light in connection with the financing of the "New Building."

A leading White bank in Nashville, had consented to become the depository of the funds to be used in the construction, but on learning that not only had a Negro architect drawn the plans but a Negro contractor had been engaged to erect the building, refused to have anything at all to do with the matter. The Building Committee then made application to a Negro Bank and were accepted.

Thereby the race is enabled to point with pride to an edifice which is almost wholly a "race production" from start to finish.

Meeting of the Peace Commissions at Memphis, Tennessee, March 19, 1918

The parent body never slackened its effort to have denominational peace—White Baptists, north and south, sympathized with us, and sought to help us.

Upon call the three commissions, one from the Southern Baptist Convention, one from the National Baptist Convention (Incorporated), and one from the National Baptist Convention (Unincorporated), met to consider and propose a basis of union for the two National Baptist Conventions. There were present for the commission of Southern Baptist Convention, O.L. Hailey, Secretary; A.J. Barton, Ben Cox, A.U. Boone, Rufus W. Weaver, W.E. Atkinson, J.B. Grambrell; from the commission of the National Baptist Convention (incorporated) T.O. Fuller, A.R. Griggs, Joseph A. Booker, C.T. Walker, C.H. Parrish, L.K. Williams, W.H. Moses; and from the National Baptist Convention (unincorporated), D.B. Gaines, George W. Alexander, S.R. Prince, John W. Hurse, J.L. Harding, E.W. Bowen, and S.S. Jones.

A.U. Boone was elected chairman and O.L. Hailey secretary of the commission.

After devotional service it was decided by unanimous vote to allow the commission from each of the National Conventions to present its views as to what would be an acceptable basis of unification and consolidation. W.H. Moses spoke for the National Baptist Convention (incorporated) and John N. Franks for the National Baptist Convention (unincorporated).

After conference it was agreed that a committee of three be appointed, one from each of the three commissions, to take the statements presented by the spokesmen, to give them consideration and to formulate a tentative basis of agreement. By mutual consent and by appointment of the chair the committee consisted of W.E. Atkinson, S.S. Jones, and L.K. Williams. Commission adjourned to meet at 3:30 p.m.

Afternoon Session

Commission called to order by Chairman A.U Boone. The report of the committee on basis of agreement was presented, considered seriatim, amended and adopted as follows:

Basis for the unification of the Negro Baptists of America and for the consolidation of the National Baptist Convention (Incorporated) and the National Baptist Convention (Unincorporated) unanimously adopted at Memphis, Tennessee, Tuesday, March 19th, by the Joint Commission composed of the Commissions of the Southern Baptist Convention and the two National Baptist Conventions.

The Joint Commission composed of the commissions appointed by the Southern Baptist Convention, National Baptist Convention (Incorporated), and the National Baptist Convention (Unincorporated) recommends unanimously the following as a basis for the settlement of the differences between the latter two bodies and for their consolidation:

1. That the Charter of the National Baptist Convention (Incorporated) be surrendered and annulled.

2. That the lawsuit now pending against the National Baptist Publishing Board be dismissed as soon as these agreements are approved by the two National Baptist Conventions, with the understanding that the right of denominational ownership and control of all institutions and boards is hereby recognized and that said ownership and control in each individual case shall be determined and established at the earliest time possible after consolidation by such methods as may be necessary.

3. That the Executive Boards of the two National Baptist Conventions be requested to approve these articles within the next two months and provide that the two conventions meet this year in the same city, in separate conventions, on the same day, for the final and complete ratification of this agreement; that said ratification in the coming session of each convention shall take precedence over all other matters after the usual opening preliminaries.

4. That immediately after the ratification as set forth above, this joint commission shall name a chairman and other officers of said united convention who shall preside over the joint session for consolidation.

5. That the united convention appoint a committee to confer with a committee of the Southern Baptist Convention about the differences concerning the location of the National Baptist Theological Seminary.

6. That the Southern Baptist Convention appoint a permanent advisory committee of nine, with which the Executive Committee, or any other committee or board of the said united convention may at any time confer.

By motion a committee of three was appointed, one from each commission, to present the findings of this meeting to the officers of each of the National Baptist Conventions and to their Executive Boards. The committee consisted of O.L. Hailey, T.O. Fuller, and D.B. Gaines.

It was decided to report the conclusions of the joint commission to a mass meeting of the Colored brethren who had come together from all over the United States and had spent two days in prayer and devotion at the First Baptist Church (Colored) and who were waiting to hear the report from the Peace Meeting. At the request of Chairman A.U. Boone, the report of the joint commission was read by W.E. Atkinson and was most heartily and enthusiastically approved by the mass meeting. The commission adjourned subject to the call of the chairman.

A.U. BOONE, Chairman
O.L. HAILEY, Secretary

There have been three most eventful days during the fifty years' life of the National Baptist Convention. The first, when a group seceded at the session in September, 1897. The second, the seceding of the National Baptist Publishing Board, September session in Chicago, 1915. Third, the election of the tenth president of the Convention at the session held in St. Louis, 1922.

The first to go was at Boston, forming the Lott Carey Convention. Many of the leaders of that group were being employed as colporteurs and Sunday school agents, by organizations of our White brethren or teachers in the American Baptist Home Mission Society schools; men who were opposed to Negroes printing Sunday school supplies for their own children for reasons not acceptable to those who did so believe.

Among the leaders in this effort were Drs. Calvin S. Brown, Albert W. Pegues, and Samuel N. Vass, of North Carolina; Drs. John W. Kerby, Richard Spiller, Philip F. Morris, John M. Armstead, and A. Binga, Jr., of Virginia; Doctors W.M. Alexander, and W.J. Howard of Maryland. The Colored members and faculties of the Virginia Union and Shaw universities, were among the most outstanding leaders of that split. The author being very active in those days, followed them up so closely in an effort to have them return, little or nothing was done to organize their meeting till in Baltimore in 1899.

Virginia Baptists, in the meantime had split, and the writer sent out postal cards to friends containing the following:

"Lexington, Va., May 17

My dear Brother:

Dr. Spiller and the old guard routed hoof, and dragon, and the friends of our Publishing Board, made leaders of Virginia Baptists .... Prof. G.W. Hayes, Drs. R.H. Bowling, W.F. Graham and B.F. Fox led the convention."

One of these cards went to Dr. J.A. Booker, Ark., which he considered such good news, he had it appear in the *Baptist Vanguard.* This was read to the Baltimore Lott Carey meeting in my hearing, and I was openly denounced and with our missionary, J.I. Buchanan, fresh from Africa, was forced from the meeting by such blistering sarcasm and vilification as I had never heard before, without any chance to explain or make a defense—and so unusual for Baptists all because I believed Negro writers could write for us as well as Negro preachers could preach for us.

They knew, whatever else we differed about, the Convention was a unit on foreign missions; hence, foreign missions was made the slogan in their attempt to organize for wrecking the National Baptist Convention. To get the force of this withdrawal, one must remember our Sunday School Publishing Board issued the first series of Sunday school supplies for January, that year, which received the applause of Negro Baptists everywhere. So when the Sunday School Publishing Board came to the Boston meeting with such a gladsome report, it threw these hired men into consternation and to this day they can give no good reason for splitting. After organizing they sought to link up with the American Baptist Missionary Union and the following will explain results. However, we are glad these brethren through a large delegation consisting of Drs. P.F. Morris, J.A. Witty, W.T. Johnson, A.W. Pegues, and G.S. Brown, returned to the Convention in 1905 at Chicago, asking to be enrolled as the First District Convention of the National Baptist Convention. They were received on their own terms.

The agreement read and adopted, concluded with the following: "Upon the adoption of this preamble and agreement between the National Baptist Convention and the Lott Carey Convention herein effected, a consolidation between the two bodies is formed, and we pray that the great Head of the church may bless them both in this happy consummation." The records say, "By motion the Convention adopted the compact." Dr. C. S. Brown, president of the Lott Carey Convention was recognized and addressed the Convention, thanking all that "peace" had been agreed upon. The *National Baptist Convention Journal 1905*, page 115 for some reason known among themselves the agreement was never kept by our brethren, and from year to year they have attempted to enlarge their borders and in some cases decry the efforts of the parent body, but as Baptists we have gone on, each working in his line, with but little friction.

Through the efforts of the Foreign Mission Board, Dr. Brown their president, was kept as a member of our board, and he attended the National Baptist Convention till 1921. Dr. Alexander, their corresponding secretary, died in 1920, and Dr. A. Graham was elected as corresponding secretary. During the intervening years they have been chartered incorporated, not as a convention but a society.

In 1922, the president and secretary of the Lott Carey Convention went to Liberia on a tour and inspection. It was reported they saw nothing in that Negro republic to praise, and in their report to their convention they said such ugly things against Liberia, that the government took it up with the U.S. government and a public apology was demanded, otherwise their workers would have been banished. As a good Baptist and citizen, the secretary of the Foreign Mission Board of our National Baptist Convention expressed himself freely in print and pulpit, as to the conduct of the Lott Carey Commission, touching Liberia. For this, the officials of that convention for the first time met the unincorporated convention in Norfolk, Virginia, 1923, and formed a corporation with them, which act caused much confusion in their ranks.

Long before this incident, however, because of our persistent agitation (1880-1896) and a growing desire among growing Negro Baptists for writers of their own who could interpret their feelings, their belongings, and our racial aspirations, no number of hirelings could stop the project.

The second of these events took place in September, 1915, in Chicago, Illinois, when the Sunday School Publishing Board seceded and withdrew. This has been referred to as a split, but it was not strictly speaking a split for the reason that six boards, the Woman's Auxiliary and all the officers of the National Baptist Convention remained with the National Baptist Convention.

A full account of this unfortunate happening will be found in the discussion on the National Baptist Publishing Board.

The third eventful day occurred in St. Louis, Mo., December, 1922, when we elected Dr. L.K. Williams, the present incumbent, the 10th president of the National Baptist Convention. It was September 22, 1922 when we were slated to meet in Los Angeles,, Calif., that a most extensive and destructive railway strike broke out, only a short time before the date for our meeting, paralyzing traffic and making it very dangerous to travel. But worst of all for us, President Elias Camp Morris, D.D., Ph.D., died during this controversy between the railroads and their employees.

The Executive Board met August 25, in Memphis, Tenn., in the First Baptist Church, Dr. T.O. Fuller, Pastor, with our sick president presiding, and called off indefinitely the meeting of the Convention which was slated to be held in California.

The strike having ended only 12 days later the Board met again; this time in Helena, Arkansas, immediately after the funeral of Dr. Morris, and issued a call for the National Baptist Convention to meet in St. Louis, Mo., on December 6, 1922. Dr. Morris had served as president from September 1894 till his death, September 5, 1922. Who should succeed him was the question to be settled in St. Louis. The candidates as announced were: Wesley G. Parks, D.D., LL.D., Philadelphia Pa., who had by the death of Dr. Morris become president; Peter James Bryant, D.D., of Atlanta, Ga.; William H. Moses, D.D., of New York City; Moses W.D. Norman, D.D., LL.D., of Washington, D.C., and Lacey K. Williams, D.D., of Chicago, Ill. For more than two months, the campaign was carried on. Much bitter feelings developed as it raged; the ugliest things ever said by one preacher about another were said by some of these brethren against their opponents.

Finally the day for the meeting came, and large delegations gathered in St. Louis from every part of our country. The enrollment showed 1800 delegates present. The several camps organized their forces on Tuesday and worked from Wednesday at 10:00 a.m. on through Thursday, all day, the second day for the election of officers, remaining in session until after 11 o'clock Thursday night. The hall was very cold and though we were without food or rest the voting went on, hour by hour. Finally the list of candidates narrowed down until it was Dr. Parks and Dr. Williams. No man living wishes to ever again go through such a nerve-racking siege. At 10:45 p.m., the tellers announced L.K. Williams' election. Ten years, or even five years earlier, the National Baptist Convention could not have stood such a strain, it would have split from the effects of such a controversy, but our men had grown wiser. In addition to this, there was no Bible or denominational principle involved in the case, so men shook hands and like all good Baptists should do, accepted the majority rule decision and all was well. Before the session was over, all previous bitterness gave place to a brotherly business session, which lasted during the remaining four days. In spirit the National Baptist Convention has long since faithfully adopted two great mottoes; First, "A man's gift maketh room for him," (Prov. 18:16); second, "Where no insult is intended there is no injury done."—Fred Douglass. In good old Baptist fashion, the winners and losers forgave and forgot and at this hour one brother who spent twenty years belittling and decrying Negro Baptists' efforts to produce their Sunday school literature is receiving a good monthly salary from the National Baptist Convention, while another who was his main ally and who to destroy our printing interest coined the expression, "Negroes' backs and White men's brains"—and this, at the time it was said, was the hardest to explain and overcome than all the blows dealt us—is now heading one of our boards at $4000 per year. Still a third one, who pulled off his coat and collar and lowered his suspenders with rolled up sleeves, did more than any man among them in 1915 to confuse, destroy, and crush our work, now draws a salary of $250 per month. In real truth, Negro Baptists are more united in their work at this writing than they have been for many years. Larger things are being projected and accomplished than ever before. They rejoice in a publishing House costing seven hundred thousand dollars ($700,000) and which, with its equipment, is well worth a round $1 million. The first unit of the American Baptist Seminary for training preachers is finished; it will accommodate fifty students. This school has been opened for the past three years with a strong faculty and a growing student body. It is possibly the largest and most ambitious project of the National Convention. During 1925 was the drive for a million twenty-five cent pieces to enlarge our Foreign Mission work, which was accomplished December 1926.

It is gratifying to know that every school fostering Christian education for the group in the various states of the country, report 1928-29 as the largest years' enrollment of the entire existence. Indeed it is reported that more than 18,000 of the brightest young men and women of the race are enrolled in various colleges in the United States. Indeed God and the Baptists are moving on.

In consequence of this increasing tendency towards liberality and mutual sufferance, we are projecting larger enterprises and accomplishing greater results in the various states, in the nation, and in foreign parts. For instance, we are adding a new building to our Training School, remodeling of our B.Y.P.U. headquarters, quadrupling our gifts to the Foreign Mission Board in three years, and filling all our denominational schools to overflowing.

And our greatest effort, the New Publishing House—the most elaborately furnished and equipped, complete, and up-to-date structure owned by Negroes in the whole world, costing in round numbers $1,000,000—is now finished and was formally opened and occupied October 19, 1925, when it was estimated that 2,000 or more persons visited it per day for six days. It was dedicated April 1926, and the following was the program observed:

SOUVENIR PROGRAM DEDICATORY SERVICES
Morris Memorial—Home Sunday School Publishing Board, National Baptist Convention, U.S.A., Nashville, Tennessee, April 20-25, 1926

PROGRAM
Tuesday Evening, APRIL 20, 1926, 8 O'CLOCK
Spruce Street Baptist Church, Eighth Ave., N.

Rev. R.B. Robert, D.D., *President*, Tennessee Baptist M. and E. Convention, presiding—Alternate, Rev. W.A. Taylor, D.D., Washington, D.C.

Praise Service—Led by Prof. Edward Boatner, of Boston, *Chorister* National Baptist Convention. Mrs. A.M. Townsend, Nashville, Music Editor and Director Sunday School Publishing Board, *Organist*.

Prayer . . . . Rev. Joseph Keill, *Pastor*
Zion Baptist Church, Nashville

Devotional Address . . . . Dr. J.T. Brown, *Editor-in-Chief*,
Sunday School Publishing Board, Nashville

Address—(Thirty Minutes) . . . . Dr. Sutton E. Griggs, Memphis, *President*
American Baptist Theological Seminary

Alternate . . . . Rev. Albert J. Greene, D.D.
Maryland

Addresses (*Fifteen Minutes*):
Dr. T.O. Fuller, Tenn.—Alternate, Dr. B.J.F. Wesbrook, Ind.
Dr. D.V. Jemison, Alabama—Alternate, Dr. J.S. Brown, North Carolina.
Dr. Geo. W. Robinson, Iowa—Alternate, Dr. J.B. Adams, New York.

Fraternal Greetings:
> Dr. J.A. Martin, *Secretary-Treasurer* C.M.E. Publishing House.
> Dr. W.M. Wilson, *Representative* Primitive Baptists.
> Dr. J.L. Hudgins, Cumberland Presbyterian Publishing House.

Presentation Visiting Ministers.

Wednesday Evening, April 21, 1926, 8 O'CLOCK
Spruce Street Baptist Church, Eighth Ave., N.

Editor Wm. H. Steward, American Baptist, Kentucky, presiding.—
Alternate, Mr. H.I. Monroe, *President* Baptist State Sunday School
Convention, Kansas.

Praise Service .... Led by Prof. Edward Boatner

Prayers .... Rev. A.W. Porter, *Pastor*
15th Ave. Baptist Church, Nashville

Devotional Address .... Dr. W.S. Ellington, *Pastor*
First Baptist Church, East Nashville

Address—(*Thirty Minutes*) .... Dr. J.C. Austin, Chicago
Chairman, Foreign Mission Board, N.B.C.

Alternate .... Dr. R.L. Bradby, Michigan

Address (*Fifteen Minutes*):
> Dr. E. Arlington Wilson, Texas—Alternate, Dr. T.J. King, Virginia.
> Dr. I.A. Thomas, Illinois— Alternate, Dr. J. Francis Robinson, Mass.
> Dr. J.A. Marshall, Miss.—Alternate, Dr. J.W. Boykin, S.C.

Fraternal Greetings:
> Dr. Henry A. Boyd, *Secretary-Treasurer*, National Baptist Publishing Board.
> Dr. E.B. Williams, A.M.E. Zion Publishing House.
> Dr. J.W. Barton, *Agt.* M.E. Publishing House, South.

Presentation Visiting Ministers.

REV. AARON BARBOUR, D.D.
Galveston, Texas

Rev. Aaron Barbour was born in Texas and there he started his ministerial life. He pastored the Macedonia Baptist Church, Galveston, Texas for 33 years. It was not the largest in size or numbers, but led Texas Baptists in gifts to mission and education. For 28 years he was president of the Texas Sunday School Convention. At times he seemed rough and uncouth, but beneath it all was a great soul. His four children— three boys, college men, two preachers, one a lawyer; and the daughter a teacher. Dr. Barbour was a great pastor and wise leader. He died August 15, 1921.

REV. C. H. JOHNSON, D.D.
Indianapolis, Ind.

Dr. Johnson was born in Louisana and began his ministry as a boy preacher chaperoned by an uncle. Being a good singer he developed into a fine preacher and spent most of his ministry in Indianapolis though he pastored for some years in Boston. On returning to Indianapolis to pastor another church he and Dr. Wesbrook became great friends and though Dr. Wesbrook was a successor to Dr. Johnson, they were indeed brothers and chums. Charlie Johnson, as those of us who knew him best loved to call him, has done a wonderful work in the world. He passed to his reward in the year 1929.

MRS. MAMIE E. STEWARD

The wife of "Uncle Billie," editor of the American Baptist. She was a music teacher in Simmons University for years and a leader among our Baptist women in all Kentucky for a number of years. She was always regarded as one of the exemplary wives and mothers in the state. She lived to see not only her own children call her blessed but her grandchildren.

REV. H. W. BOWEN, D.D.

Dr. Bowen was born in Mississippi, October 12, 1862, died in Chicago, Ill., May 28, 1928. Dr. Bowen was for years president of the State Convention and pastored some of the leading churches in all Mississippi. He was a worthy leader and a great preacher.

Thursday Evening, April 22, 1926, 8 O'CLOCK
Spruce St. Baptist Church, Eighth Ave., N.

Rev. J. Franklin Walker, D.D., *President* Ohio Baptist State Convention presiding.—Alternate, Rev. W.M. Taylor, D.D., Louisiana.

Praise Service .... Led by Prof. Edward Boatner

Prayer .... Rev. J.R. Statton, *Pastor*
Fairfield Baptist Church, Nashville

Devotional Address .... Dr. W.T. Amiger, *Dean*
American Baptist Theological Seminary, Nashville

Address (Thirty Minutes) ... . Dr. W.H. Moses, New York
Campaign Director, National Baptist Convention

Alternate .... Dr. P. James Bryant, Georgia

Addresses (*Fifteen Minutes*):
Dr. Joseph A. Booker, Ark.—Alternate, Dr. J.H. Hughes, N.J.
Dr. Jno. E. Ford, Fla.—Alternate, Dr. G.D. Griffin, Fla.
Dr. E.W. Perry, Okla.—Alternate, Dr. O.C. Maxwell, Mo.

Fraternal Greetings:
Mr. Ira T. Bryant, *Secretary-Treasurer* A.M.E.S.S. Union.
Dr. James A. Allen, Christian Church Publishers.

Presentation of Members Sunday School Publishing Board by Secretary Townsend.

Friday Evening, April 23, 1926, 8 O'CLOCK
Ryman Auditorium

Part I—"Musicale Extravaganza" .... 200 Voices
Direction Prof. Edward Boatner, Boston;
assisted by Mrs. A.M. Townsend, Nashville.

Part II—Introduction of Speaker . . . . Mrs. Mary H. Flowers
Manager, Fireside Schools, Nashville

Address . . . . Miss Nannie H. Burroughs
Corresponding Secretary, Woman's Auxiliary, National Baptist Convention; *President*, National Training School for Women and Girls, Washington, D.C.; *President*, National League of Republican Colored Women.

Part III—Moving Pictures . . . . .Prof. W.G. Hynes
National Exhibitor in charge

Presenting:
    (1) National Baptist Convention, 1905, Chicago.
    (2) National Baptist Convention, 1925, Baltimore.
    (3) Activities Sunday School Publishing Board, Nashville.

Saturday, April 24, 1926
Sight-seeing.

Sunday, April 25, 1926, 2:00 P.M.
Ryman Auditorium
Dr. A.M. Townsend, *Corresponding Secretary* Sunday School Publishing Board, Master of Ceremonies.
    (*Visiting ministers will please take seats on the platform.*)

Praise Service—Led by *Prof.* Edward Boatner, and Chorus 200 Voices

"Prayer"—Marchetti . . . . Chorus

Invocation . . . . Rev. P.A. Callaham, D.D., *Pastor*
First Baptist Church, Eighth Ave., N., Nashville

"Build Thee More Stately Mansions"Matthews . . . . Chorus

Devotional Address . . . . Dr. S.N. Vass, *Secretary*
Religious Education, Sunday School Publishing Board, Nashville

Music (Spiritual) . . . . Chorus

Responsive Bible Reading led by Rev. J.W. Bailey, D.D., Texas.

Leader.—If it had not been the Lord who was on our side, now may Israel say;

Congregation.—If it had not been the Lord who was on our side, when men rose up against us:

Then they had swallowed us up quick, when their wrath was kindled against us:

Then the waters had overwhelmed us, the stream had gone over our soul:

Then the proud waters had gone over our soul.

Leader.—Blessed be the Lord, who hath not given us as a prey to their teeth.

Congregation.—Our soul is escaped as a bird out of the snare of the fowlers: the snare is broken, and we are escaped.

Altogether.—Our help is in the name of the Lord, who made heaven and earth. Ps. 124.

Leader.—They that trust in the Lord shall be as mount Zion, which cannot be removed, but abideth for ever.

Congregation.—As the mountains are round about Jerusalem, so the Lord is round about his people from henceforth even for ever. Ps. 125.

Altogether.—He that goeth forth and weepeth, bearing precious seed, shall doubtless come again with rejoicing, bringing his sheaves with him. Ps. 126:6.

(Note.—This verse was the text of the first sermon preached by the Rev. Spiller of Norfolk, Va., in the organization of the Baptist Foreign Mission Convention in 1880 whence came the National Baptist Convention, U.S.A.)

Hymn—"Before Jehovah's Awful Throne" (Hymn No. 1)
Congregation led by Chorus.

Prayer . . . . .Dr. J.R. Jamison, *President*
Arkansas Baptist State Convention

"O Holy Lord"—Dett . . . . Chorus

Fraternal Greetings—
  Representatives Other Publishers of Religious Literature.

Presentation Visiting Ministers.

Music (Spiritual) . . . . .Chorus

Offertory Address . . . . Dr. W.F. Graham, Philadelphia
                    Chairman, Finance Committee, N.B.C.

DEDICATORY OFFERING
Dr. R.B. Hudson, *Secretary* National Baptist Convention, in charge.
(*Finance Committee.*—Dr. J.B. Singleton, Rev. Ambrose Bennett, Rev. Wm.
Haynes, Hon. S.P. Harris, Rev. E.M. Seymour.)

Solo—1—"Save Me 0 God"—Randigger.
     2—"Some Day" . . . . Prof. Edward Boatner

Introduction of Speaker . . . . Dr. E.W.D. Isaac, *Cor. Sec.*
                    B.Y.P.U. Board, Nat'l Bapt. Convention, U.S.A.

Dedicatory Sermon . . . . Dr. L.K. Williams, Chicago
                    President, National Baptist Convention, U.S.A.

Music . . . . Chorus

Processional March to New Building in following order:
          Capt. J.T. Shelby, Marshal of the Day.
     1—Led by the N.C. Davis Band and the Chorus, singing "On
     ward Christian Soldiers."
     2—Churches, each under banner and in line as follows:
     Superintendent; the Sunday school; the church members and
     friends; the Pastor, Deacons and Officers.
     3—Visiting Ministers.
     4—Members Sunday School Publishing Board.
     5—Editorial Staff of S.S. Publishing Board.
     6—Building, Committee in uniform dress.
     7—President Williams and Officers of the National Baptist
        Convention in uniform dress.

CONCLUDING EXERCISE AND SERVICES AT THE BUILDING
Corner Fourth Ave.., N., and Cedar St.

Dr. L.G. Jordan, *Historian* N.B. C., in Charge

Rasing National Flag ("Old Glory"), with Band playing "The Star-Spangled Banner" (Song No.3.) Congregation joining in the chorus.

Raising Flag of Sunday School Publishing Board with Song "Mine Eyes Have Seen the Glory" (Song No.4.), Congregation led by Band.

Prayer . . . . .Rev. J.C. Fields, D.D., Nashville
Chairman, Sunday School Publishing Board

Song—"Builder of Mighty Worlds" (Hymn No.2), Congregation led by Chorus.

Pantomime of producing a finished book from beginning to end by departments . . . . Dr. L.G. Jordan

Silver Offering —
Presenting the completed and equipped Building with offering, to the National Baptist Convention, U.S.A., by the Building Committee—Dr. E.M. Lawrence, *Chairman*.

Acceptance of the completed and equipped Building and offering, for the National Baptist Convention . . . Dr. L.K. Williams, *President* National Baptist Convention, U.S.A.

Dedication and Consecration Service

Hymn—"Holy, Holy, Holy" . . . . Congregation led by Chorus

Master of Ceremonies.—"I was glad when they said unto me, Let us go into the house of the Lord."

Ministers.—"Our help is in the name of the Lord, who made Heaven and earth. Except the Lord build the house, they labor in vain that build it."

Master of Ceremonies.—"I have hallowed this house which thou hast built, to put my name there forever, and mine eyes and mine heart shall be there perpetually."

Ministers.—"Praise ye the Lord, praise God in His sanctuary."

Congregation.—"Praise Him in the firmament of His power"

Master of Ceremonies.—"Praise Him for His mighty acts"

Ministers.—"Praise Him according to His excellent greatness."

Congregation.—"Let everything that hath breath praise the Lord."

All together.—"Praise ye the Lord."

Master of Ceremonies.—"The Lord gave the word: great was the company of those that published it."

Ministers.—"All scripture is given by inspiration of God and is profitable for doctrine, for reproof, for correction, for instruction in righteousness; That the man of God may be perfect, throughly furnished unto all good works."

Master of Ceremonies.—"Thy word have I hid in my heart, that I might not sin against Thee."

Congregation.—"Thy word is a lamp unto my feet, and a light unto my path."

Master of Ceremonies.—To the glory of God, our Father, by whose favor we have built this House,
     To the honor of Jesus, the Christ, the Son of the Living God, our Lord and Saviour:
     To the praise of the Holy Spirit, source of life and light.

Congregation.—"We dedicate this House."

145

Master of Ceremonies.—"For the worship of God through the publication and dissemination of pure, edifying, secular and religious literature; For the support and the distribution of the Bible, the Book of books"

Congregation.—"We dedicate this, the E.C. Morris Memorial Publishing House, to the glory of God and the service of man."

Ministers.—"For the fostering of Christian Education, Home and Foreign Missions;
For the better development of Christian ministers, second rank and lay leaders and workers in our churches, Sunday schools and other church departments,"

Congregation.—"We dedicate this House."

Master of Ceremonies.—"For the building of a sane race respect; For the promotion of habits of thrift, economy, and race self-reliance;

Congregation.—"We dedicate this House."

Ministers.—"For the fostering of patriotism;
For aggression against evil:
For the support of all that is good;

Congregation.—"We dedicate this House."

Master of Ceremonies.—"For the promotion of universal peace;
For the building of a world's Christian brotherhood;
Finally, for the bringing in the Kingdom of God in this earth;

Congregation.—"We dedicate this House."

Master of Ceremonies.—"As a tribute of gratitude and love, a free-will offering of thanksgiving and praise from those who have tasted the cup of salvation, and experienced the riches of thy grace;

Congregation.—"We, the people of the National Baptist Convention, U.S.A., now consecrating ourselves anew, dedicate this entire House in the

146

name of the Father, and of the Son, and of the Holy Spirit, Amen, Amen!"

Dedicatory Prayer .... Dr. C.H. Parrish, Louisville
Statistician, National Baptist Convention

Choir and Congregation.—Glory be to the Father, and to the Son, and to the Holy Spirit; As it was in the beginning, is now and ever shall be world without end, Amen.

Turning Over Building To Custodian

Turning over the completed and equipped Building and offering to the Sunday School Publishing Board, as Custodian ...... President L.K. Williams

Response of Acceptance .... Dr. A.M. Townsend
Corresponding Secretary, Sunday School Publishing Board

Song—"Praise God from whom all blessing flow."

Benediction.

IMPORTANT ANNOUNCEMENT
Prof. Boatner and the Chorus of 200 Voices
will give a Radio concert
Sunday night, April 25th,
at the First Baptist Church,
Dr. W.F. Powell, Pastor.
"Tune in" on station WCBQ—242 Meters
at 8:30 o'clock,
and enjoy this closing feature of the Dedicatory Services.

Telephone or wire congratulations
on the Radio program
to Dr. A.M. Townsend,
Secretary, Nashville, Tennessee.

SONGS FOR THE OCCASION

No. 1.

"Before Jehovah's awful throne,
Ye nations, bow with sacred joy;
Know that the Lord is God alone;
He can create, and he destroy.

"We are his people, we his care,
Our souls, and all our mortal frame;
What lasting honors shall we rear
Almighty Maker, to thy name?

"We'll crowd thy gates with thankful songs,
High as the heavens our voices raise;
And earth, with her ten thousand tongues
Shall fill thy courts with sounding praise.

"Wide as the world is thy command,
Vast as eternity thy love:
Firm as a rock thy truth shall stand,
When rolling years shall cease to move."

No. 2.

"Builder of Mighty worlds,
How poor the house must be,
That with our human, sinful hands
We may erect for thee!

"In thy blest name we gather here,
And consecrate the ground;
The walls that on this rock now stand,
Thy praises shall resound.

"May many a soul, from death redeemed,
In heav'nly regions fair,
With joy exclaim, "I learned the path
To God and glory there!"

No. 3.   "Oh, thus be it ever
When freemen shall stand,
Between their loved homes
And the war's desolation;

Blest with victory and peace,
May the Heaven-rescued land
Praise the Power that hath made
And preserved us a Nation!
Then conquer we must,
When our cause it is just;
And this be our Motto:
In God is our trust!

CHORUS   "Tis the star-spangled banner;
Oh, long may it wave,
O'er the land of the free,
And the home of the brave!"

No. 4.   "Mine eyes have seen the glory
Of the coming of the Lord;
He is trampling out the vintage
Where the grapes of wrath are stored;
He hath loosed the fateful lightning
Of his terrible swift sword;
His truth is marching on!

CHORUS   "Glory! Glory! Hallelujah!
Glory! Glory! Hallelujah!
Glory! Glory! Hallelujah!
Our God is marching on!

"He has sounded forth the trumpet
That shall never call retreat;
He is sifting out the hearts of men
Before His judgment seat;

0 be swift, my soul, to answer Him!
Be jubilant my feet!
Our God is marching on!

"In the beauty of the lillies,
Christ was born across the sea,
With a glory in His bosom
That transfigures you and me;
As he died to make men holy,
Let us die to make men free:
While God is marching on!"

Another sign of progress is found in the completed first unit of our American Baptist Theological Seminary, at a cost of $50,000. This is an outright gift of the Southern Baptist Convention, and was opened September 24, 1924.

With the beginning of 1930, our material growth is a wonder, but so many of the leaders deplore what seems a spiritual dearth. The indications are that we like other Christians are suffering from the desperate darings of the dying out-lawed liquor traffic. Only ten years ago our Nation wrote prohibition into its constitution and many otherwise good people are said to be violators of the constitution of our great country in an effort to belittle this law just as the murderer and the thief goes on violating "Thou shall not." Records show that the 150 years of the existence of this government, two thousand amendments have been offered to our constitution and only nineteen have been added. Once an amendment has been added, it is hard to repeal it. It has taken from twenty to fifty and two hundred years to thrash out whether we should add an amendment or not. The millions now in school who never saw an open saloon and who have been taught at the fireside, in school and from the pulpit, how the liquor traffic robbed millions of money, home, character, and then sent the soul wailing in hell will soon have charge of this country. So the hope is we shall not only have a Bone Dry United States, but in time a Bone Dry world. So pronounced are these present signs of a growing tendency to lawlessness and unusual crimes, many are the prayers of the spiritual minded, and special soul-saving meetings are being projected during the early life of the new year.

REV. CHAS. H. PHILLIPS, D.D.
Virginia

A most sympathizing preacher. His ability to persuade men was unsurpassed. He gave his life unsparingly to the holding of revival meetings, and many, many happy souls, in many parts of our country, owe their spiritual birth to his faithful untiring service.

REV. GRANVILLE L.P. TALIAFERRO

Dr. Taliaferro was born in Christiansburg, Va., educated at Union University. He served as pastor at Shiloh Baptist Church, Williamsport, Pa., from which point he was called as the second pastor of the Holy Trinity Baptist Church in Philadelphia, Pa., where he did his biggest work, without salary consideration. He led them in erecting a new building using the institutional plan, which was new at that time. He owned and edited the *Christian Banner* which did more to call the attention of Negro Baptists to men who would possibly never have been known but for the efforts of Dr. Taliaferro and the *Christian Banner*. He served as editor till the day of his death, August 13, 1916.

He organized The Banner Publishing Co., The Banner Real Estate Co., and

The Northern Aid Society, an insurance company. He was the only Colored director in the Republic Trust Co. He was active in all lines of endeavor for the progress of the Negro.

REV. A.P. DUNBAR, D.D.,
S.C.

Died in Columbia. Successful pastor and organizer of Second Calvary Baptist Church, Columbia. Was known as a good businessman, having organized an insurance company which still exists.

REV. J.J. DURHAM, M.D., D.D.
Of **South Carolina**

Born near Woodruff, S.C., and died at Columbia. Graduated from Fisk University in 1880—receiving his A.B. degree, and in 1885, his A.M. degree from the same school. He was a graduate of Meharry Medical College. He was president of the South Carolina Baptist State Convention, and pastor of Second Calvary Baptist Church, Columbia. He opposed denominational control, but favored board control, hence the National Baptist Publishing Board split off in 1915 over that issue; he went with them and was very bitter till his death. He was a strong reasoner, powerful in debate, and withal a great preacher.

HOLY TRINITY BAPTIST CHURCH
Philadelphia, Pa.

Holy Trinity Baptist Church, Philadelphia, Pa., was organized in 1891 with 43 members. It now has a membership of over two thousand, and is energetic in its activities for denominational demands.—*Home and Foreign Fields.*

MINUTES

OF THE
Baptist Foreign Mission Convention
OF THE
United States of America

HELD IN

MONTGOMERY, ALA.

NOVEMBER 24, 25, 26, 1880

ELDER W.W. COLLEY, Corresponding Secretary

RICHMOND, VA.

Companion Printing Company, Knoxville, Tenn.

President Elder .... W.H. McAlpine, Arkansas
First Vice President .... Elder J.W. Patterson, Virginia
Second Vice President .... Elder F.R. Howell, North Carolina
Third Vice President .... Elder R.N. Countee, Tennessee
Fourth Vice President .... Elder E.K. Love, Georgia
Fifth Vice President .... J.W. Muse, Mississippi
Sixth Vice President .... Elder E.H. Hooks, Texas
Seventh Vice President .... Elder G. Robinson, Arkansas
Eighth Vice President .... Elder P.H. Williams, Ohio
Ninth Vice President .... Elder J. Marks, Louisiana
Tenth Vice President .... Elder A. Foster, Alabama
Eleventh Vice President .... Elder James Page, Florida
Secretaries .... Elder J.M. Armstead, Tennessee;
                                    Elder G.H., Dwelle, Georgia
Treasurer .... Elder E.G. Corprew, Virginia

EXECUTIVE BOARD

Elder W.A. Bunch .... Salem, Ala.
Elder P. Hatchett .... Little Rock, Ark.
Elder G.H. Dwelle .... Americus, Ga.
Elder J. Marks .... New Orleans, La.
Elder T. L. Jordan .... Columbus, Miss.
Elder C. Johnson .... Raleigh, N.C.
Elder P.H. Williams .... Middle Port, Ohio
Elder C.P. Hughes .... Shelbyville, Tenn.
Elder C.B. Marton .... Jefferson, Texas
Elder C.H. Carey .... Abington, Va.
Elder J.W. Patterson .... Danville, Va.
Elder D. King .... Norfolk, Va.
Elder A.N. Buck .... Halifax, N.C.

CONSTITUTION

Preamble and Constitution of the Baptist Foreign Mission Convention of the United States of America:

* * * *

Whereas it becomes necessary and is our duty to extend our Christian influence to advance the kingdom of Christ, and as African Missions claims our most profound attention and feeling that we are most sacredly called to do work in this field and elsewhere abroad, therefore, we the representatives from the various churches, Sunday schools, and societies of the Baptist denomination in the United States, do solemnly organize ourselves in a Convention for the above named objects; we agree to the following Constitution:

Article I.

This Convention shall be styled and known as the BAPTIST FOREIGN MISSION CONVENTION of the UNITED STATES of AMERICA.

Article II.

The principle object of this CONVENTION shall be the diffusion of the GOSPEL OF JESUS CHRIST, on the Continent of AFRICA, and elsewhere abroad, that the Providence of God may direct.

Article III.

The membership of this Convention shall be annual or life, any member of a Baptist church, in good standing may become an annual member by paying the sum of five dollars, annually, and a life member by paying the sum of fifty dollars, in annual installments of five dollars for ten consecutive years.

Article IV.

All messengers from Baptist churches, Sunday schools, women's missionary associations, conventions, association and the annual and life members shall be recognized as members at the present and next regular meeting of this Convention. The basis of representation shall be one delegate from every church and one for every 1000 members or a fraction of the first 1000. They are to contribute according to their ability, to the fund of the Convention, and two delegates from each association or convention and one for every 2,500 members or a fraction thereof above the first 2,500 contributing to the funds of the Convention.

Article V.

The officers of this Convention shall be a president and one vice president from each state represented in this Convention and said vice presidents shall be president of the work of this Convention in their state and so considered by this Convention. Also two secretaries and a treasurer who shall be elected at every annual meeting of this Convention and hold their office until their successors are chosen, and no one shall be chosen President more than twice consecutively.

Article VI.

Fifteen judicious and experienced brethren shall be elected at every regular meeting of the convention, who shall form or constitute the Executive Board of this Convention; five of whom shall constitute an Executive Committee with full power to use all means necessary to secure the objects of this Convention during its recess, and who shall be responsible to the Convention for all their actions.

Article VII.

It shall be the duty of the Board of the Convention to take such steps as may be necessary to secure church, association, and state organizations for developing an interest in Foreign Mission,and securing cooperation with this Convention by raising means and otherwise.

Article VIII.

A majority of the Board shall be located at some central point.

Article IX.

The Board shall make an annual report of all its transactions to this Convention, giving a full account of all its doings during the interval of the meetings of this Convention, giving the condition and prosperity of our mission fields; the number of missionaries employed by them and what salaries they receive and other information in their possession that will assist the Convention to judiciously carry out its object, and they shall not form any organic cooperation with any other body.

Article X.

The president shall preside at all meetings of the Convention; he shall preserve good order, enforce the rules, and decide all questions of order, but any member may appeal from his decision to the Convention whose decision shall be final. In the event of the death of the president or his resignation, any one of the vice presidents by the request of the Executive Board may fill his place.

Article XI.

The treasurer shall receive and hold all monies, bills, deeds, and bequeaths belonging to this Convention; pay all orders issued by the Board at their regular meetings, and signed by the president and secretary of the same. He shall for the faithful discharge of his duties and the security of the Convention in its property, give such bonds as may be agreed upon by the Board; and his books may be free to the inspection of any officer of the Convention and any member of the Board. He shall make a quarterly report to the Board and an annual report to the Convention, giving an account of all moneys received and paid out by him, to whom, what for, and the general condition of the treasury.

Article XII.

All officers, boards, missionaries, and agents appointed by the Convention or Executive Board shall be members of some regular Baptist church in union with the churches composing this Convention.

Article XIII.

The bodies and individuals composing this Convention shall have the right to specify the objects to which their contributions shall be applied; but when no such specifications are made, the Convention shall make the appropriation at its discretion.

Article XIV.

The Convention shall meet at such time and place as shall be agreed upon at a preceding meeting. Special meetings of this Convention may be called by the president at the request of the Executive Board; or in case of his death or removal from office, by any one of the vice presidents.

Article XV.

This Constitution is only provisional, and is intended to meet the exigencies of the hour and may be abridged or amended at any regular meeting of this Convention by a majority vote of the same.

PROCEEDINGS OF 1880

Morning Session—Wednesday, November 24th.

The Baptist Foreign Mission Convention of the United States of America, assembled with the First Baptist Church of Montgomery, Ala., according to the call of Wednesday, November 24th, 1880.

Rev. W.W. Colley announced at 11:30 a.m., that the brethren would spend thirty minutes in praise and prayer.

Rev. R. Spiller of Norfolk, Va., sang to God's praise, "All Hail the Power of Jesus' Name."

Rev. E.G. Corprew of Portsmouth, Va., offered prayer, also Rev. M. Tyler of Alabama, and Rev. P.H. Williams of Ohio. Rev. W.W. Colley then called the Convention to order at 12 p.m., and after reading the call, on motion of Rev. Corprew, Rev. Colley was made president *pro tem,* and on motion of Rev. R. Spiller, Rev. J.M. Armstead of Tennessee, was made secretary *pro tem.* Rev. W.H. McAlpine of Alabama, read the following welcome address from the Alabama delegation and on motion it was ordered spread on the face of the minutes:

Dear Brethren:

The Alabama delegation met at 10 a.m., ordered that the following address of welcome be presented to this body as expressive of our heartfelt welcome, and hearty cooperation with the movement to have a Foreign Mission Convention. We hail with much joy and delight, the time of this meeting, because here we hope and expect to meet the representative men of the denomination from all over these United States; and become better acquainted with one another as one "household of faith;" to know more of each other's work, plans, views and desires, and by counsel one with another, to better carry forward the work of our Lord and Master. Again, because it seems to be the dawn of a brighter day upon the great question of giving Africa the gospel of Christ. As those who are prime movers in the calling of this body, have settled upon Alabama, her Capital, and the first Colored Baptist Church, as the place of holding this first meeting, we feel it a duty upon our part to tender to you the heartfelt welcome of the 100,000 Colored Baptists of Alabama. In behalf of the 600 churches, 30 associations and general state conventions, we tender to you our most heartfelt welcome and pledge to you our hearty cooperation in all lawful and Scriptural measures to carry forward the work for which you assembled.

We leave to the pastor of this church to extend the particular welcome of his city and people; as to other work for which this meeting has been called, we would say upon our part, that we feel deeply impressed with its importance, and that such a convention as you propose to organize, seems to us, really, the only practical way that the states can carry forward successfully, the foreign mission work.

We would say further, that in the planning and prosecution of this work you will have as much as is in us, our heart, mind, and money.

As to organization, plans and means for carrying on the work, we feel these are questions of great weight and importance, and upon the wisdom of these plans depends the future success of the work, but we have some modesty in suggesting ways and means. We feel, however, that this body is fully competent to the task and shall rejoice if we can become of any use, as humble instruments in the great work before you.

REV. M. TYLER, Moderator.
REV. J. WILHITE, Secretary.

Rev. J.A. Foster also delivered an address of welcome in behalf of his church and the citizens of Montgomery.

The following delegates made short and well-pointed addresses expressing the status of their state in regard to the mission to be accomplished:

Revs. R.N. Countee, of Tennessee; J.W. Patterson, of Virginia; H.W. Bowens, of Mississippi; E.K. Love, of Georgia; J. Marks, of Louisiana; F.R. Howell, of North Carolina; P.H. Williams, of Ohio; C.B. Martin, of Texas; George Roberson, of Arkansas; Miss E.F. Cassidy, of Iowa; and Miss J.P. Moore, of Illinois.

On motion it was ordered that the names of the delegates be enrolled.

The president appointed the following members as a Committee on Constitution and By-laws:

Revs. W.H. McAlpine, H. Woodsmall, E.K. Love, J.W. Muse, E.G. Corprew, R.N. Countee, C. Johnson, J. Marks, W.W. Colley, C.B. Martain, P.H. Williams, Miss J.P. Moore, and Miss E.F. Cassidy. The president appointed Rev. Spiller to preach at this church at 7:30, assisted by Rev. C.P. Hughes. Prayer by H. Woodsmall. The Convention adjourned to 7:30 p.m.

Evening Session

The Convention was called to order by Rev. J.A. Foster, and devotional services were conducted by Elder C.P. Hughes, consisting of singing hymn No. 648, reading Isaiah 35th chapter, and prayer.

Elder R. Spiller of Norfolk, Va., being introduced preached an able sermon from Psalm 126:6. "He that goeth forth and weepeth, bearing precious seed, shall doubtless come again with rejoicing, bringing his sheaves with him."

Collection $12.20. Benediction by Elder W.A. Burch, and the Convention adjourned to reassemble at 9 a.m.

SECOND DAY—Morning Session
Thursday, November 25th.

President Colley presiding and reassembled the Convention at 9:30 a.m.

Sang hymn, "We Will Rest in the Valley." Prayer by J.W. Patterson. Wednesday's journal was then read and approved, after which the Convention took recess until 1 p.m.

At 1 p.m., the president called the Convention to order and announced that the Committee on Constitution was ready to report.

The committee submitted the following which was adopted. (See constitution.)

The president appointed the following named members as a Committee on the Selection of Officers: Revs. J.W. Patterson, A.F. Owens, P.T. Hatchett, W.A. Brinkley, Hon. A.A. Blake, Revs. F. Hoods; F. Howell, H.W. Bowen, P.H. Williams, J. Marks, Miss E.F. Cassidy, and Miss J.P. Moore.

Rev. P.H. Williams of Ohio, was appointed to preach at this church at 7:30 p.m., assisted by Rev. J. Marks of Louisiana.

The president introduced Dr. S.W. Marston of St. Louis, Mo., who led in prayer.

On motion the Convention adjourned to 7:30 p.m.

Evening Session

President Colley in the chair. Rev. J. Marks read 103rd Psalm, sang hymn No. 1141, and offered prayer. Hymn 590 was sung, Rev. P.H. Williams of Ohio, being introduced, preached from Hebrews 8:25. Prayer by Rev. M. Tyler. Collection, $13.01.

The Committee on the Nomination of Officers for the ensuing year, submitted the following:

President, Revs. W.H. McAlpine, of Alabama; first vice, J.W. Patterson, of Virginia; second vice, F.R. Howell, of North Carolina; third vice, R.N. Countee, of Tennessee; fourth vice, E.K. Love, of Georgia; fifth vice, J.W. Muse, of Mississippi; sixth vice, F. Hooks, of Texas; seventh vice, G. Robinson, of Arkansas; eighth vice, P.H. Williams, of Ohio; ninth vice, J. Marks, of Louisiana; tenth vice, J.A. Foster, of Alabama; eleventh vice, James Page, of Florida.

Secretaries, Revs. J.M. Armistead, of Tennessee; G.H. Dwelle, of Georgia; Treasurer, E.G. Corprew, of Virginia.

Respectfully submitted,

J.W. PATTERSON, Chairman.

The president announced the following members as a committee to select an Executive Board for the ensuing year:

Revs. P. Guinn, R. Spiller, G.H. Dwelle, Prof. M.W. Alston, Revs. J. Marks, C.B. Marton, Miss E.F. Cassidy, Revs. P.H. Williams, J. Sims, Miss J.P. Moore, Revs. A.N. Buck, R. Ramsey.

On motion Rev. C.H. Carey of Virginia, and P. Mathes, of Alabama, were appointed to conduct the president elect to the chair, who on taking his seat mapped out explicitly the course for the delegation to pursue to expedite business. Sang the doxology. "Praise God From Whom All Blessings Flow."

Benediction by Rev. P.H. Williams. Adjourned to 9 a.m., tomorrow.

THIRD DAY—Morning Session
Friday, November 26, 1880.

President McAlpine in the chair, called the convention to order at 9 a.m., Rev. R. Ramsey of Mississippi, conducted the devotional services, read Psalm 100, sang hymn No. 725 and offered prayer. Thursday's journal was read and approved.

The president announced the following committees:

On Finance—Revs. C.P. Hughes, A.F. Owens, J.W. Muse.

On Time and Place—Revs. R. Spiller, A.F. Owens, and G. Robinson.

On Devotional Services—Revs. J.A. Foster, R.N. Countee and F. Hooks.

On Printing—Revs. J.M. Armstead, C.H. Dwelle and W.W. Colley.

On Preparing Certificates for Delegates—Prof. G.W. Curtis, Rev. C.H. Carey and P. Mathes.

On Ways and Means—Revs. E.G. Corprew, W.W. Colley, E.K. Love, R.N. Countee, J.W. Patterson, J.A. Stewart and H. Bowens.

We, your Committee to Select and Locate the Executive Board, submit the following:

We have selected Richmond, Va., for the location of the Board, and present the following named brethren for the said Executive Board: Revs. W.A. Burch, Selma, Ala.; P. Hatchett, Little Rock, Ark.; G.H. Dwelle, Ga.; John Marks, New Orleans , La.; T.L. Jordan, Columbus, Miss.; C. Johnson, Raleigh, N.C.; P.H. Williams, Middle Port, Ohio; C.P. Hughes, Shelbyville, Tenn.; C.B. Marton, Jefferson, Texas; C.H. Carey, Abingdon, Va.; J.W. Patterson, Danville, Va.; D. King, Norfolk, Va., R. Spiller, Norfolk, Va.; A.N. Buck, Halifax, N.C.; W.W. Colley.

Respectfully submitted, P. GUINN, Chairman.

The Committee on Time and Place submitted the following:

That this Convention hold its Second Annual Session with the Mt. Zion Baptist Church, Knoxville, Tenn., Wednesday before the fourth Lord's Day in November, 1881, and that Rev. John Marks, of Louisiana, preach the Annual Sermon; alternate, Rev. C.O. Booth, of Alabama. Missionary Sermon by Rev. W.W. Colley, of Virginia; alternate, Rev. A.F. Owens, of Alabama, R. Spiller, Chairman.

Evening Session

The president called the Convention to order at 7:30 p.m. Sang, "Pass Me Not 0 Gentle Saviour." Prayer by Elder P. Guinn of Tennessee.

Rev. W.W. Colley, late missionary to Africa, then delivered an able and impressive address on "African Mission."

The Committee on Ways and Means made the following report which was adopted. Be it Resolved, (1) That each state convention, general association, woman's missionary society, Sunday school convention, and district association, organize a Foreign Mission Board, with the necessary officers to prosecute the work of missions within the bounds of said associations and conventions.

(2) That said boards request the different churches and Sunday schools to give collection once every quarter for African missions, and the same be forwarded to the vice president of this Convention in each state, he to give his receipt for the same, and forward at once to the general treasurer of this Convention, and he forward a receipt for the same to the vice president.

(3) That the Executive Board of this Convention appoint a corresponding secretary, whose duty it shall be to travel over the various states and collect means for African missions and the board pay him a liberal compensation for his service.

(4) That the board strive to raise as soon as practicable, $5,000 to establish a mission house in Africa.

(5) That the Executive Committee of the Board confer with the Foreign Mission Board of the Virginia Baptist State Convention, relative to the transferring of their work in Africa under Rev. S. Cosby, to this Convention, and that the vice president of each state have the work of mission published in the denominational organs of his state when it can be done free of charge.

REV. E.G. CORPREW, Va., Chairman
REV. R.N. COUNTEE, Tenn., Secretary

The Executive Board submitted the following report which was adopted:

Montgomery, Ala., November 26th, 1880

Mr. President and dear Brethren:

We, the board, beg leave to submit the following:

According to the duties imposed upon us, we met this evening at 6 p.m. Prayer was offered by Rev. J.W. Patterson of Virginia. We elected as chairman of the board, Rev. W.A. Burch of Selma, Ala., and Rev. C.H. Carey of Abingdon, Va., as secretary.

On motion, Elder W. W. Colley was employed as correspondent secretary of the Convention at a salary of $1,000 per year.

On motion, the treasurer was requested to give a bond of $1,000 for the faithful discharge of his duty. The following bills were ordered paid:

The sexton, $5.00; secretary, $25.00; board for delegates,$7.00; and the First Baptist Church replace this $7.00 for board.

REV. W.A. BURCH, Chairman
REV. C.H. CAREY, Secretary

Rev. F.R. Howell offered the following resolution which was adopted:

Resolved, That the Executive Board of this Convention requests all the officers and Executive Committees of the various state conventions and general associations, where Foreign Mission Boards have not been organized, to act with the vice presidents of the convention in each state, as a committee on Foreign Missions.

2. That said committees request the officers and Executive Committees or the various associations and Sunday school conventions in their various states to act as a committee on Foreign Missions in their respective bodies.

3. That they make an effort to secure the cooperation of all pastors, Sunday school superintendents, editors, principals of schools, missionaries, and the representatives of the various denominational interests and awaken an interest in organizing and raising money for the work in Africa.

4. That the Executive Board of this Convention be further instructed to prepare suitable circulars explanatory of the objects of the Convention, giving facts about Africa and also such blanks as may be needed to supply those who may agree to aid in the work. Special instruction should be furnished the sisters of our churches in regards to the organization of women's mission circles in the churches.

The following brethren were appointed messengers to other bodies: Southern Baptist Convention—Revs. T.L. Jordan and R. Ramsey.

Virginia State Convention—Rev. R. Spiller.

Virginia Sunday School State Convention—Rev. C.H. Carey.

American Baptist Publication Society—Revs. J.W. Patterson and C.O. Booth.

American and Foreign Bible Society—Rev. C. Johnson.

The Missionary Union—Rev. W.H. McAlpine.

The New England Convention—Rev. W.W. Colley.

On motion all the members of this Convention were made messengers to the Baptist organizations in their respective states.

Rev. J.W. Patterson offered the following:

Resolved, That the hearty thanks of this Convention are hereby tendered to pastor and members of this church, and the Baptist citizens of Montgomery generally for kindness and hospitalities to the members of the Convention and for the interest manifested; also to the railroads which have favored the delegates with reduced rates.

FINANCE REPORT

We, your committee, beg leave to submit the following:

Alabama Baptist State Convention	$25.00
Muscle Shoals Sabbath School Convention	5.00
Eufaula District Sabbath School Convention	2.00
Union Sabbath School Convention	18.65
Bowen Baptist Association	1.70
Colored Bethlehem Association	10.00
First Baptist Church, Birmingham	1.00
Evergreen Baptist Association	2.50
Sabbath School Foreign Mission Society of Marion	4.00
East Alabama Sabbath School Convention	.75
Havehill Baptist Church, Midway	1.00
Friendship Baptist Church	.75
S.M. Reeves, Greenville	2.00
Mt. Olive Church, Clarke Co	5.00
A. Johnson	1.00
Uniontown Association	5.00
New Cahaba Association	4.00
2nd Baptist Church, Marian	5.08
Hopewell Baptist Church, Marian	3.00
Shelby Springs Association	1.00

Bethel Baptist Church, Monroeville 75
Antioch Baptist Church, Monroeville 75
C. Woods 50
Through Selma Baptist Missionary Society; Mr. Cunningham by
   Rev. C. Long 10.00
Mt. Pleasant Association 6.60
Free Mission Association, by Rev. C. Travis 10.75
New Mt. Gilead 2.55
Mt. Olive, Pine Jackson 3.90
Rev. G.M. Jackson, Eleven Grove 1.00
M.E. Church, East Port 55
Juka Church, East Port 30
Liberty Church 1.55
Carter Branch 1.85
Cherokee 1.80
No. 1, Zion 1.15
Total from the above society 43.80
Rehoboth Church 1.00
Mount Zion Church, Tallahassee 1.00
Alabama District S.S. Convention 10.00
Alabama District Association 10.00
Uniontown Sabbath School, Perry Co 2.50
Collection during the session 41.20
Mrs. Blanche 75
               Total from Alabama $211.00

VIRGINIA

Zion Baptist Church, Portsmouth $5.00
Union Baptist Church, Nansemond 5.00
Portsmouth, Norfolk and Berkley Sabbath School Union 5.00
Second Sabbath School, Portsmouth 3.40
The Sisters of Zion Church, Portsmouth 1.50
Zion Sister of Convention 1.00
Zion Sabbath School Mission Society 5.00
Bute St. Church, Norfolk 5.00
Bank St. Baptist Foreign Mission Society, Norfolk 3.50
Bank St. Baptist Church Singing Association, Norfolk 1.50
               Total. $35.90

MISSISSIPPI

Mount Olive Sabbath School, Holmes Co.	$1.00
Mount Olive Sabbath School, Holmes Co.	3.00
Mount Mariah Sabbath School, Holmes Co	1.10
Mount Valley Church, Holmes Co.	2.00
Shady Grove Sabbath School, Holmes Co.	4.50
Rose Bank Sabbath School, Holmes Co	3.00
Holly Grove, Sabbath School, Holmes Co	1.00
Straw Camp Sabbath School, Holmes Co.	1.00
Surficeville Church, Cohomo County	1.00
Oak Ridge Church, Cohomo County	1.00
Total.	$18.60

ARKANSAS

St. Paul Baptist Church, Pine Bluff	$5.00
Chapel Baptist Church, Pine Bluff	1.00
Hurricane Baptist Church, Pine Bluff	1.00
Antioch Baptist Church, Jefferson Co.	2.00
Chapel Baptist Church, Jefferson Co	1.00
Third Baptist Church, Helena	2.00
Total	$12.00

NORTH CAROLINA

North Carolina State Convention	$10.00

LOUISIANA

Fourth and Sixth District Sabbath School Institute, New Orleans	$6.00
Women's Mission Society	2.00
Total	$8.00

TENNESSEE

Middle Baptist Church, Memphis	$2.50
Middle Baptist Church, Sabbath School, Memphis	2.50
Beale Street Church, Memphis	5.00
West Tennessee, East Arkansas and North Mississippi Association	10.00
Total	$20.00

FLORIDA

First Church, Tallahassee, Fla. $1.00

Grand Total $317.06

Respectfully submitted—J.W. Muse, A.F. Owens, and C.P. Hughes.
On motion the Convention adjourned to meet with the Mount Zion
Baptist Church, Knoxville, Tenn., Wednesday before the fourth Lord's
Day in November, 1881.

REV. W.H. McALPINE, of Marian, Ala., President
REV. J.M. ARMSTEAD, of Knoxville, Tenn., Secretary

LIST OF DELEGATES

Alabama

Delegates from State Convention—Revs. M. Tyler, C.O. Booth, W.H.
McAlpine, J. Wilhite, J.P. Barton, A.F. Owen, W.R. Pettiford, A. Cun-
ningham, W.J. Stevens, W.A. Burch, P. Underwood, Wallace Allen, E.K.
Love, and P. Matthews.

Uniontown Association . . . . Revs. W.H. McAlpine, S. Dozier
Muscle Shoals Association and S.S. Convention . . . Rev. J.F. Thompson
Dallas County Association . . . . . Revs. Peter Underwood, D. Boyd,
H. Blevens, C.L. Brooks
Eufaula S.S. Convention . . . . Rev. J. Wilhite
Antioch Association . . . . .Rev. S. Fanteroy
Colored Bethlehem Association . . . . Rev. A. Cunningham
Pine Grove Association . . . . Revs. E. Thornton, C. Thornton
Alabama District Sunday School Convention . . . . . . H.A. Loveless,
R.M. Tyler
East Alabama Sunday School Convention . . . . Rev. P. Barton
Eufaula Association . . . . Rev. R. Fenn, J.D. Maddox
Shelby Springs Association . . . . Rev. H.S. Williams
First Church, Birmingham . . . . Rev. A.C. Jackson
Mt. Zion Church . . . . Rev. I.J. Jones
Mt. Canaan Church . . . . Rev. J.P. Barton
Alabama District Association . . . . Revs. M. Taylor, J.A. Fortier,
George Washington

167

Mt. Gilard and Pleasant Hill Churches . . . . .Rev. A.A. Scott
New Hope Church, Sherman . . . . Rev. W.M. Merritt
Marian Church and Sunday School . . . . Revs. W.H. McAlpine,
J.W. Curtis, N.R. Nickerson
Everdale Church . . . . Rev. G.J. Brooks
Friendship, Batesville . . . . Rev. J.D. Maddox
Midway Church . . . . Rev. A. Rivers
Mt. Olive Church and Cedar Fork . . . . .Rev. D. Small
Bethel . . . . Rev. C. Cosby
Baptist Lily and Mt. Olive . . . . Rev. C.P. Cain
Town Creek . . . . Sidney Ross
Roxana . . . . Rev. Smart Taylor
Old Elim . . . . Curtis Woods
First Baptist, Wetumpka . . . . L.P. Moore
St. Philips Street, Selma . . . . Rev. W.A. Burch
Bethel and Antioch Churches . . . . Rev. Josiah Davidson
Mt. Zion, Clairborn, Union Chapel
and Barlow Bend . . . . Rev. A. Johnson
Mt. Zion Sunday School, Hawkinsville . . . . W.M. Boykin
Marion Baptist Foreign Mission Society . . . . J.W. Curtis,
N.R. Nickerson

Selma Baptist Missionary Society—H. Woodsmall, D.T. Gully, D.L. Prentice, Mrs. A.A. Bowie, D.A. May, Eli Adams, M.W. Alston, C.W. Childs, Miss E.F. Cassidy, Mrs. Della Pettiford, Deacon Charles White, Revs. W.A. Burch, C.O. Booth, Charles Goldsby.
Uniontown Sunday School Convention—Rev. W.R. Pettiford

Arkansas
Revs. George Robinson, Pine Bluff;
P.H. Hatchett, J. Sims, Little Rock.

North Carolina
Revs. F.R. Howell, C. Johnson, Raleigh;
A. Buck, Charles Smith, Halifax.

Georgia
Revs. E.K. Love, Thomasville; D.H. Dwelle, Americus;
A.A. Blake, East Point.

Florida
Rev. James Page, Tallahassee.

Louisiana
Rev. J. Marks, Miss J.P. Moore, New Orleans.

Mississippi
Revs. R. Ramsey, Meridian; J. Harvey, Winona;
J.W. Muse, Macon; H.W. Bowen, Oxford;
A.J. Dent, Pontoto; G.W. Allen, Oklahoma;
F.E. Plummer, P.L. Fraxtius, Jackson;
Daniel Webster, Meridian; T.L. Jordan, Columbus.

Ohio
Rev. P.H. Williams, Middleport.

Texas
Revs. C.P. Martin, Jefferson; F. Hooks,
Texarkana; E. Barnes,
W.A. Walton, Navasota.

Tennessee
Revs. J.M. Armistead, Knoxville; P.
Guinn, Rodersville Junction; C.P. Hughes,
Shelbyville; J.A. Steward, Murfreesboro; W.A.
Brinkley, R.N. Countee, Memphis.

Virginia
Revs. J.W. Patterson, Danville; E.G.
Corprew, Portsmouth; C.H. Carey, Abingdon;
R. Spiller, D. King, Norfolk.

LIST OF PLEDGES

Alabama
Cross Keys and Bethel Baptist Churches, G.C. Cosey, Pastor. . $10.00
C.J. Brooks 5.00
Everdale Church, Selma 5.00

Baptist Lilly and Mt. Olive Churches, C.P. Cain, Pastor 4.00
Rehoboth and Mt. Zion Baptist Churches, T. Smith, Pastor ... 4.00
Second Baptist Church, Selma, H. Blevens, Pastor 5.00
Sabbath School Convention, Selma, C.S. Brooks, Delegate .. 5.00

Mississippi

Missionary Union Baptist Church, T.L. Jordan, Pastor $10.00
Mt. Olive Association, Rev. Ambrose Henderson, Moderator . 10.00
General Baptist Missionary Association 25.00
Zion Association, J. Harvey, Messenger 10.00
Spring Hill Association 10.00
New Prospect Baptist Church 5.00
Chapel Grove Baptist Church 5.00
Chapel Hill Church —Pastor Rev. B.P. Price, Paid 2.00
Mt. Zion, Murfreesboro, Tennessee .... $ 5.00
Stone River Association 5.00
East Tennessee General Association 15.00
Texas Association 25.00

The total collection at the Montgomery Church should read $41.20

OFFICERS FOR THE ENSUING YEAR

President, Rev. W.H. McAlpine .... Selma, Ala.
First Vice President, Rev. J.Q.A. Wilhite .... Eufaula, Ala.
Second Vice President, Rev. E.C. Morris .... Helena, Ark.
Third Vice President, Rev. R.D. Dunbar .... .Jacksonville, Fla.
Fourth Vice President, Rev. W.H. Tilman, Sr. .... Atlanta, Ga.
Fifth Vice President, Rev. G.W. Walker .... New Orleans, La.
Sixth Vice President, Rev. R. Ramsey .... Meridian, Miss.
Seventh Vice President, Rev. C. Johnson .... Raleigh, N.C.
Eighth Vice President, Rev. F. Brown .... Greenville, S.C.
Ninth Vice President, Rev. J.A. Stewart ..... .Murfreesboro, Tenn.
Tenth Vice President, Rev. J.M. Dawson .... Williamsburg, Va.
Eleventh Vice President, Rev. R.H. Boyd .... Palestine, Texas
Treasurer, Rev. R. Spiller .... Norfolk, Va.
Secretaries, Rev. J.M. Armstead ....Knoxville, Tenn.
             Rev. P.F. Morris................... Lynchburg, Va.
Statistical Secretary, Rev. H. Williams, Jr.......... Petersburg, Va.

Corresponding Secretary and Traveling Agent, Rev. W.W. Colley . . .
. . . . Richmond, Va.

FOREIGN MISSION BOARD

President, Rev. A. Binga, Jr. . . . . Manchester, Va.
Secretary, Prof. J.E. Jones . . . . Richmond, Va.
Rev. Wm. Troy . . . . Richmond, Va.
Rev. C. Johnson . . . . Raleigh, N.C.
Rev. F. Brown . . . . Greenville, S.C.
Rev. W.H. Tilman, Sr. . . . . Atlanta, Ga.
Rev. R.D. Dunbar . . . . Jacksonville, Fla.
Rev. J.Q.A. Wilhite . . . . Eufaula, Ala.
Rev. R. Ramsey . . . . Meridian, Miss.
Rev. J.A. Stewart . . . . Murfreesboro, Tenn.
Rev. G.W. Walker . . . . New Orleans, La.
Rev. R.H. Boyd . . . . .Palestine, Texas
Rev. J.A. Taylor . . . . Richmond, Va.
Rev. H. Williams, Jr. . . . . Petersburg, Va.
Rev. J.M. Dawson . . . . Williamsburg, Va.
Rev. R. Spiller . . . . Norfolk, Va.
Rev. J.W. Patterson . . . . Danville, Va.
Rev. E.C. Morris . . . . Helena, Ark.
Rev. W.W. Colley . . . . Richmond, Va.
Rev. W.H. McAlpine . . . . .Selma, Ala.
Rev. P.F. Morris . . . . Lynchburg, Va.
Rev. John Jones . . . . Liberty, Va.
Rev. J.E. Farrar . . . . Richmond, Va.
Rev. Holmes . . . . Richmond, Va.
Rev. J.B. Smith Concord . . . . Depot, Va.
Rev. L.A. Black . . . . Petersburg, Va.
Rev. J.H. Dickerson . . . . Petersburg, Va.

STATE EXECUTIVES

Alabama

Rev. J.A. Foster, Montgomery   Rev. D.C. Coleman
Rev. J.A. Burch, Selma   Rev. M. Tyler
Rev. A.F. Owens, Mobile   Rev. W.R. Pettiford
                Rev. A.C. Jackson, Birmingham

171

Arkansas

Rev. George Robinson, Pine Bluff

Rev. L.J. Hayward

Rev. E.C. Morris, Helena

Rev. J.G. Bailey

Rev. B. Rose

Rev. E. Neeley

Rev. W.B. Gibson

Florida

Rev. James Page, Tallahassee

Rev. John Jimmerson, Jacksonville

Rev. ---- Bell, Palatka

Dr. G.A. Fish, Live Oak

Rev. John Pitter, Monticello

Rev. J. Brown, St. Augustine

Rev. --- Thompson, Lake City

Mississippi

Rev. W.H. Bowen, Oxford

Rev. T.L. Jordan, Oxford

Rev. G.W. Harris, Columbus

Rev. T.R. Crump

Rev. S.J. Hunt

Rev. P.Martin

Rev. Daniel Webster, Meridian

North Carolina

Rev. F.R. Howell, Raleigh

Mrs. Sallie Hayward, Raleigh

Rev. W.A. Green, Raleigh

Mrs. C.L. Young, Oxford

Rev. N.F. Roberts, Raleigh

Rev. Ransom, Franklinton

Mrs. Hattie Shepard, Raleigh

Tennessee

Rev. W.A. Brinkley, Memphis

Rev. N.G. Merry, Nashville

Rev. R.N. Countee, Memphis

Rev. A. Nickerson, Chattanooga

Rev. S.M. Dickerson, Murfrees.

Rev. S. Thompson, Smyrna

Rev. C.C. Russell, Loudon

Texas

Rev. C.B. Martin Jefferson

Rev. F. Hook, Texarkana

Rev. W.A. Walton, Navasota

Rev. A.R. Griggs, Dallas

Rev. W.M. Massey, Waco

Rev. J. Fountain

Rev. I.S. Campbell

Georgia

Rev. J. M. Jones, Atlanta

Rev. W. J. White, Augusta

Rev. A.A. Blake

Rev. E.K. Love, Thomasville

Rev. Frank Quales, Atlanta

Rev. G.W. Wheeler, Cassandra

Rev. E. Cole, Atlanta

Virginia

Rev. H. Herndon, Charlottesville Bro. Jacob Warren, Norfolk
Rev. D. King, Norfolk   Bro. H.W. Swann, Danville
Rev. C.H. Carey, Abingdon   Mrs. Amanda Holmes, Richmond
Rev. Thos. Washington, Matthews

LIFE MEMBERS

Elder W.W. Colley, Richmond, Va.; Elder J. Clemons, Knoxville, Tenn.
Elder J.M. Armistead, Knoxville; Deacon S. Campbell, Knoxville,Tenn.
Deacon R. Banks, Knoxville, Tenn.
Elder S.M. Dickerson, Murfreesboro, Tenn.
Elder W.P. Fennick, Gallatin, Tenn.
Elder R.H. Boyd, Palestine, Texas;
Elder A. Nickerson, Chattanooga, Tenn.
Elder R. Ramsey, Meridian, Miss.

ANNUAL MEMBERS

Elder R. Spiller, Norfolk, Va.
Elder P.F. Morris, Lynchburg, Va.
Elder A. Binga, Jr., Manchester, Va
Elder James H. Holmes, Richmond,Va.
Deacon J.E. Farrar, Richmond,Va.

FIRST DAY—Morning Session
November 23, 1881

The Baptist Foreign Mission Convention of the United States of America held its Second Annual Session with the Mount Zion Baptist Church, Knoxville, Tennessee, Rev. J.M. Armistead, Pastor, commencing November 23, 1881.

1. The Convention was called to order by the president, Rev. W.H. McAlpine, of Selma, Ala., at 10 o'clock a.m., after which the president read 122nd Psalm.

2. Prayer by Rev. W.W. Colley, Corresponding Secretary and Travelling Agent of the Convention.

3. Sang hymn, "Zion Stands With Hills Surrounded."

4. The president then briefly addressed the Convention as to its duty and what is expected of religious bodies when they meet in communities like this; viz., that the Spirit of Christ is expected to characterize the

delegates not only while they are assembled in convention, but in the families where they stop; which he hoped would be the case. He then called attention to the great purpose for which the Convention was organized.

5. On motion, Rev. P.F. Morris, of Lynchburg, Virginia, was elected assistant secretary pro tem.

6. The Committee on Enrollment announced the following named delegates. (See list of delegates.)

7. On motion, the chair appointed the following Committee on Permanent Organization:

Revs. J.W. Patterson, Virginia; J. Marks, Louisiana; C.C. Russell, Tennessee; J.Q.A. Wilhite, Alabama, and J.M. Jones, Georgia.

8. While the committee was out, an informal conference was had, and Revs. D. Webster, of Mississippi; T. Washington, of Virginia; W.A. Brinkley, of Tennessee; R. Spiller, of Norfolk, Virginia; R.D. Dunbar, of Jacksonville, Florida; and J.A. Taylor, of Richmond, Virginia, addressed the Convention.

9. Rev. R. Spiller then sang "All Hail the Power of Jesus' Name."

10. At this juncture the Committee on Permanent Organization reported as follows. *(See list of officers.)*

11. On motion, the report of the Committee on Permanent Organization was adopted.

12. The president made some appropriate remarks on the compliment shown by the Convention in making choice of him to preside over their deliberations.

13. On motion, the following order of business was adopted. *(See Order of Business.)*

14. The chair proceeded to appoint the following committees:

15. On Finance—W.H. Tilman, Sr., P. Guinn, H. Williams, and J.M. Armistead.

16. On Communication—J. Marks, D. Webster, Geo. Robinson, E.K. Love, and E.C. Morris.

17. On Religious Exercises—J.M. Armistead, W. Jones, and A. Wade.

18. On Missionaries and Mission Fields in Africa—W.W. Colley, G. Robinson, Prof. J.E. Jones, J.A. Stewart, C.C. Russell, R.D. Dunbar, D. Webster, and Wm. Troy.

19. On Obituary—H. Williams, Jr., Prof. J.E. Jones, and Wm. Troy.

20. On Ways and Means—J.Q.A. Wilhite, E.C. Morris, J.M. Jones, John Jones, R. Ramsey, A. Nickerson, S.M. Dickerson, G.W. Walker, R.D. Dunbar.

WASHINGTON STREET BAPTIST CHURCH
Paducah, Kentucky

Washington St. Baptist Church entertaining the General Association of Kentucky. This remarkable church was established and was the place where George W. Dupee in the mighty wrought. The strength of Kentucky as a Baptist stronghold is due in a large measure to the life and works of Dr. Dupee.He pastored this church in the days of slavery, and one time because of some advice given his people and which was reported unfavorable by a White listener he spent the night in weeds daring not to go to anyone's home, and on advice of a White lawyer friend, stole aboard a steamer and went to Cincinnati where he remained until the close of the war. Among his successors was Rev. J. W. Hawkins who subsequently pastored at Lexington, Ky., and died during the session of the National Baptist Convention in 1910. Brother Hawkins was greatly blessed in that he has two sons in the ministry; one in Chicago and the other in Gary, Ind. The present pastor, Rev. W. K. Wall, is one of the strong young men of his day and is built on the foundation laid by the father so that Washington Street Church still holds her place as a soul-saving and character-making agency among the great churches of our time.

21. On Time and Place for next meeting—W.H. Tilman, Sr., R.D. Dunbar, J.B. Smith, R. Ramsey, and B. Dorsey.

22. On Printing—J.M. Armistead, P.F. Morris, and W.W. Colley.

23. On Foreign Mission Board—W.W. Colley, P. Guinn, E.C. Morris, D.W. Coleman, J.M. Jones, R. Ramsey, J. Marks, G. Phillips, W.A. Brinkley, T. Washington, and R.D. Dunbar.

24. On motion, the Convention adjourned with prayer by Rev. P. Guinn, and benediction by the president.

Evening Session

25. 7 p.m., religious exercises conducted by Rev. Wm. Troy of Virginia, and J. Marks of Louisiana. Rev. Troy announced hymn No. 811, which was sung by the congregation; read Matthew 5th chapter, then offered prayer and sang hymn, "All Hail the Power of Jesus' Name."

26. The president then introduced Rev. J. Marks of Louisiana who preached the Introductory Sermon from Matthew 5:15-16, subject, "The Light of the World."

27. Collection, $14.38.

28. On motion, the following were appointed Committee on Revision of the Constitution—Revs. W.W. Colley, H. Williams, Jr., E.C. Morris, J.E. Jones, H.W. Bowens, E.K. Love, and Wm. Troy.

29. On motion, it was agreed that no delegate be allowed to leave the Convention without a formal excuse.

30. On motion, the Convention adjourned by singing doxology; benediction by Rev. W.H. Tilman, Sr.

SECOND DAY—Morning Session
Thursday, November 24th

31. The Convention was called to order at 9:00 a.m., with President McAlpine in the chair.

32. Religious services were conducted by Rev. R.E. Cole, who read 102nd Psalm.

33. Prayer by Rev. W.H. Tillman, Sr.

34. The Committee on Obituary submitted the following:

Memorial

We, your Committee on Obituary, beg leave to report with regret the death of Revs. Solomon Cosby, our missionary to Africa, and E.G. Corprew, our late treasurer.

As mortals, we are subjects of decay, and each day we are called upon to record the ravages of the grim monster, Death. At this meeting of our Convention we must append to the list of departed ones, the names of Revs. Solomon Cosby and E.G. Corprew. These have recently fallen at their posts in their calling to the work of the ministry. These servants of the Most High God have stood firm in the faith of the gospel of Christ; filling other positions of trust, and greatly beloved by the people. Rev. S. Cosby was our missionary to Africa. His zeal and intelligence made him a power in the world in welcoming the gospel of God's dear Son to thousands in a benighted land, and his labor on earth has ended, but his spirit now lives in heaven.

We can truly employ the blessed words of Jesus and say, "Well done, good and faithful servant." They have entered into the joys of their Lord. We do not honor the dust of the departed ones, but yet we think the graves of those servants of Christ should be honored by stones or marble slabs with engraved memory that may pass to generations yet to come. We extend to bereaved families of our departed brethren, our sympathy. We do most humbly bow to the will of our heavenly Father, while we feel the great loss we are now sustaining by the hand of death but believe all things work together for good.

> H. WILLIAMS, Jr.,
> J.E. JONES
> Wm. TROY

35. Very touching remarks were made by Revs. J.W. Patterson, Wm. Troy, and J.A. Taylor.

36. On motion Rev. J.M. Dawson was appointed to conduct Thanksgiving Services.

37. At this juncture Rev. R. Boyd of Texas, and Rev. P. Singleton of Virginia, were admitted to a seat.

38. Revs. Dawson and J.W. Patterson then occupied the pulpit. Rev. J.M. Dawson read 107th Psalm. Prayer by Rev. Patterson. Sang Hymn No. 989.

39. Rev. Dawson then preached a very interesting sermon from 107th Psalm, subject, "The Goodness of God."

40. Prayer by Rev. J.A. Foster.

41. On motion it was voted that Rev. J.W. Patterson and H. Williams, Jr., write the biographies of Revs. Solomon Cosby and E.G. Corprew; and that J.E. Jones, P.F. Morris, W.W. Colley, and E.K. Love be a Committee on Ways and Means to have the work published.

42. Rev. G.W. Brewer, of the *Baptist Beacon*, and Judge A.T. Cottrell were introduced.

43. The corresponding secretary's report was called for, and not being ready, was deferred until tomorrow.

44. The treasurer's report was called for and, not being ready, was deferred until tomorrow.

45. On motion, Revs. J.A. Taylor, J.M. Jones, and E.C. Morris, were appointed as an Auditing Committee.

46. The Committee on Revision of the Constitution submitted their report which was received.

47. On motion the first, second, third, and fourth Articles were adopted.

48. The hour having arrived, the Convention adjourned with benediction by the president.

49. The president reassembled the Convention at 7 p.m. Revs. W.W. Colley and E.C. Morris occupied the pulpit. Rev. E.C. Morris announced hymn No. 862 and read 90th Psalm.

50. Prayer by Rev. W.W. Colley; sang hymn No. 854.

51. The president introduced Rev. Colley, who preached an able Missionary Sermon from Isaiah 54:5, "The God of the whole earth, shall he be called...."

52. Prayer by Rev. G.W. Brewer, Editor of the *Baptist Beacon*.

53. Collection, $11.65. Adjourned with benediction by Rev. Colley.

THIRD DAY—Morning Session
Friday, November 25th, 1881.

54. The president called the Convention to order at 9 a.m.

Religious exercises conducted by Rev. C. Johnson, of North Carolina.

55. The minutes of the previous day were read and approved.

56. The Committee on the Revision of the Constitution continued its report with the Fifth Article. It was so amended that messengers and delegates were made annual members.

The remainder was adopted as reported by the committee, and on motion it was adopted as a whole.

57. On motion of Rev. P.F. Morris, the editors of the various Baptist papers were requested to note in their editorials, the sermons preached before this Convention during the present session. *(Adopted)*

58. On motion the recording secretary was ordered to keep on file a complete record of all the proceedings of each session of this Convention.

59. The corresponding secretary's report being called for, he proceeded to read—after which it was received to the Auditing Committee. *(See Corresponding Secretary Foreign Board and Auditing Committee's report.)*

60. The Committee on Ways and Means for the publication of biographies of the lives of Revs. E.G. Corprew and Solomon Cosby, presented the following report which after much discussion was adopted, and the Committee requested to lay the same before the respective bodies referred to in the report. *(See report No. 2.)*

61. The Committee on Ways and Means submitted the following report, which was adopted. *(See report No. 3.)*

62. On motion, Revs. W. Coley, H. Williams, Jr., and Wm. Troy were appointed as a Committee on Charter and Seal.

63. At this juncture Revs. C.H. Strickland, of the White Baptist church, and J.B. Johnson of the M.E. church, appeared on the floor and were introduced. Dr. Strickland made some interesting remarks and expressed his wish that the work of the Convention would be successful.

64. On motion the Convention adjourned with benediction by the president.

Evening Session—7 p.m.

65. The president on the chair.

66. Two communications were read before the Convention—one from Rev. A. Binga, Jr., which was ordered to be spread over the minutes; also one from the Knoxville College, wishing the Convention to visit it before adjournment. *(Accepted.)*

67. The Auditing Committee made the following report which was adopted. *(See Treasurer and Corresponding Secretary and Auditing Committee's Report No. 1.)*

The hour having arrived for religious services, Revs. H. Williams,

Jr., and L.A. Black of Virginia, occupied the pulpit.

Rev. L.A. Black announced hymn No. 383, "Why Should the Children of the King Go Mourning?"

68. Rev. H. Williams, Jr., read Matthew 10th chapter. Rev.Black offered prayer, sang hymn No. 281.

69. The chair then introduced Rev. H. Williams, Jr., of Virginia, who preached an able sermon from Matthew 24:14.

70. After the sermon Rev. Wm. Troy led the Convention in prayer.

71. An opportunity was given for persons to become annual or life members.

ANNUAL MEMBERS:—Rev. P.F. Morris of Lynchburg, Virginia, R. Spiller, Norfolk, Virginia.

72. LIFE MEMBERS—Revs. W.P. Fennick, Gallatin, Tenn., $3.00, first installment; A. Nickerson, Chattanooga, Tenn., $3.00.

73. Collection, $13.30.

74. On motion the Convention adjourned with benediction by Rev. H. Williams, Jr.

FOURTH DAY--Morning Session
Saturday, November 26th, 1881

75. At 9:30 a.m. the president was in the chair.

76. Religious exercises were conducted by Rev. G.W. Harris, who sang hymn No. 40, read first Psalm and led the Convention in prayer.

77. The Committee on Communications made their report which was received and referred to the Committee on Printing.

78. The Committee on Time and Place reported that the time of meeting be the second Wednesday in June, and that the place of meeting be left to be fixed by the Foreign Mission Board, as there are several invitations before us and time is needed to know which is the best. Be it also

Resolved, that Rev. P.F. Morris, of Lynchburg, Virginia, preach the Annual Sermon , and the Missionary Sermon be preached by Rev. J.M. Armistead of Knoxville, Tenn.

Respectfully submitted,
J.M. JONES, Chairman.

79. On motion Rev. J.W. Patterson was added to the committee and the report recommitted.

80. Rev. Wm. Troy offered the following resolution which was adopted and referred to the Committee on Charter and Seal. (See Resolution No. 1.)

81. The Committee on Fields and Missionaries reported, which was received, and on motion the matter was referred to the Foreign Mission Board.

82. The Committee to Nominate the Foreign Mission Board for the ensuing year, submitted the following report which was adopted. *(See F.M.B.)*

83. The Finance Committee made the following partial report, which was adopted and the money turned over to the treasurer:

We, your Committee on Finance, beg leave to submit the following: The amount of money received up to date, $586.32. Collection during the setting of the Convention, $49.35.

H. WILLIAMS, Jr.,
P. GUINN,
W.H. TILMAN, Sr.,
J.M. ARMISTEAD

84. The Committee on Religious Services made the following report for tomorrow's services:

MT. ZION BAPTIST CHURCH

Sabbath school mass-meeting at 9:30 a.m. Address by L.A. Black of Petersburg, Va.

Preaching at 11 a.m. by Rev. J.W. Patterson of Danville, Va.; 3 p.m., Rev. Wm. Troy of Richmond, Va.; 7:30 p.m., Rev. W.H. McAlpine, Selma, Ala.

GILFIELD BAPTIST CHURCH

At 11 a.m., Rev. R.H. Boyd of Palestine, Texas; 3 p.m. Rev. R.E. Cole, Atlanta, Ga.; 7:30 p.m., Rev. J.A. Foster, Montgomery, Ala.

SHILOH PRESBYTERIAN CHURCH

At 10:30 a.m., Rev. P.F. Morris of Lynchburg, Va.; 3:00 p.m.,Rev. J.M. Dawson, Williamsburg, Va.

KNOXVILLE COLLEGE

At 10:30 a.m., Rev. E.K. Love of Thomasville, Ga.; 7:30 p.m.,Rev. S.M. Dickerson of Murfreesboro, Tenn.

LOGAN'S CHAPEL A.M.E. CHURCH

At 11 a.m., Rev. J. Jones, Liberty, Va.; 3 p.m., Rev. S.M. Jones, Atlanta, Ga.; 7:30, Rev. R. Spiller, Norfolk, Va.

AUSTIN CHAPEL M.E. CHURCH

At 11 a.m., Rev. J.A. Taylor, Richmond, Va.; 7:30, Rev. H.W. Bowen of Mississippi.

EASTPORT M.E. CHURCH

At ll a.m., Rev. W.P. Fennick, Gallatin, Tenn.; 3 p.m., Rev. J.B. Smith of Concord Depot, Va.; 7:30, Rev. A.C. Jackson, Birmingham, Ala.

85. Rev. P.F. Morris offered the following resolution which was adopted. *(See Resolution No. 2.)*

86. The Committee on Fields and Missionaries reported as follows: Your Committee on Fields and Missionaries believes that the work of location and employment of missionaries properly belong to the Foreign Mission Board: therefore be it

Resolved, that it be turned over to the above named board.

T. Washington, B. Ramsey, D. Webster, G. Robinson, W.W. Colley, Committee.

87. Rev. Wm. Troy offered the following resolution which was adopted, with the amendment that Rev. Troy be added to the committee mentioned in the resolution. *(See Resolution No. 3.)*

88. Rev. W.J. White of Augusta, Ga., editor of the *Georgia Baptist*, appeared on the floor, was introduced and invited to a seat.

89. After some remarks by Rev. White the Convention adjourned with prayer by Rev. P. Guinn.

FIFTH DAY—Sabbath Services
November 27, 1881

90. At 9:30 a.m., the delegates assembled with the Mt. Zion Baptist Sabbath School; after the usual exercises, and the recitation of the lesson, addresses were made by Revs. W.H. McAlpine, W.J. White, W.W. Colly, and S.M. Dickerson; the latter having with him a $14.00 Sabbath-school library, a contribution was raised and the library presented to the above named Sabbath school for which a vote of thanks was returned.

91. The hour of 11 o'clock having arrived, Revs. Wm. Troy of Richmond, and J.W. Patterson of Danville, Va., occupied the pulpit. After music by the choir; reading Job 38, and prayer by Rev. Wm. Troy, Rev.

Patterson preached an eloquent sermon from Job 38:31, "Canst thou bind the sweet influences of Pleiades, or loose the bands of Orion?"

Prayer by Rev. W.W. Colley. Doxology by the choir, and benediction by Rev. J.W. Patterson.

92. At 3 p.m., Revs. Patterson and Troy occupied the pulpit; music by the choir. Rev. Patterson offered prayer. Rev. Troy preached an able sermon from —————. Prayer by Rev. J.A. Foster. Doxology by the choir, and benediction by Rev. Troy.

93. 7:30 p.m., long before the hour of service every seat was taken, and every available place occupied. After the usual opening exercises, Rev. W.H. McAlpine preached an able sermon from Matthew.

94. Rev. J.W. Patterson moved that as the Mt. Zion Baptist Church has contributed about $100 for African Missions during this session of the Convention, that her pastor, Rev. J.M. Armistead, be made a life member, which motion prevailed.

95. The following brethren paid the first installment for life membership: Mr. Samuel Campbell and Rev. J. Clemmons, of Knoxville, Tennessee.

96. Rev. Wm. Troy, of Richmond, Va., offered the following resolution which was adopted. *(See Resolution No. 4.)*

SIXTH DAY—Morning Session
Monday, November 28, 1881.

97. At 9 a.m., the Convention was called to order by the president. Religious exercises were conducted by Elder E.K. Love of Georgia, who read 23rd Psalm, sang hymn No. 555. Prayer by Elder Wilhite of Eufaula, Ala.

98. The finance committee made the following report which was adopted. *(See Report No. 6.)*

99. On motion, the following Executive Committees were appointed. (See Executive Board.)

100. On motion, the Convention adjourned to meet Wednesday before the second Lord's Day in June, 1882. Sang hymn, "Blest Be the Tie That Binds." Prayer by Elder J.M. Armistead. Benediction by the president.

W.H. McAPLINE, President
J.M. ARMISTEAD, Secretary

REPORTS OF COMMITTEES
(No. 1)
Report of Corresponding Secretary
(Foreign Mission Board-Auditing Committee)

Dear Brethren:

We take pleasure in submitting to you this, our annual report. One year ago we organized in the city of Montgomery, Ala., for the purpose of having the gospel preached to the heathen of the world, and more especially to those of Africa, that long neglected and almost forsaken country. Some 300,000,000 of souls in that land are today stretching forth their hands for the gospel: "What shall we do?" Shall we turn a deaf ear to their cries? God forbid! For the time has come when we must put forth every effort to rescue the perishing. We have no time to be idle; they are dying, and Jesus has commanded us to go and preach to them His gospel. Is it not our duty to go hastily and rescue the perishing? The answer that comes up from every member of this Convention—We are determined, by God's help, to send them the bread of life.

At your last session, you, by resolution, requested the Virginia B[aptist] S[tate] C[onvention] to transfer to you their missionary, Rev. Solomon Cosby, and work in Africa.

Last May, at the annual meeting of the Virginia B.S.C., the matter was brought before the above Convention, and after explanations by the Board of this Convention, it was cheerfully done. But ere the arrangements had been perfected, the sad news of Brother Cosby's death spread all over this commonwealth, and the people of the United States were caused to mourn their loss of one whose combined Christian endowments are not easily found in our enlightened country. Brother Cosby was an energetic Christian gentleman. His labors in Africa were attended with much success. Our loss is his eternal gain. This was not the only misfortune your Board met. Soon after it had chronicled Brother Cosby's death, it was informed that our beloved brother and treasurer of this Convention, Elder E.G. Corpew, was no more. Both of these brethren during the Conventional year fell asleep in Jesus, and language is inadequate to pay to their memory such a tribute. Suffice it to say that death found them on the field, and they died in the triumph of faith, and are now resting from their labor. One went from the burning sands of Africa, the other from America. Long since both have joined in eternal praise to Him who liveth forever and maketh intercession for His saints.

Your Executive Committee met after the death of Elder Corprew, and

THE BAPTIST HOSPITAL
Monrovia, Liberia, West Africa

Since mission work began in West Africa back in 1821, and Liberia was founded, "Medicine, medicine, more medicine!" has been the cry. For the want of quinine and the doctors, many worthy men and women—men and women who went to save others—fill unmarked graves.

In 1919 under Dr. Amiger as superintendent, the Foreign Mission Board organized the Jordan Nurse Training Home and School for its missionaries in Liberia and rented a building in Monrovia at $25.00 per month, and Dr. Amiger fitted it up for the purpose. In sending Dr. Sisusa out, the Board equipped him with a medicine chest kit of surgical instruments and an operating table, 60 miles further down the coast. With organized efforts of our good women, the Board under the leadership of Dr. J.E. East and the best organized band of pastors in and about Philadelphia, Pa., during the past seven years have built and equipped the hospital. In 1928 the first dentist died, and Dr. Dinkins our first resident physician who conducted the finishing of the building had to return home, because of poor health. A nurse, Miss Ruth Occomy, was the sole person to care for our first venture.

Miss Carrie V. Dyer of Massachusetts, who spent many years as a teacher in Roger Williams, and with Dr. Teft, organized the Hartshorne Memorial Seminary in Richmond, Virginia. Miss Dyer helped more men and women who went forth as leaders among our people in the South, than possibly any other teacher, save Miss Johanna P. Moore. Her niece, Miss Teft, to memorialize this good woman, donated $5,000 to this hospital. The Foreign Mission Board voted to make the hospital the Carrie V. Dyer Missionary Hospital, and it is doing its work on the west coast of Africa.

appointed Elder R. Spiller treasurer pro tem for the unexpired term caused by the death of Brother Corprew. Elder Spiller will consequently furnish you in his report as to the condition of the treasury.

CORRESPONDING SECRETARY

Your corresponding secretary has traveled through many of the states and has done a noble work; though the results of his labors may not be so vivid at present, yet as time rolls on it will be seen. It is impossible at present to calculate our success by dollars and cents; but as we grow older and the cause is more extensively presented to the people; we shall be better prepared to calculate upon our success.

MISSIONARIES

Your Board desires that at least two missionaries be appointed this year for the African field.

The Board has endorsed the action of the North Carolina State Convention in appointing Rev. J. O. Hayes missionary to Africa. North Carolina has promised at least $400 toward his support. Other missionaries should be appointed as soon as possible and be allowed to labor in this country for a few months under the direction of the corresponding secretary; they would thereby become acquainted with the people and gain their confidence, and they would do much in raising means for this great cause we represent. Your corresponding secretary feels that such a course would be the result of great good.

Your corresponding secretary in his travels has not simply confined his visits to the Colored Christians of this country, but has entered some of the best White pulpits, and has thereby interested them and gained much of their confidence and some of their money; some have also promised that should we fail to raise the amount necessary to send out missionaries and carry on our operations the coming year in Africa, that they will aid us in securing the deficiency.

Your Board feels that care and discretion should be made in the appointment of missionaries, that none should be put on the field simply on account of the zeal that they may have for the Master's cause, but such as give themselves to study and preparation; those who possess a preeminent Christian character; such men, only such, will accomplish the great aim of this Convention.

THE FIELD

Your Board is not aware of the field that you shall recommend for our operations, but were it in our power to say, we should not hesitate in proposing the field recommended by Brother Cosby—the Dahomey country, where cannibalism and idolatry of the darkest nature predominate. A letter has just been received from Rev. W. J. David, a former comrade of our corresponding secretary in Central Africa, setting forth the possibilities for mission work in the kingdom of Dahomey. But our missionaries should be allowed a few months to acclimate in the public of Liberia, where they can have the attention of a civilized physician and Christian homes.

VISITS

The following are the state conventions, associations, and churches visited by your corresponding secretary:

CORRESPONDING SECRETARY'S REPORT

Connecticut
First Colored Baptist Church, Norwich, Rev. R.D. Wynne 15.00
Central Baptist Church, Norwich 5.00
Georgia
Second Baptist church, Atlanta, W.H. Tilman, Sr. 7.00
Friendship Baptist Church, Atlanta, Frank Quarles 10.00
Macedonia Baptist Church, Atlanta, Rev. C.O. Jones 2.00
Massachusetts
Union Baptist Church, Cambridge, Rev. J.H. Carter 6.00
Joy St. Baptist Church, Boston, Rev. Peter Smith 4.75
Twelfth Street Church, boston, Rev. L.G. Waldon 12.00
First Colored Baptist Church, W. Newton, Rev. J.L. Dart 11.00
Maryland
North Street Baptist Church, Baltimore, Rev.Harvey Johnson 32.50
Second Baptist Church, Baltimore, Rev. A. Brown 12.00
Calvary Baptist Church, Baltimore, Rev. P.H.A. Braxton 8.09
North Carolina
North Carolina Sunday School State Convention, Raleigh,
    Rev. N.F. Roberts, President 11.00

White Baptist Church, Franklinton, Rev. McManaway .... $ 3.30
First Colored Baptist Church, Franklinton, Rev. M.C. Ransom ... 8.00
First Colored Baptist Church, Franklinton, Rev. M.C. Ransom 33.68
First Colored Baptist Church, Oxford, Rev. M.C. Ransom 22.00
Neuse River Ass'n, Goldsboro, Rev. A.B. Williams, Moderator ... 19.30
First Colored Baptist Church, Goldsboro, Rev. A.B. Williams 3.75
Wake Forest Baptist Church, Wake Forest 20.00
Kennusville Ass'n, Warsaw, Rev. Thomas Parker, Moderator ... 11.50
White M.E. Church, Kennusville 1.30
Magnolia Baptist Church, Magnolia, Rev. Henry Lee 4.50
North Carolina State Conv. Raleigh, Rev. C. Johnson, President .. 10.00
First Colored Baptist Church, Wilmington, Rev. A.M. Conway ... 14.34
Ebenezer Baptist Church, Wilmington, Deacon Davis 10.23
Presbyterian Colored Church, Rev. Sanders, Wilmington 6.18
First White Baptist Church, Wilmington, Rev. J.B. Taylor 12.11

Rhode Island
Kongdon Street Baptist Church, New England Convention,
    Rev. A. Ellis 8.30

South Carolina
First White Baptist Church, Rev. Vass, Spartanburg 9.72
Springfield Baptist Church, Rev. Fred Brown, Greenville 14.60

Virginia
Mount Nebo Baptist Church, Rev. A. Burkley, Farmville 11.21
First Colored Baptist Church, Deacon W. Washington, Fredericksburg 35.00
First Baptist Church, Rev. B.H. Porter, Stauton 14.00
Norfolk Union Association, Rev. J.M. Dawson, Moderator,
    Williamsburg 20.15
First Baptist Church, Rev. J.W. Patterson, Danville 7.50
Bute Street A.M.E. Church, Z.T. Watkins, Norfolk 7.50
St. Luke A.M.E.P. Church, Rev. William Lewis 11.00
A.M.E. Church, Rev. Haynes, Danville 4.50
Court Street Baptist Church, Rev. P.F. Morris, Lynchburg 5.00
Bethany Baptist Association, Rev. Joseph Gregory, Moderator,
    Franklin 25.00
Churches in New England, Darlington 15.00
                      Total $506.78

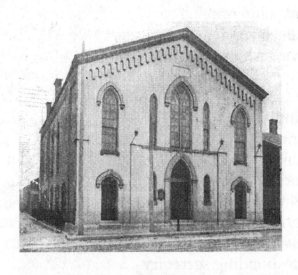

LAMPTON STREET BAPTIST CHURCH
Louisville, Ky.

Several of the very strongest preachers of all Kentucky
served here. C. C. Bates gave many years and was followed by
Rev. J. M. Williams. Dr. Williams has made the church materially and influentially. He is moderator of one of the most outstanding associations in the state and has hearty interests in all
denominational affairs. Lampton Street Church is one of
Kentucky's best institutions.

REPORT OF THE TREASURER, REV. R. SPILLER,
FROM
NOVEMBER 26th, 1880 TO NOVEMBER 26th, 1881
Receipts—1880-1881

Nov. 20—At Montgomery, Ala. . . . . $ 317.06
By treasurer, during year 205.13
By corresponding secretary, during year 506.75
By Finance Committee 652.42
By W.W. Colley, life membership 30.00
Total $1711.39

Amount in F[oreign] M[ission] treasury, Virginia . . . . $ 800.00
Amount in F.M. treasury, North Carolina 53.00
General Baptist Association, Mississippi 25.00
Amount on hand, Alabama 25.00

Amount on hand, Tennessee 20.00
Amount on hand, Texas 100.00
       Amount cash, in F.M. treasury $1394.33

Disbursements

Printing and compiling minutes .... $ 115.00
300 cards and printing the same 4.50
2500 circular letters 18.25
250 postal receipts 3.12
2,000 one cent stamps 20.00
Stationery for corresponding secretary $7.14
Traveling expense of corresponding secretary 172.05
Expenses of corresponding secretary .... <u>1000.00</u>
Total disbursements $1340.00
By cash on hand 371.00

     We, your Auditing Committee, have examined the above reports and found them correct.

               Signed:
               J.M. JONES, J.A. TAYLOR,
               E.C. MORRIS,
               Committee.

(No. 2.)
Report of Committee on Ways and Means of Publication

     We, your Committee on Ways and Means, beg leave to submit the following report: We suggest,

     1. "That the history containing all the facts available connected with the lives of Revs. E.G. Corprew, our former treasurer, and Solomon Cosby, late missionary to West Coast Africa, be written by the brethren appointed by this Convention for that purpose.

     2. "That the material, when gotten into shape, shall be given into the hands of the corresponding secretary of this convention, and that he be authorized to enter into an arrangement with the American Baptist Publishing Company of Philadelphia, to have as many copies published as he thinks can be disposed of.

     3. "That the corresponding secretary in his travels, and the members of this Convention in their fields of labor, do all they can to sell these biographies when they shall have been published.

     4. "That as much money as is necessary for furnishing stationery to

be used by the brethren in writing these sketches, and also for defraying all expenses incident to their publication, be advanced by the Virginia Baptist State Convention and Shiloh Association.

5. "That all money realized from the sale of these over and above actual expenses, go into the treasury of this Convention, to be used for the purpose of erecting a chapel in West Africa, in memory of Revs. Solomon Cosby and E.G. Corprew."

E.K. LOVE

J.E. JONES

P.F. MORRIS

W.W. COLLEY

(The committee, Prof. J.E. Jones, and Rev. P.F. Morris were requested to bear the request of this Convention as contained in these resolutions.)

(No. 3)
Report of Committee on Ways and Means

Whereas the success of our African Mission work depends almost wholly upon a thorough plan for interesting all the churches in all of the states by giving them the needed information, and giving them such plans as they must have for raising and collecting means;

Resolved (1), That an Executive Committee of seven brethren-sisters included—be appointed in all the states connected with this Convention, whose duty it shall be to organize Foreign Mission Societies, get missionary sermons preached, and thus aid our corresponding secretary in organizing and interesting the people for this great work.

Resolved (2), That each committee in its state is hereby instructed to work in union with such state organizations as may exist, and help them, when possible, secure these ends. These Executive Committees are hereby empowered to add to their number and appoint such help in their several states as may, in their judgment, help them to succeed in their work. The chairman of each committee shall write for such help and information from.the corresponding secretary as he may be able to give them.

Resolved (3), That each state represented in this Convention is hereby requested, through these committees and with their help, to raise the sum of $500 (five hundred dollars) and as much more as possible, towards the support of one missionary in Africa, and to help build houses, schools, and churches; and to help pay the interpreters through whom the missionary must preach to the heathen.

Our sisters are hereby especially called upon in all the states to help us in this great work.

All money sent to our treasurer, Rev. R. Spiller, Norfolk, Va., for Africa will be thankfully received.

From all churches, Sunday schools, missionary societies, associations, and conventions of every kind, and all persons wishing to help this great cause, and for all such money, the treasurer will send a printed receipt; and the names of the above will be printed in the minutes of the Foreign Mission Convention.

Resolved (4), That the Foreign Mission Board of this Convention be hereby empowered to appoint Rev. J.0. Hayes of North Carolina, who is now in Africa, as our missionary; and the North Carolina State Convention see that not less than $400 (four hundred dollars) be raised in that state for his support and that they do their best to raise, in addition, $100 (one hundred dollars) toward helping to build for him a house to live in.

The Foreign Mission Board is hereby empowered to appoint other missionaries and to open up such field or fields in Africa, as they may find best, and as soon as possible.

J.Q.A. WILHITE, E.C. MORRIS, J.M. JONES,
JOHN JONES, R. RAMSEY, A. NICKERSON,
S.M. DICKERSON, G.W. WALKER, R.D. DUNBAR,
Committee.

(No. 4.)
Report of Finance Committee

We, your Committee on Finance, beg leave to submit our report. Received from November 23rd, to date, November 28th, the following amounts:

Alabama

Eufaula Baptist District Association $5.00
Eufaula Baptist District Sunday School Convention 2.50
Dallas County Baptist Sunday School 1.00

Mt. Olivet and Cedar Fork Baptist Churches 7.00
Snow Creek Baptist Association 6.00
White Hall Baptist Sunday School, Loundes County 5.00
Mt. Nebo Baptist Church 1.00
Pine Grove Baptist Association 5.00
St. Phillips Baptist Church, Selma 3.25

Alabama Baptist State Convention 18.50
Woman's Baptist Missionary Society 2.00
First Baptist Church, Montgomery 5.00
Elder J.A. Foster, Montgomery............................. 1.00
Total $62.25

Arkansas
St. Paul Sunday School, Pine Bluff $5.00
Harrison Baptist Church, Pine Bluff 1.00
Middle Baptist Church, Pine Bluff 1.00
Elder John Jackson, Pine Bluff 1.00
Central District Baptist Association 25.00
Various Baptist Churches, East Arkansas 14.50
Third Baptist Church, Helena 5.00
Liberty Mall Baptist Church, Toledo 1.00
Total $53.00

Georgia
Pleasant Grove Baptist Church, Cassandra $1.00
Foreign Missionary Society, Thomasville 5.00
Total $6.00

Louisiana
Sixth Baptist Church, New Orleans .... $ 5.00
Austerlity Street Baptist Church, New Orleans 6.00
St. John's Baptist Church, Iberville Parish 5.00
Total $16.00

Mississippi
Pleasant Grove Baptist Church .... $ 5.00
Octabe Baptist Church 5.00
Elder Daniel Webster, on his life membership 5.00
Total $15.00

Tennessee
West Tennessee, East Arkansas and North Mississippi Baptist
    General Association .... $ 67.75
Beal Street Sunday School, Memphis 30.00
West Tennessee Sunday School Convention 12.05

Washington Street Baptist Church, Memphis	5.00
Washington Street Baptist Church Sunday School, Memphis	3.00
Stone River Baptist Association	3.00
General Baptist Association, East Tennessee	77.05
Elder J.M. Armstead, Knoxville, life member	30.00
R. Banks, Knoxville, on his life membership	3.00
Mt. Zion Baptist Church, Knoxville	53.69
Gilfield Baptist Church, Knoxville	1.31
M.E. Church, Knoxville	1.72
A.M.E. Church, Knoxville	10.29
Total	$301.86

Texas

Central Missionary Baptist Association	$10.00
Elder R.H. Boyd, on his life membership	3.00
Total	$13.00

Virginia

First Baptist Church, Danville	$5.00
Third Baptist Church, Petersburg	
Third Baptist Church Missionary Society, Petersburg	5.00
Harrison Street Baptist Church, Petersburg	25.00
Harrison Street Baptist Church Missionary Society, Petersburg	10.00
Sisters of Charity, Petersburg	1.00
Gilfield Baptist Church, Petersburg	17.00
Long Mountain Baptist Church, Campbell County	17.28
Long Mountain Ladies' Foreign Missionary Society	8.00
Mt. Shiloh Baptist Church, Appomattox County	13.20
Mt. Obed Baptist Church, Appomattox County	5.00
Second Baptist Church, Matthews County	2.00
Western Grove Baptist Church, Norfolk County	4.00
Colley Missionary Society, Richmond Institute	5.00
Second Baptist Church, Richmond	4.00
Second Baptist Church Missionary Society, Richmond	10.00
Female Missionary Society, Richmond	5.00
Union Norfolk Baptist Association	5.00
Court Street Baptist Church, Lynchburg	3.00
Court Street Baptist Missionary Society, Lynchburg	1.50
Mrs. Mary Davis, Lynchburg	1.00
Williamsburg Baptist Church	1.00

Fincastle Baptist. 1.00
Fincastle Baptist Church Sunday School. 1.00
Mt. Tabor Baptist Church, Henrico County 4.25
Cedar Hill Baptist Church, Nottoway County. 1.00
Poplar Lawn Baptist Church, Nottoway County. 3.63
Little Bethel Baptist Church, Nansemond County. 5.00
Second Baptist Church, Suffolk. 5.00
First Baptist Church, Fredericksburg. 9.00
Elder W.W. Colley, life member, Richmond. 30.00
Bloomfield Baptist Church, Dinwiddie County. 1.50
Total. $121.58

Recapitulation

Received from churches, Sunday schools, Sunday School Conventions,
   Baptist State Conventions, Baptist Associations, Missionary
      Societies, and individual donations. $608.47
      On life memberships. 75.00
      Two life memberships. 60.00
         Total $683.4
         Respectfully submitted,
         J.M. ARMSTEAD, P. GUINN,
         HENRY WILLIAMS, Jr.
         Knoxville, Tenn., November 28th, 1881.

RESOLUTIONS
(No. 1.)

Rev. Wm. Troy offered the following resolution, which was received and referred to the Committee on Charter and Seal:

Whereas this Convention is to be a chartered body, and there are inconveniences to which this body may be subjected: therefore to avoid usurpation of power on the part of the Board, trustee, or trustees, be it

Resolved, That the committee appointed by this Convention be, and is hereby instructed to have the charter so worded that the Convention shall have full and complete control over the property of this organization, papers, moneys, etc., and that it shall be so understood that if any trustee or trustees shall do any act or thing that may in any way hinder or trammel the work of this Convention, they shall be forthwith dismissed and other competent men appointed in their place, who will serve according to work and dictation of this body.

(No. 2.)

Rev. P.F. Morris offered the following resolution, which was adopted in view of the great demand and necessity to send the gospel to Africa, and that the present facilities of our churches to give are not such as will enable this Convention to meet this demand and necessity. Therefore, this Convention does most earnestly request all churches, where our corresponding secretary may have an opportunity to visit, give all of the proceeds to him arising from lectures delivered by him, for that purpose.

(No. 3.)

Rev. Wm. Troy offered the following resolution, which was adopted, with the amendment that Rev. Wm. Troy be added to the committee mentioned in the resolution:

Whereas the spirit of the gospel destroys all geographical and sectional lines, therefore be it

Resolved (1), That this Convention express its hearty wish to solicit the cooperation of all regular Baptists of this land to join in the efforts to spread gospel light and spiritual intelligence in the land of our fathers.

Resolved (2), That we can see no reason why there should not be a perfect unanimity of effort and action upon the part of all New Testament churches in the one aim to preach the gospel to the heathen: Further be it

Resolved (3), That a circular letter be sent from this body to the various associations and conventions and missionary bodies, to join in this great missionary enterprise.

Resolved (4), That we do most earnestly feel the need of our old and experienced ministers; their wisdom and zeal would do us good in furthering the cause of God and humanity.

Resolved (5), That Prof. J.E. Jones, Revs. P.F. Morris, and Wm. Troy be requested to write the above named circular letter to the various missionary bodies, churches, and association.

(No. 4.)

Rev. Wm. Troy, of Richmond, Va., offered the following resolution which was adopted:

Whereas in God's mercy, we, as a Convention and a Christian body, have been kindly treated in the dwelling of our brethren in the city of Knoxville; we, therefore, tender to all in every household and family who have administered to us and our brethren, our most hearty thanks, praying that the God of all peace may pour out His grace upon all.

We also send cordial thanks to the agents and superintendents of all railway companies who favored our delegates in the reduction of rates on their several railroads; be it

Resolved, That a copy of these expressions of thanks be forwarded to the various companies and published in the press of this city.

To the Committee on Printing

Please spread the following on the face of the minutes.

I have received the following amount from churches, Sabbath schools, societies and individuals:

Pleasant Hill Baptist Church, Fagatt, Miss.	3.80
Fort Lenel Baptist Church, Virginia	1.00
Macedonia Baptist Church, Mississippi	3.00
Grafton Baptist Church, Middlesex, Va	2.00
Third Baptist Church, Hampton, Va	5.00
Second Baptist Church, Hampton, Va.	1.00
Second Baptist Church, Montgomery, Ala.	3.15
Providence Baptist Church, King William's Co., Va	2.08
Bute Street Baptist Church, Norfolk	2.00
Ebenezer Baptist Church, Luna Landing, Ark.	1.00
Pleasant Grove Baptist Sunday School, South Hampton, Va.	1.00
Bank Street Baptist Sabbath School, Norfolk, Va.	2.00
Rising Mt. Zion Baptist Sabbath School, Richmond, Va.	1.00
A.J. Taylor, Richmond Institute, Va.	1.00
Baptist Church, Fauquier Co., Va.	1.00
Gravel Hill Baptist Church, Prince Edwards Co.	1.00
The Sisters Foreign Mission Society, Stonewall, Palmico Co., N.C.	2.00
Quero Baptist Church, Powhatan Co., Va.	1.00
Jerusalem Baptist Church, Caroline Co., Va.	15.00
Fifth Baptist Church, Richmond, Va.	5.00
Bethlehem Baptist Church, Pittsburg, Texas	4.85
William Boswell, Chattanooga, Tenn.	5.00
Bethesda Baptist Church, Marshall, Texas	5.00
Bute Street Baptist Church, Norfolk, Va	10.00
Zion Baptist Church, Portsmouth, Va.	5.00
Bethlehem Baptist Church, Cumberland Co., Va.	1.00
Rev. A.N. Buck, Halifax, N.C.	2.00
Miss Kate A. Dabney, Richmond Va.	1.00

Rev. Charles Smith, Scotland Neck, N.C. 5.00
Rev. R.Y. Rundey, Spartanburg, N.C. 1.00
Rev. E. Watts, Louisa C.H., Va. 1.00
Miss Ella M. Townley 1.00
Second Baptist Church, Suffolk, Va. 5.00
Little Bethel Baptist Church, Chucatuck, Va. 5.00
First Baptist Church, Fredericksburg, Va. 9.00
St. Paul's Chapel, Stonewall, N.C. 8.00
Shiloh Baptist Church, Southhampton Co., Va. 5.00
St. Mary's Baptist Church, Southhampton Co., Va. 4.00
Bank Street Baptist Missionary Society, Norfolk 2.00
Union Baptist Sunday School, Glouchester Co., Va. 1.00
Clanerdon Baptist Church, Sampson Co., Va. 1.15
Oak Grove Baptist Church, Hopedate, Ark. 2.35
Mount Zion Baptist Church, Isle of Wight Co., Va. 1.00
Bacon Castle Sabbath School, Surry County, Va. 1.00
Mount Sinai Baptist Church, Nansemond Co., Va. 4.00
Piney Grove Baptist Church, Nansemond Co., Va. 4.00
Morning Star Baptist Church, Nansemond County, Va. 5.00
Mount Sinai Missionary Society, Nansemond Co., Va. 4.00
Union Baptist Church, Northhampton Co., Va. 1.50
Rev. D. Cunningham, Hampton, Va. 5.00
Bible Class R., Bank Street Sabbath School, Norfolk, Va. 1.50
Mrs. G. Wilson, Norfolk, Va. .... .50
Cedar Creek Baptist Church, Enfield, N.C. 7.70
Peter Ruffin, Norfolk, Va. 5.10
Young Men's Missionary Society, Norfolk, Va. 5.20
Young Missionary, Zion Baptist Church, Norfolk, Va. 1.00
Foreign Mission Singing Association, Norfolk, Va. 4.05
Norfolk, Portsmouth, and Burkley Sunday School Union 5.00
S.P.G.A. of R. Department of Va. 2.00
Sabbath school, Foreign Missionary Society of the Springfield
    Baptist Church, Augusta, Ga. 10.00
Bethel Baptist Church, Longview, Texas 4.20
J.H. Baptist Church, Longview, Texas 1.60
Macedonia Baptist Church, Foreign Mission Society, Nansemond
    Co., Va. 1.07
Mount T. Baptist Church, Clinton, Miss. 1.00
Mt. Lenel Baptist Church, Corno, Miss. 2.00

Philadelphia Baptist Sabbath School, Camden Co., N.C. 2.00
Lone Star Baptist Church, Arkansas Co., Ark. 1.00
Love Rest Baptist Church, South Bend, Ark. 1.00
Mr. T.A. Holloman, Starlia, Miss. .... <u>5.00</u>
Total 224.80

This money did not come into the treasurer's hands in time to be reported to the Convention, but will be reported when it meets again.

R. SPILLER, Treasurer of the Baptist Foreign Mission Convention of U.S. of A., No. 99, Scott Street, Norfolk, Va.

TO THE FOREIGN MISSION CONVENTION
OF THE UNITED STATES OF AMERICA,
ASSEMBLED AT KNOXVILLE, TENN.

Manchester, Va., November 13, 1881.

Dear Brethren:

I regret very much that I am prevented from meeting with you on account of business engagement. But I assure you, you shall have my hearty cooperation in the grand work so well commenced. Success to you.

Yours in Christ,

A. BINGA, Jr., Chairman of the Foreign Mission Board of Virginia

P.S. Our faithful and beloved treasurer, Rev. E.G. Corprew, is no more. Owing to the fact that we have not settled up with his estate, we are unprepared to send the money we expected to have sent. But after we shall have settled up, we will be prepared to send the money which we have.—A.B.

EXTRACT

Brother Colley: Say to the brethren for me, that Virginia has firm hold of the rope, and will hold on while any one whom you may appoint "goes down in the well."—A. Binga.

CIRCULAR LETTER

To the Ministers, Churches, Associations, and Conventions of the United States of America:

In compliance with the request of the Baptist Foreign Mission Convention of the United States of America, we send forth this letter praying that it may meet the approval of the brethren and inspire their hearts to work and give of their material substance, in order that the heathen of Africa may have the gospel of the Son of God proclaimed to them. We have organized ourselves into the Baptist Foreign Mission Convention for the ostensible purpose of evangelizing and Christianizing the "Dark Continent." Our motto is, "AFRICA FOR CHRIST."

Because of peculiar relations existing between the Afro-Americans and the Africans in our Fatherland, we regard this work preeminently the work of the American Negro. We do not hold or argue that this work is SOLELY the work of the Negro; to do so would be doing wrong because of the fact that it would be contrary to the genius of Christianity. Still we hold that the circumstances surrounding the Negro point to him as the leader in the work. A careful consideration of the "Plans of Salvation" leads us to certain conclusions, and we do not think it amiss to state, at least, a few of them in this connection.

1. We believe the gospel is designed for the whole world. Believing this to be a fact we think that the members of our churches should expand their views to the entire range of the purposes of God, and put forth efforts commensurate with the whole extent and amplitude of His design. Whatever degree of strength, moral or financial, any of your churches possess it should immediately be put forth for the good of Africa. This will increase the efficiency of the church law of reflex action. Christ died for all. A ransom for all is the ground upon which we base our claim of missions for all. "Ask of me, and I will give thee the heathen for thine inheritance and the uttermost parts of the earth for thy possession," Psalm 2:8.

2. [We believe] [t]hat God wills to employ human instrumentalities for the carrying out of His design with the regard to the salvation of the world. "Ye shall be witnesses unto me, both in Jerusalem and in all Judea, etc." The sons of Africa must believe on the Son of God. "They cannot call on him, etc."

3. We state that churches are to furnish the missionaries. No church can come up to the full measure of duty which does not keep the cause of missions and missionary enterprises constantly before the mind and near the heart of every individual member. Ethiopia is stretching out her hands unto God. The Macedonian cry comes to us from beyond the waters. We want all the local associations, state conventions, and all the churches in these if possible to ally themselves with the National Baptist Foreign Mission Convention. Rest assured of this fact, no convention, association, or church can excuse itself from this Foreign Mission work on the ground that it is engaged in doing Home Mission work. Home Mission work nor past efforts cannot excuse any convention, association, church, or individual member from present obligations to the Foreign Mission work. We call upon all the friends of the Saviour to cooperate with us in

this great work of presenting the gospel to the heathen of Africa. Do not wait to see if the Convention is going to be a success but come join us and help TO MAKE IT a success. Any convention, association, church, society, or individual can at any time aid us in this undertaking by sending donations to the treasurer, Rev. Richard Spiller, No. 99 Scott Street, Norfolk, Va.; or corresponding secretary, Rev. W.W. Colley, No. 19 West Leigh Street., Richmond, Va. Now is the time; to delay is to fail in carrying out the plans of the Master with regard to Africa. WE CANNOT, WE MUST NOT FAIL in this work. Africa MUST BE REDEEMED. The Negro must be the most prominent character in her redemption, therefore, we call upon all the Baptist churches of all sections of this country to help us in the name of the Master and our common religion. Give now; give constantly, praying for the blessing of God to follow and crown the giving.

P.F. MORRIS
WILLIAM TROY
JOS. E. JONES

NOTICES

The next session of the Baptist Foreign Mission Convention will be held with the Second Baptist Church, Atlanta, Ga., Wednesday before the second Lord's Day in June, 1882.

We had overlooked the fact that Rev. Wm. Troy, of Richmond, Va., was elected auditor of the Convention, hence the same does not appear in the list of officers.

We received from C.B. Martin, $10; from Rev. F. Hook, $20. The sums will be duly acknowledged at the meeting of the Convention in June.

PREAMBLE AND CONSTITUTION OF THE BAPTIST FOREIGN MISSION CONVENTION OF THE UNITED STATES OF AMERICA

WHEREAS, It is our duty to advance the kingdom of Christ by going into all the world to preach His gospel to all kindreds, tribes, and tongues, and

WHEREAS, The benighted condition of more than three hundred millions of souls in Africa, now held in chains of the grossest idolatry, cannibalism, domestic slavery, and every species of superstition, claim our most profound attention and help, and

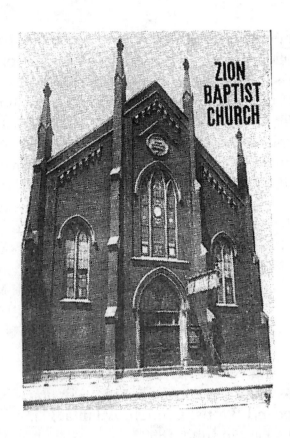

According to data furnished by Mr. Geo. W. Hayes, Zion Baptist Church is the second oldest Negro Baptist Church in Cincinnati. It was organized early in 1843, by persons who received their letters from the Union Baptist Church, December 9, 1842.

Rev. Wallace shelton came from Columbus, Ohio, as its first pastor. A horse was purchased in order that Brother Shelton might carry on his missionary labors more successfully, and it was through his untiring efforts that churches in Xenia, Dayton, Springfield and Columbus were organized.

Brother Shelton was ordained on October 8, 1883. On October 17, 1843, he was elected as pastor of Zion Baptist Church. The first meeting place of the church was on the south side of Plum Street. This was its meeting place for many years, and doubtless this was the location from which it became active in the Underground Railroad System.

In 1867, Zion built the first "big brick church" among Negroes in Cincinnati and for many years this was the finest structure of Negro churches in the Middle West. Rev. Shelton pastored here until 1874. Some good men have led Zion during the intervening years. Zion is now pastored by Rev. B. F. Reid. During his pastorate all debts against the church have been paid; an apartment house next door to the church, with fifteen rooms and five baths, has been purchased; a church bus is operated, conveying children and old persons to and from the church; a church school registering seventy-five persons has been going on for the past two years. A church library is opened daily and is the only one of its kind in Cincinnati and vicinity, and the largest Daily Vacation Bible School in Southern Ohio, regardless of color, is the one conducted in Zion Baptist Church. The future is indeed promising.

WHEREAS, God has commanded us to "go," and is giving us all ripened means for this work, therefore, we, the representatives from the various churches, Sunday schools, and missionary societies of the Baptist denomination in the United States of America, now assembled in the city of Montgomery, State of Alabama, November 24, 1880, do most solemnly organize ourselves into a convention for the above named object. We do agree to the following Constitution:

TITLE
Article I. This Convention shall be known as the "Baptist Foreign Mission Convention of the United States of America."

OBJECT
Article II. The object of this Convention shall be the diffusion of the gospel of Jesus Christ on the continent of Africa and elsewhere abroad, as God may direct.

LIFE MEMBERSHIP
Article III. The membership of this Convention shall be annual or life. Any member of a Baptist church in good standing may become an annual member by paying the sum of thirty dollars in annual installments of three dollars for ten consecutive years. Any church, Sunday school, and all religious societies may make life members by paying the sum of thirty dollars to this Convention.

MEMBERSHIP BY REPRESENTATION
Article IV. All messengers from Baptist churches, Sunday schools, missionary societies, woman's missionary societies, associations, and conventions, shall be recognized as annual members of this Convention. The basis of representation shall be one delegate from every church, and one for every one thousand members, or fraction of one thousand above the first thousand that contributes according to their ability to the funds of this Convention. Each association of churches and each convention may have two delegates; and one for every twenty-five hundred members, or fraction of twenty-five hundred so contributing to the funds of this Convention.

OFFICERS
Article V. The officers of this Convention shall be a president and one vice president from each state represented in this body; a recording

secretary, a statistical secretary, a corresponding secretary, and a treasurer, all of whom shall be elected at each annual meeting of this Convention, and hold their offices until their successors are chosen; and no one shall be elected president more than twice consecutively. The officers of the Convention shall be annual or life members of this organization.

BOARDS

Article VI. Twenty-seven judicious and experienced brethren, including all the officers of this Convention, shall form or constitute a Board of Foreign Missions, 15 of whom shall constitute a Board of Managers, with full power to use all means necessary to secure the objects of this Convention during its recess, and said Board shall be responsible to this Convention for all its actions. Members attending the meetings of this Convention, and leaving before the work of the Convention is finished and the Boards are appointed and organized, will not be put upon the Boards as they will not be present to help organize said Boards and to attend to the business of this Convention.

DUTY

Article VII. It shall be the duty of the Board to take such steps as may be necessary to secure church, associational, and state organizations for developing an interest in Foreign Missions, and securing cooperation by raising means and otherwise.

LOCATION

Article VIII. Richmond, Virginia, shall be the headquarters of the Foreign Mission Board, at or near which point, a quorum of the Board of Managers shall be located.

WORK

Article IX. The Board shall make an annual report of all its transactions to this Convention, giving a full account of all its doings during the interval of the meetings of this Convention; giving the condition and prosperity of our mission fields, the number of missionaries employed by them, what salaries they receive, and such other information as may be in their possession as will assist the convention in carrying out its objects. The Board shall not form any organic cooperation with any other body without the action of the Convention.

BONDS

Article X. The treasurer shall receive and hold all moneys, bills, deeds, and bequests belonging to this Convention, pay all orders issued by the Board at their regular meetings, and signed by the president and secretary of the same. He shall for the faithful discharge of his duties and security of the Convention, give such bonds as may be agreed upon by the Board; and his books may be free to the inspection of any officer of the Convention, and any member of the Board. He shall make a quarterly report to the Board and an annual report to the Convention, giving an account for all moneys received and paid out by him, to whom, what for, and the general condition of the treasury.

QUALIFICATION
Article XI. All officers, boards, missionaries, and agents appointed by this Convention, or by the Foreign Mission Board, shall be members of some regular Baptist church, in union with the churches composing this Convention.

DONATION
Article XII. The bodies and individuals composing this Convention shall have the right to specify the object or objects to which their contributions shall be applied, but when no such specifications are made the Convention shall make the appropriation at its discretion.

MEETINGS
Article XIII. The Convention shall meet at such time and place as shall be agreed upon at a preceding meeting, which time shall not be later than the second Thursday in October. Special meetings of this Convention may be called by the president, at the request of the Foreign Mission Board.

AMENDMENTS
Article XIV. This constitution may be amended at any regular meeting of this Convention by a two-thirds vote of the same; provided the change desired was presented in writing at a previous meeting.

ORDER OF BUSINESS

Time of Meeting
Meet each day at 9 a.m.; adjourn at 1 p.m. Reassemble at 3 p.m.; adjourn at 5:30 p.m. Meet at 8:30 p.m.

FIRST DAY'S SESSION—Wednesday, June 28

9:00 A.M.—Enrollment of delegates; appoint the following committees: first, on Permanent Organization; second, on Finance; third, on Communications; fourth, on Religious Exercises; fifth, on Ways and Means; sixth, on Obituaries; seventh, on Time and Place of next meeting; eighth, on Foreign Mission Board.

During the appointment of the above committees, an Informal Conference may be held.

12:00 P.M.—Report of Committee on Permanent Organization.

Evening Session—8:30 P.M.

Introductory Sermon by Rev. E.K. Love.

SECOND DAY'S SESSION—Thursday, June 29

9:00 A.M.—Report of the Committee on Obituaries.

10:00 A.M.—Report of Foreign Mission Board through the corresponding secretary and treasurer.

Evening Session--8:30 P.M.

Sermon on Foreign Missions by Rev. J.M. Armistead.

THIRD DAY'S SESSION—Friday, June 30

9:00 A.M.—Consideration of report of Committee on Ways and Means.

11:00 A.M.—Consideration of the report of the corresponding secretary and treasurer.

12:30 P.M.—Hear report of Committee on Religious Exercises.

Evening Session--8:30 P.M.

Africa considered. First, Map Exercises; Second, Moral Condition; Third; What the Religious World Is Doing for Her; Fourth, The Duty of the Colored Christians to Africa; Fifth, The Best Way to Perform This Duty.

FOURTH DAY'S SESSION-Saturday, July 1

9:00 A.M.— Hearing report of Committee on Finance.

10:00 A.M.—Report of Committee on Time and Place of Next Meeting and Preachers.

11:00 A.M.—Report of Committee on Printing.

12:00 P.M.—Appointing corresponding messengers.

FOURTH DAY'S SESSION-Saturday, July 1

President .... Rev. J.Q.A. Wilhite, Eufaula, Ala.
1st Vice President ....Rev. J.A. Foster, Montgomery, Ala.
2nd Vice President ....Rev. E.C. Morris, Helena, Ark.
3rd Vice President .... Rev. R.D. Dunbar, Jacksonville, Fla.
4th Vice President .... Rev. W.H. Tillman, Sr., Atlanta, Ga.
5th Vice President ....Rev. G.W. Walker, New Orleans, La.
6th Vice President .... Rev. R. Ramsey, Meridian, Miss.
7th Vice President .... Rev. C. Johnson, Raleigh, N.C.
8th Vice President .... Rev. F. Brown, Greenville, S.C.
9th Vice President .... Rev. J.A. Steward, Murfreesboro, Tenn.
10th Vice President .... Rev. J.M. Dawson, Williamsburg, Va.
11th Vice President .... Rev. R.H. Boyd, Palestine, Texas
Treasurer. .... Rev. R. Spiller, Norfolk, Va.
1st Secretary ....................W.R. Pettiford, Union Springs, Ala.
2nd Secretary .... Rev. J.M. Armstead, Portsmouth, Va.
Statistical Secretary .... H. Williams, Jr., Petersburg, Va.
Cor. Sec'y and Traveling Agent ...... Rev. W.W. Colley, Richmond, Va.

FOREIGN MISSION BOARD

President , Rev. A. Binga, Jr., Manchester, Va.; Secretary, Prof. J.E. Jones, Richmond, Va.; Rev. W.H. McAlpine, Selma, Ala.; Rev. Wm. Troy, Richmond, Va.; Rev. W.A. Green, Raleigh, N.C.; Rev. W.R. Mason, Weldon, N.C.; Rev. J.M. Jones, Atlanta, Ga.; Rev. R.D. Dunbar, Jacksonville, Fla.; Rev. H.N. Bouey, Selma. Ala.; Rev. R. Ramsey, Meridian, Miss.; Rev. J.H. Stewart, Murfreesboro, Tenn.; Rev. Thomas Luke, Shreveport, La.; Rev. S.H. Smith, Fort Worth, Texas; Rev. A.J. Taylor, Richmond, Va.; Dr. Fields Cook, Alexandria, Va.; Rev. H. Williams, Jr., Petersburg, Va.; Rev. R. Spiller, Norfolk, Va.; Rev. J.W. Patterson, Danville, Va.; Rev. E.C. Morris, Helena, Ark.; Rev. W.W. Colley, Richmond, Va.; Rev. P.F. Morris, Lynchburg, Va.; Rev. John Jones, Liberty, Va.; Rev. J.E. Farror, Richmond, Va.; Rev. J.H. Holmes Richmond, Va.; Rev. J.B. Smith, Concord, Depot, Va.; Rev. E.K. Love, Thomasville, Ga.; Rev. J.W. White, Augusta, Ga.

LIFE MEMBERS

Rev. W.W. Colley .... Richmond, Virginia
Rev. J.M. Armistead .... Portsmouth, Virginia
Rev. S.M. Dickerson .... Murfreesboro, Tennessee

Rev. R.H. Boyd .... Palestine, Texas
Rev. R. Ramsey .... Meridian, Mississippi
Rev. J. Clemons .... Knoxville, Tennessee
Rev. W.P. Fennick .... Gallatin, Tennessee
Rev. A. Nickerson .... Chattanooga, Tennessee
Rev. H. Williams .... Macon, Georgia
Deacon R. Banks .... Knoxville, Tennessee
Deacon S. Campbell .... Knoxville, Tennessee

ANNUAL MEMBERS
Miss Pennie Jarrett .... Macon, Ga.

MINUTES
FIRST DAY-Morning Session
June 28, 1882

The Baptist Foreign Mission Convention of the United States of America, held its Third Annual Session with the Cotton Avenue Baptist Church, Rev. H. Williams, Pastor, Macon, Ga., commencing June 28, 1882. The President, Rev. W.H. McAlpine, called the Convention to order at ten o'clock, and conducted the devotional exercises. After reading and singing, Rev. C. Johnson of North Carolina, led in prayer. In the absence of Rev. J.M. Armstead, the secretary, W.R. Pettiford, acted secretary *pro tem*. The president, W.H. McAlpine, at this point addressed the Convention, making some very practical remarks: among which, he said that we, to a large extent, were without experience in a work of this kind; that our experience of managing our conventions and associations was not sufficient alone to warrant our success in a work so large as this. He called upon the brethren to address themselves to the work as men; not for each one to see how often he could get the floor, or how many resolutions he could have his name signed to, but be men in the highest sense of the term; such manliness as will show itself in well arranged plans presented for the more thorough organization of the work.

List of Delegates
On motion the names of the delegates were enrolled as follows:

Alabama—The Alabama Baptist State Convention, Revs. J.Q.A. Wilhite, W.H. McAlpine, J.A. Foster, H.N. Bouey, W.R. Pettiford; First Baptist Church, Montgomery, J.A. Foster; Benevolent Society, First Baptist Church, Montgomery, J.A. Foster; Foreign Mission Society, Montgomery, Brother

Church; Union Springs, W.R. Pettiford; Eufaula Foreign Mission Society, S.S. and church, J.Q.A. Wilhite; Eufaula District Sabbath School Convention, Rev. A.D. Gachett; Opelika Baptist Church, Rev. T. Glenn.

Arkansas—Arkansas Baptist State Convention, Revs. E.C. Morris, Helena; J.C. Carbin, Pine Bluff.

Florida—First Church at Jacksonville, Rev. R.D. Dunbar; Pensacola, Rev._____ Dozier.

Louisiana—Four Baptist churches and Sunday schools, and four societies; Rev. Thomas Luke, Shreveport; Antioch African Foreign Mission Society, Rev. Luke Allen, Shreveport.

Mississippi—Meridian Baptist Church, Rev. R. Ramsey; Foreign Mission societies, Rev. Daniel Webster.

North Carolina—The North Carolina Baptist State Convention and Sisters' Foreign Mission society of First Baptist Church, Raleigh, and Sisters' Foreign Mission society of the state, Rev. C. Johnson, Raleigh.

South Carolina—Greenville Baptist Church, Rev. F. Brown, Greenville.

Georgia—Georgia Baptist State Convention, Rev. W.J. White, J.C. Bryant; G.H. Dwelle, Elias Tosin, R.R. Watson, C.T. James, Brother A.A. Blake, Revs. John Williams, Clark Guilmore, Henry Jackson, L. Williams, Macon Baptist churches; Cotton Avenue Baptist Church, Rev. H. Williams; Mt. Olive Baptist Church, Rev. J.H. Davis; First African Baptist Church, Savannah and Sabbath school, Brethren C. DeLamotta, J.H. Brown; Calvary Baptist Church, Rev. Allen Clark; Thomasville Sunday School, Rev. E.K. Love, Thomasville; Rev. S.A. McNeal, Augusta.

Texas—Texas State Foreign Mission Board, Rev. W.W. Colley; Mt. Gilead Baptist Church, Rev. S.H. Smith; Forth Worth Baptist churches, Revs. Jones and Griggs.

Virginia—Virginia Baptist State Convention, Rev. A. Binga, Jr., Dr. Fields Cook, Rev. Richard Spiller, Rev. J.H. Presley; The Colley Missionary Society, Rev. J.H. Presley. West Virginia Baptist State Convention appointed C.H. Payne.

The president appointed the following committees:

1. On Programme—W.W. Colley, W.R. Pettiford, C. Johnson.
2. On Permanent Organization—Revs. F. Brown, E.K. Love, C. Johnson.
3. On Devotional Exercises—H. Williams, J.H. Davis, E.J. Tatem.

During the absence of the Committee on Programme, the Convention held an Informal Conference, in which Revs. R. Spiller of Virginia, Thomas Luke of Louisiana, F. Brown of South Carolina, J.A. Foster, Alabama; T. Glenn of Georgia; E.K. Love of Georgia; H. Brown of Savannah; Rev. J.H. Presley of Richmond; W.W. Colley of Virginia; [and] Brother G.W. Washington of Alabama, made speeches that showed a marked interest in the work, not only of themselves, but that the people were interested in their several states where they lived. Brother Colley felt that the interest in foreign missions was rapidly growing in all the states in which he had traveled. He said that in many localities the White brethren manifested a lively interest in our African work. Several of the brethren suggested plans by which the work might be carried on. Others spoke of their being impressed that the Colored Christians of America were being led by the overruling providence of God to a great and glorious work in our fatherland, and of their confidence in God's continuing this work by us, until it shall reach the summit of success when all the sons and daughters of Africa shall have the gospel preached unto them.

On motion, Rev. E.K. Love was appointed to preach the annual sermon at 8 1/2 o'clock.

Adjourned by benediction to 3 o'clock p.m.

The Convention was called to order by the president at 3 o'clock p.m; Rev. J.Q.A. Wilhite of Eufaula, led in prayer. The Committee on Order of Business reported, and a number of copies were ordered printed. The Committee on Permanent Organization suggested the officers of this Convention for the ensuing year.

After some discussion on a proposition to amend the Constitution, the Convention adjourned at 8½ o'clock, p.m.

Evening Session—8½ o'clock p.m.

Rev. E. K. Love of Georgia, by request of Rev. H. William, the pastor, made the following address of welcome on behalf of Cotton Avenue Baptist Church of Macon, Ga.:

Dear Brethren of the Foreign Mission Convention of the United States:

With all our hearts we welcome you; we welcome you to our hearts; we welcome you to our homes; we welcome you to our house of worship; we welcome you to our means. We have had but a short time to prepare for you. We heard that you were to meet in Atlanta, Georgia, and we rejoiced that Georgia had the honor of entertaining the messengers of God, coming to us laden with good news of the precious gospel of the Son of God. We think it a blessed privilege to have the pleasure of your presence. Your work is our work. We are laborers together in the Master's vineyard. We are called upon by our blessed Lord to engage in the glorious work of sending the gospel of Christ to the perishing millions of Africa. Our aims, our

VERMONT AVENUE BAPTIST CHURCH
Washington, D.C.

Here the pious and persistent Jno. H. Brooks began work in the District of Columbia with seven members in 1865. He organized the Fifth Baptist Church, June 5, 1886. After eighteen years he left for the Glory Land, leaving a membership of 1500. Then came that resourceful, preaching dynamo, Geo. W. Lee, out of North Carolina, witty, sarcastic, and withal, a sweet dispositioned pastor. In a single revival more than 500 persons professed a hope in our Lord, and 262 were baptized into the fellowship of Vermont Avenue Baptist Church. Under his care the name was changed from the Fifth Baptist Church to its present name, and $35,000 put in its remodeling. He was a great friend to Africa, and lover of missions. Born January 5, 1857; died February 6, 1910. When he took his flight for Beulah, he left 4000 members enrolled. Then came Rev. J.E. Willis who, baptized, licensed, and ordained by Dr. Lee, was a great favorite with his people. Born in Orange County, Va., May 3, 1875; died in Washington City, leaving 6000 members, and now Rev. Chantise T. Murry, D.D., one of our young and well equipped men, who is reckoned a great preacher and good pastor, is in charge.

211

cause, and hopes are one; one family we dwell in him. Viewing the surroundings we consider your visit a godsend. Providence shapes all things for the best. If it had been the best for you to have met in Atlanta, God would no doubt have brought you there. He doeth all things for the best. Your work is a noble one. We feel happy to be counted worthy to labor with you in this grand and glorious work. You are laying the foundation for future greatness. Coming generations will rise up and call you blessed. We trust to be of service to you. If we cannot enter into the discussions and help you devise plans to perfect this work, we are thankful to know that we can hold up the prophet's hands. If we cannot preach and bear the glad tidings far away, we can be humble armor-bearers. Every pulsation of our heart beats for the teeming millions of Africa groping in ignorance dark as the night. Only permit us to join you in the good work, that we may share in the reaping by and by. If you are defeated we will suffer with you. If the ship in which you have embarked sinks, we pledge you our word that we'll go under with you and share your fate. Our interest is common, and our destiny shall be the same. We welcome you because you are servants of the Most High God, and are engaged in His cause. We feel that the redemption of suffering Africa depends largely, if not wholly, upon the Colored people of this country. We welcome you thrice to our hearts, homes, and pockets, praying that the good Lord will give you great success in your labors of love and that the redemption of Africa may be the fruits of your labors. We are yours for Africa.

At this point, by request, Brother J.H. Brown of Savannah, made the address of welcome on behalf of the state of Georgia, in which he made us feel that at an early day Georgia would be thoroughly aroused and would fill her place in the army as it marches for the redemption of Africa.

The president called upon Rev. A. Binga of Virginia, to respond to these addresses of welcome on behalf of the Convention, which he did in a very appropriate manner.

After singing hymn No. 723, and prayer by Rev. J.A. Foster of Alabama, Rev. E.K. Love proceeded to preach the Annual Sermon from Mark 16:15. The sermon brought clearly to our view our duty in giving the gospel to Africa. It also made us see the importance of sending the gospel as the chief means of the redemption of Africa. Prayer by Rev. H.N. Bouey of Selma. A collection of $5.00 was taken, and the following Committee on Finance was appointed: Brothers G.W. Washington of Montgomery; C.L. DeLamotta of Savannah, H. Williams of Macon. Adjourned.

SECOND DAY'S SESSION
Thursday, June 29—9 a.m.

President in the chair. Prayer by Brother C.L. DeLamotta of Savannah. The following committees were appointed:

On Ways and Means, Revs. W.W. Colley, W.J. White, W.H. McAlpine, A. Binga.

On Communications, Rev. H.N. Bouey, G.H. Dwelle, J.A. Foster.

On Boards, Revs. E.K. Love, J.C. Bryant, G.H. Dwelle, C. Johnson.

On Obituaries, Revs. J.C. Bryant, W.H. Tillman, R. Ramsey.

The following resolution offered by Rev. A. Binga of Virginia, was adopted:

"Whereas, We feel that the Constitution of this Convention is defective, therefore,

Resolved, That at the hour of 3 1/2 o'clock p.m., this Convention consider the propriety of appointing a committee of nine to revise the present Constitution of this body.

Resolved, By this Convention, that we furnish a synopsis of our proceedings for publication to any paper that may call upon us for such.

F. BROWN, S.C."

Revs. Wm. Sloppy, S. Cornelius, J.B. Borden, Alex Cowmew, and C. McCarty were introduced to the Convention and invited to seats. Rev. C. McCarty of the Presbyterian church was invited to address the Convention, and made encouraging remarks.

The Committee on Preaching reported as follows:

Rev. T. Glenn to preach at Mt. Olive Church at 8 1/2 o'clock; Rev. F. Brown of South Carolina, at St. Paul A.M.E. Church, at 8 1/2 o'clock; Rev. Thomas Luke of Louisiana, at Siloam Church, Unionville, at 8 1/2 o'clock; Unionville Baptist Church, Rev. Luke Allen, at 8 1/2 o'clock; Fulton Church, Rev. Daniel Webster of Mississippi at 8 1/2 o'clock.

COMMITTEE—Revs. H. Williams, E.J. Tatem, J.H. Davis

The Committee on Obituaries read their report.

We, your Committee on Obituaries, beg to make the following report:

By the Providence of Almighty God, the faithful and venerable servant Rev. Frank Quarles, has been called away. He departed this life at Flushing, N.Y., December 3, 1881. As he was a member of the Executive Committee for Georgia, appointed by this Convention, we recommend that this Convention spend some time in memorial services, and that prayer be made for the bereaved family.

COMMITTEE—J.C. Bryant, R. Ramsey, W.H. Tillman

After the reading of the report some time was spent in memorial services. A number of brethren spoke of the qualities which happily met in Brother Quarles, and we rejoice to know that these qualities well-nigh controlled the motives, aims, and life of our departed brother. When his Christian character was recalled to our minds by those who knew him best, we felt a consecrating influence stirring in our souls, wooing us to live for that which is alone worth living—the service of the Master and the redemption of the souls of men. Then hymn No. 1118 was sung: "Servant of God, Well Done," Prayer by the Rev. A. Binga, Jr., of Virginia. Adjourned to 3 p.m.

Afternoon Session
3 o'clock p.m.

Devotional exercises conducted by Rev. H.N. Bouey of Selma, singing hymn No. 480. Prayer by Rev. R. Ramsey. The hour having arrived for considering the propriety of revising the present Constitution, after some discussion the following brethren were appointed to revise the Constitution and report at the next session of this Convention: Revs. H.N. Bouey, R. Ramsey, W.H. McAlpine, Luke Allen, W.J. White, W.W. Colley, A. Binga, Jr., C. Johnson.

A Committee on Time and Place, and Preachers was appointed for the next session: Revs. J.A. Foster, A.D. Gachett, Allen Clark, and R.R. Watson. Adjourned by prayer.

Evening Session
8 ½ o'clock

Hymn No. 862 was sung. Rev. W.H. Tillman led in prayer, after which Rev. Dr. Fields Cook of Alexandria, Virginia, preached the Missionary Sermon from 2 Cor. 2:18, 19. His delivery was easy, and being ripe in experience he furnished much instruction in his discourse. Rev. R. Spillet of Virginia, offered prayer. A collection of $7.70 was taken up, and after Brethren J.H. Brown of Savannah, and G.W. Washington of Montgomery, were granted leave of absence the Convention adjourned.

FRIDAY'S SESSION
Friday, July 30—9 a.m.

Vice president, J.A. Foster, in the chair. The 90th Psalm was read. Elder T. Glenn of Columbus, offered prayer. On motion, Revs. H.N.

Bouey, W.H. McAlpine, [and] W.J. White were made a committee to recommend such papers or journals as may be the organs of this body. Committee on Boards reported. Rev. R.A. Hall of the A.M.E. Church, was introduced to examine the treasurer's books: Revs. A. Binga, W.H. McAlpine, H.N. Bouey. At this juncture, Rev. C. McCarty of the Colored Presbyterian church, by previous invitation, gave some of their plans of raising money and doing missionary work, one of which was to organize the ladies into societies to do missionary work. We think the plan of organizing the ladies of our churches into Home and Foreign Missionary Societies, is a good one, and hope that every pastor will organize a Missionary Society in his church, to do home and foreign missionary work.

FOREIGN MISSION BOARD
Report of Corresponding Secretary, Rev. W.W. Colley

With pleasure we present to you our semi-annual report. Although we have had only about six months to prosecute the work since the last meeting, the real progress made is equal to that of twelve months of any previous year. This is seen in the fact that states heretofore not visited have been visited, and are being organized. Some states have taken hold of the work and are trying to make it a success. Again, communities have been recently organized into Foreign Missionary Societies, for the purpose of helping to send the gospel of the Son of God to the three hundred millions of poor, naked heathen mothers , children, and fathers of Africa. Some of these societies have just been organized, and therefore will not be able to report much money at this session of the Convention. More than 154 missionary societies have been organized in the different states; and with an average of $7 from each one of these, foreign mission work will receive annually $1,078, which is equal to the support of two missionaries, as given by the Southern Baptist Convention when Brother David and your corresponding secretary were their missionaries in Central West Africa. The drought of last summer, which was so universal, has been so much felt by the churches, as well as otherwise, that your travelling agent has been compelled to give all free lectures on Africa; therefore not being able to collect as fast as heretofore. Your travelling agent has labored with the Executive Committees in seven states during the past six months.

He has traveled 4,792 miles in the prosecution of the work. The Executive Committee (some of them) has accomplished incalcuable good in the way of organizing their states. These committees are of so much importance that we recommend the appointment of an additional committee of seven in some of the states; especially Texas, Louisiana, and Tennessee, and possibly Mississippi and Georgia. The deepest interest is manifested by the churches of Texas; and with one year's work by your agent in that state, will receive means enough to support a missionary in Africa. At a recent meeting of the State Foreign Board of Texas, it was decided to ask the Foreign Mission Board of this Convention to allow Texas to send and support one missionary in Africa, as soon as they can raise the sum of $500 for that purpose. We are of the opinion that the foreign mission work of the Christian churches of the Nineteenth Century is the most encouraging of their labors, and that the results in the foreign fields are more than ten times those of the home fields. We are satisfied that our converts at home cost not less than $10, while those of the foreign field (Africa) will not amount to more than $.50.

At a regular meeting of the Foreign Mission Board, in January, held in the study of Rev. J.H. Holmes of Richmond, Va., our missionary, Rev. J.0. Hayes of Africa, was instructed to go as soon as practicable, to the Kingdom of Dahomy, and to send the Board plans for a church and chapel for our missionaries at that point.

A quarter's salary ($125), was sent him, and $50 to pay travelling expenses from Monrovia to Whydah.

Missionary Heard From

A letter was received, dated April 14th, 1882, Brewerville, Liberia:

My dear Brother—I have just returned from a jungle town, which brought me in contact with a dozen or more of heathen towns; and of the number of towns, I found only one person who could speak the English language, and he was a boy who looked to be about eight or ten years old. I asked him where he learned to speak English and he told me he had been going to Mr. D.A. Day's Mission.

Brother Hayes being off on a tour among the heathen when orders of the Board reached Africa, we could not hear from him in time to make a report as full as it should be.

When Brother Hayes returned from this town, it being so near the rainy season, that it would not be safe to commence the trip to the Kingdom of Dahomy until near about the close of the rains, which will be about the month of October. Our missionary is now living in a house made of leaves, poles, and logs. The Board needs money to build a house for the missionaries to live in, and a church for the heathen. In addition to the $175 sent to the missionary in Africa, by the Board of B.F.M.C., the sisters' missionary societies of North Carolina have forwarded $100 more, making the total of $275.

The Board at its meeting in January appointed Rev. J.H. Presley of the Richmond Institute to assist the corresponding secretary during the summer in presenting the cause of Africa to the churches throughout the country, and to help in organizing missionary societies in the churches and Sunday schools among our people. The Board has made and placed in the hands of the treasurer and president of the Board, suitable stub books to be used for receipting the business of the Board. At the same meeting of the Board, we adopted the rules of the Southern Baptist Foreign Mission Board to govern our missionaries in Africa.

In reviewing the past, and considering the present, we are compelled to look for great things in the future. We believe the redemption of Africa is to be brought about by the Colored people of America; and as followers of that Conqueror who has never lost a battle, let us fight manfully in the foreign mission cause, until we have taken Africa for Christ.

Yours for Africa,

W.W. COLLEY

Cor. Sec. and Travelling Agt.

Visits

The following are the places visited by your corresponding secretary:

Arkansas—The First Colored Baptist Church, Rev. R.B. White, Little Rock, $10.00; A.M.E. Church, Elder Phillips, $6.00; First Baptist Church, Rev. R. Lawson, Argenta, $2.10; Branch Normal School, J.C. Corbin, President, Pine Bluff, $3.00; St. Paul Church, Rev. Robinson, Pine Bluff, $20.60; First White Baptist Church, Dr. Mayes, Little Rock, $1.75; Mt. Pleasant Baptist Church, Rev. P. Hatchett, Little Rock, $6.25. Total $49.88.

Georgia—First Baptist Church, Rev. H. Williams, Macon, $8.60; Mt. Olive Baptist Church, Rev. J.H. Davis, Macon, $4.05; First Baptist Church, Rev. G. Gibbons, Savannah, $9.96; Second African Baptist Church, Rev. A. Ellis, Savannah, $9.29; Mt. Zion Baptist Church, Rev. Weston, $1.70; Fulton Baptist Church, Deacon Jones, Macon, $5.30. Total, $38.90.

Louisiana—Leland University, J.F. Morton, President, $1.50; Baptist Church, Rev. G. Walker, New Orleans, $12.25; Sister John Mark, $1.30; Galilee Baptist Church, Rev. Thomas Luke, Shreveport, $8.75; Antioch Baptist Church, Rev. Luke Allen, Shreveport, $25.30; M.E. Church, Rev. R. Thompson, Shreveport, $5.75. Total, $54.80.

North Carolina—First Baptist Church, Rev. W.A. Green, Raleigh, $15.58; Second Baptist Church, Rev. F.R. Howell, Raleigh, $7.70; First Baptist Church, Rev. F.H. Wilkins, $5.59; Stokes Hall, Durham, $11.64; First Baptist Church, Rev. A.A. Powell, Greensboro, $6.60. Total, $47.11.

South Carolina—Springfield Baptist Church, Rev. F. Brown, Greenville, $2.80; M.E. Church, Rev. J.B. Middleton, Greenville, $2.15. Total $4.95.

Texas—Mt. Zion Baptist Church, Deacon R. Cartham, Texarkana, $19.45; Macedonia Baptist Church, Rev. C.B. Martin, Jefferson, $6.45; M.E. Church, Rev. Logan, Jefferson, $4.75; Union Baptist Church, Rev. N. Beekam, Jefferson, $7.15; First Baptist Church (White), Rev. S.A. Hayden, Jefferson, $8.00; Bethesda Baptist Church, Rev. L. Luke, Marshall, $13.38; Wiley University, W.H. Davis, President, Marshall, $4.10; Bishop College, S.W. Culver, President, Marshall, $1.45; F.C. Long, Marshall, $1.00; First Baptist Church (White), Rev. E. Clemmons, Marshall, $6.10; M.E. Church, Rev. Peter May, Marshall, $11.05; West End Baptist Church, Rev. R.H. Boyd, Palestine, $11.50; Antioch Baptist Church, Rev. J.B. Dunda, Palestine, $6.50; Market Hall, H.J. Curry, Palestine, $4.00; Abner and P.H. Grose, Maskom, $5.30. Total, $118.18.

Virginia—First Baptist Church, Rev. J.H. Holmes, Richmond, $28.50. Total collection by the Corresponding Secretary, $360.25.

The Convention then adjourned to 3 o'clock p.m.

Afternoon Session

Rev. F. Brown conducted devotional exercises at 3 o'clock, p.m. Prayer by Rev. Luke Allen, of Louisiana. By its representative, Rev. J.A. Foster, the Benevolent Society of the First Baptist Church, Montgomery, became a member of the Convention and donated five dollars. The Committee on Time and Place, and Preachers for the next session only made a partial report.

The following are to preach the Annual Sermons at the next session:

Introductory Sermon by Rev. A. Binga, Jr. of Virginia; alternate, W.H. McAlpine of Alabama. Missionary Sermon by Rev. H.N. Bouey of Selma, Ala.; alternate, Rev. E.K. Love of Georgia. The appointing of the time and place for the next meeting was left in the hands of the corresponding secretary W.W. Colley, who will report in due time.

Report of Committee on Ways and Means

Your committee seeing the necessity of devising some means to interest our denomination in the work of African missions, recommend

1. That the conventions, associations, churches, societies, etc., be requested to employ such means as they find best by organizing societies,

soliciting subscriptions, etc.

2. That each state represented in this Convention be requested to raise the sum of $500, or as much more as possible towards the support of missionaries in Africa.

3. That the ladies be, hereby, especially called upon in all the states to help us in this work.

4. That all churches, Sunday schools, missionary societies, etc., be requested to send their money to the treasurer, Rev. R. Spiller, Norfolk, Virginia, and that he send them a printed receipt.

5. That the corresponding secretary of this Convention be hereby instructed to put himself in correspondence with the executive officers of all the conventions and associations of the United States, to secure their cooperation.

We further recommend that our ministers, churches, and the public at large, receive and aid our corresponding secretary and agent Rev. W.W. Colley, and his assistant, Rev. J.H. Presley, in the prosecution of their work of raising funds for our Convention wherever they may go.

W.J. WHITE	A. HARRIS	W.H. McALPINE
W.W. COLLEY	A. BINGA, JR.	

Report of the Treasurer

The treasurer of the Board made the following report:

Amount brought over from last meeting of the Convention at Knoxville, November, 1881, $371.33. Amounts received from churches, societies, Sunday schools, and friends during this year, $151.52; from corresponding secretary Rev. W.W. Colley $360.25. Total amount received since last Convention, $511.77. Total including amount brought over from last year $882.10. Paid during the year $532.00, leaving in hands of the treasurer $350.10.

> R. SPILLER, Treasurer
> F.M. Con., U.S.A.

Report of the Auditing Committee

The Committee on Auditing the treasurer's report, beg to report that they have examined all receipts and disbursements, and find them correct.

> Respectfully submitted,
> W.H. McALPINE
> A. BINGA
> H.N. BOUEY, Chairman

Report of Finance Committee

Alabama—First Baptist Church, Montgomery, $5.00; Culwell Baptist Church, Selma, $1.40; Hamburg Baptist Church, $2.50; Rev. David Duke's Church, $1.85; Mt. William Baptist Church, $1.75; Greenville Baptist Church, $1.00; Mt. Meigs Baptist Church, $1.30; Ridgeville Baptist Church, $1.00; Eagle Grove Baptist Church, $2.00; The Uniontown Church, $8.00; Lower Peach Tree Baptist Church, $1.85; Union Springs Baptist Church, $5.20; Elizabeth Church; $2.50; Lowndesboro Church, $8.00; Macedonia Church, $3.00; Ebenezer Church, $3.00; The Bethel Association, $15.00; The Brown's Valley Association, $4.00; The Foreign Mission Society, Montgomery, $5.00, Eufaula Foreign Mission Society, $5.00; First Baptist Church Sunday School, Montgomery, $2.00; Ladies' Sewing Society, Union Springs, $2.00; Eufaula Foreign Mission Society Sunday School, $5.00; Eufaula District Sunday School Convention, $2.00; Mt. Meigs Sabbath School, $1.50; Alabama District Sunday School Convention, $5.00; Little Cedar Sunday School, $.85; Ebenezer Sunday School, $.40 cents; Second Ebenezer Sunday School $1.00; First Baptist Church, Montgomery, $10.70; Second Baptist Church, Montgomery, $3.10; Bethel Baptist Church, Montgomery, $1.00; Shelby Iron Works Baptist Church, $1.80; Good Hope Baptist Church, $2.55; Good Hope Sunday School, $1.00; Hopewell Baptist Church, $1.50; Hopewell Sunday School, $1.00; Shady Grove Baptist Church, $3.90; Bethel Sunday School, Lawrence Co., $2.00; Good Hope Church, Buena Vista, $.70; Friendship Church, $2.20; Total $128.35.

Arkansas—Rev. I. G. Bailey, $2.00; Rev. B. Jackson, $2.00; Sister D. Thompson, $5.00; Mt. Zion Baptist Church, Little Rock, $5.00; Third Baptist Church, Little Rock, $5.00; Desoto Lodge of the G.W.O. of O.F., $10.00; United Sons and Daughters, $1.00; Elder D. l. Jordan, $1.25; Third Baptist Church Sunday School, $2.50. Total, $33.75.

Mississippi—Rev. D. Webster from the following societies and churches: New Hope Church, Meridian, $2.50; New Hope Sabbath School, $2.00; New Hope Sisters' Society, $2.00; Pleasant Grove Church, $1.00; Pleasant Grove Sabbath School, $1.00; Pleasant Grove Sisters' Society, $1.00; Gailer Church, $1.00; Gailer Sabbath School, $1.00; Pine Grove Church, $1.00; Golden Grove Church, $1.00; Concord Church, $1.10; Concord Church Sisters' Society, $1.00; Okatibber Society, $1.00; Okatibber Sabbath School, $1.00; Mt. Zion Church, $1.00; Mt. Moriah Church, $1.00; Mt. Moriah Sisters' Society, $1.00' New Hope Church, Lauderdale Springs, $1.00; New Hope, Suba, $1.00; Shiloh, $1.00; Poplar Sisters' Society, $1.00; Pleasant Grove Church, $1.00; Green Hill Church, $1.00; Green Hill Sabbath School, $1.00; Green Hills Sisters'

Society, $1.00; Shiloh Church, $1.00; New Hope Church, $1.00; Mt. Zion Church, $1.00; Pleasant Grove Church, $1.00; Elizabeth Church, $1.00; Elizabeth Sisters' Society, $1.00; New Hope Church's Society, $1.00; New Hope Sabbath School, $1.00; Pleasant Grove Church, $1.00; Garfield Church, $1.00; Garfield Church Sisters' Society, $1.00; New Hope Church, $1.00; New Hope Sisters' Society, $11.05; Sun Mount Church, $.55; Shiloh Church, $1.35. Total, $46.45.

Louisiana—Antioch Africa Missionary Society, $5.05; Mt. Zion Church, $1.00; Freemen Association, New Orleans, $4.00; Ladies' Association, New Orleans, $1.00; Galilee Baptist church, 50 cents; Greenwood Church, $.50; Bethlehem Church, 50 cents; Evergreen Church, $.50. Total, $13.05.

North Carolina—First Baptist Church, Raleigh, $9.91.

South Carolina—Springfield School, $3.00.

Texas—Pleasant Hill Foreign Mission Society, $2.00; Red Bank Foreign Mission Society, $5.00; Colley Missionary, Marshall, $3.26: Mount Gilead Church, $2.50; Seyene Baptist Church Sunday School, $2.00; Seyene Association, $5.25. Total, $20.01.

Georgia—Foreign Mission Society, First Baptist Church, $2.00;First African Baptist Church, Savannah, $5.25; First African Baptist Church Sabbath School, $4.00; F. Mission Society, Thompsonville, $1.50; Fulton Foreign Mission Society, Macon, $1.20; collected at Macon, $11.70; Mt. Olive Branch Church, $.70. Total, $25.65.

Virginia—Foreign Mission Society, Second Baptist Church, Richmond, $5.00; Loyal Baptist Church, Danville, $3.88; First Baptist Church, Danville, $13.30; Big Bethel Church, $3.15; Piney Grove Baptist Church, $1.10; Foreign Mission, Second Baptist Church; Richmond, $5.00. Total $26.43. Grand total, $281.07.

RESOLUTION

Resolved, That so much as has been paid by the Cotton Avenue Baptist Church of Macon to the Convention be accepted as a part payment on life membership of Rev. H. Williams, the pastor of this church; and whatever donation may be sent to the Board by this church, shall be credited to his life membership.—McAlpine.

On motion of Rev. R. Spiller, it was ordered that the clerk be paid $30.00 for compiling the minutes of the Convention.

Ordered that the sexton be paid $3.00 for his services.

MT. CARMEL BAPTIST CHURCH
Washington, D. C.

This church was once pastored by Dr. Gibbons, who was succeeded by Rev. W. H. Jernagin, D.D., who led these people from their old church on "L" Street, N. W., to this splendid building, which was purchased from the Presbyterians. Woodrow Wilson held membership in this church [before it changed hands] during his incumbrance of President of the United States. It is one of the most outstanding churches of our denomination.

Report of Committee on Communications

The Committee on Communications made their report which was adopted as follows:

1. The Calvary Baptist Church of Madison, Georgia, sends its pastor as a delegate, and wishes the Convention great success.

2. The Louisiana Freedmen's Baptist Association sends four dollars ($4.00), and assures your Convention of its continued support and prayers.

3. The missionary sisters of Louisiana Freedmen's Baptist Association, sends one dollar, ($1.00) and pledge themselves to do more by the Lord's help.

4. The Auxiliary Women's Foreign Mission Society of the First Baptist Church of Raleigh, N.C., sends the gratifying fact to the Convention that they have sent to Rev. J.0. Hayes in Liberia, $100, and assures the Convention of their hearty cooperation as fellow laborers.

5. Rev. Daniel Webster of Meridian, Miss., states that he has organized over one hundred auxiliary societies, and turns over $46.30. His report is encouraging and he promises to increase his efforts.

6. The First African Baptist Church and Sabbath School of Savannah, Georgia, donated to the Convention $9.25. The church sending $5.25, and the Sabbath school $4.00, and express a deep interest in the work of the Convention.

7. The Sisters and Brothers' Benevolent Society of Montgomery, Ala., sends $5, desiring to aid the missionaries in Africa.

8. The Beet Street Baptist Church of Norfolk, Va., sends $20, bidding the Convention God-speed in the glorious work of evangelizing Africa.

9. Rev. G.W. Gates of Miss., writes informing the Convention that the Missionary Baptist Convention of Mississippi regretted very much its inability to meet the Convention at this session, and states that its Convention will meet July the 18th, 1882, at Vicksburg, Miss.

10. The Colley Foreign Mission Convention in Bishop College, Texas, sends $3.26, and expresses much interest in the work of redeeming Africa.

11. The Fulton Foreign Mission Society of Macon, Ga., donates $1.20.

12. The Second Baptist Church Foreign Mission Society of Virginia, states that they have sent $50.00, and now sends $5.00 for the African mission work.

13. The Mount Gilead Baptist Church of Fort Worth, Texas, sends $2.50 and Rev. S.H. Smith with the association of their prayers.

14. The Texarkana Sunday School sends $2.00, and the Red Bank Sunday School sends $1.00.

15. The Colley Missionary Society, Richmond, Va., sends $5.00; and Rev. J.H. Presley, delegate.

16. The Loyal St. Baptist Church, Danville, Va., sends $3.88, and promises to do the best they can in future for the African work.

17. The First Baptist Church of Danville, Va., sent $13.30, and J.H. Presley as delegate.

18. An extract of a letter from Rev. P.F. Morris to W.W. Colley, will show that the Virginia Baptists are yet leading the way in the foreign mission work:

Lynchburg, Va., June 19, 1882

Rev. W.W. Colley:

The Baptist State Convention of Virginia ordered all money in its treasury for foreign mission purposes to be drawn out at the instance of the chairman of the State Foreign Mission Board.

The amount is between $1,300 and $1,400.

Your colaborer,
P.F. MORRIS

The following extract is from Rev. C.H. Carey, Pastor of the First Baptist Church of Abingdon, Va.:

Abingdon, Va., June 26, 1882

Rev. W.W. Colley:

We are at work for the cause in Africa. Our church has agreed to give $100 at any time when called for—money in the bank. The churches of the association are going to do their best this year for Africa. Your society is doing all they can for the cause. They have some money for you. I told them to try to raise $100 by the middle of next month.

Yours in Christ,
C.H. CAREY

The Mt. Zion Church at Caddo Parish, La., has agreed to take a collection every fifth Sunday in the year for the African Mission.

On motion three thousand copies of the minutes were ordered printed. At this juncture Rev. W.H. McAlpine, president of the Normal and Theological School, Selma, Ala., was granted an opportunity to speak of his school work. He gave quite a favorable report of the educational work in Alabama.

Report of Committee on Preaching for Sunday, July 2nd

Presbyterian Church—11 a.m., Rev. R. Spiller, Virginia; 3 p.m., Rev. A. Binga, Jr.; 8½ p.m., Rev. W.W. Colley.

A.M.E. Church—11 a.m., Rev. H.N. Bouey; 8½ p.m., Rev. W.H. McAlpine.

Cotton Avenue Baptist Church—11 a.m., Rev. D. Webster; 3 p.m., Rev. J.A. Foster; 8½ p.m., Rev. W.R. Pettiford.

Fulton Baptist Church—11 a.m., Rev. F. Cook.

Mt. Olive Baptist Church—11 a.m., Rev. Luke Allen; 3 p.m., Rev. A.D. Gachett; 8½ p.m., Rev. R. Ramsey.

Corresponding Delegates

Resolved, 1. That all members of this Convention who shall be present at any of the State Conventions be authorized to act as corresponding delegates; and that the minutes of this session be used as credentials.

2. That the corresponding secretary and agents of the Board be made corresponding messengers to the several State Conventions; or write communications to them and do what they can to interest them in this work.

Thanks

WHEREAS, The M. and E. Railroad, and the M. and C. Railroad have granted reduced rates to all delegates passing over their lines, therefore be it

Resolved, That the thanks of this Convention be tendered to them for their kind consideration.—Bouey.

Resolved, That the Convention does hereby tender its heartfelt thanks to the members of the churches and citizens of Macon for their kindness to us as delegates while in their city.—W.H. Tilman.

Closing

Hymn No. 1068 was sung with much feeling while the parting hand was given. Prayer by Rev. Allen Clark. Rev. W.W. Colley then continued prayer for our missionary in Africa, Rev. J.O. Hayes. The song, "Over the Ocean Wave, Far, Far, Away," was the closing exercise, which touched our sympathies. The Convention adjourned to meet at the time and place named by the Board.

REV. J.Q.A. WILHITE, President
W.R. PETTIFORD, Secretary

Board Meeting

Macon, Ga., July 1, 1882

The Foreign Mission Board was called to order by the president, Rev. A. Binga, Jr., of Virginia. After singing and prayer by Rev. C. Johnson, Brother A. Binga, Jr., was re-elected president of Board, W.R. Pettiford acting clerk.

Order of Business

Resolved, That we consider the business of the Board in the following order:

1. Present missions in Africa and other missions.
2. The field of labor.
3. Regular meetings, when, how, and where.
4. How should the corresponding secretary conduct the work?
5. Finance, W.H. McAlpine.

The following resolutions were adopted, and other business transacted as noted:

Whereas, It is historically true that the Republic of Liberia, with her adjacent equatorial countries, is the opened door to Central Africa; and

Whereas, more than 30,000 Americans, Liberians, and West Indians—many of whom are Christians and the Baptists forming an aggressive and ruling factor of them; and

Whereas, It is a fact that these Baptists have in Liberia a Missionary Convention with a Managing Board for carrying on a mission work directly among the heathen; and since it is a fact that the Liberian government with her armies would always give the surest possible protection to all Christian missions in or adjacent to her territory; and

Whereas, a union of the Baptists of Liberia is desirable, therefore be it

Resolved, That a committee of three be appointed to correspond with the Liberian Board, proposing cooperation and the terms.

—H.N. Bouey.

Ordered that the corresponding secretary ascertain from Rev. J.O. Hayes, Liberia, whether or not he has accepted the appointment of our Foreign Mission Board; if so, what date his salary commenced, and request him to remain in Liberia and not go to the Kingdom of Dahomy, as heretofore requested; also to confer with the Liberian Foreign Mission Board, proposing cooperation with them and the terms of such cooperation. On motion, Revs. W.W. Colley and H.N. Bouey, were made a committee to formulate plans to propose to the Liberian Board upon which they may work, and submit such plans to the Board, with the reply of the Liberian Board.

Resolved, That the communication of the Foreign Mission Board in Texas, asking the privilege of furnishing a man and his salary for the mission field in Africa, be referred to the corresponding secretary.

On motion the question of mission fields was laid upon the table until the next meeting.

Resolved, That the Foreign Mission Board meet monthly for the transaction of business.

On motion that corresponding secretary was allowed a clerk.

Resolved, That the salary of the corresponding secretary shall be one thousand dollars, out of which he shall pay his assistant, W.H. McAlpine.

On motion Revs. W.W. Colley and A. Binga were appointed a committee to count the money and turn it over to the treasurer. Adjourned.

REV. A. BINGA, Jr., of Va., President

W.R. PETTIFORD, of Ala., Act. Clerk

Circular Letter

To the Ministers, Churches, Associations, and Conventions of the United States of America.

In compliance with the request of the Baptist Foreign Mission Convention of the United States of America, we send forth this letter, praying that it may meet the approval of the brethren and inspire their hearts to work and give of their material substance in order that the heathen of Africa may have the gospel of the Son of God proclaimed to them. We have organized ourselves into a Baptist Foreign Mission Convention for the purpose of evangelizing and Christianizing the "Dark Continent." Our motto is, "Africa for Christ." Because of the peculiar relations existing between the Africo-Americans and the Africans in our fatherland, we regard this work preeminently the work of the American Negro. We do not hold or argue that this work is solely the work of the Negro; to do so would be doing wrong because of the fact that it would be contrary to the genius of Christianity. Still we hold that the circumstances surrounding the Negro point to him as the leader in the work. A careful consideration of the plans of salvation leads us to certain conclusions, and we do not think it amiss to state at least a few of them in this connection. 1) We believe the gospel is designed for the whole world. Believing this to be a fact we think that the members of our churches should expand their various views to the entire range of the purposes of God, and put forth efforts commensurate with the whole extent and amplitude of his designs. Whatever degree of strength, moral or financial, any of our churches possess, it should immediately be put forth for the good of Africa. This will increase the efficiency of the church by the law of reflex action. Christ died for all. A ransom for all is the ground upon which we base our claim of missions for all. "Ask of me, and I shall give thee the heathen for thine inheritance, and the uttermost parts of the earth for thy possession" (Psalm 2:8). This is his mediatorial claim to every man. This leads us to state: 2) That God wills to employ human instrumentalities for the carrying out of his design with regard to the salvation of the world. "Ye shall be witnesses unto me, both in Jerusalem and in all Judea," etc. The sons of Africa must believe on the Son of God. "They cannot call him of whom they have not heard." 3) We state that churches are to furnish the missionaries. No church can come up to the full measure of duty which does not keep the cause of missions and missionary enterprises constantly before the mind and near the heart of every individual member. Ethiopia is stretching out her hands unto God. The Macedonian cry comes to us from beyond the waters. We want all the local associations, state conventions, and all the churches, if possible, to ally themselves with the National Baptist Foreign Convention. Rest assured of this fact, no convention, association, or church, can excuse itself from this foreign mission work on the ground that it is engaged in doing home mission work. Home mission work or past efforts cannot excuse any convention, association, church, or individual member from the present obligations to the foreign mission work. We call upon all friends of the Saviour to cooperate with us in this great work of presenting the gospel to the heathen of Africa. Do not wait to see if the Convention is going to be a success, but come join us and help to make it a success. Any convention, association, church, society, or individual can at any time aid us in this undertaking by sending donations to the treasurer, Rev. Richard Spiller, No. 99 Scott St., Norfolk, Va., or corresponding secretary, Rev. W.W. Colley, No. 19 West Leigh St., Richmond, Va. Now is the time; to delay is to fail in carrying out the plans of the Master with regard to Africa. We cannot, we must not, fail in this work; Africa must be redeemed. The Negro must be the most prominent character in her redemption, therefore we call upon all the Baptist churches of all sections of this country to help us in the name of the Master and our common religion. Give now, give constantly, praying for the blessing of God to follow and crown the giving.

HOLY TRINITY BAPTIST CHURCH
Philadelphia, Pa.

Holy Trinity Baptist Church, Philadelphia, Pa., was organized in 1891 with 43 members. It now has a membership of over two thousand, and is energetic in its activities for denominational demands.—*Home and Foreign Fields.*

HISTORY OF THE FOREIGN MISSION CONVENTION
OF THE U.S. OF AMERICA

1. This Convention was organized November 24, 1880, First Baptist Church, Montgomery, Ala.; Rev. W.H. McAlpine of Marion,Ala., President; Rev. W.W. Colley of Virginia, Corresponding Secretary and Traveling Agent; Rev. E.G. Corprew of Virginia, Treasurer; Rev. J. Armistead, Secretary.

2. Second meeting in 1881, at Knoxville, Tenn., November 23rd-28th, Rev. W.H. McAlpine, President; Rev. W.W. Colley, Corresponding Secretary and Traveling Agent; Rev. R. Spiller of Virginia, Treasurer, Rev. J.M. Armistead, Secretary.

3. Third Annual Session in 1882, at Macon, Georgia, June 28th-July 1st., Rev. J.Q.A. Wilhite, President; W.W. Colley, Corresponding Secretary and Traveling Agent; Rev. R. Spiller of Virginia, Treasurer; W.R. Pettiford of Alabama, Clerk.

P.M. MORRIS, WILLIAM TROY, JOS. E. JONES

(From the Baptist Convention of North Carolina.)

On the 25th day of October 1879, in Cedar Grove Baptist Church, Newbern, North Carolina, this Convention endorsed and appointed Rev. J.0. Hayes as a missionary for Western Africa, and pledged itself to pay him annually a salary, and during the year 1880 Brother Hayes traveled and labored as missionary in the state, and raised what money he could for the work. He had been preparing for the work in Africa for a number of years. In October, 1880, he met the Convention in Warrenton, North Carolina, and urged upon the brethren of that body that they must do something to help him go to his chosen field of labor; thereupon the Convention appointed a delegation to attend the Foreign Mission Convention that was appointed in Montgomery, Alabama, on the 24th of November, 1880, to see if any money could be had towards helping to support him in his mission. Brother Hayes also sent a letter to the Convention. His letter was received, and the Board commenced making the arrangements, and early in 1881 the Sisters' Foreign Mission Society offered him one hundred dollars ($100) from the Society toward his salary, and he accepted their offer as an auxiliary to the Convention, and on the 15th of June, 1881, he sailed from New York and reached Liberia on the 23rd of July following.

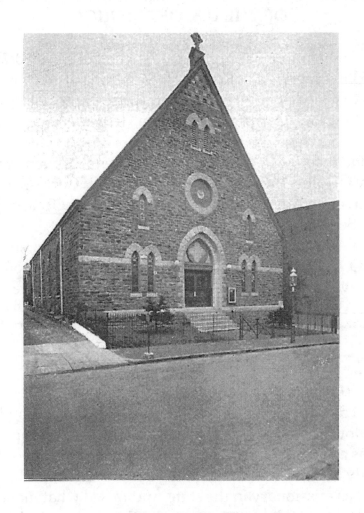

MT. ZION BAPTIST CHURCH

The Mt. Zion Baptist church of Germantown, Pa., was organized into a church in December 1884, with ten members. They were encouraged and helped by Cherry Street, the old mother church of Philadelphia. They called as their first pastor, Rev. Morton Winston, D.D., who had received his training from John Jasper of the Sixth Mt. Zion Baptist Church, Richmond, Va. Brother Winston grew with his church and became a power as a pastor and preacher. Mt. Zion grew to be the most outstanding church in that part of Philadelphia. Dr. Winston virtually gave his entire ministerial life of thirty-eight years to this church. His successor is the Rev. _____ Lamb, D.D., a man of pleasing personality, splendid Christian, and with all he is said to be a good pastor.

MINUTES

OF THE
Fourth Annual Session

OF THE
Baptist Foreign Mission Convention

OF THE
UNITED STATES OF AMERICA

HELD WITH THE
First Baptist Church, Manchester Virginia

SEPTEMBER 19-22, 1883

Rev. J.A. Foster, President, Montgomery, Ala.

Rev. R. Spiller, Treasurer, Queen St., Norfolk, Va.

Prof. J.E. Jones, Corresponding Secretary
No. 816 N. Second St., Richmond, Va.

Rev. Holland Powell, Travelling Agent, Hampton, Va.

Portsmouth, Virginia

Virginia Baptist Companion Publishing Company
1883

CONSTITUTION

Preamble and Constitution of the Baptist Foreign Mission Convention of the United States of America.

WHEREAS, It is our duty to advance the Kingdom of Christ, by going into all the world to preach his gospel to all kindred, tribes, and tongues; and,

WHEREAS, The benighted condition of more than three hundred millions of souls in Africa, now held in chains of the grossest idolatry, cannibalism, domestic slavery, and every species of superstition, claims our most profound attention and help; and,

WHEREAS, God has commanded us to "go," and is giving us all needed means for this work, therefore, we, the representatives from the various churches, Sunday schools, and missionary societies of the Baptist denomination in the United States of America, now assembled in Montgomery, State of Alabama, November 24, 1880, do most solemnly organize ourselves into a Convention for the above named object.

We do agree to the following Constitution:

Title

ARTICLE I. This Convention shall be known as the "Baptist Foreign Mission Convention of the United States of America."

Object

ARTICLE II. The object of this Convention shall be the diffusion of the gospel of Jesus Christ on the Continent of Africa and elsewhere abroad, as God may direct.

Membership

ARTICLE III. The membership of this Convention shall be annual or life:

Anyone who is a member of a regular Baptist church, in good standing may become an annual member of this Convention by paying the sum of one dollar annually.

Any one in good standing in a regular Baptist church may become a life member by paying the sum of twenty dollars at the time of enrollment, or five dollars for four years consecutively.

Membership by Representation

ARTICLE IV. All messengers from Baptist churches, Sunday schools, missionary societies, women's missionary societies, associations and conventions, shall be recognized as annual members of this Convention.

The basis of representation shall be one delegate from every church, and one for every one thousand members, or a fraction of the first thousand. They are to contribute according to their ability to the fund of this Convention. Each association of churches and each Convention may have two delegates; and one for every twenty-five hundred members or a fraction of the first twenty-five hundred, so contributing to the funds of this Convention.

Officers

ARTICLE V. The officers of this Convention shall be a president, and one vice president from each state represented in this body; a recording secretary, a statistical secretary, a corresponding secretary, and a treasurer, all of whom shall be elected at each annual meeting of this Convention, and hold their offices until their successors are chosen. All delegates shall be eligible to office.

Boards

ARTICLE VI. Twenty-seven judicious and experienced brethren, including all the officers of this Convention, shall form or constitute a Board of Foreign Missions, fifteen of whom shall constitute a Board of Managers, with full power to use all means necessary to secure the objects of this Convention during its recess, and said Board shall be responsible to this Convention for all of its actions. Members attending the meetings of this Convention, and leaving before the work of the Convention is finished and the Boards are appointed and organized, will not be put upon the Boards, as they will not be present to help organize said Boards and to attend to the business of this Convention.

Auditors

ARTICLE VII. Two auditors shall be elected out of the delegation present at the time of meeting, who shall audit the account of the treasurer and enter a certificate on his book.

Location

ARTICLE VIII. Richmond, Virginia, shall be the headquarters of the Foreign Mission Board, at or near which point, a quorum of the Board of Managers shall be located.

Work

ARTICLE IX. The Board shall make an annual report of all its transactions to this Convention, giving a full account of all its doings during the interval of the meetings of this Convention; giving the condition and prosperity of our mission fields; the number of missionaries employed by them; what salaries they receive, and such other information as may be in their possession as will assist the Convention in carrying out it objects. The Board shall not form any organic cooperation with any other body without the action of this Convention.

Bonds

ARTICLE X. The treasurer shall receive and hold all moneys, bills, deeds, and bequests belonging to this Convention [and] pay all orders issued by the Board at their regular meetings, signed by the president and secretary of the same. He shall, for the faithful discharge of his duties and the security of the Convention in its property, give such bonds as may be agreed upon by the Board; and his books may be free to the inspection of any officer of the Convention and any member of the Board. He shall make a quarterly report to the Board and an annual report to the Convention, giving an account of all moneys received and paid out by him, to whom, what for, and the general condition of the treasury.

Qualification

ARTICLE XI. All officers, boards, missionaries, and agents appointed by this Convention, or by the Foreign Mission Board, shall be members of some regular Baptist church in union with the churches composing this Convention.

Donation

ARTICLE XII. The bodies and individuals composing this Convention shall have the right to specify the object or objects to which their contributions shall be applied; but when no such specifications are made, the Convention shall make the appropriation at its discretion.

Meeting

ARTICLE XIII. The Convention shall meet at such time and place as shall be agreed upon at a preceding meeting which time shall not be later than the second Thursday in October. Special meetings of this Convention may be called by the president, at the request of the Foreign Mission Board.

Provision

ARTICLE XIV. This Constitution may be amended at any regular meeting of this Convention, by a two-thirds vote of the same; provided the change desired was presented in writing at a previous meeting.

———

ORDER OF BUSINESS

TIME OF MEETING—Meet each day at 9 a.m., adjourn at 1 p.m. Reassemble at 3 p.m., adjourn at 5 p.m. Meet at 8 p.m.

FIRST DAY'S SESSION

Wednesday, Sept. 19, 1883

9 a.m., Enrollment of Delegates. Appointment of the following committees:

1. On Permanent Organization.
2. On Finance.
3. On Communications and Ordinations.
4. On Religious Exercises for Sunday.
5. On Best Mode of Interesting, Organizing, and Carrying Forward the African Mission Work in all the States.
6. On Obituaries.
7. On Time and Place of Next Meeting.
8. On Printing and Publications.

During the appointments of the above committees, informal speeches may be made of ten minutes each by speakers on mission work in their respective states.

12 o'clock p.m. Report of Committees on Permanent Organization.

Night Session

8 o'clock p.m. Introductory Sermon by Rev. J. Smothers, assisted by W.H. McAlpine.

SECOND DAY'S SESSION

Thursday, September 20th

10 o'clock a.m. Report of Foreign Mission Board through the corresponding secretary and treasurer. Remarks by Rev. C.H. Payne.

Night Session

8 o'clock p.m. Sermon on Foreign Missions and Ordination by Rev. R.N. Countee, assisted by W.H. Wiley. Ordaining prayer by Rev. C.H. Corey, D.D. Charge by Rev. W.A. Brinkley. Presentation of Bible by Rev. A.H. Davis. Hand of fellowship by Rev. C. Johnson.

THIRD DAY'S SESSION

Friday, Sept. 21st

9 o'clock a.m. Consideration of report of Committee on Best Mode of Interesting, Organizing, and Carrying Forward the African Mission Work in all the States, opened by Rev. J.M. Armistead.

11 o'clock a.m. Consideration of reports of corresponding secretary and treasurer. Remarks by Rev. H.W. Bowen.

12:30 o'clock p.m. Hear report of Committee on Religious Exercises for Sunday.

8 o'clock p.m. Africa considered.

1. What the Religious World Is Doing for Her.
2. The Duty of the Colored Christians to Africa.
3. The Best way to Perform This Duty.

Discussion opened by W.W. Colley and William Troy, Sr.

FOURTH DAY'S SESSION

Saturday, September 22nd

9 o'clock a.m. Hearing Report of Committee on Finance. Remarks by Rev. John Marks.

10:35 o'clock a.m. Report of Committee on Time and Place of Next Meeting and Preachers.

11:30 o'clock a.m. Report of Committee on Printing and Publications, Rev. William T. Dixon.

12 o'clock m. Appointing Corresponding Messengers.

LIFE MEMBERS

Virginia

Rev. W.W. Colley .... Richmond
Rev. J.M. Armistead .... Portsmouth
Rev. A. Binga, Jr. .... Manchester
Mrs. Rebecca Binga .... Manchester
Rev. J.H. Presley .... Richmond

Tennessee

Rev. S.M. Dickerson .... Murfreesboro
Rev. W.P. Fennick .... Gallatin
Rev. A. Nickerson .... Chattanooga
Rev. J. Clemmons .... Knoxville
Deacon Robert Banks .... Knoxville
Deacon S. Campbell .... Knoxville

Texas

Rev. R.H. Boyd .... Palestine

Mississippi

Rev. R. Ramsey .... Meridian

Georgia

Rev. H. Williams .... Macon

ANNUAL MEMBERS

Virginia

Miss E.A. Black
Mrs. Kitty Wooden
Rev. C.H. Payne .... Richmond
Miss M.A. Thornton .... Hampton
Mrs. Emma Armistead .... Portsmouth
Rev. H.W. Dickerson .... Petersburg
Rev. J.A. Taylor .... Richmond
Mrs. A.L. Wallace .... Richmond
Mrs. Georgia Colley .... Richmond
N.H. Baynes .... Richmond
Deacon J. Warren .... Norfolk
Rev. R. Wells .... Richmond
Deacon H.H. Osborn .... Richmond
Rev. J.H.A. Cyrus .... Port Royal

Tennessee

Rev. R.N. Countee .... Memphis

Alabama

Rev. G.J. Brooks .... Selma

North Carolina

Rev. C. Johnson .... Raleigh

MINUTES

FIRST DAY-Morning Session

September 19th, 1883

1. The Baptist Foreign Mission Convention of the United States of America, held its Fourth Annual Session with the First Baptist Church, of Manchester, Va., commencing September, 1883.

The president, Rev. J.Q.A. Wilhite of Eufaula, Ala., being absent, vice-president, Rev. C. Johnson, of Raleigh, N.C., called the Convention to order at 10 o'clock a.m., and on invitation, Revs. P.F. Morris of Lynchburg, and R. Spiller of Norfolk, Va., conducted the devotional exercises.

2. The letter of welcome of the First Baptist Church, Manchester, Va., was read by the pastor, Rev. A. Binga, Jr., and responded to on behalf of the Convention by Rev. R.N. Countee, of Memphis, Tenn.

3. Special prayer was offered for the progress of African missions.

4. On motion of Rev. A. Binga, Jr., of Manchester, the following list of delegates was enrolled:

Alabama—First Baptist Church, Birmingham, Rev. W. R. Pettiford. St. Phillips Baptist Church, Selma, Rev. W.H. McAlpine and G.J. Brooks. Dallas County Association, Camden, Rev. D. Boyd; State Convention, Rev. J.Q.A. Wilhite.

Arkansas—North Arkansas and West Texas Baptist State Convention.

Georgia—African Baptist Church Sabbath School, Savannah, C .L. Delamotta.

North Carolina—First Baptist Church, Charlotte, Rev. A.A. Powell and Deacon W.P. French.

RALEIGH—Rev. C. Johnson. Cedar Grove Association, Rev. J.R.Cozart.

New York—New England Baptist Missionary Convention, Rev. W.T. Dixon.

Mississippi—Mississippi State Convention, Rev. J. Smothers, Port Gibson; Rev. G.W. Gale, Greenville; Rev. John Smith, Natchez; Rev. A.H. Davis, Edwards; General Association, Rev. R. Ramsey, Meridian; Second Baptist Church, F.M.S., Macon, Rev. H.W. Bowen Ladies Missionary Society, Columbus, Rev. T.L. Jordan; Missionary Society, Shuqualak, J.A. Sandas.

Louisana—New Orleans, Bazel Darsel, Dorseyville, Louisiana Southern Association, New Orleans, Rev. J. Marks, G.W. Walker, B. Dorsey.

Tennessee—East Tennessee General Association, Knoxville, Rev. C.C. Russell, Deacons R. Banks and J.W. Hamby.
Washington Street Baptist Church, Memphis, Rev. W.A. Brinkley.
Tabernacle Baptist Church Sabbath School, Memphis, Rev. R.N. Countee.
First Baptist Church, Woodland, Rev. H. Smith. First Baptist Church, Brownsville; Ministers and Deacons'
Meeting of West Tennessee, Rev. T.J. Searcy.

Virginia—First Baptist Church, Manchester, Rev. A. Binga, Jr., and Deacon J.H. Carter.
Second Baptist Church, Richmond, Rev. William Troy. A.T. Grimes, J. Johnson.
First Baptist Church, Hampton, Rev. Y. Jackson.
Southside Rappahannock Association, Rev. R. Berkeley.
Zion Baptist Church, Chesapeake, Rev. William Thornton.
Bethel Baptist Church, Gloucestor Co., Rev. J.W. Booth.
Zion Baptist Church, Portsmouth, Rev. J.M. Armistead.
Presley Missionary Society, Norfolk, Deacon J. Warren. Grove Baptist Church, Norfolk, Co., Rev. H. Powell.
Third Baptist Church, Female Missionary Society, Hampton, Rev. H.P. Weeden.
First Baptist Church, Williamsburg, Rev. J.M. Dawson, J. Carey.
Rock Branch Baptist Church, Dinwiddie Co., Rev. J.J. Jones.
Pleasant Grove Baptist Church, Prince George Co., P. Coleman, Mrs. R. Steward. Banister Association, Halifax Co., Revs. C.S. Coleman, J.T. Russell.
Fifth Baptist Church, Richmond, Rev. D. Tucker.

Colley Missionary Society, Richmond Institute, C.H. Carey, D.D.Long
Mountain Baptist Church, Campbell Co., Rev. J.B. Smith.
First Baptist Church, Sandy Bottom, Middlesex Co., Rev. J.W. Scott.
Virginia Baptist Sunday School Convention, Revs. A. Binga, Jr., J.E. Jones.
Buffalo Baptist Church, Halifax Co., Rev. D.W. Sims.
Mt. Zion Baptist Church, Staunton, Rev. R.H. Porter.
Berean Valley Association, Rev. G.W. Deskins, A. Jordan.
Ebenezer Baptist Church, Portsmouth, Rev. A.H. Lewis.
Jerusalem Baptist Church, Caroline Co., Rev. S. Todd.
Macedonia Baptist Association, Rev. G.W. Daggett.
Second Baptist Church, Manchester, Rev. D.E. Robinson, M. Goode.
Norfolk Union Baptist Association, Hon. P.J. Carter, Revs.
J.M. Dawson, Wm. Thornton.
St. Steven Baptist Church, Caroline Co., Rev. E. Freeman.
Baptist State Convention, Revs. J.H. Holmes, R. Wells, William
Troy, Sr.
Shiloh Association, Rev. J.E. Brown.
West Virginia—First Baptist Church, Quinnimont, Rev. M.S.G.
Abbott.
Mt. Olivet Baptist Association, Rev. W.H. Wiley.
Hasadiah Association, Revs. P.F. Morris, N. Jordan.
Valley Association, Rev. J. Jones.

5. On motion of J.M. Armistead, the Convention adjourned until 3
o'clock p.m. Benediction by the president.

Afternoon Session, 3 P.M.

6. The Convention was called to order by vice president, Rev.
C. Johnson, prayer by Rev. M. Elliott.

7. Minutes of the morning session read and approved.

8. On motion of A. Binga, Jr., the Convention took a recess for the
meeting of the Board until 6 p.m.

9. At 6 p.m., the Convention was called to order by vice president,
Rev. C. Johnson.

10. The following Order of the Business was adopted. (See Order of
Business.)

11. The vice president appointed the following committees:
On Permanent Organization—Revs. J. Smothers, J.M. Dawson, Wm. Troy,
A.A. Powell, C.L. Dellamatta, W.A. Brinkley, W.T. Dixon, C.C. Russell, J.
Marks, W.H. Wyley.

FIRST BAPTIST CHURCH
Montgomery, Alabama

This old building has been replaced by a large modern building. In this frame meeting house our Baptist forebears met and organized the convention whose fifthieth anniversary we celebrate August 1930.

On Ordination—Rev. R. Spiller, J.W. Boothe, A.H. Davis.

12. Adjourned. Prayer by Rev. John Jones. Evening Session, 8 o'clock P.M.

13. The Convention was called to order by vice president, Rev. C. Johnson, to listen to the Introductory Sermon by Elder A. Binga, Jr., at whose request, Rev. J. Smothers, of Mississippi, was substituted and after devotional exercises by Rev. W.T. Dixon of Brooklyn, N.Y., the vice president introduced Rev. J. Smothers, who proceeded to preach from I Cor. 3:11. Collection $10.15.

14. The chair appointed the following committees:

On Communications—Revs. W.W. Colley, J.M. Armistead, J.E. Jones, J.R. Cozart, R.H. Porter, A.H. Davis, C.H. Payne, T.L. Jordan, and Deacon Robert Banks.

On Religious Exercises for Sabbath—The pastors and deacons of Manchester and Richmond.

15. Adjourned. Benediction by Rev. W.T. Dixon.

SECOND DAY—Morning Session, 9 o'clock a.m.
September 20th, 1883

16. Vice president C. Johnson called the Convention to order. Devotional exercises were conducted by Rev. J.A. Foster of Alabama.

17. Minutes of the afternoon and evening sessions were read and approved.

18. The vice president appointed the following committees:

On Best Mode of Interesting, Organizing, and Carrying Forward the African Mission Work in the States.—Revs. J.A. Foster, W.W. Colley, H.P. Weeden, H.W. Bowen, A.A. Powell, W.T. Dixon, J.W. Hamby, M.S.G. Abbott, H.H. Osborne. *On Obituary*—Revs. John Jones, R. Ramsey, T.J. Searcy. *On Time and Place*—Revs. P.F. Morris, H. Smith, C.L. DeLamotta, W.H. McAlpine, J. Marks, C.H. Payne, A.A. Powell. *On Printing and Publication*—Revs. J.M. Armistead, W.W. Colley, A.A. Powell.

19. The Committee on Permanent Organization made the following report:

We, your committee, offer the following named brethren as officers for the ensuing year:

President—Rev. J.A. Foster, of Montgomery, Ala.

Secretary—Rev. J.M. Armistead, of Portsmouth, Va.

Assistant Secretary—Rev. R.N. Countee, of Memphis, Tenn.

Treasurer—Rev. R. Spiller, of Norfolk, Va.

Statistical Secretary—Rev. A.A. Powell, of Charlotte, N.C.
Corresponding Secretary—Rev. W.W. Colley, of Richmond, Va.
20. Adjourned. Prayer by Rev. F. Cook.

Afternoon Session, 3 P.M.
REPORT
OF FOREIGN MISSION BOARD
AND CORRESPONDING SECRETARY

We present to you our fourth annual report, which covers about thirteen months of work. We are glad to report that, notwithstanding the difficulties the Board has had to meet in organizing and carrying forward its work for Africa, that there has been and is manifested an interest in this work of African Missions, the root of which is running downward in the hearts of the ministers, members, associations, conventions, and states all the time, as they receive knowledge and light upon the subject of missions and the needs of three hundred millions of dying souls in Africa. Already the Board is receiving Christian men and women, with money and clothing for this great and grand work, but the time is not distant, when we shall have means by the thousands for the work among the Africans as we now have for the work among our people in southern states of America.

Progress of the Work in the United States

This feature of the work is difficult to measure, but we do report that through the corresponding secretary and general agent with the help of the assistant agents, Brethren J.H. Presley and J. Coles, also with the help of other good brethren including the editors of the little paper *African Missions,* and Brother C.H. Payne, who helped us to organize the State of West Virginia; through the above and our state Baptist papers, we have interested the ministry, we have stirred up the churches, organized missionary societies, brought into the Board money and clothing, brought new states into the Convention and ready to sail for Africa.

The states of Louisiana, Mississippi, North Carolina, West Virginia, and East Virginia all have organized state Foreign Mission Boards, which are doing a good work organizing their respective states. It will take at least three years or more to get all these states properly organized, after which the grandest results will follow, for the salvation of Africa. In the above states, the churches through their annual bodies are all organizing societies to help the foreign missions. Louisiana and Mississippi both have other ministers now waiting to be appointed to the active service in Africa. It is the intention of the United States F.M. Board to have each state through its own convention, etc., to carry on the work within themselves by the agent's appointment of their own state.

Recommendations for the Home Part of the Work

The Board of Foreign Missions recommends that whatever agents the state conventions may appoint be requested to organize societies in all the states to teach the churches how to give to help both home and foreign missions; also that the corresponding secretary secure the aid of all the ministers as far as possible directly and through their respective state conventions and state foreign mission and executive boards.

We recommend that every state organize a State Foreign Mission Board of its own state convention and that such state conventions and boards make their reports to this Foreign Mission Convention, and this United States Foreign Mission Board, through the year and at every annual meeting. We further recommend that all such agents and ministers, conventions, and boards, send to this Foreign Mission Board and its secretaries for any information about the African missions. We further recommend that all ministers and teachers of the different states, feeling their call to labor in Africa under this Convention, shall come recommended by the state conventions and boards of which they are members, by church relation.

We recommend that the blank form of Constitution now used by many of the states for missionary societies be printed on the back of the minutes of this Convention that the churches may organize from it.

We recommend that all ministers, missionary societies, churches, and friends subscribe for and read the *African Missions*. We further recommend that the corresponding secretary prepare a leaflet containing an appeal for help and urging the cooperation of all Baptists in the interest of African missions and have it bound in as many minutes of State Baptist organizations as possible; and that the corresponding secretary secure the use of the state papers as far as possible to publish the workings of the Board and Convention.

Special Help in the Work

With the approval of the Board, your corresponding secretary has been publishing at his expense a paper called, *African Missions*, which paper has gone into the hands and homes of from seven to fifteen hundred, monthly; thereby increasing the interest in African missions a thousandfold. This paper has cost your corresponding secretary, out of his own pocket to date $127. The corresponding secretary pays his private secretary, Rev. Wm. Troy, the sum of $60 per year at present. While organizing the work of missions in the state of Mississippi during this present year, the secretary found it to be absolutely necessary for the success of the work to employ Revs. D. Webster and A.H. Dixon, ministers of the above state at cost of $75, out of the secretary's pocket, making a total of $262. The amount is found in the subjoined table.

Work of the Assistant Agents

Brethren Presley and Coles, notwithstanding the labors of these brethren have been short and confined to the State of Virginia, yet the grand amount of good done may be seen by the following statements:— Rev J.H. Presley collected $446.14 as three months' work; converts, 122. Bro. J.J. Coles collected $101.14.

Work in Africa: After supporting Rev. J.0. Hayes as our missionary in Africa for more than one year, the Board withdrew its support in January last, Brother Hayes having written the Board that he had decided to work under some other board or person. He also wrote the Board that he would return the last money ($125) sent him, but has never done so. Very soon after the above action of both Bro. Hayes and the Board, he again changed his mind and has been writing every month, asking the Board to reappoint him. He is now willing to work for us. Rev. James 0. Hayes has been under the appointment of the Board for six months during the conventional year just passed, for which time he has made no report of his work done for us among the heathen. We believe, however, that Bro. Hayes has fully seen his mistake (this he has continued to write the Board), and that possibly if he is appointed for another year, he would succeed as our missionary. We recommend the appointment of Rev. J.H. Presley and wife as active missionaries to Africa, and that they sail by the twentieth of December 1883. The Board also recommended Brethren J.J. Coles and H. McKenney to study in the Liberia College as prospectus missionaries.

Amounts collected by the agents are as follows:

Mississippi
Baptist Church, R. Ramsey. $14.25

Baptist Church, (White). 3.00
Mt. Pleasant Church, H.W. Harris. 2.65
Jerusalem Baptist Church, B.J. McElroy. 4.35
Antioch Baptist Church, G. Hunter. 4.00
Concord Baptist Church, G. Hunter. 17.30
Editon Church, W.F. Blackwell. 1.00
White Baptist Church, J.H. Crundy 7.15
First Baptist Church, A. Lewis 11.75
White Church, Rev. Killis 55
Mt. Hope Baptist Church, M. Dunbar 14.70
F.M. Society, Mrs. A. Black 3.50
M.E. Church, James Parks 12.70
McCaughin, Miss Adele 1.00
Zion Baptist Church, Wm. Howell 9.00
Rose Hill Baptist Church, R. Pollard 7.60
Pres. Seminary, Charles Ayer 5.00
First Baptist Church, H. Bailey 2.70
Colley Missionary Society, Mrs. E.V. Mason 5.00
Presley Missionary Society, Mrs. Jacobs 2.80
Pilgrim Baptist Church, A. Goodman 18.30
Baptist Church, J.H. Nicklas 12.30
White Baptist Church, L.M. Stones 4.45
Baptist Church School, J.H. Nicklas 50
N.S.M. Society, J.H. Sanders 6.55
White Baptist Church, Mississippi Association 3.35
Baptist Church, Deacons' Association 4.35
Second Baptist Church, H.W. Brown 23.00
P.M. Society, J.H. Sanders 1.50
Johnson, Mr. Colber 1.50
M.E. Church, G. Brooks 6.80
Mariah Baptist Church, A.J. Bush 6.00
Mt. Zion Church, Mrs. Annie Nickolson 5.00
Zion Hill Church, H. Bryant
White Church, Mr. Churchill 25
Third Baptist Church, T.L. Jordan 36.75
Boldwyn Baptist Church, I.S. Hampllen 50
Boldwyn Baptist Church, A.W. Silas 1.50
Mission Society, St. Paul 11.35
Deacon Morris Watson 1.85

Oak Grove Church, D.C. Mitchell 10.90
St. John Baptist Church, I. Coleman 5.05
Baptist Church, Henry Green 11.35
M.E. Church, D.W. Calvert 8.00
Baptist Church, W. Chiles 3.65
C. Hill Baptist Church, John Leigh...................... 2.05
Black Jack, T. Lesone 16.05
16 Section Baptist Church, Carveline 2.75
Mt. P. Baptist Church, Robert John 2.50
Baptist Church, McAlerter 19.50
Daniel Baptist Church, L.T. McAlarter 11.75
New Baptist Church, R. Lewis 21.70
Ohio Second Baptist Church, A. Henderson 14.65
P. Valley Baptist Church, McMillian 5.15
C.H., J.H. Sykes 1.75
T.C. Baptist Church, S. Peterson 10.00
Olin Baptist Church, John Lyde 13.00
St. James Baptist Church, S. Gain 3.00
Baptist Church, Jack James 28.45
School, R.J. Larory 3.80
F. View Baptist Church, George King 8.00
P. Grove Baptist Church, Joe J. Lawrence 15.80
Brownridge Baptist Church, John Lyde 12.10
N. Cedar Baptist Church, Peter Minor 7.50
Abbott Baptist Church, J.W. Eyele 12.50
S. Baptist Church, S. Peterson 7.75
Mt. Baptist Church, J.W. Eyele 7.55
F.M. Society, J. Hudson 1.20
Mt. Horrot Baptist Church, E.G. Bland 18.70
State Convention, G.W. Gayles 14.10
A.M.E. Church, O.A.L.
P.G. Baptist Church, C. Hunter 12.75
Colley and Presley Missionary Society, Mrs. Jacobs, Pres. 14.25
Help, H.P. Jacobs 5.80
Zion Baptist Church, John Smith 11.00
P. Baptist Church, E. Dickerson 7.05
                                              Total $642.25

Louisiana

Baptist State Convention, John Marks $23.10
                                              Total $23.10

Ohio

Mount Mariah Church, S. Nanly $2.25
P. Creek Baptist Church, I. Bryant 11.05
Total $13.30

North Carolina

E. Dotson $1.00
Baptist Church, J.0. Crosby 19.25
Baptist Church, W.M. Reid 4.03
Total $24.28

Virginia

First Church, J.M. Dawson $17.85
Third Church, P.H. Weeden 2.15
Zion Church, A.H. Cumber 5.40
Third Church, W.D. Dickerson 2.07
Grove Church, H. Powell 1.54
Ashland, W.P. Clark 8.00
Union Church, C.C. Kemp 1.70
Divine Church, M. Bowler 2.90
Suffolk Church, A.H. Lewis 23.00
Smithfield Church, A.C. Green 13.75
Berkley Church, Rev. Lewis 7.68
Atlantic City Church, M. Bowler 7.45
Association, Hasadiah 16.11
Mossing Grove Church 5.33
Total $127.15

West Virginia

Association, C.H. Payne $18.42
Zion Church, A.M. Thomas 15.05
First Church, D. Streetton .... .50
Baptist Church, E. Edmonson 1.00
H. Robinson .... .50
Society, T.H. Norman 34.60
First Church, H. Rice 8.00
W.J. Pawish 1.00
John Stern 5.00
White Sulphur Springs, W.H. Wiley 10.58
First Church, W.H. Dunning .... .50
Zion Church, C.H. Payne 14.00
White Church, T.C. Johnson 9.17

S. Goodlove .... .50
C. Bank 1.00
J.M. Jasper .... .50
First Church, N. Bennett 20.60
M.E. Church, J.G. Taylor 6.50
Q.K. Smith 5.75
White S.M.E. Church 12.00
Quinniment, Rev. Abbott 4.30
Baptist Church, W. H. Wyley 1.30

Washington, D.C.

Missionary Society, Julia A. Pierce 1.30
   Total $171.27
   Total collected by the corresponding secretary $950.73
                                                     389.31

63. The Treasurer submitted the following report which was adopted: Treasurer in account with the Baptist Foreign Mission Convention of the United States of America from June 30th, 1882—September 19th, 1883.

To balance in hand of treasurer. $350.10
To amount received at last Convention 281.07
July 17th, Seyrien Baptist Church, Texas 5.25
July 17th, Seyrien Sunday School 2.00
August 7th, Rev. W.H. McAlpine, Selma, Alabama 30.50
September 4th, First Baptist Church, Birmingham, Alabama . 5.00
September 4th, Woman's Missionary Society, Alabama 2.00
September 4th, Sunday School First Church, Birmingham, Ala. . 2.00
September 4th, Rev. J.B. Poole, Buffalo Springs, Va. 23.88
September 18th, Zion Hill Baptist Church, Seguin, Texas 3.00
September 18th, Springfield Baptist Church, Webster Co., Miss. ... 5.00
September 18th, Zion Missionary Baptist Church, Winona, Miss. 7.00
October 27th,.Rev. C. Johnson, Raleigh, N.C. 75.00
October 26th, Eastern Fork Assn., Castalian Springs, Tenn. ... 10.00
October 26th, Rev. W.F. Fennick on life membership 3.00
November 27th, Seguin Baptist Church, Seguin, Texas 3.75
1883 May 30th, St. Phillips Sunday School, Selma, Alabama .. 5.00
July 31st, Coal Valley Baptist Church Society, West Va. 20.30
August 26th, Rev. C. Johnson, N.C., for Rev. J.0. Hayes 75.00
1882 Nov. 10th, From Bethesda Baptist Church 5.00
                                Total received $893.85

1882 June 30th, By amount paid Rev. J.0. Hayes, salary for 3
months $125.00
1882 June 30th, Paid to Rev. W.W. Colley for printing 2.00
1882 June 30th, Paid to the order of D. Webster 8.00
1882 June 30th, Paid to the order of W.R.Pettiford,Secretary . . 30.00
1882 June 30th, Paid to the order of Edward Lewis, Sexton . . . 3.00
1882 June 30th, Paid to the order W.W.Colley printing & tr. . 196.35
1882 August 11th, Paid to the order of Prof. J.E. Jones for
travelling 5.10
1882 August 11th, Paid to the order of Rev. R. Spiller for
stationery 8.00
1882 August 11th, Paid to the order of Rev. W.W. Colley 200.00
1882 September 15th, Paid to Rev. R.A. Pettiford for printing
minutes 90.00
1882 January 17th, Paid to Rev. W.W. Colley, salary 150.00
Total paid out $817.45
Balance in hand of treasury, including $17 due by Rev. E. G.
Corprew, former treasurer . . . . $ 76.45

RICHARD SPILLER, Treasurer

64. On motion, Revs. W.H. McAlpine, Wm Troy, and F. Cook, were appointed to nominate a corresponding secretary.

65. The Committee on Printing, reports as follows, which was approved:

We, your Committee on Printing, recommend that the secretary have 300 copies of minutes printed and distributed among the organizations here represented.

J.M. ARMISTEAD, W.W. COLLEY, H. POWELL
Committee.

66. The Committee on Nominating a Corresponding Secretary presented the names pf Rev. D. Morris of Lynchburg, and Rev. C.H. Payne of Richmond, Va.; and on balloting, Rev. C.H. Payne was elected.

67. On motion, the following named brethren were appointed to preach the next annual sermons:

Introductory Sermon—Rev. A. Binga, Jr. of Manchester, Va.; alternate—Rev. John Marks, of New Orleans, La.

Missionary Sermon—Rev. W. T. Dixon, of Brooklyn, N. Y.; alternate—Rev. W. A. Brinkley, of Memphis, Tenn.

THE EVERGREEN BAPTIST CHURCH

This aggressive, up-to-date and front-line church was called together by Rev. Aaron Wells and organized August 16, 1878. There were only a handful then. Following him came Israel A. Carter, its second pastor, who for a number of years molded the character and shaped the destiny of this great church. In 1923, Rev. J.E. Evans became pastor. Under his leadership the old frame church gave way to a new building and at a more desired location. And so Evergreen has continued to spread and grow until today it is one of the most aggressive churches not only in Louisiana, but in all our country. Its pastor, from his godly life and prepared sermons, is constantly injecting great enthusiasm for kingdom advancement in this great congregation. As an official in this National Baptist Convention, no distance is too long, no expense too great but what Evergreen sees that the pastor, Rev. J.E. Evans, is on hand when denominational counsellors are needed.

68. The following were appointed as messengers to corresponding bodies—Rev. W.T. Dixon of N.Y., to the New England Baptist Convention and the rest of the delegates to the state organization of the states represented by them.

69. Rev. W.T. Dixon offered the following resolution which was approved:

Resolved, That for the generous hospitality of the First Baptist Church of Manchester, Va., and their dear pastor, as well as the congregation, choir, and friends, we hereby tender our most sincere and grateful thanks for their kind entertainment of our Convention.

Resolved, That for the faithful reports of meeting in the Richmond Whig, we hereby offer our satisfaction and gratitude for recognition in their columns of the same.

Resolved, That for the constant and cheerful service of the sexton of the church we give him the sum of eleven dollars.

Resolved, That the packages of goods received for distribution among the heathen in Africa be duly acknowledged in our minutes, and humble thanks are hereby tendered the donors of the same, remembering that they who give to the poor, lend unto the Lord.

70. On motion of R. Spiller, the secretary was allowed $27.50 for compiling the minutes.

71. On motion the sexton and ice bill were ordered paid.

72. On motion of W.T. Dixon, the Convention adjourned to meet with the First Baptist Church, Meridian, Mississippi, Rev. R. Ramsey, Pastor, Wednesday before the fourth Lord's Day in September, 1884. Prayer by Rev. H.H. Mitchell.

A.J. FOSTER, President

J.M. ARMISTEAD, Secretary

Appendix

FORM OF CONSTITUTION FOR MISSIONARY SOCIETIES

OUR MOTTO—*"Go Ye Therefore, and Teach All Nations"*

Whereas, it is the duty of every Baptist (colored) in the United States to give to the support of home and foreign missions, therefore, be it

Resolved, That we organize ourselves into a Missionary Society for the above objects and adopt the following Constitution:

Article 1. This society shall be known as the Baptist Missionary Society of the _____ Baptist Church of_____.

Article 2. The object of this society shall be to raise means to send the gospel of God to the perishing heathen of Africa, and to sustain the educational and state mission work.

Article 3. The officers of this society shall be a president, treasurer, recording and corresponding secretaries, whose duty shall be the same as are common to such officers. The officers shall be elected annually, from among the male and female members of the same.

Article 4. The business meetings of this society shall be monthly. The monthly fee shall be _____ cents. The money shall be divided between the educational, state, and African missions.

Article 5. This society shall have missionary sermons preached on every 5th Lord's Day, and oftener if possible, that the members may be informed and interested in mission work—the collection of that day to go for missions. The members are requested to secure and read such books and papers as will furnish information on missions generally.

Article 6. The president shall have power to call meetings whenever in his judgment the interest of the society demands them.

In case the president or any officer neglects his or her duty, any member of the society shall have power to call a meeting and carry forward the work of the society. In case an officer is absent the president or acting president may appoint. In case the officer is dead or resigns, the society shall elect.

Article 7. The money raised by this society shall be used for no other purpose than those named in the constitution.

Article 8. Persons who are not members of any church, may become members of this society, and nine members, including officers, shall constitute a quorum with power to act.

Article 9. A printed RECEIPT shall be given for all moneys sent to the Educational, State, and Foreign Mission Board, or to agents in the name of the Convention.

OFFICERS FOR THE ENSUING YEAR

President, Rev. J.A. Foster, Montgomery, Alabama.
First Vice President, Rev. W.T. Dixon, Brooklyn, New York.
Second Vice President, Rev. J.M. Dawson, Williamsburg, Va.
Third Vice President, W.A. Brinkley, Memphis, Tennessee.
Fourth Vice President, Rev. W.H. Wyley, White Sulphur Springs,West Virginia.
Fifth Vice President, Rev. C. Johnson, Raleigh, North Carolina.
Sixth Vice President, Rev. R. Ramsey, Meridian, Mississippi.

Seventh Vice President, Rev. J.W. White, Augusta, Ga.

Eighth Vice President, Rev. G.W. Walker, New Orleans, Louisiana.

Ninth Vice President, Rev. S.H. Smith, Fort Worth, Texas.

Tenth Vice President, Rev. R.D. Dunbar, Jacksonville, Florida.

Eleventh Vice President, Rev. F. Hooks, Pine Bluff, Arkansas.

Twelfth Vice President, Rev. W.R. Pettiford, Birmingham, Alabama.

Thirteenth Vice President, Rev. D.M. Pierce, Darlington, South Carolina.

Secretary, Rev. J.M. Armistead, Portsmouth, Virginia.

Assistant Secretary, Rev. R.N. Countee, Memphis, Tennessee.

Statistical Secretary, Rev. A.A. Powell, Charlotte, North Carolina.

Corresponding Secretary, Rev. J.E. Jones, N.P. 816 North 2nd St., Richmond, Virginia.

Travelling Agent, Rev. H. Powell, Hampton, Virginia.

Treasurer, Rev. R. Spiller, Norfolk, Virginia.

FOREIGN MISSION BOARD

President, Rev. A. Binga, Jr., Manchester, Va.; Secretary, Prof. J.E. Jones, Richmond, Va.

Rev. W.H. McAlpine, Selma, Alabama; Rev. Wm. Troy, Richmond, Va.; Rev. W.A. Green, Raleigh, N.C.; Rev. C.L. DeLamatta, Savannah, Ga.; Rev. R.D. Dunbar, Jacksonville, Fla.; Rev. H.N. Bouey, Selma, Ala.; Rev. R. Ramsey, Meridian, Miss.; Rev. C.C. Russell, Knoxville, Tenn.; Rev. Thomas Luke, Shreveport, La; Rev. S.D. Smith, Fort Worth, Texas; Rev. J.A. Taylor, Richmond, Va.; Dr. Fields Cook, Alexandria, Va.; Rev. H. Williams, Jr., Petersburg, Va.; Rev. R. Spiller, Norfolk, Va.; Rev. J.W. Patterson, Danville, Va.; Rev. E.C. Morris, Helena, Ark.; Rev. W.W. Colley, Richmond, Va.; Rev. P.F. Morris, Lynchburg, Va.; Rev. John Jones, Liberty, Va.; J.E. Farrar, Richmond, Va.; Rev. J.H. Holmes, Richmond; Va.; Rev. J.J. Smith, Concord Depot, Va.; Rev. E.K. Love, Thomasville, Ga.; Rev. R. Griggs, Dallas, Texas; Rev. J.W. White, Augusta, Ga.; Rev. J.H. Armistead, Portsmouth, Va.

Rev. W.W. Colley and wife, Rev. J.H. Presley and wife, missionaries; and Rev. J.J. Coles of Va., Rev. H. McKenney, of Miss., sailed for Africa, December 1st, 1883, on the Bark Monrovia, at 9:45 o'clock a.m.

Chapter VII

"The fathers who planned and laid the foundation of this organization built wiser than they knew, and the reorganization which took place at Atlanta, Ga., was really the fruit of that first planting, and was the active beginning of the work of the Negro Baptists in a systematic way. Prior to that time, the activities of Negro Baptists were almost wholly confined to making disciples and building churches." E. C. Morris, 1916.

WORKING AGENCIES
OF THE NATIONAL BAPTIST CONVENTION

The National Baptist Convention is working harmoniously with all the great standardized Christian organizations throughout the whole world.

Negro Baptists who believe in God, in their own possibilities, and who love the right, are uniting in a bigger and better program for the glory of God, the development of the group and the good of the entire world.

THE FOREIGN MISSION BOARD—organized November, 1880, following the founding of the Foreign Mission Convention, the oldest of the Convention's working agencies, Rev. A. Binga, Jr., was its first chairman, has had an interesting history. Rev. W.W. Colley of Virginia was its first corresponding secretary and traveling agent. He served three years as secretary. Rev. J. Anderson Taylor, likewise of the Old Dominion State, succeeded him as financial secretary or field agent, when Rev. Colley who taught the Negro Baptists that they could organize in a national body, and who led the way, went to Africa as their first missionary in 1883. A leading spirit in the original body, Prof. J.E. Jones, was chosen for the work of corresponding secretary of the Board. The personnel of this Board continued unchanged for the greater part of the next decade. In 1893 the Rev. J.J. Coles, who for thirteen years had served as a missionary in West Africa, on his return to the States, was elected at the Washington, D.C. meeting of the Convention, which was held in the Vermont Avenue Baptist Church, to the position of field secretary in place of Rev. Taylor, who resigned to enter the pastorate. But Rev. Coles had come back to America with a constitution weakened by the fevers and rigors of the climate in the African bush; he fell sick and soon after died, but his wife, Mrs. Lucy A. Coles, who still lives in Richmond, Va., by request of the Board carried on his work until the next session of the Convention which took place in Montgomery, Ala., in 1894. Rev. Lucius M. Luke was elected by the Board as field agent of the Foreign Mission Board in January 1892, and later on in September, 1895, at Atlanta, Ga., was made its corresponding secretary in the reorganization. His term of office was destined to be short-lived. He was in the midst of preaching service in the Fifth Street Baptist Church, Louisville, Ky., when he was suddenly stricken with a mortal illness. He died that day, December 30, 1895, having served only three months. A strange coincidence in connection with the circumstances is that he was expounding the gospel with "The Day of Reckoning" as a subject, from the text: "How much owest thou my Lord?" when he was summoned to his reward. Few who ever heard his earnest plea for Africa can forget it.

It was February 13, 1896, when Rev. L.G. Jordan, then pastor of the Union Baptist Church, Philadelphia, was elected corresponding secretary of the Foreign Mission Board. The new secretary entered upon the work burdened with many handicaps. To begin with, the $13.00 left in the treasury of the Board by Dr. Luke had been spent by the Board at Louisville in scattering announcements of the election of and what would be expected of the new secretary. The Union Baptist Church, bidding its pastor Godspeed in his new undertaking, contributed $11.00 toward its support. Besides this there was a meager office equipment consisting of the following articles left by Dr. Luke for the carrying on of the task: one office stove, one small antiquated writing desk, three chairs, and one minute book, which was turned over to the department by a former corresponding secretary *pro tem*, Mrs. Lucy A. Coles. As has been stated elsewhere, the former members of the Board which had been located at Richmond, Va., had become offended and failed to report at the Montgomery or Atlanta meetings. Consequently there were no records of previous work available either as a guide to future activities or as reference.

For nearly twenty-six years Secretary Jordan labored to bring the needs of the millions of benighted non-Christians in Africa to the attention of their brethren in America, and in pursuance of his duty crossed the ocean four times on personal trips of investigation made to Africa, and two to South America and the West Indies, and six to Europe in the interest of our work. In 1904, Secretary Jordan organized the Native Association in South Africa and established proper relations between the English Baptists working in that part of the continent and the National Baptist Convention. In 1906, the secretary secured government recognition and standing for our missionaries in South America and in three of the West India[n] [i]slands. In 1915 accompanied by Dr. C.H. Parrish, a former chairman of the Board, he visited the scenes in Jamaica where George Leile performed his marvelous ministration to West Indian slaves, in token of which the monument in honor of Leile was erected 1916 at Savannah, Ga. In 1917, against the wishes of his board, he made a perilous trip to West Africa, despite the threatened dangers of submarine warfare, taking with him three missionaries. While on this visit, March 11th, he dedicated the Bible and Industrial Mission building at Grand Bassa, the largest and most costly at that time of any of the edifices at any of the stations in West Africa operated by the National Baptist Convention. It was during this visit also that President Daniel E. Howard of the Republic of Liberia caused the Liberian government to express its appreciation of the work which the secretary had done and was still doing to benefit Africa. In an impressive ceremony at Monrovia, the capital of the Republic, he was made "Knight Commander of the Liberian Humane Order of African Redemption," an organization which looks forward to the day when the Dark Continent shall come into her own and was given a beautiful medal as a token of recognition. During the term of office of Secretary Jordan more than two hundred students were brought to this country from Africa and other lands to receive training, and a gratifying number have gone back home after graduation or training to aid in the spread of the gospel in their native lands. Some of these students were placed in one of our Baptist schools, some in another, until at one time, there was a foreign student training for service in the majority of the states in our great Union. During Secretary Jordan's incumbency, the board was enabled to purchase nearly a thousand acres of land and to build substantial brick buildings thereon for churches and homes in Central Africa; a valuable lot in Cape Town on which a modern school building of stone and concrete has been built with forty different church sites in South Africa, besides 670 acres which are being put to good use at Suehn, Grand Bassa, Royesville, and other points in West Africa, by means of coffee trees, eleven thousand of which were planted at the one time, and palm trees and similar profitable products. The coffee plants, for instance, bearing three crops each year and bearing continuously for a period of fifty years; the many varieties of palms. In Central America, good buildings at Turrialba, Madre de Dios, Port Limon, and other points in Costa Rica bear witness of the work accomplished in that field.

After nearly twenty-six years of unremitting toil without the respite of even a single vacation (although vacations had more than once been suggested and even voted by both the Foreign Mission Board and the National

Baptist Convention for Secretary Jordan), he found himself on the verge of a breakdown. Tired mature revolted, and over the united protest of his brethren, he resigned his post. As a token of the high esteem which the National Baptist Convention bore for the retiring secretary, upon the recommendation of the Foreign Mission Board, the National Baptist Convention at the Chicago session in 1921 voted that Dr. Jordan should have the honorary title of Secretary Emeritus (the first occasion in the life of the Convention where this title has been bestowed), besides a pension of $1200 per year during his natural life. It should be stated here, however, that Dr. Jordan regularly donates one-half of this sum, $600, to the work of foreign missions, by contributing it to the treasury of the Board through Secretary East, as soon as it is tendered to him.

Dr. W.T. Amiger, who served as superintendent of Mission Work in Africa for three years, had this to say concerning the prosecution and conduct of the foreign work of the National Baptist Convention: "So well had the work been planned, and so strategically located by Dr. Jordan that after four years, since he turned the affairs of the Board to a younger man, his successor has not been put to the necessity of building a single house." Dr. J.C. Austin, Chairman of the Foreign Mission Board, in an address before the Sunday School and B.Y.P.U. Congress at Wichita, Kansas, in 1925, said, "We should love and revere forever Dr. L.G. Jordan, who through sweltering blood and tears blazed the way for twenty-six years on the Foreign Missionary field."

After tendering his resignation, Dr. Jordan made the motion that Rev. J.E. East be elected in his stead. Rev. East was directly a product of the Foreign Mission Board in the following manner: He was the only convert in a meeting conducted by the evangelist, J.W. Carr, was baptized by Dr. George B. Howard into the membership of Ebenezer Baptist Church, Pittsburgh, Pa., who for many years represented Pennsylvania as a member of our Foreign Mission Board. Also Rev. East was helped through the Virginia Seminary and College and through the Nyseck Mission School of New York by Dr. W. W. Brown, a successor to Dr. Howard, who was also a member of our Foreign Mission Board. Dr. Brown to this day delights to say:

"When I was pastoring in Roanoke, Va., back in 1898, Brother Jordan visited me bringing John Chilembwe from Central Africa. The coming of that African into my home brought me face to face as never before with my responsibility for the redemption of all the world and especially Africa. In my willingness to, and fear not to obey God , I owe the large places God has allowed me to fill. As my eyes were opened more and more, I found no debt on the church I pastored nor any amount due me, so compelling, that I turned aside from having my church pay the salary, in part or in whole of a missionary since 1907."

With the background of this fine preparation, Rev. East had gone as a missionary to South Africa and worked for the Foreign Mission Board of the National Baptist Convention; he was therefore well acquainted with the field; its needs and outlook. Enthusiastic and devoted to the missionary enterprise, Dr. East has justified the expectations of the denomination in appointing him for the work. He was elected in September 1921, and in the nine years of his service has so rallied the churches that contributions to the work have grown from $41,337.14, donated in 1921, to over $115,000 as per his report in 1929.

We must not close this account of the "Senior Board" of our Convention without mentioning that while we have never received aid from any of the organizations of our White brethren for foreign mission work, yet we have had some noteworthy donations from individuals of the other race. In 1910 a Mr. M.C. Treat for three consecutive years gave us donations averaging $1200 per year, to be applied on the salaries of the missionary, Rev. D.E. Murff, South Africa, and a native worker, Rev. John Chilembwe, British Central Africa. The following year (1911) Miss Caroline G. Ewen of New York gave the board by will the sum of $50,000, with five annuitants or beneficiaries to be provided for therefrom. The metropolitan newspapers, in an effort to belittle the work of the conscientious Baptists and to disparage the necessity of saving Africa, featured this legacy in this manner: "A crazy woman left by will, $75,000 for a 'Cats' Home and Senegambians—with all the needy children of the city left out." This will in question stipulated that the five pensioners were to receive from $300 to $600 each year from this fund, but our attorney advised that should we secure this amount, these payments would soon consume the principal. Just at this point a nephew of our deceased friend instituted a suit to break the will, alleging mental incapacity of his aunt. Fearing that this will might be broken, we were advised to compromise with the nephew. Accordingly a settlement for 15% was effected. The five annuitants ranging in ages from forty to sixty-five years were next bargained with and the sums paid them were from $1,500 to $6,000. When the whole transaction had been cleared up, it was discovered that the Foreign Mission Board was to receive about $11,000, and that was paid at intervals through a period of ten years. However, the gift enabled us to pay all outstanding obligations on our splendidly equipped headquarters at 701 S. 19th Street, Philadelphia, without the cost of one cent to the Board. The building was dedicated under the name of "The Caroline G. Ewen Building." In 1925, more than

OLIVET BAPTIST CHURCH
Illinois

This is one of the oldest churches in Illinois, and was first known in Harmon Court as far back as 1888. From there they moved to 27th and Dearborn, and it was our privilege to march with them beside the present pastor in a body from there to their present church home. some of the strongest men in the Baptist ministry served them; men like Richard DeBaptist, H. H. White, J. F. Thomas and E. J. Fisher, before they secured Dr. L. K. Williams, the present pastor. The activities of this church are regarded as the best organized among our churches and having an enrolled membership of more than 10,000. It is claimed to be the largest protestant church in the world. The house in which they worship was the leading Baptist church among White Baptists for a number of years, in which some of the great characters in this and the old world preached. Dr. P. S. Henson was possibly the last pastor before it was purchased by Olivet.

a third of the entire amount was paid to Secretary J.E. East.

The Foreign Mission Board is an active member of the Foreign Mission Conference of North America and Canada, which body meets yearly and enjoys the fellowship and inspiration which comes from information about mission work the world over. A worthwhile monthly magazine, *The Mission Herald*, founded March 1896, is published in the interest of missions. Yearly the work of this Board enlarges its scope and influence. They stress the Pauline plan for raising funds for the work, as set out in I Corinthians. Great efforts were made for the building of a hospital in Liberia and have been realized. Also the idea for the establishment of a great central industrial school in West Africa has met with wonderful response from the pastors and people of our denomination.

THE HOME MISSION BOARD was organized in 1895, and is in cooperation with the Southern Baptist Convention, by whose aid it maintains workers in all of the southern states. The American Baptist Home Mission Society cooperates with us in maintaining workers to look after the needs of our people in the states North, East, and West. With a large number of competent workers, it is enlarging its work, under the management of Secretary A.D. Williams, D.D., of Atlanta, Ga.

THE EDUCATIONAL BOARD, organized in 1893, is in cooperation with the Southern Baptists, and is now projecting the National Baptist Theological Seminary in Nashville, Tenn., which opened its doors in September 1924. What Rochester and Crozer Seminaries are to the Northern Baptists, and what the Southern Baptist Seminary is to the Southern Baptists, under God, the American Baptist Theological Seminary will be to Negro Baptists. Through the untiring efforts of a member of the Southern Convention, Dr. O.L. Hailey, a man of large faith in the future of our group, and a firm believer in the ultimate triumph of the gospel, this seminary is a donation from the Southern Baptist Convention. Many of those who organized and crystallized sentiment for that gift, like the late Drs. Burleson, Gambel, Prestage, and Eaton and several others, were of slavery days and believed in many of the traditions of the South as touching the Negro. However, as Christians they remembered us as brethren, and knowing our needs for a ministry despite all the past, they arose to help us to meet this need. In years to come, the historians will ask, "How did it happen?" They will be told. Back before 1909, these great leaders gave Rev. Sutton E. Griggs a hearing before their Convention, in behalf of their Negro brethren. Brother Griggs arose to the occasion and with the fondness of a faithful lover, and the devotion of a loving mother, and the zeal of a saint, he pleaded our cause and won for us the sympathy of this great Convention and caused these Baptist leaders to acknowledge an unpaid debt, and the American Baptist Theological Seminary came forth.

The noble sons of those great Baptist leaders are standing by the pledge of their fathers, and the Seminary is in the early morning of its helpfulness to the millions of Negro Baptists throughout the earth. By this gift, these good people are helping us to secure a larger number of competent, trained, unselfish leaders for our growing churches and expanding denomination. Our Educational Board also endeavors to aid the institutions planted by the American Baptist Home Mission Society, and the various denominational schools in the several states, by helping in their drives, counselling with their faculties and otherwise.

The American Baptist Theological Seminary
It was the purpose of the donors to call the institution the National Baptist Theological Seminary. But when our brethren of the unincorporated convention at the Memphis meeting refused to accede to any sort of peace terms, they hurriedly organized and incorporated that name. So far, however, they are operating no school under that title now. The following are the members of the first Boards.

Governing Board—O.L. Hailey, John L. Hill, E.P. Aldredge, John D. Freeman, W.M. Wood, Hight C. Moore, Chas. E. Little, Ryland Knight, E.L. Atwood, A.J. Barton, A.U. Boone, and E.Y. Mullins. These men were selected by the Southern Baptist Convention. From the National Baptist Convention the following were chosen: C.H. Parrish, L.K. Williams, R.B. Hudson, S.N. Vass, E.M. Lawrence, D.W. Cannon, E.W.D. Isaac, John Hope, W.A. Bowren, E. Arlington Wilson, R.L. Bradby, A.M. Townsend, J.H. Henderson, T.O. Fuller, E.B. Topp, E.H. McDonald, P. James Bryant, Sutton E. Griggs, S.E.J. Watson, R.T. Pollard, John Goins, J.A. Booker, C.A. Greer, and Wm. Haynes.

The Holding Board—The following brethren have been selected to represent the Southern Baptist Convention; namely, I.J. Van Ness, A.B. Hill, W.M. Gupton, E.A. Pickup, B.R. Kennedy, Albert Ewing, A.M. Nicholson, and W.F. Powell. From the National Baptist Convention the following were chosen: W.S. Ellington, S.P. Harris, J.D. Crenshaw, J.T. Brown. So far as the Southern Baptist Convention is concerned, the following is about the history so far. The National Baptist Convention had been in conference with the Northern Baptist Convention concerning the establishment of a Theological Seminary. When they found no way on their joint undertaking, it was abandoned.

Originating With O.L. Hailey

In 1912 at the Texas Convention, which met at Houston, O.L. Hailey was made chairman of a committee to advise the Convention how they might help the Negro Baptists in Texas. There being two conventions in Texas, and the White Baptists not desiring to take sides in a matter of division among themselves, the report recommended the holding of certain Bible Institutes over the state to which any interested person was invited to come.

O.L. Hailey held the first of these institutes, and from year to year conducted an institute. Dr. J.W. Bailey was corresponding secretary of the Negroes at the time. Afterwards, Dr. J.E. Knox became his successor. Dr. Knox raised the question with Dr. Hailey as to the building of a Seminary for Negro Baptist preachers. After a very extensive correspondence with both White and Colored Baptists, it was agreed to raise the question with the Southern Baptist Convention, which met in St. Louis in 1913.

Dr. E.Y. Mullins was asked to introduce the resolutions which provided for a commission of nine men from the Southern Baptist Convention to meet with a commission of nine men from the National Baptist Convention to canvass this subject and report. Rev. S.E. Griggs spoke to the resolutions with telling effect. From the Southern Baptist Convention, the following were appointed:

E.Y. Mullins	Benjamin Cox	B. F. Riley
O.L. Hailey	W.E. Atkinson	G. W. McDaniel
A.J. Barton	J.M. Frost	J. J. Bennett

From the National Baptist Convention, the following:

T.J. Searcy	E.B. Topps	W. G. Parks
A.R. Griggs	Joseph A. Booker	
T.O. Fuller	John Goins	

These brethren met in Nashville and agreed that the building of a seminary ought to be undertaken. They fixed the initial contribution from the Southern Baptist Convention at $50,000.

When the Education Commission of the Southern Baptist Convention projected a $15,000,000 campaign, the sum allocated to the Seminary was advanced to $150,000.

But in 1915 there was a division in the National Baptist Convention. The commission of the Southern Baptist Convention asked that they be appointed on mediation. Meanwhile, the work concerning the Seminary was suspended. The final result of the efforts at mediation was the agreement that the Southern Baptist Convention would cooperate with whoever would recommend the principle of "Denominational Control." The incorporated National Baptist Convention unanimously agreed to this, and the unincorporated National Baptist Convention declined to agree to this principle. That caused the Southern Baptist Convention to cooperate with the incorporated Convention, but there was no intention or purpose to deny the unincorporated brethren the privilege of attending the Seminary, if they so chose.

At Atlanta in 1919, the Southern Baptist Convention projected what has come down in history as "The Seventy-five Million Dollar Campaign." In this attempt the Seminary was to receive $200,000.

Location

This brought the commission face to face with the question of location. They asked various cities to offer bids for the location. Among the cities named were Louisville, Kentucky; Memphis, Tennessee; Nashville, Tennessee; Little Rock, Arkansas; Shreveport, Louisiana; New Orleans, Louisiana; and Atlanta, Georgia.

At first it was decided to locate at Memphis, but Memphis failed to put their bid in satisfactory shape. Meanwhile, Nashville offered a site and sympathetic cooperation.

The result of this was that the Seminary was located at Nashville. A site of forty-three acres was provided by the Colored Baptists and their friends, where the Seminary building is now located.

O. L. Hailey was called from his pastorate in Dallas, Texas, to come to Nashville and take charge of the enterprise and secure the erection of the building and the organization of the Seminary. He came to Nashville, July 1, 1919, and has been the general secretary of the undertaking from that time until the present.

The building was furnished and the school opened in September 1924. It has continued to function up to the present. The first class numbered twelve, the last class numbered forty-four.

The Southern Baptist Convention pays all the expenses incurred by O.L. Hailey in any way, and then they pay one-third of the maintenance of the school as such.

The Education Board of the National Baptist Convention had been seeking to foster denominational education. They were lending this encouragement to the several denominational schools in the states, but in 1920 they agreed to major on the Theological Seminary, and are now in active cooperation with the Seminary.

The joint commission was discontinued as such, when the Seminary was organized. The organization of the Seminary provides for two boards; one, the Holding Board, composed of twelve men—eight from the Southern Baptist Convention, and four from the National Baptist Convention. The Board of Directors consists of thirty-six men—twenty-four from the National Baptist Convention, and twelve from the Southern Baptist Convention.

The Southern Baptist Commission constituted their commission on the American Baptist Theological Seminary, naming the brethren from the Southern Baptist Convention, belonging to both boards as the commission of the Southern Baptist Convention on the American Baptist Theological Seminary.

They handle the funds coming from the Southern Baptist Convention and expend their part of the money in the conduct of the Seminary.

The sympathy and cooperation have been gradually extending and deepening, until today the Seminary is thoroughly incorporated in the joint undertaking of the Southern Baptist Convention and the National Baptist Convention.

THE B.Y.P.U. BOARD, organized in 1899, is an important factor in the lives of the young people of our churches, since it affords them opportunity for using whatever talent they may possess in planning public speaking, teaching, and soul-winning. This department has proved to be the training ground for developing efficient leaders. At the headquarters of the Board, 409 Gay Street, Nashville, Tenn., literature is printed and B.Y.P.U. merchandise such as caps, pennants, arm-bands, banners, badges, buttons, and gowns are manufactured. The pastors so greatly evaluate the work of the B.Y.P.U. that a live energetic B.Y.P.U. Convention exists in every state where Baptists are operating through organized channels. Dr. E.W.D. Isaac, secretary of this Board, is regarded as a man of unusual ability, far-sightedness, and clear thinking, who exerts a personal influence and power second to none in the Convention.

Besides carrying on the work of the B.Y.P.U. Board, Dr. Isaac is active in the work of both Roger Williams University and the American Baptist Theological Seminary as well as being a member of the Building Committee of the Sunday School Publishing Board. For years, he held Bible Conferences under the auspices of the Board in different sections of the country, and by this means thousands of persons enrolled as members of the "Systematic Bible Readers' Course" which entails the pledge that each member will read a portion of the Scripture daily. The great Sunday School and B.Y.P.U. Congress, an inspired idea of the secretary, is a great success; it meets annually and represents over eighteen thousand Sunday schools and 557 district conventions, not to speak of ten thousand B.Y.P.U.'s. Dr. Isaac began this work without funds, but by dint of his competency as a writer, preacher, and orator has made this one of the most efficient of our National Baptist Convention's agencies. The property holdings of this Board are estimated to be worth over $40,000.00. Dr. Isaac, its secretary, who is now the active senior secretary, having served continuously for twenty-five (25) years, is a large influence upon the life of the National Baptist Convention.

THE WOMAN'S AUXILIARY CONVENTION, was organized at Richmond, Virginia, in 1900, as an auxiliary to the National Baptist Convention with special emphasis on mission work. As their name implies, they help in all departments of the National Baptist Convention, but their chief objective and enterprise is The Training School for Women and Girls, which the auxiliary founded and chartered in 1910 at Lincoln Heights, Washington, D.C. It is now called The Lincoln National Seminary for Women and Girls. This change was made because of the fact that the United States Government had recently erected a penal institution in the National Capital, a reformatory for wayward girls, which is called "THE NATIONAL TRAINING SCHOOL FOR GIRLS," and much confusion of an unpleasant nature to our institution had arisen on account of the similarity. When the school was organized, our women were a unit as to interest in this school—but in time, some good woman in nearly every state organized a training school of some kind, thereby weakening the states' aid for their one big effort, The National Training School at Washington, D.C. This made the task of trustees and president all the harder. Since 1915, there has been some confusion as to the ownership of this school. The upheaval at Chicago in Baptist affairs, mentioned elsewhere in this book, set our women to "looking after their fences," to determine the exact relationship of this school to the Woman's Auxiliary of the National Baptist Convention. For nearly ten years, though the president gathered many influential White friends for the school, our women have found cause for aloofness and divided support. Things are simmering down and the outlook is much better at this writing.

On the recommendation of President L.K. Williams, July 1925, there was to be a nationwide drive for our Women's Convention. Their school stands second to none in its particular sphere among us and is the biggest organized effort of women in our group. Miss Nannie H. Burroghs, A.M., is Secretary of the Woman's Convention and Principal of the Training School, which is regarded as a model for cleanliness and discipline by many who know the school. An up-to-date steam laundry and a community store is maintained by the school and gives many a worthy girl an opportunity to help herself.

THE BENEFIT BOARD was organized in 1913 to insure our ministers, to raise and create a fund for the protection of aged and dependent ministers and other Christian workers of the denomination, and to maintain a home for the same. Though this board has the constituency and the finest opportunity in the world for becoming the second best of our home base agencies, at this writing, the outlook is not bright for so needy an institution. Not a board nor an auxiliary of the National Baptist Convention has had money raised by the Convention for its work. They were all organized, named, and pushed by the parent body. They were given the confidence of the churches which was and is a bigger asset than any other gift the Convention could make. What is true of their work is true of all congregational religious bodies. The agencies finance the parent body. This board hopes to so direct its affairs as to be the strongest asset of the denomination. Rev. Hogan of Pensacola, Fla., is secretary.

THE STORY OF THE
NATIONAL BAPTIST PUBLISHING BOARD

It was in 1891 at Dallas, Texas, that the National Baptist Convention voiced the longing for a publishing plant more fully than ever before, but nothing definite was decided. At Savannah in 1892, a resolution was passed authorizing the establishment of a denominational publishing house. All three of the Baptist conventions were holding sessions in the city at the same time, and there was considerable discussion as to the possibilities of this enterprise. In 1893 when the next of these anniversaries was held in Washington, D.C., it was in the meeting of the American National Convention, Dr. Michael Vann in the chair, a thorough review and discussion of the plan for printing literature for Negro Baptists by Negro Baptists was participated in by Drs. E.C. Morris, E.K. Love, E.J. Fisher, M.W. Gilbert, W.B. Johnson, C.L. Puree, and others. Dr. Morris' paper on "The Demand for a Negro Baptist Publishing House," brought great applause and Dr. John H. Frank offered the following resolution:

"Resolved, by the American National Baptist Convention in annual session assembled, that a special committee, one from each state and territory here represented to be selected by the respective delegation and appointed by the president with five from the country at large, be and are hereby authorized to effect plans for and proceed to the organization of the American National Baptist Convention Publication Company and Book Establishment, to be operated under the direction of Rev. C.L. Puree, Alabama; Rev. John H. Frank, Kentucky; Rev. G.W. Lee, Washington, D.C.; Rev. G.B. Howard, West Virginia; Rev. E.C. Morris, Arkansas; Rev. M.W. Gilbert, Florida; Rev. E.J. Fisher, Georgia; Rev. H.C. Green, Louisiana; Rev. H.W. Bowen, Mississippi; Rev. C. Johnson, North Carolina; Rev. P.F. Morris, Virginia; Rev. Alexander, Maryland; Rev. H. Watts, Texas; Revs. A.M. McEwen, C.H. Parrish, W.B. Johnson, A. Binga, E.K. Love, at large."

Sentiment was being formed in favor of this movement; the Baptists felt that like the spies Joshua and Caleb, they were well able to carry out this project successfully, but it was not taken up immediately. At the next session of the Convention (1894) in Montgomery, Alabama, an important question occupied the attention of the three groups: Was it wise to spend time and energy in maintaining three separate religious bodies with identical aims covering practically the same scope in their activities and all enlisting the sympathies of the same groups of earnest churches and pastors who attended the annual sessions? The consensus of opinion was that a merging of the three conventions would be a long step forward. But there were present a number of men who, for one reason or another, preferred the existing status of affairs. In the face of the debate over the proposed merger, the matter of a printing plant was relegated to the background, but a resolution was passed and a committee appointed to draft plans for a federation of the bodies. In the 1895 session at Atlanta, Georgia, the much heralded consolidation was finally affected; the oldest, largest, and most popular of these bodies, the Baptist Foreign Mission Convention absorbed the other two groups, the American National Baptist Convention and the National Baptist Educational Convention. A resolution was adopted and a committee appointed to draft plans for the amalgamation. The understanding was that the new organization, thence forward to be known as the National Baptist Convention, would take over the interests and complete all unfinished business of the former National Baptist bodies. This then gave the publishing enterprise, which had been held in abeyance, a chance to be brought up again.

We have spoken of the long and persistent agitation up to 1896 which was the direct result of a growing desire among Negro Baptists for religious writers of their own—writers who could interpret our feelings—who knew our racial aspirations, understood our yearnings. The failure of the American Baptist Publication Society to adhere to the original agreement for using some Colored writers, increased this desire many fold. Therefore, in September 1896 at St. Louis, Missouri, this Board was organized as a part of the Home Mission Board known as the Publishing Committee. The then secretary of the Home Mission Board, Rev. R.H. Boyd, D.D., was also to act as secretary of the new board to be. Nine men were in charge of this Board including the secretary himself, who, as mentioned elsewhere, in later years claimed the institution as his own property. In spite of protests from some of the brethren, this writer among them, the National Baptist Convention trustingly created this board as an equal, in deference to the wishes of Secretary Boyd. This serious mistake proved disastrous and greatly tormented us later. This writer contended then, as he contends now, that there is but one National Body and that all other bodies were simply auxiliaries or agencies through which the main body functions.[13] But not so with our Sunday School Board. When organized, the Convention permitted it to be organized under the caption, "The National Baptist Publishing Board." It was chartered as such, operated and controlled as same under the management of the self-perpetuation board of nine men. The success of the plan was remarkable and was due largely to the fact that it had the

---

[13]In accordance with this belief, the writer had the charter of the Foreign Mission Board drawn to read, "The Foreign Mission Board of the National Baptist convention," etc. In like manner the constitution of the Home Mission Board reads, "The Home Mission Board of the National Baptist Convention,"etc. [pp.271f.].

NEW HOPE BAPTIST CHURCH

New Hope is the oldest and most outstanding church of the group in Waco, Texas. Rev. Stephen Cobb is recorded as the first pastor. Following him came Revs. Wm. Massey, Abner Taylor, L.G. Jordan, James A. Dennis and the present pastor, Rev. Dr. —— Jenkins, D.D. Brother Jenkins has served this church for quite twenty years, moving them from the church built by this author in 1888, to what is one of the most beautiful meeting houses in the denomination. Modern in architecture and organization and withal a great people—Baptist through and through.

The above is a typical Negro home of other days. This was loaned us through the kindness of the Sunday School Publishing Board of the Southern Baptist Convention. Millions of our group have moved out of this form of house. In Memphis we were shown fourteen blocks of the most beautiful and up-to-date homes belonging to Negroes as may be found anywhere in the world. We were also told that there were six or eight other sections not quite so large, but just as beautiful, in other divisions of that great city. It is interesting to know that the American Negro in religion and material things is setting examples for Negroes in all parts of the world.

interest and tutelage of some of the most promising and outstanding men of their day and generation. As a consequence when our Publishing Committee issued its first series of Sunday school supplies, it became popular in a day, and came nearer to receiving the united patronage of the entire brotherhood than has any enterprise before or since. Fostered and supported by our constituency, hungering for its twenty years, it grew amazingly, and rapidly became the most efficient, influential department of the National Baptist Convention. In the language of many of its critics, it was "the most arrogant department of the whole Convention.

By reason of its favorable advantages and consequent prosperity, it was enabled to supply its managers with abundant funds with which it is said some among us were corrupted and became disloyal to the interests of the parent body. When the leaders of the National Baptist Convention created the Publishing Board they anticipated and expected that it would furnish to the National Baptist Convention the same type of service that the Publishing Board of the Southern Baptist Convention was rendering to their parent body.

In spite of being dubbed "Thankless ingrates who bite the hands that have fed them all these years," by opponents, each succeeding year saw an increase in the number of publications until the National Baptist Publishing Board was able to report in 1915 that $158,298.33 had passed through the secretary's hands during the fiscal year and by his own figures $2,400,000 were handled during his incumbency. This was all very gratifying to those members of the Convention and friends of the secretary who assured the doubting Thomases that since the secretary in his annual reports always acknowledged the Convention's ownership of the National Baptist Publishing Board, built up as it was through the patronage, good will, and confidence of the pastors and churches of the Convention, there could be no possible cause for alarm or complaint.

President E.C. Morris' recommendation that a separation be effected between the Publishing Board and the Home Mission Board was stubbornly fought by Secretary Boyd, who served in a double capacity as secretary and treasurer of both Boards, and used state missionaries as book agents. For ten long years the Convention was kept in turmoil and dissension over the question: "Who owns the Publishing House?" Two camps of followers were developed—the one believing in the propriety of Board control, another believing that the Convention which created the Board should control its creature. (In accordance with this belief the writer had the charter of the Foreign Mission Board drawn to read: "The Foreign Mission Board of the

National Baptist Convention," etc. In like manner the constitution of the Home Mission Board reads: "The Home Mission Board of the National Baptist Convention," etc.)

The Publishing Board

Footnotes:

(Anent the matter of the defeat in the plans of the National Baptist Convention and its publishing plant, it should be stated and clearly understood that lack of space prevents the use of the vast number of records of court proceedings, original letters, sworn statements, newspaper excerpts and other publications which furnish a detailed account of the entire transaction but must appear in a later edition of this book. So many persons still live who took an active part in this unfortunate occurrence that it will be only necessary to narrate as briefly as possible the story of the seceding Board.)

At the outset in 1896, in St. Louis, the whole publishing enterprise was put in charge of a Publishing Committee under the Home Mission Board. Dr. R.H. Boyd of Texas, corresponding secretary of the Home Mission Board, went to Nashville, Tenn., to begin the publication of Sunday school literature which Negro Baptists were demanding, and in spite of the opposition from the agents of the American Baptist Publication Society seemed determined to put over. Dr. Boyd's first task was to pry loose Negro Baptist attachment to the products of the Publication Society, and turn their allegiance towards their own enterprise. This he proceeded to do; gifted and attractive in person, a witty resourceful debater, trained by a long and hard contest in Texas conventions, he had acquired the nickname "splitter," and by his study and practice of law in Texas he foresaw possibilities which even the most far-visioned of his brethren failed to see at first. His skill in winning the confidence of White people secured for us through him the aid of Dr. J.M. Frost, secretary of the Baptist Sunday School Board of the Southern Baptist Convention, and of Mr. S.W. Meeks of the University Printing Press Company. With their cooperation in providing electroplates and other assistance, the first issue of *The Sunday School Teacher* and quarterlies ever printed by Negro Baptists was brought out in January 1897 and occasioned great rejoicing.

In the meantime there were still those who strove with might and main to stem the tide which having ebbed from the American Baptist Publication Society, was turning to Negro literature in an overwhelming torrent, and year by year grew more and more popular. Efforts to ridicule the literature by calling attention to typographical errors found in early issues, or as the mechanical quality of the output improved, to stigmatize the work as not being done by Negroes after all, but simply "Negro backs and White men's brains," an expression of derision which had great weight with the less thoughtful among the brethren.

As far as is known, our Publishing Board made no contributions to any of the departments of our Convention, no matter how dire the need for religious, educational or mission work. The wave of disappointment, distrust, and sorrow was intense in its premonition of disaster. Thereupon two camps of thought developed—the one believing in the propriety of Board control in denominational affairs, insisting that their rule should be undisturbed save for the annual report to the Convention; the other denying the right of the Board to hold such power. In an unskillful attempt to make wrongdoers atone and to retain our already weakened tenure on the property of the Convention, the battle waxed warmer for years. Ominously gathering clouds of dissatisfaction and dissension seen faintly on our horizon at the New Orleans meeting in 1910, brought heaviness of heart to an army of Baptists throughout the country. At that session it was charged that the secretary of the Publishing Board, in order to shift attention from the Convention's protests against his methods, assayed to "sidetrack" this subject by having Dr. C.T. Walker of Georgia nominated for the presidency to the Convention. This was an unfortunate occurrence, for while thousands of good men admired and respected Dr. Walker as an ideal minister, a Christian statesman, and a real "big brother" to his comrades, yet, as a punishment to the Publishing Board, the delegation in a measure humiliated this splendid man by almost ignoring the nomination. (See page 46, *Journal of the National Baptist Convention, 1910*.)

So determined was the Convention that the whole idea of confiscating its controlling interests by the Board and Board agents should be abolished utterly, that in Rooseveltan language, the Board and its secretary were "beaten to a frazzle." But no further steps were taken by the Convention to follow up this advantage. Had the Convention completed its task of quelling insubordination and insisting upon obedience to its mandates, the Convention, just at this juncture, would have been spared the great loss of its Publishing House many years later if not altogether.

The Home Mission Board then as now, which received assistance from the Southern Baptist Convention to maintain colporteurs, missionaries, and struggling churches, derived great benefit spiritually, mentally, and temporally from the efforts of the men who travelled, visiting the most rural churches in various sections of the country, selling and giving away books and periodicals which were the direct product of their own publishing house. At first it seemed very fortunate that the two Boards were functioning under the one secretary. It seemed a very happy circumstance that our literature could have such adequate channels of distribution.

This feeling might have continued indefinitely had it not been for a certain situation which became more and more obnoxious as years rolled on—that no matter how prosperous the business became, the secretary never could seem to find a way to pay off the mortgages which members of his own family held against what the Convention thought was its own property.

During the years the Convention's problems have been many and grievous. Most of the solutions have come to us through the experimental "trial and failure" process. But how well the lessons learned thereby the future alone will tell. One of these came from the discussion of what is recorded in our minutes as "The Purdy Matter," which controversy, originating in Tennessee, was brought up year after year to be aired on the floor of the Convention hall. Finally a motion was passed that the matter be taken back to the local authorities and that in the future no local dispute be brought to the attention of the Convention, thereby was saved much time for the settlement of questions affecting the people as a whole. Another instance is found in the matter of investigation into the affairs of the Boards. It was because for many years the secretary of our National Baptist Publishing Board always demurred when asked for a complete statement of Board matters, that the plant was finally lost to us. His objection was that to make public such a statement would ruin the business; he would be embarrassed with demands for payment of bills which were not troublesome at the time and could not obtain the credit needed to prosecute the work. We wish to stress the fact that from the time the Publishing Board was chartered, not quite two years after the enterprise was begun, to the bitter end, there were always those who favored the idea of informing the brotherhood as to the exact status of their publishing business. They murmured when they noticed that the secretary seemed unwilling to allow the Board to clear off the debt to him, to his wife, or to the institutions under his control. They complained that in buying property from his wife for the Publishing Board, he paid her only one dollar and procured a deed—a promise to give full title when the remainder of the $2,000 was paid—but that he would not pay off this mortgage in spite of the increasingly large sums of money which his yearly reports showed that he was handling. These brethren inquired why the secretary was willing to show the deeds which were unimpeachable but never had any documents to show where any releases had been made.

They recounted over and over that the main building on the corner of 2nd Avenue and Locust Street was bought for $10,000; that, in his capacity as treasurer the secretary had paid the debt down to $2,400; that he was ordered to finish paying the debt, but that on the contrary three years later it had increased to $5,000. They wondered why. They were dissatisfied over the management of matters in what they called the "Boyd and Beckham Building," next to the main building. They noticed and commented on the fact that although it was not as important as the main building, Secretary Boyd charged $150 per month ($1800 per year), while for years the main building was rented for $50 per month—$600 per year. They had an unshakable conviction that the only difference was that the $600 was paid to another landlord, whereas the other rent was his own profit. They insisted that the Convention should order the secretary to either sell that lot and building to the Convention or sell the Publishing House lots so that all of the Convention's property should be together. It was the third lot, belonging to his wife that he only paid enough on to get the deed on the record ($1.00), and they could not see why he could not pay his wife more than $1.00 on that third lot out of the more than $2 million which his last reports to them showed that he had handled. The brethren complained also about the copyrights of the *Sunday School Commentaries* and *Baptist Hymnals* being in the secretary's own name and good for 28 years, to the extent that he was asked to transfer these copyrights to the Board. Concerning some of these copyrights he defended his action, but he simply begged for time to carry out the wishes of the Convention about others of the rights in question. It was these apprehensive members of the Convention that saw to it that a charter was gotten out whereby the Convention could force the secretary to meet the wishes of that body. They were prepared to withstand the vigorous protests against a charter that the secretary voiced and said that his horror to the idea of having a chartered Convention was camouflage, pure and simple. However, the influence of these Doubting Thomases was too weak; the charter was finally set aside in deference to their respect for the horrified secretary. Nor were they taken entirely by surprise when the next move was announced: the declaration that the National Baptist Convention did not create the Publishing House but that he himself together with eight other persons created it; that the Convention had no authority over it and never had any. But too many of the men who listened to the assertion remembered when and why the Convention began the movement for publishing our own literature, and the tide turned completely at this new phase of the dispute. They recalled the occasion when Dr. E.K. Love of Savannah offered the resolution inaugurating the publishing of literature written by Negroes for Negroes. Like a tidal wave the significance of the secretary's annual reports—always made as in humility and apparently with a desire to do the Convention's will, but never fulfilling; the repeated promises to obey; the delays year after year and the resistance against the Convention's charter—all became transparent. Too late the entire Convention saw that which a few disquieted souls had seen for nearly a score of years. But the result was all the institutions built up by means of the good will, patronage, and cooperation and confidence of the churches composing the National Baptist Convention must now be owned and controlled by the Convention, amenable to the will of that body.

After the defection of Dr. Boyd, the National Baptist Convention chose Attorney S.P. Harris of Arkansas, for secretary of the new board which bears the name of the Sunday School Publishing Board of the National Baptist Convention. Owing to some differences of opinion between him and the auditor of the Convention, he only served one year.

In September 1916, many of our leaders, including the veteran secretary of the B.Y.P.U. Board Dr. E.W.D. Isaac; Dr. S.E. Griggs, editor of the *Beacon Light*; and Rev. L.K. Williams, president of the Texas Baptist State Convention were imbued with the idea that Rev. L.G. Jordan, then secretary of the Foreign Mission Board, could fill this place to the great advantage of the Convention. They insisted that Dr. Jordan, being a contemporary and personal friend of Dr. Boyd, would know best how to quell the turmoil into which the former secretary had plunged our Convention. Accordingly at the Savannah, Georgia, meeting of the Convention in 1916, the Publishing Board elected Dr. Jordan to succeed Attorney Harris. This action did not meet with favor from President Morris who expressed his opinion that the Foreign Mission work would suffer if its secretary were taken away at this period in its activities. Under great pressure from President E.C. Morris, and from an aspirant to the position and from the field secretary of the American Baptist Publication Society as well, the National Baptist Convention urged the Publishing Board to rescind its action and to allow Dr. Jordan to continue with the Foreign Mission Board. Thereupon Dr. Jordan withdrew, throwing his strength to Rev. Wm. Haynes of Tennessee, who was elected. Dr. Haynes brought to the office a fine reputation, much influence, and personal credit in the business world. He was a successful pastor, the treasurer of Roger Williams University, and an alumnus of that institution. Within four years Secretary Haynes had accomplished a vast amount of work in so organizing the Board as to secure more adequate headquarters and to meet the growing demand for Sunday school supplies. It must be kept in mind, the courts gave the seceding Board everything we had gathered for eighteen years even to our name. So, without even a pencil or a mailing list, the Convention started all over again.

In 1920 at the Indianapolis session, Rev. A.M. Townsend, D.D., the present secretary, succeeded Dr. Haynes. Like all secretaries of boards, Dr. Townsend had to plan, organize, and direct the affairs of his Board. Of the five men selected to this position before, he was the first college man elected. He brought to the office the experience of a teacher, the steady nerve of the physician, the patience of the tried pastor, and withal a disciplined mind which enabled him to see at a glance the great harvest of over twenty years' sowing, ripe and wasting for want of a reaper properly equipped with sickle. Thus panoplied, a building was born in his mind and visualized larger and yet larger till he told it to the architect who got it on paper, and then the contractor, and now we have it. Quite the greatest undertaking by our Sunday School Publishing Board is our new building, which cost quite $700,000 and is known as "The Morris Memorial Building." The cornerstone was laid Sunday, May 18, 1924; the house was finished and opened for inspection October 19-26, 1925. It is significant that the plans were drawn by Negro architects, McKissack and McKissack. (See description in folder.) It has been refinanced and is now solely the property of the National Baptist Convention.

Some Data on the National Baptist Publishing Board

For data on the National Baptist Publishing Board controversy see the *Journal of the National Baptist Convention*:

1904 Secretary Boyd requested President Morris to have the resolution touching his recommendation laid over, for another year. (Page 31.)

Dr. Boyd's brother, Rev. W.L. Dickson, offered resolution that the above request be granted. (Page 164.)

See report of Committee on President's Recommendations. (Page 165.)

1905 President again recommends separation of Boards. (Pages 157, 158.)

Rev. A.T. Stewart offers resolution on same matter. (Pages 162, 163.)

Rev. W.H. McAlpine offers similar resolution.

FIRST BAPTIST CHURCH
Memphis, Tenn.

The records of Negro Baptists organized in Western Tennessee are in possession of this church. Rev. T.O. Fuller, D.D., one of the secretaries of the National Baptist Convention, and who always ranks first in Negro Baptist leadership, is pastor. In many ways this is a model New Testament church.

Chapter VIII

Often we come upon plants which refuse to give out this sweetness so long as their parts are unbroken and unbleeding, but which will quickly yield up their odors when bruised. So it is with men. It is worthy of notice that these dark days of slavery gave birth to some strong Colored preachers.

Charles O. Boothe

A GLANCE AT THE HARD-SHELL BAPTISTS AND THEIR INFLUENCE

The upheaval in the sixteenth century over religion caused by the Reformation served in a very vital way to call the attention of all who professed to love the Christ, to the sufferings, persecutions, and tortures which Baptists had endured during all the long preceding centuries. Since those never to be forgotten days, the principles held and taught by Baptists have replaced much of the sordid godless spirit of religion everywhere. The spirit of republics and democracies, so many of which died in the making, but all aided in awakening the consciences of the masses in all lands, until they saw the heartless tyranny of the "union of church and state" exposed until enlightened Christianity choked the monster to death. Baptists have grown in influence, and by their prayerful adherence to the teaching of the Scriptures, they have won "power with God and with men," 'til all religious sects have engrafted into their various creeds many Baptist ideas, making for freedom and liberty to serve God without persecution as set forth in the Scriptures. Baptist ideas of the Bible—the Bible alone as a guide for human conduct—have gained headway and a broad plain on which cruelty and barbarism had such a sway in stifling the right to serve God according to the wishes of an individual or group have narrowed and narrowed until the thing for which Baptists gladly submitted to indescribable tortures and martyrdom in a large way, parallel Baptists in many of their views as set forth in the New Testament. The heartless doctrine of how to keep the church and state united, held and taught through all the centuries and which has been the ground for so much sorrow in the world, are twofold and set forth in the *History of Protestants and Romanists* as well; "Whose is the government—His is the religion."

That horrid old monster, "Religious Bigotry," with teeth still filled with human flesh and his fangs smeared with human gore, lived, thrived, held political and religious influence in the name of Christianity; but thank God it is dying, not already dead, and in its grave will go the faggot, the whip, the thumbscrew, racial difference, color discrimination, and all instruments of religious intolerance.

With malice toward none, and with charity for all, "every Baptist should know what a heritage of religious freedom his forebears contributed to the world of mankind and manfully contend for the faith, once delivered to the saints."

The beginning of American Baptist foreign missions can be directly traced to three men: George Leile, Adoniram Judson, and Luther Rice. The first of the three being a Negro, historians with one or two honorable exceptions have left him out of the picture. We have dealt with this first missionary elsewhere. On the other hand the opposition owes its inception and growth and finally the rise of the "Hard-Shell" Baptist group, to three men: Rev. John Taylor of Kentucky, Rev. Daniel Parker of Illinois, and Rev. Alexander Campbell of Virginia. Since the year 1802 home mission work had been carried on under Baptist auspices "for distant parts of our frontier settlement," but the distinctly foreign mission work in America was organized and enthusiastically undertaken about 1812 under the guidance of Judson and Rice. Rev. Adoniram Judson, Jr., was born in 1788 of Congregational parents in Massachusetts. In 1810 he resolved to become a missionary to the heathen. While still in college, Judson with five others, including the devout and consecrated Rice presented to the General Association a memorial, written by Judson, which expressed their desire to go to a foreign field. However, fearing that for lack of funds the association might decide not to send anyone because there were six applicants where none were expected, two of the would-be missionaries erased their names from the list. One of these was Rev. Luther Rice. The board accepted Judson and the other three. It was while on the ocean that Judson became convinced that immersion was the only Scriptural form of baptism and in consequence he insisted on being baptized immediately on reaching his destination. The story of his labors in India, of his bereavement, of his persecutors and imprisonments is well known. Many missionaries have, by his example of courage, complete consecration, and dauntless zeal, been inspired to carry on to success the work so nobly begun. His life and efforts in India were powerful factors in advancing missionary work in Africa. In April 1850,

Judson died at sea after a long illness and was buried the same day. His sufferings influenced the cause as potently as his labor—and the same fact is true of the other great missionary pioneer Luther Rice. Rice was born in 1783, like Judson, in Massachusetts and of Congregational parents. From his youth he was devout and a vigorous church worker. He early resolved to become a minister, thereby incurring the wrath of his father and alienating family and friends. While in college he decided to give himself to foreign mission work and undertook to provide for his own expenses and outfit, travelling day and night in the dead of a New England winter, because the Board which was sending Judson and the three others could not finance Rice also. Like Judson, he had a life of hardships, made more lonely in that the young lady to whom he was engaged renounced her vows to him when he persisted in his determination "to carry the gospel to heathen lands."

He never married and was reviled and cursed by his father, vilified by his opponents, estranged from those whom he loved best, but was untiring in his journeys to arouse the Baptists and organize them for their responsibilities to the heathen. He kindled interest in missionary education and endeavor throughout the country and against him "Hardshellism" arrayed all its hosts. His long life of unremunerated toil ended in 1830, but the project of "sending the gospel" was no longer an experiment; hundreds of churches, associations, conventions, schools, seminaries, and other agencies for cooperative work were witnesses that he had wrought well.

No history pertaining to the Baptist denomination can be closed without chronicling, however briefly, the revolt within the ranks which was led by opponents of the foreign missionary movement, which took on enlarged proportions following the acceptance by Rev. Adoniram Judson, Jr., and Rev. Luther Rice, of the New Testament doctrine and immersion as the only Scriptural baptism while enroute to India as missionaries under the Congregational Board. This opposition had its rise about the year 1812. Previous to this the Baptists in the United States numbered only 180,000 and had 48 associations.

The close of the Revolutionary War found the country flooded with the influences of infidelity and blasphemy, made popular by the French officers who had assisted the patriot cause. Free-thinking and a kind of religious apathy, the latter reaching even into the churches and pulpits, were widespread. Gradually a reaction set in which finally developed into a great spiritual awakening that swept the country like a tidal wave. Especially on the frontier where the grossest ribaldry had flourished, men felt the deepest conviction of their sins. Strange phenomena were witnessed in the camp meetings during this great revival of religion; the Baptists did not join in these general camp meetings—hence their ranks were but little affected. They escaped the weird symptoms which accompanied the services held in the camp meetings—the visions, trances, convulsions, and spasms of "barking," "rolling," "tumbling," "running," "laughing," and many similar exercises which took place in the religious gatherings of this period.

The battle for religious liberty being practically won, Baptist missionary activity received a great impetus at this time, but was met with determined objections and violent hostility from "those of their own household." Dissension arose in the denomination, and foreign missions was the rock on which they finally split.

With the overwhelming success that followed this missionary activity, there arose a violent and powerful opposition. Two camps developed among the Baptists: One side taught that the commands of the Savior must be implicitly obeyed in giving the gospel to the heathen; the other faction advanced many arguments against this view and laid stress upon the doctrine that no special preparation was necessary to be an effective preacher, thus conflicting directly with all that Rice was doing in the way of fostering religious education.

Perhaps the most aggressive of these hostile leaders was Daniel Parker. Whether true or not, tradition says that Parker had applied for appointment as a foreign missionary but had been rejected, and thenceforward became a bitter enemy of missions. He was unlearned and ignorant and of very poor antecedents. However, he had a very strong native intellect and a talent for invective that never failed to touch the sympathies of the common people among whom he worked. He was the chief exponent of the "Two Seed" theory, a form of predestination carried to the utmost extreme. He taught that among the children of Adam and Eve were found some who were called to be the sons of God from the beginning, and these were the elect, the seed of Christ. All other human beings were condemned—being the seed of the Devil and for them there could be no salvation. God had indeed created all, but the Devil had begotten some and these ought to go to their father, and therefore no true Christian ought to help to send the Scriptures to those who were doomed to be eternally lost. The Bible societies and missionaries were running in opposition to the will of God. He exerted himself to the utmost to induce churches everywhere to have nothing to do with them.

Taylor, on the other hand, has been characterized as "the only true Baptist" in these ranks. A pamphlet which he published in 1819 did untold harm among the churches—the more so that John Taylor himself was a man of deep piety and godly life, who was universally known and respected. He was thoroughly in earnest in his belief that the sovereignty of Baptist churches was endangered by the new missionary societies. He feared the domination of a ruling class and contended that these missionaries might, if given credence and power, usurp the prerogatives that belonged to God alone.

Alexander Campbell, the missionaries' most formidable enemy, had the idea that the missionaries were purely self-seeking and mercenary. Campbell was an educated man, with a tremendous genius for ridicule and held up the missionary undertaking to the scorn of the world, with a biting sarcasm and a piercing satire that has never been equalled in Baptist phalanxes. So many persons listened to his speeches and read his articles that the whole denomination suffered visibly. His followers have continued in small numbers to the present day, but are now pursuing most of the policies that their great leader so vehemently attacked.

CHRONOLOGICAL REPORT
OF THE NATIONAL BAPTIST CONVENTION, U.S.A.

1880 Founding of the Baptist Foreign Mission Convention, November 24, at Montgomery, Ala., through efforts of Rev. W.W. Colley, who gave up work with the Southern Baptists to do this.

1881 Circular letters sent to all associations and missionary bodies, inviting them to join in the missionary enterprise.

1882 Rev. and Mrs. J.H. Presley appointed missionaries to Africa, and Bros. J. J. Coles and H. McKinney elected to study in Liberia as prospective missionaries.

1883 154 missionary societies organized among the women in the churches with a view of strengthening home and foreign mission sentiment. The Convention's first six missionaries sailed in December.

1884 First donation —100 pieces of clothing — from First African Baptist Church, Savannah, Ga. Convention greatly edified by native African boy who sang and recited the Lord's Prayer in his native dialect.

1885 Baptist women of Kentucky gave $12 for yearly tuition of child in Vey tribe. Pension of $25 monthly voted Rev. Colley for faithful service.

1886 Consolidation of Foreign Mission Convention with Western States and Territories Convention; offer of cooperation with White society refused because they failed to do for Africa what this body has done. American Nat'l Baptist Convention organized, led by Dr.W.J.Simmons in St. Louis.

1887 Agreement to meet at same time and place with Foreign Mission Convention.

1888 Proposal for opening mission in Colombia, S. America; Rev. J. Anderson Taylor, delegate; sent to World's Conference, London, England.

1889 Copy of poem, "Course U. S. Government Should Take on Rum Trade in Congo," ordered printed and a copy sent to President of the U.S.A., Washington, D.C.

1890 Vote to organize a Women's Foreign Mission Convention and committee appointed to draft plans for same. Death of Wm. J. Simmons.

1891 Resolution to observe the Lord's Day while attending World's Fair, although activities will be open regardless of Sundays.

1892 Movement for a separate women's national organization discouraged, instead special time given for women to speak on phases of our work, in this and every annual meeting.

1893 Committee of men from each state appointed to plan for a Publication Co. and Book Establishment. Organizing of National Baptist Educational Convention in Washington D.C.

1894 Vote to continue mission work among Veys, though stations have been totally destroyed by war. Plans laid in Montgomery, Ala., for one National Baptist body.

1895 Merger of three conventions to form the National Baptist Convention in Atlanta, Ga. Death of Dr. L.M. Luke.

1896 Election [of] Rev. L. G. Jordan, Secretary Foreign Mission Board. Home Mission Board authorized to begin publishing literature because Negroes were debarred from contributing to White Sunday school periodicals, which all would study.

1897 Meeting in Boston. Heard Publishing Board's first report. Because it was a success, Lott Carey brethren planned organization and with-drew.

1898 National Baptist Publishing Board secured a charter. Convention voted to ask churches for monthly donations and each fifth Sunday collection for foreign missions.

1899 B.Y.P.U. Board organized. National Baptist Convention voted to establish a fund for education of Africans in this country to return to Africa as missionaries.

1900 Formation of Baptist Women's Missionary League, auxiliary to National Baptist Convention. Against much protest, plans of cooperation were made and offering of $9 was given by the Convention.

1901 First contribution from Women's Board of $75. Provisions for a National Baptist Convention weekly newspaper; Constitution amended to provide for auditor for this body.

1902 Stampede in Shiloh Church, Birmingham session; mistaking cry,

"Fight"and of "Quiet" for "Fire," resulting in 100 deaths, within 30 minutes.

1903 Home Mission Board authorized to provide for the reception of money contributed to aid churches in bankruptcy or needing assistance.

1904 Resolution that a Board be elected with headquarters to be agreed upon, which shall build an Aged Ministers' Home.

1905 Endorsement of appeals for exhibits for Jamestown Exposition. Forty delegates sent to first Baptist World Alliance, London, England.

1906 Land obtained and National Training School founded by Women's Convention at Washington, D.C.

1907 Convention passes resolution pledging pulpits, voices, and votes against the separate coach laws in all states.

1908 The secretary of the Benefit Board recommended the moving of the Board from Helena, Ark., to Mound Bayou, Miss. So gripping was the president's annual message that Dr. R.H. Boyd offered a motion that it be put in pamphlet form. Dr. Hawkins, president of the entertaining church, died during the session.

1909 Twenty-five delegates chosen to represent at Ecumenical Mission-
ary Conference in Edinburgh, Scotland.

1910 Committee of Investigation appointed to lay before Publishing Board matter Convention deemed important and wished looked into.

1911 Committee on State of the Country appointed to study conditions of Negroes in various sections and report findings annually— 3 ministers and 3 laymen.

1912 Resolution to allow additional year to enable Publishing Board to comply with the wishes of the Convention.

1913 Committee appointed to gather facts, compile and write history of the race and denomination; entitling them to all receipts from sale of same for first five years and 50% of net proceeds thereafter, remainder to be used for mission work in Africa. Committee to bear all publishing expenses.

1914 Convention recorded itself against election by suspension of rules; resolutions passed reaffirming former acts, giving Convention charge of Boards.

1915 Secession of Publishing Board; organization of unincorporated convention.

1916 B.Y.P.U. Board and S.S. Board unite in a joint Congress.

1917 Men and women's Sunday school classes organized into Abemelech and Deborah units.

1918 Peace Commission appointed to effect reunion of Baptists—from Southern, National, and unincorporated conventions.

1919 Resolution that the Budget System be adopted by the National Baptist Convention.

1920 Efforts made to cooperate with American Home Mission Society in northern territory.

1921 Change of charter of Foreign Mission Board; election of Rev. East as secretary on resignation of Dr. Jordan on account of ill health.

1922 Deaths of Drs. R.H. Boyd and E.C. Morris and the election of Dr. L.K. Williams to President of the National Baptist Convention.

1923 California meeting of Convention unprecedented in its history for harmony, numbers, and good feeling among brethren.

1924 Laying of cornerstone of Publishing House in Nashville session. Theological Seminary at Nashville dedicated.

1925 Creation of Historical Department; material to be printed by the Publishing Board and sales proceeds to go to Sunday School Publishing Board which is to house and finance said department.

1926 Dedication of Morris Memorial Building, home of the Sunday School Publishing Board of the National Baptist Convention. Resolution ordering the compilation of a Baptist Directory and Manual. Benefit Board requested to organize and submit plan for pensioning old and retired ministers.

1927 Policy of National Voice outlined. Report on establishment of Tuberculosis Hospital. Benefit Board ordered domiciled at St. Louis. Standard Baptist Directory and Pastors' Guide issued by Sunday School Publishing Board.

1928 Delegates sent to Baptist World Alliance, Toronto, Canada. Plans made and committees appointed for a Golden Jubilee Anniversary, celebrating fifty years of continued organized work, to be held in Chicago, Ill., August 14-25, 1930. By vote of Jubilee Commission during Sunday School and B.Y.P.U. Congress in Charleston, S. C., the whole Jubilee celebration was put in the hands of President of the National Baptist Convention.

1929 Plans completed for Jubilee.

DEPARTMENT OF COMMERCE, WASHINGTON
CENSUS OF RELIGIOUS BODIES: 1926
Negro Baptists

Washington, D.C., July 24, 1928.—The Department of Commerce announces that, according to the returns received, there were in the United States 22,082 Negro Baptist churches in 1926, with 3,196,823 members, as compared with 21,071 churches and 2,938,579 members reported in 1916. The figures for 1926 include data for the National Baptist Convention, U.S.A., Inc.; National Baptist Convention, Unincorporated; 243 churches which were reported with the Northern Baptist Convention in 1916; and a number of independent Negro Baptist churches. As a number of the churches affiliated with more than one Convention, it was not deemed advisable for the bureau arbitrarily to assign them to one or the other of the Colored Baptist conventions; however, approximately ninety percent of the whole number of Negro Baptist churches are affiliated with the National Baptist Convention, U.S.A., Inc.

The total expenditures for 1926, as reported by 20,210 churches, amounted to $19,476,981, including $16,211,927 for current expenses and improvements, $2,444,067 for benevolences, missions, etc., and $820,987 not classified. The total expenditures reported by 19,988 churches in 1916 were $8,361,919. The value of church edifices (including furniture and equipment), as reported by 19,834 churches for 1926, was $103,473,259, which may be compared with $41,184,920 reported by 20,117 churches in 1916.

Of the 22,082 churches reporting in 1926, 4,410 were located in urban territory (incorporated places of 2,500 inhabitants or more), and 17,672 were in rural areas. Of the total membership, 1,246,527 were in the urban churches and 1,950,296 in the rural churches; and of the total expenditures, 4,187 urban churches reported $11,554,870 and 16,023 rural churches, $7,922,111. The value of church property reported by 4,013 urban churches was $69,452,224, and that reported by 15,821 rural churches was $34,021,035.

Sunday schools were reported by 18,756 churches of this denomination in 1926, with 148,077 officers and teachers and 1,121,487 scholars. The number of officers and teachers in the Sunday schools as reported for 1916 was 123,817 and the number of scholars, 1,181,270.

The more important data for the Negro Baptists are shown by states in the following table. All figures for 1926 are preliminary and subject to correction.

NOTE: *See table, end of Chapter XI.*

REV. PRINCE JONES

Moderator Northwest Baptist Association, Texas. He was the immediate predecessor of Rev. L.K. Williams, D.D., president of the National Baptist Convention, as pastor of Mt. Gilead Baptist Church, Fort Worth, Texas.

REV. P. H. HUGHES

Rev. Hughes, an eloquent preacher of Clarksville, Texas; former pastor of Mt. Gilead Baptist Church, Fort Worth. Began his ministry in Texas and went to his reward from Texas.

REV. I. TOLLIVER, TEXAS

Rev. Tolliver was born and reared in Texas and was most outstanding evangelist of his day. He finally moved out of Texas and became pastor of the Liberty Baptist Church in Washington, where he died.

Chapter IX

"Our independent church government can be both a hindrance and an advantage. If we fail to use our restrained powers with the proper Bible limitations and allow our independence to be the means in the hands of corrupt men of filling our pulpits with bad materials, or on the other hand permit ignorance to triumph over knowledge, drive our intelligent people from us, and disgust the refined and truly moral who would cast their religious fortunes with us, we are alone to blame."—William J. Simmons, D.D., Field Secretary, American Home Mission Society, April 1896.

CONSOLIDATED AMERICAN BAPTIST MISSIONARY CONVENTION

1868

The Convention met with the Second African Baptist Church, at Savannah, Georgia, on the 13th of August, 1868 [with] the president Rev. Richard DeBaptiste in the chair. The Introductory Sermon was preached by the Rev. Emanuel Cartwright of St. Louis, Missouri, from Romans 1:15. "So, as much as in me is, I am ready to preach the gospel to you that are at Rome also."

Extracts From Annual Report

Though our work the past year has been comparatively meager, yet we have great reason to be thankful to God for His goodness in that He has permitted us to do what we have in the glorious work to which He has called us. There has been a general stagnation in every department of business life, compelling almost everybody, more or less, to abandon labor for general good, and give attention to family, personal, and local interests. Churches have found themselves unable to send forth their usual gifts, and benevolent merchants have been forced to say, "You must excuse me from giving, this year."

This commercial and consequent financial dearth is traceable to political disruptions, and the generally unsettled state of the country. In this respect the evil effects of our late Civil War have been felt by us all in educational and missionary as well as commercial and political enterprises. But when we look over the South and see four millions (4,000,000) of our once enslaved and sorely abused brethren now standing up and rejoicing under the unfurled and waving banner of freedom; building their own churches and dedicating them to God, and ordaining their own preachers and choosing their own legislators and their own governors, as one of the results and the very best of all the good effects of the Civil War, then we too are constrained to join with them in the anthem of joy and praise, and say, "Glory to God in the highest."

As the circulation of money is always governed by the degrees of activity in business, and as business has been dull, your Executive Board has not been able to raise one-tenth as much money for missionary purposes as would have been raised by the same effort if it had been made under more favorable circumstances, or without the hindrances mentioned and yet to be mentioned. Our whole receipts for the year, including the amount collected at the last annual meeting of the Convention, have amounted to not more than twelve hundred dollars ($1200).

Our expenditures have amounted, during the same time, to $1,500.

Adding to this our old missionary debt gives the sum of $2,800 as our liabilities or indebtedness the past year.

Now, in view of our own numerical greatness and the large gifts of our White friends for the support of missionary and education enterprises among us as a people, and for our Southern brethren in particular, the amount of our receipts appears shamefully insignificant.

Foreseeing or apprehending that we would not be able to raise the amount of money absolutely necessary to pay all the brethren employed as missionaries and agents in the several states and districts, and believing it unwise and detrimental to the progress of the Convention to increase its debt, your Board was obliged to make the appointments conditional. The main condition was that those accepting appointments should find for themselves local support till otherwise provided for, excepting such appropriations, from time to time, as the Board or Convention might find itself able to make without any serious embarrassment. To this there has been no objection; and how faithfully and successfully these good missionary brethren have continued and labored in their respective fields under such discouraging circumstances, their own statements and figures yet to be submitted, will tell in detail.

They have preached over a thousand sermons, baptized thousands of hopeful converts, and organized about sixty new churches.

Brother Campbell, of Texas, has reported 440 that he himself has baptized. Brother S. White, of Virginia, has baptized over 500.

Work To Be Done

Having reviewed what has been done, we now call your attention to the work that lies before us as a Colored National Baptist Convention, and to the methods recommended for its successful prosecution. The field that we are called upon to occupy embraces every one of the late slave states and includes hundreds of thousands of souls yet to be converted. The Baptist influence and interest in these states are already great, and a decent respect for the faith we hold and the principles we advocate as Christians and the messengers of God sent by His Son Jesus Christ, and upheld by the Holy Spirit, enjoin it upon us to go forward with renewed zeal, and preach to all and baptize as many as shall be converted to God through our instrumentality. They are of our own family and social household. They have full confidence in us and, therefore, constantly call us to come unto them with the bread of life, and teach them how and in whom to believe, and how to live as well as how to die.

How To Do It

The methods recommended for our success are, first, the cultivation of a more zealous missionary spirit by the pastors and churches of the Convention. The churches must be trained to give for the support of missions—domestic and foreign—else we shall be insufficient for the great work before us.

The delegates to the Convention usually become deeply interested in missions during its session, but forget to take up collections, and bid Godspeed to the Board during the year. How can your Board do, unless you furnish it means to do with? To appoint an Executive Missionary Board, and then close your doors and hearts and pockets against it, is to act inconsistently, and, to an enlightened mind, supremely ridiculous. No church represented in the Convention should be contented to live through the year without sending up an offering for the support of missions. Let us see this year that missionary collections shall be no more neglected than those taken to sweeten our coffee and tea.

Next, we most respectfully recommend the adoption of such measures as shall secure the best use of the means given by our White Baptist friends of the North and elsewhere, for religious and educational purposes among us as a people. Their gifts are large and cheerfully and hopefully given;

but from the remoteness, peculiarities, and exclusiveness of the channel or agency, these gifts do not produce the desired good. Thus we are exposed to the shame of having it said that our White friends have spent much on us to improve us, but entirely failed. Therefore, we urge you to adopt measures by which the agents of moneys collected from our White friends for the promotion of the Colored Baptist missionary interest in the United States, shall be compelled to respect the wishes and best good of our people in their appropriations.

Quarterly Collection

Your Board would further recommend the taking up of quarterly collections by all the pastors and missionaries of the Convention, as the first and most successful step toward the necessary, desirable, and praiseworthy end of self-reliance. The fact that we must become more self-reliant is too plain and the neglect of it too threatening for us to stand idle or passive. Our White brethren, with the exceptions already mentioned, are bound together, as such, for the defence and perpetuity of their own distinctive interests. They are true to themselves. They not only retain all they have, but draw much more from us than they appropriate directly to us. Thus in a pecuniary point of view, their burden is greater than their relief, although they profess to help us. It is necessary therefore, for us to seek and find resources among ourselves; to apply the rewards of our own labor to the development of our own religious and social interests by the use of our own native instrumentalities.

First: We must give more attention to the cause of...

Ministerial Education

For this purpose there ought to be a fund created and fostered by the Convention or its Executive Board. We recommend, therefore, that a collection be taken up annually, on the third Lord's Day, in October, in every one of our churches. God is now making large and promising accessions to our ministry, and calls upon us as old veterans to drill them and fit them for good captains and generals in the army of the Lord. In order to obey God and do this, we must have money, which these collections will supply.

Second: We recommend that the second general and annual collection be the...

Support of Missions

[This is to] be taken up annually, on the third Lord's Day of January, after preaching by the pastor or agent on the subject of mission.

Third: We also recommend that there be created a...

Church Building Fund

[This is] to be sustained and increased by annual collections, to be taken up on the third Lord's Day of April. We ought to be more interested, as a denomination, in the accumulation of church property. Our brethren in small country towns are generally compelled to go through the land, begging from house to house for means to put up a small church building in which to worship God when, if they had houses of worship, they could soon call together people enough to build for themselves, and be more independent. Going from place to place, they are often humbled and insulted, and the denomination exposed to the contempt or ridicule of others who have better systems for building their churches. Brethren, we beseech you in the name of God, for whom you profess so much love, to suffer this to be no longer, without earnest, faithful effort to stop it. If all the churches of the Convention give annually and liberally for this Church Building Fund, we can stop this disgrace to which we are now so much exposed.

Fourth: We further recommend the fourth or last annual collection be taken up as long as necessary for...

General Purposes

[This is] to be used at the discretion of the Board. The other collections, being designated, and sacred to the ends for which they are designated, cannot be used for anything else. At the expense of about $4,000, your Board could purchase lots of ground and erect suitable buildings and offices in which to conduct the business of the Convention. This is very desirable and economical, and the funds for general purposes could be applied to this and for incidental expenses, including salaries of officers.

Report of Committee on Missionaries and Fields

Whereas, There are many oppositions to the proclaiming of the gospel of Jesus Christ, many claiming that it should be moulded and turned to suit the tastes and fancies of man, keeping the people in ignorance and darkness, and covering the welfare of the people with a cloud of issues not pertinent to the salvation of the soul, therefore,

Resolved, That we hereby commend to and request of our pastors and missionaries, to preach unflinchingly, in its purity, the everlasting gospel, without conferring with flesh and blood, for "Woe unto him who preaches not the gospel."

Resolved, 2d. That the destitute places in the following states be occupied as missionary field; viz., Maryland, Virginia, North Carolina, South

Carolina, Georgia, Florida, Mississippi, Louisiana, Texas, Missouri, Arkansas, Tennessee, Kentucky, California, Delaware, New England States, and the District of Columbia. Also the present missionaries in the field not necessary to be changed be continued in their respective fields.

Resolved, 3d. That we request of our churches to let their pastors occasionally go in the surrounding country and perform missionary labor, and the churches aid their pastors in such labor, but bearing their expenses, and the pastors be empowered to take up collections on the fields to defray their expenses back home. Furthermore, the said pastors must not only have the permit of their churches, but the sanction of the Board of this Convention.

Resolved, 4th. That we hereby urge upon our pastors and churches not to neglect the collections for our missionaries, and further that all of our pastors be required to preach, occasionally, missionary sermons.

Resolved, 5th. That agents be appointed in each state, whose duties shall be to collect funds for the convention and superintend the fields in their respective states, under the direction of the Executive Board.

Resolved, 6th. That Elder N.G. Merry be appointed missionary and agent for Pennsylvania, New Jersey, and New York; 2d, Elder G.W. Dupee, for Massachusetts; 3d, Elder Thomas Jefferson, for Missouri; 4th, Elders Abraham Merry and John Smith, for Mississippi; 5th Elders John Randall and William Shorter, for Louisiana.

The next meeting of the Convention will be held on Thursday before the third Lord's Day in September, A.D. 1869, at 11 o'clock a.m., with the Washington Street Baptist Church, Paducah, Kentucky. The following are to be the preachers:

Introductory Sermon—Rev. John Cox, of Savannah, Georgia; alternate, Rev. N.B. Frierson, of Farmville, Virginia. Missionary Sermon, Rev. Jesse F. Boulden, of Natchez, Mississippi; alternate, Rev. W.J. White. Widow's Fund Sermon, Rev. Sampson White, of Virginia; alternate, Rev. A. Henderson. Doctrinal Sermon, Rev. Richard DeBaptiste, of Illinois.

OFFICERS OF THE CONVENTION

President
Rev. Richard DeBaptiste .... Chicago, Illinois

Vice President
Rev. Nelson G. Merry .... Nashville, Tenn.

CONSOLIDATED AMERICAN BAPTIST MISSIONARY CONVENTION
1869

The third annual meeting was held with the Washington Street Baptist Church at Paducah, Kentucky, Thursday, September 19th, 1869, the president, Rev. R. DeBaptiste, in the chair.

Rev. N.B. Frierson, of Murfreesboro, Tennessee, alternate to Rev. John Cox, of Savannah, Georgia, deceased, delivered the introductory discourse. Text, 1 Cor. 1:10,—"Now I beseech you, brethren, by the name of our Lord Jesus Christ, that ye all speak the same thing, and that there be no divisions among you; but that ye be perfectly joined together in the same mind and in the same judgment."

Extracts From Annual Report

During the past year the work of the Convention has been limited by want of means. No appointments with the exception of collecting agents, have been made, beyond what was recommended at the last annual meeting. But the brethren that have been in the field have been greatly blessed in their labors, as their annual reports will show. They have travelled far into the interior of Virginia, North Carolina, Alabama, Mississippi, Tennessee, Kentucky, Missouri, and other fields, and preached the gospel day and night to the multitudes found in sin and darkness. When they had no money to pay their fares on the public conveyances, none with which to buy bread for themselves whilst on their long, tedious, and often perilous journeys, still they girded their loins as faithful ambassadors of Jesus Christ, constrained to preach deliverance to the captive and went forth proclaiming salvation to every creature, as set forth in the divine commission. Tens of thousands have heard the Word through our missionaries, and thousands have been baptized in the name of the Holy Trinity. The increase during the year has necessitated the erection of new meeting houses, many of which have been built or commenced since our last meeting.

The Sunday school cause, also, has received more than usual attention in the different states. Your Board has aided, as far as possible, every effort to create a deeper and purer interest in our Sunday schools. We felt the need of a Sunday school paper. In order to meet this want, and put our Sunday schools and brethren throughout the land into communication with one another, and thus form a more perfect union, your corresponding secretary, with the approbation and encouragement of your Board and the Free Mission Society, commenced at his expense the publication of a first-class Sunday school and juvenile paper called the *Sunbeam*, humbly praying to God that it might beam on all who are in darkness, and warm every cold and melt every frozen heart; and God has abundantly blessed the enterprise. The *Sunbeam* was started last December without one bona fide subscriber, and now it has a circulation of over 6,000 copies. Twenty-nine thousand two hundred copies, or 116,800 four-column pages, have been printed and circulated since its commencement, the good results of which are almost incalculable. Pastors and superintendents and teachers, both of the North and of the South, have testified to the *Sunbeam*; and the learned, pious, and experienced ministers of our body, who know the wants of our youth, are regular contributors to its columns.

Your Board has been exceedingly financially embarrassed. The quarterly collections, recommended at the last annual meeting, have not been taken up and forwarded to the treasurer. But of this it is necessary to take a liberal view. The churches, generally, are new, as regards liberty and independence, and are not sufficiently trained to give for missions beyond their local demands, and the exceptional instances wherein they would, they are found to be poor and unable. Nearly all the means they could command, above the requirements of personal comforts, have been as much needed at home as abroad. Hence, but little has found its way to your treasurer, whose heart has wept with friend, because he had not the means to pay the missionary and incidental bills of the Convention.

Your Board must have money to work with, or else it must remain inactive, and our cause be worse than if the Convention did not exist. From the fact there are about twenty other missionary and educational societies, representing all denominations, and laboring ostensibly for our education and evangelization, it is no easy matter to raise our money outside of ourselves for the support of our missionary enterprises, unless we can show our claims upon the charity of the public to be stronger than the claims of these societies professing to work for us, and to do for us what we feel we can better do for ourselves.

Our Work

What shall we do, and how shall we do it? are questions that claim our serious attention, and your Board would most respectfully urge upon you at this session of the Convention to resolve upon a proper solution of these questions, and follow up the resolutions by faithfully doing what you resolve to do. The religious and educational development of our brethren is the great work that lies immediately before us. Both of these interests claim of us all it is possible for us to do to promote them.

Educational

Hitherto, we have left the educational work among our people to be done by others and have contributed to other organizations, both religious and secular, for the support of this work while it was right at our doors, and could have been done by us fully as well, and at far less expense. Both duty and denominational interest require us to undertake and maintain a purely educational work in connection with our missionary work. On the one hand, these are three distinct interests; but on the other they are mutually dependent, sympathetic, and cooperative.

We recommend, therefore, that you appoint an Educational Board, who shall immediately take charge of and conduct the educational work to be carried on in connection with the Convention. We recommend further that, in order to save expense in salaries of officers, the managers of the Educational Department be the same or from among those that shall fill the Missionary Board, as far as practicable and judicious. This additional work will require additional labor, for which you or your Board must provide, in the employment of assistants for your corresponding secretary.

Your Board would again respectfully call your attention to the propriety of meeting biennially, instead of annually. Many of the delegates give ten times as much to railroad and steamboat companies, to attend the annual meetings of the Convention, as they give the Convention for the support of missions. This fact denies that we feel that interest in the purposes of the Convention, and have that wisdom, power of management, and business capacity we claim to have. It is like giving ten dollars for a money purse to carry ten cents. If, therefore, you meet biennially, and require your Board to publish annual reports, as now done, you would save hundreds of dollars that might be spent in the support of missionaries and teachers in the destitute regions of the earth, while nothing material would be lost to the Convention by the change.

State Organizations

The pastors in the different states have labored faithfully, earnestly, and very successfully in the work of organizing associations and state conventions, according to the recommendation of this General Convention. Where the organization has been completed and is in operation, we have had proof that we must look upon this as a work absolutely necessary. The State of Virginia is fully organized, and the State Board very harmoniously and efficiently cooperates with the General Board. The churches and associations communicate with the Convention through the general State Board. This concentrates and simplifies the work, and at the same time gives promise of greater efficiency. But while this is the case in the State of Virginia, other states are not so well organized, and the leading brethren of them seem not to see and understand the importance of such thorough organization and cooperation with the General Board of the Convention. Several of the brethren, who take the lead in the states in which they reside, manifest a want of interest that endangers the good of the Convention of which they are members, and for which, at their annual visitations, they profess great regard.

Permanent Offices

As the collections for general purposes recommended at the last annual meeting did not come, your Board has been unable to negotiate for grounds and buildings, for permanent offices, as was intended. But it is still the purpose of your Board to secure permanent buildings for offices, etc., that the Convention, or its Board, like other national societies, may have a permanent resting place, or foothold, and thus give character to itself.

A special Committee on Education was appointed, consisting of George W. Dupee, N.G. Merry, R.L. Perry, H.L. Simpson, J.F. Boulden, R.T.W. James, and W.E. Walker. They presented the following report, which was adopted:

"Your Committee on Education has carefully and prayerfully considered the propriety of organizing and putting into operation at once an Educational Department of this Convention, as recommended by the Executive Board, and do conclude that it is to the good of this Convention, as well as our duty to the hundreds of thousands whom the Convention represents, to enter upon this important work at once, as suggested. If we are called upon as a body to spread the gospel, we are also called upon to spread intelligence, that it may be intelligently received. Therefore we recommend that the Executive Board be, and they are hereby directed to organize, or cause to be organized, an Educational Department of this Convention, officered by efficient and educational men who will at once begin the work of collecting the necessary means and organizing and sustaining schools under the patronage of this Convention.

"That the Board, or the corresponding secretary, bring this matter before General O.O. Howard, Commissioner of the Freedmen's Bureau, and request him to aid in this work, with such funds and other means as may be at his command as Commissioner of the Bureau, and thus help us to maintain schools among the 250,000 of our brethren whom we represent, and for whose good, temporal and spiritual, we are working.

The receipts into the treasury from all sources, during the year amounted to $21,213.51. The expenditures, to $21,197.14, leaving a balance of $16.37 in the treasury.

The next meeting of the Convention will be held in Wilmington, N.C., on Thursday, September 22nd, 1870. The following appointments were made:

Introductory Sermon—Elder R.M. Duling; alternate, Elder Wm.T. Dixon.
Missionary Sermon—Elder W. Shelton; alternate, Elder R.T.W. James.
Widow's Fund Sermon—Elder G.W. Dupee; alternate, Elder A.W. Jackson.
Doctrinal Sermon—Elder Sampson White; alternate, Elder W.E. Walker.

OFFICERS OF THE CONVENTION

President
Rev. R. DeBaptiste .... Chicago, Illinois

Vice-Presidents
Rev. E. Cartwright .... Missouri
Rev. N.G. Merry .... Tennessee
Rev. J.F. Boulden .... Mississippi
Rev. W.H. Banks .... North Carolina

Corresponding Secretary
Rev. Rufus L. Perry .... New York

Recording Secretary
Rev. R.T.W. James .... Kentucky

Treasurer
Deacon Isaac Bagwell .... New York

Board of Managers
W.T. Dixon .... Brooklyn, N.Y.
Matthias Vanstay .... Brooklyn, N.Y.
S. Bundick .... Brooklyn, N.Y.
G.W. Dupee .... Paducah, Ky.
W. Shelton .... Cincinnati, Ohio
H.L. Simpson .... Brooklyn, N.Y.
Henry William .... Brooklyn, N.Y.

CONSOLIDATED AMERICAN BAPTIST
MISSIONARY CONVENTION
1870

The fourth annual meeting (since the consolidation) was held with the Ebenezer Baptist Church, at Wilmington, N.C., on Thursday, September 22nd, 1870. The vice president, Rev. E. Cartwright, of St. Louis, Mo., in the chair. The Introductory Sermon was preached by Rev. W.T. Dixon, of Brooklyn, N.Y., from Matt. 28:19, 20.

Extracts From Annual Report
Another year of our missionary history has passed away and left us

rich with the blessings of God, to whom we ascribe all honor and all praise for whatever of success we have had in our efforts to lead our perishing fellow men to Christ, who invites every poor blind sinner to come unto him and receive his sight and drink freely of the waters of life, and live forever. Six thousand hopeful converts have been buried with Christ in baptism this year by our missionary teachers. To us the Lord is good. Thirty years have elapsed since the American Baptist Missionary Convention was organized, and four years since it formed an organic union with the then Northwestern and Southern Baptist Convention, prefixing the word "Consolidated" to designate the union. The first Introductory Sermon was preached by our venerable brother, Rev. Sampson White, in the year of our Lord, 1841, in the Abyssinian Church, New York City.

Then our resources were small, both of men and money; but ever since then we have been steadily planting and watering, and God has been giving a most glorious increase. Our ministry and our churches have been redoubled a hundred times, and the accessions to the churches of our body more than five hundred times redoubled. Then the walls of Southern Babylon were strong and impregnable, and our field of labor was limited; but, like the walls of Jericho, slaveholding Babylon has fallen to rise no more, and the captives are being led out. Now our field is the world, and we are being everywhere recognized as men called of God and fitted for all the duties and responsibilities and all the rights and privileges of other men.

The ratification of the Fifteenth Amendment to the Constitution of the United States has removed from us all the political disabilities of color and previous condition of servitude.* * * This we have gained since our last anniversary. God, through His great mercy and His overruling providence, has done it all—not for Himself, but for us, that we might be and do what is pleasing in His sight.

State Organizations

Our missionaries and the elders of the several southern states have been busy completing their state organizations. Cooperative work is easy and successful in the states that have been thoroughly organized, as Virginia and some other states have become. Your Board has urged all the states to form state conventions as fast as possible, and bring their official machinery and state operations into harmony and cooperation with the Consolidated Convention. It is desired that every state have its own local organized working force, and that the state organization be an organic part of the national organization—that is, the Consolidated American Baptist

Missionary Convention. In this national body, all our missionary and educational work should be so concentrated that all our strength and fitness and the results of our labors may readily appear.

Educational Department

According to the recommendation of the Board last year and the order of the Convention at its last annual session, the Executive Board met immediately after the adjournment at Paducah, Ky., and thoroughly organized an Educational Department to the Convention, making it a distinct organization with its own official and executive functions. It was efficiently officered by the election of Rev. Henry L. Simpson as president; Rev. James Poindexter as vice-president; Rev. Rufus L. Perry as corresponding secretary; and Deacon Isaac Bagwell as treasurer, with headquarters at Brooklyn, N.Y., with the Convention. It has an Executive Board of eleven persons, including the executive officers and a general superintendent of education.

The organization of this department is one of the wisest movements that has been made the past year. Hitherto we have zealously labored to send the gospel to the spiritually benighted, without giving proper attention to the capacity and thorough fitness of those whom we engaged to carry it. The result of this neglect on our part has been the toleration and propagation, if not also the organization, of errors and superstitions dangerous to the soundness and strength of our faith and our works. Though organized but one year, the department has made considerable progress. An institute has been planted at Richmond, under the principalship of Rev. William Troy. This has had, during the year, over one thousand students. Schools have been planted in Tennessee and Mississippi, and as fast as our receipts will warrant it, we will enter and establish institutions of learning under good Colored teachers in all the late slave states. Under your Educational Department, between seven hundred and eight hundred persons have been more or less instructed the past year.

The funds we hoped to get from the Freedman's Bureau were not obtained; the support hitherto given to the Colored schools of the South by the Bureau is now cut off by the limitation, and Congress has made no further provisions. This throws us upon our own resources, and such help as we can get from our White friends of the North.

There are at present under appointment by the Convention 51 missionaries, as follows: in Arkansas-1, California-1, Colorado-1, District of Columbia-1, Georgia-4, Illinois-4, Kentucky-3, Maryland-2, Mississippi-7, Missouri-4, New Jersey-1, New York-3, North Carolina-1, Ohio-4,

Pennsylvania-1, Tennessee-8, Virginia-5.

The receipts for the year were $26,044.02; the expenditures, $26,006.80, leaving a balance in the treasury of $37.22.

The next meeting of the Convention will be held in Brooklyn on Thursday, Oct. 12th, 1871.

OFFICERS OF CONVENTION

President
Rev. Richard DeBaptiste . . . . Chicago, Ill.

Vice Presidents
Rev. N.G. Merry . . . . Nashville, Tenn.
Rev. S. Bundick . . . . Brooklyn, N.Y.
Rev. W.E. Walker . . . . Trenton, N.J.
Rev. W.H. Banks . . . . Wilmington, N.C.

Corresponding Secretaries
Rev. Rufus L. Perry . . . . P.O. Box 602, Brooklyn, New York
Rev. W.T. Dixon . . . . P.O. Box 602, Brooklyn, N.Y.

Recording Secretary
Rev. H.L. Simpson . . . . Brooklyn, N.Y.

Treasurer
Isaac Bagwell . . . . P.O. Box 602, Brooklyn, N.Y.

Board of Managers
Henry Williams . . . . Brooklyn, N.Y.
Isaac Bagwell . . . . Brooklyn, N.Y.
Matthias Vanstay . . . . Brooklyn, N.Y.
Rufus L. Perry . . . . Brooklyn, N.Y.
J.L. Perry . . . . Brooklyn, N.Y.
W.T. Dixon . . . . Brooklyn, N.Y.
H.L. Simpson . . . . Brooklyn, N.Y.
Samuel Harris . . . . Brooklyn, N.Y.
James Alfred . . . . Brooklyn, N.Y.
J.F. Corprew . . . . Portsmouth, Va.
Frank Quarles . . . . Augusta, Ga.
J. Poindexter . . . . Columbus, Ohio

CONSOLIDATED AMERICAN BAPTIST
MISSIONARY CONVENTION
1871

The fifth annual meeting (since the consolidation) was held in the Concord Street Baptist Church, Brooklyn, N.Y., October 12, 1871. Rev. William Troy, President, in the chair. Introductory Sermon by Rev. W. Shelton, From Rev. 21:14.

The Executive Board Said in Their Report:

The American Baptist Free Mission Society has continued to manifest its good feeling toward our Convention. It has stood ready to help us forward at every opportunity. No steps have been taken to bring societies in any closer union, but the Free Mission Society seems disposed to yield in favor of our Convention in all missions among our brethren where it is concerned. The mission and mission property at Port au Prince, Hayti, have been turned over to our Convention by the Free Mission Society, and the original legal papers relating to the property are now in the hands of your treasurer. The relations between this Convention and the American Baptist Home Mission Society are now pleasant and amicable. Your Board and their Board have a perfect understanding, the one respecting the rights of the other, and laboring with mutual encouragement in the work of mission and education in the South. This is true, also, of the American Bible Union. Rev. Dr. Wyckoff, the Corresponding Secretary of the Bible Union, has repeatedly assured your corresponding secretary of the readiness of the Bible Union to distribute the Bible primer through our Convention among the brethren in the interior parts of the South, and keep on hand in our office such primers and revised copies of the New Testament for persons who, in our judgment, ought to have them. This he is enabled to do by donations from friends for that purpose. The proposition for a union between the American Baptist Free Mission Society and the Consolidated American Baptist Missionary Convention was referred to the Executive Board, with instructions to report at the next annual meeting. The following passed respecting our superannuated ministers:

Resolved, That we do establish a permanent fund for the relief and support of all superannuated ministers of this Convention, and that we do most earnestly urge each and every minister, church, auxiliary society, Sunday school, and corresponding body to contribute yearly to this sacred fund.

The following respecting agencies for raising funds was adopted:

Resolved, That four efficient and energetic ministers of this Convention be appointed to canvass the entire country and solicit pecuniary aid for the Convention, and report monthly to the corresponding secretary the situation of the fields and the amount of money collected, remitting the same. Be it further

Resolved, That this Convention appoint missionaries and agents of this body, that each state may be fully represented in a united cooperation of all the ministers of this Convention.

MISSIONARY WORK

Thirteen missionaries have been employed who have preached 2,562 sermons, baptized 1,492 persons, collected for mission purposes $25,240, travelled 16,703 miles, organized 6 churches, and ordained 30 men to the ministry.

OFFICERS

President

Rev. William Troy .... Richmond, Va.

Vice-Presidents

Rev. Charles Graham .... New York
Rev. E. Cartwright .... Missouri
Rev. F. Quarles .... Georgia
Rev. W.H. Banks .... North Carolina

Recording Secretary

Rev. William T. Dixon .... Box 602, Brooklyn, N.Y.

Corresponding Secretary

Rev. Rufus L. Perry .... Box 602, Brooklyn, N.Y.

Treasurer

Samuel Harris, Esq. .... P.O. Box 602, Brooklyn, N.Y.

Executive Board

W. Troy	Samuel Harris
C. Graham	H. Williams
R.L. Perry	J. Alford
W.T. Dixon	L.A. Grimes

CONSOLIDATED AMERICAN BAPTIST
MISSIONARY CONVENTION
1872

The sixth annual session (since the consolidation) was held in the meeting house of the First African Church, St. Louis, Mo., October 17, 1872. In the absence of the president, the vice-president Rev. E. Cartwright, called the Convention to order. The annual sermon was preached by Rev. J.H. Magee of Cincinnati, Ohio. Text, 1 Cor. 7:31. The annual report of the Executive Board contains the following statements:

During the past six years, we have employed 209 missionaries, including reappointments. Their labors have extended over twenty-four states, embracing 1,188,896 square miles, and a Colored population of 4,500,000 souls. They have travelled 102,489 miles, preached fully 15,000 sermons, and baptized 12,023 hopeful converts. Ninety-five new churches have been founded, and forty-six schools organized. We have collected through our several agencies and paid to these missionaries, directly and indirectly, the sum of about $94,000. During the past year, 14 missionaries have been employed, who have reported 623 weeks of labor, 1,868 baptisms, and more than $30,000 raised and expended on the several fields. The receipts of the treasurer, for the year, amounted to $4,039.03. Of this amount $2,633.60 was designated by the donors for educational purposes, and $130.21 for the printing department; leaving but $1,265.92 for the general fund.

The Haitian Mission

"On the first day of June, we commissioned Rev. J.L. Andrews and Sister Andrews, his wife, of Wilkes-Barre, Pa., as our agents and missionaries to Hayti, and directed them to get ready to go out and take charge of the mission and mission property at Port au Prince. But they were authorized to collect funds before going, to put the mission in order or to purchase and take out the frame of a new chapel. As soon as they accomplish this, they propose to enter and engage in the work of teaching and preaching Jesus. Sister Andrews has resided in Hayti. She understands the manners and customs of the people and is an excellent French scholar. Thus she is well fitted for this particular field of labor, in connection with her husband, who is a regularly ordained and a thoroughly educated Baptist minister. So the prospects for soon having an interesting mission in Hayti, are very encouraging." A recommendation from the Executive Board relative to arranging the various mission fields into districts, we referred to a committee, who presented the following report which was adopted:

"1. Southeastern District—Embracing Maryland, the District of Columbia, Virginia, West Virginia, and North Carolina, with board and secretary at Richmond, Va.

"2. Southern District—Embracing South Carolina, Georgia, Florida, Alabama, Mississippi, and Louisiana, with local board and district secretary at Savannah, Ga.

"3. Southwestern District—Embracing Missouri, Arkansas, and Texas, with local board and district secretary at St. Louis, Mo.

"4. Middle District—Embracing Tennessee and Kentucky with local board and district secretary at Louisville, Ky.

"5. Western District—Embracing all the territory north of the Ohio River and west of the chain of lakes, with a local board and district secretary in the city of Chicago.

"6. Eastern District—Embracing all the New England and Middle States, with a local board in the city of Philadelphia; all subject to the general board, to which all reports must be made for combined publication."

The Committee on Widows' Fund reported, recommending that the Widows' Fund be hereafter under the immediate control of our Missionary Board, who shall care for it in common with the other departments of our work, annually reporting its condition as now required by the trustees under the old laws; and that every pastor connected with this Convention be requested to urge this particular duty upon the attention of his church, from time to time, taking up contributions for the same, in common with other branches of our works of benevolence.

A recommendation from the Committee on Education was also adopted, urging the churches to sustain to the extent of their ability, the Educational Department as managed by the Consolidated American Educational Association.

The next session of the Convention will be held at New Orleans, La., Nov. 11, 1874, Rev. Rufus L. Perry to preach the Introductory Sermon.

OFFICERS

President
Rev. Richard DeBaptiste

Vice-Presidents
Rev. Charles Graham .... New York

Rev. Moses Broyles . . . . Indiana
Rev. J.H. Magee . . . . Ohio
Rev. E. Cartwright . . . . Missouri
Rev. Henry Williams, Jr. . . . . Virginia
Rev. Lewis Norris . . . . Kentucky
Rev. N.G. Merry . . . . Tennessee
Rev. Benj. Burke . . . . Alabama
Leonard Crimes . . . . Massachusetts

Corresponding Secretary
Rev. Rufus L. Perry

Recording Secretary
Rev. Amos Johnson

Treasurer
Samuel Harris, Esq.

Executive Board

C. Graham	Samuel Harris
H. Williams	William Emory
G. W. Talbott	William Spellman
Jacob Day	G. B. Smith
	W. T. Dixon

CONSOLIDATED AMERICAN BAPTIST
MISSIONARY CONVENTION
(1865)

1873

The seventh annual session (since the consolidation) was held at Philadelphia, Pa., Nov. 7, 1873. The annual sermon was preached by Rev. Wm. T. Dixon. Text, Isaiah 60:22.

The treasurer's report showed receipts amounting to $7,161.97; expenditures $7,120.87.

The report of the Executive Board says:

"During the last seven years, we have appointed 238 missionaries, including those reappointed. Their fields of labor extended over twenty-four different states. They have reported 112,497 miles travelled; over 17,000 sermons preached, and 15,206 hopeful conversions. They have aided in the building of 102 new meeting houses and organized fifty-six schools. We have collected and paid to these missionaries, directly and indirectly, about $100,000. Besides this we have given employment to thirty-seven other Colored persons in our educational and printing departments.

"We have had 45 missionaries employed the last year; for periods ranging from three to twelve months. These included every one of the Southern States. The only missionary work done in the North has been done by the officers of the Convention, Rev. Edmund Kelly laboring in New England and three White missionaries and agents.

"The Haitian Mission remains the same, excepting an increase of interest in the little church at Port au Prince. Rev. J.L. Andrews and Sister Andrews, who were appointed as missionaries and teachers for this field, were appointed first because Sister Andrews was familiar with the local language and the manners and customs of the people; and, secondly, because they impressed your Executive Board with the belief that they could easily raise money enough in this country, and before going out, to erect a suitable building on our lots in Port au Prince for preaching and school purposes. In this they have failed, and they are now in doubt as to whether they will go out at all. Their commissions have expired by limitation, and the Board has not renewed them. They have collected about $800. This money has been turned over to our treasurer and used in domestic work.

"During the last year the Educational Department of the Convention was incorporated under the laws of the State of New York, as an independent organization; but it has been in no wise changed in its mode of operation and cooperation with the Convention. So, practically, it is yet a department of the Convention. The executive officers of this department are officers of the Convention, which saves the salaries of one set of officers to be used for other purposes. Teachers are sent south, and schools organized on a self-sustaining basis as fast and as extensively as the gifts of friends for educational purposes will allow.

"The printing department of the Convention is now in successful operation, and bids fair to become self-sustaining. We have our own printing office, our own type, our own Baptist compositors, our own presses, our own church organ under our own business and editorial management. All the work, physical and mental, done in this department, with one exception, is done by persons of our own race, and mostly of our Colored Baptist family.

"The following resolutions were adopted:

"Resolved, That we request the Executive Board to send a deputation to Hayti, as soon as practicable, to ascertain the present condition of the seven Baptist churches, which were organized by the late Rev. Arthur Warring.

"Resolved, That the same deputation ascertain the value of the property in Port au Prince transferred to this society by the American Baptist Free Mission Society."

The next meeting will be held at New Orleans, La., Nov. 12, 1874.

OFFICERS

President
Rev. Richard DeBaptiste .... Chicago

Vice-Presidents
Charles Graham .... New York
Robert A. Pinn .... Pennsylvania
Moses Broyles .... Indiana
J.H. Magee .... Ohio
E. Cartwright .... Missouri
Henry William, Jr. .... Virginia
Lewis Norris .... Kentucky
N.G. Merry .... Tennessee
Benjamin Burke .... Alabama
William Jackson .... Rhode Island

Corresponding Secretary
Rev. Rufus L. Perry .... Brooklyn, N.Y.

Recording Secretaries
Amos Johnson .... Missouri
Rev. W.T. Dixon, Assistant

Treasurer
Samuel Harris, Esq. .... Brooklyn, N.Y.
Executive Board
C. Graham   Samuel Harris

H. Williams	William Emory
G. W. Talbott	W. T. Dixon
Jacob Day	William Spellman
	G. B. Smith

CONSOLIDATED AMERICAN BAPTIST
MISSIONARY CONVENTION
(1865)

1874

The annual meeting was held at New Orleans, La., Nov. 11. The Introductory Sermon was preached by Rev. R.L. Perry, from Psalm 27:3. The Missionary Sermon was preached by Rev. J.F. Boulden, from Matt. 4:23, and Matt. 10:6,7. The Educational Sermon was preached by Rev. Mr. Walker, N.J., from Mark 16:15-20, and 2 Tim. 11:15.

From the Annual Report of the Executive Board, we take the following:

"Since the union of the Colored churches of the North with the Colored churches of the South, we have appointed in twenty-four states 277 missionaries; they have travelled 554,000 miles, and report 19,390 sermons, 5,510 conversion as the result of their labor, and 17,277 conversions as the result of cooperative labor; beside, the agencies of the Convention have aided in building 115 new meeting houses; organized 126 day and Sunday schools, on a self-sustaining basis. The Convention has raised and appropriated to the various persons employed $11,000 including fifteen persons in the printing department.

"The relations to the American Baptist Home Mission Society and Bible Union are as amicable as could be expected, yet there ought to be a more efficient cooperation with the first named Society.

"The Hayti Mission remains in the same state as when last reported. Rev. J.L. Andrews and wife have failed in their efforts to raise the necessary funds. They have, however, raised $900, one-half of which was paid to them for their services; the other applied to the domestic work.

"The Printing Department is in successful operation. The *National Monitor* is regularly published, and in successful operation. It only requires the support of the denomination to render it not only self-sustaining, but a source of revenue. We have our own type, our own compositors, our own presses, our own editors and managers. We have issued 76,000 copies, at a cost of $2,680.

The Convention adjourned to meet at the call of the Executive Board.

OFFICERS

President
Rev. William Gray .... Greenville, Miss.

Secretary
W.C. Phillips .... Chicago, Ill.

Corresponding Secretary
Rev. R.L. Perry .... Brooklyn, N.Y.

Treasurer
Samuel Harris, Esq. .... Brooklyn, N.Y.

Chapter X

*Just as other races have left their impress upon the world, so must we.
All the civilizing forces that touch and mould us are intended to be
productive of these results, and we are set down in history as a success
or a failure as we do or not arise to the best use of our opportuntities.—
E. K. Love, D.D.*

*Praise is as good for a race as for an individual, but flattery is not good
for either. Booker T. Washington, A.M., Tuskegee.*

LEADERS IN SOCIAL SERVICE, BETTER RACE RELATIONS, AND HUMAN UPLIFT

Many of the wisest and best laymen of our group have been, and
are now, members of Baptist churches. We mention a few gathered here
and there.

John W. Work.—Writer and interpreter of Negro songs; a teacher
at Fisk and president of Roger Williams.

Geo. W. Williams, Ohio—The most outstanding racial historian;
author, *History of American Negro.*[14]*

Booker T. Washington, West Virginia.—Founder of Tuskegee Institute and "Father of Industrial Education."*

Robert R. Moton, Virginia.—Principal of Tuskegee Institute, one of
our most outstanding tribunes.

William H. Steward (Uncle Billy), Kentucky.—Editor of the oldest
Negro Baptist newspaper.

Benjamin J. Davis, Georgia.—Astute politician, outspoken editor,
leader of the Negro Press Association.

Mary B. Tolbert.—Saved Anacostia, the home of Frederick Douglass,
as a shrine for the race.*

---

[14]*History of the Negro Race in America from 1619 to 1880,* by George Washington Williams
(1849-1891), G. P. Putnam's Sons, *circa* 1882. Ed.

Nannie Helen Burroughs, D.C.—Tucked away an idea for ten years from which she produced the largest training school for girls among us conducted by women. Called one of the most eloquent and charming orators among women.

John Mitchell, Jr., Virginia.—The Fighting Editor.*

Maggie L. Walker, Virginia.—The only woman banker of the race and a leader of women.

Carter G. Woodson, D.C.—Reliable and one of the race's most extensive historians.

Charles C. Spaulding, N. C.—A shrewd financier and insurance wizard.

G. W. Trenholm—Credited with revolutionizing the educational world for Negroes and making the state school a college.

Jennie V. Porter, Ohio—One of the state's greatest organizers and teachers—planned and manages a million-dollar city institution.

William H. Wright, Kentucky—A lawyer, successful insurance organizer, and banker.

Anthony Overton, Illinois.—Organizer of our largest national bank; a safe financier and extensive manufacturer.

William Roseborough, Texas.—Composer of anthems and other church music.*

Adolphus Humbles, Virginia.—Trustee, capitalist, and promoter of Christian education.

Robert B. Hudson, Alabama.—Teacher, financier, and scribe of large mold. Secretary of National Baptist Convention.

John C. Asbury, Pa.—Shrewd lawyer, statesman, and banker.

T.C. Windham & Bros., Ala.—Most widely known builders and construction company in our group; builders of our Sunday School Publishing House.

A. Floyd Gambol, West Virginia.—Yale Medical graduate, first Negro physician in West Virginia.

Charles H. Brooks, Pennsylvania.—Always loyal; a leading promoter, churchman, and insurance broker.

John Hope, Georgia.—President Morehouse College, gentlemanly in bearing; a cautious, sane, and safe leader.

Charles E. Points, Virginia.—Banker for twenty years; treasurer of Baptist church with one discrepancy of three cents in his favor.

G. Edward Dickerson, Pennsylvania.—Churchman of large mold and lawyer.

FIRST BAPTIST CHURCH
Danville, Ky.

First Baptist Church, Danville, Ky., was organized in 1846. One hundred twenty-three members having served in the White Baptist church, was set apart the first Saturday in August by the white Baptist church as an independent organization and the recognition services followed on Sunday. The first pastor, Rev. Jordan Meaux, then Rev. Henry Green; Rev. Isaac Slaughter was the third pastor in this historical church, who served for 26 years. Rev. Wallace Fisher and Rev. S. Livingston each served a short time and was followed by J.E. Woods, D. D., who served them for 32 years and passed to his reward early in 1930. Under Dr. Woods this church became one of the most modern and attractive churches in all Kentucky. Dr. Woods became the second president of the National Baptist Convention, Unincorporated, which was organized in Chicago in 1915. He had large interest in political affairs of the state.

REV. PETER VERTREES
Gallatin, Tenn.

Born some years before the Civil War in Edmondson Co., Ky. He was one of the early students of Roger Williams University and was a teacher and a preacher. He was once principal of South Gallatin Public School; president of two leading benevolent societies in his home town, and for sixty years pastor of the First Baptist Church. He served as contemporary with Merry and Vann in Tennessee Baptist affairs. He died Jan. 18, 1926, beloved and honored by those among whom he lived and served so long.

REV. JARED M. ARTER
Washington, D.C.

Rev. Jared M. Arter, Ph.B., D.D., formerly president West Virginia Industrial School, Theological Seminary and College, and principal Hill Top Graded School, from Sept. 1, 1908, to June 15, 1915. He departed this life in 1928. Mrs. Maggie Arter, his faithful wife, has spent her whole life in helping the National Training School at Washington, D.C., where she now has charge of the laundry plant.

Wm. Harrison, Illinois.—A real church and Sunday school worker, former judge, and an eloquent orator and Assistant Attorney General of Illinois.

Watt Terry, Massachusetts.—Pioneer in large financing; a wealthy real estate dealer.

D.A. Dorsey, Florida—Hotel keeper, fine businessman, and capitalist.

Albert Jones.—Licensed preacher, called the largest lime grower in the world; licensed river captain; a capitalist.

Prof. Charles S. Thompson.—Superintendent Sunday school and large realtor and broker. These three Floridians' combined wealth amounts to more than $4 million.

F.M. Woods, Maryland.—Known as an executor of large capacity; superintendent of our public schools in Baltimore.

Marse S. Calloway, Maryland.—Realtor of large proportion.

Shedrick B. Turner, Illinois.—Lawyer and statesman; member of Illinois legislature.

Julius B. Ramsey, Illinois.—A good financier; Field Secretary, Tuskegee Institute.

Edw. D. Pierson, Texas.—Possibly the race's largest and most efficient accountant; auditor National Baptist Convention.*

Plato and Evans, Kentucky.—Contractors and builders. Erected Simmons University boys' building and Greater Antioch Baptist Church, Cincinnati, Ohio.

T.G. Ewing, Tennessee.—Attorney of the National Baptist Convention for years.*

W.L. Cansler, Tennessee.—Principal city schools, secretary of National Baptist Convention for eight years.*

Mack N. Rodgers, Texas.—Leader in fraternal organizations, Auditor of National Baptist Convention.*

R.A. Williams, Illinois.—Founder and organizer of a strong fraternal organization; very outstanding realtor.

William E. King, Illinois.—Attorney-at-law, representative in Illinois legislature.

Ed. W.D. Abner, Colorado.—Physician and head of one of America's largest benefit associations.

John L. Webb, Arkansas.—Organizer and leader of the state's largest fraternal racial organization.

Dr. Lewis, Illinois.—First and only teacher we furnished for the University of Chicago.

Edward Berry, Ohio.—A real lover of the denomination and a large giver to Christian work.

Max Yeargan, North Carolina.—Y.M.C.A. worker. Now working in South Africa.

R.H. Rutherford, District of Columbia.—Founder and organizer of a prosperous growing financial institution.

Walter W.H. Cassell, Pennsylvania.—A growing businessman and a contender for the faith.

Finley J. Wilson, District of Columbia.—Editor and leader of one of the largest fraternal associations in the United States.

Gregory W. Hayes, Virginia.—Great scholar, good teacher; a maker and leader of men.*

Alexander Terrell, Texas.—Former blacksmith, treasurer for many years of State Convention.* His son of the same name succeeded him.

Dr. A.M. Moore, Durham, N.C.—Pioneer professional and businessman of Durham; physician, financier, philanthropist, insurance magnate; outstanding Sunday school and church worker; superintendent of White Rock Baptist Church Sunday School for more than thirty years; superintendent and founder of Lincoln Hospital; trustee of Shaw University. Left a legacy for Shaw of $5,000.

Dr. J.B. Davis, Louisburg, N.C.—Prominent physician; president, State B.Y.P.U., Sunday School worker. Was instrumental in securing high school for Negroes.

Chas. C. Spaulding, Durham, N.C.—President, North Carolina Mutual Life Insurance Company; president, Mechanics and Farmers Bank of Durham and Raleigh; president, Mortgage Company of Durham. Leader in all big business interests in North Carolina, financier, insurance wizard. President, North Carolina Welfare League; deacon, White Rock Baptist Church; ex-president, Baptist State Convention.

Dr. E.E. Smith, Fayetteville, N.C.—Principal of State Normal School at Fayetteville for forty years; ex-Minister to Liberia; pastor; treasurer of the Baptist State Sunday School Convention; trustee of Shaw University.

Many, many more outstanding Baptist laymen engaged in the work

---

*Deceased. [That is, at the time of initial publication in 1930. Many more have passed since. Ed.]

of human betterment may be found in every community where our group abounds.

Baptists as a World Power

A few years ago Mr. P. Whitwell Wilson wrote in the magazine section of the *New York Times*:

"To any one who recalls what were the splendors of ceremonial religion, Roman Catholic and Protestant, which once adorned with a divine sanction the banished thrones of the Old World, it is indeed strange to be told that Warren Gamaliel Harding, Charles Evans Hughes and David Lloyd-George should belong, all of them, with John D. Rockefeller, to a 'sect' once so despised, so persecuted and so poor, as the Baptists. Let Lady Sneerwell cease her ribaldry at the staggering thought that of these four men, sons of the Baptist churches, the first is the elected head of a sovereign state, wealthier by far and not less proud than were the French of King Louis XIV; the second is this elected sovereign's minister, who is charged with responsibilities which would have surpassed the utmost ambition of a Richelieu; as Prime Minister of England, the third is endowed with a prestige compared with which the pretentions of Cardinal Wolsey sink into insignificance; while the fourth, as monarch of commerce, has founded like the Medici or the Rothschilds, the richest family in the world, and administers revenues which but yesterday would have been envied by many a first class state. All these are Baptists, and among them they are ruling, under democratic sanctions, one-third of the human race.

It means that over the palaces of emperors, the castles of nobility, the mansions of the merchant, the fortresses of the militarist, the colleges of the erudite, and the cathedrals of the ecclesiastics, those humble folk, who were immersed in the chilly yet soul-cleansing waters of the River Jordan, who prayed the more zealously in their chapels because they were excluded from parliament and the universities, who were too Puritan even for the Puritans, have at last established their civic claim. God hath indeed put down the mighty from their seats, and hath exalted them of low degree! The stone which the builders of modern civilization so contemptuously rejected, the same has become the head of the corner! Such an achievement of prosperity, commercial, political, social, is unparalleled."—F.F. Brown.

"FROM YESTERDAY'S SLAVES"

Yesterday—A.D. 1619　　　　　**Today—A.D. 1930**

Today there are in the United States among the children of Yesterday's slaves:

Negro Chemists 175
Negro Civil and Mining Engineers 167
Negro Authors 580
Negro Dentists 638
Negro Inventors 1,010
Negro Lawyers 1,200
Negro Nurses 2,600
Negro Physicians and Surgeons 4,300
Negro School Teachers 48,000
Negro Judges 1,000

METROPOLITAN BAPTIST CHURCH
Walker Avenue, Memphis, Tenn.
This church was organized by Rev. P.J. Jackson, pastored by Dr. T.J. Searcy till he died. Then came Dr. A.M. Townsend. Dr. S.A. Owen is now pastor, under whose care this splendid building was erected.—*Home and Foreign Fields.*

Chapter XI

To be filled with the Holy Ghost does not consist of sound, as some think, but obedience to Christ.—George W. Lee, National Baptist Magazine, *April, 1896.*

There has been great progress in Baptist principles since the Reformation of the sixteenth century. Throughout the Protestant world there has been steady approximation by nearly all other denominations to many Baptist principles, very materially narrowing the once broad margin dividing us from other people.— Selected.

That man that does not use the few opportunities he has would not likely use many if they were granted him. The man who had the one talent had the same chance that the others had, but he did not use it; hence was regarded as an unprofitable servant. Even the one talent he had was taken away from him and given to the faithful who took care of their opportunities and talents.—J.A. Brooks, A.M., President, Arkansas Baptist College.

THE WORK OF THE AMERICAN BAPTIST HOME MISSION SOCIETY
FOR THE NEGROES OF THE UNITED STATES

By Rev. H.L. Morehouse, D.D., LL.D., Corresponding Secretary of the Society.

(Dr. Morehouse wrote this article upon request of Dr. Boyd for an outline for Baptist History published in 1911. We are reproducing the article because of its thorough presentation of the claims of the society.)

The American Baptist Home Mission Society was organized in New York City in 1832, shortly after the last Northern state had passed an act abolishing slavery within its borders. In 1833 the Anti-slavery Association was organized for the purpose of ridding the land of slavery by constitutional enactments of the general government. Discussion on the subject waxed warm and broke out in meetings of the Society. The climax came in the meeting at Philadelphia in 1844 when Dr. Bartholomew T. Welch, of New York, answered the question of Dr. Richard Fuller, of Baltimore, "What would you do if you had the power?" The reply which electrified the great audience was this: "Do? Do? Proclaim throughout all the land, to all the inhabitants thereof. That is what I would do." The next year the Southern Baptists withdrew from the Society, as also from the Baptist Missionary Union, and organized the Southern Baptist Convention—naturally, from that date until the war, for about twenty years the Southern States were closed against Society. "When the Almighty opened the doors of access to the freedmen, the Society was swift to enter and for almost fifty years has maintained its distinctive work on their behalf. Before the war, its announced policy was that its missionaries should "deliver their message to every creature within their reach—the rich and the poor, the bond, and the free."

The Society Hears the Call to Christianize the Slaves

During the war, from 1861-1865, the Society took high grounds concerning the significance of the great struggle, declaring their conviction "that Divine Providence is about to break the chains of the enslaved millions in our land" and that "the Divine Hand most distinctly and most imperatively is beckoning us to the occupancy of a field, broader, more important, more promising than has ever yet invited our toils." This was early in the great struggle. In 1862, when the Society directed its Executive Board "to supply with Christian instruction, by means of missionaries and teachers, the emancipated slaves—whether in the District of Columbia or in other states held by our forces."

On January 30, 1862, the Board had taken the initiative in a preliminary inquiry into the condition of the Negro refugees within the Union lines. During the next three years, its missionaries and teachers were sent to various points occupied by the Union forces in the District of Columbia, in Virginia, North Carolina, South Carolina, Tennessee, Mississippi, and Louisiana.

The Society Loyal to the Government During the War

In the darkest hours of the conflict, in 1864, the Society adopted a series of resolutions expressing its unshaken faith in the triumph of the government and pledging its loyalty of the great president Abraham Lincoln, to whom a special committee of prominent men was sent with its message of cheer and hope and to whom he made a noble reply. During this period, of course, the work of missionaries and teachers was of the simplest sort. The spelling book and the Bible were the principal textbooks. Missionaries were teachers and teachers were missionaries.

A Definite Policy as to Work Among Freedmen

Immediately after the war, when emancipation had become an accomplished fact, a more definite policy was adopted by the Society to which Baptists of the North had committed this work for freedom. It expressly declared that its workers in the South must be men "emphatically loyal to good government and to God and who feel the strongest and tenderest sympathy with downtrodden humanity." Its plans were the appointment of general missionaries to win men to Christ and to gather them into churches; to impart education to all in order that they might read and understand the Scriptures; and to instruct ministers through classes organized at central points.

Noble Men and Women Give Themselves to the Work

The Northern Baptists were profoundly moved to do their part in the uplift of the newly-emancipated race. Some of the best men and women of their churches gave themselves heroically to the task, leaving homes and good positions there for life and toil among the lowly. Among these were Rev. Henry Martyn Tupper, D.D., founder of Shaw University, Raliegh, N.C.; Rev. Chas H. Corey, D.D., of Richmond, Virginia Theological Seminary; Rev. G.M.P. King, D.D., of Wayland Seminary, D.C.; Rev. D.W. Phillips, D.D., of Roger Williams University, Nashville, Tenn.; Rev. Lyman B. Tefft, D.D., of Hartshorn Memorial College, Richmond, Va.; Miss Sophia B. Packard and Miss H. E. Giles and Miss Luch H. Upton, of Spelman Seminary, Atlanta, Ga., an many others of like spirit. Dr. Nathan Bishop, for a while corresponding secretary of the Home Mission Society, when criticized for his deep interest and liberal gifts to this work, made this noble reply: "I expect to stand side by side with these Colored men on the Day of Judgement. Their Lord is my Lord, they and I are brethren; and I am determined to be prepared for that meeting."

The Preparation of Christian Leaders Emphasized

The dominant theory of the Society in this work, from the outset, has been that emphasis must be laid upon the training of competent, consecrated Christian leaders for the uplift of the race; and that Christian culture and character are fundamental thereto.

Hence, its efforts have been concentrated chiefly on Christian education for this purpose. At the same time, all through these years, many missionaries to the Negroes have been in the Society's service, mostly Negroes themselves, in the Northern and Western States, as well as in the South.

Schools Established for the Training of Negro Leaders

Schools, most of which have become strong institutions, were established under the Society's auspices as follows: Maryland Seminary, Washington, D.C., 1864 (now consolidated with the University at Richmond, Virginia); Richmond Institute, Virginia 1865, which developed into Virginia Union University in 1896; Shaw University, Raleigh, N.C., 1865; Roger Williams University, Nashville, Tenn., 1865; Leland University, New Orleans, La., 1865; Augusta Institute, Georgia, which was started in 1867, transferred to Atlanta, 1879, and now called Atlanta Baptist College; Benedict College, Columbia, S.C. 1870; Natchez Seminary, Mississippi, 1877, transferred in 1882 to Jackson and now known as Jackson College; Bishop College, Marshall, Texas, 1881; Spelman Seminary, Atlanta, Ga., 1882. Besides these schools, there are a number of others that were started by Negro Baptists that for many years have had the benefit of generous aid from the Society, both in the support of teachers and in their building enterprises, as Alabama Baptist University, Selma Ala.; State University, Louisville, Ky.; Arkansas Baptist College, Little Rock, Ark; Western College, Macon, Mo.; Howe Normal and Bible Institute, Memphis, Tenn.; Waters Normal Institute, Winston, N.C.; Walker Institute, Americus, Ga.; and Florida Baptist Academy, Texas. Several other minor institutions have also received help. The Mather School at Beaufort, S.C., has been maintained mainly by the Woman's American Baptist Home Mission Society, which also has given largely for the maintenance of Spelman Seminary and has supported teachers in other schools.

Helping the Negro to Help Himself

The Society has extended its aid to these schools, mostly of a secondary character, in order to develop the spirit of self-help and administrative ability on the part of the Negro Baptists, and had been gratified at the results attained. About sixty Negro instructors are annually under appointment by the Society, and one of the foremost of the Society's schools has a Negro president.

The Influence of the Schools Upon the Race

It has been greatly to the advantage of the Negro in the South to have been brought in contact with a large number of devoted Christian teachers from the North deeply imbued with the missionary spirit, with high ideals of character and service. Many of these have made a profound impression upon their pupils, about 80,000 of whom have been enrolled in the institutions aided by the Society. Their ever-widening influence is incalculable in the transformation of conditions in homes, in social circles, in churches and Sunday schools, in public schools, in religious work and moral reforms, in missionary enterprises, and in many other respects. Many of the foremost preachers of the gospel and others prominent in the denominational activities of the Negro Baptists, received their training in these Christian institutions.

The Principle Upon Which the Society Has Worked

The Society has proceeded upon the theory that the Black man has essentially the same nature and endowments as those of the White man, though in many respects the higher qualities have been undeveloped; and that is the duty of the race that has attained to the highest degree of civilization to help its unfortunate brothers onward and upward. Results have fully justified its faith and its works. Emphasis has been laid on the making of character rather than on making better servants for the White race. The educational work has been mostly of an academic grade, though a goodly number of students have pursued successfully the college course. Theological instruction has been given in the higher institutions, usually in connection with intellectual training in the academic work; a two years' course in English being provided for those desiring to take it. The one higher theological school is Richmond Theological Seminary, a department of Virginia Union University, whose course of study corresponds in its general features to that of theological seminaries at the North. The Leonard Medical School of Shaw University at Raleigh, N.C., has a superior faculty, a four years' course of study, and has made a creditable record. About $25,000 is to be expended soon by the Society in providing better equipment, which will give it a front rank in institutions of this sort in the South. At Spelman Seminary there is a Nurse Training School in connection with the McVicar Hospital Building. There also is an excellent Normal Teachers' Training Department. At several other schools special attention is given to the training of Christian teachers for the nearly two million of Negro children in the South, who must be taught chiefly by those of their own race. Industrial instruction has long been given in several schools to a considerable extent for both sexes. The missionary spirit has been stimulated, pupils being impressed with the idea that education is not merely an accomplishment for personal advancement, but the means whereby its possessor may become more useful to the world and the better serve his Maker.

In 1895, as a result of a conference at Fortress Monroe, between representatives of the American Home Mission Society and upon the initiative of the latter body, a plan for holding institutes for Negro Baptist ministers was worked out and put into effect in several Southern States, with great benefit. Besides these two organizations, the cooperation of the White and of the Negro Baptist Conventions in each state was secured; thus bringing them into closer Christian relationships. The general direction of the work was in the hands of the Negro Baptist Conventions and the missionaries representing them. Through the disinclination of some of the White organizations to continue appropriations for this work, it has discontinued in several states. The Home Mission Society is now, 1910, contemplating another method with the same end in view; namely, the establishment of summer schools for several weeks directly after the close of the regular work of the year, when Negro preachers can occupy vacated rooms in the school buildings and at small expense receive helpful instruction.

Splendid Buildings of the Institution

Very substantial and commodious are most of the school buildings erected by the Society. At Virginia Union University there are six imposing stone structures; at Shaw University seven of brick; at Benedict College five brick and three frame buildings; at Atlanta Baptist College, three of brick and a fourth in process of erection; at Spelman Seminary eight of brick; at Jackson College, four of brick and one frame; at Bishop College, five of brick and two frame. When the buildings of Roger Williams University at Nashville, Tenn., were destroyed by fire in 1905-6 it was decided best to dispose of the site, which had become quite valuable, and to apply part of the proceeds for the re-establishment of the school in another location and under the immediate auspices of the Negro Baptists of the State.

The Value of School Property and Cost of Maintenance

The annual cost to the Society for the maintenance of this educational work is about $140,000; the value of the school properties which it has been instrumental in securing is nearly or quite $1 million and its total expenditures for the uplift of the American Negro, since emancipation have been in round numbers $4.5 million. These large figures, however, represent but part of the investment given by the administrative officers of the Society and by presidents of institutions and their associates, in the aggregate hundreds of years of thought and talent and energy and the best that could be laid upon the altar for Christ in connection with this service.

THE WORK OF THE AMERICAN BAPTIST PUBLICATION SOCIETY AMONG THE COLORED PEOPLE

By S.N. Vass, D.D., Litt.D., former Superintendent for Colored Work of the Society but now Secretary of Religious Education of Sunday School Publishing Board, National Baptist Convention, Inc., U.S.A.

Dr. Vass wrote this article upon request of Dr. R.H. Boyd in 1911 for the work on Negro Baptist Church History published by Dr. Boyd. We are reproducing the article because of its very thorough presentation of the work of the Society.

The first service rendered by the American Baptist Publication Society to the Negro people was when the race was still in slavery and unable to help itself. It is a fact that needs no long argument to prove that the southern White people were, in thousands of cases, very kind and considerate of their slaves, and taught our people their first lessons in Christianity, in many instances gathering them into Sunday schools and encouraging them to connect themselves with churches. The result was that at emancipation there were hundreds of churches among the Colored people, while still others worshipped with the White people. The Baptist Publication Society was an important factor among the White Baptists in those early days, for it must be remembered that the Society was organized on southern soil, and Southern Baptists had no other publishing house for years but the society. It is safe to say that the Society with its tracts and broadening literature must have contributed very largely to the triumph of spirit over flesh in the master, thus leading him to treat his slaves with kindness, and finally to teach them to know Jesus. In those days noble southern White people by the hundreds had such interest in their former slaves as to labor to their utmost to save them.

When the race was in slavery the Society was not the strong organization that it is today, but it made the largest use of its limited resources. As soon as the slaves were liberated, their condition was so deplorable as to secure for them the sympathies of the northern people, and the officers of the Society began to see as never before the service God would have them render. At that time Dr. Benjamin Griffith was the General

Secretary, and a more sincere and helpful friend the Colored people never had. He saw the Colored race as the most needful and at the same time the most promising mission field in America. His convictions were so strong that he succeeded in interesting others, using his personal friendships and family relations to make friends for the race and thus secure means to carry out his program of help. The Crozers and Bucknells came to his assistance, and by their princely donations by gifts of many others, the Society was for the first time placed upon a permanent and safe basis for the great work it has accomplished since that time. It is exceedingly probable that the Society would never have been the power it is today, unless God had moved upon the hearts of Dr. Griffith and a few others in the North to build up great resources and strength in order that the Society might render the necessary help to the Colored people, and also the White people in the impoverished Southland. Strictly speaking, the great work of the Society began after the slaves were set free. Thus the immense resources of the Society tell the story of the great interest of the Society in the freedmen, and of the great work undertaken in their behalf.

If success ever crowned the efforts of any agency at work among the Colored people, it crowned those of the Baptist Publication Society. As to how helpful it had proven to the race, and just the part it has taken in bringing about the unprecedented progress of the race, the persons most competent to bear witness are the leaders of the Negro race.

In bearing the greetings of the Negro Baptists to the American Baptist Publication Society in its annual session at Dayton, Ohio, 1906, Dr. E.W.D. Isaac, one of the most distinguished and experienced leaders of the Negro race made use of these words: "It is difficult to find a Negro Baptist preacher who had not been helped in some way by this Society, and who does not stand ready and willing to acknowledge the good it has done to him." It is a strong statement but wholly endorsed by all Negro Baptist preachers North and South. If this is so, it tells a great tale in a few words for the Negro preachers have ever been the leaders among the people, and to help them was the surest and best way to help the people. Since Dr. Griffith made the start of helping Negro preachers with the gifts of books suitable to prepare them to discharge their duties more faithfully and intelligently, more than a half million dollars have been expended in gifts to the poor, especially the poor preachers of the Negro race, for this work started with our freedom. Over ten thousand preachers have been thus helped with libraries worth $20 each upon an average. These books went into the hands of men in charge of churches and who had great influence over the people. They shaped their preaching and helped the people to better living in their homes.

It is a notorious fact that but few of the preachers at emancipation had any training in school to speak of, and thousands owe nearly all their stock of knowledge to the work of the Society.

The Sunday school missionary work of the Society started in 1867, and since that time nearly fifteen thousand schools have been organized, and these were largely among the Colored people. The result is that the Negro race is better provided with Sunday schools than any race in America. This fact shows how thoroughly and wisely the Society did its work. This work of organizing fell into the hands of able Negro leaders appointed by the Society to prosecute it, and they succeeded most handsomely in their work. They succeeded the more because of the thirst of the Negro race for light and knowledge, and the Sunday school offered them the best chance to learn. As a general thing these schools did the work of the day school. Thousands learned how to read and write in them, and many of these men became preachers and are among the leaders of the people. The Sunday schools have contributed largely toward the general intelligence of the race, and the Society took care of this work almost alone for years and years and is even now supporting it and rendering invaluable aid in this direction.

The work of the Society has been among the people, the masses and the leaders. It has gone to the people and has not waited for the people to come to the Society, nor even to the church and Sunday school. It has gone into their home and around the fireside, and by its excellent publications, and by it colporteurs and through its missionaries, it has instructed and inspired the people.

The Publication Society has taken an important part in the organization of nearly all kinds of Negro Baptist bodies. It started with Sunday schools. These afterwards grew into Baptist churches. These churches banded themselves together into associations, later on into state conventions, and finally into national conventions. The very first state convention was organized through the efforts of the Sunday school missionary of the Society in North Carolina, whose name was Rev. Edward Eagles. The state convention in South Carolina was planned and organized by Dr. E. M. Brawley who was the Society's missionary at the time. Even in cases where the actual missionaries of the Society did not organize the convention, they either took important part or others were inspired through their efforts to do so.

The organization of state Sunday school conventions and county and district Sunday school bodies as a general thing represented the direct work of the Society. In North Carolina, Dr. A. Shepard, the Society's missionary, effected the organization. In Virginia Dr. Walter H. Brooks took the lead in doing the same work while in the service of the Society. In Georgia, Dr. W.J. White at one time, and Dr. E.K. Love at another, looked after church and Sunday-school work. In Alabama Dr. C.O. Boothe, later Dr. R.T. Pollard and others; in Texas Dr. E.W.D. Isaac and others; in Louisiana by Dr. W.H. Brooks and Dr. S.T. Clanton; in Kentucky Dr. Wm.H. Steward. We might go on and name some of the most distinguished men in the race that were in the service of the Society, men of ability who gave a good account of themselves, the Society being the power behind them. Finally when the National Convention was organized the representative of the Society, Dr. E.M. Brawley, rendered great help to Dr. Simmons in organizing the body, and this was later on rewarded by his election as the second president of the body.

The Baptist Publication Society has all the time believed in organizing the Negro Baptists for work. It realized that eventually they would have to take care of their own mission and educational work, and it has tried to help the race to help itself, not help the race to work apart from the Society but in cooperation with it, as long as possible. To show how wise it was in this plan, one single preacher in North Carolina is said to have been so inspired by the organization of the state work that in his lifetime he is credited with having organized some three hundred or more churches and Sunday schools. Much of this indirect work was done by the Society, perhaps the largest part of its service after all was inspiring others to take up the work.

After these bodies had been organized, they very naturally drifted into educational rather than Sunday school missionary organizations by reason of the fact that the public schools of the South did not meet the educational needs of the race. But though the Negro Baptists ought by now to be able to take over their own Sunday school missionary work and bear all the expenses of the same, there is hardly a convention in the country that is fully meeting this need, and if these conventions were the only dependence for carrying forward aggressive Sunday school mission work, the cause would greatly suffer. The fact is that nearly every convention in engaged in raising money to establish and support some institution of learning; these conventions are doing great good in this way but are not doing as much as they ought to do for Sunday-school work. The Publication Society has noted this condition, and realizing the need of both Sunday-school and regular work, it is helping in both as best it can by providing missionaries to do the Sunday school work while the conventions devoted their money to school work. Thus the Society deserves much credit for the education work that has sprung up among us in almost every county in the South. These schools may not do much, but they are a hopeful sign. The Society still works through the Sunday school as the hope of the race. It is in fact a great university with millions of children as scholars in every part of the country. It sees such great possibilities yet for the race that it is still working to organize every inch of territory. Fifty-two Sundays in the year represent fifty-two days in school, the best school on the earth. The average school for Negroes in not as long as this, and after all it is a question as the whether the Society is not doing more to educate the masses of the Negro children than the public schools. Certainly it is doing far more to teach right ideas of character and life.

When the work first started among the Colored people, reliance had to be placed upon preachers chiefly to reach the people, and the children had to be taught in the Sunday school. Now the general intelligence of the race has increased to such an extent that there are thousands who are greatly influenced by literature, good or bad, and the grown people of today also supply many such readers. The older people are passing away. A new generation is upon the stage, and the Sunday school offers a means of reaching this "New Negro" even better than the pulpit.

It has come to pass therefore that in addition to its colporteur, tract, and publishing work, the Society is especially addressing itself to save the young Negro and is using the Sunday school and Bible institute and Correspondence Training School to help to that end. It employs a superintendent of field work among the Colored people who, in cooperation with the Sunday school missionaries of the Society in the different states, and also in cooperation with workers from other bodies in all the states, is devoting his entire time to improving the condition of the schools already established, inspiring the teachers and workers and all other Christians who attend Bible institutes held in every part of the country to study the Bible more thoroughly. The method employed is to gather the people into institutes to hear normal lectures on the Bible which, while given in the simplest possible way, illustrate and enforce at the same time methods of study and teaching, and also impart a knowledge of the Bible. This is a kind of work that we people are not able to carry on for ourselves, and the Society has rendered an invaluable aid to the race by supporting these workers on the field.

Dr. A.J. Rowland is the general secretary of the Society, and the missionary and Bible secretary is Dr. Robert G. Seymour. Both of these men have a noble record of interest and helpfulness to the Negro race, Dr. Seymour being perhaps the first northern man to begin a school for Negroes in Louisiana after Emancipation. Dr. Rowland has manifested the keenest interest in all that concerned the race and is such a sincere friend of the race that he takes the risk of being misunderstood by the few, knowing that time will bring them around to his way of thinking. He has ever stood for self-help on the part of the race, but he believes this can be wisely done without pursuing a course that would alienate the friends of the race either in the North or the South.

Space will not allow a full account of the work of this great society for the Negro race, but everything possible has been done, and much has been possible. It is almost, if not quite true, that the Society has done a better work for the Negro people than for the White people. If it could only have impressed itself and its work upon the White races in this country as it has upon the Colored people, the outlook would be a thousand time better today. But what does this fact mean to us? It means that we should ever love this great institution and teach our children to love it, for perhaps there in not another body in the world that has done as much to help the whole race rise to our present position of progress and hope.

TABERNACLE BAPTIST CHURCH

Oklahoma City, Oklahoma

This church was organized in — received the greatest support in those far off days under the ministry of Rev. Jacob Bennett. Dr. W. H. Jernagin who now heads our young people's work and Judge Wm. Harrison, Assistant Attorney General of Illinois also served this church as deacon and superintendent of its Sunday school. Tabernacle Church has trained some good men who now serve the denomination in various parts of the country. Rev. W. H. Perry, D.D., the present pastor is president of the State Convention, and is recognized leader of the Oklahoma Baptists. It was the resolutions offered by Dr. Perry and prepared by the National Baptist Convention that fixed the status of the Historical Department of the National Baptist Convention.

STATISTICS FOR THE NEGRO BAPTISTS, BY STATES

State	Number of Churches		Membership		Expenditures: 1926		Value of Church Edifices: 1926	
	1926	1916	1926	1916	Churches Reporting	Amount	Churches Reporting	Amount
Total	22,082	21,071	3,196,823	2,938,579	20,210	19,476,981	19,834	$103,473,259
Urban	4,410	-------	1,246,527	---------	4,187	11,554,870	4,013	69,452,224
Rural	17,672	-------	1,950,296	---------	16,023	7,922,111	15,821	34,021,035
New Eng.								
Mass.	25	4	5,396	1,474	25	101,003	24	477,500
R. Island	8	1	1,621	30	8	28,048	8	164,000
Connecticut	26	---------	5,518	--------	26	92,393	25	742,000
Mid. Atlantic								
New York	111	43	46,823	5,652	107	672,530	93	4,868,435
New Jersey	159	106	41,129	18,149	149	824,234	146	3,473,222
Penna.	303	166	100,202	40,398	283	1,218,270	231	7,411,419
No. Central:								
Ohio	272	178	73,922	27,978	252	942,546	241	4,244,636
Indiana	161	52	30,388	10,412	136	284,248	134	1,734,664
Illinois	259	184	83,839	23,224	238	740,262	199	3,880,540
Michigan	81	18	24,883	1,229	77	292,454	67	1,703,455
Wisconsin	8	1	2,184	26	5	31,576	8	145,500
No. Central:								
Minnesota	8	2	1,436	478	8	23,399	8	81,600
Iowa	39	34	3,701	2,520	38	49,962	36	237,150
Missouri	244	282	42,299	41,218	236	340,436	223	2,373,919
N. Dakota	3	------	27	_____	-------	**	------	**
Nebraska	11	------	2,062	-------	10	28,115	10	223,950
Kansas	136	118	15,243	13,477	129	186,083	133	1,353,850
No. Atlantic:								

Delaware	8	------	1,575	--------	8	15,727	5	139,500
Maryland	99	88	33,062	29,405	90	306,628	83	1,503,046
Dist. of Col.	83	60	41,262	29,405	82	433,492	69	3,068,458
Virginia	1,610	1,403	316,095	276,544	1,584	1,536,569	1,557	10,491,231
W. Virginia	299	235	24,166	16,238	282	309,311	190	1,516,281
N. Carolina	1,316	1,373	106,807	212,019	1,107	944,629	1,201	4,920,289
S. Carolina	1,364	1,353	235,224	255,479	1,337	796,448	1,312	4,615,947
Georgia	2,900	2,774	381,312	400,214	1,797	1,010,177	2,202	6,650,906
Florida	884	1,038	98,194	69,865	839	762,256	777	3,485,974
E. S. Central: Kentucky	589	703	83,837	98,052	577	616,110	527	3,570,184
Tennessee	896	744	138,605	108,650	873	741,851	833	3,845,974
Alabama	2,415	2,156	364,565	311,103	2,361	1,791,325	2,254	7,603,818
Mississippi	2,314	2,527	226,989	287,796	2,281	872,817	2,239	3,641,884
W. S. Central: Arkansas	1,375	1,472	134,720	174,157	1,331	784,151	1,252	3,077,433
Louisiana	1, 311	1,418	132,743	146,720	1,251	668,825	1,194	3,275,174
Oklahoma	559	495	47,363	42,408	532	344,862	476	1,385,419
Texas	2,071	1,991	234,056	291,243	2,023	1,398,713	1,955	5,965,272
Mountain: Idaho	3	------	105	---------	--------	**	-----	**
Wyoming	5	1	157	39	5	3,406	4	15,000
Colorado	15	12	2,298	2,020	15	33,830	15	110,800
New Mexico	9	1	408	12	9	7,743	8	16,000
Arizona	12	----	817	-------	10	18,550	9	40,100
Pacific: Washington	7	6	681	404	5	16,515	7	79,000
California	76	32	10,654	2,316	73	191,392	69	1,237,770
Other States*	8	------	455	-------	11	16,195	10	101,950

*States having less than 3 churches (or less than 3 churches reporting expenditures or value of church edifices).
**Included in the amount shown for "Other States."
NOTE--Similar statements have been issued for 197 Religious Bodies, and others will be given out as soon as the figures are available.

SECOND BAPTIST CHURCH
Los Angeles

We have no data at hand as to age, former pastors, etc. Rev. T. L. Griffith, D.D., formerly of Iowa, has served here during the past decade, and under hid godly leadership this splendid edifice was finished and dedicated, January, 1928.

By a careful survey of the beautiful places of worship shown in our pages, from New York, through Washington, D. C., southward and westward, it can be seen Negro Baptists are alive and very active any and everywhere their lot is cast on mother earth.

Chapter XII

Our Baptist predecessors contended for the faith, and thus handed it down to us. The scene before the Sanhedrin in Jerusalem, when Peter and John were commanded to preach no more about Jesus was reenacted many time in their experiences. When commanded to preach no more as they had done, and to stop crying out against error and sin, and burying in baptism converts in the likeness of Christ, they, in the spirit of the apostle, would say: "Whether it be right in the sight of God to hearken unto you more than unto God judge ye. For we cannot but speak the things which we have seen and heard."— E.M. Brawley, D.D., The Negro Baptist Pulpit.

The message of God to the world is the everlasting gospel. It is no new upstart doctrine—an afterthought of God. It is as old as eternity, yet as new as the last sun's rays that kiss the morning flower.—Z.D. Lewis, D.D., late pastor Second Baptist Church, Richmond, Va., July, 1896.

He who fights with the pen must dip it into the ink of caution because written language lives longer than spoken language and can be so accurately referred to. "Words are things and a little drop of ink falling upon a piece of paper produces that which makes thousands, perhaps millions, think.—W.E. Holmes, A.M., President Central City College, Ga.

THE TRUTH AND SUGGESTED REMEDIES
ON A VITAL SUBJECT

Not many years ago it was considered that a Negro who expressed opinions differing from those of the average White man in the South was either saucy, impudent, or arrogant, and could be all.

But immediately after, and one of the results of, the Atlanta race riot came the organization of the Commission on Interracial Cooperation, under the direction of Dr. W.W. Alexander. This organization for the discussion of relations between the two races has steadily increased in influence and power and has gradually extended its scope to cover the whole country.

Today the better class of White citizens in all parts of the land are giving serious thought to problems along this line and cooperating in the effort to improve conditions. The Southern Baptist Convention has projected this idea in every definite and constructive way. *Home and Foreign Fields*, their missionary magazine, opens its columns yearly to men of our group as well as to those of their own group for the publication of articles dealing with subjects which make for better racial understandings. These invited men are expected to speak frankly and fearlessly their views on these racial subjects in the hope that to know and observe the truth, will make a group, a race, a nation free as well as an individual. The May number (1930) contains some strikingly illustrated contributions with pictures of Negro churches, schools, and individuals. All of these deserve to be passed down to posterity as a matter of historical record. Simple justice to the Southern Baptist people demands that facts be given showing that they, along with others in the country, are aiding in lifting the Negro to higher planes of usefulness both spiritually and materially. We are reprinting in this book four of these articles; each will tell its own story and serve a good purpose.

Baptists have in all the past taken the part of the oppressed. So now when public sentiment must be made to see it is wrong for the strong to oppress the weak, Drs. Barton, van Ness, Aldridge, Hailey, and their contemporaries who lead in Southern Baptist affairs are following the teachings of some of the best men—Baptist men—who ever lived.

I knew Drs. Rufus L. Burleson, J.B. Gamble, T.T. Eaton, E.Y. Mullins, and many others who labored with them and always worked to soften unchristian criticism against our group.

Baptists, Black and White, because of their interpretation of the Bible, love of fair play, and love for eternal principles of right, are always right in the crisis.

Thank God for our friends.

THE PLEA OF THE SELF-RESPECTING NEGRO—
"NOT CHARITY, BUT CHANCE"

By Rev. A. Clayton Powell, Pastor of Abyssinia Baptist Church,
New York City

Two little ugly, ill-clad Black boys were standing on the platform of a Southern railroad station when an express train rolled in. The throbbing, massive engine made a tremendous appeal to their imagination.

One boy said, "I wish I was a White man so I could run that thing like he runs it."

The other little fellow said, "If the White man will only give me a chance I'll run it, as Black as I am."

The latter boy tells us how the White man can help every sensible ambitious Negro to help himself. The self-respecting Negro is not asking for charity, but he is asking for a chance to help himself.

The White people, North and South, have been very generous in their contributions to Negro schools, churches, and social agencies. The Colored people would be woefully ignorant today had it not been for the millions contributed by these good friends for the mental development of the race.

There are only two worthwhile educational institutions in America receiving their chief financial support from Negroes. One of these is living just beyond the poverty line, and the other is living at a poor, dying rate.

Hampton, Tuskegee, and Spelman, Morehouse, Fisk, Virginia Union, and all the healthy colleges and schools of the Southland represent the generosity of the White man. According to the best statistics obtainable the Negroes have paid only 10 percent of the cost of their education during the last sixty-five years. The other 90 percent, of course, has come from White people.

While we give our White friends a unanimous vote of thanks, this kind of charity cannot and should not go on forever. It is bad for the White man and worse for the Negro. The Negroes of this generation are not asking for more financial help, but they are pleading for opportunities to help themselves. Like our little Black brother, they are saying, "Give us a chance and we will run this engine two or three generations hence."

If we are going to make upstanding, self-supporting men out of these sixty-five year old children, who have been a drag on our social order more than half a century, we must give them the same opportunities or development along all lines which other Americans enjoy.

Perhaps there is not a man living who knows the desires, ambitions, and aspirations of the Negro better than myself. For sixty-five years I have lived with them in log cabins, shanties, ox carts, mule wagons, on bicycle, and in automobiles.

For twenty-two years I have been with them in the largest and most congested Negro center on earth. I administer to at least 4,000 Negroes every week. The 8,500 members of my church represent the highest intelligence and the lowest ignorance—the richest and the poorest of my race.

I am, therefore, speaking with authority which comes from long years of the most intimate contact, South and North, when I say that Negroes want equality, and nothing else will satisfy them, and that nothing else will help them to help themselves out of their present low estate.

By equality, I do not mean that bugaboo of "social equality" which is constantly played up by politicians and too often by the press and pulpit. This pernicious doctrine has, perhaps, done more than any other one thing to keep the Negro from rising and to hamper him in every phase of progress.

When a Negro applies for admission to a university where the White students predominate it is said that he is seeking "social equality." When he attempts to move into a decent neighborhood, he is checked by the argument of "social equality." When he applies for a position beyond that of elevator boy, porter, butler, for which he is qualified by experience and education, he is stopped by the "social equality" wall. When he tries to secure a Pullman ticket or a stateroom on a ship that he may rest comfortably he is refused it on the ground of "social equality." When he seeks a political appointment in the state and federal governments the papers and politicians raise a howl about "social equality." When the general term "social equality" fails to halt his progress his enemies will be sure to check him by the terrible specter of "social intermingling and intermarrying of the races."

The desire on the part of Colored men to cross the line in their quest for female companionship has been greatly exaggerated, to the detriment of the Negro's progress. During the last thirty-eight years I have united more couples in marriage, perhaps, than any other Negro minister in the North. In all those years I have had only ten interracial marriages—four in Connecticut and six in New York. In five cases Colored men were united to White women, and in the other five cases White men were joined to Colored women, and these did not represent the best in either race. Because there is no law in these states against intermarriage of the races, these ten straws should indicate the way the wind is blowing. I have learned from many years of experience that Colored men are satisfied with their own women.

When 9,999 Negroes out of 10,000 plead for equality, the thought of association with White women does not cross their minds. What they really desire and what they are contending for is equality of opportunity in the struggle of life. They want equality of living conditions. They want a decent place in which to live and rear their children.

Negro communities are woefully neglected by city governments. Ashes, rubbish, garbage, dead cats and dogs are allowed to remain on the streets for days and often for weeks. No man can retain his self-respect in such an environment. And even the White section of such a city cannot be healthy when the laws of sanitation are thus flagrantly neglected in the Colored section.

Negroes are a gregarious people. Other things being equal they had rather live in communities by themselves than to be scattered over White settlements. Let White landlords keep in good repair houses in which Negroes live, and let the White city officials keep the streets clean in Negro communities, and there will be no more riots and bloodshed as in Chicago, St.Louis, and Detroit caused by Colored people moving into White neighborhoods.

Negroes want the same educational opportunities that other groups have in America. Where long practice has made it a habit of segregating Negroes in schools, it has been found that these schools are inferior in every respect to the schools provided for White pupils. If we are going to help the Negro to make the best of himself, these segregated schools must have equally prepared instructors, the same curriculum, and appropriations for their maintenance. It is not the separate school that the Negro objects to, but the separate inferior school.

If we ever expect the Negroes to reach the place where they will shoulder their own burdens and carry them like men, we must give them an equal opportunity with other American groups to improve their economic status. Negroes should not forever be forced to remain Pullman porters and firemen if they are qualified by experience and education to become conductors and engineers. No man wants to run an elevator for twenty years if he has fitted himself by training to fill a better position. The graduates from Tuskegee, Hampton, and other trade schools should not be compelled to do unskilled work simply because they are Black.

Color prejudice not only sees that the Negro is confined to unskilled labor, regardless of his qualifications, but it makes sure that he does not receive the same compensation that other men receive for the same work.

An employment agency on Sixth Avenue [in] New York displayed the other day the following on its bulletin board:

"An elevator boy wanted—
Colored; hours 8:00 a.m. to 8:00 p.m., daily,
$65 per month.
"Elevator boy wanted—
White; hours 8:00 a.m. to 7:00 p.m., daily,
$90 per month."

Even in New York it costs an elevator man 365 hours of extra labor and $300 a year to be Colored. No one but a Black man can feel the degrading influence of this discrimination based absolutely upon color, which carries with it the implication of inferiority with a vengeance.

This is not the end of the story. The elevator White man in New York pays 25 percent less house rent than the elevator Colored man.

Why should a Negro in Christian American be paid one price for his labor and another man a better price for the same work with fewer hours? This custom prevails all over "our land of the free and home of the brave," and in itself is grossly unfair, and certainly does not help in any way to help the Negro to help himself.

How can the Negro with such an unjust wage system ever become financially strong enough to walk alone? If this disparity of wages between White and Colored continues, the Colored man will never begin to educate his children, build his churches, and support his schools.

Mr. John D. Rockefeller, Jr., is showing America how to give the Negro a chance. Three years ago he built the Paul Lawrence Dunbar Apartments in Harlem, N.Y., at a cost of about $3,500,000. These buildings cover a city block and contain 512 apartments. These apartments were sold to reputable Colored families with a small cash payment of $50 a room, and a monthly payment averaging $14.50 per room. Of that amount $7.69 is applied to the principal and interest and $6.81 to upkeep. These apartments house about two thousand Negroes and the order and sanitation are 100 per cent. The forty employees are Negroes directed by a Colored graduate from Harvard.

The Dunbar Bank, financed by Mr. Rockefeller, is located in these buildings. The twenty-four employees of this bank are Colored, except the four White executives. The salaries of the Colored men range from $720 to $3,000 per year. Neither the apartments nor the bank is a philanthropy, but a business proposition, pure and simple.

It is probable that every intelligent salaried Negro received his education, in part, from the charity of the Rockefeller family, but now Mr.

John D. Rockefeller, Jr., is giving these Negroes a chance to become self-supporting and self-respecting. The children of these Negroes will not have to be educated by White philanthropy. Mr. Rockefeller undoubtedly believes that it is manifestly unfair to stigmatize Negroes with inferiority and then deny them an opportunity to prove that they have qualities equal to other groups.

The world is not old enough yet for me to say that there are not any superior races.

A little more than two thousand years ago Caesar said that the Nordic people were so inferior that they were not fit for slaves. If Caesar were living today he would be elected president of the International Ananias Club.

At this stage of racial development it behooves us to be a little careful about calling this race superior and that race inferior, for fear that a few centuries from now some of us might be elected vice-president of the same club.

May I suggest that in the midst of this trying situation, when our patience is taxed to the utmost with practical things, that we turn this question of race inferiority and race superiority over to the biologists and sociologist for about five hundred years?

There are a lot of backward races on the earth today and the Negro race is one of them. In mental development and industrial progress the Negro people are centuries behind the White people, but it will require hundreds of years to prove that the Negro is naturally inferior to anybody. Give the Negro the same chance for a few centuries that the White man has had for nearly two thousand years, and then sit in judgment on him.

The Negro in America has had only sixty-five years to show what he can do, and the fair-minded White people, North and South, are unanimous in saying that he has wrought miracles of progress, and this progress has been in an environment which at times was exceedingly unfriendly.

The Negro is not asking for any special favors, but he is pleading for fair play, footway, and elbow room while he "runs the race with patience" and "work out his own salvation with fear and trembling."

SOUTHERN CHRISTIANS AND THEIR NEGRO NEIGHBORS

*By Rev. Will W. Alexander, Director of Commission on
Interracial Cooperation, Atlanta, Ga.*

There are many angles from which southern White people view their Negro fellow citizens. The new industrial South thinks of them in terms of their contribution to economic development. Politicians, ever aware of the presence of Negroes, have spent much time and eloquence in an endeavor to determine their political status. Our public health leaders think of them in terms of sickness and high death rates. Social workers are interested in the dependent, neglected, and delinquent Negroes for whom institutions must be provided and relief found.

An increasing number of White Christians, however, are seeing in the presence of nine million Negroes in the South the supreme test of our religion. The number holding this viewpoint is increasing. For one reason, southern church people have been interested in foreign missions, and race relations in America has a direct bearing on missionary work. The vast majority of the peoples to whom our southern missionaries have gone are Colored. The shrinking of the world has brought to these non-Christians the world over a familiarity with American life. A world-wide Colored press, not too friendly to things White, plays up to these millions of Colored people in all parts of the world any injustices due to color prejudice in America.

Moreover, the followers of Christ's great competitor, Mohammed, boast that through the vast Moslem world there is no color prejudice. A traveler in Mohammedan lands finds the claim to be true. It is not strange, therefore, that recently an influential Negro churchman said in a public address, "I am not sure but that Mohammedanism offers the Negroes of the world more than Christianity. Mohammedanism has made for racial friendliness, while the most violent race prejudices are found in Christian lands." Of course many answers could be made to this statement, but they would not satisfy this man or millions of others, who see White Christian nations snatching the lands of Colored people in various parts of the world, and in other places interested mainly in "keeping them in their place." They remember that a famous slave ship was named *The Jesus*, and that one of the great slave traders left many words of Christian piety written on board a vessel, the filthy hold of which was crowded with Black men and women from Africa to be sold for a profit in White Christian lands.

Southern White Christians are, therefore, in a position of great responsibility and influence in relation to the world-wide spread of the gospel. In their attitudes to their Colored neighbors they have the power to help or hinder the movement which Christ died to establish. To demonstrate that the spirit of the founder of our religion can dominate race relations in the South is the greatest service southern Christians can render the spread of the gospel in non-Christian lands. In nine million Negro neighbors Jesus Christ is putting us to a great test, and is offering us a great opportunity to testify to the non-believing world that He is all that we claim for Him. If contemporary Christianity can establish justice and good will between White and Colored people in America, it can win the world. If it cannot solve the race problem in America, it may as well keep out of Africa and Asia.

Unfortunately, in the past many of our church people have not been aware of the fact that their Negro neighbors are a test of their fidelity to Jesus. One suspects that our pulpits and our Bible schools have had too little to say about the subject. The writer grew to manhood in a southern community with a Christian church at its center. Yet, so far as he can remember, there was never an intimation that the gospel of Christ furnished the basis for one's attitude to Negro neighbors. Our ministers were experts in telling amusing stories about Negroes, but the indifference and even hostility of many Christian people toward any effort to improve Negro life were never challenged by them.

The growing concern about the race situation on the part of southern White Christian leaders is one of the most hopeful aspects of a tense race situation throughout the world. Never before were so many White Christians in the South outspoken in their desire to find what it means to practice Christian neighborliness toward Negroes. This is noticeable particularly among the women and the young people. The Woman's Department of the Interracial Commission is cooperating with organizations of church women and with more than a million members who are studying and working to the end that more and more race relations in the South may be determined by the spirit of Christ. Whenever our young people have been given a chance to express themselves they have manifested an open-mindedness and concern which promises much good for the future. More than one hundred colleges in the South are offering courses in race relations as part of their regular work. These classes are being attended by thousands of our best students eager to prepare themselves for this delicate task of southern citizenship.

Too frequently when the denomination has built a school or supported a missionary for work among Negroes, it is assumed that the situation has been met. These things are very easily done. The more difficult and more important work is to enable White and Colored neighbors to live together in good will and genuine helpfulness. In this White people present as much of a problem as Colored. It is often easier to get Negroes educated than to get these White people to be just, patient, and friendly to their Negro neighbors. For educating and evangelizing Negroes the denominations have a program; toward the adjustment of White and Negro neighbors the local churches are only beginning to have a slight interest, and an effective race relations program for the local church is yet to be developed.

Race relations based upon Christian principles is something to which the rank and file of church people must be committed. The weakness of the present strategy of the southern churches is that work having to do with Negroes is left largely to the general denominational agencies. The work of these is important but they can never do the thing most needed. It is in hundreds of local communities where justice must be established. What is needed can be done only by local pastors through personal effort and through intelligent church members sent into the community to work for schools, legal protection, better houses, and a more adequate economic opportunity for their Negro neighbors. In the last ten years a few of our best preachers and laymen are doing this very thing through local interracial committees. In these committees White and Colored men and women of good will are seeking year by year to bring into the situation more justice, more understanding, and more of the spirit of Christ.

The significance of the Interracial Movement is that southern people have taken the initiative in it. At the moment, it is their best answer to the demands of the difficult situation which confronts them. It is an effort to establish justice in the everyday common life under the assumption that if we apply justice to the present situation, wisdom will be given with which to meet the future.

One very important result of these committees has been that in a new sense hundreds of White and Colored neighbors have come to know each other. The life of our fathers had in it many fine friendships between White and Colored people. This was easy for them. Their lives were interwoven in an intimacy that endured from the beginning of life to its close. They were literally "members one of another." The years since 1865 have destroyed this. Today, the more intelligent and self-reliant Negroes become, the less contact they have with intelligent White people. Too often the most influential White people know only the most backward Negroes. IF WHITE

345

AND NEGRO PREACHERS KNEW EACH OTHER AND WORKED WITH EACH OTHER AS DO WHITE AND NEGRO BOOTLEGGERS THERE WOULD BE NO RACE PROBLEM IN THE SOUTH. At the present time the contacts between the two races are too largely at the bootlegger level. In the interracial committees the better elements are assuming a responsibility that has all too long been left to the worst.

There are many White people who have friendly attitudes to any individual Negroes with whom they come in contact. This is commendable, but often such persons are indifferent to the miserable housing, poor sanitary conditions, and inadequate schools provided for Negroes by the community. Individual friendliness must be supplemented by community justice in the division of taxes, the administration of the law, and in economic fairness. Here is the real test of White friendship for Negro neighbors and of our loyalty to Jesus.

The interracial communities have grown out of the obvious fact that what neither White nor Colored leaders can do alone can be achieved by a joint effort. White people, however genuine their good will, cannot do for their Negro neighbors the things they most need. Negroes, like others, must do most things for themselves. This means that a group of people only sixty-five years from slavery and a few hundred years from a very primitive life must compete for their place in the most complex and rapidly changing civilization ever seen upon this earth. It means that a minority of one in ten of our population are of another color and handicapped by limitations of training and experience, as well as by the social traditions growing out of slavery. They must compete, however, at every turn with a White majority who has wealth, political power, cultural background, technical training, and the attitude and habit of domination. In London, during the war, the busses had to be manned by girls, so that the men could go to the front. When the air raids came the streets were darkened but the traffic had to move. As the busses would pass each other in the dark, one girl would cry across to the other, "Are you there?" "Yes," would come the reply. "Then stick it," the first would answer back. More than anything else Colored people in their struggle need from their White neighbors frequent and unmistakable evidences of friendly interest and confidence. The best service White people can render Negroes is to believe in them. Men can do their best only in an atmosphere of confidence.

Neighborly helpfulness between White and Colored people would be much easier if we could be rid once for all of the terms "social equality" and "intermarriage." These twin "fears" are often offered as the justification for indifference and injustice to Negroes. Yet, Negroes have never asked for either. Their demand for a full chance in life is not to be denied by attributing to them some aspiration to which they repeatedly denied. Much intermingling of the racial stocks has already taken place in the South. It has not come about through "social equality" or "intermarriage." It is in large part the result of slavery and the degradation of one race by another. No evil ever results from the practice of justice, and the White man who withholds justice to Negroes for fear it will do harm is denying the deepest ethical principles of religion. Only good will come to both Negroes and Whites from the efforts to do justice and love mercy. Good will and justice are always safe for everybody concerned. The only safe cause for the future is justice and good will in the present.

Many White people have said, "Southern White people are the Negro's best friend." If we are, it is of the utmost importance that Negroes themselves find it out. There are thousands of Negroes who have never had one reason to suspect that any White people are their friends. They know White people mainly in the police, the men who run the street cars, and men who collect the rent and their kind. There is nothing in these contacts which would indicate friendships. To create an atmosphere of friendship that expresses itself in deeds of justice is a task for which Christian men and women are supposed to be particularly fitted.

In race relations, as in other things, it is deeds, not words, that count. Sermons on brotherly love must be tested by what happens in the everyday life. I know a rural county with a large Negro population where the most orthodox and earnest gospel is preached by White Methodist and Baptist preachers. Yet, when the school tax is divided by a White school board of church members, $57 per year is set aside for each White and $1.52 for each Negro child. The difficulty in such a community is that this gospel is not translated into deeds. The application of the gospel to life calls for the expenditure of energy, the wearing out of shoe leather, for tireless patience, and undiscourageable belief that right is so important that it cannot finally be defeated. In nothing is this truer than when a White Christian in a southern community tries to be a good neighbor to his Colored fellows. Speeches, however sincere and eloquent, can accomplish little in a situation of this sort. Only constant courage and patient work can count for anything here. To this difficult and essentially Christian task, increasing numbers of southern Christians are giving themselves. They are, however, still in the minority. To increase their number is a most important work of the church.

THE "NEGRO PROBLEM" A MISSIONARY CHALLENGE

Editor, *The Home and Foreign Fields*

With a sense of deep gratification we present in this number of *Home and Foreign Fields* a symposium dealing with relationships between the Colored people and the White people of the South. The articles presented have been sought from representative thinkers of both races, and wide liberty has been given for untrammeled expression of honest opinion. It is significant that we have reached the point where such a thoughtful, sober presentation can be made without offense to either group. Twenty-five years ago this would not have been possible.

Our chief concern is with the missionary aspect of the subject, for the Christian solution of the "Negro Problem" by Southern Baptists constitutes a missionary challenge of utmost consequence. The vast majority of those whom we are seeking to reach with our missionary message belong to the Colored races—either Negroid or Mongoloid. If we can find no satisfactory and successful way of Christianizing these people of another race in our midst, we thereby declare our incapacity for being used of God in the largest measure in Christianizing the multitudes of Colored peoples of other lands.

The "Negro Problem" is a challenge to overcome race prejudice. The antipathy of one race toward another is deep-seated and universal. It seems to be a part of our inheritance of original sin. At its heart are selfishness and fear—the instinctive desire to get and keep the best for ourselves and our children, and the fear that those who belong to another group than our own may secure the advantage. Only the grace of God in human hearts can extinguish this flame of antagonism toward those of another race. Have we enough of that grace? If not, we stand ashamed in the presence of Christ, whose love knew no racial bounds, and who died for all men of every tongue and color alike.

The "Negro Problem" is a challenge to the sincerity of our Christian profession. We declare our allegiance to Christ and our committal to his worldwide program. We say that he is sufficient for the salvation of all men everywhere. We declare that he is both Savior and Lord, and that having trusted him for salvation we yield ourselves to him for service. When he commands us to go into all the world and make disciples of every creature, we acknowledge His right to command and our duty to obey. If, then, we call him Lord, why do we do not the things he has commanded us? Do we not cast serious aspersion on our sincerity when we sing, "I'll go where you want me to go, I'll do what you want me to do," and deliberately close our eyes to the underprivileged, neglected, unreached Black people at our very doors?

The "Negro Problem" is a challenge to our belief in the Bible. God tells us in Genesis that the human race originated from one family. From it came all the "races" by direct descent. Some were more privileged and have progressed more rapidly than others. In this sense there are "superior" and "inferior" races. But if all came from the original stock, then all belong to the same human family, and education, civilization, Christianization, can ultimately bring any race up to the level of any other race. For us to act as if the Negro were below the human level, as if he had no soul of immortal value, as if we had no racial kinship with Him whatever, is to declare our practical unbelief in the Word of God, no matter how we may shout our orthodoxy from the housetops.

The "Negro Problem" is a challenge to our sense of social justice. It is noteworthy in the several articles in this number from Negro leaders that their plea is not for charity but equality of opportunity. The bug-bear of "social equality" is gradually disappearing. As the Negroes progress and become self-respecting and self-supporting they shrink with as much repugnance as do White people from race amalgamation. The well-bred, informed, skilled, right-thinking Negro is proud of his race and is determined to maintain racial purity for his children. This he can do only as he is given a fair deal in the industrial and educational world. The Negro resents the vicious industrial system that compels him to live in back alleys, to work for cheap wages, and to send his children to inferior schools. He cannot believe that this is the Christian spirit—and he is right. Not color but worth must ultimately determine equality of opportunity, and we stultify our Christian conscience and cast reflection on our sense of Christian justice when we seek to hold the Negro down and "keep him in his place" just because he is Black and we are White. It is even more important for us, as the dominant race, to do right than it is for the Negro to receive fair treatment, for thus alone can we convince the non-Christian world of the superiority of the religion which we would propagate.

The "Negro Problem" is a challenge to our spirit of Baptist cooperation. Quite naturally Northern Baptist extended their aid to the Negroes of the South following the war between the states. Southern Baptist were prostrate, and the people of the North felt a peculiar responsibility for the "freedmen" whose emancipation had been achieved at such tragic cost. Time has made many changes, and today Southern Baptists are not the poverty-stricken and scattered people they were sixty-five years ago. Yet the simple fact is that we have not done much for our Negro brethren. In 1918, a joint committee of Northern and Southern Baptists was proposed for the consideration of Negro education in the South, and especially theological education. On motion of Dr. E. Y. Mullins seven brethren of the Southern Baptist Convention were named to meet with a similar group from the Northern Baptist Convention for fraternal conference. Two meetings were held, but for some reason the matter has never been pressed. Since Northern Baptists and Southern Baptists have so great interest in common in this matter, would it not seem wise for a new committee to be appointed?

The American Baptist Theological Seminary, located at Nashville, Tennessee, is Southern Baptists' most ambitious and far-reaching effort to help our Negro brethren, but it limps along with inadequate equipment and support and is scarcely touching the surface of the need for a trained Negro ministry. Here is an enterprise in which far-seeing Baptists both North and South may join, the success of which would mean more for Negro Baptist progress in the South than perhaps any single thing that could be achieved. Surely the spirit of cooperation should find its best expression in this effort on the part of White Baptists, North and South, to do something permanently worthy and fruitful in meeting the one greatest need of our Colored brethren—the preparation of a trained religious leadership.

Read with open mind and sympathetic attitude these remarkable messages dealing with this many-sided "problem" in the pages of this magazine. Then in earnest spirit turn to Him who is Lord of all life, saying, "What wilt thou have me to do?"

A SQUARE LOOK AT THE NEGRO QUESTION

New Movements Taking Place Among the Negroes

By Rev. E. P. Alldredge, Secretary Survey, Statistics and Information, Baptist Sunday School Board, Nashville, Tennessee

There are six sufficient and compelling reasons why Southern Baptists must always have a more vital interest in, and a deeper concern for, the welfare of the Negroes of America than any other White denomination in the nation.

Vital Interests of Southern Baptists in the Negroes

(1) Because of the 11,500,000 Negroes (approximately) now in America, perhaps 90 per cent of them still live here in the South in the bounds of the Southern Baptists Convention; (2) because of the 5,500,000 (approximately number) of Negro church members in America, almost 61.5 per cent of them are Baptists and, therefore, are fellow workers with us in the kingdom of God; (3) because, historically speaking, our White Baptist fathers in the faith did more to bring the whole Negro race in America to Christ than any other denomination, and these Colored Baptists of today are our peculiar heritage, bequested to us by Colored Baptist pioneers of the South; (4) because of the 6,000,000 Negroes in America (approximately) who are not Christians. Perhaps 5,500,000 of them live here in the South and constitute our first great, inescapable Home Mission task; (5) because, if won to Christ, perhaps four out of every seven of these 5,500,000 unreached and unevangelized Negroes in the South would join their brothers in black and become Baptists; (6) because thus far in their history, no racial group has shown itself more responsive to the gospel appeal as presented by Baptists than have the Negroes of the South. If, therefore, Southern Baptists have any obligation in behalf of any racial group on earth, we certainly may not escape the obligation which we owe, under God, to the Colored people of the South.

We can best discharge this great obligation however, if we understand something of the great changes, something of the new movements, which are taking place among the Negroes of our country. I propose therefore, to call attention to six of the great new movements among the Negroes of America—all of which have taken place since 1916 and 1917.

1. New Increase in the Negro Population

It will be worthwhile to note in the beginning the changes which have come to the Negro population in the South and the nation within the last decade. Here is the situation in brief:

Negro population in America in 1910 9,827,763
Negro population in America in 1920 10,463,131
Net gain in the decade (9.9 per cent) 635,368

If we bring these figures down to the decade of 1916 to 1926, using the estimate of the Bureau of the Census, we have the following approximate figures:

Negro population in America 1916 10,208,689
Negro population in America 1926 10,868,577

Ten years net gain (6.4 per cent) 659,888

Since 1910, and particularly since 1918, there have been several great migrations of the Negroes from the South. The question arises therefore as to whether the South has made any net gain in Negro population since 1910 and if so, how much? Unhappily, the figures for the 1930 census are not yet in hand, and we must rely upon the figures for 1920—though we have good reason to believe that the 1930 census will show even larger migrations to the North and East than are shown in the 1920 census. Here, then, are the comparative figures as to the number of Negroes in the South in 1910 and 1920:

Negroes in the South (S.B.C. territory) in 1910 8,842,424
Negroes in the South (S.B.C. territory) in 1920 9,033,100
Net gain in the South (S.B.C. territory) in decade 190,676 (2.1%)

This indicates quite clearly that the Negro population in the nation as a whole during the decade of 1910-1920 showed over four times the gain of the Negro population in the South. That is to say, while the North and the East showed a net gain of 444,692 in Negro population, the South with nine-tenths of all the Negroes of the nation, showed a net gain of only 190,676 in the ten years.

2. New Gains in Negro Church Work.

Another question of vital interest is: How far has Negro church work kept pace with the growth of the Negro population during the last decade? Here are the interesting and illuminating figures given by the Bureau of the Census, covering this point:

Negro Church members in 1916 4,602,805
Negro Church members in 1926 5,203,487
Net gain for ten years (13.05 per cent) 600,682
Average yearly net gain for the decade 60,068

Now, here is something quite remarkable. We know of nothing like in any other nation or among any other racial group—that while the Negro population (1916-1926) had a net gain of 659,888, the Negro churches won to God and added to the churches 600,682 persons!

But this is not all! The total contributions of the Negro churches in America increased from $18,529,827 in 1916, to $43,024,259 in 1926—a net gain of almost 150 percent!

Nor is this all! Southern Baptists have been severely criticized for putting so much money into new church houses, etc., in recent years; but the census figures show that the Negro churches of America have put an average of $11,897,265.80 a year of the past ten years into new and remodeled church houses, their total church property now standing at the magnificent figure of $205,782,628!

3. New Racial Aspirations and Demands.

But the Negroes of the South and the nation have not only experienced great population changes and remarkable growth in all forms of church work, since 1917 in particular, they have come forward with new racial aspirations and demands.

These new aspirations and demands, moreover, are being voiced not by small racial groups of agitators, as heretofore, but by the pulpit and the press of every Negro denomination in America, by the Negro teachers and doctors and lawyers as well as the Negro journalists, authors, politicians, and propagandists of the nation. In fact, up to April, 1917 it may be said that the Negro leaders of America were divided into two groups, with the "conservatives" following Booker T. Washington's ideas, outnumbering the radicals 1,000 to 1; where since 1919 there are perhaps fewer than one hundred outstanding conservative Negro leaders in America. So that today, for all practical purposes, the eleven and a half million of Negroes in America are all radical. (Figures estimated.)

We can find a concrete illustration of this change in the new radical demands set forth by a prominent church leader in 1918—demands which have since been agreed upon and voiced by all groups of Negro leaders in the nation. In fact, these demands are now regarded by most of the Negro leaders as being distinctly conservative:

The Negro's Fourteen Demands

"1. The privilege of voting at all elections and holding office, the same as enjoyed by the Whites.

"2. Better educational facilities in the South—the same as given to White youths.

"3. Abolition of 'Jim-Crowism'—the same accommodations and privileges granted to Negroes as to Whites, on all common carriers.

"4. Discontinuance of unjust discriminations and color segregation in the various departments of the government service.

"5. Military training for Colored youths, the same as for Whites without discrimination or segregation.

"6. Removal of all restrictions on the promotion of Negro soldiers and sailors not likewise imposed on the Whites.

"7. Abolition of the peonage system in the South by whatever name and whatever form it exists.

"8. Establishment of the same wage scale for blacks as for Whites.

"9. Better housing provisions for Colored employees in all industrial establishments—equal to that for the Whites.

"10. Sanitary conditions of the Negro sections of the towns and cities to be equal to that of White sections.

"11. The unfortunate and criminal Blacks to receive the same treatment before the law as the Whites—both in the matter of arrest and trial and in the matter of punishment.

"12. The abolition of lynching and mob violence.

"13. The recognition of the Negroes' rights and fitness to sit on juries.

"14. Equal opportunity to labor in the line of his talents as the Whites, and an equal enjoyment of the fruits of his labor."

4. New Racial Leadership.

A still more disturbing and disquieting shift among the Negroes of America is to be found in their almost complete change of leadership. From 1880 to 1916, for example, the leadership of the Negroes of America apart from a small, noisy, and pestilential group of radical Whites in the North, was almost wholly confined to the Colored Baptist and Methodist preachers and the Colored school teachers of the nation. Behold the complete and radical change of leadership today! The present Negro leadership may be summarized as follows:

The Negro public press—comprising a daily or two, perhaps 20 magazines, and over 300 weekly journals. Many of the ablest and best educated race leaders in America will be found giving direction and life to the Negro public press today.

The Negro educators and men of letters. In 1895, only Paul Lawrence Dunbar, the poet, and Booker T. Washington, the educator, had come to national distinction and world-wide attention; whereas today the Negro poets, dramatists, musicians, fiction writers, historians, sociologists, artists, actors, and educators of national repute in America have grown into scores if not hundreds. Countee Cullen, for example (himself a noted and highly gifted young poet), in his *Caroling Dusk*[15], lists thirty-six outstanding Negro

---

[15]*Caroling Dusk*, by Countee Cullen, Harper & Bros., 1927. Ed.

poets in America today; while Alain Locke, another noted poet, fills a magnificent volume of 450 pages with the story of *The New Negro*[16] in fiction, poetry, drama, music, art, folklore, etc. And the great Negro teachers, educators, and educational executives, like President Mordecai W. Johnson, of Howard University; President R.R. Moton, of Tuskegee, and others, have not only grown in number and increased in honors and influence among the Negroes and Whites of America, but like the Negro men of letters, have become more and more disassociated from the churches and their former co-laborers, the Colored preachers of the nations.

The Leaders of New Race Institutions and Organizations. In recent years a number of race institutions and organizations have come into existence, the influence, leadership, and power of which have tended more and more to overshadow the Negro churches and the Negro ministers. When a great racial difficulty or problem arises in America today, for example, the eleven and a half millions of Negroes no longer look to their churches for guidance and help; on the contrary, they turn to the National Association for the Advancement of Colored People; and they no longer hearken to the voice of their preachers, but they listen to the commands of W. E. B. DuBois and James Weldon Johnson—DuBois being the Moses and Johnson being the Joshua of the "Children of Ham" in America.

5. New Church Affiliations Sought.

All unknown to most of our people in the South (who imagine they know all about the Negroes), a group of Negroes have launched a movement to do away with the separate churches for the Negroes—and this movement is making decided headway. To illustrate my meaning, let us recall the historical fact that it was the insistence of the Baptist leaders of the early days upon separate churches for the Negro slaves who had become Christians towards Baptists. The more the Episcopalians, the Methodists, and others opposed separate churches for the Negroes, the more the converted slaves left their "master's faith" and went pell-mell to the Baptists.

Behold the change today, when large groups of Negro Christians, in many sections of the nation, are passing by even the very best Negro churches and hot-footing it to the outstanding and socially high-standing White churches! For this same reason also large numbers are breaking away from non-Catholic churches and going over to the Roman Catholic churches, which not only allow the Negroes to worship along with the Whites in many down-

---

[16]*The New Negro*, by Alain LeRoy Locke (1886-1954), *circa* 1925. This work was reprinted by Atheneum Press in 1983. Ed.

town churches here in the South as in the North, but which command them thus to worship with the Whites or the Whites worship with the Negroes. The whole country has been made familiar with a Brooklyn pastor (Episcopalian) who created a national stir and almost disrupted his church by requesting Negro Episcopalians to cease passing by their own splendid race churches in order to impose themselves upon his White church. And the *New York Times* of February 18, 1930, gives a half-column story of how the Negro pastors in New York City withdrew all connection with the Federated Ministers' Conference of that city on account of a report on the religious situation in New York and vicinity which contain these words:

"Commenting on Negro migrations from Harlem to outlying districts, such as Elmhurst and Corona in Queens, the Hobart report said: 'There have been instances where churches have almost been put out of business by these sudden movements....If the Negro will stay in one place, then the church will know its future problems.'"

The Negro ministers in New York City not only considered this statement to be an affront, but refused all overtures to return to the Federated Ministers' Conference until the White ministers surrendered and came together and passed the following confession and retraction:

"We never have stood and do not stand for the segregation of the Colored people of this city. The same right of free movement belongs to them as to all others of our fellow citizens.

"We are opposed to race prejudice and desire to do anything in our power to remove it.

"We desire to work in the closest cooperation with our brethren in the Colored churches in promoting closer fellowship between the Colored churches and the other churches of the city, realizing how essential this cooperation is to the extension of the kingdom of God in this city.

"We repudiate any statement that may have been or implied contrary to the above declaration."

6. New Demands for Trained Negro Ministers

Thus it will been seen that we have come to a new day and a new crisis, racially and religiously; one of the gravest that has come to the Negroes of America since Reconstruction days. A whole race of eleven to twelve millions of people have turned radical overnight—that is, radical as compared with the views held by Booker T. Washington and the Negro race leaders of his day. And, as radicals everywhere and in all ages have been accustomed to do, the eleven and a half millions of Negroes in America have changed

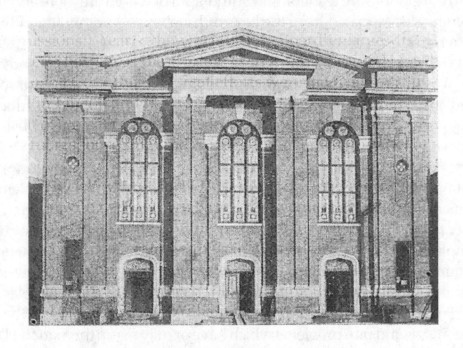

SECOND BAPTIST CHURCH
Indianapolis, Ind.

This is reported to be the oldest Negro Baptist Church in all Indiana. It was for years the center of Baptist activities in that great city. Some great men have served as pastors here.

The building is the nearest to a complete concrete building of any of our church homes.

Following Dr. B. J. Prince in 19___ came Rev. B. J. F. Westbrook, D.D. Under his pastorate the basement was razed and new plans drawn and for years work went forward till this beautiful building graces Michigan Avenue.

Dr. Westbrook, with his faithful wife, attended the best University in Indiana. Now he heads the Evangelistic Board of the National Baptist Convention.

leadership, almost wholly—deliberately pushing the conservative educators, along with the churches and preachers, into the background, and exalting the radical editors of the Negro public press, the group of Negro literati who designate themselves as the New Negroes, and the great radical Negro educators, race leaders, and authors, all of whom are more and more becoming disassociated from the Negro churches and uninfluenced by the Negro ministers.

What can be done about it? How can such a situation be met and dealt with? I maintain that, apart from the building up of a large group of consecrated and highly trained Negro ministers, there is no adequate solution to this new and difficult and delicate race problem and kingdom problem that has developed here in the South and the nation within the last ten years.

The only possible and adequate agency for meeting, mastering, and molding the issues of the present and the future interracial problems of America is a 500 per cent increase in the number of deeply spiritual and highly trained young Negro ministers. These men and these men only, for example, can create and hold intact a Christian race attitude in the hearts and minds of the eleven and a half million Negroes of this nation; and these men, and these only, can per force bring the impact of the principles and program of the Christian religion to bear upon the settlement of all the race antagonisms and race problems which have or may rise in this nation. These men and these alone, moreover, can keep in touch and cooperate with the Christian-minded White leaders and preachers of the nation who can and must build and maintain a Christian race-attitude in the hearts and minds of the White race toward their weaker brothers in black.

And still more serious is a well-known fact, vouched for by Professor Monroe Work of Tuskegee and other authorities, that upon the average one thousand highly trained young Negro preachers are needed every year to fill vacancies occurring in the main Negro churches in America; whereas all the Negro and all the White schools and theological seminaries in America combined are turning out perhaps not more than 100 each year!

We do not like to prophesy evil for our nation and for the cause of Christ; but unless the main Christian denominations in America, and the Baptists in particular, go about the task immediately of finding and training and sending out something like 500 to 750 additional young Negro ministers of the highest type every year, then we must be ready to face three positive perils within the next thirty to fifty years:

(1) The new leadership of the Negro race in America will soon pass completely out from all Christian influences and principles.

(2) With paganistic, political leaders as their only guides in racial and national affairs, there will also take place a great national mass movement of the Negroes away from the churches—wholesale drifts into agnosticism and atheism on the part of the educated groups and wholesale lapses into ancestral paganism on the part of the uneducated masses.

(3) When great, acute racial problems and violent antagonism arise in the future, what agency will then be able to grapple with the situation, restore racial peace and build again a covenant of good understanding and brotherhood between the races? There will be none!

In conclusion, let me say what every Christian student of race relations in America knows only too well, that unless the main great denominations of White Christians, and the Baptists in particular, aid the Negro denominations in this matter—aid them far more largely and constructively than has been considered necessary heretofore—this great emergency cannot begin to be met. The Negroes of America are even now weighing anchor and making ready to launch out upon the deep of an untried sea under new and adical leaders. To wait for another decade even is to see them out and largely beyond the reach of Christian influences! We must act now, or else miss our last and greatest opportunity to Christianize the Negro race!

AN OPPORTUNITY IN BLACK

By Rev. C.M. Thompson, Jr., Pastor First Baptist Church,
Barboursville, Ky.

Two men stood watching a fire. The flames were rapidly destroying the combined resources of both men. One was a young man. Upon the other were marks of age. But the man whose business life was still in the future turned in disgust and read the history of his effort in terms of calamity. The older man seemed to see beyond the darting streaks of light and smoke. He refused to see defeat in this unexpected occurrence. A dream came to him and he saw upon that very spot a larger and more modern plant, accomplishing his ambition in a better way. The young man moved away into failure. Disaster cleared the way for the larger ideas of the second one.

So it is with peoples. "According to your faith be it unto you," the Master says today as well as in the days of his flesh. Too long White men have spoken the language of "problems" and have missed the larger meaning of the Black man in their midst. Was God lacking in wisdom when he permitted millions of people of a decidedly different color to be brought to our shores and kept here through the years? Are people who erect their homes and build their churches and fulfil their work and seek the larger life, a problem in our midst? Rather they are an "opportunity, and opportunity in black."

There is no problem for Christian-minded people. Even apparent difficulties are but disguised opportunities. But are these people, found in every community, a difficulty? Their ancestors, brought to our warmer climate, by their labor contributed their part to the wealth of the Old South. The New South has come, and with the passing of the years the grandchildren and the great-grandchildren of this folk have been born among us. They furnish now a rare opportunity for the Christian White people of our nation. Let us study this opportunity.

What people have touched such depths of spiritual power in their songs as have these people? They have met the sin of gossip with song: "You can talk about me just as much as you please, but I'll talk about you down on my knees." When the load got heavy and the burdens seemed too much, they crooned: "Swing low, Sweet Chariot, coming for to carry me home." They feared becoming Pharisees and in song they found their safety: "It's not my father nor my mother but it's me, O Lord, standing in the need of prayer. It's not my sister nor my brother but it's me, O Lord, standing in the need of prayer. It's me; it's me; it's me, O Lord, standing in the need of prayer." They put to music the ambition for peace decades before the World War made the White man hate bloodshed. "I'm going to learn to war no more," mothers and fathers and children have sung round every cabin door in Dixie.

There is no tonic for hearts that are spiritually hungry like the singing of a group of down-South Negroes. They sing from their souls. You go from such an experience fed for many days to come. There is strength found in no other place. But their spiritual powers will not be kept unless these spiritual resources are conserved in the lives of the young. Jazz and the stage and the dance hall are taking this same talent and making anything but a blessing to the race and the world out of it.

Education need not remove these spiritual powers which the plantation darkly possessed. Education in many instances has merely heightened this remarkable insight into spiritual values. Listen to this Christian rebuke, given in such a way that you love its author. It came from the heart of a Colored man who died in his twenty-fourth year.

BEALE AVENUE BAPTIST CHURCH
Memphis, Tennessee

The "old Beale Street Baptist Church" was organized May 31, 1866, the year following the Civil War. It seems that its first pastor was Rev. (African Bailey) Bailey who was said to be a powerful preacher. Following him came Rev. R.N. Countee and among his successors were Revs. P.J. Jackson, T. Nightengale, and Rev. Clement. This great church is the mother of many daughters in and about Memphis. It has had a stormy history especially since the days of Countee who became a leading anti-Secret Society believer. In 1923, after twelve years litigation, the building became the property of the Solvent Savings Bank & Trust Company and was finally purchased from them by the New Prospective Baptist Church. The people who were still connected with the old church at this time took membership with the new owners who renamed the church the New Prospect Beale Street Baptist Church, with Rev. Benjamin J. Perkins, D.D., pastor. The building has been remodeled at great cost and is looked upon as the first church of that great city. Dr. Perkins has added many activities to the church so that old Beale Street Church is reincarnated and will live on as an agency for the dissemination of the gospel and the betterment of human society.

"Brother, come,
And let us go unto our God,
And when we stand before him,
I shall say:
'Lord, I do not hate.
I am hated.
I scourge no one.
I am scourged.
I covet no lands,
My lands are coveted.
I mock no peoples.
My peoples are mocked.'
"Brother, come
And, brother, what shall you say?"

—Joseph Seaman Cotter, Jr.

Or read with another of their poets the thought which came to him on reading, "Lead Kindly Light."

"Lead, gently, Lord, and slow,
For, oh, my steps are weak
And ever as I go,
Some soothing sentence speaks.

"That I may turn my face
Through doubt's obscurity
Toward thine abiding place,
E'en though I cannot see.
"For lo, the way is dark;
Through mist and cloud I grope,
Save for that fitful spark,
The little flame of hope.

"Lead gently, Lord, and slow,
For fear that I may fall;
I know not where I go
Unless I hear thy call.

"My fainting soul doth yearn
For thy green hills afar;
So let thy mercy burn--

362

> *My great, guiding star.*   —Paul Lawrence Dunbar.

There is genius in a race which has poets such as these. Truly such a people are a spiritual opportunity. Educated mentally and spiritually they will bless and sweeten the world. Not a problem they, but an opportunity.

But all this latent ability is of little value until it is brought under the sway of Christ. How can these thousands of boys and girls coming on hear unless they have preachers? How can preachers go to them unless they are sent? How can these thousands swarming into the cities and industrial areas be brought into contact with the gospel unless churches are provided? How can the educated multitudes which are being enlightened in our schools for Colored children be reached unless they have ministers who speak to them the language and thoughts of education? The answer to these questions must in a very large measure be made by the White man.

Our Colored people are an opportunity of still another type. God calls Christian people to the task of carrying the gospel to the ends of the earth. The continent of Africa was part of that world to which our Christ calls us. Who is better fitted to go into that great land than those people who, generations ago, came from its shores? Deep beneath the surface the heart of the American Black man is at one with those who live in their hutted villages on the Congo. Our American Colored folk are the logical missionaries for that vast continent. They speak the language and understand the traditions and can interpret Christ to them because they, Black men, have found Christ as a Black man sees and knows him.

It is essential that this point be observed. In one of the northwestern states a general denominational worker was spending the night in a Swedish home. A little grandmother spoke very broken English. She had lived the greater part of her life in the native land and still looked back to the homeland with longing. In the course of the evening they talked of Jesus. "Jesus Christ is Swedish, God is Swedish," she confided. But her more Americanized daughter corrected her. "Jesus was a Jew and God belongs to all people," was the statement in response. But the little old lady got her New Testament and showed the words of Jesus in her Swedish tongue. "And God talks to me in Swedish, too," was her way of closing the discussion.

The Black man knows the language of God as spoken to him. God does speak to the Black man in ways which are foreign to his White brother. God calls upon him and touches his life at different levels of experience. Let us redeem the Colored folk of our Southland and let them go out to quicken with the gospel their own flock, still bound in primitiveness and sin.

Thank God for this opportunity in black. Thank God for these people who, in the providence of God, have been placed beside us in our towns, cities, and rural sections. They have trusted us through the years. They loved our parents and our grandparents. They served them with faithfulness and love. Shall we not with equal faithfulness and love, in the best way we know, give to the descendants of the mammies and the uncles who loved their ol' missus and master the priceless gift which we possess—the gospel of the Son of God?

We have not fully seen this blessing which God has given us. It is ours, but we must accept it. It is God's opportunity awaiting us, but we must enter the door. It is not a problem, but part of God's glorious, divine plan.

HOW CAN WHITE BAPTIST CHURCHES HELP THE NEGRO BAPTIST CHURCHES OF THEIR COMMUNITY?

By Rev. John E. Briggs, Pastor Fifth Baptist Church
Washington, D.C.

For generations the White people have been interested in the spiritual welfare of the Negroes, and the labor spent among them has been very gratifying. There never has been a time so ripe for the White race to do constructive work among them as at present. It seems to be our obligation to continue to encourage, help, and instruct the Colored preachers so that they may develop and become honored and worthy men in their community.

In order to do effective work of this kind it is necessary that ministers of the White race should become acquainted with the Colored pastors and leading members and cultivate their friendship. The Negro race, while different in many respects from the White race, is putting great emphasis upon education today, and is endeavoring to produce an educated ministry. More and more of them believe that in spite of years spent without educational or other advantages, if the better class are given equal advantages, they can produce leaders worthy of recognition.

We should preach for Colored people from time to time. With all their advantages of the present day, they have a tendency to use an unnecessary amount of form and ceremony in their services. Everything is carried out in the most elaborate manner. Each speaker tries to outdo the other in his manner of expression. It seems to be an inborn trait with them, which, with the knowledge they are acquiring, like the pendulum of a clock, is swinging them far to an extreme of flowery speech and outward form. In spite of this aim to make an impression on the audience, the pastors are fundamentally sound. They have the real spirit, and it would benefit them greatly to have us preach for them occasionally, conducting more simple services, which combine control, dignity, and simplicity. Their extravagance, which some might term childishness, is not that, for those who have worked with them learn and appreciate the effort back of it all which is to convince the world that they are capable of doing things.

It would be to their advantage if there could be an exchange of visits at associational meetings and other denominational gatherings. It might be well for them to be officially appointed, but if that seems unwise or inexpedient, let it be done voluntarily on the part of either or both. There was a time when the Colored race came into more general contact with the best class of White people; there was a closer association with what we considered the better way of doing things. If they do not come in contact with the people of our churches they have as little chance of knowing our race at its best as we have of knowing and appreciating the efforts their best people are putting forth. It would not be fair to judge a race that has made as much progress as the Negro race has by associational contacts with day laborers, or with the ignorant and the worst element in general.

Negroes are naturally Baptists. It is not our problem to make them Baptists, but to keep them Baptists. As Dr. J.B. Gambrell used to say, "Give a Negro a five-cent New Testament and a conscience in good working order, and nine times out of ten he will be a Baptist." A leader of the Negro race said that "if you find a Negro who is not a Baptist it is usually because some White man has been tampering with him." One of the honored and successful pastors of a great Negro Baptist church recently stood before the Columbia Association of Baptist Churches and pleaded for more fellowship and cooperation between the White and Colored Baptists of Washington, D.C. He said, "The Catholics want us and are willing to spend any amount of money to get us; the Episcopalians and Presbyterians and others are bidding for us. They will compass land and sea to proselyte people. Why is it that you White Baptists do not encourage us and cooperate with us more? Both our preachers and members need and want it and will welcome it. Brethren, encourage us more to be true to the faith once for all delivered to the saints. It is greatly to be regretted that we do not understand each other and help each other more."

My observation is that the Negroes are weak in the two following points:

The Sunday School. Churches with large church memberships have very small Sunday schools. They have teachers who may be public school teachers, but they have no training in Sunday school work. They are developing few leaders, particularly for religious education. While there are some in the more progressive churches that realize the need of such training, up to the present time it is not being stressed. Teachers' meetings are general, but not the Worker's Council, nor the Teacher-Training Class. Oftentimes the pastor is the only one fitted to teach; an architect who designs a building, not necessarily a church plant. They are such a class. More often than not, from a standpoint of building, their equipment is poor. When they put up new buildings they employ and do not generally conduct a religious census with its attendant advantages, nor do they keep a good record system, and even when they have departmental work they do not use graded literature.

However, our own *Conventional Normal Manual* has proved a delight to a certain class of women who went through it and are the proud possessors of their diplomas. If some of our own churches that are capable would meet groups composed of members of different Colored churches, and teach the book, sending back trained teachers to the different Sunday schools, it would help greatly to show them what the present day Sunday school should be. Recently an effort has been made on the part of the Negro Y.M.C.A. to teach a Sunday School Manual, but the women teachers need it as well. They are losing boys and girls in the teen-age just as we are. They need to know what is best for their children just as much as we need to know what is best for ours.

Missions. We should inspire them to greater missionary effort. If they would measure up to their ability they could take over all the work we are doing in Africa, and do more besides. They are weak on tithing, and while they will and do give, their contributions depend largely upon the money they obtain in various ways. In order to create a greater missionary spirit in the years to come, their leaders should be studying Home and Foreign Missions, as our leaders are doing, but they lack the teachers. In one instance a White woman is starting to teach a class of seven or eight Negro women. A chapter will be taught each week from our present *Home Study Book.* The class consists of women from different churches and they are so eager to begin that they can scarcely wait for the first lesson. At the same time they are taking a mission study course in *From Jerusalem to Jerusalem*, and in this way these two books will be introduced into a half dozen different churches in the locality. The way to get their boys and girls interested in mission work is to start them now, beginning with the Sunbeam age and carefully training them along this line. They have done little so far.

What they need is a plan of missionary education for their young people. Personal service, White Cross, and Stewardship, are new fields which they are willing to enter but lack the necessary leaders. They need consecrated men and women from our churches to teach them; those who are not handicapped by fear of criticism—for there is more or less of it on both sides, and probably will be until God's children everywhere realize that He "hath made of one blood all nations of men for to dwell on all the face of the earth, and hath determined the times before appointed, and the bounds of their habitation; that they should seek the Lord, if haply they might feel after him, and find him."

SIXTH AVENUE BAPTIST CHURCH
Birmingham, Ala.

In its early days when it was a small frame building, J. Q. A. Wilhite pastored this people. At his death they secured the service of Rev. John W. Goodgame, D.D., who led them in the building of this great church which is one of the most outstanding agencies of Baptist efforts and services in all Alabama.

RACE RELATIONS—A TEST OF VITAL CHRISTIANITY

By Rev. Vernon Johns
President Virginia Theological Seminary and College
Lynchburg, Va.

"We are agreed that at no point is our vital Christianity being tested today more than at the point of our attitude toward the Negro in our midst." How true! A cartoon in a Negro journal some months ago showed a celebrated White evangelist, of the rather pronounced and militant type, waging a terrific onslaught against sin. The preacher had knocked booze under the ropes; gambling had taken to its heels; Sunday movies and baseball were on the run, and a score of other sins lay prostrate and mangled in the wake of the divine tirade. But in the midst of these battered and broken evils there stood a huge, gawky giant marked "Race Prejudice," holding in his hands, "discrimination—corruption—unequal wages—ropes—torches," and the like, as he grinned complacently and said concerning the holy warrior: "He never even looked at me!"

The publishers of *Home and Foreign Fields,* by devoting a number to race relations, are proving themselves free from such religious blindspots. And this delightful vision is followed by an inquiry as to what White Christian men and women can do to help the more disadvantaged race within their midst. The answer to the question takes the form of two further inquires. First, What does the Negro need? and second, How can White Christians help to met that need?

The late Dean Bosworth, speaking of the difficulties which beset the first president of Oberlin College, said, "His task was simple. He had everything to get." This statement may be aptly applied to the condition of the Negro. One of Bert William's Colored preachers, addressing his Sunday congregation, is made to say that he needs everything "from a hat down and from an overcoat in." The Negro, in common with other groups and even more desperately than they, needs the means for physical subsistence. "A man must live before he can philosophize," and this is equally true of men in humbler vocations. "Jesus," says Professor Rauschenbush, "did not ignore the elemental needs of humanity. He was never so 'spiritual' as some of his followers."

The White Christian may well be reminded that the problem of material existence is much more acute for the Negro than for himself. The White race in America has been given two and one-half centuries in which to get for themselves all that was worth having before the Negro entered the struggle in his own right. In these business acquisitions the more advanced race had also the free, forced service of his dark brother. There must have been built during these long years numerous fortunes, or the foundations of numerous fortunes, which are still intact; or, which if broken up, passed exclusively into the hands of White people. While a large percentage of White people have inherited much from the past, about all that the Negro has had passed on to him from his forebears was a large doctor's bill, burial fee, or the responsibility of providing for a number of orphans. The Negro who would otherwise accumulate wealth is often burdened with inheritance of a deficit from his direct ancestors, or heavy dependencies in the lateral branches of his family.

Or let us take the Negro and the Caucasian who start out side by side to win their way. They may seem to have equal opportunities, but this is only "seeming," as will appear on analysis. Suppose the two set out to live by selling books, notions, or nursery stock. The White agent need not limit his canvass to White homes. In fact, he is apt to canvass the Negro community first. The Negro, on the contrary, would be guilty of an outrage if he called at the home of White neighbors in the same capacity. In one instance, a rather adventurous Colored brother did call at a White home with some such purpose. He was not certain of the name of the occupant, so he said to the little boy who met him at the door, "I presume this is where Mr. Hemmings lives." The little Nordic ran into the house with surprise and disgust crying, "O, mama, look! Here is a Negro at our door presuming."

It is not necessary to mention the fact that there are numerous positions in which the Negro may not hope for the opportunity to earn the means of living. It is appropriate to suggest here that to refuse one the right to earn a living is indirectly to deny him the right to live. In many instances, also, the Negro renders highly valuable service to industry with little hope of anything above very meager reward. I once had charge of the funeral of a Colored man who had served for thirty years in a large and very prosperous industry. His White employer was present and remarked that there was not a person in his employ whose service had meant more to the firm than that of the deceased. But the deceased had never earned more than fourteen dollars a week.

In these times when unemployment is increasing the hardship of the Negro hand, and the ready-made positions by which educated Negroes had lived are crowded, White Christians may help the Negro by remembering the specific difficulties which confront him in his efforts to subsist. But always here the assistance should take the form of opportunity instead of alms. To what extent can White Christians help their Negro neighbors get a fair portion of the opportunities which the community provides for people to subsist and thrive? If the Negro has the strength to labor, or the mind to direct, will these be welcomed by White Christians who have charge of the community's life, or will they be discountenanced because the owner is dark of surface?

> *"Yet he has made dark things*
> *To be glad and merry as light!*
> *There is a little dark bird, sits and sings,*
> *And a dark stream ripples out of sight—*
> *Dark frogs chant in the safe morass,*
> *And the sweetest stars are made to pass*
> *O'er the face of the darkest night.*

Again, White Christians can help the Negroes in their community by exercising the teaching functions. The Negro is required to measure up to the White man's standard of civilization. No allowance is made for his handicaps when he comes to the bar of either justice or public opinion. To the contrary, both tribunals beat the White delinquent with rods—and [the] Negro delinquent with scorpions. But think how deprived the Negro has been of the natural opportunity to prepare for the social responsibility which is a part of civilization. During the long eventful years when American institutions were being designed and constructed, the Negro lacked both freedom and responsibility. The invaluable social experience and education which came to White Americans out of that long, vast sacrificial, creative enterprise were denied the Negro by the nature of his circumstance. No one can ever tell what damage was done to our preparation for the ordeal of citizenship and responsibility now upon us, when we were deprived of the privilege of growing up with the nation of which we are now a part. We have crossed the same seas and the same wilderness with our White brothers. But he crossed as adventurer and we as slaves. We knew that the discoveries and creations would belong all to him. How could we be alert? We labored knowing that labor brought us neither pay nor promise. How could we make our efforts joyous? Our White brothers have the genius of American civilization in their blood and fiber because they were free men, privileged with responsibility in the making of it. Now the Negro, come of age, must learn the difficult language of American civilization which the White race learned as children.

Nothing is more evident than our need of instruction at this point. We cannot build institutions as a race and promote our group life as long as the Negro cares more for a hundred dollars which he owns individually than he cares for a million-dollar institution which we own together, or a hundred million-dollar institution which we might own. The Negro has made some progress as an individual, but still has little sense of commonwealth. The White man can give us valuable lessons here. I think White people genuinely interested in the improvement of Negro life would do well when the opportunity is presented to describe to Negro groups the steps in the process by which our great social and political organizations have come to be, portraying especially the adventure, cooperation, and sacrifice involved.

Finally, White Christians can help the Negro by more contact with his religious life in an effort to make Negro religion more an instrument of vision and power, and less matter of display and fruitless emotion. And by all means, White Christians, help to make the law in your community an instrument for the Negro's protection instead of his persecution. How, forsooth, can a man respect a thing which never touches him except to his degradation? I know of no better words with which to close than these lines addressed by a Negro poet, from Georgia, to White America:

> *How would you have us—as we are?*
> *Or falling 'neath the loads we bear?*
> *Our eyes fixed upward on a star,*
> *Or gazing empty at despair?*
> *How would you have us, men or things?*
> *With courage firm, and footsteps fleet,*
> *Strong, willing sinews in you wing?*
> *Or tightening chains about your feet?*

We have come from nothing to something, materially; from zero to thousands of dollars credit—commercially and financially—from a condition of servility to one of intelligent manipulation of our own affairs; from consumers to producers.

W. BISHOP JOHNSON, D.D., LL.D.,
Editor of *Baptist Magazine* in 1901.

REV. FELIX G. DAVIS
Texas

Born and died in Texas. Among the early educated ministers of the state. Graduated from Roger Williams University, Nashville, Tennessee, and was a strong, real Baptist preacher.

NEW HOPE BAPTIST CHURCH
Meridian, Mississippi

As far back as 1865 the author remembers when there sat on a hill in the western part of Meridian a large frame church surrounded by pine trees. This was the first church into which our little wandering feet treaded when we were fresh from slavery and old enough to hear the story of the Lord. Rev. Rent Ramsey was its moderator and the first preacher we remember hearing. The mental picture of this pastor and church hung on the walls of my memory has served me a good purpose all the years of my life. I was born within fourteen miles of this church.

The present pastor, Rev. W. G. Wilson, a strong, courageous, and with all known as a Baptist preacher of conviction and destined to keep this historical old church in line with its day. Rev. D. Webster was its first Negro pastor.

WHEN AND WHERE NEGRO BAPTISTS HAVE MET NATIONALLY, SINCE THEIR FIRST ORGANIZATION IN 1840

AMERICAN BAPTIST MISSIONARY CONVENTION, ORGANIZED 1840

Place	President	Preacher of Introductory Sermon	Text	Secretary	Year
New York, N. Y.	Rev. H. Lincoln	Sampson White	Amos 8:2		1841
Philadelphia, Pa.	Rev. H. Lincoln	Sampson White	John 17:18	Rev. B. M. Hill	1842
Philadelphia, Pa.	Rev. H. Lincoln	Jeremiah Asher	Mal. 2:2	Rev. B. M. Hill	1843
Providence, R. I.	William Williams	William Jackson	2 Tim. 2:2	Rev. B. M. Hill	1844
New York, N. Y.			Matt. 24:14		1845
Philadelphia, Pa.	Rev. Daniel Sharp	Thomas W. Allen	Psalm 167	Rev. Solomon Peak	1846
Baltimore, Md.		Leonard A. Grimes	John 2:17		1848
Philadelphia, Pa.	Hon. George N. Briggs	H. H. Butler	Heb. 12:1	Rev. Edward Bright	1849
Philadelphia, Pa.	Hon. George N. Briggs	Leonard Black	1 Tim. 1:15	Rev. Edward Bright	1850
Brooklyn, N. Y.	Hon. George N. Briggs	Edmund Kelley	Matt. 3:9	Rev. Edward Bright	1851
Boston, Mass.	Hon. George N. Briggs	Jeremiah Asher	John 3:5	Rev. Edward Bright	1852
New Bedford, Mass.	Hon. George N. Briggs	Leonard A. Grimes	Col. 1:28	Rev. Edward Bright	1853
Philadelphia, Pa.	Hon. George N. Briggs	Edmund Kelley	Luke 2:14	Rev. Edward Bright	1854
Philadelphia, Pa.	Hon. George N. Briggs	Chauncey Leonard	Heb. 10:12, 13	Rev. Wm. Shailer	1855
New York, N. Y.	Hon. George N. Briggs	Sampson White	Acts 8:40	Rev. Wm. Shailer	1856
Boston, Mass.	Hon. George N. Briggs	Jesse F. Boulden	Lam. 3:22	Rev. Wm. Shailer	1857
Philadelphia, Pa.	Hon. George N. Briggs	James Underline	Heb. 9:16,39	Rev. Wm. T. Brantley	1858
Newbury, N. Y.	Rev. Chauncey Leonard	Edmund Kelly	Luke 24:46	Rev. Wm. Jackson	1859
New York, N. Y.	Rev. Wm. Spelman	T. Doughty Miller	Luke 12:20	Rev. T. D. Miller	1860

SOUTHERN AND NORTHWESTERN MISSIONARY BAPTIST CONVENTION, ORGANIZED 1864

N. B.: No minutes.

THE CONSOLIDATED AMERICAN BAPTIST MISSIONARY CONVENTION, 1866

Place	President	Preacher of Introductory Sermon	Text	Secretary	Year
Philadelphia, Pa.	Rev. Richard Vaughn			D. H. Crosby	1852
Boston, Mass.	Rev. Henry Thompson			D. H. Crosby	1853
	Rev. Jeremiah Asher			Wm. Jackson	1855
	Rev. L. A. Grimes			C. Leonard	1856
	Rev. C. Leonard			James Underline	1857
	Rev. C. Leonard			Wm. Jackson	1858
	Rev. S. White			Wm. Jackson	1859
	Wm. Spellman			D. Miller	1860
	Rev. R. De Baptiste			R. Perry	1872
	Rev. Amos Johnson			Wm. T. Dixon	1877

BAPTIST FOREIGN MISSION CONVENTION, U. S. A., ORGANIZED NOVEMBER 24, 1880

Place	President	Preacher of Introductory Sermon	Text	Secretary	Year
Montgomery, Ala.	Rev. W. H. McAlpine	Elder R. Spiller	Ps. 126:6	J. M. Armstead	1880
Knoxville, Tenn.	Rev. W. H. McAlpine	J. Marks	Matt. 5:15, 16	J. M. Armstead	1881
Macon, Ga.	Rev. W. H. McAlpine	E. K. Love	Mark 16:15	W. R. Pettiford	1882
Manchester, Va.	Rev. J. Q. A. Wilhite	J. Smothers	1 Cor. 3:11	J. E. Jones	1883
Meridian, Miss.	Rev. J. A. Foster	A. Binga, Jr.,	Acts 16:9	H. H. Mitchell	1884
New Orleans, La.	Rev. W. A. Brinkely	J. E. Jones	2 Peter 3:18	S. T. Clanton	1885
Memphis, Tenn.	Rev. J. A. Foster	A. S. Jackson	2 Tim. 2:21	J. J. Spelman	1886
Little Rock, Ark.	Rev. A. S. Jackson			J. J. Spelman	1887
Nashville, Tenn.	Rev. A. S. Jackson	W. J. Simmons	Isaiah 61:1	J. J. Spelman	1888
Indianapolis, Ind.	Rev. E. K. Love	C. T. Walker	Luke 9:13	S. T. Clanton	1889
Louisville, Ky.	Rev. E. K. Love	Prof. J. Edmond Jones	Romans 1:16	S. T. Clanton	1890
Dallas, Texas	Rev. E. K. Love	A. S. Jackson		S. T. Clanton	1891
Savannah, Ga.	Rev. A. R. Griggs	E. W. D. Isaac, Sr.	Luke 24:27	S. T. Clanton	1892
Washington, D. C.	Rev. E. K. Love			S. T. Clanton	1893
Montgomery, Ala.	Rev. E. C. Morris			S. T. Clanton	1894

Place	President	Preacher of Introductory Sermon	Text	Secretary	Year
Atlanta, Ga.	Rev. E. C. Morris			W. H. Steward	1895
St. Louis, Mo.	Rev. E. C. Morris	A. S. Jackson, D. D.	Joshua 13:1	W. H. Steward	1896
Boston, Mass.	Rev. E. C. Morris	W. Bishop Johnson	Mark 16:30	W. H. Steward	1897
Kansas City, Mo.	Rev. E. C. Morris	W. M. Gilbert	Matt. 9:37, 38	W. H. Steward	1898
Nashville, Tenn.	Rev. E. C. Morris	W. H. Bowling, D. D.	Deut. 10:17	W. L. Cansler	1899
Richmond, Va.	Rev. E. C. Morris	A. M. Johnson, D. D.	Rev. 3:8	W. L. Cansler	1900
Cincinnati, Ohio	Rev. E. C. Morris	E. R. Carter	Psalm 72:17	W. L. Cansler	1901
Birmingham, Ala.	Rev. E. C. Morris	E. M. Cohron	Psalm 2:8	W. L. Cansler	1902
Philadelphia, Pa.	Rev. E. C. Morris	Jos. A. Booker, D. D.		W. L. Cansler	1903
Austin, Texas	Rev. E. C. Morris	W. E. Gladden	Acts 1:8	W. L. Cansler	1904
Chicago, Ill.	Rev. E. C. Morris	W. W. Brown, D. D.		W. L. Cansler	1905
Memphis, Tenn.	Rev. E. C. Morris	C. H. Parrish, D. D.		W. L. Cansler	1906
Washington, D. C.	Rev. E. C. Morris	B. Tyrell, D. D., Ph. D.		W. L. Cansler	1907
Lexington, Ky.	Rev. E. C. Morris	M. W. D. Norman, D. D.		R. B. Hudson	1908
Columbus, Ohio	Rev. E. C. Morris	R. Kemp, D. D.	Romans 3:29	R. B. Hudson	1909
New Orleans, La.	Rev. E. C. Morris	A. S. Jackson		R. B. Hudson	1910
Pittsburg, Pa.	Rev. E. C. Morris	C. A. Ward	Rom. 1:14, 15	R. B. Hudson	1911
Houston, Texas	Rev. E. C. Morris	G. A. Goodwin	Luke 5:4-11	R. B. Hudson	1912
Nashville, Tenn.	Rev. E. C. Morris	C. H. Parrish	Ex. 5:1; Ps. 6:8-13	R. B. Hudson	1913
Philadelphia, Pa.	Rev. E. C. Morris	G. W. Rayford	Acts 10:44	R. B. Hudson	1914
Chicago, Ill.	Rev. E. C. Morris	Rev. L. K. Williams	Isa. 60:1	R. B. Hudson	1915
Savannah, Ga.	Rev. E. C. Morris	Rev. W. M. Taylor	Psa. 121; Mark 9:5	R. B. Hudson	1918
Muskogee, Okla.	Rev. E. C. Morris	J. W. Ribbons, D. D.		R. B. Hudson	1917
St. Louis, Mo.	Rev. E. C. Morris	W. M. Taylor	Psalm 121	R. B. Hudson	1918
Newark, N. J.	Rev. E. C. Morris	Rev. T. J. Goodall	1 Cor. 3:11	R. B. Hudson	1919
Indianapolis, Ind.	Rev. E. C. Morris	Rev. O. C. Maxwell	Col. 3:16	R. B. Hudson	1920
Chicago, Ill.	Rev. E. C. Morris	J. C. Austin	Gen 12:2	R. B. Hudson	1921
St. Louis, Mo.	Rev. W. G. Parks	Rev. L. K. Williams	Rev. 1:17;18	R. B. Hudson	1922
Los Angeles, CA	Rev. L. K. Williams	Mordecai Johnson	Luke 6:26-28	R. B. Hudson	1923
Nashville, Tenn.	Rev. L. K. Williams	Rev. C. A. Ward	Rev. 6:2	R. B. Hudson	1924
Baltimore, Md.	Rev. L. K. Williams	E. Arlington Wilson		R. B. Hudson	1925
Ft. Worth, Texas	Rev. L. K. Williams	J. C. Jackson	Micah 4:1	R. B. Hudson	1926
Detroit, Mich.	Rev. L. K. Williams	Rev. T. S. Boone	Gen. 1:1; John 1:1-13	R. B. Hudson	1927
Louisville, Ky.	Rev. L. K. Williams	Rev. W. H. R. Powell	Matt 5:3	R. B. Hudson	1928

375

WEST CHESTNUT ST. BAPTIST CHURCH
Louisville, Kentucky

This church was organized in 1886. Rev. Wm. Johnson, D.D., Pastor. Dr. Johnson has pastored this church 32 years and is one of the most popular pastors in the city of Louisville. He has recently remodeled W. Chestnut making it an up-to-date church, be it said with credit to Dr. Johnson. He has aways known how to gather about him well prepared helpers, as doctors, lawyers and other professional men. West Chestnut St. Church has a beautiful future and a strong preacher.

AMERICAN NATIONAL BAPTIST CONVENTION, ORGANIZED AUGUST 25, 1886

Place	President	Preacher of Introductory Sermon	Text	Secretary	Year
St. Louis, Mo.	Rev. W. J. Simmons	W. A. Burch	Isaiah 28:16		1886
Mobile, Ala.	Rev. W. J. Simmons				1887
Nashville, Tenn.	Rev. W. J. Simmons			J. L. Cohran	1888
Indianapolis, Ind.	Rev. W. J. Simmons			J. L. Cohran	1889
Louisville, Ky.	Rev. W. J. Simmons			J. L. Cohran	1890
Dallas, Texas	Rev. W. M. Brawley			W. H. Steward	1891
Savannah, Ga.	Rev. M. Vann			W. H. Steward	1892
Washington, D. C.	Rev. M. Vann			W. H. Steward	1893

THE NATIONAL BAPTIST EDUCATIONAL CONVENTION, ORGANIZED SEPTEMBER, 1893

Place	President	Preacher of Introductory Sermon	Text	Secretary	Year
Washington, D. C.	Rev. A. Williams			W. B. Johnson	1893
Montgomery, Ala.	Rev. A. Williams			W. B. Johnson	1894

LOTT CAREY BAPTIST FOREIGN MISSION SOCIETY, U. S. A.

Place	President	Preacher of Introductory Sermon	Text	Secretary	Year
Washington, D. C.	P. F. Morris			A. W. Pegues, D. D.	1897
Washington, D. C.	C. S. Brown, D. D.	H. H. Mitchell, D. D.	Deut. 11:24	A. W. Pegues, D. D.	1898
Baltimore, Md.	C. S. Brown, D. D.	J. E. R. Miller, D. D.	Rev. 14:6	A. W. Pegues, D. D.	1899
Alexander, Va.	C. S. Brown, D. D.	J. Milton Waldron, D. D.	Matt. 13:38	A. W. Pegues, D. D.	1900
Philadelphia, Pa.	C. S. Brown, D. D.	R. D. Winn, D. D.	Mark 16:15	A. W. Pegues, D. D.	1901
Washington, D. C.	C. S. Brown, D. D.			A. W. Pegues, D. D.	1902
Winston-Salem, N. C.	C. S. Brown, D. D.	R. Spiller, D. D.	Gen. 49:10	A. W. Pegues, D. D.	1903
Pittsburg, Pa.	C. S. Brown, D. D.	A. A. Graham, D. D.	John 9: 4	A. W. Pegues, D. D.	1904
	C. S. Brown, D. D.			A. W. Pegues, D. D.	1905
Richmond, Va.	C. S. Brown, D. D.	J. H. Lee, D. D.	Neh. 6:3	A. W. Pegues, D. D.	1906
Portsmouth, Va.	C. S. Brown, D. D.			A. W. Pegues, D. D.	1907
Pittsburgh, Pa.	C. S. Brown, D. D.	C. C. Somerville, D. D.	John 20:21	A. W. Pegues, D. D.	1908
Washington, D. C.	C. S. Brown, D. D.	R. C. Quarles, D. D.	John 10:16	A. W. Pegues, D. D.	1909
Durham, N. C.	C. S. Brown, D. D.	J. A. Whitted, D. D.	Gen. 4:9	A. W. Pegues, D. D.	1910
Lynchburg, Va.	C. S. Brown, D. D.			A. W. Pegues, D. D.	1911
Wilmington, N. C.	C. S. Brown, D. D.	J. H. Moore, D. D.	Luke 9:33	A. W. Pegues, D. D.	1912
Portsmouth, Va.	C. S. Brown, D. D.	F. W. Williams, D. D.	Exodus 14:15	A. W. Pegues, D. D.	1913
Washington, D. C.	C. S. Brown, D. D.	W. H. Stokes, D. D.	Isaiah 54:1-3	A. W. Pegues, D. D.	1914
Raleigh, N. C.	C. S. Brown, D. D.	S. N. Vass, D. D.	1 Kings 19:9	A. W. Pegues, D. D.	1915
Richmond, Va.	C. S. Brown, D. D.	W. T. Johnson, D. D.	Matt. 16:15	A. W. Pegues, D. D.	1916
Baltimore, Md.	C. S. Brown, D. D.	J. C. Taulton, D. D.	Exodus 14:15	A. W. Pegues, D. D.	1917
Portsmouth, Va.	C. S. Brown, D. D.		Songs of Solomon 6:10	A. W. Pegues, D. D.	1918
Rocky Mount, N. C.	C. S. Brown, D. D.	J. H. Randolph, D. D.	Isaiah 15:17	A. W. Pegues, D. D.	1919
Washington, D. C.	C. S. Brown, D. D.	P. J. Wallace, D. D.		A. W. Pegues, D. D.	1920
Portsmouth, Va.	C. S. Brown, D. D.	B. F. McWilliams, D. D.	Phil. 4:19	A. W. Pegues, D. D.	1921
Newark, N. J.	C. S. Brown, D. D.	W. B. Hayes, D. D.	Acts 26:19	A. W. Pegues, D. D.	1922
Charlotte, N. C.	C. S. Brown, D. D.	J. E. Kirkland, D. D.	John 12:21	A. W. Pegues, D. D.	1923
Homestead, Pa.	C. S. Brown, D. D.	A. Hobbs, D. D.	Gen. 17:19, 20	A. W. Pegues, D. D.	1924
Washington, D. C.	C. S. Brown, D. D.	A. W. Brown, D. D.	John 3:16	A. W. Pegues, D. D.	1925
Norfolk, Va.	C. S. Brown, D. D.	D. E. Over, D. D.		A. W. Pegues, D. D.	1926
Brooklyn, N. Y.	C. S. Brown, D. D.	C. H. Clark, D. D.	Matt. 5:47	A. W. Pegues, D. D.	1927
Richmond, Va.	C. S. Brown, D. D.	S. L. McDowell, D. D.	Acts 16:9	A. W. Pegues, D. D.	1928
Winston-Salem, N. C.	C. S. Brown, D. D.	J. C. White, D. D.		A. W. Pegues, D. D.	1929
Columbia, S. C.	C. S. Brown, D. D.	J. L. Pinn, D. D.	Acts 10th Chap.	J. H. Moore, D. D.	1930

NATIONAL BAPTIST CONVENTION, UNINCORPORATED. ORGANIZED 1915

Place	President	Preacher of Introductory Sermon	Text	Secretary	Year
Chicago, Ill.	Rev. E. P. Jones			T. J. King	1915
Kansas City, Mo.	Rev. E. P. Jones			T. J. King	1916
Atlanta, Ga.	Rev. E. P. Jones	Rev. E. W. Bowen	Rom. 13:12	C. P. Madison	1917
Little Rock, Ark.	Rev. E. P. Jones	Rev. E. R. Carter	Matt. 11:6	C. P. Madison	1918
Norfolk, Va.	Rev. E. P. Jones	Rev. C. T. Dorroh	Not stated	C. P. Madison	1919
Columbus, Ohio	Rev. E. P. Jones	Rev. C. P. Madison	John 9:4	C. P. Madison	1920
New Orleans, La.	Rev. E. P. Jones	Rev. L. Drane	1 Cor. 3:11	C. P. Madison	1921
Nashville, Tenn.	Dr. E. P. Jones	Rev. J. A. Royal		C. P. Madison	1922
Ft. Worth, Texas	Dr. E. P. Jones	Rev. J. H. Eason	Prov. 18:24	C. P. Madison	1923
Chicago, Ill.	Dr. J. E. Wood	Rev. J. W. Winn	Matt. 28:18, 20	C. P. Madison	1924
Kansas City, Mo.	Dr. J. E. Wood	Rev. C. H. Clark	Mark 12:7	C. P. Madison	1925
Indianapolis, Ind.	Pr. J. E. Wood	Rev. J. W. Hurse	2 Cor. 4:4	C. P. Madison	1926
Denver, Colo.	Dr. J. E. Wood	Rev. I. M. Hendon	Matt. 28:19, 20	C. P. Madison	1927
Shreveport, La.	Dr. J. E. Wood	Rev. G. L. Prince	Prov. 29:18	C. P. Madison	1928
Norfolk, Va.	Dr. J. E. Wood			C. P. Madison	1929

Chapter XIII

OUTLINES OF BAPTISTS' STANDINGS BY STATES

Alabama

Number of churches--2,022; number of ordained ministers--1,500; number of baptisms--14,075; total membership--214,231; number of schools--1,852; enrollment--106,267; church buildings--1,500; parsonages--50; total value of property--$3,191,700; associations--109; state conventions--2.

In Alabama there are 289,772 White Baptists, totaling 504,003 Baptists in the state.

Arkansas

Number of churches--1,428; number of ordained ministers--922; number of baptisms--14,075; total membership--108,000; Sunday schools--1,400; enrollment--48,918; church buildings--1,500; parsonages--10; total value of property--$928,00; associations--31; state conventions--1.

District of Columbia

Number of churches--69; number of ordained ministers--165; number of baptisms--100; total membership--39,878; Sunday schools--69; enrollment--4,800; church buildings--60; parsonages--3; total value of property--$2,075,000; associations--1; state conventions--2.

In the District of Columbia there are 14,545 White Baptists, totaling 54,423 Baptists in the district.

Florida

Number of churches--1,510; number of ordained ministers--600; number of baptisms--6,000; total membership--125,000; Sunday schools--1,300; enrollment--30,059; church buildings--639; parsonages--70; total value of property--$2,000,000.

In Florida there are 117,418 White Baptists, totaling 242,418 Baptists in the state; state conventions-2.

Georgia

Number of churches--3,846; number of ordained ministers--5,362; number of baptisms--26,595; total membership--552,010; Sunday schools--2,829; enrollment--167,034; church buildings--3,800; parsonages--22; total value of property--$13,692,200; state conventions--1.

In Georgia there are 414,415 White Baptists, totaling 966,425 Baptists in the state.

Illinois

Number of churches--337; number of ordained ministers--376; number of baptisms--3,370; total membership--347,000; Sunday schools--348; enrollment--260,250; church buildings--337; parsonages--200; total value of property--$1,674,000; state conventions--2.

In Illinois there are 94,996 White Baptists, totaling 441,996 Baptists in the state.

Indiana

Number of churches--127; number of ordained ministers--181; number of baptisms--690; total membership--36,000; Sunday schools--118; enrollment--43,030; church buildings--85; parsonages--12; total value of property--$1,000,000; state conventions--2.

In Indiana there are 86,559 White Baptists, totaling 122,559 Baptists in the state.

Kansas

Number of churches--139; number of ordained ministers--187; number of baptisms--689; total membership--21,000; Sunday schools--120; enrollment--11,070; church buildings--139; parsonages--25; total value of property--$1,475,300; associations--6; state conventions--1.

In Kansas there are 59,308 White Baptists, totaling 80,308 Baptists in the state.

Kentucky

Number of churches--589; number of ordained ministers--439; number of baptisms--2,365; total membership--90,000; Sunday schools--521; enrollment--28,306; church buildings--560; parsonages--20; total value of property--$1,000,000; state conventions--1.

In Kentucky there are 318,984 White Baptists, totaling 408,984 Baptists in the state.

Louisiana

Number of churches--1,377; number of ordained ministers--525; total membership--126,981; Sunday schools--1,265; enrollment--63,090; church buildings--1,200; total value of property--$1,715,300; state conventions--2.

In Louisiana there are 126,951 White Baptists, totaling 253,932 Baptists in the state.

Maryland

Number of churches--69; number of ordained ministers--85; baptisms--746; total membership--17,000; Sunday schools--15; enrollment--1,616; church buildings--46; total value of church property--$500,000; associates--3; state conventions--1.

In Maryland there are 224,664 White Baptists, totaling 241,664 Baptists in the state.

Michigan

Number of churches--40; number of ordained ministers--36; number of baptisms--727; total membership--14,111; number of Sunday schools--28; enrollment--1,856; meeting houses--31; parsonages--13; total value of property--$1,314,500; associations--1; state conventions--1.

In Michigan there are 57,941 White Baptists, totaling 72,052 Baptists in the state.

Mississippi

Number of churches--2,210; number of ordained ministers--585; number of Sunday schools--1,028; total membership--400,000; enrollment--111,058; church buildings--2,000; parsonages--250; total value of property--$1,937,000; associations--64; state conventions--3.

In Mississippi there are 224,664 White Baptists, totaling 624,664 Baptists in the state.

Missouri

Number of churches--269; number of ordained ministers--353; number of Sunday schools--244; number of baptisms--1,447; enrollment--85,100; church buildings--288; parsonages--10; total value of property--$1,345,000; associations--16; state conventions--1.

In Missouri there are 224,793 White Baptists, totaling 313,773 Baptists in the state.

New Jersey

Number of churches--179; number of ordained ministers--210; number of baptisms--1,430; total membership--37,704; Sunday schools--51; enrollment--5,647; church buildings--164; total value of property--$3,613,700; associations--4; state.

In New Jersey there are 68,314 White Baptists, totaling 106,018 Baptists in the state.

New York
Number of churches--122; number of ordained ministers--146; number of baptisms--517; total membership--16,242; church buildings--74; total value of property--$1,312,600; associations--1; state conventions--2.

In New York there are 185,926 White Baptists, totaling 202,168 Baptists in the state.

North Carolina
Number of churches--1,421; ordained ministers--1,200; total membership--200,000; Sunday schools--1,123; enrollment--75,507; church buildings--1,177; parsonages--78; total value of church property--$1,451,000; associations--48; state conventions--1.

In North Carolina there are 368,191 White Baptists, totaling 586,191 Baptist in the state.

Ohio
Number of churches--268; number of ordained ministers--406; number of baptisms--1,998; total membership--65,000; number of Sunday schools--279; enrollment--19,300; church buildings--264; parsonages--31; total value of church property--$2,980,700; association--5; state conventions--2.

In Ohio there are 92,888 White Baptists, totaling 157,888 Baptists in the state.

Oklahoma
Number of churches--410; number of ordained ministers--380; number of baptisms--1,260; total membership--58,000; number of Sunday schools--200; enrollment--20,000; church buildings--380; parsonages--20; total value of church property--$650,000; associations--12; state conventions--2.

In Oklahoma there are 128,763 White Baptists, totaling 186,763 Baptists in the state.

Pennsylvania
Number of churches--135; number of ordained ministers--341; number of baptisms--694; total membership--50,000; number of Sunday schools--27; enrollment--10,000; church buildings--100; parsonages--6; total value of church property--$1,210,000; associations--4; state conventions--1.

In Pennsylvania there are 158,974 White Baptists, totaling 208,974 Baptists in the state.

South Carolina

Number of churches--1,420; number of ordained ministers--750; number of baptisms--1,250; total membership--200,000; number of Sunday schools--1,306; enrollment--86,356; church buildings--1,337; parsonages--10; total value of church property--$1,400,000; associations--64; state conventions--2.

In South Carolina there are 223,448 White Baptists, totaling 423,448 Baptists in the state.

Tennessee

Number of churches--783; number of ordained ministers--634; total membership--190,000; number of Sunday schools--700; enrollment--33,679; church buildings--695; parsonages--35; total value of church property--$1,126,000; associations--37; state conventions--2.

In Tennessee there are 277,743 White Baptists, totaling 467,743 Baptists in the state.

Texas

Number of churches--1,752; number of ordained ministers--1,095; number of baptisms--7,500; total membership--215,000; church buildings--1,659; parsonages--100; number of Sunday schools--1,619; enrollment--82,617; total value of church property--$1,868,000; associations--51; state conventions--4.

In Texas there are 490,051 White Baptists, totaling 605,000 Baptists in the state.

Virginia

Number of churches--900; number of ordained ministers--1,000; number of baptisms--800; total membership--275,000; number of Sunday schools--900; enrollment--140,000; church buildings--900; parsonages--12; total value of church property--$2,900,000; associations--36; state conventions--2.

In Virginia there are 225,243 White Baptists, totaling 500,000 Baptists in the state.

HOWE INSTITUTE

Howe Institute is now a part of Roger Williams University, Memphis, Tenn. Dr. T. O. Fuller is the leading spirit, and hopes to make a greater Roger Williams.

West Virginia

Number of churches--266; number of ordained ministers--350; number of baptisms--740; total membership--26,300; number of Sunday schools--350; enrollment--12,800; church buildings--210; parsonages--16; total value of church property--$775,000; associations--9; state conventions--1.

In West Virginia there are 76,201 White Baptists, totaling 102,501 Baptists in the state.

Shenandoah Valley (Free Baptists)

Number of churches--30; number of ordained ministers--25; number of baptisms--75; total membership--1,500; church buildings--30; parsonages--5; total value of church property--$63,000.

*Only Totals of White Baptists in the U. S. Are Included in These Findings.

GRAND TOTALS

UNITED STATES

Number of churches--55,603; number of ordained ministers--40,477; number of baptisms--341,585; total membership--8,729,025; number of Sunday schools--47,223; enrollment--5,496,439; church buildings--49,140; parsonages--8,485; total value of church property--$471,758,600; associations--2,135; current expenses--$62,481,118; beneficence--$14,162,887; total--$76,644,005.

CANADA

Number of churches--1,286; number of ordained ministers--884; number of baptisms--5,452; total membership--141,384; number of Sunday schools--1,163; enrollment--108,542; church buildings--1,503; parsonages--512; total value of church property--$5,892,700; associations--40.

MEXICO

Number of churches--95; number of ordained ministers--75; number of baptisms--660; total membership--6,147; number of Sunday schools--73; enrollment--3,613; church buildings--44; parsonages--16; total value of church property--$1,006,400; current expenses--$40,004; associations--6; beneficence--$27,540; total--$67,544.

GRAND TOTALS, 1929

Number of churches--56,965; number of ordained ministers--51,428; number of baptisms--347,697; total membership--8,876,516; number of Sunday schools--48,459; enrollment--5,564,266; church buildings--59,257; parsonages--9,616; associations--2,178; total value of church property--$478,367,800; current expenses--$64,561,134; beneficence--$14,876,936; total--$79,073,079.

BAPTISTS IN THE WORLD

EUROPE
Total Churches--8,157; Pastors and Missionaries--4,790; Members--1,636,366; Scholars in Sunday schools--645,882.

ASIA
Total Churches--3,231; Pastors and Missionaries--1,645; Members--359,160; Scholars in Sunday schools--185,062.

AFRICA
Total Churches--1,247; Pastors and Missionaries--390; Members--78,751; Scholars in Sunday schools--38,588.

AUSTRALIA
Total Churches--474; Pastors and Missionaries--392; Members--34,088; Scholars in Sunday schools--44,736.

Grand Total--Churches 7,139; Pastors and Missionaries--58,195; Members--11,040,321; Scholars in Sunday schools--6,531,804.

TEN YEARS' GROWTH OF THE NEGRO CHURCHES, 1916-1926
A remarkable disclosure set forth in the 1926 Census of Religious Bodies relates to the growth and present standing of the Negro churches

in the United States. Confining ourselves to the decade of 1916 to 1926, let us notice six outstanding features of the growth of the Negro churches in the United States:

1. Growth of Negro Church Organizations

We can best get a bird's eye view of the situation, perhaps, by first noting the growth of the Negro church organizations. Briefly summarized, the main facts are as follows:

In 1916 there were 19 distinct Negro denominations, whereas in 1926 there were 24.

In 1916, moreover, there were Negro churches affiliated with 21 White denominations, whereas in 1926 there were 30 White denominations which included Negro churches in their numbers.

During this decade the total number of Negro churches passed from 39,592 in 1916 to 42,585 in 1926, a net gain of 2,993 Negro churches.

The gains in Negro church members were equally striking, for while the total Negro church membership in the United States in 1916 stood at 4,602,805, by 1926 it had reached 5,203,487, a net gain of 600,682, or 13.05 percent; whereas the growth of the entire Negro population of the United States (1910-1920) amounted to only 635,368, or 6.46 percent. We know of no people who have excelled this achievement.

The total contributions of the Negro churches, for all purposes, at home and abroad, moreover, mounted up from $18,529,827 in 1916 to $43,024,259 in 1926, a clear net gain of $24,494,432 for the ten years, which is practically 150 percent net gain for the ten years.

As part of the contributions of the Negro churches, we note also that the value of their church property increased from $86,809,9700 in 1916 to $205,782,628 in 1926, a net gain of $118,972,658, or about 135 percent, for the ten years, which means that the Negro churches of America put an average of $11,897,265.80 into new and remodeled church houses every year for the past ten years! Truly this is a remarkable record—for any race or any people!

2. Growth of Negro Church Members

This brief summary of the achievements of the Negro church organizations in the United States, during the decade of 1916-1926, will doubtless help us to appreciate a detailed study of the remarkable growth of the church members of the Negro churches. State by state, we present in the accompanying table ("Growth of Negro Church Members") this interesting and engaging part of the story.

GROWTH OF NEGRO CHURCH MEMBERS, 1916-1926

STATES	Negro Church Members		Ten Years' Gains/Losses (%)
	1916	1926	
Alabama	475,140	557,231	82,091/ 17.27
Arizona	532	2,199	1,667/ 313.34
Arkansas	242,199	201,240	*40,959/ 16.91
California	6,906	25,763	18,857/273.05
Colorado	4,448	6,188	1,740/ 39.11
Connecticut	6,292	10,593	4,301/ 68.35
Delaware	10,989	12,459	1,470/ 13.37
District of Columbia	48,377	72,382	24,005/ 49.62
Florida	138,055	190,893	52,838/ 38.27
Georgia	581,724	538,093	*43,631/ 7.50
Idaho	50	205	155/310.00
Illinois	49,633	137,131	87,498/ 176.28
Indiana	20,883	49,704	28,821/ 138.01
Iowa	5,313	8,577	3,264/ 61.43
Kansas	21,842	28,292	6,450/ 29.53
Kentucky	137,211	127,126	*10,085/ 7.35
Louisiana	209,843	248,797	38,954/ 18.56
Maine	None	None	
Maryland	87,179	97,025	9,846/ 11.29

Massachusetts	8,610	13,882	5,272/ 61.23
Michigan	8,469	46,231	37,762/445.88
Minnesota	2,629	3,702	1,073/ 40.81
Mississippi	403,881	348,425	*55,456/ 13.73
Missouri	75,792	82,207	6,415/ 8.46
Montana	310	228	*82/ 26.45
Nebraska	2,070	5,163	3,093/149.42
**Nevada	61	154	93/152.45
New Hampshire	None	None	————
New Jersey	38,839	71,221	32,382/ 83.37
New Mexico	231	710	479/207.35
New York	43,921	114,543	70,622/160.79
North Carolina	359,380	431,333	71,953/ 20.02
North Dakota	None	27	27/ N/A
Ohio	49,053	119,529	70,476/143.67
Oklahoma	59,967	68,379	8,412/ 14.02
Oregon	291	832	541/185.91
Pennsylvania	108,672	177,532	68,860/ 63.36
Rhode Island	2,590	3,465	875/ 33.78
South Carolina	447,084	405,614	*41,470/ 9.27
South Dakota	18	142	124/688.88
Tennessee	196,022	226,823	30,801/ 15.71
Texas	396,157	351,305	*44,852/ 11.32
Utah	86	269	183/212.79
Vermont	None	None	———

Virginia	328,230	378,742	50,512/ 15.39
Washington	1,204	2,280	1,076/ 89.36
West Virginia	21,853	32,754	10,901/ 49.88
Wisconsin	575	3,699	3,124/543.30
Wyoming	189	398	209/110.58
Totals	4,602,800	5,203,487	600,687/ 13.05

*State shows losses.
**These figures cover scattered groups in several states where few or no Negro churches are found.

In seven of the states it will be noted there were decided losses in Negro church membership, viz., Arkansas, Georgia, Kentucky, Mississippi, Montana, South Carolina, and Tennessee. In all these cases, however, the losses were due to one cause—migration of the population—and not to any failure of the Negro churches. So that what was loss to the seven states just mentioned was entirely offset by the gains of the following states, viz:

Illinois gained 87,498
Indiana gained 28,821
Michigan gained 37,762
New Jersey gained 32,382
New York gained 70,622
Ohio gained 70,476
Pennsylvania gained 68,860

As already noted, the total net gain of Negro church membership in the United States (1916-1926) was 600,786, or 13.05 percent, as compared to a total net gain of 635,368, or 6.46 percent, to the entire Negro population of the United States, an achievement not surpassed by any other racial group or any other body of Christians in America.

3. Comparative Growth of Negro Population and Negro Church Members

As throwing still further light on the remarkable growth of the Negro churches, as indicated in their increasing membership, we present herewith in parallel columns the last known Negro population statistics state by state, and the latest report of the Bureau of the Census on the Negro church membership. Unfortunately we do not have any very reliable estimates of the Negro population state by state since 1920; whereas, the latest reports of the membership of the Negro churches is for the year 1926. Attempting to use these figures as comparable will necessitate adding the probable growth of the Negro population for the six years dating from 1920. With these allowances in mind, let us note some interesting facts in the accompanying table:

Probable Negro population in U.S. in 1926 10,868,577
Negro church members, all faiths, in 1926 5,203,487
Unchurched Negroes in U. S. in 1926 5,665,090
Percent of Negroes in the churches in 1926 .... 47.87%
Percent of Negroes not in any church 52.13%
Percent of total population (White and Colored) in U.S. who were
    not identified with any church in 1926 .... 53.48%

NEGRO POPULATION AND NEGRO CHURCH MEMBERS IN U. S.,
1920 AND 1926, RESPECTIVELY

States	Negro Population in 1920	Negro Church Members, 1926	Unchurched Negroes, 1926
Alabama	900,652	557,231	343,421
Arizona	8,005	2,199	5,806
Arkansas	472,220	201,240	270,980
California	38,763	25,763	13,000
Colorado	11,318	6,188	5,130
Connecticut	21,046	10,593	10,453
Delaware	30,335	12,459	17,876
District of Columbia	109,966	72,382	37,584
Florida	329,487	190,893	138,594
Georgia	1,206,365	538,093	668,272
Idaho	920	205	715

Illinois	182,274	137,131	45,143
Indiana	80,810	49,704	31,106
Iowa	19,005	8,577	10,428
Kansas	57,925	28,292	29,633
Kentucky	235,938	127,126	108,812
Louisiana	700,257	248,797	451,460
Maine	1,310	None	1,310
Maryland	244,479	97,025	147,454
Massachusetts	45,466	13,882	31,584
Michigan	60,082	46,231	13,851
Minnesota	8,809	3,702	5,107
Mississippi	935,184	348,425	586,759
Missouri	178,241	82,207	96,034
Montana	1,658	228	1,430
Nebraska	13,242	5,163	8,079
*Nevada	346	154	192
New Hampshire	621	None	621
New Jersey	117,132	71,221	45,911
New Mexico	5,733	710	5,023
New York	198,483	114,543	83,940
North Carolina	763,407	431,333	332,074
North Dakota	467	27	440
Ohio	186,187	119,529	66,658
Oklahoma	149,408	68,379	81,029
Oregon	2,144	832	1,312

Pennsylvania	284,568	177,532	107,036
Rhode Island	10,036	3,465	6,571
South Carolina	864,719	405,416	459,105
South Dakota	832	142	690
Tennessee	451,758	226,823	224,935
Texas	741,694	351,305	390,389
Utah	1,446	269	1,177
Vermont	572	None	572
Virginia	690,017	378,742	311,275
Washington	6,883	2,280	4,603
West Virginia	86,345	32,754	53,591
Wisconsin	5,201	3,699	1,502
Wyoming	1,375	398	977
Population Growth	405,446	----------------	405,446
Totals	10,868,577	5,203,487 47.87%	5,665,090 52.13%

*We have no reliable estimates of Negro population by states since the 1920 census; hence we use the figures for this year and add the probable growth for the six years following 1920.

4. Negro and White Church Members Compared

It is perhaps a well-known fact that the Negro population of the United States is not growing as fast as the White population, at least for the last decade for which we have accurate statistics (1910-1920). For while the Negro population, as has just been noted, increased from 9,827,763 in 1910, to 10,463,131 in 1920 (a net gain of 635,368), this gain was not in keeping with the growth of the White population of the United States. So that the percentage of Negroes in the total population of the United States in 1920 was actually less than it was 1910, the percentage being 9.9 percent for 1920, as compared to 10.7 percent for 1910.

This raises the very interesting question: How does the growth of the membership of the White churches compare with the growth of the White population, on the one hand, and with the growth of the membership of the Negro churches, on the other hand? Perhaps we can best summarize the answer of these questions as follows:

White population in 1916 (estimated) 91,808,623
White population in 1926 (estimated) 106,262,240
Net growth of White population, 1916-1926 14,453,617
Percentage of White population growth, 1916-1926 .... 15.7%
White church members in U.S., 1916 37,324,054
White church members in U.S., 1926 49,292,405
Net gain of White church members 11,968,351
Percentage of gain of White church members 32.06%
Negro population in U.S., (estimated) 1916 10,208,689
Net gain of Negro population (estimated), 1926 10,868,577
Net gain of Negro population (estimated), 1916-1926 659,888
Percentage of gain of Negro population, 1916-1926 .... 6.46%
Negro church members in U.S., 1916 4,602,800
Negro church members in U.S., 1926 5,203,487
Net gain of Negro church members 600,687
Percentage of gain of Negro church members 13.05%

From this summary two facts are outstanding: (1) The growth of White church members during the ten years (1916-1926) was 32.06 percent, as compared to the growth of 15.7 percent for the White population for the same period, while (2) the growth of the Negro church members was 13.05 percent, as compared to the growth of 6.46 percent for the Negro population. In both cases the gain of the churches, White and Colored, in the United States was over twice the gain of the population, and the respective gains are about equal. The Negro churches, however, come out of the decade with this distinct advantage, that while their church gains almost wholly covered the entire Negro population gains, the White churches, in spite of their large gains, fell behind the gains of the White population by 2,485,216.

The accompanying table ("Church Members: Negroes and Whites in the United States, 1926") not only gives the latest known comparative statistics, state by state, covering both the White and Colored church memberships of the United States, but it gives the additional interesting information that of the 54,495,822 total church members in the United

States in 1926, 49,292,405 (90.45 percent) were Whites and 5,203,487 (9.55 percent) were Negroes. In this connection it is interesting to note that the White population comprised 90.1 percent of the total population of the United States in 1920, as compared to 9.9 percent for the Negro population.

CHURCH MEMBERS: NEGROES AND WHITES IN THE UNITED STATES, 1926

STATES	White Church Members	Negro Church Members	Total Church Members
Alabama	659,939	557,231	1,217,170
Arizona	150,887	2,199	153,086
Arkansas	420,067	201,240	621,307
California	1,541,748	25,763	1,567,511
Colorado	346,675	6,188	352,863
Connecticut	945,865	10,593	956,458
Delaware	97,683	12,459	110,142
District of Columbia	166,499	72,382	238,871
Florida	337,572	190,893	528,465
Georgia	812,091	538,093	1,350,184
Idaho	162,474	205	162,679
Illinois	3,220,823	137,131	3,357,954
Indiana	1,333,112	49,704	1,382,816
Iowa	1,071,575	8,577	1,080,152
Kansas	738,286	28,292	766,578
Kentucky	924,378	127,126	1,051,504
Louisiana	788,211	248,797	1,037,008
Maine	204,092	---------	204,092
Maryland	661,021	97,025	758,046

Massachusetts	2,486,322	13,882	2,500,204
Michigan	1,740,792	46,231	1,787,023
Minnesota	1,278,481	3,702	1,282,183
Mississippi	452,304	348,425	800,729
Missouri	1,499,071	82,207	1,581,278
Montana	152,159	228	152,387
Nebraska	556,260	5,163	561,423
Nevada and "other states"	19,615	154	19,769
New Hampshire	223,674	--------	223,674
New Jersey	1,910,363	71,221	1,981,584
New Mexico	214,827	710	215,547
New York	6,681,604	114,543	6,796,147
North Carolina	975,550	431,333	1,406,883
North Dakota	304,936	27	304,963
Ohio	2,746,967	119,529	2,866,496
Oklahoma	512,704	68,379	581,083
Oregon	251,899	832	252,731
Pennsylvania	5,034,518	177,532	5,212,050
Rhode Island	447,930	3,465	451,395
South Carolina	467,192	405,614	872,806
South Dakota	294,480	142	294,622
Tennessee	791,248	226,823	1,018,071
Texas	1,929,209	351,305	2,280,514
Utah	369,322	269	369,591
Vermont	161,123	---------	161,123

Virginia	763,621	378,742	1,172,363
Washington	381,942	2,280	384,222
West Virginia	499,352	32,754	532,106
Wisconsin	1,469,365	3,699	1,473,064
Wyoming	62,577	398	62,975
Totals	49,292,405 90.45%	5,203,487 9.55%	54,495,892 100%

5. Negro and White Church Members in the South

We have been at some pains to ascertain the facts about the comparative standing of the Negro and White church members in the several states within the bounds of the Southern Baptist Convention. In the accompanying table ("Church Members in the South: White and Colored") we are presenting the results of our studies. The table shows an utterly different situation as compared to that of the nation as a whole. For example, in the United States, as we have just seen, 90.45 percent of all church members, in 1926, belonged to White churches; whereas, in the South (Southern Baptist Convention territory) only 75.38 percent of the church members belonged to the White churches. On the other hand, in the nation as a whole, only 9.55 percent of the church members belonged to Negro churches; whereas 24.62 percent of the church members in the South (Southern Baptist Convention territory) were Negroes.

To state the case another way, there were 5,203,874 Negro church members in the United States in 1926; whereas 4,362,806 of these were here in the South. There are other points of especial interest in the table presented herewith—such as the standing of the Negro church membership in the several states, etc.

CHURCH MEMBERS IN THE SOUTH: WHITE AND COLORED, 1926
(This includes the several states in the bounds of the Southern Baptist Convention.)

STATES	White Church Members	Negro Church Members	Total Church Members
Alabama	659,939	557,231	1,217,170
Arizona	150,887	2,199	153,086
Arkansas	420,067	201,240	621,307
District of Columbia	166,499	72,382	238,871
Florida	337,572	190,893	528,465
Georgia	812,091	538,093	1,380,184
Southern Illinois	805,206	34,282	839,488
Kentucky	924,378	127,126	1,051,504
Louisianna	788,211	248,797	1,037,008
Maryland	661,021	97,025	758,046
Mississippi	452,304	348,425	800,729
Missouri	1,499,071	82,207	1,581,278
New Mexico	214,827	710	215,547
North Carolina	975,550	431,333	1,406,883
Oklahoma	512,704	68,379	581,083
South Carolina	467,192	405,614	872,806
Tennessee	791,194	226,823	1,018,017
Texas	1,929,209	351,305	2,280,514
Virginia	793,621	378,742	1,172,363
Totals	13,361,543	4,362,806	17,724,349
Percentage of church members	75.38	24.62	100
Percentage of populations	76.2	23.8	100

**MAKING SAFE THE FUTURE
OF AMBITIOUS NEGRO YOUTHS**

The new Trades Hall in course of erection, National Training School for Women and Girls, Nannie H. Burroughs, president, Lincoln Heights, Washington, D.C. Only two of the three stories have been completed.—*Home and Foreign Fields*.

NEGRO CHURCH MEMBERS: BAPTIST AND OTHER FAITHS, 1926

STATES	Total Negro Church Members	Negro Baptists Church Members	Other Negro Church Members
Alabama	557,231	364,565/65.42	192,666
Arizona	2,199	817/37.15	1,382
Arkansas	201,240	134,720/66.94	66,520
California	25,763	10,454/40.57	15,309
Colorado	6,188	2,298/37.13	3,890
Connecticut	10,593	5,518/52.09	5,075
Delaware	12,459	1,575/12.64	10,884
District of Columbia	72,382	41,262/57.00	31,120
Florida	190,893	98,194/51.44	92,699
Georgia	538,093	381,312/70.86	156,781
Idaho	205	105/51.21	100
Illinois	137,131	83,839/61.13	53,292
Indiana	49,704	30,388/61.13	19,316
Iowa	8,577	3,701/43.15	4,876
Kansas	28,292	15,243/53.87	13,049
Kentucky	127,126	83,837/65.94	43,289
Louisiana	248,797	132,743/53.35	116,054
Maine	None	None	--------
Maryland	97,025	33,062/34.07	63,963
Massachusetts	13,882	5,396/38.87	8,486
Michigan	46,231	24,883/53.82	21,348
Minnesota	3,702	1,436/38.78	2,266
Mississippi	348,425	226,989/65.14	121,436

Missouri	82,207	42,299/51.45	39,908
Montana	228	None	228
Nebraska	5,163	2,062/39.93	3,101
*Nevada and "other states"	154	50/32.46	104
New Hampshire	None	None	--------
New Jersey	71,221	41,129/57.74	30,092
New Mexico	710	408/57.46	302
New York	114,543	46,823/40.87	67,720
North Carolina	431,333	206,807/47.94	224,526
North Dakota	27	27/100	--------
Ohio	119,529	73,922/61.84	45,607
Oklahoma	68,379	47,363/69.26	21,016
*Oregon	832	250/30.04	582
Pennsylvania	177,532	100,202/56.44	77,330
Rhode Island	3,456	1,621/46.78	1,844
South Carolina	405,614	235,224/57.99	170,390
South Dakota	142	None	142
Tennessee	226,823	138,605/61.10	88,218
Texas	351,305	234,056/66.62	117,249
Utah	269	155/57.62	114
Vermont	None	None	--------
Virginia	378,742	316,095/83.45	62,647
Washington	2,280	681/29.86	1,599
West Virginia	32,754	24,166/73.78	8,588
Wisconsin	3,699	2,184/59.04	1,515

Wyoming	398	157/39.44	241
Totals	5,203,487/ 100	3,196,623/ 61.43	2.006,864/ 38.57

*Includes those scattered in states where no Negro churches exist.

6. Baptist Leadership Among the Negroes

It has long been known that Baptists are far in the lead of all denominations among the Negroes. It will be surprising to some to learn, however, that Baptist leadership among the Negroes is being challenged and cut down, to some extent, in the last two decades.

Three things apparently account for the failure of the Baptists to hold and sustain their former overwhelming leadership of the Negro church forces. In the first place, the Methodists, Presbyterians, Lutherans, Catholics, and Congregationalists are spending vast sums, year by year, in aggressive programs of evangelization, education, and social betterment of the Negroes. They are, on the whole, winning multiplied thousands from Baptist homes to these other denominations.

In the meantime only the Northern Baptist Convention, among the White Baptist denominations, is making any serious attempt to aid the Negro Baptists of America; the Southern Baptist Convention, apart from its attempt to help establish and maintain the (Negro) American Baptist Theological Seminary, has done nothing worthy of attention for the Negro race within the last twenty years.

In 1918 or earlier, a third disintegrating movement for Baptists set in among the Negroes of the United States—wholesale migrations to the North, East, and West. A careful study of the population table already presented in this chapter reveals how very serious have been the losses to all the denominations, and to the Baptists in particular, from the migrations of the Negro population.

Nine Negro Methodist Denominations

Referring again to the gains of the Methodists among the Negro population of America, it may be interesting to present here the (1926) statistics of the nine Negro Methodist denominations of the United States. We should bear in mind, however, that large numbers of Negro churches affiliate directly with the (White) Methodist Episcopal Church and are not noted in this summary. The forces of the nine Negro Methodist bodies in 1926 were as follows:

Negro Methodist denominations 9
Churches 11,913
Church members 1,221,988
Church houses 10,857
Pastors' homes 3,182
Value of church property $69,044,110
Total contributions, 1926 .... $15,180,917
Sunday schools 10,865
Enrolled in Sunday schools 775,636

Negro Baptist Forces in United States

The accompanying table ("Negro Church Members: Baptists and Other Faiths"), however, makes it quite clear that Baptists still have a distinct and commanding leadership among the Negroes of the United States. Summarizing the facts set out in the accompanying table, for example, we note the following situation in 1926:

Total Negro church members in U.S., 1926 5,203,487
Baptist Negroes 3,196,623
Percent of Negro church members who were Baptists, 1926 ...61.43%
Negroes belonging to all other churches 2,006,864
Percent of Negro church members affiliated with non-Baptist
  churches 38.57%
Total Baptists (White and Colored), 1926 8,440,922
Negro Baptists, 1926 3,196,623
White Baptists, 1926 5,244,299

GROWTH OF BAPTIST AND OTHER MAIN DENOMINATIONS IN THE UNITED STATES, 1916-1926

Only once every ten years may we know with reasonable certainty the comparative growth of the various denominations in the United States. For many of the smaller denominations never publish their own statistics; also many of the minor groups in the larger denominations, like the Baptists, Methodists, etc., make reports of their statistics only to the Bureau of Census every ten years. For this reason it is partially impossible to ascertain either the actual or the comparative progress of the various religious bodies in the United States, except by reference to the reports of the Bureau of the Census.

For this reason, it is all the more necessary and important, as well as vital and interesting, that we get a clear understanding of these reports of the Bureau of the Census as they pertain to the religious life and progress in the United States.

In the summary which follows, therefore, we present first the ten years' growth of the Baptists as the leading non-Catholic denomination in the United States; and then we compare with the Baptists the records of the ten other main denominational bodies, compiling the figures in each case from the reports of the Bureau of the Census and letting them largely speak for themselves.

1. High Points of Baptist Growth

In the accompanying table ("Ten Years' Growth of the Baptists of the United States and the World") will be found some surprising and many vitally interesting things. Let us note, for example, the following:

Baptist Sunday school growth, counting all groups of Baptists, together, did not keep pace with the growth of the churches, the gain of the churches being 2,254, with 1,287,609 increase in the number of church members, whereas there was a net gain of only 236 Sunday schools, with 810,142 additional pupils enrolled.

The Baptist Young People's Unions had a splendid gain, the number of unions increasing during the ten years by 12,303, or about 45 percent, while the young people enrolled in these organizations had a net increase of 313,821, or 31,382 every year of this decade.

While the number of church houses did not increase very much (only 487 for the ten years), there were 2,760 additional pastors' homes built and a sufficient number of the church houses rebuilt entirely or remodeled throughout to bring about an amazing increase in the value of church property. The statistics indicate, for example, that Baptist church property in the United States had a net increase of $295,709,538 (about 139 percent) for the ten years (1916-1926), or $29,570,953 a year for this entire decade.

The contributions of Baptists, both to local church work and to the great causes of missions, education, and benevolence, likewise had over 100 percent net gain during the ten years. The proportion of these gifts going to missions, education, and benevolence remained about the same throughout the decade; that is, practically $4.00 were given to local church work to every $1.00 that was given to missions.

The number of Baptist schools and colleges showed a net gain of only eight for the ten years, but the number of students and the property and endowment of the schools and colleges showed a hundred percent net gain or more. Hospital property, on the other hand, increased from $2,000,000 to more than $15,000,000 in the ten years. Likewise the orphanage property had a net gain of almost three hundred percent.

It is the best and most encouraging record which the Baptists of the United States have made in any decade in their history. A summary of this record is presented in the accompanying table:

TEN YEARS' GROWTH OF THE BAPTISTS OF THE UNITED STATES AND THE WORLD, 1916-1926

(Note: White and Colored Baptists of all groups are considered.)

ITEMS	1916	1926	Ten Years'Gain
Churches	57,938	60,192	2,254
Ordained Ministers	38,204	*50,112	1,908
Total Members	7,153,313	8,440,922	1,287,609
Sunday Schools	47,653	47,889	36
Enrolled in Sunday Schools	4,351,454	5,161,596	810,142
B. Y. P. U.'s	26,812	39,115	12,303
*Enrolled in B. Y. P. U.'s	643,488	957,309	313,821
Church Houses	51,794	52,281	487
Pastors' Homes	5,826	8,586	2,760
Value Church Property	$212,383,697	$508,093,235	$295,709,538
Gifts to Local Church Work	$ 31,729,953	$ 79,713,094	$ 47,983,141
Gifts to Missions, Education and Benevolence	$ 8,297,166	$ 19,166,001	$ 10,868,835

Total Contributions, All Purposes	$ 40,027,119	$ 98,879,095	$ 58,851,976
*Theological Schools	15	18	3
*Students	1,449	3,010	1,561
*Colleges (Jr. & Sr.) Univs.	102	108	6
*Students	41,030	61,506	20,476
Academies and Institutes	118	117	-1
*Students	3,481	18,391	14,910
*Total Schools and Colleges	235	243	8
Total Students	45,960	82,907	36,947
Total Ministerial Students Total Value, School Property	3,481	5,621	2,140
Endowment	$99,608,885	$194,666,870	$95,057,985
Homes for the Aged	23	23	------------
Value of Homes	*$ 690,000	$ 2,343,500	$ 1,653,500
Hospitals	20	36	16
*Patients Cared for 33,418	37,800		71,218
*Value Hospital Property	2,000,000	15,393,800	13,393,800
Orphans' Homes	20	33	13
*Value of Property	$ 1,500,000	$ 5,629,900	$ 4,129,900
*Children Cared for	3,200	5,130	1,930
Baptists of World	8,245,693	10,692,083	2,446,390

*These items were obtained from official Baptist sources but are not presented in the reports of the Bureau of Census.

2. Membership Growth and Standing of Main Denominations

We next present in the accompanying table ("Ten Years' Membership Gains of Main Denominations," etc.) the comparative growth and

THE WALKER MEMORIAL BAPTIST CHURCH
New York City

This is among the leading churches of greater New York. It is named in memory of the late B. H. Walker, a former pastor. Rev. John W. Saunders is now the aggressive spiritual pastor. Under his care the church has gone forward by leaps and bounds and is recorded among the fundamental Baptist churches of our Zion.

standing of the main denominational groups in the United States as of the year 1926.

Numerical Standing of Main Denominations, 1926

Arranged according to their numbers in 1926, it will be seen that the twelve main denominational groups in the United States stood as follows in 1926:

1.	Roman Catholics	15,814,253
2.	Baptists	8,440,922
3.	Methodists	8,070,619
4.	Lutherans	3,966,003
5.	Presbyterians	2,625,284
6.	Episcopalians	1,859,086
*7.	Campbellites	1,811,309
8.	Congregationalists	881,696
9.	Reformed Churches	617,551
10.	Mormons	606,561
11.	Holiness Churches	493,460
12.	United Brethren	395,885

TEN YEARS' MEMBERSHIP GAINS OF MAIN DENOMINATIONS IN THE UNITED STATES, 1916-1926

Denominations	Members In 1916	Members In 1926	Ten Years' Gains and Losses
Adventists (5 groups)	114,915	146,177	31,262--27.20%
Baptists (18 groups)	7,153,313	8,440,922	1,287,609--18.00%
Campbellites (2 groups)	1,543,965	1,811,309	267,344--17.31%
Congregationalists	809,236	881,696	72,460--8.95%
Eastern Orthodox (Greek Catholics, 7 groups)	249,840	259,394	9,554--3.82%
Episcopalians	1,092,821	1,859,086	766,265--70.11%
Friends (Quakers, 4 groups)	92,379	91,326	Loss 1,053-- 1.14%
Holiness Churches (24 groups)	207,721	493,460	285,739--137.60%
**Lutherans (22 groups)	2,467,516	3,966,003	1,498,487--60.73%

Menonites (17 groups)	79,363	87,164	7,801--9.83%
Methodists (19 groups)	7,166,451	8,070,619	904,168--12.6%
Mormons (2 groups)	462,329	606,561	144,232--31.19%
Presbyterians (9 groups)	2,255,626	2,625,284	369,658--16.39%
Reformed Churches (4 groups)	527,971	617,551	89,580--16.96%
United Brethren:	13,363,543	15,814,25	2,450,710—18.33%
Roman Catholics* (3 groups)	367,934	395,885—3	27,951—7.59%
Totals--16 (139 groups)	37,954,923	46,166,69—0	8,211,767--21.63%

* Only "communicants" are here counted among Roman Catholics.
** All baptized Lutherans in the United States, both infants and adults, are counted in the government figures.

Numerical Gains of Main Denominations

Arranged according to their total net gains during the ten years under review (1916-1926), the respective records were as follows:

1. Roman Catholics, net gain 2,450,710
2. Lutherans, net gain 1,498,487
3. Baptists, net gain 1,287,609
4. Methodists, net gain 904,168
5. Episcopalians, net gain 766,265
6. Presbyterians, net gain 369,658
7. Holiness Churches, net gain 285,739
*8. Campbellites, net gain 267,344
9. Mormons, net gain 144,232
10. Reformed Churches, net gain 89,580
11. Congregationalists, net gain 72,460
12. Adventists, net gain 31,262
13. United Brethren, net gain 27,951

*We do not use the designation "Campbellites" with any intended disrespect or animus, but because we know of no other designation by which we can group "the Disciples of Christ" with "the Churches of Christ."

Percentage of Net Gains of Main Denominations

If we now view these main denominational groups from the standpoint of the percentage of their respective gains during this decade (1916-1926), a wholly different line-up appears, as follows:

1. Holiness Churches had 137.6%
2. Episcopalians had 70.1%
3. Lutherans had 60.73%
4. Mormons had 31.19%
5. Adventists had 27.2%
6. Roman Catholics had 18.33%
*7. Baptists had 18.00%
8. Campbellites had 17.31%
9. Reformed Churches had 17.00%
10. Presbyterians had 16.39%
11. Methodist has 12.61%
12. Congregationalists had 8.95%
13. United Brethren had 7.59%

*Baptist membership gains during this decade were cut down seriously by certain former errors and inflations in the number of Negro Baptists in 1916.

3. Baptists Lead Methodists by 370,303 and More

For years now it has been the custom of Dr. H.K. Carroll, the great Methodist statistician, to publish a yearly report of the churches of the United States, in which he seems always careful to bring his own denomination out well in the lead of all non-Catholic bodies. We have publicly called attention to the fact that some parts of Dr. Carroll's figures were based upon estimates which were misleading so far as Baptists were concerned. It will be a particular interest therefore to notice how the government figures smash Dr. Carroll's estimates to pieces and incidentally leaves the Baptists where the 1916 Government Census left them—well in the lead of all non-Catholic bodies in America.

Attention should be directed to the fact that we have not included the German Baptists (Dunkards) in the Baptist group below. Why or by whom they were formerly dissevered from the Baptists, while Baptists were made to pack and carry for the "Free Will Baptists (Bullockites)," with 36 members in the whole United States, and the "Two-Seed-in-the-Spirit Predestinarian Baptists" (who are simply one of the many kinds of "Hardshell" Baptists or "Primitive" Baptists), with 304 members in the whole nation—just why or by whom this arrangement of Baptist bodies was ever effected no one seems to know. Certainly we can find no ground for such grouping and classification. Leaving out the German Baptists (Dunkards), however, it will be noted that in 1926 Baptists were 370,303 in the lead of Methodists; whereas, if these be included in the Baptist group (as I hold they should), then Baptists were 528,551 in the lead of the Methodist group in 1926.

The Twenty-three Baptist Bodies

The 23 Baptist bodies here reported are not 23 Baptist "denominations," but only 12 denominations at most. But here is the list:

Northern Baptist Convention	1,289,966
Southern Baptist Convention	3,524,378
Negro Baptists	3,196,623
General Six Principle Baptist	293
Seventh Day Baptists	7,264
Free Will Baptists	79,592
United American Free Will Baptists Church (Colored)	13,396
Free Will Baptists (Bullockites)	36
General Baptists	31,501
Separate Baptists	4,803
Regular Baptists	23,091
United Baptists	18,903
Duck River and Kindred Associations of Baptists (Baptist Church of Christ)	7,340
Primitive Baptists	81,374
Colored Primitive Baptists	43,978
Two-Seed-in-the-Spirit Predestinarian Baptists	304
Independent Baptist Church of America	222
American Baptist Association	117,858
Total, not including German Baptists	8,440,922

Brethren, German Baptists (Dunkers):

Church of the Brethren (Conservative Dunkers)	128,392
Old German Baptists Brethren	3,036
The Brethren Church (Progressive)	26,026
Seventh Day Baptists (German, 1728)	144
Church of God, New Dunkers	650
Grand total Baptists in the United States, 1926	8,599,170

SUNDAY SCHOOL AND B.Y.P.U. CONGRESS,
NATIONAL BAPTIST CONVENTION
Charleston, South Carolina, June 1929.—*Home and Foreign Fields.*

The Nineteen Methodist Bodies

The 19 Methodist bodies here listed are not 19 Methodist "denominations" in the usual meaning of that word, but perhaps not over 10 denominations at the outside. The list follows:

Methodist Episcopal Church	4,080,777
Methodist Protestant Church	192,171
Wesleyan Methodist Connection (or Church) of America	21,910
Primitive Methodist Church in the United States of America	11,990
Methodist Episcopal Church, South	2,487,694
Congregational Methodist Church	9,691
Free Methodist Church of North America	36,374
New Congregational Methodist Church	1,229
Holiness Methodist Church, Lumbee River Conference	459
Reformed Methodist Church	390
African Methodist Episcopal Church	545,814
African Methodist Episcopal Zion Church	456,813
Colored Methodist Protestant Church	533
Union American Methodist Episcopal Church	10,169
African Union Methodist Protestant Church	4,086
Colored Methodist Episcopal Church	202,713
Reformed Zion Union Apostolic Church	4,538
Reformed Methodist Union Episcopal Church	2,265
Independent African Methodist Episcopal Church	1,003
Total Methodists, 1926	8,070,619

THE STORY OF THE SILVER BLUFF CHURCH AND INFORMATION ABOUT NEGRO BAPTISTS IN EARLY TIMES

By Walter H. Brooks, D.D.

Because of the vast amount of research entailed in preparing this story and of the long years of faithful service by Dr. Brooks, I believe it should be given a permanent place in the records of the Negro Baptists. Therefore, for permanency, it is here included. A great many incidents and dates are stated and restated in this volume, some for the sake of emphasis and others for the want of time for eliminations and transfers.

In speaking of the beginning of Negro churches in the United States, those of the Baptist faith must not be forgotten. Nor must we err in thinking that the first churches of this faith were planted at the North. It is true there were Negro Baptists in Providence, R. I., as early as 1774, and doubtless a great deal earlier, but they had no church of their own. Indeed, there is absolutely no trace of Negro Baptist churches, at the North, which existed prior to the nineteenth century. The oldest Negro Baptist churches, north of Mason and Dixon's Line, are the Independent or First African, of Boston, Mass., planted in 1805; the Abyssinian, of New York City, planted in 1808; and the First African, of Philadelphia, Pa., planted in 1809.

Negro Baptists churches, unlike other Negro churches, had their beginning at the South, and at a somewhat earlier date.

The first church of Negro Baptists, the very first and oldest, so far as authentic and trustworthy writings of the eighteenth century establish, was constituted at Silver Bluff, on Mr. Galphin's estate, a year or two before the Revolutionary War.

It continued to worship there, in comparative peace, until the latter part of 1778, when the vicissitudes of war drove the church into exile, but only to multiply itself elsewhere. Moreover, the work at Silver Bluff began afresh with the cessation of hostilities, and was more prosperous than ever in 1791.

But you ask, "Where is Silver Bluff?"

Silver Bluff was situated on the South Carolina side of the Savannah River, in Aiken County, just twelve miles from Augusta, Ga. All there was of it in September 1775, seems to have been embraced in what Rev. William Tennett. of Revolutionary fame, styled "Mr. Galphin's Settlement."

Nevertheless, as it lay in the track of the Revolutionary forces—and was for a time a center of supplies to the Indians, who had their habitation in that quarter, living in treaty relations with the colonists—Ramsey, Carroll, Drayton, and others give it a place on the map of South Carolina. Indeed, so identified was Silver Bluff with the Galphins, their interests, and their influence, that by 1785, it was known far and near as Galphinton. Fort Galphin was here. Bartram, who visited in 1776, declares that Silver Bluff was "a very celebrated place," and describes it as "a beautiful villa," while the picture which Jones in his history of South Carolina gives of Silver Bluff, to say the least, is animating.

Rev. David George, who was one of the constituent members and the first regular pastor of the Silver Bluff Church, is our authority in regard to the early history of this flock. We made the following extracts from letters of his, which we published in London, England, in connection with other foreign correspondence, during the period 1790-1793:

"Brother Palmer, who was pastor at some distance from Silver Bluff, came and preached to a large congregation at a mill of Mr. Galphin's; he was a very powerful preacher."* * * "Brother Palmer came again and wished us to beg master to let him preach to us; and he came frequently." * * * "There were eight of us now, who had found the great blessing and mercy from the Lord, and my wife was one of them, and Brother Jesse Galphin. * * *"Brother Palmer appointed Saturday evening to hear what the Lord had done for us, and next day, he baptized us in the mill stream." * * *"Brother Palmer formed us into a church, and gave us the Lord's Supper at Silver Bluff." * * *"Then I began to exhort in the church, and learned to sing hymns." * * * "Afterwards the church advised with Brother Palmer about my speaking to them, and keeping them together."   * * * "So I was appointed to the office of an elder, and received instruction from Brother Palmer how to conduct myself. I proceeded in this way till the American War was coming on, when the ministers were not allowed to come amongst us, lest they should furnish us with too much knowledge." * * *"I continued preaching at Silver Bluff, 'till the church, constituted with eight, increased to thirty or more, and 'till the British came to the city of Savannah and took it."

The first clear conception of time which we get from these extracts in regard to the origin of the Silver Bluff Church, is where Mr. George speaks of being left in sole charge, as Liele and Palmer may no longer visit Silver Bluff, lest in so doing they should impart to the slaves of the settlement a knowledge which, in the then prevailing conditions, would result in their personal freedom and, consequently, in great financial loss to their masters. This undoubtedly was not later than November 1775, when the Earl of Dunmore issued on American soil a proclamation of emancipation, in which the Black slaves and the White indentured bondmen, were alike promised freedom, provided they espoused the cause of England in its struggle with the colonists. How well these slaves understood and appreciated the proffered boon may be inferred from a letter which was written by Mr. Stephen Bull to Col. Henry Laurens, President of the Council of Safety, Charleston, S.C., March 14, 1776. In that letter he says: "It is better for the public, and the owners, if the deserted Negroes who are on Tybee Island be shot, if they cannot be taken." By this means, as he informs us, he hoped to "deter other Negroes from deserting" their masters. According to Mr. Bull's representation, the Negroes along the Savannah River were abandoning their masters and going to the British in scores an hundreds, to the detriment of their owners, and the menace of the cause of American independence.

Rev. George Liele, although not a runaway slave, appears to have had some liking for the Tybee River as a place of abode, and it is probable that when he could no longer visit Silver Bluff, and was not in camp with Mr. Henry Sharp (who had not only given him his freedom, but also taken up arms against the Revolutionists), he resorted to Tybee Island to preach the gospel of Christ to the refugees there assembled. At any rate, when Liele appears in Savannah, Ga., as a preacher of the gospel, his biographer declares "He came up to the city of Savannah from Tybee River."

The next hint which we get from the statements of the Rev. David George, in regard to the time when the Silver Bluff Church was planted, is where he says, that Rev. Mr. Liele preached at Silver Bluff both before and after the organization of the church. Happily Liele himself refers to Silver Bluff as a place where he used to preach. Mr. Liele also informs us that he became a Christian about two years before the American War, but did not immediately connect himself with a church; that, when he did join, he became a member of Rev. Matthew Moore's church in Burke County, Ga.; that he was a member of this church about four years; that this membership terminated with the evacuation of Savannah; that he preached at Yamacraw and Brumpton Land about three years; and that he went to Jamaica, in the West Indies, in the year 1782.

Let us consider carefully these facts, with reference to time. The three years, which preceded 1782, were 1781, 1780, 1779. This brings us to the evacuation of Savannah by the Americans, within two days, as the British captured the city December 29, 1778. The four years which preceded 1779 were 1778, 1777, 1776, 1775. We understand from Mr. Liele's statements concerning himself, therefore, that he became a member of Rev. Matthew Moore's church at the close of the year 1774, or the beginning of 1775, but was converted at the end of the year 1773, and let a whole year or nearly so, pass before becoming a church member.

It is probable that Mr. Liele did not wait to be received into the fellowship of a church before going from plantation to plantation to tell his fellow slaves of the blessing of salvation which he had experienced. He may have thus declared the love of Christ at Silver Bluff as early as 1773, as Burke County, Ga., in which he lived is in part, practically adjacent to Aiken County, S.C., in which was Silver Bluff. Accordingly, we are warranted in concluding that the Negro Baptist church at Silver Bluff was constituted not earlier than 1773, not later than 1775.

In making these deductions, we are not ignorant that the year 1777 has been designated as the time of Liele's conversion; 1778 as the time when he united with Rev. Matthew Moore's church, and four years later, or 1782, as the time when his membership in that church ceased.

In explanation of this view its advocates insist that the three years in which Liele preached at Brumpton Land and Yamacraw are included in the four years during which he was a member of Rev. Matthew Moore's church. According to this claim, the Silver Bluff Church could not have been planted earlier than 1777 nor later than 1778.

We do not share this view for good and sufficient reasons. When Liele in 1779 went to Savannah to reside, during the British occupancy, he became separated from Rev. Matthew Moore's church, and the people of Burke County, Ga., for all time. With the British troops he entered Savannah, as the Americans had evacuated it at the very close of the year 1778; with the British he remained in Savannah during his three years' stay in that city; and with a British officer he left the country in 1782, for Kingston, Jamaica, British West Indies, where he spent the remainder of this life. His four years' connection with the Rev. Mr. Moore's church, therefore, must have preceded the year 1779, covering the time from the latter part of 1774 to the latter of 1778.

As Rev. George Liele informs us that he became a Christian about two years before the American War, those who place his conversion in the year 1777, are compelled to reckon the beginning of the Revolutionary War from the year 1779. Errors are hard things to substantiate and

FIRST BAPTIST CHURCH
Baltimore, Md.

This historic church is 109 years old having been formed in 1821, though it took organized form 9 years later. Among the mighty leaders who wrought in Baltimore was Dr. Allen and P. C. Neal. The present pastor, one of our very best young men, Rev. Wm. H. Young, B.Th., D.D. The remodeled building is a beauty. Dr. Young took work with them in 1928 and accomplished this $29,000 job in 10 months. The old First Church is modern and well equipped in a training camp for Christian service.

force men to choose between strange dilemmas. But, in explanation of this absurdity, it's claimed that the Revolutionary War did not make itself manifest, in Georgia and South Carolina until about the year 1779; and the Negroes of Georgia and South Carolina, in speaking of it, would refer to that year as the beginning of the war. But as a matter of fact, the Revolutionary struggle in South Carolina and Georgia was manifest from the very first. Thus the biographer of Rev. Abraham Marshall, of Kiokee, Ga., having informed his readers that the subject of his sketch was ordained to the work of the gospel ministry May 20, 1775, adds, "Just as he had chosen his life work, the Revolutionary War broke out, and Georgia became a scene of violence and bloodshed. During almost the entire struggle, the people were subject to the combined outrages of Britons, Tories, and Indians."

Thus, too, the biographer of Gov. John Houston's trusted slave, Andrew C. Marshall, writes, "The embargo having taken effect in Savannah at the opening of the Revolution, fifteen merchants of that city agreed to give him a purse of $225.00 if he would carry word to several American vessels that lay in a bay on the lower seaboard, in which achievement he was successful."

The expression "the opening of the Revolution," in this passage, refers to the year 1775, and not to 1778-1779, for the British attacked the city of Savannah as early as March 3, 1776, and would have captured it if they had not been repulsed by the Americans.

The English agents and their American allies (the Tories) and the Cherokee Indians, who resided in the neighborhood of Silver Bluff and made it the commercial mart it was in colonial times, took up the cause of the British against the Revolutionists from the very beginning of the war. Accordingly, the Hon. William H. Drayton, of South Carolina, on August 30, 1775, urged the sending of foot-soldiers and mounted men to the vicinity of Augusta, Ga., to protect the interest of the patriots, and chasten their foes.

Eight days later, September 7, 1775, the Rev. William Tennett of South Carolina, wrote in his journal as follows: "Went ten miles to New-Savannah, where I had appointed a meeting of inhabitants, in hopes to draw an audience out of Augusta, from Mr. Galphin's Settlement and Beach Island, but most of the men having marched with Mr. Drayton, and Mr. Galphin being from home, I had but few."

To this same neighborhood Col. Andrew Williamson led a large force of South Carolinians in defence of the American cause some time later, and General Griffith Rutherford with 2,400 men reinforced him September 1776.

In review of all these statements—in regard to the time when the

Revolutionary War began to make itself manifest in Georgia and South Carolina—we conclude that when the Rev. George Liele says he was converted to Christianity about two years before the Revolutionary War, he refers to the year 1773, and his visits to Silver Bluff were at an end by the summer of 1775. We are, therefore, driven back to our first affirmation; namely, the Negro Baptists Church at Silver Bluff, S.C., was organized not earlier than 1773, not later than 1775.

The writers who have insisted that Mr. Liele united with Rev. Matthew Moore's church in 1778, and terminated that membership in 1782, have followed what is undoubtedly an erroneous inference.

Liele said, "I continued in this church about four years till the `vacuation." But as the expression seemed to Dr. Rippon indefinite, in some particulars, he sought information from persons, who were supposed to be capable of guiding him, and added five words to the statement of Liele, which made it read as follows:

"I continued in this church about four years, till the 'vacuation"—of Savannah by the British.

Dr. Rippon is careful to state that "Brother George's words are distinguished by inverted commas, and what is not so marked, is either matter compressed, or information received from such persons to whom application had been made for it."

It is easy enough to see how the inference was drawn, for in one of his letters Mr. Liele says, "Our beloved Sister Hannah Williams, during the time she was a member of the church at Savannah, until the `vacuation, did walk as a faithful, well-beloved Christian."

Here there is no room for doubt. Liele speaks in this case of the evacuation of Savannah by the British, July 1782, but in the former instance the only evacuation of Savannah, which harmonizes with the story of his own life and the events and circumstances of his time and those of his associates, is the evacuation of Savannah by the Americans, December 29, 1778.

Mr. Geo. Galphin—Patron of the Silver Bluff Church

The planter and merchant on whose estate the Silver Bluff Church was constituted is deserving of special mention in connection with the story of that people. We learn from White's history of Georgia, that "George Galphin was a native of Ireland, emigrated soon after manhood to America, and died at Silver Bluff, his residence, on the Savannah River, in South Carolina, on the second of December, 1782, in the seventy-first year of his age." Mr. N.W. Jones, in his history, quotes Mr. William Bartram as saying that Mr. George Galphin was "A gentleman of very distinguished talents and great liberality."

The spirit of justice and kindness, it appears, was manifest in all his dealings with the peoples of the weaker races, who were daily about him. The Red Man and the Black Man alike saw in him a man of kindly soul. David George, who was ever a British subject, described his former master as an "anti-loyalist." Mr. Jones, speaking as an American, pronounced him a "patriot." Neither spoke of him except to praise. A master less humane, less considerate of the happiness and moral weal of his dependents, less tolerant in spirit, would never have consented to the establishment of a Negro church on his estate. He might have put an end to the enterprise in its very incipiency. But he did not. He fostered the work from the beginnings. It was by his consent the gospel of Christ was preached to slaves who resided at Silver Bluff. It was by his permission the Silver Bluff Church was established. It was he who permitted David George to be ordained to the work of the gospel ministry. It was he who provided the Silver Bluff Church with a house of worship, by suffering his mill to be used in that capacity. And it was he who gave the little flock a baptistery, by placing his millstream at their disposal on baptizing occasions. But we are satisfied that he had no conception of the far-reaching influence of these deeds of kindness.

The truth is, the Galphins appear to have been masters of the patriarchal type. Thomas Galphin, under whose beneficence the work at Silver Bluff was renewed in post-bellum time, was, as we shall see, as much the benefactor and protector of Rev. Jesse Peter, as Mr. George Galphin had been to David George before and during the earlier stages of the Revolutionary War. State Papers, Indian Affairs, Vol. I, G. No. 2, p. 32, reveal the fact that John Galphin was an Indian interpreter and a friend of the Cussetahs. It is indeed suggestive that in 1778 these Indians wished a Negro whom Mr. John Galphin owned to be a messenger with one of their men to the Whites.

The Silver Bluff Church in Exile
With the fall of Savannah at the very close of the year 1778, the Silver Bluff Church completed the first stage in its history. For at that time Mr. David George the pastor, and about fifty other slaves whom Mr. Galphin had abandoned in his flight, went to Savannah to find safety and freedom under the British flag. Later Mr. George returned to South Carolina and abode for a time in the city of Charleston. Thence in 1782, he sailed to Nova Scotia, in company with not less than five hundred White persons, who were adherents of the British cause.

In Nova Scotia he abode ten years, preaching the gospel of Christ to the people of his own race who had found their way into that portion of the continent, in large numbers, after abandoning their homes in the United States.

These labors were performed amid hardships and persecutions, but in faithfulness to God and suffering humanity. In prosecuting his mission, he preached in Shelburn, Birchtown, Ragged Island, and in St. Johns, New Brunswick. So pronounced was the opposition to his labors in New Brunswick, that he found it necessary to invoke the protection of the civil authorities. How well he succeeded in doing so may be imagined from the subjoined statement:

> *"Secretary's Office, Fredericktown, 17th July, 1792, I do hereby certify that David George, a free Negro man, has permission from his Excellency, the Lieutenant Governor, to instruct the Black people in knowledge, and exhort them to the practice of the Christian religion. Jno. Odell, Secretary."*

It should excite in us no surprise that Mr. George was opposed in his labors in this new home, for, as Mr. Lorenzo Sabine declares, "The original population of this colony was composed almost entirely of the Loyalists of the Revolution." They had not changed their views in regard to the rights of Negroes by being removed from a land where the two races had hitherto sustained the relation of master and slave. The real surprise lies in the fact that the secretary of the province was himself a preacher, a minister of the Episcopal church, and a former resident of the State of New Jersey. It is needless to state that the Rev. Jonathan Odell did Rev. David George a splendid service, when he gave him the above mentioned certificate.

So effective were the arduous labors of Mr. David George that he is enrolled among the pulpit pioneers, in Mr. Bill's history of Canadian Baptists. He was certainly first to plant a Baptist church at Shelburn, as well as a number of feeble beginnings elsewhere.

But Canada was only a temporary home to Mr. George and to others from the States. Accordingly, he took a colony of Blacks to Sierra Leone, British Central Africa, in 1792.

Of this colony Mr. G. Winfred Hervey, A.M., remarks,

"The first settlers of Sierra Leone were what they needed to be, men of bravery. They consisted of about 12,000 Colored men who had joined the British forces in the American Revolution. At the close of the war they went to Nova Scotia, but the climate proving too unfriendly to them, they were, in 1792, transported to Sierra Leone."

One of the first things that Mr. George did after reaching Africa was to plant a little Baptist church, which was composed of Colored persons from America who had arrived in their fatherland by way of Nova Scotia.

In order to stimulate in the English people an intelligent interest in the colony of Sierra Leone and secure for the Baptist cause in Freetown the sympathy and aid of English Baptists, Mr. George took a trip to London, England, shortly after establishing himself on the continent of Africa.

It was this visit to the metropolis of the world which doubtless more than anything else facilitated the collection and publication of many facts then existing and ascertainable, in regard to Colored Baptist preachers and their churches in the eastern and western hemispheres. In visiting Europe, Rev. Mr. George took with him letters of commendation from persons of recognized standing in England. The Rev. John Rippon, the distinguished London divine, thus speaks of Mr. George, after investigating his standing: *"Governor Clarkson, in the most unreserved manner, assured me that he esteemed David George as his brother, and that he believed him to be the best man, without exception, in the colony of Sierra Leone."*

Had the Silver Bluff Church done nothing more than produce this one earnest Christian man, this faithful preacher of Christ, this potent factor in the planting of a colony under the English flag, it would not have existed in vain. But it did more.

The Silver Bluff Church Revived

When peace had been restored, and the Revolutionary forces, British and American, had been disbanded or recalled, Silver Bluff began to assume once more the conditions which existed between master and slave in colonial times. Once more, too, the Galphin place became a center of Christian activities, and the Negro Baptists of Silver Bluff were more numerous than ever.

The man whom God used in resuscitating the work at Silver Bluff was the Rev. Jesse Peter who, according to an old custom of applying to

Rev. Aaron Wells
One of the pioneer preachers of Louisiana.

J. S. Borders, N. J., born in Mississippi. His ministry extended into Oklahoma, New Mexico and New Jersey. He passed to his reward during 1929. He was the father of H. T. Borders, the successful and energetic man now pastoring Hopewell Baptist Church, Newark, N. J.

This great church has the largest seating capacity of any Baptist church among us. The present pastor is the Rev. J. E. Kirkland, D.D., known as one of the most outstanding preachers among the young men of his day.

the slave surname of the master, was better known as Jesse Galphin, or Gaulfin. Having been connected with the Silver Bluff Church from the very first, and only separated from it during the Revolutionary War and the period of readjustment immediately thereafter, Jesse Peter was eminently fitted, at least in one particular, to take up the work at Silver Bluff which the Rev. David George had resigned in the year 1778. He knew the place, he loved the people. Silver Bluff was his home, and there he was held in high esteem. Moreover, he possessed what is essential to ministerial success everywhere: deep sincerity, seriousness of purpose, knowledge of the Word of God, an excellent spirit, and capacity to deliver with profit and pleasure the message of truth and mercy. Mr. Jonathan Clarke and the Rev. Abraham Marshall (we knew him personally) have left on record beautiful testimonials of his work and his worth.

Why this young man, who had obtained his freedom by going to the British at the fall of Savannah, in 1778, remained in America to resume the condition of slave after the Revolutionary War is not known. It is known, however, that, unlike Rev. George Liele and Rev. David George, men of adventurous spirit, the Rev. Jesse Peter was not inclined to wander far from the scenes and sounds of his South Carolina home. If indeed he ever traveled beyond Kiokee, Ga., in the one direction, and the city of Savannah, in the other, we have failed to note the fact. It is known, too, that he had an indulgent master, and it is possible that he preferred a state of nominal slavery, under his protection, to a fancied state of want and hardship in a foreign land. Or it may be he was willing to die for Christ, and so deliberately entered again into the old condition of bondage in order to enjoy the privilege of preaching Jesus where Liele and George had labored in other days.

Jesse Peter's Ordination

It is to be presumed that Rev. Jesse Peter was regularly ordained to the work of the gospel ministry. We take this view because he exercised the duties and privileges which ordination implies without being ever called in question for doing so. Moreover, his three years' association with Liele and George in Savannah during the British occupancy afforded him ample opportunity to be publicly and regularly consecrated to his life-work. Certainly Abraham Marshall of Kiokee, Ga., would not have associated himself with Jesse Peter in the ordination of Andrew Bryan of Savannah in 1788, if Jesse Peter had not himself been ordained to the work of the ministry.

Visiting Pastor

Such were the conditions in the earlier stages of Rev. Jesse Peter's pastorate at Silver Bluff that he did not reside at his old home but came and went as a stated visitor. Accordingly, Mr. Jonathan Clarke, writing from Savannah, Ga., December 22, 1792, says, "Jesse Peter (whose present master is Thomas Galphin) is now here and has three or four places in the country, where he attends preaching alternately".

Rev. George Liele, writing from the West Indies in 1791, had said to Rev. Joseph Cook of South Carolina, "Brother Jesse Gaulphin, another Black minister, preaches near Augusta, in South Carolina, where I used to preach."

Referring to him, Rev. George White in his *Historical Collections of Georgia*, speaks as follows: "On the 20th of January, 1788, Andrew, surnamed Bryan, was ordained by Rev. Abraham Marshall, and a Colored minister named Jesse Peter, from the vicinity of Augusta."

Benedict, referring to Rev. Marshall in the same connection, states that "He was accompanied by a young preacher of color, by the name of Jesse Peter, of Augusta."

From these testimonies, it is evident that Rev. Jesse Peter was a non-resident pastor of the Silver Bluff Church from 1788 to 1792, if not for a longer period.

Henry Francis

During the first period of Rev. Peter's pastorate at Silver Bluff, another slave who lived in that locality began to preach.

Rev. Andrew Bryan, writing from Savannah, Ga., December 28, 1800, refers to him in the following manner: "Another dispensation of Providence has greatly strengthened our hands and increased our means of information: Henry Francis, lately a slave of the widow of the late Col. Leroy Hammond, of Augusta, has been purchased by a few humane gentlemen of this place, and liberated to exercise the handsome ministerial gifts he possesses amongst us, and teach our youth to read and write." He adds, "Brother Francis has been in the ministry fifteen years, and will soon receive ordination."

According to Rev. Bryan, the Rev. Henry Francis was a half-breed, his mother being White, his father an Indian, but I find in a letter, written by another from the city of Savannah, May 23, 1800, that he is characterized as "A man of color, who has for many years served Col. Hammond, and has handsome ministerial abilities."

The question easily suggests itself, Was Henry Francis a member of the Silver Bluff Baptist Church, when, in 1785, he began to preach? We infer that he was from certain known facts as to his place of abode and his opportunities for church membership:

1. He lived in the immediate neighborhood of Silver Bluff. Rev. William Tennett informs us that the Hammond place was in South Carolina, four miles from Augusta, Ga., and Lossing, Rev. Marshall, and others, that Silver Bluff was also in South Carolina, twelve miles from Augusta. It was easy, therefore, for Henry Francis to attend divine service at the Silver Bluff Church.

2. It was the custom of the slaves on the neighboring plantations to attend preaching at Silver Bluff during the pastorate of David George, and the custom doubtless prevailed in Jesse Peter's pastorate. If Henry Francis attended church at Silver Bluff, he did only what other slaves of the neighborhood did.

3. But what is more, there was no other Baptist church, White or Colored, in the neighborhood for Francis to join. Marshall's church at Kiokee, Ga., was twenty miles above Augusta, while Botsford's meeting house, in the opposite direction, was "25 or 30 miles below Augusta." In Augusta itself, there was no Colored Baptist church until 1793, and no White Baptist church until 1817. To our mind the conclusion is inevitable that Henry Francis, in 1785, was a member of the Negro Baptist church at Silver Bluff, South Carolina.

4. In reaching this conclusion, we have been not a little influenced by the fact that when Henry Francis was formerly ordained to the gospel ministry at Savannah, Ga., seventeen years after he had commenced to preach, and when he was an officer in the Colored church at Savannah, the ordination sermon was not preached by Dr. Henry Holcombe, of the White church of the city, nor by Bryan of the First African, but by Rev. Jesse Peter, pastor or the Silver Bluff Church. We can account for the deference shown Rev. Jesse Peter on this occasion only on the presumption that Henry Francis was converted, baptized, and licensed to preach at Silver Bluff, and Jesse Peter was the instrument which God had used in bringing these results to pass.

If we are correct in these views, the Ogeechee African Baptist Church, on the Ogeechee River, fourteen miles south of Savannah, organized in the year 1803, is more indebted to the Silver Bluff Church for her first preacher and instructor of youth than to any other church.

Jesse Peter as Resident Pastor

Of Jesse Peter's ministry at Silver Bluff as a resident pastor, we are not well informed. In a letter written from Kiokee, Ga., May 1, 1793, Rev. Abraham Marshall speaks of him as follows: "I am intimately acquainted with Jesse Golfin; he lives thirty miles below me in South Carolina, and twelve miles below Augusta. He is a Negro servant of Mr. Golfin, who, to his praise be it spoken, treats him with respect."

Jesse Peter, then, was resident pastor of the Silver Bluff Church in the early spring of 1793.

From another source we learn that the membership of the Silver Bluff Church, at this time, was sixty or more.

The Church at Augusta

Here we lose sight of the Silver Bluff Church, just as the First African Baptist Church, of Augusta, Ga., better known as the Springfield Baptist Church, comes into being. Jesse Peter had secured standing and recognition for the First African Church, at Savannah, Ga., and Henry Francis had been ordained for the Ogeechee Church by him and Andrew Bryan and the Rev. Henry Holcombe, and it is natural that he would wish for his work at Silver Bluff the standing and recognition which had been secured for the work in and about Savannah, Ga.

In order to obtain this boon and have his work in touch with that near the seacoast, it would be necessary to transfer its place of meeting from the state of South Carolina to the state of Georgia where he had a friend who was able to bring things to pass. It is in this way alone we account for the beginning of the First African Baptist Church at Augusta at the very time when the Silver Bluff church disappears. The curtain falls on the Silver Bluff Church, with Rev. Jesse Peter as pastor, when the church is reported as in a flourishing condition. The curtain rises and again we see a flock of devoted Christians, with Jesse Peter as pastor, but they are twelve miles away from Silver Bluff, South Carolina, receiving the regulating touches of the Rev. Abraham Marshall (White) and another White Baptist minister, which give the body standing and influence as the First African Baptist Church of Augusta, Ga.

Here is what Benedict says of the body. "This church appears to have been raised up by the labors of Jesse Peter, a Black preacher of respectable talents, and an amiable character. It was constituted in 1793 by elders Abraham Marshall and David Tinsley. Jesse Peter, sometimes called Jesse Golfin, on account of his master's name, continued the pastor of this church a number of years, and was very successful in his ministry."

If, as we presume, the Silver Bluff Church is still with us in another meeting place and under a new name, the oldest Negro Baptist church in this country today is that at Augusta, Ga., having existed at Silver Bluff, S.C., from the period 1774-1775 to the year 1793, before becoming a Georgia institution.

The First African Baptist Church, of Savannah, Ga.

The story of the Silver Bluff Baptist Church would not be complete without reference to the Negro Baptist Church at Savannah, Ga., which existed before Andrew Bryan became a Christian.

Neither Dr. E.K. Love, the late pastor of the First African Baptist Church, nor Rev. James M. Simms, of the Bryan Church, have intimated, in their respective histories, that Savannah had a Colored Baptist church before the 20th of January, 1788. Nevertheless, the fact remains that during the British occupancy, that is, from the year 1779 to the year 1782, there was at Savannah, Ga., an African Baptist Church.

If the Colored people of Savannah had been without a Baptist church during 1779-1782, it would have been strange indeed. For Rev. David George led a company of fifty or more fugitive slaves from Galphinton, S.C., into that city at the close of the year 1778; and this company, it is reasonable to infer, included a considerable part, if not nearly all of the members of the Silver Bluff Church.

Devout Christians who had enjoyed such privileges as slaves, and that for years, in South Carolina would scarcely be satisfied without them in Georgia as free men, when they had with them three preachers of the gospel, David George, George Liele, and Jesse Peter, men of their own race and denomination; men from the vicinity of Augusta who had figured in the planting and growth of the Silver Bluff Church.

We are glad that we have historical data, which establish the fact, that there was a Negro Baptist church in Savannah, during 1779-1782, and the Colored Baptist ministry, which had made itself felt at Silver Bluff for the centuries to come, was now embraced in the church at Savannah. But in this church, it will be seen, George Liele, the eldest of the trio, was the pastor, and not David George. Mr. Liele, as servant of the British officer who has given him his freedom, could secure for the church recognition and influence at the hands of the military government then in possession of Savannah, which neither David George nor Jesse Peter could obtain. Mr. Liele was with a man who had influence with the British government. David George and Jesse Peter, as strangers and fugitives, were unknown to that government and without influence. It is in this way we account for the fact that Liele and not David George, was pastor of the church. Under ordinary circumstances, the Silver Bluff element, which we fancy included nearly the whole church at the beginning, would have insisted upon having their old pastor. In hunting for facts which make it manifest that Savannah, Ga., had a Colored Baptist church prior to 1788, we have consulted the testimony of persons who were connected with the church at the time, and that of persons of recognized standing who were contemporaneous with them and competent to testify.

Mr. Joseph Cook, of Euhaw, Upper Indian Land, South Carolina, in a letter to Dr. John Rippon, London, England, dated September 15, 1790, uses the following language; "A poor Negro commonly called Brother George, has been so highly favored of God, as to plant the first Baptist Church in Savannah, and another in Jamaica." As Hervey, Cox, Phillipo, and others who have noticed missionary efforts of Negro Baptists in the West Indies inform us that Rev. George Liele left the United States in 1782 and began preaching at Kingston, Jamaica, British West Indies, in 1784, it is evident from Mr. Cook's letter that the church which Liele planted at Savannah existed prior to 1782.

Mr. Cook is corroborated by F.A. Cox, D.D., LL.D., who, in speaking of Rev. George Liele in his history of the Baptist Missionary Society of England, states that "He had been pastor of a Colored congregation in America."

A paragraph, which we take from the *History of the Propagation of Christianity Among the Heathen,* is of the same nature. It refers to the church of which Mr. Cook speaks in this manner:

"'The first Baptist preacher in Jamaica was a black man named George Liele, who, though a slave, had been the pastor of a Baptist church in Georgia. He was brought to Jamaica about 1782.' Mr. Liele, on his own behalf, testified that there was a Colored Baptist church in Savannah, Ga., during the British occupancy, and mentions by name at least three of its members, who were not in this country, after the British withdrew their forces from Savannah, 1782. In a letter to Mr. Joseph Cook, written from Jamaica, in 1790, Mr. Liele refers to one of these members in the following manner: 'Also I received accounts from Nova Scotia of a black Baptist preacher, David George, who was a member of the church of Savannah.'"

In a communication written in 1791 and addressed to the pastor of a

London church, Mr. Liele refers to one of his Jamaica members in this style: "Sister Hannah Williams, during the time she was a member of the church of Savannah, until the evacuation, did walk as a faithful, well behaved Christian."

In answer to questions in regard to Rev. Jesse Peter, Mr. Liele replied to his London correspondent as follows: "Brother Jesse Gaulphin, another black minister, preaches near Augusta, in South Carolina, where I used to preach. He was a member of the church at Savannah."

In the face of this testimony, coming from different sources, and from parties widely separated from each other who had no motive to deceive, there is absolutely no room for doubt as to the fact that a Colored Baptist church existed in Savannah, Ga., during 1779-1782.

What measure of prosperity attended the work of the Colored Baptist church at Savannah, Ga., during the years 1779-1782, we are not informed. It was well that at a time when churches in some parts were going to pieces because of the ravages of war, this little flock remained intact. We infer, however, that it did a most blessed work. Mr. Liele speaks in one of his letters of one "Brother Amos" who appears to have been a product of the Colored church at Savannah, or the older church at Silver Bluff, S.C. Amid the changes wrought in the closing day of the Revolutionary War, this Negro preacher had his lot cast in New Providence, Bahama Islands, British West Indies. According to Rev. George Liele, Amos had a membership of 300 in 1791. Benedict informs us that Amos was in correspondence with his brethren in Savannah, Ga., in 1812, and at that time the church at New Providence numbered 850.

A Remnant of Lisle's Church in Savannah
After the Revolutionary War

What portion of the Savannah church remain in America after the evacuation of the city of Savannah by the British in 1782, we are not able to state. But blessings and trials attended that portion of the flock which went abroad, and that which remained. Andrew Bryan, Hannah Bryan, Kate Hogg, and Hagar Simpson were among the last converts received into the fellowship of the Colored Baptist church at Savannah before the pastor, the Rev. George Liele, sailed for the West Indies in 1782. These and probably others, like the Rev. Jesse Peter, remained in America after the restoration of peace between the United States and the "mother country" and labored under Andrew Bryan, their new spiritual leader, for the continuation of the work, which had been so blessed of God under the labors of George Liele.

From Lisle's departure in 1782 to the time of Andrew Bryan's ordination in 1788, the little flock at Savannah, Ga., was bitterly persecuted, but its work of resuscitation and progress, was wonderful—wonderful because of the moral heroism which characterized it.

It is reasonable to suppose, however, that much of the opposition to the church at Savannah during 1782-1787 was due to the circumstances in which it had come into being, and not to real antipathy to the cause of Christ. For it must be borne in mind that it was a creature of the Revolutionary War, and of British origin, having been planted when the rightful people of Savannah were languishing in exile, or heroically struggling with the enemy in other parts of the country.

Bryan and his associates were beaten unmercifully for their persistency in holding on to the work, but they were prepared to yield their lives in martyrdom sooner than relinquish what Rev. George Liele had instituted, and it lived—lived amid the fires of persecution.

Rev. Jesse Peter, a member of the church under Liele, and, after the Revolutionary War, pastor of the church at Silver Bluff, saw what was needed to end this persecution and proceeded to change the aspect of things. He was held in high esteem by the colonists, and the Rev. Abraham Marshall of Kiokee, Ga., was his chief admirer and friend. Accordingly, he secured the services of the Rev. Abraham Marshall in making all things new. The church was organized anew, the pastor ordained to the office of a Baptist minister, and the organized church, with its preacher, brought into membership with the Georgia Baptist Association. As the Rev. Abraham Marshall was beloved by Georgia Baptists, as no other man of the state, it was enough that this church should have his official approval and recognition. Referring to this new order of things, instituted on the 20th day of January, 1788, Rev. Marshall, the one associate with Rev. Jesse Peter in the undertaking, recognized Rev. Peter as taking the initiative, when he says, "I assisted in the constitution of the church, and the ordination of the minister."

So ended the second period in the history of this church, as the dawn of it new day began—a day in which the once-persecuted servant of God could say, "We enjoy the right of conscience to a valuable extent, worshipping in our families, preaching three times every Lord's Day, baptizing frequently from ten to thirty at a time, in the Savannah, and administering the Sacred Supper, not only without molestation, but in the presence and with the approbation and encouragement of many of the White people."

Let us recapitulate. We began with the church at Silver Bluff, S.C. We were next attracted to Canada, and then to far-off Africa by the labors of David George, the first regular pastor at Silver Bluff. Again we follow a portion of the Silver Bluff Church to Savannah, Ga. In Savannah we see a church growing under the labors of Rev. George Liele, then we find Liele and Amos in the British West Indies, leading great congregations of Colored Baptists.

Once more we turn our eyes homeward, and we are attracted to the church at Silver Bluff, S.C.; to the church at Augusta, Ga., and the church at Savannah, Ga., which having endured the severest trials, rejoices in recognition and peace—the church of today.

No one can study this remarkable beginning of Baptist interest without being impressed with the fact that God reigns, and He bringeth all things to pass according to the council of His own will.

Palmer

But who was "Elder Palmer," the man who planted the first of this series of churches? David George states that he was a powerful preacher, and that he was pastor of a church some distance from Silver Bluff. We are satisfied that the church alluded to was not in South Carolina, nor in Georgia; nor were the members of the church in question, nor its pastor of African descent. It is our opinion that "Elder Palmer" was no less distinguished person than the Rev. Wait Palmer, the founder of the First Baptist Church of Stonington, Conn.

(1) It was possible that he should be the author of this remarkable beginning of Colored Baptist churches in the United States. For he was living and active during and prior to the Revolutionary period, and long before.

(2) Moreover, Rev. Wait Palmer of Stonington, Conn., was as his biographer states, "an actor in the great New Light, or Separatist movement." and in this capacity he "preached often in the destitute regions." Benedict testifies that "He became a famous pioneer in Virginia and North Carolina. (Ed. 1848, p.475)

(3) But what is more, Mrs. Marshall, the mother of Rev. Abraham Marshall of Kiokee, Ga., was a sister of Shubal Stearns, and Shubal Stearns was baptized and ordained to the work of the ministry by the Rev. Wait Palmer at Tolland, Conn., in the spring of 1751. It was but natural that, in his zeal to preach Christ in destitute regions, Palmer would visit this

Headquarters of the Foreign Mission Board, Corner Bainbridge and 19th Streets, Phiadelphia, Pennsylvania.

Since this building was purchased and remodeled the Board has bought a building adjoining it which gives them sufficient space for enlarging their headquarters.

Connecticut family and preach the gospel to any who might desire to hear it, to the salvation of their souls.

If it should be thought by some that no man would, in the circumstances, have gone on a preaching tour from Connecticut to South Carolina, it may be well to recall the fact that Rev. Abraham Marshall covered the ground in question in the year 1786, travelling both ways on horseback, preaching nearly every day during the three months he was from home. But Palmer was now in the South and not in the North, as Benedict states.

No other Palmer known to Baptists fits the case like this friend of Shubal Stearns. We shall continue to assign to him the credit of the first Negro Baptist church in America until we can find another "Elder Palmer" whose claim is absolutely certain.

Headquarters of the Foreign Mission Board, Corner Bainbridge and 19th Streets, Philadelphia, Pennsylvania.

Since this building was purchased and remodeled, the Board has bought a building adjoining it which gives them sufficient space for enlarging their headquarters.

BORN	BENEATH THIS MARBLE	DIED
March 25th	Are Deposited the Remains of Elder	September 25th,
A.D. 1783	LUTHER RICE	A.D. 1886

A minister of Christ, of the Baptist denomination
He was a native of Northboro, Massachusetts
Departed this life in Edgefield District, S.C.
In the death of this distinguished servant of the Lord,
Is "a great man fallen in Israel."

THAN HE

Perhaps no American has done more for the great missionary enterprise. It is thought the first American foreign mission, on which he went
to India, associated with Judson and others, originated with him. And
if the Burmans have cause of gratitude toward Judson for a faithful version of God's Word, so they will through generations to come arise up
and call Rice blessed; for it was his eloquent appeals for the heathen on
his return to America which raised our Baptist churches to adopt the
Burman Mission and sustain Judson in his arduous toils.

No Baptist has done more for the cause of education. He founded
The Columbian College in the District of Columbia which he benevo-
lently intended, by its central position, to diffuse knowledge, both literary and religious, through these United States. And if for want of de-
served patronage that unfortunate institution, which was the special
subject of his prayers and toils for the last fifteen years of his life, fail to
fulfill the high purpose of its founder; yet, the spirit of education, awak-
ened by his labors shall accomplish his noble aim.

LUTHER RICE

With a portly person and commanding presence,
Combined a strong and brilliant intellect,
As a theologian he was orthodox;
A scholar, his education was liberal,
He was an eloquent and powerful preacher;
A self-denying and indefatigable philanthropist.
His frailties with his dust are entombed;
And upon the walls of Zion his virtues engraved.
By order of the Baptist Convention for the State of South Carolina
This monument is erected to his memory."
—Taylor's Memoir of Luther Rice

BAPTIST EDUCATIONAL INSTITUTIONS

NAME	When Founded	LOCATION	PRESIDENT OR PRINCIPAL	Male	Female	Total
I THEOLOGICAL SEMINARIES						
1 Berkeley Baptist Divinity School	1904	Berkeley, Calif.	Claiborne M. Hill, D. D., LL. D.			
2 Bethel Theo. Sem.	1871	St. Paul, Minn.	G. Arvid Hagstrom, D. D.	7	1	8
3 Colgate-Rochester Div. School7	1928	Rochester, N. Y.	Albert W. Beaven, D. D.	5	2	7
German Dept.	1852	Rochester, N. Y.	Albert J. Ramaker, D. D., Dean	13	---	13
Italian Dept.	1907	Rochester, N. Y.	Antonio Mangano, D. D., Dean	5	---	5
4 Crozer Theo. Sem.	1868	Chester, Pa.	Milton G. Evans, D. D., LL. D.	1	---	1
5. Divinity School, University of Chicago	1866	Chicago, Ill.	Shailer Mathews, D. D., LL. D., Dean	10	---	10
6 Eastern Bap. Theo. Seminary	1925	Philadelphia, Pa.	A. K. deBlois, Ph. D., D. D., LL. D.	44	---	44
7 Evangelical Semininary of Porto Rico3	1919	Rio Piedras, P. R.	James A. McAllister, D. D.	14	2	16
8 International Baptist Seminary	1920	East Orange, N. J.	Frank L. Anderson, D. D.	7	---	7
9 Kansas City Baptist Theo. Sem.	1901	Kansas City, Kans.	Lyman M. Denton, Th. D., D. D.	7	3	10
10 Los Angeles Baptist Theo. Sem.	1927	Los Angeles, Calif.	Wm. A. Matthews, Ph. D., D. D.	6	5	11
11 Newton Theo. Institution, The	1825	Newton Center, Mass.	Everett C. Herrick, D. D.	7	---	7
12 Northern Bap. Theo. Sem.	1913	Chicago, Ill.	George W. Taft, D. D.	9	1	10
Norwegian Bap. Theo. Sem.	1913	Chicago, Ill.	Peder Stiansen, Th. M., Dean	14	---	14
13 Spanish-American Bap. Theo. Sem.		Los Angeles, Calif.	Rev. J. F. Detweiler	1	---	1
14 Western Bap. Theo. Sem.	1927	Portland, Ore.	Wm. T. Milliken, Ph. D., D. D.	2	3	5
14 Theological Seminaries				9	---	9
3 Theological Departments						
17 Theological Schools				161	17	178
II TRAINING SCHOOLS						
1 Baptist Institute for Christian Workers	1881	Chicago, Ill.	J. Milnor Wilbur, D. D.	5	19	24
2 Baptist Missionary Training School	1892	Philadelphia, Pa.	Miss W. S. Brinson, A. M.	---	7	7
2 Training Schools				5	26	31
III UNIVERSITIES AND COLLEGES						
1 Bates College	1864	Lewiston, Me.	Clifton D. Gray, Ph. D., LL. D.	38	6	44
2 Broaddus College	1871	Philippi, W. Va.	William W. Trent, A. M.	9	7	16
3 Brown University	1764	Providence, R. I.	Wm. H. P. Faunce, D. D., LL. D.	146	5	151
4 Bucknell University	1845	Lewisburg, Pa.	E. M. Hunt, D. D., LL. D., D. C. L.	57	10	67
5 Carleton College4	1866	Northfield, Minn.	D. J. Cowling, Ph. D., D. D., LL. D.	41	23	64
6 Colby College	1820	Waterville, Me.	Rev. F. W. Johnson, L. H. D.	32	3	35
7 Colgate University	1819	Hamilton, N. Y.	G. B. Cutten, Ph. D., D. D., LL. D.	72	---	72
8 Denison University	1831	Granville, Ohio	A. A. Shaw, D. D., LL. D., D. C. L.	46	15	61
9 Eastern University	1925	Philadelphia, Pa.	Charles T. Ball, Th. M.	9	7	16

438

NORTHERN BAPTIST CONVENTION

Male	Female	Total	Students for the Ministry	No. of Buildings	Total Value of Property (not Including Endowment)	Amount of Endowment	Income from Endowment	Total Income Last Year	Total Expenses Last Year	Volumes in Library	Commencement
33	30	63	25	4	$169000	$1115400	$26683	$47166	$51712	9500	May 1
44	40	84	42	3	200000	150000	7315	65258	59807	18000	May 2
71	3	74	71	2	515100	3648045	117232	138751	137147	63000	May 3
45	-----	45	45	1	150000	[Div. School] 8700		19120	18790	4000	May
7	-----	7	7	----	[Included in Colgate-Rochester Divinity School]						May
65	9	74	65	13	400000	1150000	80000	----------	----------	38000	June 4
585	131	716	585	-----	[Included in University of Chicago]			----------	----------	----------	June 5
111	39	150	138	4	800000	2000000	120000	120000	120000	12000	May 6
37	-----	37	37	13	34400	----------	----------	10153	9550	3425	May 7
30	13	43	30	5	450000	----------	----------	35561	34120	4000	May 8
77	47	124	74	3	225000	175000	----------	78000	78000	10000	May 9
45	9	54	54	2	25000	----------	----------	----------	----------	1000	May 10
65	15	80	65	6	259000	1354569	51624	84897	83981	41000	June 11
173	27	200	172	4	825000	46132	2534	52081	59779	7750	May 12
6	1	7	6		[Northern Sem.]	31000	1600	2700	2700	----------	May
15	1	16	14	----	----------	----------	----------	10058	9633	2050	13
22	19	41	20	2	70000	----------	----------	12000	12000	3000	June 14
1431	384	1815	1450	62	$4122500	$9670146	$415688	$675745	$677219	216275	
----	75	75	-----	2	$350000	$100000	$7260	$33802	$33258	5000	May 1
----	46	46	---	1	150000	65554	3562	36237	34029	3500	June 2
----	121	121	----	3	$500000	$165554	$10822	$70039	$67287	8500	
378	254	632	12	22	$1143000	$1820905	$127275	$261608	$261454	57375	June 1
83	62	145	9	5	500000	15000	900	42145	55609	3000	June 2
1492	617	2109	11	48	6347500	9931006	510395	1421779	1460000	385000	June 3
711	396	1107	20	25	2159400	1316200	62000	602000	590866	50000	June 4
423	414	837	23	19	1272300	2725904	103048	567547	569558	91300	June 5
381	249	630	19	20	985000	1440610	68826	259150	256111	70500	June 6
990	-----	990	--- --	14	3079600	4220325	134237	397319	391649	108000	June 7
457	432	889	15	22	2086400	3488060	164403	556115	562788	85000	June 8
84	42	126	43	3	100000	----------	----------	40000	41000	1200	June 9

NAME	When Founded	LOCATION	PRESIDENT OR PRINCIPAL	Instructors		
				Male	Female	Total
10 Franklin Col. of Indiana	1834	Franklin, Ind.	Homer P. Rainey, Ph. D.	19	5	24
11 Grand Island College, The	1892	Grand Island, Neb.	John Mason Wells, D. D.[9]	9	5	14
12 Hillsdale College	1844	Hillsdale, Mich.	Wm. Gear Spencer, LL. D.	19	15	34
13 Kalamazoo College	1833	Kalamazoo, Mich.	Rev. Allen Hoben, Ph. D.	20	7	27
14 Keuka College	1892	Keuka Park, N. Y.	A. H. Norton, Pd. D.	8	20	28
15 Linfield College	1857	McMinnville, Ore.	Leonard W. Riley, D. D.	19	7	26
16 Ottawa University	1865	Ottawa, Kans.	Erdmann Smith, LL. D.	16	10	26
17 Shurtleff College	1827	Alton, Ill.	Gorge Milton Potter, LL. D.	11	8	19
18 Sioux Falls College	1883	Sioux Falls, S. Dak.	Rev. Joseph A. Cooper, A. M.	10	8	18
19 Univ. of Chicago, The	1891	Chicago, Ill.	R. M. Hutchins, A. M., LL. B.	752		752
20 Univ. of Redlands	1907	Redlands, Calif.	Victor L. Duke, LL. D.	31	12	43
21 Univ. of Rochester[2]	1850	Rochester, N. Y.	Rush Rhees, D. D., LL. D.	92	19	111
School of Medicine and Denistry	1920	Rochester, N. Y.	G. H. Whipple, M. D., Sc. D., Dean	148		148
Eastman School of Music	1918	Rochester, N. Y.	Howard Hanson, Mus. D., F. A. A. R., Dir.	42	42	84
Extension Course	1916	Rochester, N. Y.	Francis J. Brown, A. M., Asso. Dir.	66		66
Summer School	1921	Rochester, N. Y.			53	53
22 William Jewell College[5]	1849	Liberty, Mo.	John F. Herget, D. D., LL. D.	21	2	23
22 Universities and Colleges				1733	289	2022

IV
JUNIOR COLLEGES

1 Alderson Junior College	1901	Alderson, W. Va.	J. A. Tolman, Ph. D.[10]	5	9	14
2 Colby Academy (for Girls)	1837	New London, N. H.	H. Leslie Sawyer, A. M.	4	8	12
3 Colorado Woman's College	1889	Denver, Colo.	Samuel J. Vaughn, A. B.	4	29	33
4 Frances Shimer School	1853	Mt. Carroll, Ill.	Rev. William P. McKee, A. M.	1	20	21
5 Rio Grande College	1876	Rio Grande, Ohio	Willard W. Bartlett, A. M.	8	5	13
6 Stephens College[5]	1856	Columbia, Mo.	James M. Wood, A. M.	14	49	63
6 Junior Colleges				36	120	156

V
ACADEMIES AND INSTITUTES

1 Bethel Academy	1905	St. Paul, Minn.	A. J. Wingblade, A. M.	8	6	14
2 Coburn Classical Inst.	1820	Waterville, Me.	Drew T. Harthorn, L. H. D.	5	4	9
3 Cook Academy	1872	Montour Falls, N. Y.	Bert C. Cate, A. B.	10	2	12
4 Hebron Academy	1804	Hebron, Me.	Ralph L. Hunt, A. B.	14		14
5 Higgins Classical Inst.	1891	Charleston, Me.	Rev. Wm. A. Tracy, A. B.	3	4	7
6 Keystone Academy	1868	Factoryville, Pa.	Curtis E. Coe, A. B.[11]	6	1	7
7 Maine Central Inst.	1866	Pittsfield, Me.	Edwin M. Purinton, A. M.	4	9	13
8 Peddie School, The	1866	Hightstown, N. J.	R. W. Swetland, LL. D.	28	1	29
9 Pillsbury Academy	1877	Owatonna, Minn.	Milo B. Price, Ph. D., LL. D.	9	2	11
10 Ricker Classical Inst.	1848	Houlton, Me.	Roy M. Hayes, A. B.	6	5	11
11 Suffield School[2]	1833	Suffield, Conn.	Rev. Brownell Gage, Ph. D.	16	1	17
12 Vermont Academy	1876	Saxtons River, Vt.	John B. Cook, LL. D.	9	6	15
13 Wayland Academy	1855	Beaver Dam, Wis.	Edwin P. Brown, A. B.	7	9	16
14 Western Pa. Classical and Scientific Inst.[6]	1872	Mt. Pleasant, Pa.	Mrs. H. R. Gregory	1	3	4
14 Academies and Institutes				126	53	179

Students			Students for the Ministry	No. of Buildings	Total Value of Property (not Including Endowment)	Amount of Endowment	Income from Endowment	Total Income Last Year	Total Expenses Last Year	Volumes in Library	Commencement
Male	Female	Total									
170	137	307	12	6	$504600	$850000	$50000	$108900	$140000	33000	June 10
101	194	295	7	11	450000	120000	3500	57320	59564	11625	June 11
201	287	488	12	23	718800	766800	50350	158876	156956	30075	June 12
225	151	376	7	16	763300	1089629	62000	194892	193272	25075	June 13
---	250	250		13	931100	224104	10173	169697	162973	12300	June 14
140	194	334	12	8	422400	835379	37461	82748	83195	12000	June 15
209	238	447	21	6	670000	642000	32500	148416	128287	15300	May 16
165	184	349	20	9	425000	570000	27165	93530	92707	19825	June 17
115	158	273	9	4	275000	225000	10470	57000	48265	8000	June 18
6878	7555	14433	685	64	37347000	50889403	2516157	5015539	5991497	1000000	Qu'r. 19
266	343	609	20	14	1737100	2754025	132444	370888	364860	21625	June 20
515	479	994	---	13	2513800	10100000	350359	566436	583657	115150	June 21
98	10	108	---	1	4113400	10500000	540237	1077579	1043690	28800	
126	273	399	---	2	4032400	5000000	354731	639197	688268	19050	
487	978	1465	---	[University	of	Rochester]	---	53339	40262	---	
131	361	492	---	[University	of	Rochester]	---	36959	32815	---	
305	128	433	64	10	738900	1123248	59514	133938	136321	35000	May 22
15131	14386	29517	1021	378	$73316000	$110647598	$5408145	$13112917	$14135624	2238200	
69	96	165	3	3	$316000	---	---	$47044	$48090	2750	May 1
-	---	150	150	---	6	200000	$150000	$12000	62000	60000	5000	June 2
-	---	275	275	---	4	513000	60000	6500	100000	100000	4000	May 3
3	209	212	---	12	476900	282294	11365	141866	108377	6000	June 4
92	67	159	10	3	178000	89000	5000	42000	42000	5000	June 5
-	---	618	618	---	13	1184600	45772	7060	438034	394442	7400	May 6
164	1415	1579	13	41	$2868500	$627066	$41925	$830944	$752909	30150	
123	159	282	20	---	[Included	in	Bethel	Theological	Seminary]	---	June 1
50	30	80	---	5	$236900	$32647	$1274	$77882	$65620	4000	June 2
140	40	180	3	2	250000	86000	4200	108197	108197	5000	June 3
232	---	232		13	386300	366226	10000	131151	118628	4000	June 4
69	70	139	1	4	134000	20000	1062	18269	18541	1700	June 5
60	---	60	3	5	179100	3000	---	41264	47592	2000	June 6
128	126	254	2	3	250000	78000	3700	37589	35872	500	June 7
350	---	350		18	1408700	206941	8270	377650	353116	11100	June 8
118	70	188	---	8	400000	386000	53000	74000	72000	2600	June 9
67	83	150	---	4	153300	25000	1727	31855	34285	3000	June 10
195	65	260	---	5	328600	433398	9063	133462	134047	---	June 11
106	80	186	1	10	500000	100000	5000	80000	86000	5000	June 12
68	73	141	1	7	402000	269900	17181	94501	94429	4975	June 13
-	---	118	118	---	2	40000	44166	2830	5752	5594	300	June 14
1706	914	2620	31	86	$4668900	$2051278	$77307	$1211572	$1173921	44175	

441

NAME	When Founded	LOCATION	PRESIDENT OR PRINCIPAL	Instructors		
				Male	Female	Total
VI						
INDIAN SCHOOL						
1 Bacone College ____	1880	Bacone, Okla. ____	Benjamin D. Weeks, D. D. __	8	10	18
59 Institutions ___ _ _				2069	515	2584

1Previous reports.
2Not under denominational control.
3Interdenominational. Property owned by The American Baptist Home Mission Society.
4Affiliated also with the Congregational and Episcopal Churches.
5Cooperating also with the Southern Baptist Convention.
6Music school only.
7Merger of Colgate Theological Seminary, founded 1819, and Rochester Theological Seminary.
8Retired. Succeeded by Clarence A. Barbour, D. D., LL. D., S. T. D.
9Resigned. George Sutherland, D. D., Acting President.
10Resigned. Succeeded by W. S. Dunlop, D. D.
11Resigned.

SOUTHERN BAP

NAME	When Founded	LOCATION	PRESIDENT OR PRINCIPAL	Male	Female	Total
I						
THEOLOGICAL SEMINARIES						
1 Southern Bap. Theo. Sem. _____	1859	Louisville, Ky._____	John R. Sampey, D. D. _____	21	---	21
2 Southwestern Bap.- Theo. Sem. _____	1908	Seminary Hill, Tex.	L. R. Scarborough, D. D., LL. D.	20	10	30
2 Seminaries _____ __				41	10	51
II						
TRAINING SCHOOLS						
1 Baptist Bible Institute, The _____	1917	New Orleans, La. __	W. W. Hamilton, Th. D., D. D., LL. D. _____	11	1	12
2 Baptist Woman's Missionary Union Training School __	1907	Louisville, Ky. _____	Mrs. Janie Cree Bose ___ _ ___	6	5	11
2 Training Schools _ __				17	6	23
III						
UNIVERSITIES AND COLLEGES						
1 Anderson College ____	1911	Anderson, S. C.____	Miss Annie D. Denmark, A. B. ____	2	21	23
2 Baylor University ___	1845	Waco, Tex._____	Samuel P. Brooks, LL. D. ____	62	24	86
College of Medicine	1903	Dallas, Tex. _____	Samuel P. Brooks, LL. D. ____	112	4	116
College of Dentistry	1904	Dallas, Tex. _____	Samuel P. Brooks, LL. D._____	40	---	40
College of Pharmacy	1900	Dallas, Tex. _____	Samuel P. Brooks, LL. D. ___	10	---	10
3 Baylor College for Women _____ _ __	1845	Belton, Tex. _____	John C. Hardy, LL. D. _____	14	44	58
4 Bessie Tift College_	1847	Forsyth, Ga. _____	Aquila Chamlee, D. D. _____	11	9	20
5 Blue Mountain Col._	1873	Blue Mountain, Miss	Lawrence T. Lowrey, Ph. D.___	7	17	24
6 Carson and Newman College	1851	Jefferson City, Tenn.	James T. Warren, LL. D._____	14	11	25
7 Chowan College _ ___	1848	Murfreesboro, N. C..	W. B. Edwards, A. M. _____	2	14	16
8 Coker College ___	1908	Hartsville, S. C.____	Carlyle Campbell, A. M. _____	14	11	25
9 Furman University _	1825	Greenville, S. C.____	W. J. McGlothlin, Ph. D., D. D. LL. D. _____	35		35

Students			Students for the Ministry	No. of Buildings	Total Value of Property (not Including Endowment)	Amount of Endowment	Income from Endowment	Total Income Last Year	Total Expenses Last Year	Volumes in Library	Commencement
Male	Female	Total									
180	125	305	8	5	1 $800000	1 $270000	1 $13000	1 $116826	1 $159592	1 2500	June 1
18612	17345	35957	2523	575	$86275900	$123431642	$5966887	$16018043	$16966952	2540250	

Founded 1850

TIST CONVENTION

Students			Students for the Ministry	No. of Buildings	Total Value of Property (not Including Endowment)	Amount of Endowment	Income from Endowment	Total Income Last Year	Total Expenses Last Year	Volumes in Library	Commencement
Male	Female	Total									
434	----	434	432	6	$2250000	$1750000	$80000	$137029	$135500	32000	April 1
309	228	537	306	4	1796000	446599	----	173256	173256	10000	May 2
743	228	971	738	10	$4046000	$2196599	$80000	$310285	$308756	42000	
134	76	210	108	23	$750000	$1000	----	$103297	$95473	60000	May 1
_ ----	139	139	----	3	327000	163728	$6584	45972	42662	1550	April 2
134	215	349	108	26	$1077000	$164728	$6584	$149269	$138135	61550	
----	275	275	----	6	$275000	$90000	$3025	----	----	5000	May 1
1154	1495	2649	114	20	1893900	541817	29941	$666940	$573028	54075	May 2
343	14	357	----	4	184400	----	----	73000	59000	5825	May
105	----	105	----	3	233500	----	----	74000	105000	1000	May
44	----	44	----	2	18000	----	----	20000	16000	----	May
----	1382	1382	----	11	1032000	532000	30652	637397	496026	25000	May 3
----	313	313	----	6	444500	80000	4798	145214	132240	10000	June 4
1	339	340	----	8	447000	300176	16000	93318	93318	11275	June 5
208	305	513	40	8	382000	522799	31368	189518	196533	12000	May 6
----	160	160	----	9	250000	100000	5000	65000	65000	9000	May 7
----	249	249	----	7	556200	535439	37765	161077	160840	11000	June 8
522	4	526	62	24	1206300	691959	120373	276749	283961	21000	May 9

NAME	When Founded	LOCATION	PRESIDENT OR PRINCIPAL	Male	Female	Total
10 Georgetown College	1829	Georgetown, Ky.	M. B. Adams, D. D., LL. D.	20	7	2"
11 Greenville Woman's College2	1819	Greenville, S. C.	David M. Ramsay, D. D.	4	30	34
12 Howard College	1842	Birmingham, Ala.	John C. Dawson, Ph. D. LL. D.	41	13	54
13 Howard Payne Col.	1889	Brownwood, Tex.	Edgar Godbold, LL. D.4	15	14	29
14 John B. Stetson Univ.	1876	DeLand, Fla.	Rev. Lincoln Hulley, Ph. D., Litt. D., LL. D.	18	14	32
15 Judson College	1838	Marion, Ala.	E. V. Baldy, D. D., LL. D.	7	26	33
16 Limestone College	1845	Gaffney, S. C.	R. C. Granberry, D. D.	5	19	24
17 Louisiana College	1906	Pineville, La.	Claybrook Cottingham, LL. D.	16	7	23
18 Mercer University	1833	Macon, Ga.	Spright Dowell, LL. D.	40	2	42
19 Meredith College	1891	Raleigh, N. C.	Chas. E. Brewer, Ph. D., LL. D.	7	36	43
20 Mississippi College	1826	Clinton, Miss.	John W. Provine, Ph. D., LL. D.	25	---	25
21 Mississippi Woman's College	1912	Hattiesburg, Miss.	J. L. Johnson, LL. D.	12	18	30
22 Montezuma College	1922	Montezuma, N. Mex.	Rev. C. R. Barrick, A. M.5	7	2	9
23 Oklahoma Bap. Univ.	1910	Shawnee, Okla.	W. W. Phelan, Ph. D.	24	9	33
24 Ouachita College	1886	Arkadelphia, Ark.	A. B. Hill, A. M.6	15	7	22
25 Shorter College2	1873	Rome, Ga.	W. D. Furry, Ph. D.	11	14	25
26 Simmons Univ.	1891	Abilene, Tex.	J. D. Sandefer, LL. D.	28	22	50
27 Tennessee College for Women	1907	Murfreesboro, Tenn.	E. L. Atwood, D. D.	7	11	18
28 Union University	1834	Jackson, Tenn.	H. E. Watters, D. D., LL. D.	20	11	31
29 Univ. of Richmond	1832	University of Richmond, Va.	F. W. Boatwright, LL. D.	34	14	48
30 Wake Forest College	1834	Wake Forest, N. C.	F. P. Gaines, Ph. D., Litt. D.	43	---	43
31 William Jewell Col.3	1848	Liberty, Mo.	John F. Herget, D. D., LL. D.	21	2	23
31 Universities and Colleges				743	433	1176

IV
JUNIOR COLLEGES

NAME	When Founded	LOCATION	PRESIDENT OR PRINCIPAL	Male	Female	Total
1 Averett College	1859	Danville, Va.	J. W. Cammack, D. D.	1	23	24
2 Bethel College	1849	Russellville, Ky.	Rev. O. W. Yates, Acting	7	1	8
3 Bethel Woman's Col.	1854	Hopkinsville, Ky.	J. W. Gaines, LL. D.		20	20
4 Bluefield College	1922	Bluefield, W. Va.	Oscar E. Sams, D. D., LL. D.	9	1	10
5 Boiling Springs Junior College	1907	Boiling Springs,	Rev. John Caylor	5	7	12
6 Burleson College	1895	Greenville, Tex.	J. A. Campbell, D. D.	14	10	24
7 Campbell College	1887	Buies Creek, N. C.	W. F. Jones	3	12	15
8 Campbellsville College	1907	Campbellsville, Ky.	J. S. Rogers, D. D.	4	16	20
9 Central College 2	1892	Conway, Ark.	W. T. Lowery, Ph. D.	6	7	13
10 Clarke Memorial College	1908	Newton, Miss.	F. S. Groner, D. D.	5	5	10
11 College of Marshall	1912	Marshall, Tex.	J. L. Creech	6	8	14
12 Cumberland College2	1889	Williamsburg, Ky.	J. L. Ward, A. M.	5	2	7
13 Decatur Baptist Col.	1898	Decatur, Tex.	M. E. Dodd, D. D.	3	9	12
14 Dodd College	1921	Shreveport, La.	John W. Crouch, D. D.	7	6	13
15 Hannibal-LaGrange College	1858	Hannibal, Mo.	Rev. C. B. Miller, M. D.	5	16	21
16 Hardin College	1873	Mexico, Mo.	M. P. L. Berry, Ph. B.	3	11	14
17 Hillman College	1853	Clinton, Miss.	B. J. Albritton, A. B.	7	6	13
18 Jacksonville College	1899	Jacksonville, Tex.	J. N. Mallory, Ph. D.	10	7	17
19 Jonesboro College	1924	Jonesboro, Ark.	R. L. Moore, Ed. D.	14	13	27
20 Mars Hill College	1856	Mars Hill, N. C.	Rev. J. W. Overall, LL. D.	6	4	10
21 Missionary Bap. Col.	1919	Sheridan, Ark.	H. D. Morton, Th. M.	5	5	10
22 Mountain Home Col.	1893	Mountain Home, Ark.	R. K. White	4	5	9
23 Norman Junior Col.	1900	Norman Park, Ga.	Rev. W. J. Jones	2	19	21
24 Pineland College	1926	Salemburg, N. C.	J. W. Jent, Th. D.	9	6	15
25 Southwest Bap. Col.	1878	Bolivar, Mo.	James M. Wood, A. M.	14	49	63
26 Stephens College3	1856	Columbia, Mo.	H. G. Noffsinger, A. M.	5	25	30
27 Virginia Intermont College	1884	Bristol, Va.	G. W. McDonald, A. B.	5	6	11
28 Wayland College	1909	Plainview, Tex.	Rev. W. C. Ferguson7	10	5	15
29 Will Mayfield	1878	Marble Hill, Mo.	J. B. Huff, A. M.	7	8	15
30 Wingate Junior Col.	1923	Wingate, N. C.	Dr. J. B. Davis	6	5	11
30 Junior Colleges				187	317	504

Students			Students for the Ministry	No. of Buildings	Total Value of Property (not Including Endowment)	Amount of Endowment	Income from Endowment	Total Income Last Year	Total Expenses Last Year	Volumes in Library	Commencement
Male	Female	Total									
199	161	360	16	7	$349100	$704624	$40023	$116526	$150368	46100	June 10
---	441	441	-----	8	650000	150000	---------	124472	118018	8000	May 11
1282	649	1931	70	10	467000	700000	40000	294000	294000	25000	May 12
368	465	833	44	10	544000	100917	3499	105547	109152	14000	May 13
300	217	517	31	17	1000000	1600000	---------	---------	---------	32625	May 14
---	280	280		12	700000	500000	30000	198717	190433	11500	May 15
---	326	326	-----	8	600000	408000	23000	109673	93512	9875	May 16
364	291	655	36	9	600000	300176	17304	124059	131759	9000	June 17
764	330	1094	70	35	1010800	735603	18859	158832	166332	39000	June 18
---	511	511	-----	10	1369700	474551	26719	234840	232562	14700	June 19
529	30	559	46	9	700000	625000	32000	92000	87000	12000	May 20
1	395	396	-----	12	450000	500000	26000	100000	98000	10050	May 21
34	38	72	10	5	552900	---------	600	119755	142526	6000	May 22
329	508	837	61	5	500000	12000	600	109435	115958	8550	May 23
186	151	337	27	14	377800	540404	30483	163319	160726	10500	June 24
---	212	212	-----	6	488800	346175	29000	147470	138489	12000	June 25
450	500	950	65	12	720400	500000	30000	280000	285000	16000	June 26
---	206	206	-----	2	359000	31440	---------	90000	89809	8000	June 27
600	713	1313	50	9	850000	200000	12000	146000	146000	13000	May 28
734	286	1020	78	11	2414200	2214958	132028	392325	390252	44075	June 29
700	---	700	84	10	602300	2264159	145972	273229	272928	33000	May 30
305	128	433	64	10	738900	1123248	59514	133938	136321	35000	May 31
9522	11374	20896	968	339	$22967700	$17425445	$975928	$5916350	$5730091	583150	
---	402	402	9	4	$450000	$25000	$1500	$101000	$101000	4500	May 1
125	28	153	23	5	213700	87652	4800	37841	40346	8500	May 2
---	177	177	-----	4	250000	11000	660	50000	50000	5000	May 3
122	37	159	6	12	600000	---------	---------	83051	64051	2700	June 4
175	110	285	32	3	270000	---------	162	36352	36349	1200	May 5
295	210	505	25	10	415000	12500	---------	51000	51000	13800	May 6
140	160	300	6	4	125000	---------	750	75000	75000	4500	May 7
---	205	205	----	4	400000	---------	---------	30000	35000	3000	June 8
120	170	290	12	5	138000	---------	---------	80000	80000	4000	May 9
72	100	172	14	7	350000	---------	---------	45000	45000	3100	May 10
174	174	348	36	4	500000	441953	---------	7000	7000	4000	May 11
85	75	160	5	4	250000	30000	24307	65000	75000	4500	May 12
---	105	105	-----	3	600000	10000	1500	52000	52000	3500	June 13
125	160	285	24	3	300000	54000	600	25000	35000	4000	June 14
---	105	105	-----	7	569800	111259	3000	46000	47000	5000	May 15
---	110	110	-----	6	100000	---------	---------	92017	146057	3500	May 16
76	107	183	17	8	126300	16000	---------	---------	---------	3000	May 17
160	180	340	26	4	300000	---------	1263	23762	25210	4025	May 18
274	214	488	41	10	368000	60000	---------	109000	109000	4500	May 19
49	117	166	21	1	45000	---------	3000	122378	119454	7000	May 20
120	86	206	13	11	150000	100	---------	13600	16800	2500	May 21
133	71	204	-----	6	252000	200000	4	27550	34173	8000	May 22
---	265	265	-----	6	165000	100000	10000	60000	52000	3700	May 23
210	395	605	50	7	262000	---------	5000	15000	15000	3500	May 24
---	618	618	-----	13	1184600	45772	---------	52499	60433	5000	May 25
---	393	393	-----	8	650000	150000	7060	438034	394442	7400	May 26
130	120	250	40	2	250000	12500	9000	130000	120000	5750	May 27
71	67	138	21	4	192000	57500	500	47100	48650	3500	May 28
112	128	240	18	5	210000	29000	3300	42934	48410	4000	May 29
101	76	177	17	4	250000	38637	2500	67000	61000	3300	May 30
2869	5165	8034	456	174	$9963400	$1492873	$78906	$2026118	$2044375	139975	

NAME	When Founded	LOCATION	PRESIDENT OR PRINCIPAL	Male	Female	Total
V **ACADEMIES** **AND** **INSTITUTES**						
1 Acadia Bap. Inst. 2	1917	Church Point, La.	Rev. Thomas E. Mixon	3	4	7
2 Alexander Schools Inc.	1925	Union Mills, N. C.	W. E. Sweatt, Supt.	1	8	9
3 Armo Bap. Academy	1918	Blue Eye, Mo.	I. L. Wilson, A. B., Th. M.	2	2	4
4 Barbourville Baptist Inst.	1899	Barbourville, Ky.	L. P. Manis	4	5	9
5 Blairsville Bap. Inst.	1905	Blairsville, Ga.	Rev. Frank A. Clarke	1	3	4
6 Blue Ridge Mission School	1916	Buffalo Ridge, Va.	J. W. H. Dyches, Th. D.	3	5	8
7 Brewton-Parker Inst.	1905	Mt. Vernon, Ga.	A. M. Gates, Sc. B.	7	5	12
8 Buchanan Bap. Mission School	1911	Council, Va.	Robert A. Henderson, A. M.	2	8	10
9 Chattahoochee High School 2	1901	Clermont, Ga.	W. L. Walker	2	2	4
10 Cosby Academy 2	1913	Cosby, Tenn.	Chas. H. Turner 8	1	4	5
11 Edisto Academy	1915	Seivern, S. C.	W. H. Cannada, Th. M.	3	4	7
12 Eldridge Bap. Acad.	1898	Eldridge, Ala.	Rev. M. W. Mims	2	3	5
13 Ensley-Howard High School	1924	Ensley, Ala.	E. E. Cox	4	1	5
14 Fork Union Military Academy	1898	Fork Union, Va.	Col. N. J. Perkins, A. B.	10	---	10
15 Fruitland Institute	1899	Hendersonville, N. C.	A. B. Miller, Th. M.	2	7	9
16 Hargrave Military Academy	1909	Chatham, Va.	Col. A. H. Camden, A. B.	11	2	13
17 Harrison-Chihowee Institute 2	1882	Seymour, Tenn.	J. L. Jeffries 9	3	2	5
18 Hazard Institute 2	1901	Hazard, Ky.	C. D. Stevens	4	5	9
19 Hiawassee Academy 2	1887	Hiawassee, Ga.	DeWitt T. Buice	3	3	6
20 Lee Baptist Inst.	1903	Pennington Gap, Va.	Romulus Skaggs, A. B.	2	3	5
21 Long Creek Acad. 2	1914	Long Creek, S. C.	Rev. L. H. Raines	2	6	8
22 Magoffin Inst. 2	1904	Salyersville, Ky.	P. T. Thompson, Th. M.	4	2	6
23 Mary P. Willingham School	1912	Blue Ridge, Ga.	Rev. A. B. Greene, A. B.	1	9	10
24 Newton Co. Acad.	1920	Parthenon, Ark.	W. T. Burdine	2	3	5
25 Newton Institute	1898	Newton, Ala.	P. W. Lett, Th. M.	2	4	6
26 North Grennville Bapt. Acad.	1892	Tigerville, S. C.	M. C. Donnan, Th. M.	2	5	7
27 Nuyaka Indian School 2	1925	Nuyaka, Okla.	Rev. L. B. Alder, Supt.	2	3	5
28 Oak Hill Bap. Acad. 1	1881	Kindrick, Va.	Rev. W. A. Hash	2	6	8
29 Oneida Bap. Inst. 1	1899	Oneida, Ky.	J. A. Burns	4	12	16
30 Piedmont Bap. Mission School	1921	Alhambra, Va.	Rev. H. C. Ruffin	2	1	3
31 Piedmont Institute 1	1909	Waycross, Ga.	W. C. Carlton, A. M.	3	6	9
32 San Marcos Baptist Academy	1907	San Marcos, Tex.	Col. J. E. Franklin, A. M.	11	15	26
33 Smoky Mountain Academy	1915	R. 9, Sevierville, Tenn.	Miss Mayme Grimes	1	4	5
34 South Mountain Industrial Inst., Inc.	1919	R. 4, Bostic, N. C.	Miss Ora Hull	1	5	6
35 Sylva Collegiate Institute 2	1898	Sylva, N. C.	N. R. Prickett	3	3	6
36 Watauga Academy	1882	Butler, Tenn.	C. A. Todd, Th. M.	1	5	6
36 Academies and Institutes				113	165	278
101 Institutions				1101	931	2032

1 Previous reports.
2 No report. Data taken from Year-Book of the Southern Baptist Convention.
3 Cooperating also with the Northern Baptist Convention.
4 Resigned to accept Secretaryship of the Missouri General Association.
5 Resigned. Succeeded by Dr. E. W. Provence.
6 Resigned. Succeeded by Dr. Chas. D. Johnson.
7 Resigned. Succeeded by J. W. Jeffries, D. D.
8 Resigned. Succeeded by Lee R. Watson.
9 Resigned. Succeeded by Roy Anderson.

Male	Female	Total	Students for the Ministry	No. of Buildings	Total Value of Property (not Including Endowment)	Amount of Endowment	Income from Endowment	Total Income Last Year	Total Expenses Last Year	Volumes in Library	Commencement
39	36	75	25	16	$65000	----	----	$15000	$15000	600	May 1
116	56	172	2	4	68000			17500	18000	2800	May 2
34	46	80	1	3	28200	$1000	$100	3789	4039	1425	May 3
65	75	140	2	3	85000	----		12000	12000	1200	July 4
28	56	84	----	2	20000	----		2800	2800	1600	May 5
72	78	150	2	3	30000	----		10000	10000	400	May 6
102	80	182	----	6.	140000	30000	1490	17713	17713	800	May 7
76	66	142	1	6	150000	----		12050	12050	1000	May 8
44	63	107	----	3	25000	1000	55	4000	3700	1000	May 9
28	25	53	2	4	30000	----	----	5000	5000	1500	May 10
38	22	60	6	4	60000	----	----	10000	10000	1500	May 11
27	35	62	2	6	100000	----	----	5000	5000	600	May 12
42	37	79	2	1	85000	----	----	16473	16694	1200	May 13
121	----	121	3	4	350000	500	20	56896	54977	600	June 14
70	70	140	4	6	140000	----	----	19000	18750	2000	May 15
182	----	182	5	4	250000			63547	63415	1100	May 16
30	35	65	3	4	90000	----		5000	5000	1300	May 17
197	153	350	1	3	185000	35000		----	----	1000	May 18
34	51	85	2	3	35000	----		3200	2300	800	May 19
50	60	110	----	3	85000	----		6000	8000	600	May 20
47	60	107	2	4	47500	----		7000	7000	900	May 21
89	75	164	----	3	125000	5000		7200	7200	1000	April 22
----	150	150	----	3	100000	----	----	22500	22500	800	May 23
41	59	100	2	3	35000	----	----	3500	3498	1400	May 24
22	30	52	8	3	100000	----	----	8227	12014	2800	May 25
40	60	100	13	7	50000	18000	1300	17282	17282	----	April 26
45	33	78	----	15	80000	----	----	1200	1200	300	May 27
45	47	92	2	4	35000	2500	----	----	----	500	June 28
195	202	397	----	6	300000	25000	----	32000	32000	7000	April 29
29	27	56	----	1	15000	----	----	3500	3500	550	June 30
117	105	222	7	2	150000	----	----	15000	12000	500	June 31
290	159	449	14	13	500000	----	----	----	----	3000	May 32
44	70	114	----	1	25000	----	----	3450	3500	500	June 33
16	21	37	----	5	7200	----	----	9063	9080	1875	April 34
35	34	69	1	4	60000	----	----	14000	14000	2000	May 35
37	55	92	----	3	30000	----	----	5670	5600	1175	May 36
2487	2231	4718	112	165	$3680900	$118000	$2965	$434560	$436212	47325	
15755	19213	34968	2382	714	$41735000	$21397645	$1144383	$8836582	$8657569	873200	

447

NAME	When Founded	LOCATION	PRESIDENT OR PRINCIPAL	Instructors		
				Male	Female	Total
I **THEOLOGICAL SEMINARIES**						
1 American Bap. Theo. Sem. 1	1924	Nashville, Tenn.		6	---	6
Central Bap. Theo. Sem.	1921	Topeka, Kans.	E. L. Scruggs, D. D.	4	2	6
2 Theological Seminaries				10	2	12
II **UNIVERSITIES AND COLLEGES**						
1 Arkansas Bap. Col.	1884	Little Rock, Ark.	Rev. S. P. Nelson, Ph. D.	8	9	17
2 Benedict College	1870	Columbia, S. C.	Rev. C. B. Antisdel, LL. D.	13	15	28
3 Bishop College	1881	Marshall, Tex.	David C. Gilmore, D. D.	15	12	27
4 Coleman College 1	1887	Gibsland, La.	M. M. Coleman, Sc. B.	9	7	16
5 Jackson College	1877	Jackson, Miss.	Rev. B. Baldwin Dansby	7	8	15
6 Leland College	1870	Baker, La.	Rev. J. A. Bacoats, A. M.	9	5	14
7 Morehouse College	1867	Atlanta, Ga.	John Hope, Ph. D., LL. D.	19	2	21
8 Morris College 1	1908	Sumter, S. C.	J. J. Starks, D. D., LL. D.	10	12	22
9 Oklahoma Baptist University 1	1912	Muskogee, Okla.		3	7	10
10 Roger Williams Col.	1866	Memphis, Tenn.	T. O. Fuller, Ph. D., D. D.	11	9	20
11 Selma University	1878	Selma, Ala.	R. T. Pollard, D. D., LL. D.	9	17	26
12 Shaw University	1865	Raleigh, N. C.	Joseph L. Peacock, D. D.	12	11	23
13 Simmons University	1873	Louisville, Ky.	C. H. Parrish, D. D., LL. D., F. R. G. S.	10	11	21
14 Spelman College	1881	Atlanta, Ga.	Miss Florence M. Read, A. B.	4	34	38
15 Virginia Union Univ.	1865	Richmond, Va.	Wm. J. Clark, D. D.	20	6	26
16 Virginia College and Theo. Sem. 1	1888	Lynchburg, Va.	Vernon Johns, D. D.	---	---	---
16 Universities and Colleges				159	165	324
III **JUNIOR COLLEGES**						
1 Central Mississippi College	1893	Kosciusko, Miss.	W. A. Reed, Jr., A. B.	2	10	12
2 Central Texas Col. 1	1901	Waco, Tex.		5	5	10
3 Florida Memorial College	1808	Live Oak, Fla.	Robert L. Holley, S. T. D.	4	8	12
4 Florida Normal and Industrial Inst.	1892	St. Augustine, Fla.	Rev. N. W. Collier, Litt. D.	7	13	20
5 Friendship Normal and Industrial Col.	1891	Rock Hill, S. C.	E. R. Roberts, D. D.	4	8	12
6 Guadalupe College 1	1884	Seguin, Tex.	C. H. Griggs, D. D.	6	7	13
7 Hayden Mem. Inst.	1904	Franklin, Va.	Rev. R. Lloyd Heck, B. D.	3	3	6
8 Houston College	1895	Houston, Tex.	Rev. Joseph Wilson, Jr.	1	2	3
9 Howe Junior College	1888	Memphis, Tenn.	T. O. Fuller, Ph. D., D. D.	3	5	8
10 Northern University 1	1913	Rahway, N. J.	W. J. Winston, D. D.	4	1	5
11 Pittsylvania Collegiate Inst.	1902	Gretna, Va.	G. W. Goode, D. D.	1	4	5
12 Seneca Junior Col. 1	1899	Seneca, S. C.		2	5	7
13 Storer College	1867	Harpers Ferry, W. Va.	Henry T. McDonald, LL. D.	7	10	17
14 Western College 1	1891	Kansas City, Mo.	Clement Richardson, A. M.	5	7	12
14 Junior Colleges				54	88	142

| Students | | | Students for the Ministry | No. of Buildings | Total Value of Property (not Including Endowment) | Amount of Endowment | Income from Endowment | Total Income Last Year | Total Expenses Last Year | Volumes in Library | Commencement |
Male	Female	Total									
41	-----	41	41	4	$200000	-----	-----	$12000	$12000	500	May 1
24	1	25	24	1	10000	-----	-----	6000	6000	3000	May 2
65	1	66	65	5	$210000	-----	-----	$18000	$18000	3500	-----
135	90	225	56	4	$100000	-----	-----	$25358	$25358	5000	May 1
174	291	465	26	15	369400	$133000	$5852	77626	77182	9500	May 2
173	307	480	27	16	304500	13797	664	121485	120869	5000	May 3
133	178	311	14	7	150000	-----	-----	-----	-----	-----	June 4
108	142.	250	80	10	146500	476	24	44382	42369	2450	May 5
40	80	120	5	6	300000	100000	6000	40000	40000	5000	May 6
455	-----	455	19	8	334900	320000	14032	117934	126848	9000	June 7
200	340	540	31	8	165000	-----	-----	40000	40000	1200	May 8
35	90	125	7	3	25000	-----	-----	23000	27000	300	May 9
105	100	205	30	7	150000	40000	2000	10000	11000	2000	June 10
147	292	439	58	8	225000	-----	-----	55537	50793	5000	May 11
149	198	347	33	17	606100	355000	19333	103011	102884	11150	June 12
127	115	242	40	4	194000	-----	-----	31376	37429	3500	June 13
-----	331	331	-----	14	894300	67502	19694	113796	113900	14000	June 15
387	228	615	70	14	760000	474672	2145	239900	228032	10250	June 14
											16
2368	2782	5150	496	141	$4724700	$1504447	$69744	$1043405	$1043164	83350	
106	204	310	6	3	$65000	-----	-----	$10000	$9766	350	May 1
93	112	205	20	4	75000	-----	-----	8000	7961	1200	May 2
76	127	203	12	7	125000	-----	-----	25000	26000	800	May 3
80	87	167	21	15	450000	-----	-----	132676	130071	2500	May 4
75	112	187	15	5	35000	-----	-----	9125	8944	500	May 5
35	72	107	5	8	150000	-----	-----	11041	10573	1500	May 6
30	70	100	1	1	18000	-----	-----	3500	3500	300	May 7
6	14	20	1	6	150000	-----	-----	-----	-----	300	May 8
101	99	200	18	7	75000	-----	-----	8500	8600	2000	June 9
58	-----	58	58	2	45000	-----	-----	11000	9500	1100	June 10
37	48	85	-----	2	50000	-----	-----	15214	15494	75	May 11
57	123	180	-----	5	75000	-----	-----	6000	6000	1500	May 12
70	110	180	1	18	400000	$100000	$5000	49645	46203	4000	June 13
60	72	132	28	3	150000	-----	-----	30000	40000	3000	May 14
884	1250	2134	186	86	$1863000	$100000	$5000	$319701	$322612	19125	

NAME	When Founded	LOCATION	PRESIDENT OR PRINCIPAL	Instructors		
				Male	Female	Total
IV **ACADEMIC GRADE**						
1 Americus Institute	1897	Americus, Ga.	F. R. Lampkin, A. M.	3	4	
2 Baptist Industrial Academy	1903	Monroeville, Ala.	H. J. Lamar	4	3	
3 Bertie Academy 1	1895	Windsor, N. C.	W. S. Etheridge	3	5	ι
4 Bluestone-Harmony High School	1898	Keysville, Va.	M. C. Rux, D. D.	3	4	7
5 Central City College 1	1899	Macon, Ga.	Rev. J. H. Gadson	4	7	11
6 Columbia Baptist Academy	1888	Magnolia, Ark.	Wm. J. Brigham, A. B.	1	4	5
7 Consolidated-White River Academy	1893	Brinkley, Ark.	C. A. Gettis	2	5	7
8 Hartshorn Memorial College	1883	Richmond, Va.	Rev. David G. Mullison	1	8	9
9 Linden Academy	1903	Linden, Ala.	George P. Austin	1	4	5
10 Mather School	1868	Beaufort, S. C.	Miss Lydia Edgerly		10	10
11 Meridian Bap. Sem. 1	1897	Meridian, Miss.	G. M. Reese, Sc. B.	3	3	6
12 National Baptist Training School for Women and Girls	1909	Washington, D. C.	Miss Nannie H. Burroughs, A. M.		10	10
13 Nelson-Merry College 1	1893	Jefferson City, Tenn.	Rev. H. J. Bailey, A. B.	3	6	9
14 Northern Neck Industrial Academy 1	1898	Ivondale, Va.	W. B. Edelin, A. M.	2	2	4
15 Prairie Normal and Industrial Inst. 1	1903	Prairie, Ala.		2	7	9
16 Rappahannock Industrial Academy	1902	Ozeana, Va.	W. E. Robinson, Sc. B.	2	5	7
17 Roanoke Institute	1896	Elizabeth City, N. C.	C. F. Graves, A. M.	4	5	9
18 Smallwood-Corey Institute 1	1906	Claremont, Va.		1	4	5
19 St. John Industrial Institute	1906	R. 3, Austin, Tex.		6	5	11
20 Sylvia Bryant Bap. Institute	1907	Atlanta, Ga.	Rev. Charles M. Clayton, A. B.	4	4	8
21 Tidewater Institute	1908	Chesapeake, Va.	J. R. Custis, D. D.	2	9	11
22 Union Bap. Inst.	1881	Athens, Ga.	C. H. S. Lyons, A. B.	3	7	10
23 Walker Bap. Inst. 1	1888	Augusta, Ga.	P. A. Evans	3	10	13
24 West Virginia Industrial Seminary and College 1	1902	Hill Top, W. Va.	H. Walden, Ph. D.	1	4	5
25 Williams and Jones University	1928	Baltimore, Md.	Rev. James A. Fry	2	1	3
25 Academies				60	136	196
57 Institutions				283	391	674

1 Previous reports.
NOTE. Several institutions, mainly of academic grade, are not included in the foregoing list because of failure to report statistics for a period of more than two years.

Male	Female	Total	Students for the Ministry	No. of Buildings	Total Value of Property (not Including Endowment)	Amount of Endowment	Income from Endowment	Total Income Last Year	Total Expenses Last Year	Volumes in Library	Commencement
51	75	126	2	8	$48500	---	---	$15615	$15390	2000	May 1
93	120	213	2	6	8000	---	---	3500	3000	100	April 2
131	243	374	---	2	15000	---	---	8000	8000	1350	May 3
40	76	116	5	7	35000	---	---	10000	9100	700	May 4
64	60	124	26	3	67800	---	---	13690	13858	4000	May 5
35	90	125	2	2	12000	---	---	3500	3200	150	May 6
21	49	70	---	3	60000	---	---	5000	5000	500	May 7
---	151	151	---	4	120000	---	---	39535	42854	2950	June 8
108	114	222	1	3	10000	---	---	3501	3501	---	May 9
---	99	99	---	8	90000	---	---	23595	22391	2000	May 10
---	67	67	---	8	20000	---	---	5680	5680	300	May 11
---	120	120	---	8	175000	---	---	48500	48120	6000	June 12
44	88	132	12	2	19500	---	---	4673	4490	300	May 13
22	73	100	2	4	20000	---	---	5107	5113	100	May 14
52	62	114	2	4	16000	---	---	3014	3014	100	May 15
34	69	103	---	4	25000	---	---	6834	6981	600	May 16
47	104	151	5	4	50000	---	---	8000	8000	1000	May 17
25	14	39	4	6	10000	---	---	---	---	---	May 18
52	110	162	10	3	250000	---	---	---	---	---	June 19
45	75	120	11	4	18000	---	---	4800	4600	200	May 20
70	83	153	4	2	47500	---	---	14366	14366	300	May 21
108	160	268	4	3	38500	---	---	8000	11000	750	May 22
147	196	343	10	3	65000	---	---	11000	15000	300	May 23
43	20	63	25	2	25000	---	---	10000	10000	200	May 24
8	4	12	8	1	---	---	---	---	---	---	May 25
1240	2327	3567	135	104	$1245800	---	---	$255910	$262658	23900	
4557	6360	10917	882	367	$8043500	$1604447	$74744	$1637116	$1646434	129875	

451

BIBLIOGRAPHY

-A-

Almanac and Baptist Register (1841-60)
American Baptist Publication Society
American Baptist Year Book (1868-1930)
American Baptist Register (1833-52) ....
.... I.M. Allen and J. Lansing Burroughs
American Slavery Debate, W.G. Brownlow vs. Rev. A Pryne.
American Baptist Missionary Convention Report of 1859-1860

-B-

Baptist, The Encyclopedia (Two vol., 1881) . . William Cathcart, D.D.
Baptist, The: (1898) .... W.H. Boggs
Baptist Succession: (1873) .... D.B. Ray
Baptist in Alabama (1840) .... Hosea Holcombe
Baptist Annual Register (1790-1802) .... John Rippon, D.D.
Baptist Library .... Thos. Westlake
Baptist Message (1911)
Baptist History (1855) .... G.H. Orchard
Baptist Annual Register U. S. (1833) .... I.M. Allen
Baptist Register Triennial (1836) .... I.M. Allen
Baptist Register (1852) .... J. Lansing Burroughs
Baptist Heritage (1922) .... Geo. E. Horr, D.D., LL.D.
Baptist and Their Doctrines (1913) .... B.H. Carroll, D.D.

-C-

Century of Baptist Missions: (1901) .... A.H. Newman, D.D.
Century of Foreign Missions: (1901) .... Sophie Bronson Titterington
Cyclopedia Col. Baptist of the (1895) .... C.O. Booth, D.D.
Century Baptist Achievement (1901) .... H.N. Newman, D.D., LL.D.

-D-

Domestic Slavery (1845) .... Cor. Rt. Rev. Richard Fuller and
Rev. Francis Wayland

-F-

Fifty Years Among the Baptists (1859) .... David Benedict
First Colored Baptist Church in N. A. (1888) .... Jas. M. Simms

-G-

General History of Baptist Denomination in American--2 Vol. (1813)
.... David Benedict
General View of the Baptists in the Past.
General View of the Past.
God Against Slavery (1857) .... Geo. B. Cheever, D.D.

-H-

History of Negro Baptists in Mississippi (1898) .... P.H. Thompson
History of First Baptist Church (1888) .... E.K. Love
History of Baptists in Missouri (1882) .... R.S. Duncan
History of Louisiana Negro Baptists (1804-1914) ....
.... Wm. Hicks, A.B., D.D.
History of Baptists (1887) .... Thomas Armitage, D.D., LL.D.
History of Kentucky Baptists (1769-1885) .... J.H. Spencer
History of Baptists--New England (1894) .... Henry S. Burrage
History of General Baptists (1656-1896) 1896 .... Jas. W. Smith
History of Baptists East of Mississippi (1896) ...... Justin D. Smith,D.D.
History of Negro Church (1921) .... Carter G. Woodson

-J-

Journal of the American National Baptist Convention (1889-91) ....
.... William J. Simmons
Journal of the National Baptist Convention, U.S.A. (1895-1930)
Journal of The National Baptist Convention, Unincorporated
origin, (1915-1928).

-K-

Kentucky Baptist History (1922) .... W.D. Nowlen, D.D., LL.D.

-L-

Lectures on the Baptist History (1877) .... Wm. R. Williams

-M-

Minutes of the American Baptist Missionary Convention (1865) Men of
    Mark (1887).
Modern Baptist Heroes and Martyrs (1911) .... J.M. Prestridge, D.D.

My Baptism (1904) .... Jas. Mountain

-N-

National Baptist Magazine (Vol. 1-7) .... W. Bishop Johnson, D.D.

-O-

Our Baptist Ministers and Schools (1892) .... A.W. Pegues, Ph.D.

Outlines of Baptist History (1911) .... N.H. Pius, D.D.

-P-

Progress vs. Baptist Principle .... Thomas F. Curtis

People Called Baptist (1919) .... George McDaniels

-R-

Religious Instruction of Negroes (1843) .... Chas. C. Jones

Religious Development of Negroes in Virginia ....
.... Joseph B. Earnest, Jr., M.A.

Reminiscences of 30 Years' Labor in the South .... C.H. Corey, D.D.

-S-

Semple's History of the Rise and Progress of the Baptists--Va. ....
.... Rev. G.W. Beale (1810) Robert B. Semple.

Southern Baptists Working Together (1925) ....
.... E.P. Alldridge, A.M., Th.M., D.D.

Struggles and Triumphs of Religious Liberty (1851) ....
.... Edward B. Underhill, Esq.

-W-

What Baptists Believe (1913) .... O.C.S. Wallace, D.D., LL.D.

Why I Became a Baptist (1902) .... Madison C. Peters, D.D.

PATHFINDERS

They lived NOBLY; wrought MIGHTILY, and passed GLORIOUSLY to their reward.

SOME NEGRO BAPTIST PATHFINDERS

-A-

Rev. Allen Allensworth, D.D. Kentucky
Born - April 3, 1843. Louisville
The great children's preacher; U.S. Army Chaplain, promoter of education, presidential elector, orator of the highest order.

-B-

Rev. Joseph A. Booker, Arkansas
Born - December 26, 1859, Portland
Died - September 9, 1925
Preacher, educator, religious writer, President of Arkansas Baptist College, Secretary of the Home Mission Board.

Rev. Jesse F. Bolden, D.D., Mississippi
Born - October 8, 1820, Delaware
Scholar, preacher, editor, organizer of the Baptists of Mississippi Valley; member of the legislature and speaker of the House.

Rev. Horace N. Bouey, D.D., South Carolina
Born - 1849
Died - 1909, Liberia, Africa
One of the pioneers of the West Africa Foreign Mission among Negro Baptists.

Rev. Wm. Beckham, D.D., Texas
Field Secretary of the National Baptist Convention; preacher, rugged, built for endurance; did more to awaken National Baptist consciousness from coast to coast than any one since its organization.

Prof. John R. Blackburn, Ohio and Mississippi
Eminent Baptist teacher, grand secretary of the Grand Lodge F.A.M., and a great Sunday school worker and promoter of the Baptist churches in Ohio.

Rev. Richard H. Boyd, D.D., Texas
Man of great native ability, pleasing personality, great lover of his family; first corresponding secretary of the Home Mission Board, first corresponding secretary of the National Baptist Publishing Board of the National Baptist Convention.

Rev. E.M. Brawley, D.D., South Carolina
Born - March 18, 1851, Charleston
Baptist scholar, rare exegete; organizer of the Florida Baptist Academy and many churches.

Mrs. Peter James Bryant, Georgia
An educator, leader of Christian women, vice president of the Women's Convention, Auxiliary of the National Baptist Convention of the U.S.A., and a consecrated, forceful character for Christ.

Rev. Jacob R. Bennett, D.D., Pennsylvania
Dr. Bennett was reared in Mississippi; attended Roger Williams; pastored in Arkansas, Illinois, and Pennsylvania. He attained great prominence in Arkansas; was a well known figure in the National Baptist Convention and once served as recording secretary of the Foreign Mission Board. He died in St. Louis on a return trip from Arkansas to his home in Chester, Pa.

-C-

Rev. Dan W. Cannon, D.D., Georgia

Able preacher, one of the educational leaders of Georgia; president of the S.S. and B.Y.P.U. Congress of the National Baptist Convention; went early to his reward.

Rev. M.C. Clayton, Maryland

Founder of the First African Church of Baltimore, Md., a versatile genius, leader and organizer of great ability, and for whom a school is named in that city.

Rev. William A. Creditt, D.D., Pennsylvania

Born - July 14, 1864, Baltimore, Md.

Died - June 10, 1921 in Philadelphia,

Great preacher, pastor, and builder of Cherry Memorial Baptist Church of Philadelphia; educator, founder and president of Downing Industrial School; among the most eloquent men of his day.

-D-

Rev. George W. Dupree, D.D., Kentucky

Born - July 24, 1826, Gallatin County

Successful pastor, moderator of the General Association of Ky.; editor and Greek scholar; prominent member of the American Baptist Consolidated Convention that met at Nashville in 1867; a man of great power in forensic arena.

Rev. D. Webster Davis, D.D., Virginia

Preacher, educator, poet, philosopher, lecturer, outstanding leader of the new generation; died young.

Rev. Richard DeBaptiste, Illinois

Born - November 11, 1831

One of the early builders of the churches of the middle west; recording secretary of the Northwestern and Southern Baptist Convention; president of the Consolidated American Baptist Missionary Convention, which was the first effort to organize the Colored American Baptist family; a distinguished preacher, ripe scholar, thoughtful preacher, and withal a great man.

Miss Emma B. Delaney, Florida

Serving in Central and West Africa

Successful African missionary builder of schools in Africa. Did much to arouse and ----- -------- ---- --- African redemption, died in middle life at Fernandina, Fla.

Rev. William T. Dixon, D.D., New York

Veteran pastor of the Concord Baptist Church; president of the New England Baptist Convention, and early organizer of the first units of the National Baptist Convention.

-E-

Rev. P. S. Evans, Mississippi

Born - November 28, 1854, Columbus

Preacher, influential Mississippi leader, secretary of a Baptist Convention, promoter of Christian education.

-F-

Rev. Peter Fossett, Ohio

Born - June 6, 1816, Monticello, Va.

Died - January 4, 1910, Cincinnati

Said to be a grandson of Thomas Jefferson, President of the U.S.; Famous preacher and one of the fathers of Ohio Baptist, great exemplar, expounder, and disciplinarian.

-G-

Rev. Daniel A. Gaddie, D.D., Kentucky

Born - May 21, 1836
Died - 1912
A tower of strength in the Kentucky pulpit; moderator of the General Association.

Rev. Aaron R. Griggs, D.D., Texas

Born - 1850, Hancock Co., Ga.
Died - 1922
Distinguished pastor, leader of Texas Baptists; promotor of Christian education, prime mover in securing the cooperation of the Southern Baptist Convention in erecting and helping operate the American Baptist Theological Seminary at Nashville; a man whose prayer life was abiding.

Rev. Geo W. Gaylas, D.D., Mississippi

Born - June 29, 1844, Wilkinson County
Eminent preacher, president of the Mississippi State Convention; member of the Board of Police; and the last Colored state senator in the Mississippi Legislature.

Rev. Leonard A. Grimes, Massachusetts

Born - November 9, 1815, Leesburg, Va.
Died - Boston, Mass., March 14, 1873
Eminent Boston pastor, great in prayer, eloquent speaker, agent of the underground railroad, one of the organizers of the American Baptist Missionary Convention 1840 and the Consolidated Baptist Convention, 1866 the leading

spirit among the Colored Baptists of the North between 1846-1873.

Rev. Matt. W. Gilbert, D.D., Tennessee

Born - July 25, 1812, South Carolina
Died - March 9, 1917, Tennessee
Among those who founded the Live Oak Academy of Florida, successful pastor having filled some of the best pulpits in his native state; New York, and Tennessee; eloquent, learned, a great preacher and teacher of men.

-H-

Prof. Gregory W. Hayes, A.M., Virginia

Born - Amelia County
Died - December 22, 1906
Distinguished educator, thorough scholar, finished orator, able lay preacher, and exegete, builder and president of Virginia Theological Seminary and College; marvelous leader of men, and enthusiast, promoter of Negro Baptist publishing concern, a national leader of far-flung vision.

Rev. U. L. Houston, Georgia

Born - February, 1825, South Carolina
Pulpit orator, successful pastor, promoter of education, one of the organizers of the Georgia State Convention and vice president, member of the Georgia Legislature; powerful preacher; free from sensationalism but practical and direct.

-J-

Rev. H. P. Jacob, Mississippi

Born - 1825
Died - Oklahoma
Great organizer of churches, associations and the convention in that state.

Rev. Harvey Johnson, D.D., Maryland

Born - August 4, 1843, Fanquier County, Va.

Died - 1923

Eminent pastor; founder and promoter of Clayton Williams Academy; vice-president of the Ministers' Conference, and vice-president of Maryland Baptist State Convention of White and Colored Baptist churches; early advocate of Negro Sunday-school literature; organizer and supporter of all the departments of the National Baptist Convention, and one of the outstanding clergymen of his generation.

Rev. Caesar Johnston, North Carolina

Born - June 23, 1832, Warren County, Died - Raleigh, N.C., August 7, 1910

First president of the North Carolina state Convention; pastor of great power; promoter of education, always a conspicuous, outspoken, and loyal member of the National Baptist Convention.

Rev. Joseph E. Jones, D.D., Virginia

Born - October 15, 1850, Lynchburg

Distinguished scholar, teacher of homiletics, Greek and other subjects in Virginia Union University; corresponding secretary of the Baptist Foreign Mission Convention, one of the units that merged in 1895 making the National Baptist Convention. No man in his generation inspired more ministers to educate themselves, and more churches to help in the education of preachers, than he.

Rev. Peter Johnson, Georgia

Born - 1802, Augusta, Ga.

Member of the Springfield Church which is possibly the oldest Negro church on the continent, he pastored in Georgia and South Carolina. Was a blacksmith by trade. Died December 20, 1881.

Pioneer Baptist preacher, successful pastor, church builder, promoter of education; a long and successful pastorate; did great work for the Baptist churches in his day.

-L-

Rev. Geo. W. Lee, Washington, D.C.

A Baptist preacher of the first magnitude; a great pastor and national Baptist leader, brilliant, intellectual; a warm-hearted, overpowering preacher; always a friend to poor sorrowing Africa.

Rev. Lucas M. Luke, D.D., Texas

Born - July 12, 1857, Caddo Parish, La.

Died - December 31, 1895

Gifted preacher; first corresponding secretary of the Foreign Mission Board of the National Baptist Convention, as now organized; loved Africa, and did much, in those far-off days, to awaken the country to African missions.

Rev. Emanuel K. Love, D.D., Georgia

Born - July 27, 1850, near Marion, Ala.

Eloquent preacher, successful pastor of the First Baptist Church of Savannah, with ---- --- --- --- --- Georgia Central, and an early advocate of publishing Negro Sunday-school literature; a great leader of men.

Rev. C.H. Lyons, Georgia

Born - June 2, 1854, Marion, Ala.

Pastor, educator, promoter of Christian education; corresponding secretary of the Georgia Baptist State Convention; intellectual, proficient in Latin, Greek, and Hebrew, well balanced, pious, eloquent and one of the noblest characters produced in Georgia.

-M-

Rev. Elias C. Morris, D.D., Arkansas

Born - May 7, 1855,
Murray County, Ga.
Died - September 5, 1922

Distinguished president of the National Baptist Convention from 1895 until his death; for a long time pastor of Centennial Baptist Church at Helena; a great pastor; Christian statesman; business man, and the most distinguished and greatest beloved leader of Colored Christians in the world, in his generation.

Rev. Andrew Marshall, Georgia

One of the most eminent, pious, God-like men that ever lived. Great pastor, evangelist, and Georgia leader. Addressed the Legislature of Georgia during the dreadful days of slavery; a man with a splendid library, and well-posted.

Rev. Nelson G. Merry, Tennessee

One of the leading spirits who organized Northern Colored Baptists with a view of having them function nationally; helped organize the American Baptist Missionary Convention in which the other district conventions consolidated; successful pastor of Spruce Street Baptist Church, Nashville. Deeply pious, highly respected; a towering national figure.

-P-

Rev. Wesley G. Parks, D.D., LL. D., Tennessee and Pennsylvania

President of National Baptist Convention, one of the leading pastors in the country, public spirited, outstanding leader of the National Baptist Convention.

Rev. William R. Pettiford, Alabama

Born - January 20, 1847, Granville Co., N.C.

Successful pastor, leading trustee of Selma University, and banker.

Rev. Rufus L. Perry, Ph. D., New York

Able editor, ethnologist, essayist, logician, profound student of Negro history, eminent Greek, Latin, and Hebrew scholar, and early organizer of Colored American Baptists.

Rev. James Poindexter, D.D., Ohio

Minister of the Gospel, great advocate of human rights, director of Bureau of Forestry of Ohio, member of Board of Education, City of Columbia, early organizer of Baptists of the Middle West.

Rev. Randall Pollard, Mississippi

Pioneer in the Baptist ministry of Mississippi. During the Civil War kept the mixed White and Colored church alive when Whites began to abandon them at Natchez.

Rev. Charles L. Puree, D.D., South Carolina, Alabama and Kentucky

Born - 1856

President of Selma University, Selma, Alabama, and Simmons University; a painstaking scholar, excellent preacher and organizer.

Rev. Nathaniel H. Pius, A. B., D.D.

Born - Texas
Died - Tennessee

Graduate of Bishop College. He became a great teacher and preacher and was a good singer - serving as chorister of the National Baptist Convention. He wrote, tho very small, the only history Negro Baptists ever had, "Outlines of Baptist History," prior to 1930.

-Q-

Rev. Frank Quarles, Georgia

Born - 1814, Virginia

Died - December 3, 1881

Pastor of Friendship Baptist Church, Atlanta. Under his leadership Friendship Church became the birthplace and the first home of Spelman Seminary, one of the best girl schools serving our group. Outstanding leader of Georgia Baptists. Moderator of Ebenezer Baptist Association, and president of the State Convention.

-R-

Rev. L.M. Robinson, Georgia

Successful pastor, powerful evangelist, church builder, leader of men. The type of man who has done marvelous work in building up Baptist churches in all parts of our country.

-S-

Rev. William J. Simmons, D.D., LL. D., Kentucky

Born - June 24, 1849, Charleston, S.C.

Died - October 30, 1890

Founder and president of Simmons University; organizer of the National Baptist Convention of America. One of the ablest preachers of the race in his day. Learned, eloquent, organizer of men and an outstanding educator.

Rev. Wallace Shelton, Ohio

Born - Virginia

Died - Cincinnati

Organizer of the Colored Baptists of Ohio. Organizer and pastor of Zion Baptist Church, Cincinnati. An outstanding leader among early Baptists of the country.

Rev. Charles Stewart, D.D., Illinois

Born - May 28, 1869, Frankfort, Ky.

Preacher, lecturer, widely known newspaper man, the finder of men. An outstanding national news reporter - known from coast to coast.

Rev. Andrew J. Stokes, D.D., Alabama

Born - July 25, 1858, Orangeburg County, S.C.

Died - September, 1924, Los Angeles, Calif.

Great pastor of First Baptist Church of Montgomery; birthplace of organized work of Negro Baptist; treasurer of the National Baptist Convention.

Rev. Richard Spiller, D.D., Virginia

Died - March 23, 1929, Durham, N.C.

Leading pastor, organizer of Virginia Baptist State Convention; one of the 151 persons who organized our work in Montgomery in 1880; promoter of education; practical, outstanding and upstanding Baptist preacher.

-T-

Rev. Wm. H. Tillman, Georgia

Born - January 6, 1830, South Carolina

Successful pastor of the great Wheat Street Baptist Church; brilliant orator, moderator of Ebenezer Association, promoter of education, denominational and Bible doctrine.

Rev. James T. Tolbert, Georgia

Born - May 28, 1830, Augusta

Successful -- -- -- -- -- preacher before the war, moderator of the Storm Branch Association of South Carolina.

Rev. E.B. Topp, D.D., Mississippi

Born - April 7, 1858, Shannon

Died - January, 1925

Successful pastor Farris Street Baptist

Church; for a short time an African missionary; promoter of Christian education; president of his State Convention.

Rev. Wm. Troy

Was among the first missionaries sent to the South by the American Baptist Missionary Convention. He went from St. Louis to Mississippi in the wake of the Union soldiers before the Civil War closed. He was regarded as a powerful preacher, an organizer and could win and hold men. He finally settled to pastoring the Second Baptist Church in Richmond, Virginia. Through some misunderstanding he withdrew from the church and organized the Moore Street Church. He was again re-called to the Second Church and again withdrew and organized the Sharon Baptist Church.

Rev. D.A. Townsend, D.D., Tennessee

Born - September 27, 1848, Franklin County

Died - December 23, 1927, Winchester, Tennessee

Dr. Townsend was one of the early educated ministers of the group. He pastored for fifty years, and during the same time taught school and served as clerk for the Elk River Association. He was the father of Dr. A.M. Townsend, Secretary of the Sunday School Board.

-V-

Rev. Michael Vann, D.D., Tennessee

Born - April 5, 1860, West Tennessee
Died - July, 1897

One of the country's ablest pastors; promoter of education; president of the American National Baptist Convention, and a public spirited citizen of great power in his day.

Rev. Randall B. Vandarvell, D.D., Tennessee

Born - 1832, Neeley's Bend
Died - December 1899

Successful self-made man; promoter of education; president of State Sunday School Convention, and of the State Convention; died in selecting place for Roger Williams University; one of the fathers of Tennessee Baptists.

-W-

Booker T. Washington, LL. D., Alabama

Born - April 18, 1856, Franklin County, Va.

Clerk 1st Baptist Church, Malden, W. Va. Founder and Principal of Tuskegee Normal School; lay preacher; loyal promoter of the National Baptist Convention, and principal speaker at each session for a number of years. An American leader in industrial education, and organizer of the Negro Business League.

Rev. John H. Washington, N.C.

First state missionary; did much to organize and unify the Baptists in North Carolina.

Rev. Charles T. Walker, D.D., LL. D., Georgia

Considered the greatest Negro preacher of modern times. He traveled all over America and a considerable portion of Europe; preached in some of the greatest churches in the world. A successful pastor; moderator of the Western Union Association, and the Walker Baptist Association; founder and promoter of the Walker Baptist College; promoter of the Y.M.C.A. movement in New York for Colored men.

Rev. Jas T. White, Arkansas

Born - August 25, 1837, New Providence, Indiana

Successful pastor of First Baptist Church, Helena; organizer of the Missionary Baptist Convention; editor; commissioner of public works; State Senator, and an eloquent preacher.

Rev. Edward D. White, D.D., M. D., South Carolina

General State Missionary; one of the founders of Morris College at Sumter; did as much for the Baptists of his state, as any man of his day and generation; beloved by everybody.

Rev. S. E. J. Watson, D.D., Illinois

Born - Texas

Successful pastor of Pilgrim Baptist Church of Chicago; Chairman of Board of Evangelism of the National Baptist Convention, and writer for the B.Y.P.U. An eloquent, outstanding character among the younger men, who went all too early to his reward.

Rev. Sampson White, Pennsylvania

Born - Virginia

One of the ablest preachers of his day; successful pastor, and a great organizer. His ministry extended over a long period of many states.

Rev. Geo. W. Williams, LL. D., Ohio

Eminent Negro Historian, author of world-wide reputation; his two volume History of the American Negro is the most extensive and widely consulted work of its kind yet written. He was a judge; advocate of the Grand Army of the Republic; minister to Haiti; novelist; scholar; magnetic orator, editor, soldier, traveler and preacher.

Rev. Henry Williams, Georgia

Born - December 10, 1843, Georgia

Great evangelist, preached in all parts of Georgia, Alabama, and many of the western states; took a leading part in building up the denomination in his state and country.

Thirty-sixth Anniversary of the National Baptist Convention held in Savannah, Georgia, 1916

Across the years God has led us to our Fiftieth Anniversary

THE BRITISH
OF THE
SECOND WORLD WAR

Angus Konstam

SHIRE PUBLICATIONS

SHIRE PUBLICATIONS
Bloomsbury Publishing Plc

PO Box 883, Oxford, OX1 9PL, UK
1385 Broadway, 5th Floor, New York, NY 10018, USA
Email: shire@bloomsbury.com

SHIRE is a trademark of Osprey Publishing, a division of
Bloomsbury Publishing Plc

First published in Great Britain in 2013 by
Shire Publications

A CIP catalogue record for this book is available from the
British Library.

Shire Library no. 739.   ISBN-13: 978 0 74781 237 1

Angus Konstam has asserted his right under the Copyright,
Designs and Patents Act, 1988, to be identified as the
author of this book.

Designed by Tony Truscott Designs, Sussex, UK
Typeset in Perpetua and Gill Sans.
Printed and bound in India by Replika Press Private Ltd.

19 20 21 22 23   10 9 8 7 6 5 4 3

COVER IMAGE
A Royal Navy officer using a sextant aboard a destroyer
on convoy protection duties, 1942. (IWM TR 92)

TITLE PAGE IMAGE
A bugler sounding a call on board the battleship *King
George V*, pictured in November 1942, while the flagship
of the Home Fleet was lying at anchor in Scapa Flow.
(IWM TR 307)

CONTENTS PAGE IMAGE
Gunners manning a 4-inch gun on board a lend-lease
'Town' class destroyer, engaged in convoy escort work.
For the gun crews, this often meant spending long hours
at their cold, exposed action stations.

ACKNOWLEDGEMENTS
Pictures are acknowledged as follows:

Imperial War Museum: cover image, title page and
pages 6, 16, 26, 38, 40, 42, 52 and 53; Orkney Library
and Archive: pages 20 (top), 29 (top), 37 (bottom) and
50 (bottom); Peter Newark Picture Library, page 28
(bottom).

All other photographs are from the Stratford Archive.

IMPERIAL WAR MUSEUM COLLECTIONS
Some of the photos in this book come from the Imperial
War Museum's huge collections which cover all aspects
of conflict involving Britain and the Commonwealth since
the start of the twentieth century. These rich resources
are available online to search, browse and buy at www.
iwmcollections.org.uk. In addition to Collections Online,
you can visit the Visitor Rooms where you can explore
over 8 million photographs, thousands of hours of moving
images, the largest sound archive of its kind in the world,
thousands of diaries and letters written by people in
wartime, and a huge reference library.
To make an appointment, call (020) 7416 5320,
or eMail: mail@iwm.org.uk.
Imperial War Museum: www.iwm.org.uk

Shire Publications is supporting the Woodland Trust, the UK's leading woodland conservation charity, by funding the dedication of trees.

CONTENTS

INTRODUCTION

A cheerful Able
Seaman manning
the twin 0.5-inch
machine-gun turret
of a motor
torpedo boat
(MTB-24), pictured
in Dover during
1942. Ratings in
Coastal Forces
craft had to
perform a wider
range of tasks than
their counterparts
on larger vessels.

IN 1939 THE ROYAL NAVY was suffering from decades of cutbacks and government parsimony. Then the Second World War came, and the service had to cope with a dramatic expansion in both the size of the fleet and the level of naval manpower. By 1945 over a million men and women had served in the Royal Navy – more than double the number who answered the navy's call during the First World War. By the war's end the Royal Navy was the largest and most powerful of Britain's armed forces.

The majority of these new recruits were 'hostilities only' sailors, most of whom had never been to sea before. They all had to be trained, both in the basics of service life, and in the specialist skills the navy required of its sailors. In return, they brought with them a fresh outlook and enthusiasm to the task, which in turn influenced the way the Royal Navy functioned. The old hands of the peacetime navy played their part in showing their new shipmates how things were done. Meanwhile experienced and trainee seamen alike were having to meet the needs of a new kind of naval warfare, fought against enemy aircraft and U-boats – threats that the peacetime Royal Navy had been ill prepared to meet.

Somehow these sailors – or those who survived – learned their trade with a relish that befitted the navy's reputation for quiet professionalism. These seamen endured the harsh conditions of the Arctic convoys, the unremitting air attacks in the Mediterranean, and the challenges posed by escort work in the Atlantic. They served on all kinds of warship, from stately battleships and aircraft carriers to lowly motor vessels too small to be given a proper name.

When called upon they fought the fires or tried to stop the flooding that could claim their ship, and, if that failed, they endured

Four crewmen line the stern of a motor gunboat, as their vessel returns to port after a patrol. In Coastal Forces, dress regulations were relaxed, and the thick off-white Coastal Forces' pullover was frequently worn.

the deadly aftermath as they fought for their own survival in oil-covered seas. Together they saw the long hard-fought war through to its conclusion, and in the process they lived up to the high reputation of a service that had a historic expectation of victory, regardless of the odds facing it. This book tells the story of these wartime sailors and reveals a little of their life and times through six years of unremitting war.

The crew of the 'Gem' class anti-submarine trawler *Cornelian*, pictured shortly after they had shot down a German bomber off Eddystone Lighthouse on 5 March 1942. This converted trawler was armed with a single 4-inch gun.

5

LEARNING THE ROPES

In THE AGE OF SAIL, recruitment into the navy was by way of the press gang or the prisons – very few sailors actually volunteered. This all changed with the introduction of steam power, and the attendant need for new skills other than the ability to 'hand, reef and steer'. From the mid-nineteenth century on, sailors were inducted into training establishments and taught the skills they needed in shore bases before they were sent to sea. Before the war sailors were first recruited as teenagers of fifteen or sixteen. They then served for twelve years from their eighteenth birthday. At this point they had the option of either leaving the service or re-enlisting for a further ten years, in order to qualify for a pension when they reached the age of forty.

New recruits were sent to boys' training establishments such as HMS *Ganges* in Suffolk. There the youngsters were first exposed to the rigours of naval discipline and were taught the basics of their new profession. One petty officer said of his early naval training: 'Imagine – fifteen years signed away by children unaware of life's meaning. Having procured the body, the service proceeds to divorce the mind of its natural environment, from every aspect of life apart from that of the naval service.' While some were eager volunteers, others were sent to the navy by their parents, or from orphanages.

Given the volatile economic climate of the inter-war years, the attraction of a guaranteed job for their sons was an attractive prospect for many parents, but not all recruits relished the prospect of a naval career. One seaman, speaking in 1941, claimed: 'Joined as a boy when I was fifteen ... My father shoved me in. I ain't forgiven the old bastard to this day!'

The routine in these establishments was notoriously harsh. One former sailor claimed that *Ganges* was worse than the prisons and Foreign Legion barracks he encountered after leaving the service. Over a third of all recruits were seamen. A fifth were stokers, who were aged eighteen to twenty-five when they joined up, as, at least in theory, their work required greater physical strength and stamina. The same age restrictions applied to recruits for the Royal Marines, for similar reasons.

Opposite:
A Petty Officer from HMS *Raleigh* near Plymouth, teaching new recruits the art of boat handling. It was felt that instruction in boatwork helped foster teamwork, professional pride and discipline. (IWM A 3141)

After basic training, these boy seamen were sent to their first ship, or sent for further training in one of a number of specialties, to become signalmen, telegraphists, writers, stewards, cooks or sick-berth attendants. Similarly, engineering artificers were selected from recruits who had already learned a mechanical trade before enlisting.

The war brought an end to this pre-war system of naval training – one that had changed little since the nineteenth century. The last intake of boy seamen was in 1940. By that time most new recruits were 'hostilities only' ratings, their numbers augmented by men drafted in from the Royal Naval Reserve. In May 1939 Parliament passed the Military Training Act, which introduced peacetime conscription for men aged twenty to twenty-one. On 3 September, when war broke out, this was replaced by the National Service Act, which expanded the age band of conscripts to include those aged eighteen to forty-one. By early 1942 the upper age bracket had been extended to forty-six. The result was a flood of potential naval recruits.

Teenage boy seamen, being instructed by a very experienced petty officer on board the battleship *King George V* in late 1940. This new battleship joined the Home Fleet in Scapa Flow on 11 December.

The main control deck in the engine room of a 'Queen Elizabeth' class battleship. While an engineering officer studies the gauges, an engineering artificer updates the engine-room log.

8

Conscripts were given the option to select the service they wanted to join. The navy then vetted these aspiring sailors and selected those with the best educational and physical qualifications. Potential recruits chose the navy for a variety of reasons: the chance to see early action, the promise of foreign travel, or even the desire to avoid the mud and blood of the trenches – still the popular perception of the way the army fought its battles. The musician George Melly opted for the navy because the uniform was 'more amusing'.

At first the vetting process was rudimentary, but by 1941 it had developed into a professional business, aimed at weeding out unsuitable candidates. Rejects were generally sent to join the army, which had lower educational requirements.

Once selected, recruits often waited for several months before they could be inducted into a naval training programme. When their orders came, they were sent a travel voucher for a one-way rail ticket and told to report to a training base. The delay early in the war was largely due to a shortage of training facilities. By 1940–1 new training bases had been opened, such as HMS *Royal Arthur*, established in a pre-war holiday camp run by Butlins.

Other bases included the pre-war establishment HMS *Ganges*, and HMS *Glendower*, built by Butlins for the navy in Pwllheli, North Wales. By the spring

A batch of new recruits, photographed on their arrival at the training base HMS *Royal Arthur*, a former holiday camp in Skegness. To judge by their age, these men are engineering rather than seaman entrants.

Wren aircraft
mechanics serving
in the Fleet Air
Arm rearm a Sea
Hurricane Mark I
with 0.303-inch
ammunition at
RNAS Yeovilton.
Wrens first took
on this important
role in late 1941.

of 1942 there were seventeen such establishments, including those used to train new ratings in the various specialties such as gunnery, signals or engineering.

Conditions varied considerably. George Melly, who was sent to *Royal Arthur*, described the way the navy transformed these holiday camps:

> Planned for the regimented pleasure of the Fair Isle jerseyed civilians of the late thirties, they needed no more than a few coats of drab paint and a whaler in the swimming pool to become wartime shore establishments. The redcoats were transformed into Petty Officers. The intercom system, through which the campers had been hi-de-hied to meals or jollied along to enter the knobbly knees competition, now barked out our orders.

In 1940 Ken Forrester from Lancashire was sent to HMS *Collingwood* near Portsmouth. His instructor was a petty officer who had seen action at the Battle of Jutland, brought back from retirement. Forrester described his experience:

> Through the next seven weeks we did route marches, workouts in the gymnasium, self defence, rope work, knots and splices, the rule of the road when sailing, such things as 'A close hauled ship you'll never see, give way

to one that's running free', 'Green to green, red to red, perfect safety go ahead', 'If upon your port is seen a steamer's starboard light of green, there's not so much for you to do as green to port keeps clear of you', and so the verses of safety went on.

We were also taken down to Portsmouth harbour for rowing instruction on 28-foot whalers with one man to each oar, followed by 32-foot cutters which needed two men to each oar. When you had done a few hours at that your poor arms didn't know what had hit them. We were taught naval terms such as 'fore' and 'aft', and 'stem' and 'stern' ('front' and 'back'), 'sheets' were ropes,

and dozens of other terms that we were to use in our daily work. Also taught was the build-up of a ship starting at the keel-hog-keelson and thereon up to the gunwales.

The time spent on basic training was reduced from almost four months to seven weeks. Then sailors progressed to learn a specialisation. A division into stokers and seamen had already been made. While some seamen remained unspecialised, most learned an additional skill, such as gunnery, signals or radar operation. In theory, the smartest entrants were selected for a more complex specialism, while those with less mental agility became gunners. In reality, seamen were drafted into the specialism that needed them most.

Leading ratings from each messdeck queue up for their mess rum ration. Half a gill was issued daily to all ratings over twenty, diluted by an equal measure of water. Non-commissioned officers drew their rum neat.

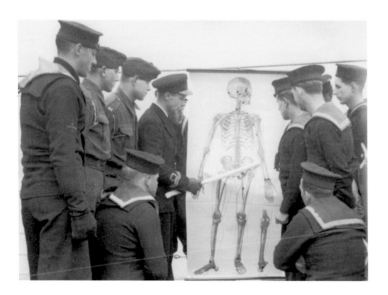

On board a cruiser a surgeon lieutenant gives a group of sailors and marines a lecture on first aid, which was considered an important part of shipboard training for all of a ship's company.

Trainee cooks attending a lecture on producing a roast meal at a Royal Naval training establishment near Portsmouth. The instructor appears to be an experienced petty officer cook.

To learn this skill, the sailors were sent to a new training base. Before the war gunnery training had been conducted on board operational warships, but in wartime that was not possible, as ships needed fully trained crews. HMS *Excellent* in Portsmouth was the principal gunnery school, although sea training was also provided on board a training ship based in the Clyde estuary.

Gunners were divided into three sub-groups – quarters ratings, layers and control ratings – each of which had a specific task to perform. Training was often done on obsolescent guns – the idea being that the principles of gunnery remained the same. Anti-aircraft gunnery was a new specialism, and this training included aircraft recognition as well as weapons training.

The Torpedo Branch ratings dealt with mines and depth charges as well as torpedoes; they included electricians as a sub-specialisation, as many of these systems were electrically operated. Another major specialism was the Communications Branch, whose training programme was followed by visual signallers and wireless telegraphists. Both specialist groups had to learn Morse code, but signallers waved flags and flashed signal lamps, while telegraphists sent and received wireless signals. The main training base for these communicators was HMS *Mercury* in Hampshire.

Radar and sonar (Asdic) operators were vital to the efficiency of a modern warship, but the number of trainees required was relatively small. After initial

Gunners inside one of the 16-inch gun turrets of a 'Nelson' class battleship perform routine maintenance checks on the turret's fully mechanised loading system. Such checks were vital to the smooth running of the guns.

training at *Mercury*, practical radar training was conducted on training craft vessels in the Irish Sea, while Asdic ratings trained in HMS *Osprey* or HMS *Nimrod* on the Clyde estuary.

While the Engineering Division was smaller than the Seaman Division in terms of naval manpower, the demands of the engineering specialisations were generally greater, and so specialist training tended to last longer. The greatest demand was for stokers. The name was a reminder of the days when warships were coal-fired. In 1939 stokers had to tend machinery rather than shovel coal. As stokers tended to be older than seaman recruits, they were more likely to think for themselves than their shipmates working topsides. Most took a pride in their engineering skills, and in their ship's machinery. A month of initial training was followed by six weeks of more detailed mechanical training in engines and boilers.

Those recruits who had previous skills or showed the most aptitude could be selected to become artificers, and competition for artificer places was steep. Once selected, these young men learned metalworking, so that they could repair machinery, and extensive theoretical and practical training in marine engineering and electrical engineering. Training lasted for four and a half years, both on land and on board ship. At the end of it most artificers emerged as highly skilled engineering petty officers.

Mechanicians were recruited from the ranks of stokers, after having served time at sea, and having shown a high degree of mechanical aptitude. They and engine-room mechanics learned advanced specialist skills, such as fitting and turning, welding or electrical wiring. Their training lasted for several months, but they emerged as useful engineers, with a practical approach that complemented the more academic skills learned by artificers. Finally there were artisans – men who had a useful peacetime skill, and who were encouraged to practise it in the navy. These men included plumbers, carpenters, painters and shipwrights. They entered as members of the Engineering Division but were diverted into their own category.

When a seaman had finished his basic training and his specialism training, he was ready to go to sea. The drafting notices were eagerly anticipated, and everyone had his own aspirations – for big ships, small ships, ships in home waters, or those serving overseas. Sometimes the choice necessitated additional

Radar operators manning a Type 279 air warning radar on board a British wartime cruiser. The development of new technologies meant that the navy required a new breed of technical specialists.

13

Almost a third of the ship's company of a warship usually comprised stokers or engine-room artificers. The badges of these two men indicate they are Stokers, 2nd Class.

An engineer petty officer and his assistant run diagnostic checks on the electrical equipment on board the submarine *Tribune* in 1942. As full uniform is being worn, the photograph must have been taken in port.

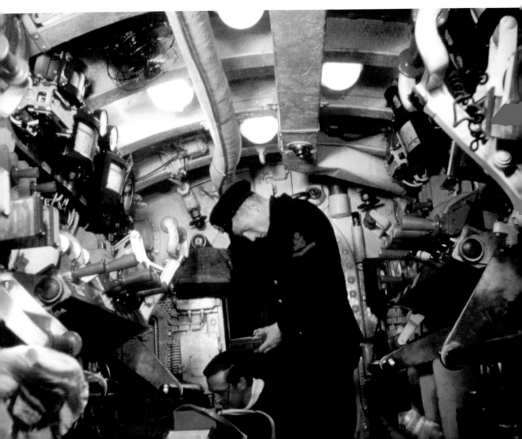

training – for instance, if the new sailor was earmarked for service in Coastal Forces, minesweepers or landing craft. After learning to be an anti-aircraft gunner, Ken Forrester received his posting:

> I got a 'draft chit' (posting) to HMS *St Christopher*, which was the Highland Hotel in Fort William, Scotland. It had been taken over by the Admiralty and was used as a training base for Coastal Forces. We went down the pier head every morning to be trained aboard Motor Launches (MLs) or Motor Torpedo Boats (MTBs) and Motor Gun Boats (MGBs). We trained on Loch Linnhe, Loch Eil and Loch Leven ... This went on until mid-January 1942, when a group of us were drafted to Manor Naval Barracks, Brightlingsea, Essex, where we remained a few days before being moved on to my first boat, which was a Harbour Defence Motor Launch (HDML).

By the time the newly trained rating was ready to join his first ship he probably thought he was a proper sailor. His new shipmates would soon disabuse him of this idea, pointing out that his training in the navy's wiles and ways had only just begun. At least, though, he was serving aboard an operational warship and was ready to play his part.

Nicknamed 'the Crab', this primitive contraption was used to train hundreds of Fleet Air Arm pilots during the war. After mastering the basics of flying on the machine, the trainee pilots would move on to real aircraft.

Naval ratings preparing their hammocks while being temporarily accommodated in the overcrowded naval barracks in Portsmouth. These barracks were used to house men waiting to join their ships.

15

BRITAIN'S SEA POWER

ARTHUR FERRIER

SUBMARINE CREW AT 'ACTION STATIONS' DURING AN ATTACK

IS YOURS!

LIFE ON BOARD

BEING SENT TO A NEW SHIP was not like a posting in the other services. A ship was a home, a community and a weapon of war, all rolled into one grey-painted package. In some ways life on board a warship was an abnormal one. It took people away from familiar surroundings, from women, and from their families. These all-male naval communities might comprise fewer than a dozen members, or be expanded into floating townships of 1,500 men. At sea the crew might remain isolated from the rest of the world for days, weeks or even several months at a time. The sailor had no option but to adapt to his environment, and to become an integral part of his ship's company. Until the Admiralty decreed it otherwise, this would be his home.

A sailor's future was determined by a drafting chit. Would he be sent to a battleship, a destroyer or a small escort vessel? Would he join the ship in Scapa Flow, Gibraltar or Portsmouth? Experienced sailors took the news in their stride. For instance, in September 1939 Stoker Frederick Wigby was at home in Kent when he switched on the radio and heard 'Mr Chamberlain announce that we were at war with Germany ... Next day the drafting office informed me I would be going to a new corvette ... I just had time to say goodbye to my wife and son.'

Elsewhere, the news that Britain was at war was received with mixed emotions. In Scapa Flow sailors of the Home Fleet heard Chamberlain's announcement broadcast over their ships' loudspeakers. Ships at sea received the news by telegram. On the destroyer *Firedrake*, the crew 'were all crowded around the loudspeaker, listening to the old boy's speech. When it finished somebody said "About bloody time too!" That was all.' This attitude was typical. Sub-Lieutenant Marwood of the destroyer *Antelope* recalled:

> We were at Portland when we received the message: 'Special telegram TOTAL GERMANY', which meant we were at war with Germany. I have to admit that those of us who had just completed all our basic training as naval officers would have been very disappointed had war not been declared.

Opposite:
The public image of the wartime Royal Navy was one of a thoroughly professional force, trained to perform their often dangerous job with skill, dedication and a sense of humour.
(IWM PST 14012)

Off Milford Haven the destroyer *Walpole* was dropping depth charges on a possible enemy U-boat within ten minutes of receiving the Admiralty's telegram.

For many sailors the routine of wartime life soon established itself. Conditions could be basic, especially in the smaller ships of the fleet. Newly trained stoker William Stonebridge recalled the conditions on board the destroyer escort *Stevenstone*:

Sailors relaxing in a messdeck on board an aircraft carrier. During 1944–5 the *Pacific Post* was the newspaper of the British Pacific Fleet and contained news from home as well as operational updates.

The Stokers' Mess was underneath the Seamen's, which was reached by descending an iron ladder. That mess-deck was your home. You had your meals there, you slept there, and you wrote your letters there. There were lockers round the outside of the mess in which you stored your belongings and, having cushions on top, served as seats. In front of the lockers were four wooden tables, two each side of the mess-deck bolted to the floor, from which you ate your meals, wrote your letters, and the same as the lockers, slept on. You used your hammock if you were going to get a whole night's sleep. Namely, if not watch-keeping or if you were on day work. There were bars running across the top of the mess to use when you slung your hammock and were suspended from the ceiling very comfortably. Space aboard ship was very cramped but like everything else, you got used to it.

Others would have considered this luxurious. During the Arctic convoys, Seaman Charles Reeve discovered that hammocks were a luxury on his cruiser.

My most vivid memories are of not being able to sling hammocks, which normally you would sleep in in harbour. This was for damage control reasons. People wouldn't want to be bumping into hammocks while they were trying to plug a hole, to put it crudely. So you had to sleep on the deck, which was up and under and all over the place. Our ship was a fairly new one, but even then you were sleeping in water and in the case of communications ratings, you weren't issued with anoraks or heavy clothing as you needn't go on the upper decks, so you just tossed up which end of you would be warm, your feet or your head. It's even true to say that breathing was difficult; sitting and lying was certainly difficult in those conditions.

The division of the ship's company into messes was a feature of naval life that Nelson would have recognised. In the age of fighting sail, a mess centred around the crew of a gun, who ate, slept and spent their leisure time beside

On warships escorting the Arctic convoys, ice had to be regularly removed from the superstructure, in order to keep the ship functioning effectively. Inevitably this involved attacking the ice with picks and axes.

Most wartime messdecks were cramped, and sailors had to adapt to living in close proximity to each other, making the most of their quarters for both sleeping and spending their off-duty time.

their gun, where a mess table could be slung. In the Second World War navy messes were usually divided by specialisation, with stokers, seamen and various other sub-divisions of the ship's company each having its own messdeck. The larger the ship, the more specialist the messdeck composition became. Artificers, petty officers and chief petty officers had their own messes, while officers tended to have their own cabins.

Usually, a mess comprised twelve to sixteen men, while boy seamen messed separately, under the supervision of a petty officer. A typical mess comprised a deal table with wooden benches, at right angles to the ship's side, a rack for crockery and clothes lockers, and another for ditty boxes, where the ratings stored their private possessions. The men slept in hammocks slung over their messes. During daytime these hammocks were lashed up and stowed in racks. There was no privacy in this environment, and, unlike in the peacetime navy, these wartime messes often contained men of a wide range of ages, intelligence and backgrounds. All had to get along with each other, for the good of the mess.

Seamen quickly learned to recognise difficult or aggressive types, and to deal with them accordingly. The author Tristan Jones described his berth on board the destroyer *Obstinate*:

> My mess was the after seamen's mess ... They were a crowd of the finest men I ever came across in my life, for all their personal peccadilloes ... I soon got to know all 15 men in my mess very well, and sorted out those to cultivate and the ones to – not to avoid – there was no such possibility on a crowded ship – slide by.

The cartoonist for *The Hatston Chronicle* putting the finishing touches to his latest work, for inclusion in the service newspaper. This young seaman and amateur artist served in HMS *Sparrowhawk*.

After accommodation, the next most important thing for most sailors was food. In larger ships, from light cruisers upwards, or in submarines, a 'general messing system' was in operation. All cooking and washing up

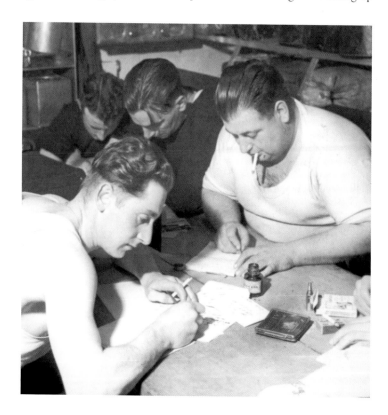

Sailors on board the small 'Hunt' class destroyer escort *Garth* write letters home during their off-duty hours. They sit at their crowded mess table, one of the few spaces available for such activities.

was centralised. Food was prepared in a galley, fitted out with all the equipment and utensils the cooks needed. When cooked, the food was passed down to a serving room in a lift. From there, it was sent out to the various messes, by means of a duty messman, chosen by rota. The men ate at their mess tables, and after the meal the duty messman washed up in the scullery adjacent to the serving room. Artificers, senior ratings and officers ate in their own dining areas, messdecks or in the wardroom.

The diet tended to be repetitive, and because of shortages portions were less generous than many would have liked. A typical day's meals would include a breakfast of tea, toast and butter, and then a lunch of meat, potatoes

The crew of the submarine *Trump* return to port after a successful patrol. Dress regulations on board submarines were lax, but many of these young men have made an effort to smarten up before entering port.

A senior rating – probably a petty officer cook – supervises the production of a meal on board a large warship, assisted by two cooks, and a pair of young sailors drafted in as pot-scrubbers.

A seaman fulfilling his regular obligation to his mess by peeling their ration of potatoes. In small ships each mess was responsible for its own cooking. Illustration by Roger Furse.

and vegetables, finished off with tinned fruit or a pudding. Afternoon tea consisted of tea, bread and jam, while supper took the form of sausage, egg and chips. On Sundays this evening meal was replaced with a salad. According to one sailor, the cabbage was often tough and overcooked, and the potatoes were invariably fried. Tinned food also lost its appeal after a few weeks. Still, wartime sailors ate reasonably well compared to civilians, whose food was strictly rationed.

On smaller ships or older vessels a 'Standard Ration and Messing' system was used. Here, the navy supplied the basic (standard) rations such as meat and potatoes, and a messing allowance. This allowance was paid to each mess, who in turn had to buy their own provisions, and cook their own meals. The cooking

ability of the seamen was not taken into consideration. A wartime sailor recalled how the system worked: 'Each mess subtracts two of its members in rotation, who, during the forenoon watch clean the place and prepare the food, cutting up meat, cleaning vegetables, making pastries…' The food was then taken from the mess table to the ship's galley, where it was cooked and then served. The results were not always of the highest quality, but most sailors soon learned to produce safe, basic food without messing things up too much.

Cooks preparing the evening meal on board a British warship. In larger ships, from cruisers up, a general messing system was used, where meals were prepared centrally. On smaller ships each mess was responsible for its own cooking.

On the destroyer *Beagle*, Seaman Ken Slee experienced this form of messing, and he highlighted the problem that arose when the messes did not have an opportunity to replenish their food supplies. At one stage in 1940 his mess

> … only had corned beef, potatoes and carrots left and his mess men decided to make a stew so that it would go further. A young recruit was given the job and was instructed to make it in the heavy mess pot. All went well until he put dough-boys into it – he added too many – and the whole of it became one solid mass, like a stone! He said to Ken 'What shall I do with it?' The answer was 'Ditch it', which he did. The language in the mess can well be imagined – no stew and no pot.

Conditions were even worse on the small escorts that protected the transatlantic convoys. On the destroyer *Bulldog*

> … the worst thing of all was our bread supply. First the crusts went green, which wasn't too bad because we could cut the crusts off. Then the inside of the bread started going green. This we covered with jam and pretended it wasn't there.
>
> After a while, when the bread really was inedible, we had to go onto what is known in the services as hardtack. This is a form of biscuit, just like a dog biscuit, and as long as your teeth were good you had no problem eating them – and if you had a cup of tea you could always dunk them to soften them up.

Sailors visiting the NAAFI canteen of HMS *Bellona*, while the light cruiser was escorting an Arctic convoy in 1944. This tiny shop sold a range of essentials, from razor blades and shaving cream to boiled sweets and soft drinks.

The crowded messdeck of a destroyer in rough seas, where, despite the crowded and spartan conditions, the sailors had to 'slide along' with their shipmates for months at a time. Illustration by Roger Furse.

Besides running out of bread, our meat supply had also been diminished, so we had to go onto another good old standby – tins of corned beef. These were 7 pounds in weight and were issued at one tin per mess (about twelve men's rations). We also had tins of sardines, which helped to

give us a variety of food and vitamins, powdered milk, and vegetables that included tinned carrots and dried haricot beans and peas which needed to be soaked overnight.

Despite all these privations, most sailors thrived in their new wartime environment. They enjoyed a sense of purpose, and a camaraderie that was unknown in civilian life. Above all, they felt they were playing their part, regardless of their role on board. Unlike in the army or air force, the entire ship's company of a warship goes to war together, and shares the same risks. Cooks, stewards, writers, signallers and stokers form just as important a part of a ship's company as the gunners and torpedo men who actually fired at the enemy. All hands were needed to save the ship if it was damaged – to shore up flooding, extinguish fires or run emergency power cables. On board a warship, everyone was in it together.

In large ships such as the battleship *Rodney*, the issue of the daily rum ration was a solemn occasion, supervised by junior officers, petty officers and marine NCOs. Each measure is carefully poured into a waiting mess can – one for each mess on board the battleship.

BACK THEM UP

A CRUEL SEA

THE ROYAL NAVY was used to fighting wars on a global scale. It had strategic interests in the Mediterranean, in the Atlantic and Indian oceans, and in the Far East. It maintained gunboats on China's Yangtze river, and cruisers based in the Caribbean. Towards the end of the war it created a Pacific Fleet, which fought alongside the US Navy during the climax of the war against Japan. The bulk of the fleet, however, was divided between the Mediterranean Fleet and the forces operating in home waters.

It was the Home Fleet that bore the responsibility for defending Britain's shores from attack, and for safeguarding the fragile lifeline of Atlantic convoys that helped keep Britain in the war. Later, the Home Fleet fought to protect the Arctic convoys, which demonstrated Allied solidarity and helped the Soviet Union repulse the German invaders. While losing control of the Mediterranean would have been a strategic setback, doing the same in home waters would have brought about Britain's defeat. Put simply, the Home Fleet was Britain's greatest wartime line of defence.

The Home Fleet was based in Scapa Flow, the same anchorage in Orkney used by the Grand Fleet during the First World War. When the war began the defences of Scapa Flow were completely inadequate. A small eastern entrance to Scapa Flow had still not been blocked on 14 October 1939, when U-47 slipped through the channel on the surface and fired its torpedoes at the unsuspecting battleship *Royal Oak*.

Stoker Herbert Johnson recalled the attack:

> At about 1 o'clock in the morning there was a phenomenal explosion – it really terrified me – and I went up to go to my action station ... We were in harbour so nobody would believe it was a torpedo.

Then, fifteen minutes later, there was another great eruption.

> We'd been hit by another torpedo, and started to list right away ... I went on the deck ... and by that time it was obvious she had leaned over quite

Opposite:
The Admiralty was well aware that the Royal Navy depended on the heartfelt support of the British people, and campaigned to maintain public awareness of the importance of the service. However, despite the impression given in this poster, large-scale fleet actions were a rarity. (IWM PST 14874)

a bit, and I thought 'What will I do now?' I noticed that an officer went over to the ship's side ... and he slid into a boat that was tied there (called a picket boat). So I followed him, and I slid down into the picket boat and watched the *Royal Oak* roll over.

Johnson was one of the lucky ones. Over two-thirds of her 1,234-man crew were lost when the battleship sank.

Wren ratings staffing the plotting table in the operations room of HQ Western Approaches, which from 1941 was based in Liverpool. The WRNS played a vital part in the smooth operation of this key naval headquarters.

A depth charge detonating astern of an escort during an anti-submarine action. Operating depth charge launchers on the pitching, rolling deck of a small escort vessel was extremely hazardous work.

The Home Fleet abandoned Scapa Flow until the defences of the anchorage were strengthened. It returned in March 1940 and soon Scapa was a bustling naval base, protected by a ring of anti-aircraft guns, anti-submarine defences and coastal batteries. It remained the Home Fleet's base throughout the war. While Scapa Flow may have been a well-placed strategic base for the navy, it was an unpopular posting for many of the sailors who had to spend much

of their war based there. An airman posted to Orkney recalled meeting a sailor on the ferry crossing from the Scottish mainland:

> I sat on deck somewhere near the prow of the ship, and a sailor returning from leave sat next to me. He hated the Orkneys; he hated that bloody Scapa Flow which was the reason for his being sent there; he'd rather be anywhere than in the bloody Orkneys; he was going to see his CO and ask for a Middle East posting; he'd rather go without leave than be up here. Life up

Sailors from the battleship *Royal Oak* leaving the ship for a run ashore in Kirkwall. This photograph was taken on 13 October 1939, the day before the battleship was sunk in Scapa Flow by U-47, with the loss of 833 of her crew.

In 1942, during Captain's Rounds on board the battleship *Rodney*, the Master-at-Arms checks the crew ten paces ahead of the captain, hoping to deal with any problems of dress or deportment before the captain can see them.

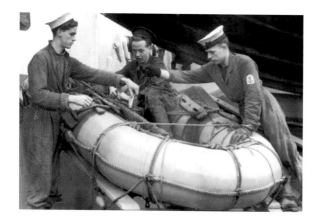

Seamen securing a Carley float during preparations for putting to sea. The sailor on the right is a leading seaman, and therefore the man responsible for supervising this mundane but essential task.

here was too bloody lonely, too bloody meagre, too bloody cold! He broke down and cried. Nonplussed, amazed and innocent, I offered him my only bar of chocolate.

The trouble was that many warships remained at anchor in Scapa Flow for months on end, and their crews rarely had the chance to visit other ships, or to go ashore. Even if they did, the delights of shore were limited: overcrowded bars where beer was rationed, a NAAFI, and a cinema or theatre where tickets were hard to get. Few sailors would have shared the opinion of a Wren stationed in the Orkney naval base of Lyness:

> To me this lonely outpost was sheer magic ... My main memory is of the sheer beauty of the lonely islands, the lovely colours of the hills, the rare wild flowers, and seabirds and seals which followed me around my coastal walks, and above all the kindly, friendly local crofters.

It was from Scapa Flow that the fleet sailed to hunt down the *Bismarck*, to escort merchant convoys to Murmansk, and to help Atlantic convoys fight

A Royal Marine band and a naval colour party are drawn up on the quarterdeck of HMS *King George V*, during a wartime visit to Scapa Flow by King George VI.

The crew of a multi-barrelled 2-pounder 'pom-pom', pictured during an Arctic convoy. The manning of upper-deck weapons of this kind was a cold and often tedious duty, but a vital one.

The bridge crew of a destroyer keep a wary eye out for German dive bombers while approaching Dunkirk in late May 1940. For many sailors the air attacks experienced off Norway and Dunkirk provided a first experience of combat.

their way through the waiting packs of German U-boats. For many 'hostilities only' ratings, their first taste of action came in April 1940, when the Germans invaded Norway. The British and French sent troops to support the Norwegians, but within weeks they had to be evacuated. In the process the warships that served as makeshift troop transports had to run the gauntlet of enemy air attacks.

In the confined waters of the Norwegian fjords it seemed as if the German dive bombers could attack without warning. A junior officer from the destroyer *Walker* wrote: 'I must say, I would rather be on land for a raid than in a ship. One feels so naked and exposed on the upper deck, and unable to dodge, and also one knows that the plane is attacking *you*.'

In the light cruiser *Carlisle* Able Seaman Hutchison described the experience in more detail:

A petty officer – the 2nd Coxswain – operating the forward hydroplane controls in the control room on board the submarine *Tribune*. He wears a typical submariner's jersey.

All one could hear was the powerful engines of the plane diving flat out through the low clouds and over the mountain top. It seemed to fill the whole sky. I then looked death — stark death — in the face for the first time in my life. I saw it release two wicked-looking black bombs. They seemed small at first and then they got larger and larger... I don't know if I was petrified or what, but I kept on looking.

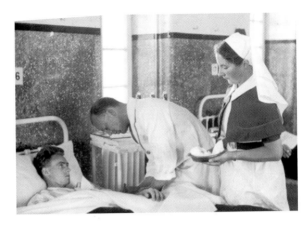

A young sailor is tended by medical staff in a wartime naval hospital in Malta. Although today these facilities might look spartan, naval hospitals were well equipped and staffed.

He watched as the bombs overshot the ship and splashed in the fjord, sending up cascades of water. That day the crew of the *Carlisle* endured a relentless six hours of near-constant air attacks.

A few weeks later, sailors experienced the same ordeal off the beaches of Dunkirk. Seaman Gordon Bonny was on board the destroyer *Worcester* when she came under air attack on her way home:

We are steaming up a narrow fairway, loaded to capacity and doing eight knots on one screw. Stukas hang above us like a flock of vultures. I look up and astern, a mass of them is coming into attack. We open fire, and, from that moment on, all I see is the breech in front of me, together with the loading numbers of the gun crew.

Stukas scream, and so do the bombs, and we've got several alongside. All hell is let loose again. The pongos [soldiers] are having a go with rifles and bren-guns. Gunner's mate is riddled with shrapnel and has collapsed down the ladder. His broken pipe lies at my feet. I think to myself, 'This is it. We can't come out of this lot.' My trainer, an LR3 from Pompey, has rolled off his seat. His guts are ripped open, and he looks a goner. A shell is being rammed home when a chunk of shrapnel smashes the handle into two parts. Ginger, the starboard-rammer number, sinks to the deck in agony, his right knee shattered. I feel a severe kick in my left buttock, there is a colossal noise — Stukas howling, bombs screaming and explosions all round.

Four of us are on the deck — silence. They're gone. I lift myself up on the breech, my left leg stiff. No Stukas astern. We look at one another in disbelief. I glance up forward and note many bodies not moving among the army. LR3's body taken down to the upper deck and covered. Only one of the gun crew is not wounded. We alter course to starboard and go aground on a sandbank. Two tugs see our plight and soon draw us off.

While at Action Stations men grabbed whatever rest they could. Here crewmen from one of HMS *Suffolk's* 4-inch anti-aircraft guns sleep while on patrol in the Atlantic in June 1941.

After Dunkirk the emphasis changed. The navy's primary task was to protect Britain from invasion. When the invasion never materialised, the main aim of the fleet was to protect Britain's maritime lifeline in the Atlantic. The same seamen who had braved air attacks off Norway and in the English Channel now watched merchant ships succumb to torpedoes in mid-Atlantic. This exposure to war helped harden the resolve of many sailors. They now realised that this was total war, to be fought to the bitter end. This new-found determination helped many endure the rigours of what came next.

The Battle of the Atlantic was arguably the longest and most arduous naval campaign of the twentieth century. Britain relied on imported foodstuffs, raw materials and fuel to service its needs. If this maritime lifeline were to be cut then Britain's surrender would be inevitable. It was a campaign

where quarter was neither asked nor given. However, while more than 3,500 Allied merchant ships were lost, and 175 warships, the Germans were unable to sever this strategically vital flow of goods. It became a war of attrition, which effectively came to an end in December 1941, when the United States entered the war. The Germans were simply unable to cope with the maritime resources available to the Allies. In the end the German Kriegsmarine sacrificed its U-boat arm in an increasingly futile attempt to alter the course of the war.

Bridge-crew ratings of the 'Scott' class destroyer *Douglas* enjoying a tea break during the escort of a convoy homeward-bound from Gibraltar to Liverpool. Yeomen and signallers formed an essential part of the bridge staff.

With hindsight these bald facts seem irrefutable. However, for those who participated in the campaign and watched ships sink all around them the outcome of the battle seemed very much in doubt. Somehow it seemed easier for the warships than for the merchant ships. As the novelist Nicholas Monsarrat put it, 'We can crack on a few revs, fling ourselves about a bit, strike back formidably if the opportunity arises, but they have to wallow along as if nothing had happened – same course and station, same inadequate speed, same helpless target.'

Sometimes the crew of an escort vessel was given a rare chance of avenging their mercantile colleagues. Stoker George Fogden recalls one such moment in May 1941, while serving in the destroyer *Bulldog*:

> We were steadily moving at about 7 knots – the usual speed for a convoy of merchant ships ... suddenly the Engine Room telegraph from the bridge clanged round to 'Full Steam Ahead' ... All of a sudden we heard a series of explosions deep below us. Our depth charges had been deployed. The Telegraph Indicator from the bridge then went to 'Stop Engines', which we carried out immediately. For a while all was quiet. We had no idea what was happening, as we were down in the bowels of the ship, but without any warning our 4.7 guns opened fire, shaking the whole ship. Then all was quiet again. We knew no more until we were relieved at midday by the next duty Engine Room watch. When we got on deck we could see we had a U-boat in tow. She had been damaged by our depth charges, and had surfaced. The crew had jumped into the water, and were picked up by other escort vessels.

In fact, *Bulldog* had managed to board and capture U-110, and with it its Enigma coding machine. Thanks to *Bulldog*, the Allies were able to crack the Germans' military codes.

Wearing their rough-weather rig, the crew of a minesweeper lower an Oropesa float (or sweep) overboard. The float supported the line used by these small vessels to cut the cables of tethered mines.

Saving men from the water was barely possible in the Atlantic. In the Arctic Ocean the chances of survival were negligible. From August 1941 the Home Fleet escorted convoys through these inhospitable waters. The merchantmen were carrying war material to the Soviet Union – tanks, planes, guns and ammunition that would help turn the tide of the war in the east. During this long and gruelling campaign the Royal Navy lost sixteen warships. One of these was the light cruiser *Edinburgh*, which was torpedoed off the Norwegian coast. Some men were trapped below decks.

Seaman John Kenny recalls: 'A seventeen-year-old seaman was trapped in the telephone room with water all around. He was in communication by voice pipe with the bridge. The Captain and others did their best to bolster his morale as long as possible by talking to him, but eventually he succumbed.' The cruiser was hit again, and this time she broke in two. The order came to abandon ship, and Kenny recalls how this was carried out with commendable order and discipline. When *Edinburgh* finally sank, she took fifty-eight of her crew down with her.

What was remarkable about the men of the Home Fleet was their ability to rise to the challenge posed by stormy and freezing seas, primitive conditions, near-constant danger, and long periods of intense discomfort and boredom. While their actions may have lacked much of the drama of the war in the Mediterranean, or the novel nature of the war in the Pacific, victory at sea was secured in the cold grey waters surrounding the British Isles, and in the icy seas from Newfoundland to Liverpool, and Scapa Flow to Murmansk.

As well as learning a skill, sailors also had to learn how to communicate or receive information. This young gunner forms a vital part of the communications chain linking the gunnery directors to the guns.

The crew of the small anti-submarine trawler HMS *Berkshire*, a patrol and escort vessel photographed in Scapa Flow during 1943. Most British sailors were in their twenties during the war.

FURY IN·THE
MEDITERRANEAN

IF THE Battle of the Atlantic was a struggle to maintain Britain's maritime lifeline, the Battle of the Mediterranean was fought to preserve Britain's Empire. During the war Britain relied heavily on imports and manpower from India, Ceylon (Sri Lanka), the Persian Gulf and East Africa, and ideally these would be transported through the Suez Canal and the Mediterranean. In 1939 the Germans posed little or no threat to this strategically important flow of goods. Instead, it was the Italians who were considered the danger, even though they were still neutral. That was why the British maintained such a large naval force in the Mediterranean. For Britain, the Mediterranean played a vital part in her global strategy. Losing control of its waters might well result in also losing Britain's link with the Empire. As Britain was dependent on the Empire for raw materials and food, that might well mean that Britain could lose the war.

For the British Mediterranean Fleet the war began on 10 June 1940, when Italy declared war on Britain and France. The following day the Italians bombed Malta – the first of over three thousand raids on the island. These air attacks would continue for almost two and a half years. At the time, Malta was one of three British naval bases in the Mediterranean. To the west lay Gibraltar, and to the east was Alexandria in Egypt. For Britain, the campaign would centre on the ability to keep the sea lanes open between these three strategic locations. Being in the middle, and just 50 miles from the nearest Italian airfield, Malta was bound to suffer the wrath of the enemy. In mid-1940 few could have expected that the 'Siege of Malta' would be so strongly prosecuted, or so costly in terms of lives and ships.

However, the first decisive action in the campaign was not against the Italians: it was the bombardment of the French fleet based in North Africa – a move designed to keep the fleet from joining the pro-German Vichy French. The French ships were shelled as they lay in port and did not stand a chance. Seaman Williams, on board the battlecruiser *Hood*, wrote home: 'We have seen our first action, but I regret to say it was against the French fleet … We had no option but to open fire.' He added: 'I must admit I felt

Opposite:
The crew of
a secondary
(anti-aircraft) gun
director on the
light cruiser
HMS *Sheffield*
during operations
in the central
Mediterranean,
pictured shortly
before the battle
of Spartiavento
in November 1940.
(IWM A2301)

A radio operator on board a wartime submarine. Specialist ratings such as radar and radio operators were given additional training and earned slightly more money than other sailors.

Flight-deck crews on board the fleet carrier *Victorious* arm Barracuda torpedo bombers and Corsair fighters, in readiness for an air strike against the German battleship *Tirpitz* in April 1944. (IWM TR 1812)

funny in the stomach when I heard the shells whistling over the top of our heads – the only pity is that it wasn't the Italians.' Rear Admiral Somerville wrote: 'We all feel thoroughly dirty and ashamed that the first time we have seen action was an affair like this.' But it was a necessary act if Britain was to defeat the enemy in the Mediterranean.

During the second half of 1940 the Royal Navy had three clashes at sea with the Italians, and in all of them the Italians withdrew before the battle reached its height. Then, in November 1940, Swordfish torpedo bombers from the fleet carrier *Illustrious* attacked the Italian naval base at Taranto, crippling three Italian battleships. For a few months it looked as if the struggle was tipping in Britain's favour. On land, the Italians were being driven back, and thousands of troops were surrendering, but these successes prompted the Germans to intervene.

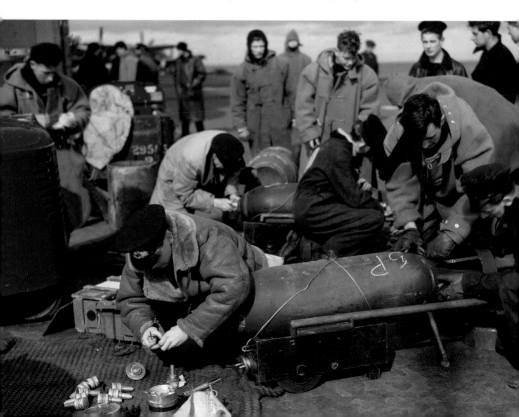

On land Rommel's Afrika Korps was formed, to support the Italians in North Africa, while the German Luftwaffe sent considerable numbers of aircraft to the Mediterranean, to bolster the Italian air force. Together, the Axis powers would dominate the skies over the central Mediterranean for the next two years. Finally, in September 1941, the Kriegsmarine sent U-boats into the Mediterranean, where they would pose a significant threat to British convoys and naval task forces.

Despite all this, the British Mediterranean Fleet remained a potent force. In late March 1941 Admiral Cunningham's ships inflicted a heavy defeat on the Italians at the Battle of Matapan, sinking three heavy cruisers and a destroyer, and crippling an Italian battleship, all for the loss of one torpedo bomber. As a teenage midshipman, Prince Philip, later the Duke of Edinburgh, manned a searchlight on board the battleship *Valiant*, when it illuminated an Italian cruiser:

> I seem to remember that I reported I had a target in sight, and was ordered to open shutter. The beam lit up a stationary cruiser, but we were so close by then that the beam only lit up half the ship. At this point all hell broke loose, as all our eight 15-inch guns, plus those of the flagship and *Barham*'s

Fleet Air Arm aircrews being briefed before a mission. These briefings ensured that everyone knew what was expected of them. On their return the survivors of the mission would also undergo a debriefing.

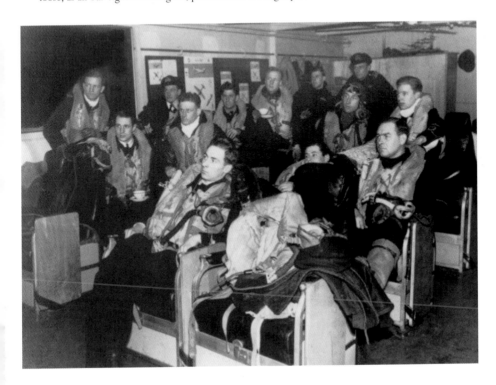

started firing at the stationary cruiser, which disappeared in an explosion and a cloud of smoke. I was then ordered to train left and lit up another Italian cruiser, which was given the same treatment.

This victory, though, would be the last for some time. Instead, the Mediterranean Fleet endured a series of fierce air attacks, at first off Greece during the evacuation of Allied troops there, and then in the waters surrounding Crete. The air attacks were relentless, but even here the navy struck back. A petty officer in the light cruiser *Dido* recalled attacking German troop transport, bound for Crete: 'Our first salvo of shells hit her fair and square amidships, and she immediately burst into flames from stem to stern. The enemy had been waving white flags at us when picked up by our searchlight, but we were out to destroy, not capture.'

Still British losses mounted. On 21 May 1941 the destroyer *Juno* was sunk by air attack, and the next day the cruisers *Gloucester* and *Fiji* and the destroyers *Greyhound*, *Kashmir* and *Kelly* were all sunk. Faced with unsustainable losses, Cunningham was counselled to withdraw his ships, rather than continue to place them in harm's way to evacuate the army. He replied: 'It takes three years to build a ship – it takes three centuries to build a tradition.' The operation continued.

There were a few lighter moments amid all the tragedy. An officer recorded a conversation he overheard on board a destroyer off Crete when a petty officer came upon a young seaman contemplating the bomb-damaged wreckage of his messdeck. 'What's wrong with you,' he demanded, above the roar of gunfire. The lad pointed a tragic finger at the debris. 'There's two bottles of pickles in there, smashed to the deck. They was unopened.' 'There's plenty more in the purser's store,' replied the petty officer. The boy nodded, inconsolable. 'That's right, but if you knowed the job we had to get our caterer to draw this lot.' Another near miss lifted the ship and dropped her, shuddering. 'He ain't pickle minded,' explained the ordinary seaman.

After Crete, the navy suffered a similar battering in the waters around Malta. While the island itself was pounded by enemy bombers, convoys running between Gibraltar and Malta endured relentless air attacks. Then in September 1941

Opposite: An Engineer Artificer acknowledging commands sent by voicepipe to the Engine Room of a British battleship. Regulations demanded that anti-flash hoods were worn when the ship was action stations. (IWM TR 312)

The breech of a port-side 15-inch gun, in one of the main turrets of a 'Queen Elizabeth' class battleship. The loading process was mechanical, but the operation was supervised by the crew on the left.

A seaman wearing a pullover, dungarees and rubber boots reports to a veteran petty officer on board a wartime destroyer. The navy relied heavily on the wisdom and experience of its senior ratings.

the first U-boats appeared. An early casualty was the light cruiser *Manchester*. Able Seaman Hindmarsh recalled the aftermath of the torpedo hit in 'A' turret:

We felt the gradual loss of speed; there was no surge of strength from astern. The noise of battle could be heard still, but growing fainter, ahead of us …The tannoy was silent. The midshipman tried to call gunnery control: no reply. The bridge: line also dead. The lighting in the turret began to dim. 'Emergency lighting!' ordered the middie. 'All guns check, check, check!' … By now there was scarcely any way perceptible on the ship. Everything had turned silent. We were waiting for the tannoy to crackle into life, or the phone buzzer to sound at the middie's elbow. But the minutes dragged on. As the minutes passed by, and turned into a full

While open bridges had been abandoned in other navies, the British felt they provided the ship's captain with a better sense of spatial awareness, particularly during an air attack. This is the bridge of a 'Southampton' class light cruiser.

half hour, then more, we noticed that the list to starboard was gradually increasing. With a hole in her side, how long might it be before the ship would heel right over, and turn turtle?

Eventually, the order came to abandon ship.

In 1942 the destroyer escort *Eridge* was escorting a Malta convoy when they were attacked by enemy aircraft. As Seaman Vic Chanter recounted:

With no air support, things looked black, and at 10:30 the main attack started. Despite valiant work by our gun crews there was little that could be done to prevent the onslaught that was hailed upon us. Because of our speed and manoeuvrability, we managed to escape damage whilst our guns tried their utmost to prevent harm to the *Glen Campbell*. Unfortunately, the almost inevitable happened, and the ship, which was put in our trust, received what turned out to be its final blow, from which it would not recover. I had seen worse destruction; tankers hit and exploding in a ball of flame, leaving no trace. *Glen Campbell* certainly disintegrated, but there were survivors and debris. Oil quickly spread over the area, and, here and there, the sea was ablaze. Not wanting to tempt fate and suffer any more casualties, the marauders flew away, leaving us to lick our wounds and pick up the pieces.

Flight-deck crew watch a Grumann F4 Wildcat fighter taking off from the fleet carrier *Formidable*, while she was operating in the western Mediterranean in November 1942.

This tragedy was repeated all too many times during the dark months of 1941–2. Eventually though, victory in North Africa, the arrival of American reinforcements and an influx of ships, aircraft and supplies all helped to turn the tide. By July 1943 the Allies were on the offensive, and Sicily was invaded. By September the Allies were established on the Italian mainland, and Italy had surrendered. While the Germans would fight on, and naval losses would continue, the Battle of the Mediterranean had been won. Now the Royal Navy was able to divert its precious naval resources to other theatres – to Europe, and the invasion of Normandy, and to the Pacific, where Britain was forming a new fleet to strike back at the Japanese.

IN EASTERN SEAS

BEFORE THE WAR, the Far East had been a relatively popular posting. The Royal Navy maintained a China Squadron based in Hong Kong, and a gunboat flotilla on the Yangtze river. Singapore, at the tip of the Malayan peninsula, was a major naval base, while Britain's imperial partners Australia and New Zealand both maintained a presence in the South Pacific. Further to the west the navy maintained a base in Ceylon, where warships could help protect Britain's maritime interests in the Indian Ocean.

The Japanese attack on Pearl Harbor in December 1941 presaged a Japanese onslaught in south-east Asia. The battleship *Prince of Wales* and the battle-cruiser *Repulse* had already been sent to the Far East, but on 10 December they were attacked by Japanese naval bombers off the eastern coast of Malaya. Both ships were lost, and 840 British sailors were killed. Stoker Bill Moss, who served in the *Prince of Wales*, was one of the lucky ones.

The aftermath of a Japanese kamikaze attack on the British fleet carrier *Victorious* off Okinawa in May 1945, when three suicide pilots crashed their planes into the carrier's armoured flight deck. Having extinguished the blaze, fire crews assess the surprisingly minor damage.

He helped launch a Carley float, which held about a dozen men. Then Moss noticed a problem:

> The float must have got punctured, as it was sinking a bit at one end ... so me and another lad went over the side and hung on to the float. Then he said, 'There's a cork mattress floating down, can you try and get to it?' We saw this mattress, which was quite a distance away and without more thought I started to swim after it ... There was no paddle with it so any paddling which was needed had to be done with bare hands. I managed to get on it, which was a bit awkward, but by this time the ship was about a mile away, as it was still afloat and had continued going away from us.

Stoker Moss continued to watch as the battleship sank, noting that 'the bow seemed to have a massive hole right through the middle and it seemed to be as clean as a whistle as though a torpedo had smashed clean through ... It was as though I was in at the death of this glorious ship.' He was fortunate to

Sailors clambering to safety from the battleship *Prince of Wales*, after she was torpedoed by Japanese aircraft off the coast of Malaya in December 1941. The crew had five minutes to abandon ship before it sank, taking 344 men with her.

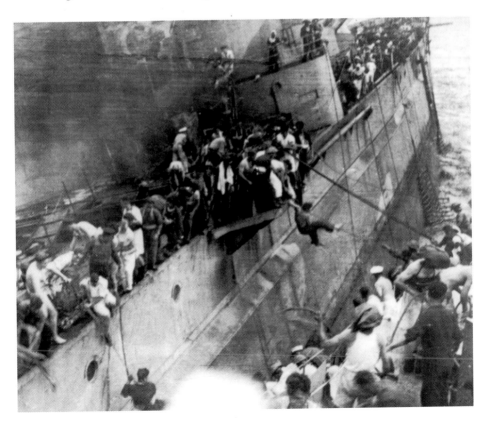

A navigating officer at work in the chartroom of a battleship. As well as officers, navigating sections included ratings, who updated charts and maintained equipment.

be picked up soon afterwards by a boat from the destroyer *Electra*. Another survivor, Commander Ward, remembered 'having experienced this dreadful attack, swimming around the *Prince of Wales* for one and a half hours among sharks before being picked up'.

Hong Kong fell on Christmas Day 1941, and then Singapore was lost on 15 February 1942. In just seven weeks, the British had been driven out of south-east Asia. Further disasters would follow. On 1 March the heavy cruiser *Exeter* was lost, and a month later the Japanese carriers entered the Indian Ocean. The light carrier *Hermes* was sunk, and on Easter Sunday Japanese carrier-based aircraft bombed Trincomalee, Britain's naval base in Ceylon. Two other victims were the heavy cruisers *Cornwall* and *Dorsetshire*. Seaman Philip Munro was on board *Dorsetshire* when the Japanese planes launched their attack:

Neptune's Court, ready to supervise the light-hearted 'Crossing of the Line' ceremony, carried out when a ship passed across the Equator. Events such as these did much to maintain the morale of a ship's company on long overseas deployments.

We had been steering south all day to rejoin the battle fleet, miles out in the Indian Ocean, when suddenly, out of the sun, like hungry lustful hawks screaming murder and death, came dive bombers. The sky seemed full of them, peeling off from their formations; black specks, each spewing a bomb from its belly as they screeched down on us.

The vicious cracks of our four-point-seven guns were drowned by the crash of heavy bombs. The *Dorsetshire* shuddered and shook as her decks and sides were blasted and torn. Chattering cannon and machine gun bullets punctured her superstructure. Bomb after bomb crashed down, and they never seemed to miss! A dozen in as many seconds, thousand-pounders, tearing the 'Old Girl's' heart out. Both starboard HA mountings were hit, the twin guns sticking out crazily at odd angles from twisted and blackened shields; a funnel gone, the mainmast hanging like a drunken blackened ghost; smoke and hissing steam everywhere.

'Keep the guns firing,' shouted the Captain. The order

was repeated down to the guns, but more than half of them were completely out of action, the remainder with sorely depleted crews ... The telephone operator rang up to the Bridge phone from his exchange in the bowels of the ship. The Yeoman of Signals answered it, and on saying who was speaking heard, 'Sorry, Bunts, but I can't get out ... my legs are gone.' The ship gave a lurch and the phone went dead.

The Captain gave the order to abandon ship, the order being passed with difficulty over the noise of battle, the hiss of escaping steam, and the moans of the wounded and dying. One man shouted out, 'Women and children first', and even the badly wounded managed a smile; it somehow broke the awful tension.

It would be two years before the Royal Navy could seek revenge. In May 1944 a joint Anglo-American carrier task force launched a strike against Surabaya in Java, and this prompted the decision to commit more ships to the war in the Pacific. In November 1944 the British Pacific Fleet was formed, based in Sydney. It was the largest wartime fleet assembled by the Royal Navy, with four battleships, six fleet carriers and numerous smaller vessels. Working in close co-operation with the US Navy, this fleet would actively take the war to the Japanese. By January 1945 it was operating in the waters of the East Indies, and in March it moved north to support the landings on Okinawa. By July the British battleship *King George V* was bombarding the Japanese mainland, and the fleet was present in Tokyo Bay, to watch the Japanese surrender.

During these dramatic events the British sailors took this new war in their stride. They were also proud of their ships, which they saw as the equal of their American counterparts. In some cases they were better: the armoured flight decks of British fleet carriers proved their worth during the kamikaze attacks off Okinawa. As the US Navy's liaison officer on board *Indefatigable* put it, 'When a kamikaze hits a US carrier it means 6 months of repair at Pearl [Harbor]. When a kamikaze hits a Limey carrier it's just a case of "Sweepers, man your brooms!"'

The last surface battle of the war was fought off Penang, when British destroyers engaged the Japanese heavy cruiser *Haguro*. A British sailor recounted the story:

All ships firing star shell flares to light up the enemy. Cruiser unaware of our presence until now. *Saumarez*

The loading of 15-inch shells aboard the battleship *Warspite*, while the battleship lay off Mombasa in March 1942. White shorts, socks and plimsolls appear to have been the approved rig of the day.

A seaman in front of 'Captain's Requestmen and Defaulters' gathering on board a destroyer, headed by the first lieutenant. As the term suggests, these hearings dealt with disciplinary matters, and also requests by crewmen for leave, transfer and pay.

going in to fire torpedoes. Other destroyers surround cruiser. *Saumarez* fired torpedoes and a second later is hit by a salvo of 8-inch shells from the cruiser. One hit in number one boiler room, one hit in wheelhouse lobby, and one hit on top of the funnel. Three hits on cruiser with *Saumarez'* torpedoes. *Venus* and *Verulam* attack, and hits observed on cruiser with torpedoes ... Then *Vigilant* goes in close and fires 4' 7" guns, hits nearly every time, and cruiser nearly down. One shell must have hit the magazine as she blew up, turned over and sank.

There were no survivors.

The Japanese capitulation on 15 August 1945 was met with jubilation throughout the fleet, as well as back home in Britain. The formal Japanese surrender came on 2 September, but by then most sailors were dreaming of going home to a country that at long last had found peace. Unlike 50,758 of their fellow sailors, they had survived six years of total war.

A flight deck crew arming a Grumman Avenger on HMS *Implacable* while the carrier was operating in the Pacific in 1945. Normal working dress regulations appear to have been relaxed.

DEMOBILISATION

During the Second World War the strength of the Royal Navy grew considerably, in terms of both ships and manpower. By 1945 it was greater than it had ever been in the service's long and proud history. Most of these sailors and Wrens were 'hostilities only' personnel, and, now the fighting was over, they expected to be demobilised. Many, especially those serving overseas, would be disappointed at the time taken to send them home.

This, though, was understandable. The navy still had extensive global commitments, and it would take time to decommission many of the thousands of warships, coastal vessels and landing craft that were now surplus to naval requirements. The Second Sea Lord Vice-Admiral Sir Algernon Willis played a prominent part in the steady demobilisation of the wartime navy, and in the planning of a new peacetime service.

Of the 860,000 officers, men and women who were serving in the Royal Navy in 1945, only 195,000 would remain two years later as part of a greatly slimmed-down force. The work of demobilisation began even before the hangovers from VJ Day had cleared. In every naval shore establishment demobilisation centres were set up and, as ships returned home, their crews were processed in batches and so released from service. A petty officer who experienced demobilisation in Portsmouth recalled:

> Fifty-six days paid leave was granted from the actual day of release. Those concerned were organised in groups to visit a local warehouse, where each individual received a free issue of civilian attire, namely two pinstripe suits. Resettlement offices were established in most districts, to advise and assist servicemen to adapt themselves to a new and, in many cases, unwelcome life… Send-offs became a routine spectacular as each demob group reached the final day. Taxis departed well adorned with boots and placards bearing words like 'Paid off!' or 'Nozzers [recruits] for Civvy Street'!

Older sailors were demobilised first, starting with pre-war ratings who had exceeded their pensionable age. As each draft left, and many ships were decommissioned and laid up, the remaining younger men were moved to other ships that were still in commission. These had been left short-handed when more senior men had been demobilised. Some 'hostilities only' ratings volunteered to stay in the service for a few extra years, serving in the minesweepers that were busily trying to remove the detritus of naval warfare from around the coasts of Europe.

This was not an easy time for many regular naval personnel. As they watched their 'hostilities only' shipmates leave many had doubts about their role in a peacetime navy. Many had already had their fill of service life or had been demoralised by tragedy, either at home or at sea. Pay was poor compared to civilian wages, and morale suffered. However, the navy began recruiting again, pay levels were increased, and gradually the manpower of what remained of the fleet regained its even keel. For many, though, the scars of war would remain with them, whether they stayed in the service or looked for new employment in 'civvy street'.

Keeping morale and fitness levels high remained a priority. Here, crewmen exercise on the flight deck of a homeward-bound aircraft carrier.
(IWM A 30981)

Adjustment was tough. For many young men, finding a suitable job presented a major hurdle. In September 1945 The Times newspaper commented on the problems facing former officers.. "Many officers are now leaving [the Forces] who, by reason of their youth, have qualified for nothing but war, but in a war which demanded youth at any price, have risen to senior positions of considerable responsibility and relatively high pay. They have acquired experience ... and they have matured even beyond their years .... but these qualities will not usually be applicable to civilian tasks until there has been a process of adaptation.

As one marine put it, 'It took me some time to settle down in civilian life. I had changed and no longer spoke the same language as previously... Life now seemed rather slow, as we had lived on a knife edge for so long, seen dreadful sights, and lost many good friends, but with patience I soon got the hang of it again.' That sense of dislocation was only to be expected. For those who had served in the wartime Royal Navy, life would never be quite the same again.

Wrens staffing a small shore base are thanked by their CEO, immediately prior to their demobilisation. (IWM A29288)

FURTHER READING

Anonymous. *The Royal Navy Today*. London, *c*. 1942.

Bacon, Sir Reginald (editor). *Britain's Glorious Navy*. Odhams, 1943.

Bigland, Eileen. *The Story of the Wrens*. Nicholson & Watson, 1946.

Howarth, Stephen. *The Royal Navy's Reserves in Peace and War*.
    Leo Cooper, 2003.

Konstam, Angus. *Scapa Flow*. Osprey, 2009.

Laffin, John. *Jack Tar: The Story of the British Sailor*. Littlehampton
    Book Services, 1969.

Lavery, Brian. *Hostilities Only: Training in the Wartime Royal Navy*.
    National Maritime Museum, 2004.

Lavery, Brian. *Churchill's Navy: The Ships, Men and Organisation, 1939–45*.
    Conway, 2006.

McKee, Christopher. *Sober Men and True: Sailors' Lives in the Royal Navy,
    1900–45*. Harvard University Press, 2002.

Prysor, Glyn. *Citizen Sailors: The Royal Navy in the Second World War*.
    Penguin, 2012.

Sumner, Ian, and Baker, Alix. *The Royal Navy, 1939–45*. Osprey, 2001.

Swaffer, Hannen. *What Would Nelson Do?* Gollancz, 1946.

Wells, John. *The Royal Navy: An Illustrated Social History, 1870–1982*.
    Sutton Publishing, 1994.

The battleship *King George V*, sketched while she was being fitted out at the Rosyth naval base on the Firth of Forth in October 1940. As with all new warships her crew joined their ship while she was nearing completion.

PLACES TO VISIT

Explosion! The Museum of Naval Firepower, Heritage Way, Priddy's Hard, Gosport, Hampshire PO12 4LE. Telephone: 023 9250 5600. Website: www.explosion.org.uk

Fleet Air Arm Museum, RNAS Yeovilton, Ilchester, Somerset BA22 8HT. Telephone: 01935 840565. Website: www.fleetairarm.com

HMS Belfast, The Queen's Walk, London SE1 2JH. Telephone: 020 7940 6300. Website: www.iwm.org.uk/visits/hms-belfast

Imperial War Museum, Lambeth Road, London SE1 6HZ. Telephone: 020 7416 5000. Website: www.iwm.org.uk/visits/iwm-london

Imperial War Museum North, The Quays, Trafford Wharf Road, Manchester M17 1TZ. Telephone: 0161 836 4012. Website: www.iwm.org.uk/visits/iwm-north

National Maritime Museum, Park Row, Greenwich, London SE10 9NF. Telephone: 020 8312 6608. Website: www.rmg.co.uk

Royal Naval Museum, HM Naval Base, Portsmouth, Hampshire PO1 3NH. Telephone: 023 9272 7562. Website: www.royalnavalmuseum.org

The Royal Navy Submarine Museum, Haslar Jetty Road, Gosport, Hampshire PO12 2AS. Telephone: 023 9251 0354. Website: www.submarine-museum.co.uk

Scapa Flow Visitor Centre and Museum, Lyness, Hoy, Orkney. Telephone: 01856 791300. Website: www.scapaflow.co.uk (Seasonal: museum closed during the winter.)

The Second World War Experience Centre, 1A Rudgate Court, Walton, near Wetherby, West Yorkshire LS23 7BF. Telephone: 019 3754 1194. Website: www.war-experience.org/index.html (A virtual rather than a physical museum, the centre collects and presents first-hand wartime testimony.)

INDEX

Page numbers in italics refer to illustrations